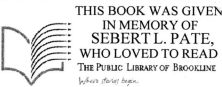
Before

THE REVOLUTION

Before

THE REVOLUTION

AMERICA'S ANCIENT PASTS

Daniel K. Richter

THE BELKNAP PRESS OF
HARVARD UNIVERSITY PRESS
Cambridge, Massachusetts
London, England

First Harvard University Press paperback edition, 2013

Library of Congress Cataloging-in-Publication Data

Richter, Daniel K.
Before the Revolution : America's ancient pasts / Daniel K. Richter.
p.   cm.
Includes bibliographical references and index.
ISBN 978-0-674-05580-3 (cloth : alk. paper)
ISBN 978-0-674-07236-7 (pbk.)
1. United States—Civilization.   2. United States—Civilization—Indian influences.
3. United States—Civilization—European influences.   4. United States—Civilization—
African influences.   5. America—History—To 1810.   6. United States—History—
Colonial period, ca. 1600–1775.   I. Title.
E169.12.R497 2011
973'.01—dc22   2010037881

To the memory of Bud Richter

Contents

Prologue

A´NCIENT. *adj.* [*ancien,* Fr. *antiquus,* Lat.]
1. Old; that happened long since; of old time; not modern.
Ancient and *old* are distinguish'd; *old* relates to the duration of
the thing itself, as, an *old* coat, a coat much worn; and *ancient,*
to time in general, as, an *ancient* dress, a habit used in former
times . . .

> "With the *ancient* is wisdom, and in length of days
> understanding." *Job.* xii. 12.

LA´YER, *n.s.* [from *lay*].
1. A stratum, or row; a bed; one body spread over another.

—Samuel Johnson, *A Dictionary of the English
Language* (London, 1755)

Layered Pasts

"WE HAVE IT IN OUR POWER to begin the world over again," Thomas Paine wrote in 1776. "A situation, similar to the present, hath not happened since the days of Noah." Citizens of the United States have frequently pretended that they lived in a land of fresh starts, a land that hardly had a past that mattered—except perhaps the era of Paine, when godlike Founders created a timeless new order for the ages. Yet Paine himself knew better. Much of his revolutionary pamphlet *Common Sense* is devoted to history lessons: on monarchy in general, on the British monarchy in particular, on the place of North America in the European imperial world, and on why, since the battles of Lexington and Concord, it all had become "superceded and useless."[1]

"Superceded" perhaps, useless Paine hoped—but certainly not gone. According to the Genesis tale evoked by *Common Sense*, Noah's ark had preserved a pair of each type of creature living in the former world. Even as the Creator "blotted out every living thing that was on the face of the ground," he "remembered Noah and all the wild animals and all the domestic animals that were with him in the ark."[2] When the vessel came to rest on the mountain, the earth's heights and valleys had been reshaped but not wholly destroyed, and Noah's offspring soon proved that they carried within them the original sin of their antediluvian forebears. At heart, then, Paine's biblical allusion was geological as well as theological. The ancient flood scoured the landscape but could not eliminate what earlier epochs had laid down. The world begun over again rested on—and took its shape from—the remains of what came before.

The history of the United States, this book argues, has a similar quality.

3

The American Revolution submerged earlier strata of society, culture, and politics, but those ancient worlds remain beneath the surface to mold the nation's current contours. The chapters below explore a geology of six sequential cultural layers defined by people I call respectively *progenitors, conquistadores, traders, planters, imperialists,* and *Atlanteans.* Each new layer spread over the older ones, but what came before never fully disappeared. Indeed, the new was always a product of the old, made from bits and pieces retained from deeper strata. The people of these now-submerged worlds may seem as lost to us, and as difficult to interpret, as the shale and fossils undergirding today's cities, farms, and McMansions. Yet to understand fully the society that grew up in North America after 1776, the cultural forms that accumulated before anyone dreamed there would *be* a United States need to be excavated—and understood on their own dynamic terms. The words "old" and "ancient," the eighteenth-century dictionary compiler and literary wit Samuel Johnson insisted, do not have precisely the same meaning. Something "old" could simply be worn out, but "with the *ancient* is wisdom."[3]

Ancient cultural layers have been accumulating, of course, since long before the days of Noah, or, as Native Americans might say, since our first ancestors came out of the ground. But the layers most relevant to our story are the ones that produced the peoples who encountered each other in the decades after 1492. The twin strata of *progenitors*—cultural tectonic plates that formed on opposite sides of the Atlantic Ocean—were themselves already half a millennium old in the era of Columbus. They took shape during a period of global warming that inaugurated what would later be called the "Middle Ages." Beginning in the decades after the year we now call 900 C.E., strikingly parallel agricultural revolutions produced strikingly different civilizational forms in North America and Western Europe. Distinctive systems of power and authority, of family and kinship, of religion and spirituality, of production and exchange took shape on the two continents. Just as important, as the climate cooled in the fourteenth century, each system began unraveling, and inherent instabilities of the two medieval syntheses came to the fore. On both sides of the Atlantic, powerful traces of the earlier orders, and of their many instabilities, remained, for better and worse, to shape all succeeding layers.

During the century after 1492, descendants of the two progenitors crashed violently together. The associated earthquakes transformed the cultural landscape everywhere from Europe to Africa to the islands of the

Caribbean and, finally, to North America. In crusades sponsored by monarchs assembling primitive states, driven by freelance warriors seeking power and wealth, and justified by zeal for spreading what was called the True Faith, Western Europeans spilled out into the Atlantic basin. The exploits of these *conquistadores*—Protestant as well as Catholic—owed more to the loyalties and beliefs of the Middle Ages than to anything we would recognize as "modern" or "capitalistic," although they nonetheless contained the germs of those later traits. Honed in late medieval campaigns in places such as Moorish Granada and Celtic Ireland, exported to such islands as the Canaries and Azores, perfected in the Spanish conquests of Hispaniola, Mexico, and Peru, and brought to fruition in disastrous English efforts to colonize at Roanoke and Jamestown, patterns of ruthless violence, enslavement, and oppressive rule of indigenous peoples laid an ugly base for all that would follow.

In North America, cultural debris thrown up from the layer of the conquistadores settled in two distinct yet overlapping strata during the late sixteenth and early seventeenth centuries. The first, the layer of *traders,* drew much of its material from patterns of exchange and political power forged by Native North America's progenitors. Some enterprising adventurers traveling in the wake of the conquistadores—most notably from France and the Netherlands, but also from England and elsewhere —meshed their economic goals with the very different ones of Native peoples. Exchanges of all sorts, from material goods to religious ideas to plants, animals, microbes, and human genes, produced hybrid communities. Yet there was little harmony in the hybridity. While handfuls of Europeans struggled to make a go of it in outposts scattered along seacoasts and rivers providing access to the continental interior, hundreds of thousands of Native Americans perished from unfamiliar diseases inadvertently brought by the newcomers. The epidemics, in combination with wars among indigenous peoples over trade routes, resources, and political dominance, left much of the countryside empty of human habitation. The Native survivors created enduring forms of interdependence with European trading partners and fashioned tools that future generations of Indian leaders would use to help their people maintain autonomy in the face of colonial expansion.

The second layer thrown up by the collisions that began in 1492 drew much of its material from patterns of land use and gendered power inherited from Europe's progenitors, as filtered through a distinctively English emphasis on patriarchal control of land and labor. For English *planters*, that emphasis on control gained urgency from religious and political upheavals in the early seventeenth-century British Isles. In the aptly named "New England," in the Chesapeake Bay region, and on Caribbean islands, waves of voluntary and involuntary exiles from Britain's troubles imported first their own families, then indentured servants, and finally enslaved Africans to agricultural colonies from which Native people were largely excluded. This exclusion set English planters starkly apart from the Dutch, French, Spanish, and indeed English traders, whose outposts remained deeply entwined with indigenous communities. Wherever Protestant English men put down family roots, agricultural production for global markets on lands held as private property became the key to prosperity and the measure of masculine self-rule. Anyone who stood in the way of these men—Native Americans, landless European newcomers, obstreperous servants and slaves, people of differing religious views, would-be English royal governors—did so at their peril.

In the mid-seventeenth century, as the stratum of the planters settled uneasily over those of the traders and conquistadores, fresh waves of state expansion flowed outward from a Europe still in upheaval. Imperfectly and violently, a new layer of *imperialists* imposed itself atop the constantly shifting colonial mass, smashing and assimilating bits of the older layers as it did so. The English and French states took the lead in this process, attempting to conquer Native Americans, the Dutch, the Spanish, and their own rambunctious colonial subjects along the way. Some Native nations— restive under the pretensions of European planters and traders alike— found common cause with some imperialists, turned competition among European states to their own purposes, and rejuvenated their ability to shape the continent's history. But for many other Indian peoples, and for many ordinary Spanish, French, and English colonists, the process was a blood-drenched disaster. Historians have given the key events of the process such orderly names as the Pueblo Revolt, King Philip's War, Bacon's Rebellion, or Leisler's Rebellion. But those terms fail to capture the chaotic terror of the imperial transition for all concerned.

Gradually, and unpredictably to most of those who lived through it, by the second quarter of the eighteenth century the violence yielded to temporarily more stable forms. Economic and political networks spanning the Atlantic bound North America ever more tightly to Europe and Africa. Thriving agricultural production rooted in the stratum of planters created a relentless demand for labor that absorbed hordes of new farmers, families, and servants—not just from the British Isles, but from continental Europe—along with even larger throngs of enslaved laborers from West Africa. The prosperity that these laborers produced for their masters reinvigorated patterns of seaborne commerce created by earlier traders. Atlantic trade became equally vital to Native Americans and to the descendants of European immigrants; the material lives of both depended on imports and exports. Continued imperial competition among Protestant England and Catholic France and Spain, meanwhile, kept alive the crusading religious spirit inherited from the conquistadores. Thus, earlier strata continued to mold succeeding ones.

The polyglot social forms of the eighteenth century defied easy categorization as "American," "European," or "African." Instead, they partook of all three identities, and of the seaborne commercial and imperial networks that tied them together across the Atlantic. The stratum of *Atlanteans* in which all North Americans found their uneasy places in a global British-dominated culture was the one that both produced, and was in turn submerged by, the new layer of the revolutionary generation that created the United States.

The revolutionaries of 1776 labored mightily to assert that the history of the United States had never been truly connected to this former Atlantean world, let alone to all the layers that undergirded it. "America," Paine insisted, "would have flourished as much, and probably much more, had no European power had any thing to do with her."[4] North America's Native peoples certainly would have agreed with the latter sentiment, but in 1750 one would have been hard pressed to find any European-American residents of Britain's—or France's, or Spain's—colonies who could have imagined such an idea. They, and their enslaved workers and their Native neighbors, lived in a transatlantic world dominated by European powers, a world so fully integrated and mutually prosperous (albeit also mutually exploitative) that the revolutionary secession of thirteen British colonies along the North American seaboard would have seemed neither possible nor desirable. By 1765, however, a long, brutal conflict known as the Seven Years War had revealed the fragility of the ties that bound the transoceanic empire, and the future seemed far less clear.

Still, despite the strains of the Seven Years War, the movement for independence from the Atlantic world caught nearly everyone by surprise. Like the antedeluvians Paine evoked in *Common Sense*, the Atlanteans of mid-eighteenth-century America "were eating and drinking, marrying and giving in marriage, until the day Noah entered the ark, and they knew nothing until the flood came and swept them all away."[5] That revolutionary flood, along with the details of individual lives such as Paine's, are the subjects of many other books by many other authors. This one traces broad patterns in the lives of generations of people who had no idea that something called an independent United States was in the future but who laid down the substrate on which we stand today. Their stories began a thousand years ago.

Progenitors

PROGE´NITOR. *n.s.* [*progenitus,* Lat.] A forefather; an ancestor
in a direct line.

—Samuel Johnson, *A Dictionary of the English
Language* (London, 1755)

ONE

Legacies of Power from
Medieval North America

THE STORIES BEGAN A thousand years ago, but *as* stories they hardly survive at all. In Chaco Canyon, in what we now call New Mexico, the remains of massive pueblos dominate the landscape. In the greater Mississippi Valley, what seem small natural hills are in fact massive earthen mounds raised a millennium ago by human hands. Who built these places and why are questions that remain shrouded in mystery. The structures in Chaco Canyon are attributed to those called *Anasazi* (a Navajo slur meaning "Ancient Enemies") or, more neutrally, "Ancestral Puebloans." The creators of the eastern earthworks are known only by the popular term "Moundbuilders" or the scholar's label "Mississippians." Fragmentary memories of these people survive in Native American stories about past migrations and conflicts, but the lack of clear references to the creators of such dramatic structures is striking. It is almost as if some trauma led to cultural amnesia among those who came later. Traditions recited at Acoma Pueblo in the early twentieth century speak of long-ago folk who were unhappy in their homes and migrated to the south. "It is not known how far they went," the story says, "but finally they stopped at a place where they went through the ceremony of forgetting . . . and left their sickness and trouble behind."[1]

This Acoma memory, like all the others, cannot unambiguously be connected to the New Mexico ruins. The stories of Chaco Canyon and the Mississippi Valley can only be pieced together from fragments of archaeological and material evidence. Most of the details and all of the voices of the human beings involved are irrevocably lost. But the sagas commenced with global climate change. In the years from about 900 to 1300 C.E., in lands around much of the northern Atlantic Ocean, summers were longer and weather more predictable than in the past or in the "Little Ice Age" that followed and that would continue into the nineteenth century. During the Medieval Warm Period, average temperatures in the Northern Hemisphere were two to three degrees Fahrenheit higher than in the previous epoch and perhaps five degrees higher than in the depths of the much less stable era that followed. On both sides of the Atlantic, climate change coincided with major shifts in the way people produced food and organized themselves to do the work. In places like Chaco Canyon and the Mississippi Valley (and France and the British Isles), these innovations formed the basis for novel social, economic, and political systems.

In both North America and Western Europe, new, often brutal, cultural syntheses emerged during the Middle Ages to codify the distinctive forms of power that men and women wielded toward one another and toward the natural world, only to enter a period of crisis when the climate cooled. When people from the two continents met each other in the sixteenth century, the terms of engagement were determined by systems of power that their respective medieval progenitors had created.

Human societies are complicated things, and they never respond in any straightforward way to alterations in the environment. Moreover, the history of climate is, to say the least, an inexact science. Researchers debate the spotty and indirect evidence bitterly, often with the contemporary politics of global warming firmly in mind, and they caution against too-easy generalizations and mechanistic assumptions about human adaptation. They also debate the causes of climate change: sunspot activity, volcanic eruptions, changes in ocean currents, human clearing of forests? Whatever the explanation, year-to-year differences could be more dramatic than long-term averages, and there were many local variations. Throughout the North American Great Plains and Great Basin and along much of the Pacific Coast, for instance, the Medieval Warm Period seems to have produced frequent droughts rather than fecund growing seasons. Still, tree-ring studies, soil and ice core samples, pollen remains, glacial moraines, and other evidence indicate that, across much of North America and Western Europe, average temperatures increased significantly enough to matter—although not nearly as dramatically as they would at the turn of the twenty-first century.

From the tenth through the early fourteenth centuries, growing seasons became longer and more reliable than they had been in the past or would be again until the nineteenth century. The most beneficial effects were on areas with a temperate "continental" climate, where a rise of a couple of degrees in average temperature could translate into several weeks of additional frost-free days in most years. Agriculture had long been known in such zones but had previously been relatively insignificant because crops first cultivated in more southerly climes were poorly adapted to local conditions. In the Americas, those southern climes were in what are today Honduras, Costa Rica, and Mexico, and those crops were the maize, beans, and squash that, for the better part of two thousand years, had supported successive densely populated civilizations there.

North America's agricultural revolution involved the spread all three crops together, and with good reason. Maize by itself is an inadequate staff of life. Consumed alone, it induces pellagra, a disease that produces skin lesions, diarrhea, and mental disorders. But a diet that combines corn and beans is a different story. Legumes are an excellent source of the essential amino acids lysine and tryptophan, whose absence is likely to result in pellagra. Maize contains almost none of either, but it does contribute the protein zein, which, when consumed along with beans, provides a particularly healthful mix of nutrients. Soaking the corn in lime or ash, as Native peoples almost always did, releases niacin, the absence of which is another major cause of pellagra. Treated maize boiled together with beans, in the ubiquitous Native American soup that Algonquian-speakers of the St. Lawrence Valley called *sagamité*, yields additional nutritional treasures, unlocking 90 percent of the considerable carbohydrates in each crop. Moreover, boiling is also the most efficient means of cooking foods that have been dried for storage, and dried corn and beans can be kept for years. Meantime, squashes, pumpkins, and gourds—which also naturally store well after harvest—provide C- and B-vitamins, to complete a remarkably well-balanced diet. A little fish or shellfish or meat from hunting (nowhere in the Americas were there large animal species easily domesticated for food) provided a nice complement, but people could survive well on the three main crops alone.

For poorly understood reasons, obscured in hotly contested archaeological evidence, it appears that the complete subtropical mix of crops did not spread anywhere north of Mexico until the eve of the Medieval Warm Period, and dispersed through most of the continent only once the climatic changes commenced. Theorists debate endlessly why societies make the difficult trade-offs necessary to become dependent on agriculture, and we will probably never know the tedious processes of trial and error by which North Americans figured out how to breed versions of subtropical plants suited to their more temperate local conditions. Only squashes and bottle gourds—the least delicate and most easily grown of the three crops— seem to have a truly ancient North American heritage; seeds dated to as early as 5000 B.C.E. have been found in today's Illinois, and seeds from about 2300 B.C.E. in Kentucky. Perhaps as early as 1800 B.C.E., the small-cobbed and not terribly nutritious variety of maize known as *chapalote,* a forerunner of popcorn, was being grown in areas of present-day New Mexico and Arizona. A related variety appeared in the Mississippi River Valley by approximately 100 B.C.E. At about the same time, or perhaps a few centuries earlier, beans grew in New Mexico. Their further spread is difficult to trace, because diners seldom left behind seeds for future archaeologists to find, but legumes appear to have traveled little beyond that region during the succeeding thousand years.

Thus, when the Medieval Warm Period began in North America, there was nothing new about the idea of growing crops. A pattern that might better be called gardening than agriculture was widespread in the Southwest and the greater Mississippi, Missouri, and Ohio river valleys during the first millennium C.E. In the latter region, an "Eastern Agricultural Complex" included a variety of domesticated and semi-wild plants —among them sunflowers, chenopodium, sumpweed, goosefoot, and pigweed—whose seeds, along with gathered hickory nuts, acorns, butternuts, various roots, and early varieties of maize, could be pounded into flour and eaten in soups and breads.[2]

Everywhere north of the Rio Grande, however, hunting, fishing, and gathering remained the primary means of subsistence. An almost universal division of labor gave primary responsibility for hunting and fishing to men, and the intricate tasks of gathering and gardening to women. This apparently was true even among the peoples who built the earliest of the massive earthworks that since have fascinated North Americans, most notably Poverty Point (dated 2200–700 B.C.E.) in Louisiana and Mississippi and Adena (1000 B.C.E.–100 C.E.) and Hopewell (200 B.C.E.–400 C.E.) in the Ohio River Valley.

Within this long North American tradition of horticultural experimentation, by at least 700 C.E., farmers in the Southwest were raising a new form now called *maiz de ocho,* or eight-rowed flint corn. Apparently the product of hundreds of years of local developments, rather than a direct import from the south, maiz de ocho had several important characteristics. Compared to chapalote and other North American predecessors, its eponymous eight rows of kernels were more plump, more numerous, and more easily ground into flour, creating a level of dietary productivity that for the first time clearly set maize apart from other cultivated and semi-wild grains. Moreover, in contrast to the 140-day growing season necessary for Central American varieties of that era, maiz de ocho could be grown in 120 days or less. And flint corn proved extraordinarily adaptable to local conditions. When temperatures warmed and growing seasons lengthened after the year 900, maiz de ocho was poised to take off, diversifying, along with its traveling companions squash and beans, in countless ways.

In the arid landscape of today's New Mexico, Arizona, and southern Colorado, the agricultural revolution depended, to one degree or another, on artificial irrigation. This was particularly true along the Gila and Salt rivers of Arizona, where, as early as 700 C.E., the people known as Hohokam ("Those Who Have Gone," in the O'odham language of the Native Southwest) were building canals to bring scarce water to artificial flood plains. Waterworks were somewhat less widespread to the east, among the people archaeologists call Mogollon, or to the north, among the Ancestral Puebloans. In all these locations, intense care was necessary to tailor the land to preserve moisture through the use of terraced gardens and other techniques. Perhaps the intensity of the labor involved explains why in the Southwest, unlike elsewhere in North America, agricultural work apparently fell to men, although the land and crops themselves seem to have remained under the control of women, who had long been in charge of vegetable foods, gathered or gardened.

In part because of this role in food production, female kin groups—extended families in which both men and women traced descent primarily through grandmothers' lines—apparently provided a central organizing principle for the many small agricultural communities that dotted the Southwestern landscape by the year 900. A group of elderly sisters, their daughters, their granddaughters, their unmarried grandsons, and their husbands and sons-in-law likely made up the households in each village. Thirty, fifty, perhaps a hundred interrelated people lived in communal dwellings gathered around ceremonial spaces. Throughout the re-

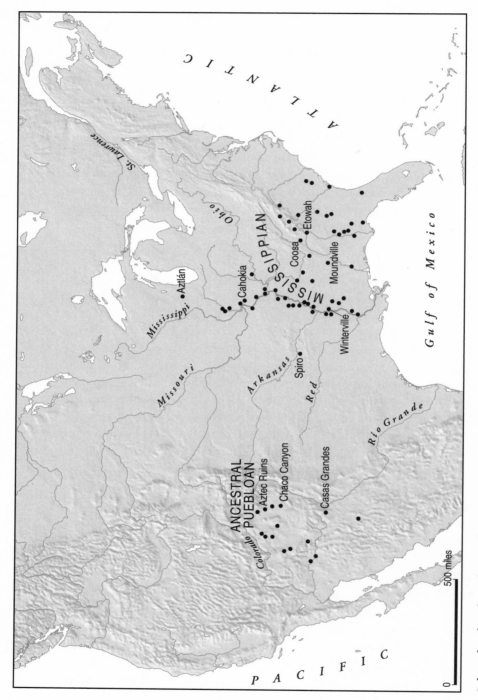

ATLANTIC

St. Lawrence

Ohio

Aztlán

Mississippi

Cahokia

Missouri

MISSISSIPPIAN

Etowah

Coosa

Moundville

Gulf of Mexico

Arkansas

Spiro

Red

Winterville

Rio Grande

ANCESTRAL
PUEBLOAN

Aztec Ruins

Chaco Canyon

Casas Grandes

Colorado

500 miles

0

PACIFIC

Selected archaeological sites of medieval North America.

gion, these buildings included the large roofed-over subterranean rooms called *kivas*. Hohokam sites included sunken ball courts and small burial mounds, both presumably inspired by Central American models. Hohokam people also excavated dwellings and storage facilities for crops, taking advantage of the earth's warming and cooling effects by submersing their large round or oval houses a foot and a half or so into the ground. Mogollon and Ancestral Puebloan peoples, meanwhile, began to build upward with stone, adobe, and scarce timber, combining housing and storage space in precursors of the multi-story pueblos of later eras.

As the Warm Period took hold, what remained, in one scholar's words, "an extremely variable . . . precipitation context" nonetheless produced "a continued favorable moisture regime" for most of the tenth century.[3] Under these conditions, Southwestern agricultural ways of life effloresced, with substantial population growth and the emergence of several remarkable urban centers. None were more remarkable than those of Chaco Canyon in what is now the Four Corners region of New Mexico. By the mid-eleventh-century, twelve "great houses," with smaller "room block" complexes interspersed among them, stretched along as many miles of the north side of the canyon. Roughly three hundred less carefully laid-out room blocks, or "unit pueblos," dotted the opposite rim. Archaeologists estimate that several thousand people lived in this core area. Tens of thousands more lived within a sixty-mile radius, where approximately seventy great houses and perhaps 5,300 villages constituted a single sphere of cultural and economic interaction. The largest of the great houses is known today as Pueblo Bonito. Constructed largely between 1030 and 1079 C.E. on a site already occupied for at least two hundred years, it contained roughly seven hundred rooms arranged in four stories, and it sheltered dozens of kivas, some apparently serving the community as a whole, others individual kin groups.[4]

The surviving physical evidence leads archaeologists to wildly different conclusions about how the families who lived in these apartments interacted with each other, about economic relationships among them, and about the degree to which Chaco Canyon was politically stratified. But a convincing case exists for a major gulf between the elite inhabitants of the great houses and the commoners who lived in the unit pueblos. Most great-house dwellers seem to have been better nourished than their unit-pueblo counterparts (if more likely to suffer from intestinal parasites and other diseases of crowded living). The great houses sat astride major junctions that controlled water resources. Their hundreds of rooms, most of which were probably used for food storage and ceremonial purposes rather than residence, mark them as central facilities for collection and re-distribution of corn, beans, and squash, most of it produced in a large hinterland where smaller great houses stood among countless still-smaller unit dwellings. An array of exotic goods from across the continent and Central America—copper and feathers from Mexico, marine shells from the Pacific Coast, turquoise and ceramic pottery from closer at hand, mica and selenite from farther away—accumulated in the great houses, with almost nothing in the unit pueblos. "Chaco Canyon became a black hole into which goods were imported but from which nothing tangible was exported," one author observes, while "Chaco society turned into a mini-empire, divided between a well-fed elite living in luxury and a less well-fed peasantry doing the work and raising the food."[5]

Differences in life continued after death. Great houses included rooms clearly designed as tombs, where the bodies of an elite few rested with an array of such exotic goods as turquoise, shell beads, rare minerals, ceremonial sticks, and pottery vessels. None of these items appear in the graves of lesser individuals, buried simply beneath the floors of their unit pueblos. At Bonito, one funeral chamber in particular testifies to the hierarchy of Chaco society. Interred in a bed of sand were two men surrounded by some thirty thousand turquoise and shell beads and dozens of ceramic vessels, all covered by a lid of planks. Above the planks lay the remains of twelve other men, whose disarticulated bones and disorderly positions suggest that they were killed during funerary rites for the favored pair.[6]

Such rituals indicate not only the gap between the powerful and the weak, but the ritual significance of great houses. They were major ceremonial centers where those adept at mobilizing the powers of the sun, the rain, and the earth performed the rites that allowed crops to grow and people to thrive. Pueblo Bonito, for instance, was laid out in two balanced halves divided by a row of rooms, possibly reflecting dualities both in relationships among kin groups and the balance of forces in the world of spirit beings. Some architectural features seem to have been designed to serve as astronomical observatories to track the passage of the sun and moon and the rotation of the skies around a northern axis. Ceremonies marking the seasons and important points in the agricultural calendar would have drawn hundreds of pilgrims from the countryside to the open spaces and kivas of the great houses.

One of the most striking characteristics of Chaco is the network of some 250 miles of roads that spreads out from the canyon, sometimes linking cities to one another, sometimes apparently providing sacred pathways to the cardinal directions. Proceeding with perfect straightness until, with a logic lost to us, making an abrupt zig or zag, the roads were cut a few inches into the earth or lined with boulders or stone walls, and they included flights of steps to surmount obstacles or descend to the canyon floor. Literally and symbolically, these roads placed Chaco Canyon at the heart of a vast web of power mobilized on behalf of the people. "A group of leaders, their kin, and retainers . . . lived in Great Houses at the exact center of the world," an archaeologist concludes. "The people supported the Lords of the Great House through levies and taxes; the Lords did not work."[7]

Yet there was much work to be done. To build just one of the several hundred rooms in each pueblo, more than forty tons of sandstone had to be cut from canyon cliffs and hauled by human effort to the construction site. To roof and floor the twelve cities in the canyon, as many as two hundred thousand large trees had to be felled with stone axes and dragged more than fifty miles from their nearest source, for nearby areas had been quickly deforested. Kivas large and small were constructed with meticulous care, with extravagant use of scarce wood for roof timbers, careful preparation of veneered stone walls, and laborious displacement of earth to build terraces and foundations and to create thirty- to sixty-foot-diameter rooms dug to a depth of six feet or more. One scholar calculates that construction of one such great kiva alone would have required nearly thirty thousand person-hours of work.[8]

Only two possibilities for mobilizing labor and resources on these scales present themselves. Perhaps there was an extraordinary outpouring of voluntary effort, motivated by a combination of religious zeal and competition among kin groups for prestige. More likely, something like slave labor, coerced from the lesser folk who lived in unit pueblos, did the heavy work. Few archaeological topics are more sensitive, or more passionately debated, than the possibility that slave labor built the great houses of Chaco Canyon. Yet, to a degree that unsettles our preferred view of the Native American past—but that is evoked by the enmity conveyed in the Navajo term *Anasazi*—the power of this society likely did rest on the exploitation of conquered and subordinated foes. A story told today among Navajo people says that a figure named Noquilpi, or the Great Gambler, lived at

Chaco Canyon and, having enslaved all of his neighbors by winning games of chance, made them build him a massive house.

Whether or not gambling was involved, the basic story of enslavement fits not only with the material disparities between great houses and surrounding dwellings but with archaeological evidence of brutal warfare in the region before the rise of Chaco and the presumed regional peace its warriors enforced. During that period of pacification, a remarkable level of violence continued, marked by what one archaeologist euphemistically calls "nonformally buried bodies, fragmented burials, and processed human remains."[9] Evidence of what can only be interpreted as bloody massacres of entire families and communities appears in many outlying settlement sites, as well as in several of Pueblo Bonito's many rooms—where victims seem to have been brought to endure public deaths that may have involved ritual cannibalism. The most compelling analyses of the admittedly ambiguous evidence suggest that armed gangs systematically employed terror and occasional mass executions to enforce the common people's support of the elite. The Acoma Pueblo story does not say, but it is tempting to speculate that such scenes were in the minds of those who "went through the ceremony of forgetting . . . and left their sickness and trouble behind."

Far to the east, similar horrors may have accompanied the rise of agricultural centers in and around the Mississippi River Valley. In this area of abundant rainfall and numerous riverside flood plains, artificial irrigation and water conservation were irrelevant. Instead, the key to the spread of corn-bean-squash agriculture was the adaptation of crops to a shorter growing season. The exact mode of transition and places of innovation may never be known, but during the onset of the Medieval Warm Period the marvelous adaptability of maiz de ocho (or some locally developed relative) allowed Native farmers to reduce the time between planting and harvest to as little as ninety days. In succeeding centuries, the original eight rows of kernels expanded to ten, twelve, or fourteen, and blue, red, white, and yellow hues signaled nearly infinite variations. New kinds of squashes and legumes also multiplied.

For easily worked flood plain soils, eastern people developed an impressively simple agricultural technology. Using only a digging stick to make a hole in which to plant the seeds and a stone hoe to build up a hill around growing plants, they planted corn, beans, and squash together in the same fields. Growing beans twined around corn stalks, while broad-leaved squash vines retarded weed infestations and retained moisture in the soil. Once the squash vines began to spread, little weeding or other tending was necessary until the crops matured. In the East, even more than in the Southwest, all of this activity occurred in a realm gendered female. In later times, women dug the hills, tended the plants, and harvested the crops. A traditional story among Creek Indians explains that the Creator originally arranged for hoes to do the chores without human assistance, but that "some wicked women passed a field where the hoes . . . were at work and made fun of them. "'Since you are not contented with my plan, henceforth do the work for yourselves,'" the Creator said, "and ever since the women have worked the fields."[10] That women did so during the Medieval Warm Period is suggested by everything from studies of female arm bones showing clear signs of hard labor to a thousand-year-old bauxite figurine found in the American Bottom region, where the Illinois, Missouri, and Mississippi rivers converge. It depicts a woman hoeing the back of the earth, which is personified as a serpent from which squash vines sprout to cover the cultivator's back.

In the American Bottom, the agricultural revolution evoked by that figurine gave birth to the greatest urban center that North America would ever see before the mid-eighteenth century. We have no idea what the place was called by its inhabitants, who might have numbered twenty thousand, but it has long been known to both Native and Euro-American people as Cahokia. The spot had been inhabited since approximately the year 700. Within a few decades around 1050, fueled by the new agriculture and, presumably, the rituals believed necessary to sustain it, Cahokia underwent a rapid transformation, its population increasing by a factor of five. The centerpiece of a massive building project was a four-sided flat-topped pyramid now called "Monk's Mound," covering sixteen acres at its base and rising at the highest of its several levels to one hundred feet above a fifty-acre earthwork plaza. Inside and outside a protective palisade wall were dozens of smaller pyramids and mounds, along with thousands of public buildings, communal houses, and storage structures. At one edge of the city, a circular arrangement of posts, built and rebuilt several times in varying configurations, tracked the movements of the sun, which during the equinoxes appeared to rise from inside the main temple pyramid.

Several smaller mound centers, usually interpreted as subsidiary towns whose chiefs owed allegiance to a paramount chief at Cahokia, dotted the 250-square-mile American Bottom area. As in the Southwest, exotic goods from all over the continent found their way to these centers. Just as great houses in the Southwest depended upon unit pueblos, the American Bottom cities and towns were supported by a network of agricultural hamlets that shared little of the urbanites' material wealth. And, like scholars of the Southwest, archaeologists of this region disagree mightily, but a strong case can be made that the residents of the hamlets were conquered and enslaved peoples. At the least, most experts agree that this was a highly stratified society, with a vast gulf between the common people and the elite.

Cahokia was among the earliest, and certainly the largest, of many such population centers that flourished along with the agricultural revolution throughout the Mississippi, Ohio, and Arkansas river valleys, the interior Southeast, and the upper Florida peninsula. Lumped together by scholars as "Mississippian," these many chiefdoms probably did not share a common language or political affiliation. Instead, they appear to have participated in local variations on three interlocking religious practices.

The first, long predating the agricultural revolution, involved death and the afterlife. For many centuries in this part of the continent, mound building had been integral to funeral rituals. Practices varied greatly across time and space, but it was common for burial to be a three-stage process extending over several years. Bodies of the deceased might be either cremated or exposed on a platform until the flesh decayed, or both, with the bones then carefully gathered and stored communally in a "charnel house," where they would be tended by religious specialists. At some point in the ritual calendar, the charnel house and its contents would be burned to the ground, and everything would be covered with earth. This process, if repeated regularly over the decades at a particular sacred spot, gradually created substantial earthworks. Many of the mounds at Cahokia and other Mississippian sites were of this sort, and were probably associated with particular lineages and clans who buried their leaders there. As in the Southwest, some high-status burials involved the wholesale slaughter of lesser folk. The corpse of one elite Cahokia man not only was placed on twenty thousand shell beads carefully arranged in the form of a bird, but was buried next to fifty-three ritually executed young women. Analysis of the victims' remains reveals that they were poorly nourished and had been born elsewhere, telling markers of captivity and enslavement.[11]

Other mounds—the most imposing ones—focused more on life than on death and, if they were not an entirely novel product of the agricultural revolution, they seem to have been central to a second set of rituals, which dealt with the forces that caused crops to grow. Embodying the four cardinal directions in their square, flat-topped shapes, carefully placed with respect to the movements of the sun, mediating between the realms of earth and sky, and renewed on a cyclical basis with additional layers of earth, such mounds and their surrounding plazas were the setting for the communal rituals that sustained life.

Presiding over realms of both life and death with a third set of religious practices were a few elite chiefs whose esoteric knowledge gave access to sources of power. Their rituals apparently centered on a "warfare/cosmogony complex," combining imagery of bloodshed and weaponry with evocations of powerful spiritual beings. Shell artifacts incised with figures bearing war clubs and severed heads, ear ornaments in the shape of human heads, fierce birdlike and serpentine beings, crosses presumably representing the four cardinal directions, hard-to-interpret "weeping eye" motifs—such things are found in high-status burials at nearly every major Mississippian center.[12] Evoking both life and death and crafted of exotic raw materials often transported from great distances, these items embodied the awe-inspiring forces chiefs could mobilize.

In ritual as well as physical life, Mississippians worked out the North American corn-beans-squash agricultural revolution in a way very different from that of their contemporaries in the Southwest. Yet these divergent cultural forms that flourished after the year 900 shared far more than their crops and their unprecedented densities of population. To an arresting degree, transforming the landscape became central to the experiences of these first large-scale North American agriculturalists. This involved more than merely planting seeds and coaxing them to grow, molding the landscape to preserve scarce moisture, and digging canals to divert watercourses. In the Southwest it entailed the quarrying of stones, the molding of mud into adobe, the transporting of rare desert timber across considerable distances, and the combination of these materials to build permanent structures that reached into the sky.

More important, it involved digging into the earth—to plant crops, to construct semi-subterranean houses, and especially to build great kivas, where the people conducted rituals necessary to channel the forces that made crops grow and the balances that kept humans and the earth working together. There is every reason to believe that these kivas, with their single central roof openings, symbolized the place from which the ancestors emerged from the underworld to populate the upper world; this is how later Pueblo peoples explained their similar structures. Among Mississippians, meanwhile, ritual transformation of the earth became almost an obsessive form of cultural work. Monk's Mound, at Cahokia, in itself contains more than twenty-one million cubic feet of earth evidently carried to the site one basket at a time. Built in a single extended operation and carefully engineered to withstand erosion, the structure would have taken an estimated 370,000 days of labor to complete.[13] Resembling inverted kivas, such mounds—and the human power that went into their construction—mediated between the world above and the world below.

To begin to understand the significance of such work, and why such complex social, political, and ritual forms evolved around it, requires going beyond archaeological remains to explore what later Native American oral traditions say about the forces involved. If, among the hundreds of language and religious traditions in North America, there were any common ways of understanding the world, they had to do with the nature of power and how it was mobilized. Everything—or rather every*one*—in this world and the next, in the underworld and the sky world, embodied, conveyed, or possessed power. Native American understandings of the precise nature of that power varied—although most would say it was a mystery—but its existence was almost universally acknowledged.

More important than the nature of power itself was that it was associated with a vast range of "persons," only a small minority of whom were humans but all of whom displayed familiar emotions, needs, motives, and moral strengths and weaknesses. Other-than-human persons included such elemental forces as the sun, the rain, the four winds, and the earth itself, along with animals, plants, streams, mountains, and any number of other actors capable of influencing the course of events. Blurring the line between such clearly other-than-human persons and human persons were, in endless cultural variety, perhaps gods with complicated personalities, perhaps ancestral progenitors who fell from the sky or emerged from the earth, perhaps culture heroes or trickster figures who might intervene in history at any time, perhaps great primordial animals such as the Bear, the Wolf, or the Turtle from which human clans descended, perhaps personal guardian spirits, perhaps even one's own soul, which could leave and return to the physical body at will. The deceased and the unborn were also beings of power whose characteristics were not quite like those of mortal human persons.

Such persons could intervene in humans' lives in a variety of visible and invisible ways. The effects could be for good or ill, or, better put, either advantageous or disadvantageous. This was not so much because other-than-human persons were inherently good or evil, but simply because they *were* persons who had their own aims and who might or might not find themselves obligated to work with others. Thus, the sun might either encourage other-than-human food plants to grow, or scorch them to withered stalks. Those plants in turn might bear fruit that human persons could eat, or refuse to do so. Similarly, deer and other animals might voluntarily give themselves up to be eaten, or make themselves scarce. The power wielded might be great or small, far more than human persons could muster on their own, or insignificant by comparison. Often the power was dangerous and could be safely dealt with only indirectly, through intermediaries and elaborate ceremonies. Whatever the case, human persons had to ally themselves with both human and, especially, other-than-human persons to channel power in productive ways. Among human persons, the brokering of alliances required interpersonal skills and character traits that nearly every later Native culture placed at the center of its moral universe: a subordination of self to community, an ability to cultivate peace, harmony, balance, consensus.

Beneath these ideals, four intertwined mechanisms undergirded the mobilization of power and the structure of leadership. First and most fundamental were the ties of kinship. The most effective source of collective power was a large multigenerational household, with the obligations of members of an extended matrilineage (or, in some societies, patrilineage, traced through the father's line) and with ever-ramifying ties of marriage linking it with other households in one's own town or in others nearby. In most cultures, lineages were part of larger groupings called clans, believed to be descended from some other-than-human ancestor, that united people across multiple communities. Such kinship ties provided power not just in sheer numbers of human persons but, more importantly, in the product of their various labors. Most of the work that mattered—farming, hunting, food preparation and storage, dozens of other daily and occasional tasks—was collective and intensely dependent on the work of other segments of the kin group. Together, women and men, old and young, wives and husbands, girls and boys, aunts and nieces, uncles and nephews fed the group, nourished its wealth, and ensured its success in the world. In such an interdependent, kin-defined world, people without kin had no defined place. Perhaps they were even other-than-human. Thus, war captives and conquered villages—as beings unrelated to the families of their the victors—were fit to be killed or enslaved, if they could not be somehow transformed into kin through ritual adoption.

The economic ties that knit households together—and that made persons without kin so alien—point toward a second source of power and alliance: economic obligations. The available archaeological and folkloric evidence suggests that exchanges of labor, goods, and other resources in medieval North America seldom occurred in a context we would recognize as "buying" and "selling." Instead, exchanges were couched in terms of "gifts." Yet this was no utopian world of generosity and harmony, for a gift can be a inegalitarian, protean social force. Young men and young women were required to give the fruits of their agricultural, hunting, gathering, and domestic labors to the larger kin group; to do otherwise would be selfish, deficient in the generosity most prized in a gift economy. The elders, in return, redistributed goods from the food, the material resources, and the social capital they controlled on behalf of the kin group, thus creating further obligations among those who received.

All gifting thus, in some sense, became competitive. Prestige, social status, and political influence went to those most visibly in a position to give material and cultural resources away, and thus to create unequal bonds of obligation. The obligations of the enslaved, who owed their lives to their captors, were incalculably greater. If this interpretation is correct, the food stores and exotic goods accumulated at Pueblo Bonito and Cahokia were markers of the importance of such places not because of their mere accumulation, but because they allowed political leaders to display their conspicuous generosity, their conspicuous control of labor and goods, and thus their ability to channel power.

The connection between material goods and personal and collective status clarifies the importance of a third source of power and alliance in medieval North American agricultural societies: the ability to control access to human and material resources outside the community, resources that went beyond what one's own kin and neighbors could supply. With respect to human persons, external resources could be channeled either through war or diplomacy. Many later North American societies drew sharp boundaries to protect the everyday world of local kin and community from these dangerous attempts to access external power, and their medieval predecessors probably did so as well. Symbolically, if not in actuality, the domestic space of the agricultural town was identified with women and insulated from the external world associated with men; as later Iroquoian-speaking peoples of the Northeast would put it, the village was female and the forest was male. Within the symbolically male world of external affairs, meantime, separate categories of leadership and ritual presided over the martial realm of war and the peaceful arena of diplomatic alliance and gift-exchange, with war chiefs and peace chiefs serving distinct roles. Later Muskogean-speakers of the Southeast even went so far as to label entire towns "red" for war and "white" for peace.

Ample archaeological evidence testifies to the ubiquity of warfare in North America: palisades and other defensive structures constructed around villages, martial imagery carved on material artifacts, weapons suited more to killing humans than to killing animals, charred and butchered bones, mass graves, the existence of subsidiary agricultural hamlets near major urban centers. At the peak of their influence, centers like Pueblo Bonito and Cahokia might have provided peace and stability within their regional domains, as North American analogues of the Eastern Hemisphere's *pax Romana*. And like the peace of ancient Rome, Native American stability apparently rested on overwhelming military force near home and constant warfare on the peripheries. If an almost universal later North American pattern is any guide, a principal measure of success in war was the taking of captives. This created a sort of forced alliance in which the power of enemies could be absorbed either symbolically through scalping, ritual execution, and in some cases cannibalism, or literally through incorporation of the vanquished into the community through adoption or enslavement. The process of extending power through warfare was enhanced by other practices, such as the presentation of captive slaves to a military ally as a gift to seal a political relationship.

Like most societies in human history, those of medieval North America glorified martial violence: they bestowed exalted social status on warriors who increased their power in these ways, and they heaped shame on those who were conquered and enslaved. But there is also every reason to believe that a countervailing ideology embracing peace was at work among both elites and commoners—at least, this is what is implied by everything we know about the ritual dualities of war and peace among the descendants of these societies. In the Southwest, the contests enacted on ball courts channeled aggressive impulses and internal social and political disputes into forms less deadly than outright warfare. Among Mississippians, the activity later known as *chunkey* must have served similar functions: in a large open plaza, contestants rolled distinctive two- to three-inch disks made of stone or ceramics and attempted to stop them by throwing wooden poles in their path. Tobacco pipes, often with bowls carefully shaped in contemplative human or other-than-human figures were prominent features of peace councils among later Native Americans; no doubt they served similar functions in medieval times. And while we can have no direct access to the oral traditions people recited as they smoked such pipes, they probably taught the virtues of peace over war, cooperation over violence. Whether listeners actually took the lessons to heart is, as always in human history, another matter.

In the peaceful realm of diplomacy rather than warfare with outsiders, the ways in which people mobilized power were largely an extension of the ways in which they did so within their local communities. Just as leaders brokered relationships—of kinship and marriage, exchange and mutual obligation—with their counterparts within and among villages, they tried to do the same with people who spoke differently, practiced different rituals, and had access to important material resources and other advantages. Precisely because such people were alien, and because they had goods and powers that were exotic, it took particular skill to make them surrogate kin and to establish ties of mutual obligation that brought exotic resources into one's community. The source of a peace leader's power—or rather of the power he mobilized on behalf of his matrilineal kin group and his community—rested on his personal ability to make connections, to forge far-flung alliances, and to establish exchange routes that brought exotic or essential goods into the community. At some point, as the alienness of languages and practices increased and as the sources of goods became ever more distant and strange, the process shifted from alliances with human persons to connections with other-than-humans. Dealing with folk whose speech was incomprehensible and whose customs seemed barbaric differed less in kind than in scale from interacting with mysterious beings who dwelled beneath salt waters a thousand miles from today's Arizona or Illinois or who lived in realms above the sky. In every case, one hoped to make the connections necessary to mobilize power.

So we can begin to understand the exotic copper, feathers, marine shell, and mineral artifacts that figure so prominently in the material goods left behind at Pueblo Bonito and in the Mississippian centers. Such "prestige goods" were visible markers of powerful connections, valuable not so much for their inherent qualities as for the human and other-than-human transactions they brought to mind. Prestige goods, one anthropologist explains, "constitute a type of inalienable wealth, meaning they are goods that cannot be conceptually separated from their place or condition of origin but always relate whoever possesses them to that place or condition." The potency of such goods comes from their association with their source, often described as "ancestral beings—creator deities, culture-heroes, primordial powers—that are credited with having first created or crafted the world, its creatures, its peoples, and their cultural skills."[14] Chiefs and other political leaders wore such items on their bodies, displayed them during ceremonies, or stored them in temples to symbolize the alliances made on behalf of their people—and they redistributed them to followers and allies to further broaden the circle of associations. Indeed, one of the principal functions of centers such as Cahokia seems to have been to disperse particularly potent goods far and wide among allied communities. Distinctive styles of ear ornaments and chunkey stones, for instance, seem to have been produced at Cahokia for this purpose.

Prestige goods, then—whether symbolizing an alliance of equals in the next town, the ties that bound lesser villages to great ritual centers, or the mysterious relationships between human and other-than-human persons—were visual displays of power, the power mobilized by a successful leader on behalf of his kin and community. Apart from the transactions in which they originated, they had little if any value. This helps to explain why, on archaeological sites, items such as shell, metal, and turquoise are most often associated with the burial of high-status individuals. When a chief died, his human and other-than-human connections died with him, or went with him to wherever the spirit of the deceased traveled next. Succeeding chiefs had to reestablish alliances, to acquire and redistribute their own symbolic exotic goods, on the basis of what presumably was a prior career of cultivating connections. This highly personalized quality of chieftainship provides the most convincing explanation for the frequent rise and fall in influence of particular towns and cities apparent in the archaeological record—a phenomenon scholars call "chiefly cycling," in which regional centers came and went over time, waxing and waning in their influence with respect to each other. Lacking a monopoly of force to defend their privileges, chiefs depended for their status on a fragile ideological consensus at home and on equally fragile sources of supply abroad that they could not directly control.[15]

Particularly for centers such as Pueblo Bonito or Cahokia, the power of chiefs and the status of cities apparently depended not only on kinship, reciprocal economic obligations, and the ability to mobilize the alliances represented by exotic goods, but also on access to esoteric knowledge, especially regarding the other-than-human forces that ensured agricultural success. Gathering together unprecedented numbers of people dependent on the produce of the soil, established in ecological niches where water was always the crucial variable (too little in the Southwest, too much on Mississippian flood plains), yet mobilizing material and spiritual powers no lesser communities could amass, chiefs and lineages who claimed to understand what was necessary to control the sun, the rains, and the ways of corn, beans, and squash took on enormous cultural importance. "Humans, animals, natural forces, and supernatural spirits were all intricately related in balanced ties of reciprocity," explains a scholar of later Pueblo society. "So long as people performed religious rites joyfully and precisely, careful that every prayer was word-perfect and full of verve, and that the ritual paraphernalia was exact to the last detail, the forces of nature would reciprocate with their own uninterrupted flow." Ceremony thus ensured that "the sun would rise and set properly, the seasons of the year would come and go, bringing rainfall and verdant crops in summer, and in the winter, game and snow."[16]

Summer and winter, rain and snow, ceased to come predictably in the Southwest somewhat earlier than elsewhere in the northern hemisphere. In both Chaco Canyon and the Mississippi Valley, dense populations had been living at the edge of the land's agricultural carrying capacity during the best years of the Medieval Warm Period. Perhaps the extraordinary religious fervor, political capital, and material resources devoted to agricultural ceremonies in both places shows a cultural recognition of just how unstable the balance was. In the arid Southwest, the balance had always been particularly delicate, and collapse appears to have come suddenly—not with the onset of global cooling in the early 1300s, but with a fifty-year-long local drought that struck the Chaco Canyon area after 1130, at the height of the Warm Period. The elite appear to have abandoned Pueblo Bonito and the other great houses of Chaco to move approximately one hundred miles north to the site known today as "Aztec Ruins," where they rebuilt their great houses and kivas and presumably continued to assert their sovereignty over common people. Within a century, those great houses too, were abandoned. One theory is that the rulers then moved hundreds of miles south to Casas Grandes (also called Paquime), in what is today northern Mexico, where they found a new local population to dominate and new sources of prestige goods to display their power.

Whatever the case, within a few generations the entire remaining commoner population of the Four Corners dispersed to more ecologically sustainable communities elsewhere. Another series of droughts struck the Southwest in the last quarter of the thirteenth century, followed shortly thereafter by two centuries of unpredictable rainfall that was the hallmark of the Little Ice Age there. All of the major Ancestral Puebloan and Hohokam urban centers were gradually abandoned in favor of new pueblos, most occupied for only a generation until the people moved on to still newer locations. These settlements tended to be fairly large and to be designed for defense in a period of military chaos. The former, stratified system of smaller supporting villages apparently disappeared in favor of a more egalitarian settlement pattern.

The fragile importance of the abandoned urban centers for ritual as well as agriculture is suggested by the Acoma tradition of those who left their homes and migrated south to leave their trouble behind and enact "the ceremony of forgetting." This particular tale is apparently not shared by neighboring modern Pueblo peoples, but it is part of a common larger cycle of stories that explain why ordinary people can no longer directly interact with the other-than-human persons known as *kachina,* ancestral beings who live half the year on earth and half the year in the underworld, who mediate between humans and spirits, and who form the clouds that bring rain to nourish crops. In the Acoma story, some kachina had been killing human people, provoking a battle in which hero figures called the Warrior Twins slew them, only to bring the spirits back to life in the form of human impersonators, or kachina dancers. Thenceforth, the other-than-human persons visited only in this indirect, ceremonial way.

Archaeological evidence confirms that a new set of rituals emerged in the thirteenth and fourteenth centuries as people dispersed from the old ceremonial sites. Depictions of kachinas first appear on kiva wall murals during this period. At the same time, open plazas that were probably used for kachina dances resembling the ceremonies that remain central to Hopi ceremonial life today became prominent features of pueblos. Egalitarian and widely participatory, with large numbers of dancers wearing masks representing countless different kachinas, these new rituals stood in stark contrast to the elite centralized ceremonies presumed to have taken place in the great kivas of Chaco Canyon. In this and countless other ways, "the remarkable shifts in Pueblo architecture, settlement, iconography, and society around 1300, when sites begin to look like modern pueblos, represent Pueblo peoples' conscious, deliberate reaction to and rejection of Chaco, distancing themselves from that bad experience."[17]

It is tempting to speculate that a similar Native American religious reformation, a similar rejection of ceremonial and political hierarchies, accompanied the abandonment of Cahokia and its environs in the early years of the Little Ice Age. But all we can do is speculate. The only certainty is that not only the city itself but the entire American Bottom area was abandoned shortly after 1300; its peoples dispersed to parts unknown, preserving no stories clearly connected to the place (although Siouan-speaking peoples of the eastern plains do have traditions of origins in the general region). One catastrophe after another had struck Cahokia during the thirteenth century: nearly fifty years of droughts, an apparent military attack that burned the main palisade, a major earthquake that damaged Monk's Mound. These events must have undermined the supernatural claims on which the power of Cahokia's chiefs rested and must have called into question the efficacy of the agricultural ceremonies over which they presided. Indeed, it seems that, for a generation or so, Monk's Mound was abandoned and that multiple decentralized rituals were taking place on other mounds within the district. Then these as well ceased.

A similar collapse of both ceremonial and political authority seems to have occurred during the fourteenth century at every other major Mississippian city. Moundville, near today's Tuscaloosa, Alabama, for instance, was, in its thirteenth-century heyday, second in size and influence (albeit a distant second) only to Cahokia. Built on a three-hundred-acre palisaded site, with the principal of its twenty-six mounds rising fifty-eight feet into the air, it had been home to approximately a thousand people and had dominated a regional population of around ten thousand.[18] By about 1350, almost all residents of the city seem to have departed, though some of the mounds apparently continued in ceremonial and mortuary use for more than a century. Parallel stories can be told of such lesser cities as Winterville, in today's state of Mississippi, and Etowah, in Georgia.

The most intriguing hints of the end of the Mississippian phenomenon comes from its westernmost major center, Spiro, in today's Oklahoma. As at Moundville, most of its once-sizable residential population apparently dispersed in the late thirteenth century, but Spiro continued to be the site of funerals and other ceremonies until approximately 1400, when a massive charnel house containing the bones of generations of chiefs and the largest store of distinctively Mississippian prestige goods apparently ever accumulated was interred in a climactic ceremony that appears to have marked the final abandonment of the site.

The textbooks say that Mississippian cultures long outlived Spiro, as simple and complex chiefdoms continued to build mounds throughout the Southeast into the sixteenth—and, in the case of the Natchez people of the lower Mississippi Valley, the eighteenth—century. Yet the great cultural efflorescence represented by Cahokia and its contemporaries came to an end with the Little Ice Age. Nothing on the scale of political and ceremonial power mobilized at the great medieval centers would ever be seen again. As in the Southwest, related but smaller-scale and less enduring political communities replaced their predecessors. And, as in the Southwest, the ceremonial life that mobilized power seems to have become more widely participatory, less centered on the esoteric knowledge of a tiny elite. As just one of many examples, in the eighteenth century everyone among the Choctaw descendants of what might well have been the inhabitants of Moundville enjoyed the several-stage burial process previously restricted to the Mississippian elite. A later Cherokee tradition seems to recall more directly the transition from centralized elitism to a more egalitarian society, in a story about the violent overthrow of a corrupt, oppressive priestly class called the *Aní-Kutání*.

Despite the disappearance of the great urban centers and the retreat from centralized hierarchy, core elements of the medieval synthesis en-

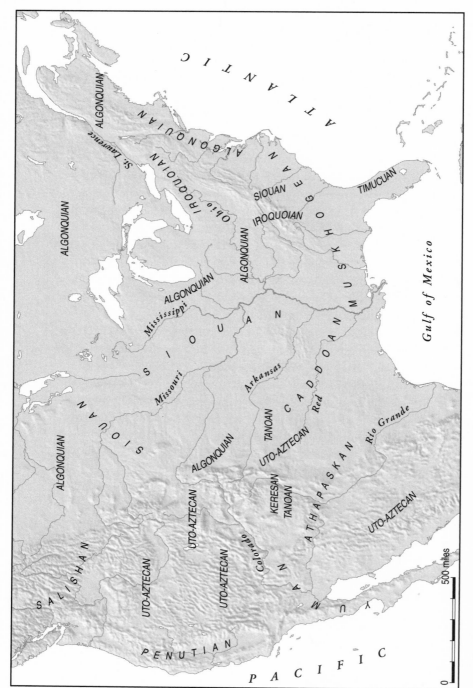

Major language families of North America, ca. 1600.

dured. Even at the peak of Mississippian power, the vast majority of the agricultural population lived not in cities but in small hamlets of a few dozen to a few hundred people, and they continued to do so throughout the fifteenth and sixteenth centuries. The agricultural revolution of the Medieval Warm Period was permanent, and continued its spread through the continent after 1300. By that time, the flood plains of the Missouri and Arkansas river systems had filled with villages of fifty to three hundred people who were the ancestors of Caddoan-speaking Arikaras, Pawnees, and Wichitas, Siouan-speaking Hidatsas and Mandans, and others. Living in communal earth lodges, mixing agriculture with bison hunting, trading and warring with hunter-gatherers from areas of the Plains unsuited to agriculture, and participating in the same far-flung prestige-goods exchange networks as had the Mississippians and Ancestral Puebloans, these peoples appear to have been organized in small-scale chiefdoms with none of the monumental ritual sites characteristic of the great population centers of medieval North America. Much the same was true of a vast swath of territory north of the Ohio River and south of the Canadian Shield, which was the northern limit for growing seasons long enough for agriculture.

During the Medieval Warm Period, then, corn-beans-squash agriculture and a way of life based upon it took permanent hold nearly everywhere the climate allowed. Agriculture was so transformative that Native American origin stories talk, almost universally, about the introduction of corn, beans, and squash as one of the founding spiritual gifts given to the original people—as if there were no time when food crops did not exist. It was as if, in the agricultural revolution, the Native American world began over again.

The major exceptions were in Alaska, much of today's Canada, the arid Great Plains, and the Great Basin of the Southwest, where agriculture was not possible, and on the Pacific Coast, where the complex chiefdoms of the ancestors of Tlingits, Tsimshians, and Haidas were based on salmon fishing rather than farming. Among the peoples of these regions, only the Algonquian-speaking hunter-gatherers of Hudson Bay and the far northeast would have much contact with Europeans before the middle of the eighteenth century. The French began building trading posts in what is now Manitoba only in 1731; Russians arrived in Alaska only in 1741; Spanish occupation of California began only in 1769. The vast majority of North American societies that encountered Europeans in the three centuries after 1492 were farmers, children of the agricultural revolutions that swept the continent beginning in the tenth century.

The timing, scope, and character of North Americans' agricultural revolutions set their diverse societies apart from the equally diverse peoples of Central America and the Caribbean. In the west, lightly populated desert expanses isolated the North American Southwest from the Valley of Mexico and the Yucatan, although constant small-scale interaction occurred. In the east, sea currents made it difficult for boats without sails to navigate the hundred miles that separated the Florida peninsula from Cuba and the other islands of the Caribbean, which had primarily been peopled by migrants paddling northward from South America. North Americans, shaped by their own histories and traditions, stood apart. Divided by language, endlessly varied in local customs and beliefs, they were nonetheless united by common substrata: subsistence patterns combining agriculture, hunting, and gathering, extended and often matrilineal kinship, long-distance trade, decentralized chiefdom forms of political organization, and common understandings of power relationships. Mobilizing power through exchanges of goods and benefits, creating the connections that brought benefits to one's people, comprehending that power flowed *through* leaders rather than from them—these were the enduring elements of North America's medieval cultural synthesis that sixteenth-century Native peoples would bring to their encounters with Western Europeans.

TWO

Legacies of Conquest
from Medieval Europe

UNBEKNOWNST TO MEDIEVAL North Americans, on the opposite side of
the Atlantic others were likewise raising monuments to a new kind of agricultural civilization. Who would at first think to juxtapose cathedrals, with
their soaring columns of stone and windows of stained glass, with the tow-
ering walls of Pueblo Bonito or the earthen mounds of Cahokia? Yet the
comparison is worth pursuing, if only because the style of Western European architecture later known as "Gothic," and the distinctive notions of
sacred landscape it created, took shape in France and England almost simultaneously with their North American counterparts and reached full
flower at the peak of the Warm Period in the mid-thirteenth century.
Usually built on ancient holy sites and often incorporating portions of
much earlier buildings, cathedrals, like temple mounds, often took generations to erect, though occasionally, like England's Salisbury or North
America's Cahokia, the work occurred in fairly short order. In relative
terms, the amounts of labor and materials mobilized with simple technologies were similarly astonishing: Salisbury needed at least 60,000 tons of
stone painstakingly hauled by oxcart from distant quarries, 2,800 tons of
timber, 32,000 square feet of glass, four hundred tons of lead, and incalculable loads of chalk-and-sand mortar. Church-building in France during
the two centuries after the year 1050 required more cut stone than did the
entire architectural history of ancient Egypt.[1]

Culturally, the comparisons are even more compelling: the soaring
spaces focusing human attention on the spirit world (and the spirit world's
attention on humans); the orientation to the cardinal points (a cathedral's

37

grand western entrance mediated between the sacred and the ordinary
and opened a vista to its screened choir and eastward-oriented great altar,
restricted to the holy men who knew its rituals); the association with the
remains of the dead (in surrounding graveyards, in crypts beneath the
floor, and particularly in the bones and relics of the exalted class of dead
known as "saints" that lent the place its power); the collections of other
rare and spiritually charged artifacts that cathedrals displayed; the calen-
drical ceremonies that drew pilgrims from far and wide; the political
power that sacred structures evoked for leaders and elite kin groups who
built them. Power moved through cathedrals even as it moved through
temple mounds or kivas, and it did so in ways rooted in an agricultural order that blossomed during the Medieval Warm Period and experienced a
crisis with the dawn of the Little Ice Age.

In Western Europe, no less than in North America, life altered dramatically in the Warm Period after the year 900; the cathedrals at Salisbury,
Chartres, and Reims were made possible by those changes. As in North
America, the transformations swept through an area that had long been on
the periphery of cultural innovation. In this respect, northwestern Europe
was to Greece and Rome as North America above the Rio Grande was
to Central America. As in North America, many developments have to
be pieced together tentatively from archaeological and other nonliterary
sources. Needless to say, environmental change was only one causal factor
among many complicated cultural processes, and there were major differences between developments on the two sides of the Atlantic—and of
course generalizations for either continent fail to hold always and everywhere. Still, there were striking parallels between North America's Mississippian and Ancestral Puebloan efflorescence and Western Europe's High
Middle Ages.
    Although some have questioned whether the term "agricultural revolu-
tion" is appropriate for Western Europe during this era, it is clear that dramatic changes in food production coincided with the Medieval Warm Period. The central innovation was the three-field system of crop rotation,
which began to take hold in much of northern Europe and Britain during
the tenth and eleventh centuries. Although historians are not as certain as
they once were about either its ubiquity or its novelty, the three-field system replaced in many areas an earlier agricultural model that Germanic

peoples of the northern parts of Western Europe had inherited from the Roman Empire. Many farmers had formerly used two sets of fields; one was cultivated and the other left fallow, and the cultivation would alternate from year to year. The main crop had been wheat, sometimes joined by plots of rye or other grains, planted in the autumn and harvested in the spring.

The new three-field pattern took advantage of climatic changes during the Warm Period to add summer crops to the ancient mix. The two-field system had always been better adapted to the wet, mild winters and dry summers of the ancient Mediterranean region than to the very different environments north of the Alps and the Pyrenees. The three-field system was not only better adapted to northern conditions, but substantially more productive than the Mediterranean model. For any given place, the three-field revolution increased the amount of land under annual cultivation by a third; a community that formerly cultivated, say, three hundred of its six hundred acres annually now farmed four hundred.[2] The transition may not have been quite as earthshaking as the replacement of North America's Old Eastern Agricultural Complex with a regime of corn, beans, and squash, but it was dramatic nonetheless. On both continents, new agricultural patterns transformed life in temperate zones.

In northwestern Europe, more was involved than new crops and a new organization of the landscape. A novel kind of yoke allowed horses to be employed as draft animals, augmenting the slower and less powerful oxen that still did much of the work. Horsepower was particularly useful in pulling improved heavy, wheeled plows, which were now frequently fitted with moldboards that turned as well as dug the soil. As these innovations spread, simple harrows made of wood also began to replace dragged thorn bushes in the chore of smoothing freshly plowed ground. An even simpler device—two pieces of wood attached together to make a flail—improved the process of threshing.

None of these changes occurred overnight, and all built upon precedents that were hundreds of years old. Nonetheless, the cumulative impact was striking. Vast areas either abandoned since the decline of Rome or never before cultivated were put into production. More important, the three-field system diversified the diet of ordinary people. Among the new summer crops were oats, barley, and a variety of legumes, including vetches, peas, lentils, and beans. The expanded availability of legumes (apparently grown previously, if at all, mostly as garden vegetables) was a major nutritional improvement to a diet formerly composed largely of daily bread. Western Europeans and North Americans discovered the virtues of the "musical fruit" at almost exactly the same time.

Most European households kept gardens, which, like the gathered vegetation of North America, contributed essential nutrients for at least part of the year. The extent to which this phenomenon was novel is unclear, and, even for the elite, the yield was what the most careful student of early medieval nutrition calls "a somewhat monotonous diet heavily oriented to members of the cabbage and onion families."[3] Most of the year, bread, gruel, porridge, and low-alcohol "small beer" dominated what, by modern medical or medieval North American standards, was an unhealthily impoverished menu. Still, the nutritional gains from Western Europe's agricultural revolution were substantial. As the system took full hold, in the eleventh through fourteenth centuries, the region's population seems to have roughly tripled.

There were countless local variations across space and time, but among that expanding European population the vast majority of people—85 to 90 percent in the thirteenth century—grew their own food in the manner just described. Much of the work was done collectively at the level of a small hamlet that, like most contemporary Native American villages, sheltered a few hundred people. Although each household claimed specific rights, plowmen's need to minimize awkward turns produced a characteristic pattern of long, narrow, deeply furrowed, common fields. In other ways, too, the expense and technological demands of working with teams of horses and heavy plows and with crops that had to be harvested quickly made separate family holdings impractical. Cultivated and fallow fields were large, scattered, and interspersed with common pastures and woodlots. All of these surrounded a village cluster of houses in which the people who worked the fields lived, a cluster whose central feature and most impressive structure was almost invariably a church. Mississippian villagers, with their houses gathered near a sacred mound and surrounded by cornfields and forest, would have understood the logic.

Despite the achievements of the agricultural system that came to dominate Western Europe, we cannot automatically conclude that it was inherently superior to the one that spread almost simultaneously through eastern North America. Maize was simply superior to wheat, at least in terms of its fecundity. One grain of European winter wheat produced only three to five grains at harvest time; modern farmers, by contrast, expect a return of one to twenty. More directly relevant, medieval North American farmers harvested, with far less labor, as many as two hundred grains of maize for each one they planted, without the laborious plowing, harrowing, sickling, threshing, and winnowing necessary for the meager European yield.[4] Meanwhile, metalworking, the harnessing of waterpower, and all the other much-vaunted technologies unknown in North America produced few visible benefits for overworked, undernourished European people whose wood- or mud-walled, thatched-roof, often chimneyless houses provided few fundamentally different indoor comforts from those of their North American counterparts—unless one counts as a comfort the sounds and smells of the cattle who sometimes shared a single roof with humans, separated from them only by a crude partition.

Such domestic animals, largely absent from North America's agricultural revolution, were a mixed blessing for Western European humans. Cheese, butter, and eggs provided crucial protein. Yet reliance on horses to do plowing and other work came at considerable cost: most of the new summer oat production went into equine stomachs. Other domestic animals—apart from pigs, goats, and fowl, who were mostly left to scavenge for themselves in the woods and thus occupied an ecological niche similar to North American deer—required similar trade-offs. Cattle (kept mostly for their labor and dairy products) and sheep (kept for their wool) could not survive just on the stubble of fallow fields; people who raised them had to set aside large tracts as pasturage and devote substantial amounts of land to fodder crops. Moreover, cattle and sheep were far too valuable to be slaughtered regularly for meat before they reached unappetizing old age or were about to starve when fodder ran short. The combination that one historian has labeled "the carbohydrates of the plough and the proteins of the forest," then, produced an inferior diet at a high cost in labor and in environmental degradation.[5]

The human costs were high as well. The new social and political forms associated with Western Europe's agricultural revolution took shape in a period of nearly constant bloodshed. Here, too, there were strong parallels with contemporary North American developments. Both sides of the Atlantic saw the glorification of war, the elevation of violence as social spectacle, and the emergence of a class of warriors that ultimately came to channel much of its aggression into highly ritualized but still deadly forms, while other voices tried to maintain a counter-ideal of peace.

But here the parallel developments of the two great medieval agricultural civilizations began to diverge. The divide had nothing to do with whether European knights or American warriors were more brutal toward their enemies; there was gore enough on all sides. Nor did it involve patterns of hereditary social differentiation; the perceived gap between an American paramount chief and a kinless enslaved captive was perhaps even more vast than that between a European lord and a serf. Instead, the key factor was a practice that both chief and captive would have found almost incomprehensible: the bizarre European custom according to which individual warriors were entitled to possess land in perpetuity, pass it on to their lineal descendants in the male line, and force others to do the work of making it productive. It is only a slight oversimplification to say that everything that makes medieval Western Europe and North America seem so incompatible derived from these intertwined practices.

Not to put too fine a point on it, the medieval Western European ruling class—all those glorified by titles and called "knights," "lords," and "kings"—were the descendants of thugs who had terrorized the region's population in the chaotic centuries since the end of effective Roman government and, most recently, since the breakup of Charlemagne's short-lived empire in the ninth century. Strong men with private armies—or rather gangs of heavily armed horsemen—offered weaker people protection from Vikings, Magyars, Muslims, and one another in exchange for increasingly onerous obligations. "The word 'protection' is used in our sources," a modern historian notes, "and if its meaning is today sometimes ambiguous, thanks to its association with the Mafia of Italy or the USA, that ambiguity would have been well understood by any early medieval lord."[6]

The protection racket extended in all directions through the system called "vassalage." The system of obligations usually labeled "feudal" encompassed what weaker parties ("vassals," a term derived from a Celtic word for "boy" or "servant") owed for the protection provided by stronger parties ("lords," from the Old English *hlaford*, "giver of loaf," provider of food).[7] At the bottom of the hierarchy, the vast majority of ordinary people owed labor, food, and everything else necessary to support their lord and his armed retainers. That lord in turn was the vassal of a greater lord, for whom he and his knights were bound to fight and to whom he owed various economic obligations. In theory, at the top of the hierarchy there should have been an emperor, heir to the caesars and Charlemagne. In practice, although a man holding that title claimed vassals throughout Central Europe and the Low Countries, there were multiple apexes at the level of those called "princes" and "kings." On every tier, lords sought opportunities to extort resources from those below them, in the form of taxes, fees, rents, and obligations that went by names such as *aid, relief, bar, heriot,* or *corvee.* Their powers rested not only on military and economic might, but on their rights to mete out justice in the manorial courts over which they presided, to appoint a priest for the village church, and to wield their vast authority in countless other ways.

In that village church, meanwhile—as in the great Christian cathedrals that, throughout Europe, served the function of temple mounds—a creed originally preached by a wandering prophet of forgiveness who had been executed in the most ignoble way mutated into a religion focused on an authoritarian judge-king who, on the Last Day, would wield his sword, cast his enemies into the fires of Hell, and grant arbitrary pardon to the few who acknowledged his lordship over all and had paid the price for their sins in this world and in Purgatory. A scene repeatedly painted above the main altars of medieval churches illustrated a passage from the Book of Revelation. "I saw the dead, great and small, standing before the throne, . . . and all were judged according to what they had done," John of Patmos said of the apocalypse he envisioned. "Anyone whose name was not found written in the book of life was thrown into the lake of fire."[8] Artists lavished far more attention on the pains of the burning many than on the joys of the saved few admitted to Paradise. Such gruesome images encouraged Europeans to give alms to the poor, to contribute to the building of great cathedrals, to feed and clothe the armies of priests, monks, and nuns who prayed for them and for sinful departed ancestors, to seek the intercession of deceased saints who had some claim on the Lord's favor, and in countless other ways to pay their feudal homage to a harsh heavenly king.

The same images also encouraged warriors to find in their arbitrary god a model for brutally slaying their enemies and literally lording it over their vassals. To wield such power, a knight needed a horse with appropriate equipage, a suit of armor, metal weapons, the free time to become well versed in their complicated use, and a variety of servants to see to his needs. The capacity of a warrior to maintain himself in this style rested on property rights to agricultural land—and rights to the labor of those who produced its fruits. "Land, in a pre-industrial society, was the source of (very nearly) all wealth," a modern study concludes. "Put simply, wealth brought you power because it allowed you to reward armed men who in turn allowed you to acquire further wealth in a variety of ways and defend the wealth you had."[9]

In theory, all land belonged to a king; English kings, especially after the Norman Conquest of 1066, were apparently more effective in exerting this claim than those on the Continent. Whatever the case, it is not too much of an overstatement to say that kings acquired land through one of three means: conquest (a polite term for murderous theft), the free grant of his liege subjects (a polite term for protection-racket extortion), or inheritance (a polite term for profiting from the thefts and extortions of one's ancestors). Warriors who fought on behalf of the king received in return landed estates, held as "fiefs," over which they in turn became lords and might carve out subfiefs they could grant to their own vassals—and so on until, in theory at least, all of society was knit together in a grand pyramid of protection and obligation. In practice, however, because fiefs and all their privileges over time became heritable (albeit subject to payments to the lord as they passed from generation to generation) and because everyone in the pyramid who mattered was well armed, the upper levels of the hierarchy had very little real leverage over the powerful men just below them. Any lord militarily and economically strong enough to build a castle on his fief and mobilize enough armed men to protect it was immune to most threats from above or below.

A king's real power, then, rested not on his mighty vassals, who were as much a threat as a support, but from his ability to maintain personal control over estates large enough to provide all the resources he needed. And those resources could be vast; in the 1230s, for example, King Henry III of England collected roughly £25,000 per year, while even the wealthiest baron was lucky to reap £1,000 and a typical knight £15 to £30.[10] Even so, the powers of kings were limited, resting more on their status as the greatest of local lords over their direct vassals than on the host of local lords who paid them allegiance; their real power to shape events was not much greater than that of a similarly honored North American paramount chief. At every point in the hierarchy, "generosity, sumptuous display, the provision of patronage and the furnishing of aid were all ways of expressing status, and they all required wealth," concludes a student of the early Western European Middle Ages who might as well have been speaking of

North America. "In return, they brought that loyalty and material and spiritual support which was the basis of power."[11]

From king to knight and at each status between, then, the keys to power were to hold and expand the lands one had, to fend off the worst forms of extortion from those above (including the king), and to extract the maximum return from those below. The vast majority of the people were so far below, that they were hardly in a position to play the game at all. The farmers the entire system claimed to protect—men who were unfree serfs, technically free "villeins," or members of the broad category lumped together as "peasants"—held their fiefs in the form of strips of land in the three-field system of their lord's estate. In return for their right to extract a meager living from those holdings, their obligation was to feed and support the lifestyle of their *seigneur*, or lord. These dues were paid in some combination of three forms—work, shares of the harvest, or money—with the first becoming rarer and the latter two more common over the decades. Perhaps as much as half of the farmer's meager yield went to his lord; from the rest, he had to feed his household and try to set aside a small surplus to exchange for things that he and his household could not produce themselves. This was no small feat in light of the fact that, in many areas, only about half the population had access to two acres of land—generally considered the bare minimum to support a household. Yet, even under the harshest conditions, peasants could find means to ward off the worst oppressions and carve out gains for themselves—if only by insisting that things be done as they always had been done. Over time, many came to hold multiple small fiefs from different seigneurs, gaining additional leverage.

And even male peasants—like all male household heads—had the right to exploit at least some other people's labor: those of their wives and dependent children. For another major difference between the two medieval civilizations—another odd characteristic of Western European society—was the radical attenuation of its kinship ties, contrasting with the close bonds that defined North American communities. If sagas, folktales, and early Roman chronicles are to be believed, the Germanic peoples of Northern Europe once had clans and lineages that, except for their patrilineal rather than matrilineal lines of descent, would have been familiar in their basic operating principles to Native North Americans. But through complicated processes of population movement, interaction with and incorporation into the late Roman Empire, and centuries of violent upheaval, nearly all of these broader connections peeled away, and the vast majority of people came to live in nuclear, rather than extended, family households. By the tenth century, even among the warrior elite, clan and lineage gave way to the simple line of patrilineal descent called the "house." For such a house, a long-ago, perhaps semifictional male ancestor who supposedly originated an iconic coat of arms preserved a pale reflection of the Bear, Turtle, or Wolf other-than-human persons who originated Native American clans.

Throughout Western Europe, residence patterns tended to be not only nuclear but "neo-local." When a couple married, instead of one spouse taking up residence with the extended family of the other, the pair established a separate new residence—albeit one still embedded in a village community of relatives. Neo-locality had several consequences for the social order and especially for the power of individual fathers, no matter how oppressed they might have been in the broader peasant scheme of things. "A man's home is his castle," it would later be said. However powerless a man might be outside his humble four walls, his pretensions to dominion over wife, children, and domestic animals paralleled those of his lord.

Yet many people never married at all, encouraged by a Roman Catholic Church that prized celibacy to leave their earthly father's home for their Heavenly Father's monasteries and convents. Those who married did so relatively late in life—at age twenty-five or beyond—largely because of the difficulty of acquiring access to the land necessary to support a household. Extending the period in which sons were subordinate to their biological fathers, late marriage emphasized the personal dominance of the household head. Keeping young women similarly subordinate before marriage, and severing most economic ties to their natal families thereafter, had the same effect. Reinforcing this subordination were Church teachings that declared unions an indissoluble sacrament (a doctrine first promulgated only in the medieval period) and legal codes that denied women the right to possess property of their own. Under England's common-law doctrine of "coverture," for instance, heritable property belonged to a woman's father or other guardian before marriage, and to her husband thereafter; as a *femme covert*, she had no independent standing in the world. Only an unmarried widow, and only as long as she remained unmarried, was exempt, as a *femme sole*, or "woman alone."

Household composition in general and the rights of women in particular, then, deeply divided the experiences of European and American kin-ship. Particularly at the upper levels of the social structure, broader kin connections within the lineal family remained very real, with varied eco-nomic responsibilities accruing to uncles, brothers, and cousins. But these relationships resembled the formal obligations that Native Americans as-sociated with members of their clan, rather than the intense, daily interac-tions with an extended lineage who shared a large common residence. Al-though various servants and unmarried or widowed relatives often joined a European conjugal couple and their children under the same roof, and al-though siblings, parents, and the rare surviving grandparent were likely to live nearby, such family life nonetheless would have appeared profoundly atomized to a Native American. On some very real level, attenuated lin-eages and neo-local residence made every European married man, no matter how poor, a ruling patriarch, in a way unimaginable in societies where more collective (but not necessarily more pleasant) patterns of age-graded and gendered power prevailed. The singular Christian command-ment to "honor thy father" had a meaning profoundly different from that of the common Native American injunctions to honor numerous "grandfa-thers" and be mindful of obligations stretching backward and forward in time through "seven generations."

The picture of medieval European society painted here is harsh—deliber-ately so, to stress how European and American societies, in many ways so parallel, also were imbued with fundamentally different basic operating principles. There were many local variations, many spaces for human initiative, and a constant need for those with power in Europe to wrap themselves in a mantle of Christian rituals and rules that, like the esoteric ceremonial knowledge of Mississippian chiefs, signified legitimacy in the minds of those they ruled.

And over time, from the tenth to the thirteenth centuries, the roughest edges and most brutal forms of exploitation smoothed. Agricultural trans-formations improved, however marginally, the lives of peasants. Military and political stability and prosperity born of the agricultural transforma-tion allowed a rebirth of long-distance exchange—with the cities of South-ern Europe, with ports throughout the Mediterranean world, and, ulti-mately, with sources of spices and other riches far to the east. This in turn spurred the gradual growth of trading towns and urban populations outside the manorial order, but not outside the protection and taxation of kings. Trade introduced money into every level of society, if not in the form of coinage, at least as a means of paper accounting. Gradually, painfully, many of the most onerous of peasant obligations were "commuted" into cash payments.

Meantime, the Latin Catholic Church—always compromised by its own status as a large landholder with many peasant vassals, by its need for military and political protection, and by the uses to which the powerful put its doctrines—nonetheless provided a moral counterbalance to the worst forms of brutality. Thousands of men and women took vows of celibacy and poverty, lived communally in monasteries and convents that were the antithesis of neo-local households, and sealed themselves off from much of the violence and exploitation around them to devote their lives to the prayers and rituals their god demanded of them in payment for the sins of humanity. And from earliest post-Roman times, the Church reminded kings and princes who claimed divine sanction that they were responsible for the material, and especially spiritual, well-being of the people they ruled. Through concepts such as the "Peace of God" and the "Truce of God," the Church imposed the ideal, and often the reality, of cessations of violence on Sundays and during holy seasons and the right of sanctuary in houses of worship.

The ubiquity of Christian values can certainly be overstated. The Church had long incorporated diverse local customs, varieties of belief, and thinly veiled pagan traditions within the universality conveyed by the term "Catholic," and there is little evidence either that most lords willingly deferred to popes and bishops or that most peasants (or lords) grasped the fine points of Christian theology. Everywhere, "cunning men," healers, midwives, witches, and alchemists dealt with an unseen world every bit as diversely populated as that of the other-than-human inhabitants of North America. Still, for all this religious variety, the idea of a spiritually and politically unitary Latin Christendom presided over by the universal spiritual monarchy of the Catholic pope as Christ's vicar on earth provided an additional point of contrast between Western Europe and North America, where ethnocentric loyalties and hatreds were more locally dispersed among countless communities who each considered themselves the only "original people."

Nothing focused this sense of pan-European unity more fully than the series of military Crusades against the Islamic powers of the Middle East that began in 1095. At a council of bishops that Pope Urban II convened in that year, the pontiff called not only for a renewal of the Truce of God but for a campaign to seize the Holy City of Jerusalem from its Muslim overlords. The text of the pope's speech has not survived, but, according to a contemporary chronicler, Urban declared that "all who die by the way, whether by land or by sea, or in battle against the pagans, shall have immediate remission of sins." Equipped with this plenary indulgence—this promised reprieve from the perils of the Last Judgment—and in hopes of carving new feudal estates from conquered territory, the crusaders could pursue a holy mission:

> Let those who have been accustomed unjustly to wage private warfare against the faithful now go against the infidels and end with victory this war which should have been begun long ago. Let those who, for a long time, have been robbers, now become knights. Let those who have been fighting against their brothers and relatives now fight in a proper way against the barbarians. Let those who have been serving as mercenaries for small pay now obtain the eternal reward.[12]

Most of those who set off for the Holy Land over the next two centuries—not only knights deflected from causing trouble at home but thousands of ill-armed idealistic peasants (in 1096) and perhaps even children (more likely young men, in 1212) would never return home, and the Latin Kingdom of Jerusalem that the crusaders established in 1099 would fall to the Muslim forces of Saladin in 1187, never to be retaken. In material terms, it was all a colossal waste of human and economic resources. Yet the enduring cultural significance of the Crusades can hardly be overstressed. As a standard textbook once put it, "Although some men undoubtedly went crusading in search of fiefs and plunder . . . or simply from love of adventure, it seems clear that the majority were moved by genuine religious enthusiasm and complete confidence that the crusade was the path of salvation." These campaigns were "the chief proof of the tremendous vitality and expansive power of medieval civilization and the most concrete illustration of the meaning of the common expression, 'an age of Faith.'"[13] Linking armed conquest to eternal salvation, infusing material striving with spiritual obligation, finding internal unity in battle with external foes, making religious bigotry an emblem of virtue, the crusading spirit became one of the most indelible components of the Western European medieval synthesis.

If the militant zealotry of the Crusades revealed major differences with the North American situation, one moderating influence on the violence at the heart of Western European society perhaps best embodies the complicated mix of parallels and contrasts between the two medieval orders. The cult of chivalry—firmly in place in Western Europe as the Crusades drew to a close—must have had its counterparts among North American warriors, who operated by equally intricate codes of manly honor on their ball courts and chunkey grounds. European chivalry involved far more than evocations of Christian unity through battle with infidels, intricate rituals of combat, pageantry of ceremonial jousts, and poetry of courtly love. Fine-tuned notions of conspicuous display, loyalty, generosity, and martial skill fundamentally distinguished the gentlefolk, the nobles, from the common herd. Although in theory these traits could be learned by those who rose to the chivalric class through military accomplishment, they increasingly came to be perceived as inherited. All men who fought in heavy armor on horseback shared a self-image that associated them with kings, princes, and great lords.

Thus, even as chivalry provided a veneer of legitimacy to the behavior of the warrior class and reduced random violence, it also entrenched an ideology of fundamental distinction, fundamentally unequal rights, between the very few who ruled and the very many who did not. And beneath it all, the system remained, at its heart, one based on violence and exploitation of land and of those who labored on it. Knights still had only one vocation and one avocation: fighting and hunting, respectively. So a tiny group of European males spent their days much as did nearly every young North American man.

Which points again to the bundle of parallel contrasts and contrasting parallels that emerged on opposite sides of the Atlantic during the Medieval Warm Period. In Western Europe, as in North America, war and bloodshed were central to the social order (albeit with very different social consequences). In Western Europe, as in North America, an elite claiming supernatural authority exacted food, labor, and other forms of tribute from the commonalty (albeit in more personally acquisitive ways). In Western Europe, as in North America, commoners supported the military and spiritual elite with the produce of their collective labor (albeit labor that was differently gendered, with men rather than women working the fields and women tending animals that were domesticated). In Western Europe, as in North America, life for the vast majority was at the same time highly lo-

calized and connected to broader networks of politics, religion, and exchange (albeit in a monetarized form that depersonalized many, but by no
means all, interactions). In Western Europe, as in North America, the lo-
calized worlds owed shifting forms of allegiance to paramount leaders
whose authority was more ceremonial than absolute, more temporary than
permanent, more dependent on religious belief than raw power (albeit
in what social scientists would call "kingdoms," historians would label
the "Holy Roman Empire," and theologians would term the "Holy See,"
rather than in "complex chiefdoms" and shared agricultural rituals). These
patterns were the legacy of Europe's progenitors.

As in North America, that legacy was transmitted and transmuted through
the ordeals of the Little Ice Age. The final great parallel development is
that, when peoples from the two continents met, their medieval syntheses
of social order and power were in crisis. The catastrophic impact of the
Little Ice Age is clearer for Western Europe than for North America.
From 1315 to 1322, extraordinarily heavy rains and cold weather washed
out crops in regions ranging from the British Isles through present-day
Germany to Scandinavia. Farm animals, as well as people, perished, both
from scarce fodder and from epidemics, probably of the viral malady rin-
derpest, which thrived in wet conditions. The devastation of cattle and
sheep herds compounded the disaster for the humans who depended on
them for dairy products, meat, and money to purchase scarce grain. Exact
figures are impossible to determine, but local studies in Flanders and England suggest death rates in 1316 alone of approximately 10 percent.[14] An
English poet-chronicler's lament still conveys the horror, even to us who
no longer recognize many of the words:

> another sorwe that spradde over al the lond;
> A thusent winter ther bifore com nevere non so strong.
> To binde alle the mene men in mourning and in care,
> The orf [cattle] deide al bidene
>   and maden the lond al bare,
>   so faste,
> Com nevere wrecche into Engelond that made men more agaste.[15]

Yet colder average temperatures, unstable weather, floods, and famine
turned out to be the least of the wrecks that made England and all Europe

aghast. A still worse sorrow spread over all the land—a kind of sorrow that Native Americans escaped, at least for the present. Between 1347 and 1351, bubonic plague, the "Black Death," spread throughout Europe. Additional pandemics struck in 1361–1363, 1369–1371, 1374–1375, 1390, 1400, and at least once a decade thereafter for the next century. The rat-borne fleas that carried the bacillus *Yersinia pestis* might have initially traveled westward from Central Asia with nomadic herders seeking new grazing territories in the midst of climatic upheavals, thence to spread still further on ships plying Mediterranean and Atlantic coastal waters. Whatever the case, the cumulative impact on already stressed Western European populations was catastrophic. By 1400, perhaps 40 percent of the population of France and 50 percent of England had perished; approximately 3,000 French and 1,000 English villages lay totally abandoned. Estimates vary widely, but by 1450 there may have been only a third as many Western Europeans as there had been in 1300.[16]

Not surprisingly, social upheavals accompanied the ecological and epidemiological disasters. Manorial lords, faced with depopulated manors and empty coffers, attempted to tighten the screws on their remaining tenants. Tenants resisted—sometimes violently, as in the peasant revolts known as the French Jacquerie of 1358 and the English Rising of 1381 —more often in ways that incrementally improved their circumstances. Nothing so dramatic as a general emancipation of the rural population occurred, but instead countless negotiations between lords and tenants gradually transformed the social order. Some villeins took advantage of periods of chaos to simply leave their seigneuries and seek opportunities elsewhere, in cities or on other estates. Remaining peasants accumulated larger holdings and extracted better terms, in many cases escaping all labor service and gaining freedom from restrictions on their rights to change residence or marry without the lord's permission. Serfdom, already rare in France by 1300, virtually disappeared in England and most of the rest of Western Europe by 1400.

Under these circumstances, seigneurs everywhere had greater difficulty finding laborers to cultivate their domains. In some cases, they were forced to employ short-term servants on annual contracts. In many others, lords essentially gave up, turning acreage over to peasant leaseholders or transforming cropland into pasturage for sheep. The largest landowners— those in the higher ranks of the political order—in one way or another managed to make their lands continue to pay. But many lesser lords could

not, and their holdings devolved to former tenants and prospering peasants. Thus, in England especially, a substantial class of freeholders—"yeomen," who owed formal obligations to no one but the king—emerged.
None of these changes happened overnight or universally, and none of the
blessings were unmixed. In particular, the liberalization of rents and other
dues occurred in a context where declining population meant ever-lower
prices for the agricultural produce that farmers ever more often had to sell
in the marketplace to meet their ever more money-centered remaining
obligations. But by the mid-fifteenth century the cumulative result was
clear. The seamless ideal of a pyramid in which all knew their place in the
hierarchy of protection and obligation became increasingly divorced from
social reality.

The new order emerging from the decay of the medieval synthesis remained predominantly rural and agricultural, but far less so than it had
been during the High Middle Ages. In 1300, Paris had dwarfed all places
on the continent, with a population of some two hundred thousand; London, Cologne, and Bruges had each housed perhaps fifty thousand. But
virtually nowhere else north and west of Italy had city life been familiar.[17]
By 1450, however, the trajectory was toward ever-larger urban concentrations. As with transformations in the countryside, the quickening of European urban life was gradual and rooted in trends that extended well back
into previous centuries. Cities had always been both integral to, and great
anomalies within, the medieval order. In many of the ways they were integral to the order, they functioned much like Pueblo Bonito or Cahokia. As
locations for cathedrals, they were sites of sacred rituals mediating life and
death. As concentrations of skilled craftsmen, they were the source of luxury items that functioned much like prestige goods. As consumers of foodstuffs, they depended uneasily on the produce of outlying villages. As
homes for merchants and ports for seaborne and riverine commerce, they
were important nodes in long-distance as well as regional trade networks.

With the activities of those merchants, the parallels between Western
European and Eastern North American cities break down—and the ways
in which cities were anomalous within the rural medieval order also become clear. The roots of the difference were money and, more broadly,
concentrations of private capital in forms other than land. Merchants and
their love of gold (not to mention their supposed association with Judaism)
made them suspect characters in the medieval world of Christendom;
their lack of conspicuous generosity and of skill in the manly arts of war

Western Europe, c. 1500.

made them the very embodiment of ignobility. But merchants and their money were also absolutely crucial—especially to kings, who found them (like unarmed urbanites in general) useful counterweights to the power and wealth of their militaristic landed vassals. And so, gradually in the tenth to thirteenth centuries, merchants had extracted city charters from kings, who exempted them from obligations to other lords in exchange for direct taxes, fees of various kinds, percentages of monopolies on particular trades, and loans and outright gifts to the royal coffers.

The vast majority of city dwellers shared almost none of the vast wealth that made the legal freedoms of the city possible, and only tiny oligarchies acquired the full freedom that allowed them a voice in governing. Powerful guilds and legal monopolies still placed great restrictions on economic and other activities. Most women and all servants and bound apprentices hardly shared any freedom at all, and, especially for the poor, cities were unhealthy places where one might better expect to die than to prosper. Indeed, for the period of general depopulation, there is no evidence that cities in general grew in terms of absolute population; most actually shrank in size between 1300 and 1450. Nonetheless, towns were becoming great magnets for people seeking the economic opportunities and personal freedoms that were so hard to win in the countryside. By the late fifteenth century, as populations throughout Western Europe at last began to grow again, a third of the people in the Low Countries (today's Belgium and the Netherlands) lived in towns, and, in Western Europe as a whole, on average 20 percent of the population made their living from crafts or trades, rather than agriculture.

The demographic and political status of cities and their residents reveals another realm in which the formerly parallel trajectories of the two continents now diverged. The Western European kingdoms that in many ways had resembled North American chiefdoms were slowly transforming themselves into something like nation-states. In 1337, the conflict later called the Hundred Years War commenced. Beginning as a convoluted family quarrel among royal claimants to suzerainty over France, it ended in 1453, after countless sieges of continental cities, with a vastly strengthened French monarchy under the victorious Charles VII. That monarchy was beginning to elicit a new kind of ethnic, perhaps even national, loyalty from its subjects. England, meanwhile—its king, Henry VI, having lost all claims on the Continent except to Calais—plunged into its own period of dynastic chaos during the Wars of the Roses. When Henry VII emerged victorious at Bosworth Field in 1485, he was able to bequeath his successors a position similar to that of their French rivals. In 1300, two closely related dynastic monarchs had asserted authority over loose conglomerations of feudal lords in France and England that were described more accurately as "communities of the realm" than as "nations." By the 1450s, both geographic and political identities had become much more strongly unified from top to bottom and had begun to resemble, in both theory and practice, modern polities.

Warfare was central to the emergence of these new entities and identities. The term "Hundred Years War" summarizes the almost constant conflict among kings that engulfed not just England and France but all the peoples of Western Europe during the transition to what we call the Early Modern era. From the fourteenth century onward, technologies and tactics steadily changed in ways that made the semi-independent bands of heavily armed horsemen who were so central to the medieval order increasingly obsolete. At safe distances of up to two hundred yards, archers could rain a deadly hail of arrows on mounted men. In closer combat, the "pike squares" perfected by Swiss armies—thousands of men who stood eighty abreast and seventy ranks deep, and moved with tight discipline— combined wielders of long iron-tipped poles in the front rows with swingers of deadly halberds in the rear to pluck knights off their horses and slaughter both men and beasts. In countless battles, massed archers and foot soldiers proved their superiority to cumbersome knights on horseback, who became even clumsier when they encapsulated both themselves and their mounts in additional armor. The full-length suits that grace so many museums today reflect the death-throes, rather than the high point, of a military technology passing into irrelevance.

Meantime gunpowder, a Chinese invention known in Europe since the thirteenth century, also began to have a major effect on warfare. Small arms (or, rather, weapons portable enough to be transported without great effort by a single person) were still too heavy and inaccurate to be of much use offensively; crossbows were more reliable. Nonetheless armies increasingly carried the new weapons, as English troops did late in the Hundred Years War. Far more significant than the wielding of small arms, however, was the development of siege artillery, which quickly made castles quaint and, by the fifteenth century, required the building of new, vastly more expensive forms of fortification designed to resist cannon fire. Again, the Hundred Years War was a turning point; on the Continent, one English fortification after another fell to French artillery. Monarchs everywhere began turning their cannon on the castles of uncooperative vassals, or at least threatening to do so. As much as anything, artillery helped to shift the balance of power toward the new political centers over which the kings presided.

Two things united these new ways of killing, conquering, and intimidating: they relied more on large numbers of narrowly trained infantrymen than on individual, highly skilled knights, and they were massively expensive—far more expensive than any mere knight or lord could afford. Only kings, and only kings ingenious enough to develop creative ways of raising unprecedented revenues, could afford them. And, in the end, even kings could not really bear the staggering costs. Artillery-resistant fortifications were astronomically expensive. When English forces captured the modest-size town of Tournai (in present-day Belgium) in 1513, the first estimates for new bastions required 60,000 feet of hewed stone, 8,000 tons of fill, 700 tons of wood, 192,000 bushels of lime, and 1,000 loads of sand—not to mention cannon to sit atop them and the labor to build them. Three decades later, the projected cost of a single Italian bastion was 44,000 ducats. There is no easy way to convert such a sum into today's currency, but this was the equivalent of several million modern dollars.[18] Once such extravagant fortresses were constructed, assaults on them required ever more powerful and numerous artillery, ever larger carts and oxen teams to transport them, ever more elaborate earthworks to protect them and their gunners, and ever more gold to pay the bills.

And then there were the costs of personnel. Major military campaigns might require 20,000 to 30,000 troops. Each solder was far cheaper to maintain than a mounted knight, but collectively drained endless ducats, livres, pounds, or crowns per month. Before the sixteenth century, no king could afford to keep substantial numbers of men under arms in peacetime—or even long enough to complete a siege or follow up a victorious battle. Late medieval and Early Modern armies thus had to be recruited ad hoc for particular campaigns, through a combination of expensive techniques. Impoverished men invariably described by their social betters as criminals and ne'er-do-wells could be lured with promises of monetary pay and booty. Commanders, similarly, could be recruited from the warrior class, but now not so much because they brought with them their own bands of loyal mounted retainers as because they could be convinced—in exchange for future payment, booty from conquest, ransom for high-status captives, or position at court—to advance their own funds to pay troops raised from their estates or dragooned under circumstances that did not bear close scrutiny.

From the perspective of kings, such techniques had the virtue of post-poning cash outlays until after the campaign was over, if not indefinitely, but they were not particularly effective in raising reliable forces. For that, only the employment of mercenaries would do. Skilled warriors willing to work for pay abounded—many of them from Swiss, Italian, or German principalities, but they hailed from all points in and outside a particular king's realm. Yet mercenaries demanded prompt payment, and, with no other loyalty, were prone to desert mid-siege if the money failed.

At the turn of the fifteenth century, an advisor to the French king, Louis XII, famously observed that three things were necessary to military success: "money, more money, and yet more money."[19] The connection be-tween finance and war inexorably drove the gradual transformation of me-dieval monarchies into Early Modern kingdoms and, eventually, nation-states. In the late fifteenth century, Isabel of Castile, Charles VIII and Louis XII of France, and Henry VII of England ingeniously wrung every penny they could from traditional manorial obligations, while inventing ef-ficient ways to track and disperse coins that flowed into their intermingled personal and official coffers. Their successors—Charles V and Felipe II, François I, Henry VIII and Elizabeth I—had to negotiate with their sub-jects in countless ways, in corteses, estates, parliaments, councils, and courts, to gain new rights of taxation, new sources of fees, new tariffs on trade, new percentages of monopolies. But such means were never enough. The one constant was that monarchs had to borrow to meet their military expenses, and to borrow from those who had money to lend: pref-erably the merchants of their own cities; if necessary, merchants in cities elsewhere, such as the Italian peninsula or the Low Countries. Slowly, something beginning to resemble what historians would later call the "fiscal-military state" began to emerge.

Through all of this, in some ways the meaning of kingship changed hardly at all. The language of feudal obligation and chivalric ideals re-mained ubiquitous. Kings fought wars for surface reasons little different from those of their ancestors—dynastic controversies over claims to a throne, personal insults, martial glory—and they still often personally led troops in battle. Intermarriage among patriarchal dynastic households ensured that kingship (and, especially, queenship) need have little relation at all to the vernacular languages and customs of those who were ruled. Holy Roman Emperor Charles V, for just one example, grew up speaking Dutch; as "Carlos I" of Spain, he barely mastered Castilian and probably never tried Aragonese or the many other languages of peoples he ruled. Kings' subjects, too, spoke multiple languages and virtually unintelligible local dialects. The standardizing influences of Shakespeare, the King James Bible, or the Académie Française had not yet been thought of. Most of those who participated in the intellectual developments known as the "Renaissance" communicated with each other in Latin, the ancient universal language of western Christendom. Meantime, the vast majority of speakers of local dialects often had only a hazy idea of what went on beyond a radius that they could walk in a day or so. In an era when maps as we know them hardly existed at all, people had no pictures in their heads to tell them what a nation looked like.

Yet, viewed from another perspective, everything had changed. Somewhere, in the complicated interactions of demographic transitions, economic transformations, the decline of feudal obligations, and the efforts of kings to find the economic and political resources necessary to wage war, emerged new understandings of the relationship between monarchs and ordinary people—at least male people with a certain level of landed property or merchant capital. Multiple levels of feudal loyalties yielded, by fits and starts, to a more direct relationship between king and subject that was still described in feudal terms but in practice was much nearer what we would call patriotism. The "protection" from violence and oppression that centuries earlier had undergirded relationships at multiple levels had come to center almost entirely on the monarchy and those who worked on its behalf. Externally, protection came in the form of those ever more expensive wars. Internally, protection came in the form of courts enforcing the supremacy of kings' laws over the patchwork of local customs and manorial privileges. Nowhere were these processes entirely successful or uniform. Even in England—where, since at least the time of the Norman Conquest, manorial courts had been enlisted in the enforcement of the king's "common law," and by 1400 royally appointed "justices of the peace" existed nearly everywhere—considerable local variation remained. But throughout Western Europe, kings now asserted—and most people accepted—a monopoly on violence. Only crowns had legitimate power over life and death: abroad through their troops, at home through the law.

These transformations from within the emerging states joined equally long-term transformations from without, as the ability of popes to focus the religious and chivalric energies of kings and knights for an imagined united Christendom faded away. Here, too, the fourteenth and early fifteenth centuries were an important turning point. First came the "Babylonian Captivity" of the papacy at Avignon from 1309 to 1377, and then the "Great Western Schism" of 1378 to 1417, when two, and briefly three, rival papacies claimed the Throne of Saint Peter. Into the power vacuum stepped kings who increasingly took upon themselves the crusader role, embracing titles such as "Most-Christian King" (used in France at least since the reign of Charles VI, 1380–1422), "Catholic King" (employed by Spanish monarchs since Pope Alexander VI first used the term in 1493), and "Defender of the Faith" (belatedly bestowed on England's Henry VIII by Pope Leo X in 1521). Henry VIII earned his title for his *Defense of the Seven Sacraments,* an attack on Martin Luther's doctrines published the same year in which Leo excommunicated the German reformer (the book was actually written by Henry's advisor Thomas More). The fact that Henry kept the title and passed it on to his successors, after his own break with Rome made him supreme head of the Protestant English Church, perhaps best symbolizes the changing balance of royal and papal power—and the shift in Europe's center of political gravity away from Rome to the new monarchies of the western periphery.

Yet core social forms forged during the Medieval Warm Period survived the long period of cultural transformation that accompanied the onset of the Little Ice Age in the fourteenth century. Patriarchal nuclear households remained the fundamental building blocks of the social order. Land—and the control of people to work it—remained the most highly valued font of wealth and political power, the most treasured resource that kings could bestow on their subjects, and the most profound basis for an unequal social order in which a very few men deemed themselves entitled to rule the vast multitude of ordinary women and men. Within that tiny elite, martial valor—channeled aggressively outward to conquer new sources of landed wealth and advance the faith—remained the true measure of nobility and preserved warfare as the main business of kings. Within that elite, and among many who hoped to emulate it, the fact that merchants and money, more than land and labor, were becoming the real engines of the economy, and far more important than landed warriors to the ability of kings to conduct that business, only made the old chivalric values that much more compelling. An *ideal* of feudalism blossomed even as the institutions and obligations that word had never adequately described crumbled around it.

On the two sides of the ocean, the cultural developments of the Medieval Warm Period and the Little Ice Age occurred without direct reference to each other, and with no one comprehending that great forces of winds and currents actually tied the two North Atlantic continents together. In a great sweeping circuit, breezes and waters circulated from the islands of the Caribbean to the eastern coasts of North America, flowing from today's Florida to Newfoundland, past Greenland, Iceland, and the British Isles to the western coasts of Spain and Portugal, and then to the Canary Islands and West Africa, before returning to the Caribbean to begin the cycle anew. Had they known about these currents (which would not be fully understood until the mapping of the Gulf Stream in the eighteenth century), religious seers everywhere would have concluded that some great spiritual force intended the two continents to be joined—awaiting only the invention of sailing technology sufficient to exploit the winds that had been provided.

Yet only on the northern fringes of the two continents can we be certain that anyone from Europe encountered anyone from America. In about the year 1000, Leif Ericsson sailed west from the island that the Norse had dubbed Greenland, a name they chose partly to make it seem attractive for settlement, partly because it was much greener in the Warm Period than it is today. Leif successively made landfall at places he called Helluland (perhaps Baffin Island), Markland (probably Labrador), and Vinland (Newfoundland, named for the grapes or, more likely, wine berries that grew there). Exploiting currents that, in far northern waters, sometimes ran counter to the main flows and allowed boats capable of sailing against the wind to travel westward, others soon followed his route. Off and on for the next few years, groups of Norse people from Greenland lived at the site today known as L'Anse aux Meadows in the north of Newfoundland, and perhaps at some other places nearby.

Icelandic sagas about Vinland, written down three centuries after the

events, say that the first encounter between Norse people and North
Americans occurred when an exploratory party led by Leif's brother Thorvald found three Native men resting under the shelter of overturned
boats. Apparently with no provocation, the Vikings captured and killed all
but one, who returned shortly with a flotilla of canoes that unleashed a hail
of arrows, one of which fatally wounded Thorvald. Later, when the Europeans returned to establish themselves at what was presumably L'Anse,
Native people showed up with furs they hoped to trade for weapons. The
Norse refused, giving them instead, according to one saga, pieces of red
cloth and, according to another, milk from their cattle. The native people
found these beasts terrifying, perhaps because the lactose intolerance
common among Native Americans led the milk to make them violently ill.
Whatever the case, within a few weeks, peaceful exchange gave way to a
pitched battle. The Norse won, but soon thereafter they abandoned their
outpost.

While there is no reason to assume that the sagas record events literally,
things did apparently go wrong quickly. The Norse called the inhabitants
of Vinland *Skraelings,* a word that roughly translates as "savages." The inhabitants' identity is uncertain, but they likely were people of the Thule
Inuit culture—whale fishers who, during the Warm Period, migrated from
Alaska eastward across the Arctic and probably reached Labrador not too
many years before the Norse did. By the thirteenth century, Thule people
had also colonized northern Greenland, where they again made contact
with Norsemen. While there is some evidence of peaceful interchange between the two groups—iron and copper of presumed Norse origin spread
through the Arctic in this period—conflict seems to have been the norm.
That conflict, along with the onset of the Little Ice Age and, doubtless,
other factors, led to the collapse of the last Norse outposts in Greenland
by the second decade of the fifteenth century.

Greenland and Labrador, then, were the places where the expanding
medieval worlds of North America and Western Europe briefly met, and
where the transforming worlds of the Little Ice Age again retreated from
each other. By the early sixteenth century, when the worlds would again
come into contact, almost no one remembered any of the previous encounters. But the Norse sagas about Vinland retained an interesting detail.
In the midst of the climactic battle against the Norsemen, a Native man
got hold of an iron axe. In one version, he and his companions, impressed
with its incredible sharpness, chop away at trees until they break the han-

dle. In another, the man swings the axe and accidentally kills a compatriot standing next to him. In both versions, the axe is then thrown as far away as possible.[20] This was a Norse story, with a Norse moral, presumably about how little Native people valued European technology. But it might just as well have been a Native story, with a slightly different moral spin on the value of things and people imported from Europe. Whatever the case, the thrown axe—a useful piece of private property wasted or an exotic prestige good acquired and then rejected—symbolizes central values bequeathed by medieval progenitors to the Europeans and North Americans who reestablished contact at the end of the fifteenth century.

German pikeman, c. 1522.

Wendat warrior, c. 1619.

3

5

4

Clockwise from upper left: Missisippian figurine of a woman holding maize and sunflower plants, which grow over her back. Three-field agriculture in Europe. Corn, bean, and squash agriculture in North America.

6

9

7

Clockwise: Temple containing the remains of deceased chiefs, Roanoke Island. Interior of Salisbury Cathedral, England, with the remains of deceased notables interred beneath the floor. Fifteenth-century European depiction of the city of Jerusalem. Modern artist's depiction of the Mississippian city of Cahokia.

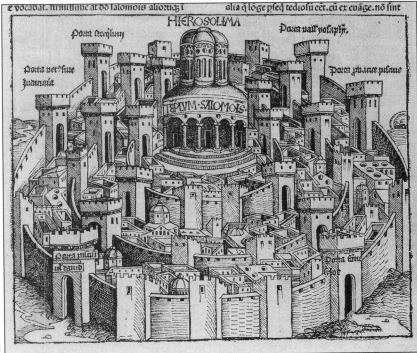

8

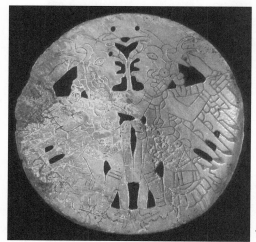

10

13

Clockwise: Power in shell—a gorget from Spiro Mound, Oklahoma. Power in print—assurance to the faithful that the flame of Protestantism cannot be extinguished, and page from the Geneva Bible, with its massive apparatus of Calvinist commentary. Power in earth and stone—the great house of Pueblo Bonito.

11

12

THE FIRST BOOKE OF

MOSES, CALLED

GENESIS.

This word Gene-fis is the beginning and generation of the creatures

THE ARGVMENT.

Mofes in effect declareth three things, which are in this booke chiefly to be confidered: Firft, that the world, and all things therein, were created by God, and that man being placed in this great Tabernacle of the world to behold Gods wonderfull works, and to praife his Name for the infinite graces, wherewith he had endued him, fell willingly from God through difobedience, who yet for his owne mercies fake reftored him to life, and confirmed him in the fame by his promife of Chrift to come, by whom he fhould ouercome Satan, death and hell. Secondly, that the wicked vnmindfull of Gods moft excellent benefits, remained ftill in their wickednefse, and fo falling moft horribly from finne to finne, prouoked God (who by his preachers called them continually to repentance) at length to deftroy the whole world. Thirdly, hee affureth vs by the examples of Abraham, Izhak, Iaakob, and the reft of the Patriarkes, that his mercies neuer faile them whom he chufeth to be his Church, and to profefse his Name an earth, but in all their affliction and perfecutions he euer affifteth them, fendeth comfort, and deliuereth them. And becaufe the beginning, increafe, preferuation and fucceffe thereof might be onely attributed to God, Mofes fheweth by the examples of Kain, Ifmael, Efau and others, which were noble in mans iudgement, that this Church dependeth not on the eftimation and nobilitie of the world: & alfo by the feruineffe of them, which haue at all times worfhipped him purely according to his word, that it ftandeth not in the multitude, but in the poore and defpifed, in the fmall flocke & little number, that man in his wifedome might be confounded, and the Name of God euermore praifed.

CHAP. I.

1 *God created the heauen and the earth.* 3 *The light and the darkeneffe.* 8 *The fyrmiment,* 9 *He feparateth the water from the earth.* 16 *He createth the funne, the moone, and the ftarres.* 21 *He createth the fifh, birds, beafts,* 26 *He createth man, and giueth him rule ouer all creatures,* 29 *And prouideth nourifture for man and beaft.*

a *Sirk of all, and before that any creature was, God made heauen and earth of nothing* Wifd. 11, 14. * Pfa. 33.6. and 136.5. ecclu. 18, 1. act. 14.15. and 17, 24.

IN the a beginning * God cre-ated the heauen and the earth.
2 And ye earth was b I without forme and void, and c darkeneffe was vpon the t deepe, and the Spirit of God d mooued vpon the t waters.

the heauen be gathered into one place, and let the dry land appeare : and it was fo.
10 And God called the dry land, Earth, and hee called the gathering together of the waters, Seas : and God faw that it was good.
11 Then God faid, h Let the earth bud forth the bud of the herbe, that feedeth feed, the fruit-full tree, which beareth fruite according to his kinde, which hath his feede in it felfe vpon the earth : and it was fo.
12 And the earth brought foorth the bud of the herbe, that feedeth feede according to his kind, alfo the tree that beareth fruit, which hath his feed in it felfe according to his kind: and God

* This word figni-fieth is the beginning and generation of the creatures

h So that we fee it is the onely power of Gods word that maketh the earth fruitfull, which elfe natu-rally is barren i This fentence is

14

Ruins of ceremonial center at Chaco Canyon, abandoned in the twelfth century.

Ruins of St. Andrews Cathedral, Scotland, destroyed by Protestants in the sixteenth century.

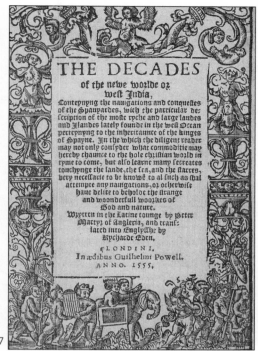

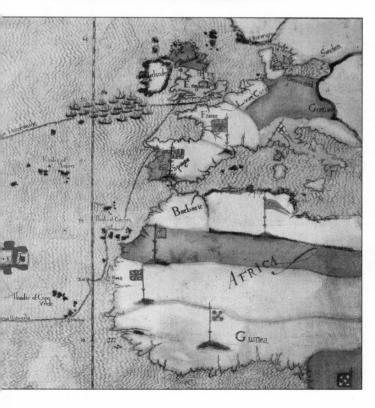

Clockwise: European readers learn of the wonders of the Americas: Flemish engraver Theodor de Bry's fanciful image of Columbus landing in the West Indies, 1594, and Richard Eden's *The Decades of the Newe Worlde,* 1555. Francis Drake riding Atlantic winds and currents, 1585.

17

19

22

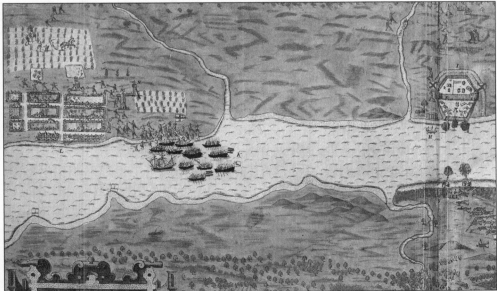

Clockwise: Wedding portrait of Fernando of Aragon and Isabel of Castile, 1469. Theodor de Bry's depiction of René de Laudonnière and Timucuan Native people at column erected in 1562 by Jean Ribault, St. John's River, La Caroline Colony. San Agustín, La Florida, besieged by Francis Drake, 1585. Spanish silver mines at Potosí.

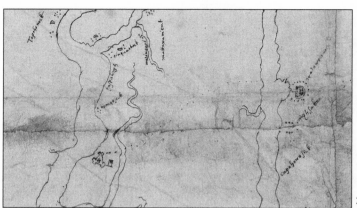

23

26

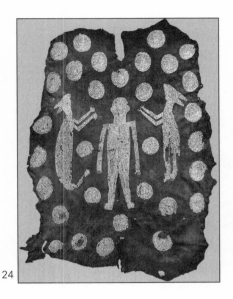

Clockwise: A 1608 sketch map of
what the English called the James
River and York River and Native
people called Tsenacomoco: the
triangular structure at lower left is
the English capital, Jamestown; the
D-shaped structure at mid-right is
the Native capital, Werowocomoco; a
dotted line traces the route between
them. "Powhatan's Mantle,"
illustrating the power of a paramount
chief. Pocahontas in London, 1616.
24 John Smith in London, 1616.

25

27

Sensationalistic European image of the attack on Virginia colonists in 1622.

Conquistadores

To CO´NQUER. *v.a.* [*conquérir,* Fr. *conquirere,* Latin].
1. To gain by conquest; to over-run; to win.

CO´NQUEROR. *n.s.* [from *conquer*].
1. A man that has obtained a victory; a victor . . .
2. One that subdues and ruins countries.

—Samuel Johnson, *A Dictionary of the English
Language* (London, 1755)

THREE

Crusades of the Christ-Bearers
to the Americas

EXOTIC ITEMS ACQUIRED from afar are often said to be a preoccupation of fifteenth-century Europeans. Yet the idea that explorers sailed off into uncharted oceans on a mad quest to find rare spices from the Far East fits neither with the nature of the new monarchies of Western Europe nor with the character of those who set out to conquer the globe on their behalf. It is revealing that the identity that Christopher Columbus fashioned for himself and his mission made no reference to spices, or axes, or any of the mercantile pursuits that the European elite derided as unworthy of true nobility. The introduction to the surviving version of the official diary Columbus presented to Queen Isabel and King Fernando ignores such things:

This present year of 1492, after Your Highnesses had brought to an end the war with the Moors, . . . because of the report that I had given to Your Highnesses about the lands of India and about a prince who is called "Grand Kahn," which means in our Spanish language "King of Kings"; how, many times, he and his predecessors had sent to Rome to ask for men learned in our Holy Faith in order that they might instruct him in it and how the Holy Father had never provided them; and thus so many peoples were lost, falling into idolatry and accepting false and harmful religions; and Your Highnesses, as Catholic Christians and Princes, lovers and promoters of the Holy Christian Faith, and enemies of the false doctrine of Mahomet and of all idolatries and heresies, you thought of sending me, Cristóbal Colón, . . . to see how their conversion to the Holy Faith might

67

be undertaken. And you commanded that I should not go to the East by land, by which way it is customary to go, but by the route to the West, by which route we do not know for certain that anyone previously has passed. So, after having expelled all the Jews from all of your Kingdoms and Dominions, . . . Your Highnesses commanded me to go, with a suitable fleet, to the said regions of India.[1]

In keeping with this crusading religious spirit, Columbus, late in his life, took to signing his name with a cryptic set of symbols that included the characters Χρο *Ferens,* combining Greek and Latin words for "Christ-Bearer"—the meaning of the name "Cristóbal" in Spanish or "Christopher" in English. As his biographer observes, the signature was "a reminder that by baptism he was consecrated to the task of carrying the word of God overseas to heathen lands."[2]

Like Columbus' Christian name and the fervor of his professed mission to the Indies, early European contacts with Americans were driven more by legacies of the decaying medieval synthesis than by the emerging world of commerce. Certainly, material gain was always a major motive, but that motive focused on subduing agricultural land and labor more than on the lust for capital and commodities. For a long time, chivalric ideals and feudal dreams retained a hold on certain European minds and behavior that outstripped the ignoble logic of mercantile trade: Quests by men who saw themselves as Christ-bearers set patterns for the earliest colonial enterprises in North America that might better be seen as the final examples of a late-medieval form of enterprise rather than as harbingers of the modern era. The centuries-long path to what we incorrectly remember as the first English colony, Jamestown, ran through the Mediterranean to the Canary Islands to the Azores to Columbus' West Indies and even to Ireland, by way of the crisis of Christendom known as the Protestant Reformation. From France and England as well as from Spain, warriors spreading their conflicting versions of the Gospel while attempting to enrich themselves and their monarchs by the conquest of territories and peoples carried Europe's unraveling synthesis to a North America similarly in crisis.

Most educated Europeans of the time knew that Columbus was wrong. They did not disagree with him about the imperative to spread Christianity and manorial overlordship to infidels and pagans or about the virtues of expelling Muslims and Jews from the homeland. Nor did they quarrel with the idea that the planet was spherical, which was common knowledge. But they did know that Columbus had severely underestimated the distance that crusaders would have to sail west around that earth to reach the coasts of Asia. From his reading of Marco Polo and other sources, the Christ-Bearer argued that the Asian continent was nearly twice as wide as it actually is and that the supposed island of "Cipangu" (a confused understanding of what we know as Japan) lay perhaps 1,500 miles off the coast of Cathay (China). Moreover, he calculated that each of the 360 degrees of global latitude spanned only about three-quarters of the distance we now know to be accurate. Combined, these errors placed Cipangu a relatively short sail west of the Canary Islands.

Yet Columbus was a far better mariner than he was a geographer. Long experience in sailing routes stretching from West Africa to Iceland gave him great skill in determining latitude with the rough instruments available and, especially, a brilliant idea about Atlantic wind patterns. Prudent seafarers preferred to sail outbound against the wind, undertaking the most laborious part of their voyage first and planning easy trips home with the breeze at their backs; this was how the Norse who had earlier sailed west toward Greenland and Vinland had operated. But skilled mariners knew that powerful opposing winds and currents made it impossible to sail directly westward from anywhere in the latitudes between the Azores and Ireland. Columbus' great insight—or foolish notion—was to head south from the Canaries, where easterly winds would carry him far to the west, trusting that somehow he could make a great circle and return via the westerlies. Thus, he intuited what would become, for centuries, the main route from Europe to the Caribbean, to Central and South America, and to the southern parts of North America: a swoop down near the coast of Africa, then across to the Caribbean, and then home across the North Atlantic. The circular winds and currents of the North Atlantic that for millennia had given Western Europe, West Africa, the Caribbean, and eastern North America a potential natural unity were at last beginning to be understood.

In this respect, Columbus was an innovator, the first of a hardy, if not by our lights entirely admirable, breed of modern explorer. Yet, while his feats inspired countless others, it is just as important to see him, along with his contemporaries, as products of a long tradition stretching back to the medieval Crusades, to the rise of the Western European monarchies, and to the poorly remembered Norse travels. Cipangu and Cathay were semi-mythical places—like almost everything else in what many scholars now consider the largely fictional travels of Marco Polo. Yet these places were no more and no less real in Western European minds than the realm of the "Grand Kahn," the fabled Indian Christian kingdom of "Prester John," or such spots as the "Isle of St. Brendan," "Antilia," "Hy-Brasil," and the "Earthly Paradise" (Columbus came to think Panama was on its outskirts), or countless other locations that decorated fifteenth-century maps and imaginations. Nor were these places much less real than Constantinople, the Crusader States of the medieval Levant (the last of these had fallen to Muslims in 1291) or, indeed, sacred Jerusalem, whose reconquest for the Church remained the ultimate goal of many Christian Europeans long after the era of the Crusades. These places, too, were known mostly from legend and word of mouth rather than first-hand experience.

Few conquistadores shared Columbus' intense spirituality and millennial visions, but all, to one degree or another, placed themselves in the crusader tradition that their monarchs had embraced as the responsibility of Christian kings. "Experience prooveth that naturally all princes bee desirous to extend and enlarge their dominions and kingdomes," a London merchant exhorted King Henry VIII. "Wherefore it is not to be marveiled, to see them every day procure the same, not regarding any cost, perill, and labour, . . . but rather it is to be marvelled, if there be any prince content to live quiet with his owne dominions." Indeed, "with a small number of ships there may bee discovered divers New lands and kingdomes, in the which without doubt your Grace shall winne perpetuall glory, and your subjectes infinite profite."[3]

Precisely because chivalric ideals had little relevance for modern pike-and-artillery warfare, they became all the more cherished by those who dreamed of far-off lands. Places in that vast unknown territory called the "Indies" that were either uninhabited or occupied by pagans rightfully belonged to the Church. It was the obligation of Christian monarchs and knights to bring them into due submission and to turn the natives' labors to the rightful profit of their godly conquerors. Such ideas took particularly strong hold in post-Columbian Castile after Pope Alexander VI granted all heathen lands west and east of an imagined line on the imagined globe to Spain and Portugal, respectively, in 1493. The Spanish and Portuguese crowns confirmed the arrangement a year later in the Treaty of Tordesillas. Under the terms of these documents, America's "native peoples were Spanish subjects waiting to be located and informed of their new status," one historian concludes. Because the non-Christian inhabitants of these lands "were royal 'subjects and vassals' before the fact, their resistance of conquest made them rebels," not freedom fighters.[4]

All of this went far beyond just the imaginations of conquistadores. Western European expansion into the Atlantic world had long-standing historical precedents. These precedents were most deeply rooted on the Iberian Peninsula, and so it makes sense that the crowns of Spain and Portugal took the lead in Atlantic expansion. The patterns stretched back at least to the Aragonese conquest from the Moors of the Mediterranean islands of Majorca in 1229 and Minorca in 1287. In both cases, the bulk of the existing Islamic population seems to have been enslaved or expelled. Their holdings were replaced by new manorial estates granted to the military commanders who had raised the conquering troops, to the merchants who financed the campaign, and to other great men whom the king of Aragón needed to reward for their political and financial favors. Still richer rewards came in the form of a papal indulgence that promised Christians who resettled conquered lands the same forgiveness of sins earned by crusaders to the Holy Land.

Similar processes of religiously justified enslavement and repopulation characterized the thirteenth-century phase of what Spaniards and Portuguese came to call the *Reconquista* of the Iberian Peninsula from the Islamic Moors. In many ways, Iberia was the western front in the Crusades; successes against Islam there helped inspire Pope Urban II to call for the first assault on the Holy Land. Slowly, with many advances and retreats, to the east, the Aragonese and the Catalans took over Valencia and Murcia. To the west, the Castilians did the same with Andalucía and Extremadura, and the Portuguese with the Alentejo and the Algarve. These latter four conquests, however, presented particular challenges. Western territories that had never been heavily populated in the first place were not so much conquered by Christians as abandoned by retreating Moors. Arid and largely unsuited to the forms of cultivation developed during Europe's agricultural revolution, such regions could not be effectively occupied without considerable creativity, hordes of imported laborers, and substantial capital. None of these resources was easily found; in the end, much of the land was used for pasturage rather than crops. Portuguese and Castilian monarchs came to see such projects less as a source of easy rewards for their loyal vassals than as troublesome burdens to their treasuries. These conquests needed to be financed by increasingly lavish grants of lands and resources to those who made it happen—foot soldiers as well as great men—for, as in all wars, everything turned on money.

When the Reconquista resumed in earnest with the rebounding of European populations in the fifteenth century, a standardized mechanism for conquest took shape. The Castilian monarch issued a license to an *adelantado*—an "advancer"—who agreed to raise the funds and troops necessary to conquer a particular castle or town for the Crown and the Church. Should he succeed, the *adelantado* could expect to receive a noble title and the rights to govern the area and its surviving population, to possess estates, and to retain a share of the plunder—in short, to become a neo-feudal manorial lord. Those he recruited to follow him, often the same kind of impoverished folk who joined any army in this era, could likewise expect a share of the booty, grants of land, and rights to command labor. Determined not to recreate the kind of overmighty vassals that had hobbled their medieval predecessors, Castilian monarchs kept their *adelantados* under relatively strict control, selling the licenses for high prices, spelling out intricate legal obligations in documents called *capitulaciones,* closely overseeing the distribution of conquered land *(repartimiento),* and claiming their *quinto*—a fifth of all booty, taxes, and mineral wealth. But nonetheless the incentives for *adelantados* were huge. A potent combination linked religious fervor, national purpose, and personal enrichment to a massive dream of feudal revival. A conquistador could envision a future as lord and master of vast domains, a landowner reaping the fruits of his conquests through the sweat of infidel brows.

Famously and symbolically for those who came after, the conquistadores took Granada in the Columbian year of 1492, expelling Islam from its last corner of Iberia, a peninsula that, as Columbus noted, would become wholly Christian when Jews were banished a few months later. But perhaps more immediately relevant to what followed in Columbus' wake—and to Columbus' role as an *adelantado*—was the fifteenth-century conquest of the Canary Islands. That archipelago off the coast of North Africa had long been known to Europeans from ancient Roman books and from the occasional medieval visit. In 1402 King Enrique III of Castile took it upon himself to grant lordship over the islands to a Norman nobleman named Jean de Bethencourt, who then raised forces to conquer the eastern islands of Lanzarote, Fuerteventura, and part of Ferro and to settle in as "King of the Canaries." Subsequent *adelantados* took the remainder of Ferro and Gomera in the 1420s and Gran Canaria in the 1470s and 1480s. In the year of Columbus' voyage, *capitulaciones* were issued for the conquest of the final islands, Tenerife and La Palma. The islands' native population, the Guanches, included agriculturalists and pastoralists who were organized, like many of their Native American contemporaries, in numerous small-scale chiefdoms. Sometimes these allied with the conquistadores against native enemies. More often they put up fierce resistance. In a long process that finally ended on the most populous island of Tenerife in 1496, the Spanish pitted the chiefdoms against one another. Over the course of the fifteenth century, as many as thirty thousand Guanches perished or were enslaved in these wars.

Enslavement, then, was part of the equation from the earliest days of Iberian expansion. That it was should be no surprise. For centuries, Christians and Muslims had enslaved each other in their wars throughout the Mediterranean basin, and the same was true for Muslims and non-Muslims in North Africa. There was, as yet, no clear association between slavery and race, although there was almost always what we would call an ethnic dimension. Thus, the words "slave" in English, "esclavo" in Spanish, and "esclave" in French all derive from the same root as "Slav," referring to the eastern European peoples who were most commonly bought and sold in the late medieval period.

Religious differences also were significant. Christians generally argued, at least in theory, that fellow Christians could not be enslaved. Unrepentant "infidels" (monotheists such as Muslims who had presumably heard the word of the Christian God and had rejected the true faith) were another matter. As for "pagans" such as the Guanches who had never known the Gospel, opinions differed. The learned might point to Aristotle's speculation that some people were simply destined to be slaves. The Church might point either to teachings that obligated Christians to convert and free benighted souls, or to Pope Clement IV's 1344 declaration that pagans whose sexual, cannibalistic, idolatrous, or otherwise objectionable behavior violated "natural law" deserved enslavement. "It is said that the barbarous people are those who live without law; the Latins, those who have law," proclaimed a textbook studied by Queen Isabel, "for it is the law of nations that men who live and are ruled by law shall be lords of those who

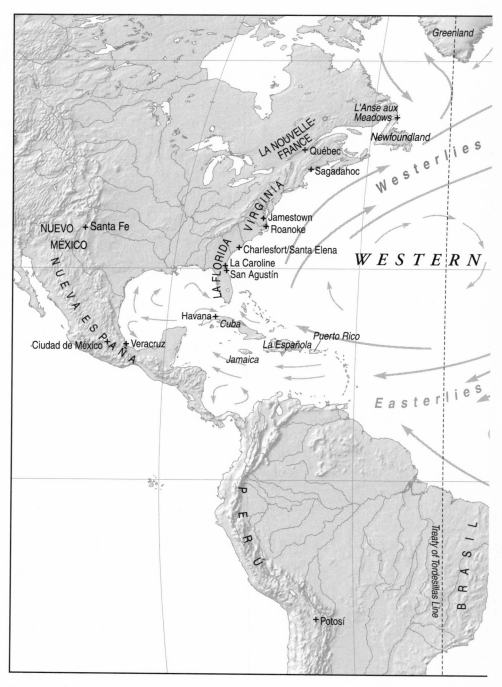

Conquistador outposts, c. 1210–1610.

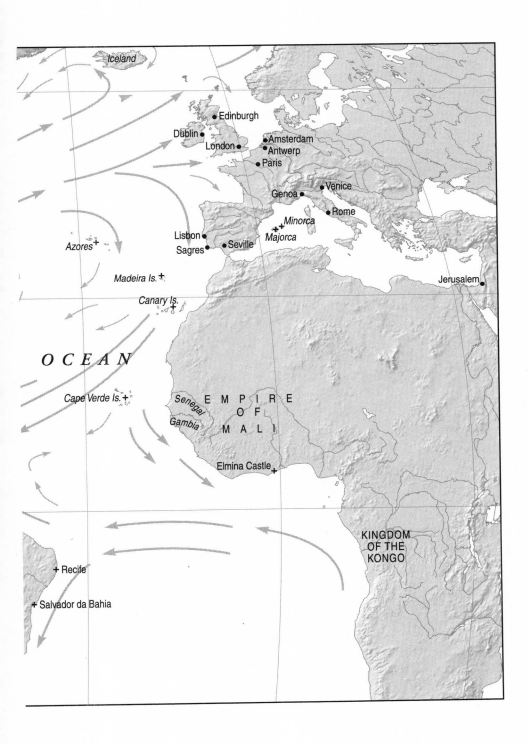

Iceland

Edinburgh
Dublin
London
Amsterdam
Antwerp
Paris
Genoa
Venice
Rome
Minorca
Lisbon
Majorca
Sagres
Seville
Azores
Madeira Is.
Canary Is.
Jerusalem

OCEAN

Cape Verde Is.
Senegal
EMPIRE
OF
MALI
Gambia
Elmina Castle

KINGDOM
OF THE
KONGO

Recife

Salvador da Bahia

have no law, because they are by nature the slaves of the wise who are ruled by law."[5]

By such lights, enslavement became the appropriate, perhaps even merciful, fate of those on the wrong end of a "just war" against rebels to the true faith and violators of natural law. Because those spared to labor for the victors deserved to die, they were, in effect, "socially dead"— kinless, nameless, rightsless property that could be bought and sold. Practice seldom measured up to theory. The socially dead stubbornly asserted their human liveliness, by running away, resisting, extracting privileges, proving their indispensability, finding ways to purchase their own freedom. The result was that relatively few people who survived long enough spent their entire lives as human property, and little systematic thought was given to such issues as the status of an enslaved woman's children. In a society in which the many forms of unfreedom embedded in the medieval European order were still familiar, the ambiguities of such enslavement fit right in. Native North Americans, with their complicated violent practices of enslavement and adoption of war captives, would have understood. So, too, would West Africans, who had their own indigenous patterns of captivity and enslavement.

For Europeans, the "just war" theory had additional messy ambiguities. Freelance conquistadores seeking booty and financial gain—and often desperately in need of ready money to pay off those who had financed their enterprises—seldom made fine distinctions between combatants and noncombatants and easily slipped over into what can only be described as slave-raiding for profit. More Guanches seem to have been captured this way than in anything that Church, Crown, or lawyers would recognize as legitimate battles, despite the promulgation in 1434 of a papal bull outlawing new enslavements and promising indulgences to masters who freed their existing slaves. Ships' captains and merchants, meanwhile—visiting various ports in the Mediterranean and, as the fifteenth century progressed, West Africa—were unlikely to ask many questions about where the slaves they bought and sold came from and what sort of "just war" in the Canaries or in the African interior had declared their social death.

Unsurprisingly, enslaved people from Africa early began showing up on newly conquered estates in the Canaries, on the Iberian mainland, and, especially, on the previously unpopulated Madeira and Cape Verde Islands being claimed during these years by the Portuguese. Nowhere was slave labor yet the dominant labor system. On the sugar plantations and in the processing mills that came to dot the eastern Atlantic islands, a mixture of tenants, small landholders, and European servants labored alongside the enslaved to carry on the unpleasant work. And it was unpleasant work indeed, best done by gangs of people engaged virtually year-round in planting, hoeing, and harvesting a crop that had to be hacked in the field and rushed to the processing mill within minutes so as not to lose its sweetness. Few would undertake such work voluntarily or survive long in doing it. Wherever they could be obtained in sufficient numbers, enslaved workers gradually became the preferred option for those who acquired land and had the capital to invest in sugar-processing equipment.

So the trade in slaves and the conquest of territory had already intertwined long before Columbus. Conquest was also, from the start, inseparable from rivalries among Western European monarchs and the ongoing development of the states they ruled. In the whole enterprise of Atlantic expansion, Castile played catch-up to its Iberian rival, Portugal. Only slightly less famed and encrusted with legend than Columbus is the figure of Portugal's Infante Dom Henrique, known in English as Prince Henry the Navigator. In the 1420s, he had already established his role as patron of maritime exploration from his court at Sagres, on the southwestern tip of the Algarve, supported by significant financial resources that came from his leadership of the community of knights called the Order of Christ. Although Henrique's precise role in fostering innovations in navigational instruments and vessel design remains debatable, his patronage surely assisted those who were perfecting such things as quadrants, astrolabes, compasses, and ships combining square and triangular lateen rigging, designed to sail both with and against the wind.

Just as significant was Henrique's role as a scholar assiduously collecting old books, maps, and stories about places believed to be in the Indies. This research inspired ships' masters to act as seaborne conquistadores to go in search of such places, to subdue them for Christendom, and to reap the profits. Appropriate to a period in which national identities still often meant less than the fading unitary ideal of Christendom and in which princes relied heavily on mercenaries to wage their wars, most of those whom Henrique attracted were not Portuguese or Iberian but from the

Italian Peninsula, especially Columbus' city of Genoa. This applies both to the ships' masters and to those who provided the bulk of the financing to outfit vessels and crews. Resident branches of Italian mercantile houses dominated the trade of cities such as Lisbon and Seville.

The merchant backers sought gold, slaves, and, yes, those spices that otherwise came overland to the Levant and then across the Mediterranean. But for Henrique and the adventurers he sponsored, the primary factors were the ongoing struggle against Islam (despite his nautical English nickname, the prince's only personal exploits abroad were three mostly disastrous land campaigns in North Africa), the glory of conquest, and the hope of making contact with mysterious islands that ancient texts and maps insisted were there. The proclaimed purpose of opening a direct sea route to Cipangu and Cathay was not so much to trade for spices as to open an eastern military front against Islam and—perhaps by making common cause with the legendary Prester John's Christian South Asian (or was it African?) kingdom—to retake Jerusalem.

Inspired by such ideas, ship masters sponsored by Henrique and others moved out into what was then more often called the "Western Ocean" than the "Atlantic." From 1420 onward, Henrique asserted dominion over the previously uninhabited Madeiras, which subsequently became the feudal domain of his Order of Christ and those it contracted to clear the islands' forests and establish manors and sugar mills there. Expeditions sent in the 1430s to find the Isle of St. Brendan stumbled instead on the unpopulated Azores, which by the 1450s had joined the Madeiras as lands distributed to the conquistadores who brought them under cultivation.

Meantime, other ships were steadily pushing ever farther down the African coast. In 1441, a Portuguese vessel returned from the region with a load of gold dust and slaves. In the 1450s Genoese mariners sponsored by Henrique sailed into the Gambia and Senegal rivers and encountered the Muslim trading empire of Mali. In the 1460s, after the Infante's death, the uninhabited Cape Verde Islands joined the Azores as Portuguese domains. In 1482, the Kingdom of the Kongo was contacted, and the Portuguese king João II, who would proclaim himself "Lord of Guinea," blessed the establishment of what became known as Elmina Castle, the soon infamous slaving entrepôt on the Gold Coast of present-day Ghana. Long before Vasco da Gama rounded the Cape of Good Hope in 1496 and proved it was possible to sail to the east, the wealth to be extracted from the coast of Africa and the Atlantic Islands had become clear. Portugal's extended Atlantic Reconquista turned irresistibly south, to West Africa—and in subsequent years, by much the same winds and currents, to Brazil.

Spain's belated rival attempts started in the same direction with the conquest of the Canaries, but then, urged in part by a 1479 treaty that yielded the African coast to Portugal, moved westward. Columbus' *capitulación* promised an unusually lofty set of hereditary titles and privileges should his expedition succeed. As "Viceroy and Governor-General over all such mainlands and islands as he shall discover or acquire," Columbus could "take and keep a tenth of all gold, silver, pearls, gems, spices and other merchandises produced or obtained by barter and mining within the limits of these domains, free of all taxes."[6] But, like previous *adelantados,* he also needed to repay enormous financial burdens from his projected tenth, obligations to his private financial backers and to the Crown, both in taxes and in repayment of an unusual direct royal investment in the enterprise. These debts had to be satisfied before anyone could even think about settling in long-term as lord of a conquered manor.

As a result, Columbus' second voyage, in 1493, brought seventeen ships and at least twelve hundred men to the island he renamed La Española (Hispaniola), where gold had in fact been found on the first voyage. The invaders sought precious metal as the only sure way to pay immediate expenses, particularly in light of the vast costs incurred for ships and men. And they were all men, a thousand or so of them to be paid wages should they ever return to Spain, two hundred of them unpaid gentlemen freelancers, most of them hoping for plundered wealth. Few of their names survive, but it is a safe bet that none planned to work a sugar mill personally should the cane plants that the expedition brought along take root. Nor, despite the presence of several Catholic friars among them, were they particularly interested in converting the Taino inhabitants to Christianity, much less in following royal orders that the natives be "treated very well and lovingly."[7]

There was some gold in the hills of Hispaniola—thirty thousand ducats' worth was rounded up from Tainos through diplomatic gift exchanges, trade, and other means and sent back to Spain with the first return fleet— but it quickly became clear that there would not be nearly enough to pay the bills, at least not if it had to be acquired in peaceful trade. Nor could hundreds of ill-fed, sick, and underemployed men long be kept waiting for the gold they had come for. Not surprisingly, within a few months the Spanish had a nice little "just war" on their hands. By early 1495, fifteen hundred enslaved prisoners had been divided equally among those Columbus shipped back to Spain for sale, those claimed personally by various conquerors, and those released because no one seemed to know what else to do with them.

Rapidly replaying processes that had taken decades in the Canaries, the Spanish pitted one chiefdom against another and within a year imposed an impossible level of tribute on almost the entire island population. On pain of death, every male over age fourteen was to deliver up a hawk's bell full of gold dust every three months. The amount was about the volume of a thimble; perhaps just as important, the tiny bells were items the Tainos had eagerly sought in trade with the newcomers. When the demands for gold were not met, more just wars followed, with a horrific death toll. From a population of perhaps three hundred thousand in 1492, an estimated one hundred thousand were dead by 1496 and two hundred forty thousand by 1508. All sixty thousand survivors were subjected to the *encomienda,* a system of forced labor that replaced the unworkable system of gold tribute in 1499. Technically, the system was neither slavery nor serfdom; in theory the Tainos were free—neither bound to the land nor heritable by their masters. Still, the *encomenderos*—Spanish colonists who gained the individual right to exploit this labor in their gold fields, farms, or sugar mills in return for the obligation to care for their charges' spiritual welfare—found a neo-serfdom to work their neo-feudal estates.[8]

That the dream of feudal revival through righteous conquest seldom came true even in this distorted form, that the Spanish Crown repeatedly tried to suppress the *encomienda* system (which would endure in some Spanish colonies until the eighteenth century), that repeated edicts against enslaving Native people issued from Iberian courts and colonial pulpits—all mattered little. Feudal dreams drove the string of conquests that followed as conquistadores poured out of their Hispaniola beachhead to conquer the islands of Puerto Rico in 1508, Jamaica in 1509, and Cuba in 1511, and, on the mainland, the territories of the Aztecs in 1521, the Incas in 1536, and Chile in 1541. With astonishing brutality and seeming ease, relative handfuls of Spaniards with their steel swords, their horses, and their war dogs—but mostly with their talent for pitting rival indigenous groups against each other and with the devastating unfamiliar diseases they unwittingly unleashed among friends and foes—reduced to

rubble the great Aztec capital city of Tenochtitlán, whose glories put Seville, Paris, or London to shame, and subdued the mountainous Incan empire of Peru.

Despite rapid depopulation from pestilence and overwork, conquered
Native peasants yielded the incalculable riches their *encomenderos* demanded. In the first century and a half after Columbus, about 181 tons of
gold and 16,200 tons of silver legally entered Spain from its new colonies,
and still more arrived surreptitiously. In the two centuries after 1565, the
great silver mines of Potosí alone yielded at least 45,000 tons of silver, and,
one seventeenth-century Spanish critic estimated, "every peso coin . . .
cost the life of ten Indians who have died in the depths of the mines." Another called Potosí "a mouth of hell, into which a great mass of people enter every year and are sacrificed by the greed of the Spaniards to their
'god.'"[9]

In this brutal environment, one *adelantado* after another read aloud in
Latin, Castilian, or perhaps a broken local language the legal document
known as the *requerimiento,* which, taking final written form in 1512, explained the Natives' duty to submit to the pope and the Catholic monarch
and threatened a well-deserved death should they rebel:

> We ask and require . . . that you acknowledge the Church as the ruler and
> superior of the whole world, and the high priest called Pope, and in his
> name the king and queen . . . our lords, in his place, as superiors and lords
> and kings of these islands and this mainland. . . .
>
> If you do so you will do well, and that which you are obliged to do for
> their highnesses, and we in their name shall receive you in all love and
> charity, and shall leave you your wives and your children and your lands
> free without servitude, that you may do with them and with yourselves
> freely what you like and think best, and they shall not compel you to turn
> Christians unless you yourselves, when informed of the truth, should wish
> to be converted to our holy Catholic faith. . . .
>
> But if you do not do this or if you maliciously delay in doing it, I certify
> to you that with the help of God we shall forcefully enter into your country
> and shall make war against you in all ways and manners that we can, and
> shall subject you to the yoke and obedience of the Church and their
> highnesses; we shall take you and your wives and your children and shall
> make slaves of them, and as such sell and dispose of them as their high-
> nesses may command; and we shall take away your goods and shall do to

you all the harm and damage that we can, as to vassals who do not obey and refuse to receive their lord and resist and contradict him; and we protest that the deaths and losses which shall accrue from this are your fault, and not that of their highnesses, or ours, or of these soldiers who come with us.[10]

That anyone really expected Native people to understand these words is doubtful. The primary audience for documents testifying that the *requerimiento* had been read was actually European: such pieces of paper testified to the Castilian court that the rules had been followed and reminded the conquistadores themselves in whose name they pretended to rule. But these threads of royal control were fragile indeed during the first generation of Spanish conquests. At last, in 1542, the Leyes Nuevas, the "New Laws" of the Indies, promulgated by Carlos V, began slowly to bring the great era of licensed mayhem to an end. The New Laws attempted to rein in the conquistadores more effectively and to define the rights of Native peoples, including a ban on their enslavement, whether or not they complied with the *requerimiento*. But what had already happened in the Americas—and much of what would follow, New Laws or not—had been fundamentally shaped by the fifteenth-century experiences of conquistadores in the eastern Atlantic islands. Dreaming of massive riches and a return to feudal glory, conquistadores set off to subdue the world for Christ and Crown, hoping to settle down as lords of their new domains, where the laborers—conquered Natives preferably, imported European tenants potentially, enslaved Africans if necessary—would cultivate the earth and enrich their new masters.

On one level, all of this had little to do with North America above the Río Grande and across the hundred miles of water that separated the Florida Peninsula from Taino Cuba. Spanish sails crossed the latter distance with ease, but nonetheless the vast swath of southeastern North America that Spanish maps labeled "La Florida," like everywhere else on the North American mainland, saw no *encomiendas,* no great estates, no significant Spanish colonization during the violent early years of the conquistadores. Only long after the colonization of Meso-America and South America had settled into a bureaucratized routine of centralized viceregal government, a tightly disciplined Church, and a predictable annual transit of armed treasure fleets bearing the silver of Peru's mines to Seville would much Castilian attention turn to North America. The crown actually explicitly forbade settlement north of the Caribbean for a few years after 1559.

The marginality of North America to early Spanish colonization was not for lack of trying—as demonstrated in 1539–1542 by Hernando de Soto's violent *entrada* among the post-Mississippian chiefdoms of the Southeast and Francisco Vásquez de Coronado's equally violent search for the fabled Seven Cities of Cíbola among the Pueblos, not to mention the exploits of such even less successful *adelantados* as Ponce de León, Lucas Vázquez de Ayllón, Pánfilo de Narváez, and Álvar Núñez Cabeza de Vaca. The problem was that there appeared to be no gold to be found, no silver or other ready riches to finance the initial expenses of sustained colonization north of the Caribbean. A permanent Spanish presence in North America became necessary only because in 1565 a group of French Protestants dared settle themselves at a place they called La Caroline on the St. John's River in La Florida. With the French heretics duly slaughtered, by 1576 only a single garrison at San Agustín seemed to the Spanish worth keeping in the northern territories it claimed.

Yet those French Protestants embody the lasting impact of Spanish conquistadores on the history of North America. "It is natural for all people, not excluding the French, to imitate the plans and actions of others," observed one chronicler of the debacle at La Caroline. "As soon as the discovery of so many riches and strange lands by the Spanish and especially Portuguese was rumored all over Europe, the maritime nations . . . felt piqued into the efforts to do the same in places where the Spanish and Portuguese had not been."[11] The major European rivals of the Iberian crowns—the French and the English—spent more than a hundred years eying covetously the rich yields of gold, silver, slaves, and other exotic commodities the conquistadores had secured and struggling to find some way "to do the same." North America seemingly could play only a secondary role—at best as a base for predatory assaults on Spanish treasure fleets, at worst as a continued source of frustration for those seeking Spanish-style wealth or a maritime short-cut to Cipangu and Cathay. Nonetheless, from it all, dreams of exploitative conquest for Cross and Crown left their stamp on the North American mainland.

Thus, any Spanish *adelantado* would have understood, and eagerly accepted, the instructions that England's Henry VII issued to the Genoa-born Venetian navigator John Cabot in 1497. In hopes of duplicating feats that Columbus and his men were just then carrying out on Hispaniola, Cabot, his sons, and their heirs received "full and free authority, leave, and power to saile to all parts, countreys, and seas of the East, of the West, and of the North" and to "subdue, occupy, and possesse all such townes, cities, castles, and isles of them found . . . , getting unto us the rule, title, and jurisdiction of the same villages, townes, castles, and firme land." All profits gained from trade to any places the Cabots conquered would belong to them, except for "one fifth of the capitall gaine so gotten," due the Crown.[12] Cabot did not return from the aptly labeled "Newfoundland" entirely empty-handed: to prove that a place where he encountered no actual people indeed was inhabited, he brought back a Native-made hunting snare and a wooden needle used to make fishing nets. But he certainly found nothing like the riches of Hispaniola. Nor did he know or care that he apparently made first landfall only about five miles from the long-abandoned Norse settlement at L'Anse aux Meadows.

Cabot never returned at all from his poorly documented second voyage, in 1498. Nearly as obscure are the activities of his son Sebastian and a handful of other English would-be conquistadores who followed Cabot's route from Bristol to Newfoundland and other points on the North Atlantic coast over the next couple of decades. Yet clearly they found neither gold, nor Cipangu, nor Cathay. That many other Europeans traced the same route to discover the bountiful fisheries of the Grand Banks hardly interested European crowns and gentleman adventurers at all. As late as 1577, Martin Frobisher complained of Newfoundlanders that "their riches are not gold, silver or precious Drapery . . . [but rather] trifles, more to be wondred at for their strangenesse, then for any other commoditie needefull for our use."[13]

The French, meanwhile, were coming to their own conclusions about the worthlessness of North America as a target for conquest or a stopping point on the way to Cathay. Sailing under a charter from King François I, in 1524 the Florentine Giovanni da Verrazano mapped the North American coast from today's Carolinas to Maine. Unlike Cabot, he saw plenty of Native people, kidnapping at least one to take back to France and trading or skirmishing with many others, but he did not find what he was looking for. "Verrazano claimed these lands for France, and at the same time demonstrated that North America was a vast land barrier, a geographical nuisance, between Europe and the riches of Cathay," a modern historian explains. "Moreover, it appeared to have much the same flora and fauna as did France: no spices, no exotic woods, no advanced civilizations surfeited with gold, silver or precious stones."[14]

Three expeditions and two short-lived colonial settlements headed by Jacques Cartier in 1534, 1535–1536, and 1541–1542 seemed to confirm Verrazano's lessons. Sailing nearly a thousand miles up the promising gulf and river the French called the St. Lawrence got one nowhere nearer to Cathay, or even to a rumored place of great riches called "Saguenay." Moreover, the Native people who lived in the sizable towns of Stadacona and Hochelaga (on the later sites of Québec and Montréal, respectively) quickly made it clear that there would be no easy conquests in the territory Cartier dubbed "Canada," after misunderstanding the Stadaconans' answer to his question about what they called the place; the term approximates the Iroquoian word for "our town." It is almost too perfect an ending to Cartier's dreams of conquest that the cargo of diamonds and gold he triumphantly displayed on his final return to France turned out to consist of quartz crystals and iron pyrite, "fool's gold."

Still, it was no fool's gold that the Spanish had found in Hispaniola and Mexico, and no fool's silver that they extracted from the mines of Peru. Little wonder, then, that when French or English people thought about the Americas, all their models, all their images of the land and its people, were based on what they had read of the Native people of the Caribbean and Meso-America. Particularly in light of the scant knowledge assimilated from the short and often violent experience of conquistadores with actual Native North Americans, "Indian" came to be synonymous with "Taino" (although few Europeans ever assimilated that proper name for indigenous islanders). All such "Indians" wore few clothes (except for the fanciful feathered headdresses that graced early printed images), were governed (if that was the word for it) by *caciques,* slept in *hammocks,* smoked their fish on *barbecues,* and traveled in *canoes* (Taino words all). All were suspected of being *cannibals,* all certainly were pagans, who either were slaves to the devil or had no religion whatsoever. And all, therefore, without question had to accept the governance of a Christian monarch, at the point of the sword if necessary.

The readers of *The Decades of the New World,* by Richard Eden—the first extended English-language book about the Americas—would have encountered a brief list of words in what readers might reasonably conclude was the one and only "Indian language." Among those words were *"Canoe,* a boat or barque" and *"Caciques,* kings or governors."[15] Published

in 1555, *The Decades* was mostly a translation of Pietro Martire d'Anghiera's Latin account of Columbus' exploits, enlivened by a few other
documents and Eden's own commentary on the land and its Native people. "One special thing I observed amongst other in reading over" Anghiera's book, said Eden in a later publication. "The cause why after the
conquest made of them, the Spaniards do in continual bondage and slavery keep them," he explained, "may thus be Englished," or translated:

> These be the Indians qualities, in respect
> whereof they deserve no liberty.

In the continent or firm land they eat man's flesh: they be more given to
sodomy than any other nation of the world: there is no order of justice
among them, they go naked, they have neither love nor honesty, they be
fools and furious, there is no truth in them, except it be for their own
profit: inconstant, without all discretion, very unkind, and lovers of novelties. . . . They be slothful, thieves, of judgement very gross and base, without all honesty and good order. Neither do the men behave themselves
loyally with their wives, nor the wives with their husbands: they be super-
stitiously given to soothsaying, as fearful as hares, filthy, eating lice, spiders,
and worms, wheresoever they find them: they have no art, nor good condition of men. . . . In conclusion, I say that God never created so corrupt a
people for vice and beastliness, without any mixture of goodness and civility: they are as blocktish as asses, making no account at all to kill themselves.[16]

What more did would-be conquistadores need to know?

They needed to know, of course, where they could get their share of the
riches, the landed estates, the docile agricultural labor force, the glories
for Crown and Cross that they imagined the Spanish had found. "How
greatly doth it sound to the reproach of all Christendom, and especially to
such as dwell nearest to these lands (as we do) being much nearer unto the
same then are the Spaniards," Eden fairly shouted at his countrymen,
"that we have no respect neither for God's cause nor for our own commodity to attempt some voyages into these coasts, to do for our parts as the
Spaniards have done for theirs."[17]

By the time Eden wrote, in the mid-sixteenth century, no one could
pretend that Christendom remained a unitary whole, and this, too, pro-

foundly shaped the fervor of Europe's conquistadores. "God's cause" was being ripped apart not only by the efforts of new monarchs to seize control over the wealth and power of the Church within their realms, but by the powerful spiritual and intellectual currents of the Protestant Reformation. Eden, in fact, wrote at a particularly fraught period in the intertwining of national monarchies and religious ferment, and was, accordingly, one of the last European authors who could unselfconsciously talk about a unified Christendom expanded through "merciful wars against . . . naked people."[18] In 1555, when Eden's words saw print, the man who a year later would become King Felipe II of Spain, was also king of England—at least for the lifetime of his wife, Mary I. She and the husband her subjects called Philip had made it their business to bring her realm back into the Catholic fold it had left when Henry VIII and his Parliament declared its independence from Rome in 1534. Mary's early death in 1558, and the accession to the throne of the resolutely Protestant and unmarried Queen Elizabeth I, irrevocably attached England's rivalry with Spain—and all questions of conquests in the Americas—to the cause of Protestantism and its struggle against Roman Catholicism.

FOUR

Crusades of the Protestants
to New Worlds

THE FIRST ARRIVALS OF substantial numbers of Europeans in North America cannot be understood apart from the spiritual fervor—and murderous violence—spawned by conflicts between Catholics and Protestants. For the better part of a century on the continent of Europe, religious rivals killed each other mercilessly in civil wars, wars among nation-states, and wars not easily put in either category. Many Protestants became convinced that they were in fact living in the End Times, that the final cataclysmic struggle between Christ and the Antichrist was unfolding before their eyes, and that their every political as well as spiritual effort must be bent to the cause. The Antichrist was none other than the pope, and his chief agent on this earth was none other than the "Catholic monarch" of Spain, first Carlos V and then Felipe II. For Protestants throughout Europe—and they were everywhere, even in Spain itself—military, political, and economic struggles against the Spanish state thus took on a cosmic significance far beyond mere lust for gold and landed estates. A kind of Protestant conquistador emerged, seeking to combat the papist with all the fervor his predecessors had devoted to combating the infidel in their Lord's struggle to bring about a new heaven and a new earth. Those who most self-consciously assumed the role were English.

But what was Protestantism? To a large degree, for Henry VIII and the many German princes who aligned themselves with the reformers Martin Luther or John Calvin, Protestantism was often little more than an alternative way to achieve the goals that Spain's Carlos V and France's François I achieved without breaking with Rome: the political power that came from the right to appoint bishops and other clergy, and the economic power that came from the right to tax or manage directly the Church's vast lands and resources. Certainly for Henry VIII, "Defender of the Faith," the primary dispute was not, initially, with core Catholic teachings. Theologically, very little changed in the nationally independent Henrician Church. Latin prevailed in most rituals. The Statute of Six Articles passed by Parliament in 1539 (subtitled "An Act Abolishing Diversity in Opinions") affirmed Catholic doctrines about the Mass, confession, and clerical celibacy. *The King's Book*, the official statement of faith of 1543, affirmed a Catholic understanding of the sacraments, endorsed prayers for the dead, and discouraged Bible reading among the laity.

All this was very much as Henry VIII wanted it. The monarch whose name was on the title page of the *Defense of the Seven Sacraments* fancied himself a serious religious scholar. On the issue of divorce, for instance—the surface issue in Henry's controversy with Pope Clement VII—one should not dismiss out of hand the sincerity of the king's belief that he had sinned by marrying Catherine of Aragón, who had been betrothed to his deceased brother, and that his divine punishment was to be denied a male heir. It is a little harder to know what to make of his supposed suggestion that one of the Ten Commandments be rewritten along the lines of "Thou shall not covet another man's wife without due recompense."[1] There is less doubt about what to make of the enormous Church wealth the Crown expropriated when it dissolved England's monasteries and convents between 1536 and 1540. Many of their lands were distributed to political supporters of the Crown, solidifying these temporarily nonviolent conquistadores' commitment to the independence of the English Church and its new head, the king.

But all this says nothing about the power of Protestant doctrines and spirituality, which developed quite apart from the actions of kings and princes and took on a life of their own. In some ways, there was little new in the ideas that would come to be called Protestant. For centuries, theologians and the occasional mystic among the lower male clergy, women religious, and laity of both sexes had debated thorny questions about the respective roles of divine grace and human works, of faith and doctrine, of scripture and tradition, of ceremony and piety, and of clergy and ordinary people. There had been endless calls to return to the pure practices of the original apostles, to improve standards of learning among the clergy, to erase superstition among the laity, to decrease the secular power of bishops and the papacy, to purge institutions of perceived corruption, to struggle with issues of sexuality and marriage. Sometimes the debates remained academic. In that tradition—if the story is true that Professor Luther tacked his Ninety-Five Theses (in Latin) next to other announcements hanging on the church door at Wittenberg in 1517—the propositions would have been intended only for his university colleagues and Church officials. Sometimes the old debates led to such permanent changes as the founding of a new monastic order, fiscal and behavioral reforms, or new models of piety and might gain their advocates recognition as "saints." More often, especially when the lower orders got too many ideas of their own, people were branded as heretics and killed.

Had it not been for the forces that were already leading monarchs to challenge Rome and for the new technology of printing that allowed ideas to spread in unprecedented ways—the Ninety-Five Theses quickly went into print in German translation, perhaps without the author's consent— Luther's proposals might well have gone the way of their predecessors, suppressed or absorbed by an ever-flexible Catholic Church. But according to one estimate, a third of German books published in the years 1518 to 1525 came from Luther's pen.[2] Thus, his calls for reform would be heard loud and clear.

The old idea that Luther rediscovered—the idea that inspired almost everything the self-styled reformers did and said—came from Paul's Epistle to the Romans. "'No human being will be justified in [God's] sight' by deeds prescribed by the law, for through the law comes the knowledge of sin," wrote Paul. "There is no distinction, since all have sinned and fall short of the glory of God; they are now justified by his grace as a gift, through the redemption that is in Christ Jesus."[3] For Luther and his followers, this was the core of the Gospel, the "Good News," although it started from the pessimistic premise that humans were so inherently corrupt that nothing they ever did could make them justified in the eyes of their creator.

The concept of justification was something similar to one we use to describe the way words line up on the margin of a page. Words could never line themselves up on their own without the external efforts of a typesetter. Neither could humans straighten their course without the external, freely given grace of God. Good works, charity, penance, praying, following laws to the nth degree—none of these things, admirable though they might be, could earn humans salvation. Certainly it did no good for the Church to set aside a special category of sinful humans called "priests" with the authority to tell other sinful humans what they must *do* to be justified before the King of Kings. It was even worse to pretend that priests could do the people's work for them through the sacrifice of the Mass, the saying of prayers for the living and the dead, and the sale of indulgences that atoned for sins. All such "priestcraft" was "works righteousness," an abominable heresy that enslaved people in a futile quest to earn the justification that could be gained only through God's arbitrary free gift of grace.

From this simple idea, many others followed logically, even necessarily, and something truly new was created. There were no sacred intermediaries between God and humans. There was no priesthood apart from the "priesthood of believers." There were no "Saints" who carried on that intermediary work from beyond the grave; all the believers were equally "saints" (and, Luther said, sinners at the same time). There were no sacraments, if by "sacrament" one meant magical acts performed by priests for the salvation of the people. There were only, for Luther, acts in which God did the work of imparting grace to the saints; only, for Calvin and many others, human acts that were symbolic reminders of that grace. Hence, at least four of the seven sacraments that Henry VIII wrote about dropped out of the picture: ordination of a special breed called "priests," confirmation of the promises made by parents and godparents at infant baptism, and last rites for the dead clearly embodied "works righteousness." These could survive only as markers of life passages. Marriage was no longer a dispensation given to weak laity by a superior celibate clergy to regulate the production of children, but a civil contract between (in theory) two equals who were (even more in theory) to express their God-given sexual desires with each other. Luther was unclear on whether confession, cleansed of its priestly intermediation and of any hint of penitential works, remained a sacrament. Only baptism and the eucharist, stripped of much of their magical quality for Lutherans, of nearly all of it for Calvinists, clearly remained. As all these ideas developed, the very definition of the "Church" was transformed. Formerly an organization of priests, monks, and nuns who interceded between God and the laity and instructed them on how to atone for their sins, it was now the gathering of believers, of the saints justified by grace. With the Roman Catholic Church removed as intermediary, the only source of authority was sacred scripture itself, which all people had to read for themselves in their own language—thus Luther's great work of translating the Bible into German.

These were very dangerous ideas. If all should read the scriptures, who was to say which reading of ambiguous and contradictory texts was correct? If grace was free, who was to say who had it and who did not? If works did not earn justification, why not let people just do as they pleased? If the elaborate church furnishings, stained glass, images of saints, decorated altars, and all the other glories of medieval cathedrals devoted to the discredited Mass and the false teachings of the pope had to be destroyed—and they were, to the extent that virtually no decorative glass, statues, or ritual vessels survived on the island of Great Britain—what was to restrain iconoclastic mobs, like the one that in 1559 took less than a week to dismantle Scotland's entire Cathedral of St. Andrews, from turning their rage on all symbols of hierarchy? If scripture was the only authority, what role was there for kings and princes, what lord could there be but *the* Lord?

The elite reformers who put forward these anarchic ideas in pulpits erected in the hollowed shells of formerly glorious church buildings always pulled back from their fullest implications. On the one hand, they repeatedly asserted, with astonishing optimism, three themes: that there could be only one divine truth, and therefore those who had received grace could never legitimately disagree on core beliefs; that, while good works could not earn justification, grace empowered the justified to do truly good works; and that, in the end, God's laws remained God's laws, and they had to be obeyed.

On the other hand, elite reformers invariably found themselves compromising even this much of the anarchic core of Protestantism, finding ways to reemphasize hierarchy and secure social order. There would be no more priests, but of course it was necessary to have a university-educated licensed ministry to ensure that orthodoxy was taught and to prevent ordinary people from taking things into their own hands. Restrictions on reading the scriptures in the vernacular could never be openly accepted, but, for instance, English lay people could be encouraged to read the Geneva Bible of 1560, whose weighty apparatus of Calvinist notes and commentaries left few interpretive issues unresolved. And someone had to enforce God's laws. For Luther himself—badly shaken by a peasant uprising in 1524—this led to a doctrine calling for almost complete submission to government authority as ordained by God, whether that authority was Catholic or Protestant or neither. The ultimate product was the purely political settlement whereby, under the Peace of Augsburg of 1555, all people in each state in the Holy Roman Empire were bound to follow the religion of their then-prince, Catholic or Protestant—the same basic idea Henry VIII imposed on England.

Followers of the younger, French-born reformer Calvin turned Luther's view of the relationship between the saints and secular authority inside out, but they could do so only by placing severe restrictions on the operation of God's free grace. Grace was indeed free, and works indeed did not lead to justification, and people indeed were inherently sinful. But, said Calvin, God also insisted on the just punishment of those who violated His laws. It followed that the vast majority of sinful human beings would endure the eternal punishment they so richly deserved. Only an elite few— "predestined" by God's mysterious grace since before the moment of Creation—would receive the gift of regeneration, and even these, some argued, could never be entirely certain during their lifetime whether they were saved or damned. Yet at least assurance could be glimpsed, and brief moments of intense spiritual communion with the divine and with other godly souls could be enjoyed.

Most Calvinists therefore placed great emphasis on the individual "conversion experience," in which the sinner recognized his or her utter depravity and, from that depth of despair, felt the first glimmering of the divine grace on which salvation entirely depended. That grace also allowed the reborn saint, however imperfectly, to obey God's laws and to perform the good works that were the product, not the cause, of salvation. The spiritual psychology that Calvinism spoke to, then, centered on intense self-examination, on wild swings between glimpses of spiritual peace and despair over one's sinfulness, and on a vital attempt to prove to oneself and others that one possessed the grace to shape one's every deed to the will of God.

About which, logically, there should have been no choice, since everything that happened was predestined by an omnipotent deity. Calvin and his successors never adequately resolved the apparent paradox, except to declare that their all-powerful god preferred to work in natural ways and to unfold his predestined plans through what appeared to be free moral choices by individuals. This voluntaristic understanding of predestination had many important implications. It was vitally necessary for believers to do all they could to discern God's plan, through scripture reading, prayer, self-examination, and attention to "providential" events that testified to the deity's design. One was put in the world for a purpose, and it was the duty of a saint to discover that purpose and fulfill it, whether as a prosperous blacksmith or as a lowly stable-keeper, a village preacher or a lofty magistrate, a great lady or a humble maidservant. This emphasis on worldly vocations undergirds what has often been called the "Protestant work ethic." But any good Calvinist knew that, although wealth might be a sign of God's favor, it might just as well be a snare laid by the devil. The real point of work was to advance God's kingdom.

And it was God's kingdom, not the realm of any earthly prince, that always had to be kept in mind. Saints not only had to live their personal lives in accord with divine will through strict conformance to the Ten Commandments, but they had a duty to ensure that the vast majority of reprobates without grace conformed too. Although it was seldom safe to say so out loud or in print, the implication was that rulers who refused to play this role, whose lives were not blameless, who persisted in "papist" or "ungodly" rule, should be overthrown if they could not be converted.

For much was at stake in the struggle between the godly and the Antichrist, with his Roman minions. Religion, politics, and international affairs wove a tangled and violent web of transcendent significance. It is no accident that the rebel Dutch burghers in the Low Countries who struggled for most of the sixteenth century to gain their independence from Felipe II were overwhelmingly Calvinists. No accident, either, that many Protestant ministers driven out of England during the brief Catholic reign of Mary I and Felipe II spent their exile with Calvin in Geneva and then returned home to complain relentlessly that Elizabeth I's state church was insufficiently Protestant, insufficiently severe in its enforcement of divine law, and insufficiently aggressive toward Catholic Spain. These efforts to purify the nation earned them the derisive name "puritan." And it was also no accident that the majority of the French colonists slaughtered by the Spanish in Florida were the variety of Calvinists known as Huguenots, whose coreligionists were at the same time involved in the early stages of the generation-long period of religious and political chaos that would culminate in the "War of the Three Henries."

When the short-lived colony of La Caroline was established in 1564, Calvinism was very much a persecuted movement in France. Although the colony's leaders, Jean Ribault and René de Laudonnière, had the protection of King Charles IX's mother and regent, Catherine de' Medici, there could be nothing officially Protestant about its mission. A French history published a few decades later said only that the colonists were "motivated . . . by different desires: some solely to see and explore the land; others to put to good use their first respite from the civil wars into which they had been led; and others because of the great hope of enjoying the prosperity and riches that had been proposed to them and which Florida promises."[4] All those involved, however, believed that among the colony's purposes would be to strike a blow against Felipe II and to provide a refuge for Huguenot Protestants.

Refuge or not, bills had to be paid; and so, as on Hispaniola six decades earlier, the search for precious metals became the colonists' first priority. In 1562, Ribault had led an advance mission to scout a location for the French colony and stake a claim to "New France." Near the mouth of the St. John's River in Florida and on Parris Island off what is now South Carolina, he erected stone columns bearing the French coat of arms; and then he sailed home, having left thirty men behind at a makeshift post called "Charlesfort." Also left behind were two young Native men originally acquired to serve as translators. These had long since jumped ship, but not before a few chats on deck had convinced Laudonnière that he could "understand the greater part of their conversations."[5] Whatever meager mastery of the local language Laudonnière acquired cannot have improved much in the nearly two years that passed before French politics allowed him to return to the St. John's River with three hundred colonists. It is difficult to know what, exactly, a paramount chief named Saturiba told him about Ribault's stone column, which the Native people had bedecked with magnolias and surrounded with baskets of corn. But according to Laudonnière, Saturiba proclaimed that a piece of silver he carried came from an up-river people called "Thimogona," that these people were his greatest enemies (indeed, that is the meaning of the word "Thimogona," which comes down to us as "Timucua," the name of the region's population). Saturiba announced that he would be delighted if the French and their firearms joined him in making war on them.

"The Spaniards in their conquests always entered into alliances, pitting one king against the other,"[6] Laudonnière later observed. So naturally he told Saturiba he would oblige, and then, as soon as his men, with the assistance of Native roof-thatchers, finished building the triangular bastions of La Caroline, he sent one of his lieutenants up the river to make an alliance *with* the Thimogonas. For these people, whose paramount chief was called Outina, presumably controlled the silver supply (most of which turned out to be scavenged from European shipwrecks) and, furthermore, claimed to know the way to copper and gold mines in the Appalachian Mountains. During the next few months, Laudonnière repeatedly refused Saturiba's demands that he attack Outina.

Matters came to a head when Saturiba's people and their allies nonetheless made war and returned with twenty-four Thimogona captives, thirteen of whom went to Outina as paramount chief, in keeping with the long-standing political importance of the exchange of enslaved prisoners. Laudonnière demanded that the slaves be released to him. When Saturiba protested that "he was not subservient to" the French, Laudonnière sent twenty armed men to seize the prisoners, thus "bringing reason to this savage and to make him understand how his bravado would only hurt him." To make matters worse, the men sent to take the liberated captives home actually fought alongside Outina against an enemy yet farther in the interior. In January 1565, Laudonnière again not only refused to join Saturiba in battle against Outina but sent aid to the Thimogonas instead.

At this point, food ran short for the colonists, who had been relying on the trade and hospitality of Saturiba to support them. Laudonnière attributed the problem to seasonal hunting that regularly took Saturiba's people away from home for several months of the year. The more likely possibility—that the Natives had decided to cut the French off—apparently never occurred to him. Meantime, Ribault's scheduled return with additional colonists and supplies was long overdue. While two separate mutinous groups sailed off in purloined vessels to raid Spanish ships or islands, starvation loomed, and the colonists determined to return to France. But they still needed food, for the present and to supply their journey. After increasingly desperate efforts to strong-arm Outina into providing it, Laudonnière kidnapped the chief, on the theory that, as the colony was to be abandoned anyway, "there was no longer any danger from making the Indians unfriendly by forcing them to furnish us with food."[7] Not surprisingly, a war ensued, and the French simply started stealing corn from neighboring villages.

Then, before Laudonnière could leave the scene of devastation he had created, in rapid succession three fleets showed up at La Caroline: first, that of England's John Hawkins, who traded much-needed provisions for some of the fort's artillery; then that of Ribault, with his long-awaited reinforcements; then that of the avenging Spanish.

In their desperation, the colonists at La Caroline might have lost track of the religious significance of their efforts, but the *adelantado* whom Felipe II had dispatched specifically to exterminate the Huguenots did not lose focus. Governor-General Pedro Menéndez de Avilés summarily executed nearly every French Protestant he found. Those who survived his assault on the fort were hanged, supposedly under a sign that read "I do this not as to Frenchmen, but as to Lutherans."[8] Apart from a few strong-looking laborers condemned to fifty years of slavery, all the professed Protestants among two large parties of other colonists whom Menéndez later tracked down were stabbed in the back with their hands tied after they learned, as the *adelantado* proudly reported to Felipe II, "how we had taken their Fort and hanged all those we found in it, because they had built it without Your Majesty's permission and because they were scattering the odious Lutheran doctrine in these Provinces." There was no doubt that he must rain "fire and blood . . . against all those who came to sow this hateful doctrine."[9] Menéndez de Avilés did not know the difference between a Calvinist and a Lutheran, but he certainly understood that he was involved in a religious as well as national crusade.

England's Elizabeth I also cared little for the differences between Calvinists and Lutherans. Like her father, Henry VIII, she demonstrated no particular enthusiasm for the fine points of Protestant theology. If she had had a conversion experience, it must have been in the dreadful moment when she first realized that her survival as queen depended on England's never again returning to the Catholic fold. In the eyes of the Church (and Spain), Elizabeth, like her short-lived predecessor, Edward VI, was the bastard child of a mother whom Henry VIII had never legally married. Since there were no offspring of the marriage between Felipe II and Henry's Catholic daughter, Mary I, the legitimate heir to England's throne was Mary Stuart (granddaughter of Henry VIII's sister), who had married King James IV of Scotland.

"Mary Queen of Scots" had never really ruled her country. Inheriting the crown as an infant, she had spent her childhood in the France of Catherine de Médicis. She had briefly been queen as the wife of François II, who was succeeded by his brother Charles IX. Mary was, then, no stranger to the intertwining of dynastic quarrels and religious warfare. In her absence from Scotland, the nobles who ruled in her name turned the country Protestant, under the influence of Calvin's disciple

John Knox. When she returned to the British Isles in 1561, a few months after François II's death, the nobles were hardly willing to yield their power to a nineteen-year-old Catholic woman who spoke French better than Scots. The many intrigues by which she was deposed in favor of her infant son James VI and wound up imprisoned south of the border in England are less important to our story than the fact that, for many Catholics inside the British Isles as well as on the Continent, she became the focus of countless schemes to depose Elizabeth and undo England's reformation.

The survival of the English monarchy therefore became inextricable from English Protestantism, and in the hot and cold wars with Spain that characterized Elizabeth's reign, England's patriotism—England's very national identity—became just as inextricable from religion. To be English was, by definition, to be Protestant. To be an English Catholic (and there were thousands of them) was more than an oxymoron. It was an act of treason against the monarch who was head of the Church of England, against the nation that was engaged in a desperate struggle with Spain, and in favor of a foreign sovereign, the pope.

Yet, much to the chagrin of those coming to be called "puritans," Elizabeth and her political and religious advisors constructed a compromise style of Protestantism that had room for nearly everyone but the most committed (and therefore all the more suspect) Catholics. A Lutheran-style state church apparatus administered by a hierarchy of bishops joined a moderate Calvinist theology reduced to thirty-nine carefully worded Articles of Faith, a Book of Common Prayer whose liturgical ambiguities nonetheless left little room for local experimentation in forms of worship, and an official Book of Homilies designed to discourage extemporaneous preaching of dangerous doctrines in favor of learned recitations of uncontroversial Calvinist dogma. Such theological obfuscations ensured that clarity in England's domestic Protestant identity and mission could come only from outside, through the struggle against Spain.

As the proclaimed leader of Catholic Europe, Spain found similar clarity. The Church's Council of Trent, which met off and on from 1545 to 1563, made major reforms in response to the various Protestant movements. While firmly rejecting every theological position put forward by Lutherans and Calvinists, the council imposed an unprecedented degree of centralization upon the diverse catholicity of the medieval Church. The new order expressed itself through the freshly standardized Tridentine

Latin Mass, which flattened most local diversity in worship, and through an insistence that no national or local authority inside or outside the Church could question the authority of the papacy. Abuses such as the easy sale of indulgences or of Church offices were suppressed. There was a great new awareness that ordinary lay people (and, for that matter, priests) needed to be seriously educated in Catholic doctrine if they were to be kept out of the hands of the Protestants. A new religious order, the Society of Jesus, or Jesuits, most notably took on this task. But everywhere universities, schools, and catechizing assumed an importance they had never had before. Still, mere education would not be enough. The Catholic Reformation insisted that heresy and superstition had to be rooted out wherever they were found, through the courts known as inquisitions (originally devised in Castile to try recently converted Muslims and Jews suspected of backsliding), and through the military conquest of states ruled by heretics such as Elizabeth.

This is where the troops of Felipe II—an ascetic and deeply pious man—came in. And this is why many Protestants were convinced that the Battle of Armageddon had begun. The unfortunate residents of Felipe's rebellious Low Country provinces, whether they were Catholic, Lutheran, or Calvinist, needed no convincing; the wartime carnage was frightful. No reliable casualty figures exist, but from 1567 to 1609 in what later became Belgium, a third to a half, and in some areas of Flanders nearly all, of the rural population was at least temporarily driven from their homes.

The embattled Low Countries were always the focus of England's late sixteenth-century struggle with the "papists." Elizabeth seldom intervened openly, apart from a disastrous experiment in the 1580s, when the Netherlands officially became a "protectorate" of England, with Elizabeth I's close associate Robert Dudley, Earl of Leicester, as its military governor-general. When Leicester provoked something of an independence movement of his own and the official military relationship came to an end, countless young English men who might in an earlier era have gone on a crusade or enlisted as mercenaries went across the North Sea to join their coreligionists in battle. So many English soldiers—among them such important figures in later North American colonies as John Smith, John Underhill, and Miles Standish—learned their craft in this way that an early Virginia official referred to "that university of ware, the Lowe Countries."[10]

Meantime, other English men harassed Spanish interests wherever they could, mostly by sea, where continued efforts to find new routes to the East, by way of Russia, or Africa, or South or North America, took on new urgency. "Sea Dogs" such as Hawkins, Francis Drake, Walter Ralegh, or Humphrey Gilbert, whose official licenses as "privateers" legalized their piratical attacks on Spanish shipping and ports, became national heroes for their actions as naval *adelantados,* who recruited and financed their brutal ventures much as did their Spanish counterparts and who bestowed on their ships such names as *Grace of God, Gift of God,* or *John Evangelist.* In all of this, North America seldom captured any particular attention, although the occasional commentator observed, in suitably Calvinist predestinarian language, that it was "probable by event of precedent attempts made by the Spanyards and French sundry times, that the countreys lying north of *Florida,* God hath reserved . . . to be reduced unto Christian civility by the English nation."[11]

Such thinking—reinforced by the success of English privateers in the Spanish Caribbean and the ever-present allure of the annual treasure fleet—led Walter Ralegh to envision a colony north of Florida, in territory he christened "Virginia" to honor his unmarried queen. Ralegh, despite the repeated charges of "athiesme" made against him, epitomized the militantly Protestant Elizabethan English conquistador. In about 1568, at the precocious age of fourteen, he left Oriel College, Oxford, to join many fellow Devonshire natives who had volunteered to fight on behalf of the Huguenots in France. Over the next few years, he dropped in and out of Oriel and London's Inns of Court, where lawyers learned their trade. Meanwhile he involved himself with the privateering and colonizing schemes of his half-brother Humphrey Gilbert and met the two great propagandists of English oversees expansion, Richard Hakluyt the Elder and Richard Hakluyt the Younger. He attracted the attention of the queen and, after stints of fighting in the Low Countries and Ireland, Ralegh became a royal favorite, showered with titles, monopolies, perquisites, and, finally in 1584, rights to a North American patent that had lapsed when Gilbert died at sea in a failed attempt to establish a Newfoundland colony the previous year.

Humphrey Gilbert's dream of North American colonization reveals how deeply neo-feudal ideals took root among English Protestant conquistadores. Like so many before him (and Ralegh after him), Gilbert and his heirs would possess any "remote heathen and barbarous lands" they could conquer, with virtually unlimited rights to govern and redistribute the territories, in exchange for delivering to the queen one-fifth of all the silver and gold they extracted from those lands.[12] Gilbert envisioned a massive North American estate where agricultural colonists would enrich him with their varied rents and feudal dues. Gentleman adventurers who made substantial investments in the project would receive minimum grants of one thousand acres, which they presumably would lease out to tenants on terms similar to those of Gilbert's own servants and free tenants. Adventurers and laborers alike would pay annual rents and be responsible for providing military service and equipment, while turning over to Gilbert two-fifths of gold, silver, and precious stones and one-tenth of all other metals.

Such emoluments, supplemented by profits gained from selling English manufactures to the colonists, were the entire business plan, apart from the riches to be gained from using the colony as a privateering base. No one thought through exactly what the colonists would grow, why any ordinary English people would want to migrate, or how the Native people were to be convinced to supply the food and other resources necessary until the imported population became self-sustaining. "Gilbert's outlook seems to have been fairly typical of that of the adventurers generally," one scholar says. "They expected to use martial rather than entrepreneurial skills to get the wealth and status they and their followers wanted," and "they did not suggest any plan for engaging settlers or American Indians in large-scale production of agricultural commodities for the market."[13]

Ralegh's aristocratic nonbusiness model was almost exactly identical to that of his half-brother Gilbert. It was as if nothing new had been learned since the days of Columbus on Hispaniola, and, as a result, the colony Ralegh tried to establish in Virginia displayed startling parallels to its unwitting predecessor at French La Caroline. Once again, there was an exploratory mission to stake territorial claims and to lure aboard potential Native translators. In 1584, Arthur Barlow and Philip Amadas, guided by Gilbert's veteran Portuguese pilot Simon Fernandes, sailed to the Outer Banks of today's North Carolina and identified Roanoke Island as the best place for a privateering base. They picked up a young man of chiefly lineage named Manteo (the name may be a variant on *mantou*, or "power"), whose Croatoan people lived thirty miles to the south of Roanoke, near modern Cape Hatteras. They also convinced a Roanoke commoner who identified himself as Wanchese (the Algonquian word means "young boy") to leave his home on the mainland just opposite the island, and then sailed home by way of Bermuda and the Azores, in hopes of taking a Spanish prize.

In London, while learning English and teaching Algonquian, Manteo and Wanchese discovered that, just as at home, chiefs received preferential treatment over ordinary people. Not surprisingly, the well-fêted elite Manteo apparently decided that an alliance with the English could turn to his people's advantage, while the ignored commoner Wanchese bided his time until he could get home. Intentionally or not, the English thus created relationships that would allow colonists to pit local leaders against each other: Manteo of the Croatoans would be Virginia's favored Outina, and Wanchese's chief Wingina of the Roanokes would be its betrayed Saturiba. As Hakluyt the Younger put it, the colonizers expected to "join with this king heere, or with that king there, at our pleasure, and may so with a few men be revenged of any wrong offered by any of them; or may, if we will proceed with extremitie, conquer, fortify, and plant in soils most sweet, most pleasant, most strong, and most fertile, and in the end bring them all in subjection and to civilitie."[14]

While Manteo said (or was optimistically understood to say) all the right things about Virginia—there was gold there and the soils were marvelously fertile—and while Ralegh's men planned the next stage of their effort, Hakluyt summed up the duties of a Protestant conquistador. "The ends of this voyage are these," he declared. "(1) To plant Christian religion, (2) To trafficke [that is, to trade], (3) To conquer." Even better would be "to doe all three." Yet "to plant Christian religion without conquest will bee hard. Trafficke easily followeth conquest: conquest is not easie. Trafficke without conquest seemeth possible, and not uneasie. What is to be done, is the question."[15]

The immediate thing to be done was to send approximately five hundred men—all men—to establish a beachhead, to find the gold that had to be there, and, under the direction of scientist Thomas Hariot assisted by artist John White, to document the natural and human resources of the area. Under the command of Ralegh's cousin Richard Grenville (whose high social status was balanced by his lack of experience in anything related to the enterprise), the expedition was star-crossed from the outset. Storms separated the ships of its first installment and provided them with an excuse to spend many weeks privateering from a makeshift fort in

Puerto Rico while consuming most of the provisions intended for the colonists; the queen diverted a second and larger installment of ships to the war with Spain; Grenville and the seasoned military veteran Ralph Lane, intended to be left with the colonists as governor, despised each other.

Once the expedition arrived at Roanoke, the men had barely begun to throw up fortifications and houses on the northern end of the island when an exploring party found a silver cup missing after they visited the mainland Roanoke village of Aquasogoc. Grenville sent a party to retrieve it—a troop of men under Amadas, who, "not receiving it according to his promise, . . . burnt, and spoiled their corn, and Town, all the people being fled."[16] Within a couple of weeks, Grenville sailed for England in search of reinforcements. Lane remained behind in charge of approximately one hundred men, most of them servants and employees of Ralegh, a few of them gentlemen adventurers, all of them waiting for their gold, their Spanish plunder, and their food, which the embattled Roanokes had somehow to be convinced to give them.

So La Caroline's story played out at Roanoke with English variations, including a long-overdue resupply fleet and unsuccessful efforts by a governor of La Florida named Pedro Menéndez—Pedro Menéndez Marqués, nephew of Menéndez de Avilés—to find the colony and expunge still more "Lutherans" from La Florida's Catholic soil. Records on what happened during the winter of 1585–1586 are spotty, but Lane's men seem to have spent most of their time exploring the Chesapeake and other potential water routes to Cathay, chasing down Native reports of pearls and gold and copper mines, spreading deadly disease (probably influenza) in many of the places they visited, and using increasingly desperate means to extort food from their Roanoke neighbors. Wingina, chief of Wanchese's Roanoke people, meantime, took on the name "Pemisapan," which connotes wary watchfulness. Whether this was a ceremonial title he would have assumed anyway or, as Lane suspected, a declaration of war, Pemisapan apparently began mobilizing an alliance against the English, and, like Saturiba before him, tried to cut off all contact by late April. Shooting soon began, and, on the first of June, Lane and his men surrounded Pemisapan and his counselors for what they pretended would be a merely verbal showdown. On Lane's signal, "Christ our victory!" the English opened fire. They went back to their fort proudly displaying Pemisapan's severed head.[17]

Within a week, a European fleet showed up, bearing not La Florida's

Menéndez Marqués but England's Francis Drake, fresh from a raid on San Agustín that had forced the Spanish governor and his garrison to retreat into the woods while the town's two hundred fifty houses—stripped of windows, locks, and similar hardware—were burned. Drake appropriated this particular iron booty, along with captured Spanish artillery, in order to grace the thriving settlement he expected to find at Roanoke. The far more substantial plunder of gold, ships, and African and other slaves that his fleet had seized from previous raids on the Cape Verdes, Hispaniola, and Cartagena was headed for England, to be sold to pay the expedition's financiers and to prove the value of Roanoke as a supply base for privateering.

The difficulty Drake had in finding an Outer Banks harbor deep enough for his ships revealed the flaw in that plan even before he discovered that Lane's half-starved colonists had so badly poisoned their relations with their Native neighbors. After much discussion, and after a hurricane had smashed or scattered much of Drake's fleet, Lane decided to pack up everyone, including the Croatoan Manteo, and head for England. The long-awaited supply ship arrived barely a week later. Shortly after that, Grenville returned to Roanoke with three ships and several hundred intended colonists, whom he inexplicably carried back to England after finding Lane's post abandoned. He left only fifteen men to hold the place. These were never seen by English eyes again. Nor were three of Lane's colonists and, apparently, about three hundred enslaved Africans Drake had with him, all of whom had been left behind in the hasty evacuation. These people were by far the largest group of Roanoke's "lost colonists."

The more famous group arrived in 1587. Despite some impressive-sounding organizational innovations, the new expedition reflected dramatically scaled-down expectations for an enterprise that had already cost Ralegh as much as £30,000, with only a portion offset by privateering prizes and no prospect of rents or other income. To minimize expenses and begin the peopling of his manorial domain, Ralegh used two forms of delegated feudal authority. With much attention to heraldic detail, he drew up a contract of rights and privileges for a "Cittie of Ralegh," a self-governing corporation composed of those who invested either their funds or persons in the colony. The document creating the corporation does not survive, but it appears that those who paid their own way but made no other monetary contribution were promised at least five hundred acres of land—a very large estate—and that financial investors could expect much larger tracts to lease to tenants. Most decisions were left in the hands of the corporation's appointed governor, John White, in consultation with twelve "assistants" appointed from the largest investors. This group—White recruited a total of 110 people, including fourteen families and various servants—was intended to settle not at Roanoke but somewhere on the Chesapeake Bay, which everyone agreed was far more likely to provide a good harbor for privateers and a better route to the still-hoped-for riches of the continental interior.

For Roanoke and its environs, Ralegh envisioned a second exercise in delegated authority. Manteo, once he had been instructed and baptized as a Protestant, would become the queen's "Lord of Roanoke."[18] As Hakluyt had said, "To plant Christian religion without conquest will be hard," but not impossible, if this co-optation of local hierarchies, a tactic long pursued by Spaniards, worked out.

Yet nothing at this latest iteration of Virginia would work out. Plagued by provision-consuming delays, White's fleet of three small ships, piloted by Fernandes, was weeks late in leaving England. After an unusually long passage to the West Indies, Fernandes spent further weeks supposedly looking for fresh water, salt, and other supplies, but apparently hoping for a chance to raid some Spanish galleons. When White's ships finally reached Roanoke, they found no trace of the previous colonists except for their largely intact houses and a single mysterious skeleton. Meantime, Fernandes, who was one of the corporation's appointed assistants, refused to take the colonists on to the Chesapeake. He did, however, agree to wait a few weeks to see things safely settled on the Outer Banks before sailing home by way of the Azores, where he hoped to find a Spanish prize ship.

Within a few days of the colonists' arrival at Roanoke, one man who strayed too far from the fort on a crabbing trip was killed. Shortly thereafter, a visit with Manteo to the main town of the Native people over whom he was to rule as lord (a piece of information that had not yet been revealed to them), yielded three disturbing pieces of information: the Croatoans would not be providing any surplus corn to support their otherwise marginally welcome guests; the straying crabber had been killed by Roanokes led by Wanchese; and the same Roanokes had done away with the men Grenville had left behind the previous year. White—who, it should be remembered, was a painter not a fighter—determined that a punitive attack was needed to show the Roanokes who was in charge. A nighttime attack on a group of people sitting around a fire at the Roanoke town of Dasemunquepeuc killed one and nearly slew several others, men, women, and children. Some of the dead were personally known to the attackers. This was because they were not Roanokes at all but kin of Manteo's Croatoans, who had discovered that their Roanoke rivals had abandoned the place for fear of English attack and had come to steal their ripening crops.

While White and Manteo—hastily baptized and invested as lord not only of Roanoke but also of Dasemunquepeuc—tried to patch things up after this fiasco, the colonists faced a hungry future, if they had a future at all. It was late August, and any supply ship from home was likely to head to their intended destination on the Chesapeake rather than the Outer Banks. To make matters worse, there was little realistic hope that Manteo could help the colonists extract food from the Natives. Their refusal to supply it, and their purloining of the crop at Dasemunquepeuc, we now know, was due to the most severe drought in the region in the previous eight hundred years. Under these Little Ice Age circumstances, the colonists unanimously insisted that White return to England with Fernandes and fetch a "present and speedy supply of certain of our known and apparent lacks and needs."[19] No one else, they believed, could do the job: White had the necessary influence with Ralegh; he could find the way back to their location; and he would indeed return, because he was leaving behind his daughter and newly born granddaughter, Virginia Dare. As every U.S. schoolchild used to know, neither White nor any other English person would see Virginia Dare or the others again.

Nearly three years later, in 1590, White finally returned. He found the word "CROATOAN" cryptically carved on the palisades of an abandoned fort from which the houses had been carefully dismantled and taken away. The long delay epitomizes the marginal place of North America in England's crusade against Catholic Spain and in its Protestant conquistadores' quest for landed wealth and glory. White had arrived in England just as war with Spain was reaching its climax. In preparation for battle with Felipe II's *armada católica*, the English government embargoed virtually all shipping, thus halting a fleet of seven supply vessels that Ralegh intended to send to Roanoke in early 1589. White managed to get permission to sail with two other ships, but these were captained by privateers so eager to chase Spanish prizes that they themselves fell victim to French raiders stalking similar prey. Similar priorities ruled a year later, when, after the defeat of the Spanish Armada, White sailed with three privateers who kept themselves very busy in the West Indies before making the quick trip to find the carved word at Roanoke. They then hastened on to the Azores in quest of Spanish prey, allowing no opportunity for further investigations. For those who sailed the ships, Roanoke or the Chesapeake had never had any appeal beyond providing a base for their lucrative plunder of enemy shipping, and they, and their Crown, were doing quite well without that base.

The motives of Ralegh, Grenville, Hakluyt, and others were more complex, but for them, too, North America was only one possible means to the broader ends of defeating Spain, spreading the gospel (if not exactly the spirit) of Protestantism, and reaping the profits of conquered manorial estates. Like the Spanish and the French before them, they largely abandoned North America for what seemed more lucrative opportunities elsewhere. As Lane had concluded when he deserted the place in 1586, "the discovery of a good mine, by the goodness of God, or a passage to the South Sea, or some way to it, and nothing else can bring this country in request to be inhabited by our nation."[20] Much more promising were Muscovy, Africa, the West Indies, and South America. Ralegh's own shifting interests were demonstrated in 1586, when he published a book entitled *The Discoverie of the Large, Rich and Bewtiful Empire of Guiana*. But more important than any of these faraway fantasy lands, were opportunities closer to home, in Ireland, where Ralegh, Lane, Grenville, and nearly everyone else involved with Roanoke were carving out lucrative estates.

Ireland was to England's conquistadores what Granada and the Canaries were to Spain's. England's equivalent of the Reconquista stretched back to the days of the Norman invasions, which had created the English Pale of Settlement in the central and eastern portion of the island. By the early sixteenth century, the Pale had shrunk to a small area in the immediate neighborhood of Dublin, and the "Old English" population had heavily intermarried with the indigenous Celts. Technically, medieval English monarchs had been "lords" but not "kings" of Ireland, which was under the effective control of an array of Anglo-Irish earls and local Celtic leaders. The former described the latter, living "beyond the Pale," as barbarians, with no legitimate right to own land. This was because they refused to recognize the authority of the English lords whose rights derived from the Norman Conquest, because their distinctive Celtic variety of Catholicism seemed virtually pagan in its deviance, and because they were semi-migratory pastoralists who did not properly cultivate the soil; Ireland was a corner of the Northern European world that the medieval agricultural revolution had never reached. English commentators were even harsher than the Anglo-Irish. Gaelic people "live like beastes, voide of lawe and all good order," declared Ralegh associate Barnaby Rich, who found them "more uncivill, more uncleanly, more barbarous and more brutish in their customs and demeanures, then in any other part of the world that is known." The duty of England, therefore, was, in the words of Rich's contemporary Peter Carew, "the suppressing and reforming of the loose, barbarous and most wicked life of that savage nation."[21]

That duty had gained a cloak of legitimacy from 1536 to 1541, when the Anglo-Irish parliament acknowledged Henry VIII as king, rather than lord, of Ireland and as head of its national church, whose monastic lands, like those of England's, were expropriated and redistributed to Protestant supporters. But not until 1565—the year that French La Caroline met its bloody end—did Elizabeth's government first assert its intention to move beyond the Pale and subject all of Ireland to English rule. These acts drove substantial numbers of Catholic "Old English" into alliance with the Gaelic Irish and joined the cause of Irish autonomy to the international struggle between Catholics and Protestants, Spain and England.

As always in the sixteenth century, financing and execution of the Irish conquest fell to private hands. In that effort, Gilbert, Grenville, and many others in their circle gained their first experience as conquistadores, attempting to create estates first in Ulster in the north and then in Munster in the southwest. Like the Iberian Reconquista, these campaigns were said merely to restore to a legitimate sovereign territories that he or she rightly possessed and to return the peasantry to proper subordination and religious adherence. Like the Indians of New Spain, the Irish were unilaterally declared the monarch's subjects, and their resistance movements (major ones occurred in 1559, 1568–1583, and 1594–1603) were labeled rebellions that had to be brutally suppressed.

And brutal the suppression was. Gilbert, most notoriously, decreed that "the heads of all those (of what sort soever they were) which were killed in the day, should be cut off from their bodies and brought to the place where he encamped at night, and should there be laid on the ground by each side of the way leading into his own tent so that none could come into his tent for any cause but commonly he must pass through a lane of heads." As a contemporary commentator understated, this induced "great terror to the people when they saw the heads of their dead fathers, brothers, children, kinsfolk and friends, lie on the ground before their faces."[22] Such terror, Gilbert as well as many of his fellow conquistadores and numerous English commentators believed, was not only necessary but justified because the Gaelic Irish were so barbarous and so irrationally resistant to civilized rule.

Gaelic lords, like American caciques listening to the *requerimiento*, were given the chance to make due submission. If they refused, their lives and their lands—three hundred thousand acres or more after the 1568–1583 rising—were forfeit. The expropriated lands would be transformed into "plantations" resettled by *adelantados* called "undertakers," who would, by force if necessary, put the surviving native population to productive work and begin their gradual progress toward civilization and Christianization. Thomas Smith, one of the most prominent of such undertakers, placed the harsh task in both predestinarian and historical terms. The Lord "did make apt and prepare" the English "to inhabit and reform so barbarous a nation as that is, and to bring them to the knowledge and law were both a goodly and commendable deed, and a sufficient work of our age." Indeed, just as in ancient times "this country of England, once as uncivil as Ireland now is, was by colonies of the Romans brought to understand the law," so now must England forcefully bring the same gifts to the Irish.[23]

Much more connected these Irish developments to North America than the fact that many of the same conquistadores were involved there and at Roanoke, that the two colonial enterprises proceeded at the same time, or that Ralegh diverted most of his attention from Virginia to the forty thousand acres of Munster lands he received after the suppression of the rising in 1583. By 1589, at least one thousand English men and hundreds of women and children had emigrated to Munster; 144 of them, half with their families, settled on Ralegh's plantation and 108 on Grenville's somewhat smaller holdings—numbers comparable to those envisioned for Roanoke. Thomas Hariot and, within a few years, John White were among the immigrants. In 1598, however, when the Gaelic tenants and laborers on these estates joined the war against the English that had been raging in Ulster for four years, everything was wiped out, just as it had been in Roanoke. "The misery of the Englishry was great," said one observer. "The wealthier sort, leaving their castles and dwelling-houses, . . . made haste into walled towns," while "the meaner sort . . . were slain, man, woman, and child; and such as escaped came all naked to the towns."[24] Brutal military campaigns restored English supremacy by 1603, but the plantation process had to begin all over again.

Despite the fact that Munster met an end much like Roanoke's or La Caroline's, the earliest seventeenth-century English undertakers continued to approach their task much as their predecessors had. If anything, Irish experiences only solidified a powerful set of expectations about the nature of colonization that had first been shaped by Iberian precedents in the Atlantic islands, the Caribbean, and Meso-America. "Plantations" were less economic than political and cultural enterprises—the landed estates that were due rewards for those who undertook the bloody work of expanding the domains of Crown and true religion. Rents and manorial dues, not particular commodities such as sugar, were to be the main source of profits. And—the conquistadores attempted to convince themselves—the most important product of a plantation was not gold or sugar but "civility." That capacious term included both the extension of English law and Protestant religion into domains formerly ruled by papists, infidels, or pagans and the forceful subordination of the native population to the new regime. As one member of Queen Elizabeth's Privy Council put it with reference to the Irish, "nothing but feare and force can teach dutie and obedience."[25]

Against this background, many aspects of English expectations for Roanoke come into clearer focus. Manteo, like a Gaelic lord who submitted to due authority and converted to Protestant religion, would bring his people into proper subordination to the English Crown. Others who resisted, like Wanchese, must be ruthlessly punished, whether they stole a mere silver cup, murdered a stray colonist, or refused the supplies necessary to support their rightful lords. The "Citie of Ralegh," like an Irish plantation, would be populated by an English elite and perhaps some imported laborers, but mostly would rely on Native tenants.

This is what most late sixteenth-century English people meant by the word "plantation." In theory, what was to be planted was not so much literal crops as the metaphorical example of English government, civility, and religion. Aristocratic lords of the manor—far from being useless obstacles to the hard work of building a colony—were, in this view, the most important component, for only they possessed the habits of command, the experience in military discipline, the authoritarian gravitas, to plant civilized government and enforce Christian behavior. Imported English artisans and servants would do their part by setting good examples for the far larger numbers of Native tenants resettled to labor on the lands of their new lords. It was Native labor, then, that was expected to make colonial estates profitable in the long run—and the Natives' descendants, if not the Natives themselves, would thank their conquerors for the gift of civilization, just as the English thanked the ancient Romans.

The chain of reasoning became clearest in the most lasting contribution of the Roanoke experience, the lavishly illustrated 1590 edition of Hariot's book *A Briefe and True Report of the New Found Land of Virginia.* "The naturall inhabitants," Hariot assured his readers, "in respect of troubling our inhabiting and planting, are not to be feared," for "they shall have cause both to feare and love us, that shall inhabite with them." Once "they upon due consideration shall finde our manner of knowledges and craftes to exceede theirs in perfection," the Natives "shoulde desire our friendships and love, and have the greater respect for pleasing and obeying us," until by "meanes of good government . . . they may in short time be brought to civilitie, and the imbracing of true religion." Hariot's only suggestion that "fear" and "obeying" might not be so easily gained was a brief admission that "some of our companie towards the ende of the yeare, shewed themselves too fierce, in slaying some of the people, in some towns, upon causes that on our part, might easily enough have been borne withall." No matter. "Because it was on their part justly deserved, the alteration of their opinions generally and for the most part concerning us is the lesse to bee doubted." Moreover, like the ancient Romans, the modern English would eventually be praised for their sternness. After many pages of Theodor de Bry's magnificent copper engravings based on John White's peaceful watercolors illustrating "the nature and manners of the naturall inhabitants," readers of *A Briefe and True Report* encountered five fanciful images of ancient Britons or "Picts," including a frightful warrior holding a severed head still dripping blood. These images, originally painted by

White on the basis of an "oolld English cronicle," were included "to showe
how that the Inhabitants of the great Bretainnie have bin in times past as
sauvage as those of Virginia."[26]

Ireland and Roanoke; La Caroline and Hispaniola; the Canaries and
Azores: against these conquistador backgrounds, it is hard to see anything
new, any really fresh start, any notable beginnings in what most people in
the United States have come to think of as the first "permanent" English colony, Jamestown. At the outset, it differed little from countless
other *adelantado* adventures that preceded it, most of which never got
off the ground. In 1606, two overlapping Virginia companies of investors—one based in Plymouth, the other in London—received grants from
King James I to establish plantations, "which may, by the providence of
Almighty God, hereafter tend to the glory of his divine Majesty, in prop-
agating of Christian religion, . . . and may in time bring the infidels and
savages, living in those parts, to human civility, and to a settled and quiet
government."[27] The Plymouth Company's short-lived colony on the Sagadahoc River in present-day Maine went the way of so many others, abandoned after less than a year. The London Company's venture, meanwhile,
was conceived as the fulfillment of Ralegh's two-decades-old plans. After
establishing a base on the Chesapeake Bay, the colonists' first three tasks
were to find gold (of which the usual fifth was due the king) or some other
source of revenue for paying initial expenses, to find a passage to the
Pacific, and to find the lost Roanoke colonists of 1587.

     That none of these goals were quickly met should trouble no one, cau-
tioned one of countless preachers and other worthies who tried to remind
the Jamestown colonists of the nobility of their cause. "Why is there not
then *present profit?*" the Reverend William Crashaw asked the colony's investors and its intended new governor, Thomas Lord De La Warre, in
1609.

> I answer, that profit is not the principal end of this action; if it were, what
> should so many of the *Nobility*, of the *Gentry*, and especially of the *Clergy*,
> have their hands in it? It is not fit for them to be *Merchants:* But the high
> and principal end being *plantation*, of an English Church and Common-
> wealth, and consequently the *conversion* of heathen, hence it is therefore
> that profit cannot be presently expected, because we are still to send more

supplies of men, munition, instruments and tools for all trades: but when there be sent so many that they are able to defend themselves, . . . and when they have built their Church and Town, . . . then it is time to *expect,* and then we are sure to *receive* such quantity of *gain,* as will give full contentment to every man for his monies adventured: and then for a *short time* of disbursements, begins *a long time* of profit.[28]

There were no quick profits to be made at Jamestown. The starving times and appalling death rates of the first winter; the subsequent unappreciated efforts of the colony's council president, John Smith, to get what he regarded as an honest day's work from his all-male collection of company employees, gentlemen adventurers (roughly a third of the first three shipments of emigrants), and gentlemen's personal servants; the renewed starving times that followed Smith's departure in 1609; the long-delayed supply ships; the brutal military discipline necessary to get anything done; the constant English-versus-Native tensions so often rooted in demands for food—all the things that appear so puzzling in isolation become predictable given the announced purposes of the colony, the expectations of the colonists, and the numbingly familiar stories of earlier would-be conquistadores. Just like their Roanoke predecessors, the colonists had packed up to abandon the place in 1610—only to be met by a fleet bearing the long-delayed De La Warre, who sent them back to their death trap on swampy Jamestown Island. By 1616, more than seventeen hundred colonists would be transported to Jamestown; a mere 351 survived to tell the tale. Perhaps the only surprising thing about Jamestown is the dogged persistence of the colony's investors and the ingenuity with which they convinced their countrymen to continue to pour resources into their ill-conceived project—£50,000 sterling by 1616—which for ten years yielded no appreciable revenue at all.[29]

But as the Reverend Mr. Crashaw reminded the investors, short-term profits were not the point. On the supposedly main business of reducing the Native population to civility, the London Company was just as doggedly innovative as it was in raising capital. Tsenacomoco, "the Densely Settled Land," as the tidewater bordering the southwestern side of the Chesapeake Bay was called in the local Algonquian language, was home to about twenty thousand Native people whose roughly 160 villages constituted more than thirty chiefdoms. The *weroances* of most of these chiefdoms owed allegiance to the *mamanatowick,* or paramount chief,

Wahunsonacock, also known as Powhatan; his title incorporated—more certainly than Manteo's—the Algonquian word for spiritual power, *manitou*. Some of the allegiances he claimed from subordinate chiefs were apparently of very long standing, others the result of recent political or military conquests. A few chiefdoms, most notably the Chickahomonies, whose territories lay in the middle of Powhatan's zone of influence, remained autonomous. There were thus many opportunities for the English to try to divide and rule, but it seemed clearly preferable to attempt first to make the principal local lord a vassal of King James.

Accordingly, in the fall of 1608, admiral Christopher Newport returned to the Chesapeake with instructions to summon Powhatan to Jamestown, invest him with a crown, and deliver gifts from the king, including a basin and a matching ewer or pitcher, a suit of clothes, and, somewhat inexplicably, a bed. Powhatan, who in the eyes of his own people had already reduced the English to *his* subordinates by capturing, ritually adopting, and then releasing the man in charge during Newport's absence, John Smith, refused to play along. Instead, he insisted that the English demonstrate their subordination by bringing the gifts to him at his capital on the York River. "If your king have sent me presents, I also am a king, and this my land," Powhatan announced; Newport was "to come to me, not I to him."[30] The admiral had no choice but to trek with fifty of his men overland to meet Powhatan, while three barges brought the presents by water.

Then, as Smith reported, "All things being fit for the day of his coronation, the presents were brought, his basin, ewer, bed and furniture set up, his scarlet cloak and apparel (with much ado) put on" Powhatan's body.

> But a foul trouble there was to make him kneel to receive his crown, he neither knowing the majesty, nor meaning of a Crown, nor bending of the knee, endured so many persuasions, examples, and instructions, as tired them all. At last by leaning hard on his shoulders, he a little stooped, and Newport put the Crown on his head. When by the warning of a pistol, the boats were prepared with such a volley of shot, that the king start[ed] up in a horrible fear, till he see [that] all was well, then remembering himself, to congratulate their kindness, he gave his old shoes and his mantle to Captain Newport.[31]

That mantle is probably the same one that survives to this day in the Ashmolean Museum at Oxford. Illustrated in intricate beadwork, a man, presumably the *mamanatowick*, stands surrounded by thirty-two spirally formed medallions, presumably representing his subordinate chiefs. Newport had become the thirty-third.

Given these conflicting struggles for dominance, it is no surprise that the two peoples were soon engaged in low-grade warfare, and that English demands for food, and Smith's efforts to induce the "fear" that characterized English rule in Ireland, were the principal grievances. When Smith, ousted in a coup and severely injured in the groin by an accidental explosion of gunpowder, left the colony in October 1609, starving colonists and fed-up Natives declared open season on each other. Unaware of how chaotic things had become, the company continued to dream of ingenious ways to incorporate the Algonquians like an Irish peasantry. New governor Thomas Gates was dispatched in 1609 with instructions to "procure from them some convenient number of their Children to be brought up in . . . [English] language, and manners." If necessary, the youngsters should be kidnapped "from their . . . Priests by a surprise of them all and detaining them prisoners." In fact, it would be neither "cruelty nor breach of Charity to deal more sharply with them and then proceed even to death with these murderers of Souls and sacrificers of gods images to the Devil."[32]

In the midst of a hot war—and a storm that delayed Gates for months in Bermuda—the scheme could never be implemented. Nonetheless, the Anglo-Powhatan conflict did come to an end as a result of a kidnapping— of Powhatan's daughter Pocahontas in 1613. Pocahontas spent the better part of a year as a hostage at Jamestown and at the English settlement of Henrico, where a clergyman instructed her in the rudiments of Protestant belief. During this time she also met John Rolfe, a twenty-eight-year-old widower who quickly became smitten with the young woman ten years his junior. Whether Pocahontas returned the feelings is unclear. In March 1614, then-deputy governor Thomas Dale took Pocahontas with him when he marched an army to burn and pillage houses in the heart of Powhatan's domain. Despite this show of force, the *mamanatowick* refused to come to terms, until Rolfe suggested a diplomatic marriage to seal an alliance. Powhatan—who had already offered "that his daughter should be [Dale's] child, and ever dwell with [him], desiring to be ever friends"—agreed. Within a few days, Pocahontas was baptized with the name "Rebecca" and married Rolfe at Jamestown.[33] "Rebecca" was the biblical name of the patriarch Isaac's wife, the mother of two nations.

The marriage marked the high point of English conquistador dreams. Not only had peace with Powhatan been secured and a high-profile con-

vert to Protestantism been made, but Powhatan's rivals the Chickahomonies had also pledged their feudal vassalage. According to colonist
Raphe Hamor, their chiefs formally promised to "be King JAMES his subjects," to be "ready and willing to furnish us with three or four hundred
bowmen to aide us against the Spaniards," and to "bring into our store
house, at the beginning of their harvest two bushels of corn a man, as tribute of their obedience to his Majesty." Moreover, their "eight chief men"
agreed to "receive a red coat, or livery from our King yearly, and each of
them the picture of his Majesty, engraved in Copper, with a chain of Copper to hang it about his neck, whereby they shall be known to be King
JAMES his noble Men."[34]

In 1616, Pocahontas, her husband, their infant son, and about ten other
delegates from Tsenacomoco began a triumphant tour of England to display the long-hoped-for success in reducing Virginia to civility. A widely
circulated engraving by Simon van de Passe depicted, in fashionable English garb, "Rebecka daughter to the mighty Prince Powhatan Emperour
of Attanoughskomouck alias Virginia converted and baptized in the Christian faith, and wife to the worthy Mr. John Rolff." Alas, Pocahontas succumbed to an unknown ailment before she could return home. Her father
died less than two years later, and English conquistador fantasies also
quickly passed away.

Ironically, her husband, John Rolfe, was as much as anyone responsible for the rapid decay of Anglo-Powhatan relations—not that there had
ever been much chance that Native love and fear of the English would
last any longer in "Attanoughskomouck" (a very approximate spelling of
"Tsenacomoco") than in Ireland. In 1613, Rolfe had shipped to England a
sample crop of tobacco, grown from seeds he had imported from the West
Indies. In that plant, Virginia at last found its substitute for gold—particularly after 1617, when the company began offering new incentives for gentlemen and would-be gentlemen to take up estates in the colony. As
in Gilbert's earlier plan, great men were offered substantial "particular
plantations," or manors they would populate with tenants. Individual emigrants received "headrights" entitling them to fifty acres each for themselves and for any person—family member, tenant, or laborer—they imported. In relative terms, Virginia's European population and economy
began to boom, from fewer than 400 in 1617 to 1,240 in 1622. These colonists, out of the more than thirty-five hundred who emigrated during
those five years, were the only ones who survived the still-ferocious en-
demic diseases.[35]

All the headrights those figures implied, and all the demands to clear prime land to plant lucrative tobacco, pressed the Native population hard—as did the arrogant assumption of English planters that the Powhatans would either take their Irish place at the bottom of the social order or get out of the way. In March of 1622, Native people led by Powhatan's kinsman and successor, Opechancanough, systematically slaughtered at least 330 English, a quarter of the colony's population. A decade of scorched-earth retaliatory warfare ensued against Opechancanough's people.[36] In that way, at least, the Chesapeake came to resemble Ireland.

The war in Tsenacomoco destroyed the London Company. In 1624 the Crown revoked the company charter and assumed direct control of the colony, or what was left of it. North America, it would seem, had once again proven its utter worthlessness as a zone for Christian conquest. And North Americans had once again proven utterly unwilling to play their assigned roles as the Picts of the modern world. "*Powhatan* the chief Lord of all the Savages, with thirty nine *Werowances,* have yielded to more than forms and circumstances of homage," and "he accepted a Copper Crown as Vassal to His Majesty," English promoter of colonization Samuel Purchas recalled, barely containing his rage. For a time,

> Temperance and Justice . . . kissed each other, and seemed to bless the co-habitations of *English* and *Indians* in *Virginia.* But when *Virginia* was violently ravished by her own ruder Natives, yea her Virgin cheeks died with . . . blood . . . , Temperance could not temper herself, yea the stupid Earth seems distempered with such bloody potions and cries that she is ready to spew out her Inhabitants: Justice crieth to GOD for vengeance, and in his name adjureth Prudence and Fortitude to the execution.
>
> . . . Disloyal treason hath now confiscated whatsoever remainders of right the unnatural Naturals had, and made both them and their Country wholly *English.*

Conquistador fantasies of ruling a grateful Native population would never entirely disappear, but they would never again dominate English thinking about North America and its indigenous peoples. "Murdered carcasses," proclaimed Purchas, "have taken a mortal immortal possession, and being dead, speak, proclaim and cry, *This our earth is truly English, and therefore this Land is justly yours O English.*"[37]

Traders

TRADE. *n.s.* [*tratta,* Italian].
1. Traffic; commerce; exchange of goods for other goods; or for money.

TRA´DER. *n.s.* [from *trade*].
1. One engaged in merchandise or commerce.

—Samuel Johnson, *A Dictionary of the English
Language* (London, 1755)

FIVE

Native Americans and
the Power of Trade

THE ENGLISH WERE IN Jamestown to conquer. The Indians thought the newcomers were there to trade, and thereby to be absorbed into Tsenacomoco. The relationship that Samuel Purchas declared dead after the war of 1622 involved not just a struggle over political power but a contest between two *kinds* of power, rooted in the separate medieval pasts that had shaped Western Europe and North America. As Purchas reminded his readers, when Newport tried to crown Powhatan in 1608, the point of the ceremony was to make the *mamanatowick* a vassal of King James. The gifts that the Englishman carried symbolized feudal domination—or would have, if only Powhatan had knelt properly to receive them. For Powhatan, however, Newport's crown, ewer and basin, clothing, and mysterious bed—all exotic goods from across the sea—evoked a different conception of power. In Native America, to acquire rare goods from distant places was to demonstrate the strong alliances that a leader could mobilize on behalf of his community. When Newport gave these goods to Powhatan, he tapped ancient patterns of political interaction that mobilized power in a familiar North American way. The political systems of conquistadores and traders overlapped at Jamestown, and they proved spectacularly incompatible.

To understand the phenomenon more fully, it is important to remember that—just as the Jamestown colonists arrived at the end of a long series of similar exploits by European conquistadores—Powhatan and his people were responding to Jamestown after a long history of encounters with Europeans and trade in their material goods. In 1607, when Newport and the

121

other English arrived, European ships and European hairy faces were rare, but hardly unprecedented, appearances on the Chesapeake. Also relatively rare, but far more familiar, were items from Europe such as the axes that figured so prominently in Norse memories of Vinland. For Native Americans, those goods were central to the experience of European contact. Contests for power that the conquistadores framed in terms of domination, Native people understood in terms of exchange. Most colonists in English Virginia failed to grasp that fact. By contrast, their contemporaries who traveled more northerly routes to the Americas—French and Dutch, as well as English—embraced the economic benefits of commerce with Native people. When these Europeans tried to exploit those benefits, they enmeshed themselves in power struggles defined on Indian terms. The results were no less violent, no less determined by warfare, than the wreckage left by the conquistadores, but they were perhaps even more crucial in giving shape to the seventeenth-century North American world.

Traders, even more than conquistadores, introduced Europe to Native North Americans. Not just on the shores of the Chesapeake but in the most remote interior regions of the continent, European goods arrived before European people did, passed along through ancient routes of exchange, alliance, and power. Archaeological evidence and European explorers' comments confirm that the items most likely to make the trip were those that most resembled the rare goods that had traveled these routes for centuries. Pieces of brass or iron cut from kettles or axeheads filled the same niches as native copper and other minerals and could be reshaped using familiar cold-working methods. Glass beads were entirely novel. Although they resembled ones long fashioned from marine shell, they had a particular power that came from their virtual indestructibility and their translucent colors, particularly blues that evoked the other-than-human realms of water and sky.

By 1607, most of those goods probably entered North America through exchanges between Native people and the scattered European outposts that had been established on the continent—in La Florida, in the Pueblo country that Spanish colonizers called Nuevo México, in Newfoundland and adjacent areas where European fishing fleets maintained permanent camps. Others came as gifts from coastal visits by explorers from Europe, booty from failed expeditions by would-be Spanish lords, or loot from shipwrecks or abandoned outposts. Most Native people encountered these items at second, third, or tenth hand, exchanged by one chief or would-be chief with another as proof of alliance with the mysterious oceanic sources from which the items came. A chief who could make direct contact with those sources and turn them to his people's benefit could become a powerful person indeed. Retold with this understanding, the story of Jamestown sounds quite different.[1]

Powhatan almost certainly wanted to become such a chief, and he was not the first among his people to make the attempt. As early as 1546, an English ship had blown into the Chesapeake Bay on a storm and found "over thirty canoes" full of Native people who already knew enough about Europeans to bring along "as many as a thousand marten skins in exchange for knives, fishhooks and shirts."[2] A more significant attempt to secure access to European goods began in 1561, when a man named Paquiquineo and two traveling companions were either kidnapped or volunteered to sail from Chesapeake Bay on a Spanish ship. For the better part of a decade Paquiquineo traveled the Spanish imperial world, sojourning in Seville (where he received gifts of clothing from King Felipe II), Ciudad de México (where he was baptized with the Christian name "Don Luis"), and Havana (where he met Florida governor Pedro Menéndez de Avilés during the staging of the campaign against La Caroline). Almost as soon as he learned enough Castilian to be understood, Paquiquineo, "a clever talker," touted "the grandeurs of his land," the willingness of his people to hear the Gospel, and his eagerness to provide "the help which Timothy gave to Saint Paul."[3] In the fall of 1570, such talk finally got him back to Tsenacomoco, along with two Jesuit priests and seven other Europeans who planned to convert the region's Native people to the True Faith.

What happened next is very much in doubt. The version usually repeated is that Paquiquineo renounced Christianity and slaughtered the missionaries with their own axes. The source of the story was a young boy named Alonso de Olmos, the only Spanish survivor of the presumed killings, to which he did not claim to be an eyewitness. The boy did, however, see firsthand a particularly appalling set of deaths. Governor Menéndez de Avilés forced Alonso to translate while a priest hastily baptized a group of Native men before hanging them from the yardarm of his ship for their supposed crimes. (Paquiquineo himself was nowhere to be found.) Perhaps a frightened Alonso—who had apparently been living contentedly with the Natives for several months—told the truth about the Spaniards' fate. Perhaps he just said what he thought the governor of La Florida wanted to hear, rather than informing him that the missionaries had simply starved to death. Their only surviving letter complains that both they and the drought-plagued Indians were desperately short of food.

Whatever the case, the kind of alliance that Paquiquineo apparently hoped to establish with powerful outsiders never came to fruition. Yet three hints in the skimpy documents suggest the centrality of European material goods to the drama. First, after Paquiquineo and the missionaries had set out from Havana to the Chesapeake, they stopped at the Spanish outpost of Santa Elena, which had replaced French Charlesfort on what is today Parris Island, South Carolina. To supply the new mission, the priests resident at Santa Elena donated "the best and richest articles . . . in the way of chalices, monstrances, and vestments and other articles besides church furnishings." Paquiquineo must have seen these items as a rich cargo of prestige goods.[4] Second, almost immediately after the missionaries set up camp in Tsenacomoco, they announced a ban on trade between Europeans and Indians, who were expected to provide food freely in support of the priests. At about this time, Paquiquineo relocated to a town some distance off and stopped communicating with the missionaries—a move they attributed to apostasy, but he, probably, to their unwillingness to establish an exchange-based alliance. Third, whether or not Paquiquineo personally killed the newcomers with axes they refused to give him, the exotic goods from Santa Elena apparently did find their way to his people after the missionaries' deaths. Menéndez's retaliatory raid was inspired by a report from a Spanish ship that Native men wearing priests' vestments had been seen beckoning Europeans to come ashore.

In 1607 no one beckoned the English ashore at Jamestown. That fact, and the wariness of Powhatan's attempt to integrate the English into his chiefdom, makes sense against the background of what had earlier happened with the Spanish. Paquiquineo was almost certainly a member of a chiefly lineage connected with Powhatan, directly or by marriage. Some have argued, unconvincingly, that he was the same man later known as Opechancanough, Powhatan's successor and leader of the war against the English in 1622. Be that as it may, Paquiquineo's long experience among the Spanish must have conveyed to Powhatan as deep (and as mistaken) an understanding of what to expect from the English as the one that Smith and Newport had gained from their reading of Spanish books and of accounts of the Roanoke and Ireland colonies. Clearly the English were dangerous to deal with, but they were also a source of great power if Powhatan could ally himself with them.

In nearly every encounter with English leaders, Powhatan dramatized his ability to mobilize the power of exotic goods. The coronation ceremony was only one of several such occasions. When Smith was captured and adopted during the winter of 1607–1608, Powhatan proposed that the colonists relocate to a territory he would assign them, where he would supply them food in exchange for "Hatchets and Copper." A few months later, when Smith paid a ceremonial visit bearing gifts of "a suit of red cloth, a white Greyhound, and a Hat," Powhatan showered the English with food-stuffs while declaring that Smith was now one of his subordinate chiefs and that the English were no longer "strangers . . . but Powhatans, and that the Corn, women and Country, should be to [them] . . . as to his own people"; this offer must have seemed particularly attractive to (or perhaps even been wishfully mistranslated by) English men bereft of both food and female companionship. Later, Newport gave Powhatan twelve large copper kettles, and on another occasion twenty swords; in exchange, the *mamanatowick* continued to provide the colonists with gifts of food. As the two sides drifted toward war in 1609, Powhatan listed the goods required to avert conflict. If Smith "would send him but men to build him a house, bring him a grindstone, 50 swords, some peices [firearms], a cock and a hen, with copper and beads, he would load his ship with corn."[5]

During the war of 1609–1614, goods continued to hold their power. At least one English raiding party "ransacked" the temple of one of Powhatan's subordinate chiefs and "took down the Corpses of their dead kings from of their Tombs, and carried away their pearls, Copper, and bracelets." Native men "stopped full of Bread" the mouths of Englishmen they slew, and sang a song mocking "Captain Newport [who] brought them Copper."[6] Even the marriage between Pocahontas and John Rolfe, which ended the war, gave Powhatan an opportunity to use traditional forms of alliance to subordinate the English. In Native America, as in Europe, the exchange of spouses, like the exchange of slaves, was a political act; Powhatan supposedly had a hundred wives in the various chiefdoms of his domain.

A revealing moment occurred when colonist Ralph Hamor visited the *mamanatowick* on behalf of Governor Thomas Dale to try to convince him to marry another daughter to the English. Powhatan refused and instead focused the conversation on prestige goods. Hamor, Powhatan complained, failed to wear on his neck a chain of pearls that the *mamanatowick* had sent to Dale for the purpose of identifying official emissaries. Moreover, the gifts the Englishman brought—"two large pieces of copper, five strings of white and blue beads, five wooden combs, ten fish-hooks, and a pair of knives"—were "not so ample . . . as formerly Captain *Newport*" had bestowed. To clarify what he expected, Powhatan "caused to be fetched a great glass of sack, some three quarts or better, which Captain *Newport* had given him six or seven years since, carefully preserved by him, not much above a pint in all this time spent." To each of the Englishmen in Hamor's party he dispensed "in a great oyster shell some three spoonfuls" of the fortified wine and then instructed Hamor to tell Dale "to send him these particular, Ten pieces of copper, a shaving knife, an iron froe to cleave boards, a grinding stone, not so big but four or five men may carry it, which would be big enough for his use, two bone combs, such as Captain *Newport* had given him . . . , an hundred fish-hooks or if he could spare it, rather a fishing seine, and a cat, and a dog." Powhatan insisted that Hamor repeat each item and, the Englishman said, "yet still doubtful that I might forget any of them, he bade me write them down in such a Table book as he showed me, which was a very fair one." Like the bottle of sack and the crown from England, the blank "table" notebook (which might or might not have come from Newport and which Hamor was not allowed to mark) was a prestige item that ratified the *mamanatowick*'s power. "He told me," said Hamor, "it did him much good to show it to strangers which came unto him."[7] The foreigners who were so impressed with Powhatan's control of exotic spiritous liquors and blank book pages were other Native people who understood the power of chiefs much better than did Hamor or Dale.

Whether Powhatan's own people remained impressed with the *mamanatowick*'s ability to control the alliances that such goods demonstrated is a different question, and the answer perhaps explains Powhatan's increasingly extravagant and exotic demands for iron plows, millstones, and domestic animals. One measure of the difficulties is the experience of a man named Uttamatomakkin, who traveled to England with Pocahontas and John Rolfe on the ill-fated voyage of 1616–1617. A shaman (the prefix *uttama-* connotes "spiritual" or "priestly"), he was a close advisor to

Opechancanough sent specifically to report on English intentions. Respected at home for his religious authority, he fell victim in England to a running joke: everywhere he went, wags said he had tried to count uncountable English men and English trees by making notches on a stick. Although, along with Pocahontas, Uttamatomakkin had an audience at the Court of St. James, he "denied ever to have seene the King," because the monarch acted nothing like a proper chief. When John Smith finally persuaded him otherwise, "he replyed very sadly, You gave Powhatan a white Dog, which *Powhatan* fed as himselfe, but your King gave me nothing, and I am better than your white Dog."[8]

Uttamatomakkin returned to the Chesapeake with nothing good to say about the English to Opechancanough or anyone else. Unsurprisingly, there is no evidence that, when Opechancanough succeeded Powhatan, he made any effort to base his status on the control of English prestige goods. Quite the opposite: he relied on a holy man named Nemattanew (known to the colonists as "Jack of the Feather"), who supposedly preached that his distinctive plumed garment protected him from the most deadly of European items, their bullets. That he nonetheless died from English gunfire during a scuffle with colonists who accused him of murdering one of their own was probably the episode that determined the timing of the 1622 attack.

The end of the Chesapeake chiefs' efforts to use prestige goods to build power in the traditional way resulted from a more basic factor than the violent refusal of the English to play along. Once substantial numbers of European and Native people began living near each other, it became virtually impossible for *any* chief to control the flow of goods to his people, even if, as Powhatan apparently tried to do, he redefined prestige in ever more esoteric directions. As early as January 1608—only a few months after the establishment of Jamestown—Smith complained that ordinary colonists and visiting sailors were trading so much metal to ordinary Indians that corn and furs "could not be had for a pound of copper, which before was sold for an ounce."[9] Archaeological excavations confirm that the jewelers and metalworkers textbooks have long derided as useless appendages to the lazy Jamestown colonists worked busily to make copper and other metal items to trade with Native people. This might have been the colony's only productive enterprise in its earliest years. All along the coasts— and soon along the interior rivers—of eastern North America, this kind of unregulated trade between commoners was bad news for chiefs like

Powhatan, whose power depended on European goods' remaining rare
and under their personal control. But the opportunities that such trade
represented—for both Europeans and Native people—were enormous.
Some chiefs found ways to turn the new conditions to their advantage.
Others did not.

Powhatan's people called Europeans *Tassantasses*, a term that roughly
translates as "strangers," perhaps because the invaders' behavior so violated assumptions about the material components of a proper alliance.
Elsewhere in eastern North America, however, the most common names
for the newcomers were words that meant things like "axemakers,"
"metalworkers," "clothmakers," or "woodworkers." "They call *English-men*
Cháuquaquock, that is, *Knive-men*," Roger Williams explained of the Narragansetts of what is now southern New England, whose stone tools were
rapidly being replaced by *"Knives, Awle-blades, Hatchets* and *Howes"*
from Europe.[10]
     Everywhere, exchanges of material goods defined political relations.
The imported things that defined new allies might have begun as prestige
goods to be displayed like Powhatan's notebook—European documents
and Native oral traditions alike repeatedly describe axeheads worn as neck
pendants by chiefs apparently unaware of their intended use—but they
quickly gained power from their utilitarian as well as political value. Iron
axeheads could be cold-worked not just into objects of display but into a
variety of cutting, scraping, and piercing instruments. More easily, sheet
copper from kettles could become raw material not just for objects of personal adornment but for any number of sharp implements and tools. Such
use of imported metal continued even as increasing supplies enabled people to use knives, axes, kettles, awls, fishhooks, and countless other items
intact for their designed purpose. Sharper, lighter, and less labor-intensive
to acquire than the stone, ceramic, or bone utensils used for centuries,
these implements became commonplace almost overnight wherever Native people got ready access to them. Woolens, too, rapidly supplemented
and replaced furs and skins for clothing and many other uses. The demand
was not exactly infinite, but intense nonetheless. Everywhere Europeans
went in North America, they found ready customers for any metal and
cloth they happened to bring with them.
     Systematic—as opposed to haphazard—trade in these items first de-

veloped not with the Spanish or English or any of the other would-be conquistadores who approached the continent by the southern route Columbus discovered, but with those who traveled the northern route that Cabot had followed in the 1490s and that forgotten Norse colonists had pioneered centuries earlier. Although gold and conquests were absent from what the English called "Newfoundland," by the opening years of the 1500s, and perhaps even decades earlier, hundreds of fishermen from all over Western Europe—English, French, Portuguese, Spanish, and Basque—discovered commodities profitable enough: whale oil and codfish. In Catholic Europe, where people were forbidden to eat meat on as many as 166 fast days annually and where few reliable, cheap sources of preserved protein were available, dried and salted fish was always in demand, but especially on the eve of the meatless season of Lent, when in France, for instance, the price of *poisson* doubled compared to other times of the year.

From the early sixteenth through the mid-twentieth centuries, there was no more bountiful fishery in the world than the Grand Banks of Newfoundland. By the 1520s, at least twenty and perhaps as many as ninety fishing boats left France alone for the area each year. Fifty years later, as many as three hundred crews of diverse origin sailed there annually. By 1615, two hundred fifty English vessels supposedly went to Newfoundland and returned with a catch worth £120,000—an enormous sum that even Jamestown's greatest promoters could never have imagined from their enterprise.[11] Two systems of preservation were used for the catch. "Wet fishery" packed the product in brine stored in the hold of the boats, and thus seldom required crews to spend much time on land. "Dry fishery," which became the preferred method for English crews by the second half of the sixteenth century, processed the fish on shore, cleaning and drying filleted slices on open-air racks before lightly salting them and packing them for shipment to customers in southwestern Europe.

These dry-fishery camps are where what is usually called the "fur trade" began. Its origins are easily imagined. Early sixteenth-century fishermen discovered that Native people were eager to barter food, animal skins, and other items for metal, glass, and cloth. Next trip, they brought along a supply of these items specifically to trade. At some point, the Europeans also learned that good prices waited in Europe for North American furs, especially for those from colder regions where animals grew the thickest coats and particularly for beaver pelts, whose fine inner hairs were ideal for processing into felt that could be made into hats. Most valuable were pelts from which the coarse outer hairs had worn away and that natural oils had softened—which is to say that old, worn skin cloaks would fetch the highest price. The French called this commodity *castor gras,* or "greasy beaver."

Long before 1600, regular summer rendezvous brought Native people to the coasts of Newfoundland, Acadia, northern New England, and the Gulf and River of St. Lawrence, where a confluence of streams at a place the French called Tadoussac became a particularly important trading center. It was not entirely clear who got the best bargain in an exchange of preworn fur clothes for possibly pre-used woolen blankets. In the early 1630s, one Native man certainly thought he had the better end of things. According to a French missionary, the man said,

> "The Beaver does everything perfectly well, it makes kettles, hatchets, swords, knives, bread; and, in short, it makes everything." He was making sport of us Europeans, who have such a fondness for the skin of this animal and who fight to see who will give the most . . . to get it; they carry this to such an extent that my host said to me one day, showing me a very beautiful knife, "The English have no sense; they give us twenty knives like this for one Beaver skin."[12]

In the years around 1600, two developments in Europe created a particular demand for such skins and—through a long chain of circumstances—put that French missionary in contact with his many-knived host: large broad-brimmed beaver-felt hats came into fashion in Europe, and, perhaps as a result, the beavers whose pelts had long been traded through Muscovy to hatters in the Netherlands and elsewhere went nearly extinct.

French merchants and the French Crown thus awakened to the profits to be made from monopolizing the furs of Canada, long scorned for its fool's gold and mundane fisheries but still claimed for the Most-Christian King as a result of Cartier's long-ago exploits. In 1578, King Henri III had issued what Spaniards would have called a *capitulación* to a nobleman named Mesgouez de La Roche, appointing him French viceroy over Canada and other so-called pagan lands. Nothing immediately came of the grant, but, twenty years later, after the end of the French wars of religion, when La Roche received a new commission from Henri IV, the document was suddenly worth something. The trade over which La Roche was granted a monopoly in exchange for reserving the king's share was no speculative proposition but a source of real profit.

The only problem was that the trade had somehow to be seized from hundreds of fishermen of diverse nations and especially from an influential group of French traders from the port of St. Malo. This a task could be accomplished neither by La Roche, from a base he had established in Acadia, nor by the successor to his grant, who tried to fortify a year-round settlement at Tadoussac, nor by the next claimant, Pierre du Gua, sieur de Monts, who received his commission in 1603 and tried again in Acadia. Coincidentally, de Monts's traders abandoned their Acadian post at almost the exact moment in 1607 when Englishmen were arriving at Jamestown.

Within a year, however, de Monts's associate Samuel de Champlain led an expedition that established a new post, whose fundamental goals could not have been more different from those of Jamestown. Unlike the conquistador fantasies and vague economic plans of virtually every previous European incursion into North America, Champlain's *entrada* had a very specific economic goal: to occupy a spot where Indian traders from the interior could be forestalled before they got downstream to the competition at Tadoussac or on the coast. That spot was very near the abandoned site of the Native town that Cartier had known as Stadacona, atop a natural fortress of cliffs where the St. Lawrence River narrowed dramatically and could be defended against European competition with a few cannon; transliterating an Algonquian term for "narrow passage," Champlain called it "Québec." At Tadoussac, Acadia, Spanish San Agustín, even English Jamestown, Native people encountered Europeans eager to sell goods as a sideline to their main businesses of fishing, conquest, or agriculture. At Québec, the Natives found Europeans whose main interest was to trade with them. Not surprisingly, relations between Europeans and Indians on the St. Lawrence took a very different course from that of their dealings on the Chesapeake.

Yet not necessarily more peaceful. Champlain quickly learned that he had set up shop in a war zone. His main trading partners were Algonquian-speaking hunter-gatherers from nearby Innu (Montagnais) and Algonquin bands and Iroquoian-speaking peoples of the Wendat (Huron) confederacy, whose agricultural villages lay hundreds of miles farther into the interior. These nations had long been at war with the Iroquoian-speakers of the Haudenosaunee, or Iroquois League, to the south; their conflicts probably caused the abandonment of Stadacona and St. Law-

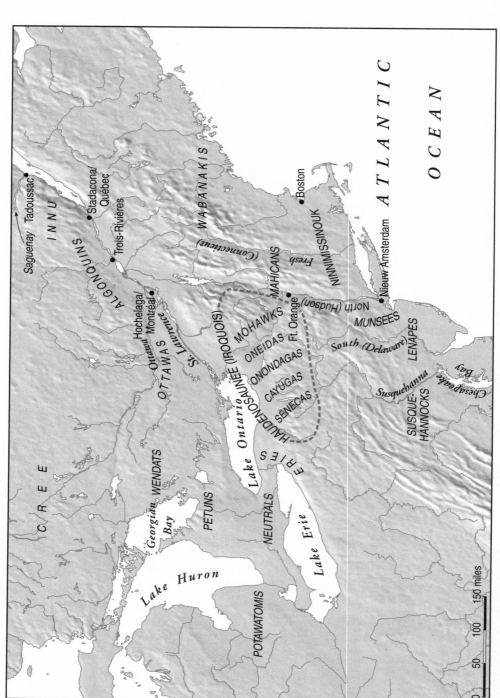

Northeastern North America, c. 1650.

rence Iroquoian towns that Cartier had encountered in the region. The French entrepôt of Tadoussac was on the eastern edge of Innu territory. Champlain's Québec was on the western edge. The largely uninhabited former territory of the St. Lawrence Iroquoians lay between Québec and the later site of Montréal (not occupied by the French until 1642). Farther west was Algonquin territory, centered on the many streams flowing into the Ottawa River, the main route to the Wendat country on the Georgian Bay of Lake Huron. This geography made the Algonquins—despite their small population, in comparison to perhaps thirty thousand Wendats—key players in both the relationship between Native peoples and the French and within the Native alliance against the Haudenosaunee Iroquois.

Since long before the arrival of Champlain and his trade, access to European goods had become central to the struggles of the Algonquins, Innu, and Wendats against the Haudenosaunee. Quite apart from the considerable attraction of iron, copper, and glass as prestige goods, trade with the axemakers promised great advantages over one's foes. Axes, French trading partners soon discovered, could be formidable weapons compared to the wooden and stone war clubs wielded by most Mohawk Iroquois, whose only metal hatchets in 1610 were those "which they sometimes win in war." More important, arrowheads fashioned from pieces of copper kettles, which Algonquin and Innu people seem to have rapidly acquired, flew straighter, farther, and with more force than what Champlain described as those "tipped with a very sharp bit of stone"—the kind still fired by most Mohawks.[13] Champlain knew all this from personal experience. Campaigning with his new allies in 1610, he pulled an ineffectual Iroquois flint arrowhead from his own neck. A year earlier he had more convincingly demonstrated the superiority of European weapons when a single shot from his musket killed three Mohawk war leaders.

As Champlain's predecessor at La Caroline had observed, conquistadores "always entered into alliances, pitting one king against the other."[14] In the early years of what colonizers grandiosely referred to as La Nouvelle-France, it was the Native people who did the pitting, using their alliance with the French against their rivals and leaving the Europeans increasingly frustrated by their lack of control over events. In language Powhatan no doubt would have loved to use, in 1636 an Algonquin chief the French called Le Borgne ("The One-Eyed") announced to Wendat chiefs who were reluctant to join a particular campaign against the Iroquois "that his body was hatchets; he meant that the preservation of his person and of his Nation was the preservation of the hatchets, the kettles, and all the trade of the French, for the Hurons." Indeed, he crowed, he was so much "master of the French" that he could not only take them back from the Wendat country to Québec but make them "all recross the sea."[15] That an Algonquin chief could make such a claim—empty or not—after nearly thirty years of French presence in the region illuminates the ways in which trade with Europeans undergirded Native political authority and shows where the real power lay.

So tenuous, in fact, was the de Monts organization's hold on power at Québec that privateers from Virginia had briefly conquered the place in 1629. (These were the English men whom the Native man considered senseless because they did not know the proper value of a beaver pelt.) Already in 1628, the French Crown had reassigned de Monts's trading privileges to a new, and presumably better-capitalized, entity of roughly one hundred investors, thus known as "La Compagnie des Cent Associés," whose first expedition to La Nouvelle-France (along with most of its initial capital investment) was captured by the same English privateers who overran Québec.

Like their English contemporaries, Les Cent Associés mixed commerce with nationalism and, especially, religious fervor. The Crown excluded Protestants from the company and its colony, and perhaps half of the investors were notably pious Roman Catholic laity and prominent clergy. Les Cent Associés were thus serious about their religious agenda, which envisioned the creation of "a New Jerusalem, blessed by God and made up of citizens destined for heaven," and made the conversion of Native Americans to Catholic Christianity a central goal.[16] The primary agents of this work were to be the great Catholic missionary order of priests who stood in the forefront of the Catholic Reformation: the Society of Jesus. Indeed, the Jesuits—who came to hold as much as a quarter of the lands distributed by the company, and whose clerical and lay personnel comprised a substantial portion of the colony's European population—were in effect the silent business partners of Les Cent Associés.

Yet secular business uneasily remained the basis of religious hopes for the colony. "These Gentlemen of the New Company have done more good here in one year than those who preceded did in all their lives," Jesuit missionary Paul Le Jeune wrote from Québec in 1635. Still, he feared "that these Gentlemen . . . may altogether or partly lose the great courage they now display, if unfortunately their trade in peltries should not always succeed."[17] For zealous Catholics like Le Jeune—whose apocalyptic sense of the importance of the work more than matched that of their English Protestant rivals—the winning of souls was all that mattered. "The burning desire of a great number of our Fathers, who find the air of New France the air of Heaven, since there they can suffer for Heaven, and there can help souls to find Heaven," Le Jeune proclaimed, was matched by "many young Nuns, consecrated to our Lord," who, "overcoming the fear natural to their sex," boarded ship "in order to come and help the poor girls and poor women among these Savages."[18]

When Les Cent Associés regained control of Québec for France by treaty with the English in 1632, Jesuit priests, already at work in the colony since 1625, assumed a prominent role in relations with the colony's Native trading partners. While cloistered nuns remained in Québec teaching Native women and tending the sick, Jesuit priests fanned out to the hunting camps of Algonquin and Innu people and took up residence in most of the Wendats' agricultural villages, becoming the primary embodiment of the French alliance everywhere they went. In this, they assumed much the same role that Paquiquineo had apparently envisioned for the Jesuits he had brought to Tsenacomoco three generations earlier. Powerful spiritual as well as diplomatic figures—with their odd (even by European standards) hairstyles, their black-robed cross-dressing, their proclaimed vows of celibacy, their chants, incense, and book-based spells—they were persons more safely allied with one's kin and community than with one's enemies.

Unlike their unfortunate predecessors in Tsenacomoco, these Jesuits well understood the importance of gift-giving to the process of building successful alliances with Native people. "All affairs of importance are managed here by presents," missionary Paul Le Jeune explained in 1636. Thus, he gave a Wendat council "a collar of twelve hundred beads . . . , telling them that it was given to smooth the difficulties of the road to Paradise." On a less public scale, another missionary in Wendat country observed three years later that the Jesuit fathers could "live happily and contentedly" if they regularly distributed "little glass beads, rings, awls, small pocket knives, and colored beads."[19] But Europeans needed more than prestige goods large and small to cement alliances in the 1630s and 1640s.

Christian converts received preferential prices on all trade goods and, after 1641, an exclusive right to purchase firearms.

By then, the French had long since ceased to be the region's exclusive source of such weapons. In 1609, within a year of the establishment of Québec (and within two years of the planting of Jamestown), an Englishman named Henry Hudson had sailed up the river that later came to bear his name. Like Champlain and the French, Portuguese, Basque, English, and other fishing crews before him, Hudson came to North America by the northern route, not the southern one favored by the Spanish. Like the Jamestown colonists and dozens of other previous *adelantados,* he sailed in search of a passage through the North American continent to the east; on two previous voyages much farther north, he had approached—and in 1610 he would enter and die in—the bay that now also bears his name. Like Jean Ribault at La Caroline and Richard Grenville at Roanoke, Hudson sailed in the Protestant cause against Catholic Spain. Like many of his predecessors—not least of them Columbus—despite the importance of his exploits to rivalries among emergent European nation-states, he sold his services to the highest bidder. His 1607, 1608, and 1610 journeys were made on behalf of royally chartered English merchants, but the 1609 expedition was sponsored by an entity known as the Dutch United East India Company—the Vereenigde Oost-Indische Compagnie, or VOC.

Which was *not* like anything that had come before. Created in 1602, during the long struggle of Calvinist forces in the northern provinces of the Netherlands to ratify their independence from the Spanish monarchy, the VOC superficially resembled earlier European conquistador partnerships: its duty was to use its own military powers to seize a trading monopoly on behalf of the nation. No previous *adelantado,* however, had received quite so sweeping a charge as the VOC, whose projected domain included all the oceans, coastlines, and islands between the Cape of Good Hope and the Strait of Magellan. This was the half the globe that, since the 1494 Treaty of Tordesillas, Catholics had considered Portugal's. Once Felipe II became king of Portugal as well as of Castile and Aragon in 1580, these realms effectively became part of Spain's empire and thus a prime target of the Dutch.

Still, it was less the scale of the VOC than several other factors that made the enterprise unlike any previous European agent of expansion. The United Provinces of the Netherlands were not a monarchy but an unequal coalition of aristocratic republics governed by a body called the States General, originally formed to coordinate the provinces' struggle for independence from the Spanish Crown. Most of the provinces also recognized the office of *stadtholder*, a quasi-monarchical military commander appointed by the dominant Dutch provinces of Holland, Zeeland, and Utrecht; at the turn of the seventeenth century, this was Maurits van Nassau, Prince of Orange. The VOC, created in wartime under these complicated political arrangements by wealthy merchants in the urban ports of Holland and, to a lesser extent, other Low Country provinces, had none of the ideological trappings of conquistador monarchy or landed manorialism characteristic of other European powers' overseas ventures. Such ideas meant little anyway in mostly urban Dutch provinces, which were so short of land that they had to steal arable fields from the sea with dikes and windmill-driven pumps. The company, then, was not handicapped by dreams of estates worked by docile peasants, nor was the conquest of territory ever its main purpose.

Instead, its focus was trade. Ships owned by the merchants who created the VOC already carried most of the commerce of France, and much of that of England and even Spain. The buying, the selling, and—especially novel as a consciously cultivated source of wealth—the transportation of goods were what the Dutch were good at. So good that those who invested in the VOC gave it financial resources no monarch or chartered French or English company could begin to match. With an initial capitalization of nearly 6.5 million gulden—then worth roughly £600,000 pounds, now worth incalculable millions of dollars or euros—the VOC immediately became a force no one could ignore.[20] And that force had one further trick up its sleeve. As the creation of so many independently powerful merchants, the VOC placed few limits on the autonomous activities of its investors. Far from being a centralized colossus, it was a loose coalition of free agents pursuing the main chance.

In their focus on trade and their political amorphousness, the Dutch people who sent Hudson to North America, perhaps more than any other Europeans of their day, found a congruence of fundamental interests with Native Americans—at least those with whom they could make successful trading alliances. Hudson set sail in 1609 barely a month before Dutch and Spanish negotiators completed the odd arrangement known as the

Twelve Years Truce. For a dozen years, the Spanish pledged to treat the
Netherlands as if they were independent states, to ignore the open practice of Calvinism there, and (under a secret codicil) not to interfere with
Dutch traders who entered Spanish colonial waters. Hudson's was among
the first of countless ships that the VOC and its constituent and noncon-
stituent merchants unleashed on the Atlantic and Pacific during the truce,
to try to take over the trade routes not just of Spain and Portugal but of
the fledgling colonial enterprises of England and France as well. Where
there were no Europeans with whom to trade, the Dutch imaginatively
sought markets with Native Americans, Africans, and Indonesians.

Like every other European ship that entered North American waters,
Hudson's found Native people already coveting the goods it carried and
already wary of the humans who sailed it. The first groups that Hudson encountered—from two of the many small communities in the lower Hudson Valley and New York Bay area—welcomed the newcomers on successive days and exchanged tobacco, currants, hemp, and other items for
knives and beads. The next day, other Native people attacked an exploratory party, killed one man, and wounded two others, presumably for
some unrecorded or unwitting provocation rooted in the fact that the
Europeans had already somehow concluded that they "durst not trust
them."[21] Similar peaceful and hostile encounters, in roughly the same two-
to-one proportion, continued throughout the voyage up and down the
river, with one significant difference. When the Europeans reached the
point at which the stream was no longer navigable, near present-day Albany, for the first time they found partners ready to exchange furs rather
than foodstuffs and specifically interested in axes as well as beads and
other "trifles." These people were probably Mahicans, speakers of an
Algonquian language distinct from that spoken downriver, who had either
participated in or knew about the kind of trade going on farther north at
Québec and Tadoussac.

Within a year of Hudson's voyage, at least one merchant house had
fitted out a ship to follow his route up what the Dutch called the "North
River," rather than the "Hudson." The expedition's specific purpose was to
trade for furs with the Mahicans and other Natives, including their neighbors to the west, the Haudenosaunee Mohawks. Other Dutch ships followed, often representing competing merchants. By 1614, the future site
of Albany had become, like Tadoussac before it, an annual gathering place
for European and Indian traders. In these same years, Dutch vessels also

opened commerce with Native people along two other great water routes into the interior, the "South" (Delaware) and "Fresh" (Connecticut) rivers. Optimists among the Dutch began referring to the entire trading orbit defined by these waterways and adjacent coasts by a name they frequently spelled *Nieu Nederlandt.* For dozens of Native chiefs and their people, however, little about the landscape or its names immediately changed. What mattered was that axes, knives, copper, glass beads, woolen cloth, and countless other things were finally available in quantities that neither the French on the St. Lawrence nor the English on the Chesapeake could yet provide.

The vague outlines of Nieu Nederlandt's trading system took clearer shape when Europe's Twelve Years Truce came to an end. As conflict between the Dutch and the Spanish resumed (a struggle that would later be considered part of Europe's Thirty Years War), in 1621 the States General chartered an entity called the Geoctroyeerde West-Indische Compagnie, West India Company, or WIC. While modeled after the VOC, the WIC was, at least in its early years, far more aggressively Protestant and nationalistic in its rhetoric and far more predatorily anti-Spanish in its privateering and trading activities than its counterpart. At the same time, while it was still a financially formidable force, the WIC lacked the huge capitalization of the VOC. With its energies focused on the profitable and militarily significant gold and slaves of West Africa, dyewoods of Brazil, and sugar of the Caribbean, the WIC never regarded Nieu Nederlandt as the main focus of its efforts. Nonetheless, the company considered its North American business significant enough to begin building permanent posts and to try to recruit sufficient colonists to defend them from the Spanish, English, and French. By 1624, the trading center on the upper Hudson had been transformed into "Fort Orange," and people had been sent to secure a more effective occupation of Manhattan, at the entrance to the river. Two years later, Nieu Nederlandt's new director-general, or governor, Peter Minuit, arrived and famously purchased that island from some Munsee chiefs who might or might not have actually owned it.

The transaction—which, it should be noted for the record, at sixty gulden, or perhaps a laborer's yearly wage, involved far more than the legendary twenty-four dollars in today's currency—was a bargain to Minuit. But the load of hatchets, knives, beads, and cloth it entailed epitomized what the Dutch arrival meant to Native people throughout the middle section of the Atlantic coast and the adjacent interior. Each kin group, it seemed, now could hope to display a collection of imported goods to rival Powhatan's. "The principal article of their household utensils is the pot or kettle in which the meat is cooked," one French chronicler observed. "They measure property by the number of kettles."[22] Iron goods also were marks of status; in the 1630s a Dutch traveler to Mohawk country described houses sporting "interior doors made of split planks furnished with iron hinges" and festooned with "iron chains, bolts, harrow teeth, iron hoops, [and] spikes."[23] Both observations capture the way that conspicuous display mixed seamlessly with practical matters of cooking and hingeing as Native people entered the new world of transatlantic trade.

Well before 1650, throughout the continent from the Gulf of Mexico to the Gulf of St. Lawrence, the practicalities of everyday Native American life came to depend on imported European goods. The changes were more evolutionary than revolutionary, often involving a direct substitution of copper kettles for earthenware pots, iron for stone axes, metal for flint arrowheads, woolens for furs in the fashioning of breechclouts and skirts. Only a few of the imports were so unprecedented that they could not easily be integrated into familiar patterns of use. Among these novelties were alcoholic beverages—a source of no end of future pain in eastern North American societies, where intoxicants had been virtually unknown. Also unprecedented were firearms, in this early period valued more for their prestige and shock value than as practical weapons for hunting and war, because bows, arrows, and clubs remained more accurately and reliably deadly than finicky smoothbore muskets.

Still, the ripple effects from relatively minor technological innovations could be profound. A simple device combining a bit of flint and steel that modern archaeologists call a "strike-a-light," for instance, made fire easily transportable for the first time. Native travelers could now expect not only to keep warm but, using lightweight copper kettles and newly efficient tools, to enjoy a hot meal and a more weathertight temporary shelter. Metal arrowheads and iron-enhanced war clubs and hatchets spawned similar, if less beneficial, chains of consequences. Largely ceremonial battles between massed armies wearing wooden armor—battles such as the one in which Champlain got his war injury—quickly became obsolete once firearms (inaccurate as they were) came into play, and once copper arrowheads proved their capacity to penetrate wooden armor, which had been proof against stone weapons. What came to be called "Indian-style" fighting—including small-scale ambushes, sharp-shooting from protected locations, avoidance of pitched battles—was an innovation developed in response to the same European technology that in former years had so transformed warfare on its home continent.

In more pacific realms, similar Native adaptations of imported technology also occurred. Imported iron tools, cloth, beads, and metal made possible an explosion of artistic and craft forms rooted in medieval aesthetic traditions. Metal knives and awls bequeathed anything carved from bone, antler, or wood a degree of detail unimaginable with stone tools. Imported glass and copper further enriched the ornamentation of everything from decorative hair combs to necklaces and ear pendants, to war clubs, to the gable ends of communal houses. Tomahawks, peace pipes, ceremonial masks, and dozens of other iconic Native American artifacts emerged from a creative mixture of imported technologies and materials with Indian traditions stretching back at least to the medieval period.

Nothing illustrates this phenomenon better than the shell beads known as wampum or, as the Algonquians and Dutch called it, *seawant*. Among the prestige goods that circulated in medieval North America, perhaps the most prized items were those made from the white central core of spiral whelks and the "black" (actually purple) shells of quahog clams. Both reflect light in extraordinary ways from infinite variations in shade and pattern. Only with the introduction of iron tools did it become possible to fashion these materials into small tubular beads finely drilled for stringing and thus to create what is called "true wampum." The technique was probably invented by Algonquian-speaking people who lived along the coasts of Long Island Sound, where both kinds of shell are most plentiful; indeed, a Native name for Long Island was Sewan Hacky, or "Wampum Island."[24] By the 1620s, Dutch traders had discovered a huge market for wampum among their far-flung Native trading partners, and they paid the Indian makers of the beads handsomely in European goods. By the late 1620s, coastal Southern New England Native communities were devoting most of their productive time to crafting tens of thousands of beads each year, which the Dutch in turn exchanged for furs from Native peoples elsewhere in the interior or along the Atlantic coast.

For Native people of the Northeast in particular, but especially for Iroquoian-speakers, wampum beads woven into strings and belts became integral to religious and political life—an efflorescence and democratization of ancient gift-giving and prestige-goods rituals. "With this wompompeage they pay tribute, redeem captives, satisfy for murders and other wrongs, [and] purchase peace with their potent neighbors, as occasion requires," said one European commentator. "In a word, it answers all occasions with them, as gold and silver doth with us." Another echoed that "their money consists of certain little bones, made of shells . . . , and these they string upon thread, or they make of them belts as broad as a hand, or broader, and hang them on their necks, or around their bodies."[25]

The idea that wampum was money also epitomizes the kind of cross-cultural product that the shell beads were. Although Dutch and English colonists did consider them to be money within their own gold-and-silver-starved communities, there is little evidence that Native people used them as a medium of exchange. Indians valued wampum as Europeans did gold, but they prized it for its beauty and its spiritual and cultural associations, and perhaps for the way its proliferation continued the egalitarian trends at work since the fall of the great Mississippian hierarchies. In wampum, then, as in the trading of fur and the selling of glass beads, cloth, tools, and weapons, the Dutch, the French, and some of the English found a lucrative—if, by the standards of Spanish treasure fleets, unromantic and niche marketed—trade in North America. Native people, for their own reasons just as deeply rooted in their economic and cultural traditions, similarly found the basis for a lucrative relationship. All the pieces should have been in place for a mutually profitable golden age. But there would be no such golden age. Instead, an entirely different class of imports from across the ocean spawned an era of catastrophic death as great as any in human history—a horrific dying that made even Christendom's Black Death seem modest.

SIX

Epidemics, War, and
the Remapping of a Continent

WHAT POWHATAN FAILED to achieve with Virginia, other Native leaders accomplished, at least briefly, with the very different European colonies of La Nouvelle-France and Nieu Nederlandt. Yet before any French or Dutch people could be successfully incorporated into the North American politics of exchange, diseases that colonists unwittingly brought with them threw everything into disarray. Smallpox was the greatest of the imported killers, but measles, mumps, chicken pox, and influenzas in their ever-evolving forms were nearly as deadly. Hemorrhagic fevers similar to Ebola might also have been part of the gruesome mix. Demographically devastated Native communities fell into a desperate spiral of conflict that made Europe's contemporary wars of religion look tame, dramatically reorganizing the political landscape of North America. For some of the temporary winners in these conflicts, the arrival of English people in territories north of Virginia was a godsend. For others, the creation of what the colonists called New England was a disaster.

Viral infections had attacked Western Europeans (and Africans and Asians) for well over a millennium and probably found their origins as agents of human disease in a much earlier round of agricultural revolutions than the ones that shaped the world of the conquistadores. When ancient humans of the Eastern Hemisphere domesticated pigs, cattle, chickens, and other livestock and began living in close quarters with them, it is likely that viruses evolved to cross the species barrier and to thrive in new

143

hosts. By 1500, Europeans, Africans, Asians, and these viruses had lived and died together for so many centuries that a rough truce had settled in the form of what were known as "childhood diseases." Most people contracted the illnesses at an early age; many survived the experience, and for the rest of their lives remained protected by antibodies they had developed in fighting off the attack. The rare adult who escaped smallpox or measles in childhood faced a much more devastating illness than his or her younger counterparts. Fully developed immune systems produced a reaction of pustules and fevers so overwhelming that these, more than the virus itself, set off a chain of secondary infections and respiratory or other failures almost certain to kill the victim.

Native Americans—with no experience of either domesticated farm animals or the viral diseases associated with them—were doubly vulnerable targets. No one was immune, and thus nearly everyone got seriously ill, none more seriously than the adults who otherwise might have nursed children back to health. The odds were frightful: half the population of a village exposed to smallpox was likely to perish in a single epidemic. The surviving half would be immune to future attacks of smallpox—either because their bodies defeated the first assault or because of some rare genetic trait that made them invulnerable—but that meant nothing when the next viral wave of measles or chicken pox levied its own, nearly equal, toll on a community now debilitated by the loss of so many productive members. Within a hundred-year period in any given location, the Native population probably shrank, on average, by 90 to 95 percent.

There is much we simply don't know, and will never know, about the Great Dying. Native oral traditions are largely silent. Perhaps a therapeutic act of forgetting suppressed the details. Perhaps the trauma was so thorough that few coherent stories could survive. Most of the devastation occurred beyond the sight of Europeans who might have recorded it, although just what happened is subject to debate. Surely, viruses passed from one Native community to another even when the Natives had no direct contact with Europeans, but how often and how easily this kind of transmission occurred is not clear. European records that do describe long-ago epidemics seldom satisfy modern medical standards of diagnosis. Issues of transmission are particularly hard to sort out. Caribbean and Central American Native people in close contact with Spanish colonizers endured multiple killing waves in the 1500s, but the extent to which these epidemics spread north of the Rio Grande or across the Florida strait is uncertain. In North America, the effect of particular epidemics seems to have been geographically spotty; one community might be devastated, while another, perhaps a political or military rival only a few miles upstream, escaped for a time unscathed.

Only two things are indisputable: that the dying began very early—so early that, by the time Europeans began interacting regularly with North Americans, many Native people were already attempting to recover from demographic disaster—and that the establishment of substantial European trader communities in the first three decades of the seventeenth century set off a particularly devastating wave of epidemics, perhaps because the traders brought with them for the first time enough sick children to keep the viruses alive on a transatlantic voyage.

As early as 1585, in Roanoke, Thomas Hariot reported that Native "people began to die very fast, and many in short space," after the English colonists visited their villages. "In some townes about twentie, in some fortie, in some sixtie, and in one six score" perished.[1] Similarly, in 1616 a French missionary said that the Native people of Acadia "often complain that, since the French mingle with and carry on trade with them, they are dying fast, and the population is thinning out."[2] In 1617, what one English colonist described as a "great mortality" struck both Jamestown and its Native neighbors. Its impact was "far greater among the Indians," who endured repeated bouts over a three-year stretch—precisely the period when the alliance promised by Pocahontas's marriage was falling apart and Powhatan himself passed away, although probably not from the epidemic.[3] The deaths in Acadia and the Chesapeake may or may not have been related to an unidentified ailment that killed thousands along the coast of New England from 1616 to 1618.

Better documented is a pandemic of smallpox that in the years 1633–1641 swept through New England, the St. Lawrence Valley, the Great Lakes region, and the continental interior at least as far south as Chesapeake Bay and as far west as the Appalachians. All of the Native peoples who were just then integrating the French and Dutch into their trading networks were horribly afflicted. The Wendat and Haudenosaunee Iroquois populations apparently declined by half in a single stroke, and similar death tolls must have struck nearly everywhere, especially among densely settled agricultural peoples. In the Connecticut Valley, nine hundred fifty of one thousand people in a single village died, Dutch traders reported in 1634, "and many of them did rot above ground for want of

burial."[4] Similar death rates were reported in Native towns near Massachusetts Bay. "Every day it is worse than before," a Wendat man said four
years later and hundreds of miles to the northwest. "This cruel malady has
now overrun all the cabins of our village, and has made such ravages in our
own family that, lo, we are reduced to two persons, and I do not yet know
whether we shall escape the fury of this Demon. I have seen maladies in
the country before, but never have I seen anything like this."[5]

No one anywhere had. A Dutch chronicler was not exaggerating when
he wrote in 1650 that "the Indians . . . affirm, that before the arrival of the
Christians, and before the small pox broke out amongst them, they were
ten times as numerous as they now are."[6] In the midst of all the death, at
least temporarily some communities fared better than others and could
take in refugees from less fortunate places where the Natives were incapa-
ble of feeding or defending themselves. Families and individuals drew on
existing bonds of kinship, marriage alliance, and trading connections to rebuild village life from the fragments that survived. They did so amid all the
processes of economic and political change that the Little Ice Age and the
new world of trade with Europeans had spawned. Surviving chiefs who
could ensure access to vital tools and weapons became nodes around
which new communities could coalesce.

In the Wendat country and elsewhere, Jesuit priests became similar
nodes—or, rather, points of attraction for some and points of repulsion for
others. With people dying in massive numbers, with Native shamans and
medical practices seemingly powerless against disease, and with Frenchmen both largely immune to and widely blamed for the illnesses they
brought, the new faith (or at least the new rituals associated with it) assumed either a desperate appeal or a hateful repugnance. Missionaries, to
their credit, fearlessly circulated among the sick and dying, dispensing water, dried fruits, and bits of sugar along with their prayers to comfort the
afflicted. Enough victims survived to make some people credit the priests'
ministrations and doctrines, explore seriously what the priests had to say,
and accept baptism.

Enough failed to survive—and, worse still, were christened at the last
moment by fathers hoping to send their souls to paradise—to convince
their kin that baptism itself killed and that the French were the cause of all
the suffering. The Wendats "cry aloud that the French must be massa-
cred," missionary Barthélemy Vimont reported in 1640. "They observed,
with some sort of reason, that, since our arrival in these lands, those who

had been the nearest to us, had happened to be the most ruined by the diseases, and that the whole villages of those who had received us now appeared utterly exterminated; and certainly, they said, the same would be the fate of all the others if the course of this misfortune were not stopped by the massacre of those who were the cause of it."[7] Yet neither side in an increasingly bitter conflict between Native Christians and non-Christians could afford to expel the Jesuit shamans or to risk the disruption of trade with Québec. In a world of constant death, no one could live without secure access to metal, cloth, and, especially, the tools of war.

For in North America, death had long produced war. It was always necessary to restrengthen one's people by rebuilding alliances and incorporating the power of captive slaves. Just as the attempted European conquest of the Americans often brought out the most violent cultural tendencies in would-be manorial lords, the combination of disease and improved weaponry sent Native American forms of organized brutality spinning out of control. Death and trade, in a macabre alliance, fueled a struggle for resources in which the most valuable prizes were human lives themselves.

Thus, the ongoing conflicts that Champlain had found himself drawn into exploded in an orgy of killing and captivity. As the great smallpox outbreaks of the 1630s were still unfolding, Iroquois war parties seeking captives to replace the dead began a series of raids on their Innu, Algonquin, and Wendat enemies that dwarfed anything seen in the past. Soon they were both regularly raiding settled Wendat villages and systematically blockading the St. Lawrence River to attack Indian traders bound for Québec. The Iroquois returned home with dozens rather than the usual handfuls of captives, along with plundered furs that would be exchanged at Fort Orange for firearms and other weapons. By the mid-1640s, French and Dutch observers agreed that Iroquois warriors had three to four hundred muskets—an arsenal that grew with each passing year. Haudenosaunee people could "obtain all things very cheaply: each of the Dutch outbidding his companion, and being satisfied, provided he can gain some little profit," French colonists complained. In particular, guns bought "from the Flemings" gave Iroquois war parties a tremendous advantage over less well-armed foes, who nonetheless had enough metal weapons and guns to exact their own frightful toll.[8]

The bloodshed entered a new phase in 1648 and 1649, when warriors from the five Iroquois nations joined forces to conquer successively all of the major villages of the Wendat confederacy. "So far as I can divine, it is the design of the Iroquois to capture all the Hurons, if it is possible; to put the chiefs and a great part of the nation to death, and with the rest to form one nation and one country," wrote Jesuit missionary Isaac Jogues as early as 1643.[9] Jogues had been captured by a Mohawk Iroquois party in 1642, escaped the next year, returned to the Mohawk country to try to establish a Jesuit mission in 1646, and would be executed as a sorcerer shortly before the Iroquois design was implemented. Hundreds of Wendats (and Haudenosaunee people) died in the struggle. Hundreds, perhaps thousands, of others were taken captive and incorporated, with varying success, into lineages of the five Haudenosaunee nations as slaves and adoptees. Others scattered to new homes in the West of the continent or to the village of Lorette, near Québec, where their descendants live today.

With the Wendats defeated, war parties from the Five Nations turned their guns on other neighbors, near and far. Great Lakes agricultural nations that spoke Iroquoian languages and shared broad cultural patterns with the Haudenosaunee were particular targets, because their captives were apt to be most easily assimilated. The people known as the Petuns, or the Tobacco Nation, fell by 1650. The nation called the Neutrals, because they traditionally allied with neither the Wendats or the Haudenosaunee, succumbed in 1651, and their neighbors the Eries dispersed in 1657. In each case, Iroquois war parties systematically attacked successive villages and forced those they captured to carry plundered furs and trade goods with them to their new homes.

Those who escaped captivity sought refuge and military allies among neighboring groups who spoke similar languages. Many Eries apparently escaped to the south, to the area between the frontiers of Virginia and La Florida, where they became known to the English as "Westos." There they brought the fierce new northern style of warfare to fresh enemies descended from the Mississippians, most of whom did not yet have firearms. Other Iroquoian-speaking survivors moved west and became known as "Wyandots" (a variant on the word "Wendat"). Algonquian-speakers settled among their linguistic kin, the Ottawas, Potawatomis, Miamis, and others—all of them, like the Wyandots and the captive-reinforced Haudenosaunee, products of the mixture of new peoples that came out of the Great Dying and the wars that followed. The Algonquian-speaking survivors called themselves "Anishanabe," which, like "Wendat," roughly translates as "the People," telling a polyglot story of displacement and reconstitution.

The Anishanabe and Wyandots, who continued to trade with the French throughout their struggles, had sufficient access to metal weapons and firearms to make them more formidable opponents of the Iroquois than some others. But La Nouvelle-France, lacking the capital, commercial expertise, and far-flung trading connections of the Dutch West India Company and its affiliated merchants, simply could not supply goods at the rates and quantities available to the Iroquois at Fort Orange.

Meantime, French colonists feared they would be the next target of the perceived Iroquois juggernaut. "If we do not go to humiliate these barbarians," concluded a French nun at Québec, "they will destroy the country and drive us all away by their warlike and carnivorous nature."[10] Approximately one hundred fifty French lost their lives in conflict with the five Haudenosaunee nations between 1608 and 1666, including six Jesuit priests remembered by their Church as martyrs. Although this was not an insignificant total for a colonial population that numbered in the hundreds rather than the thousands, spread over six decades the total is modest— less than half, for instance, the number of Virginia colonists who died on that single day in 1622. The toll was no higher because there was little incentive to eliminate the French trading centers that acted as a magnet for the Native trappers that Iroquois warriors plundered and captured. The French were meddlers in the primary fight—which was the battle among rival Indian communities for control of trade routes and, especially, human captives who could restore the population and power lost to the real enemy, disease.

In these battles, interior peoples with only spotty or indirect trade connections to Europeans hardly stood a chance—or rather their only chance was to assimilate, forcibly or voluntarily, into villages of the Five Nations. As a Haudenosaunee tradition recorded in the nineteenth century explained, "their plan was to select for adoption from the prisoners, and captives, and fragments of tribes whom they conquered . . . to make good their losses. They used the term, WE-HAIT-WAT-SHA, in relation to these captives. This term means a body cut into parts and scattered around. In this manner, they figuratively scattered their prisoners, and sunk and destroyed their nationality, and built up their own."[11] By the early 1660s, the we-hait-wat-sha seem to have comprised a majority of people who lived in the Iroquois Nations, and, in some villages, as many as two-thirds of the population might have been war captives. But even with the huge influx of newcomers, the total Haudenosaunee population never reached half its pre-epidemic level. To barely hold on, the Iroquois left vast areas once peopled by the captives virtually empty of human inhabitants.

We know about the campaigns of the Haudenosaunee because they were so minutely recorded (and sometimes exaggerated) by Jesuit missionaries. Similar scenarios played out elsewhere on the continent beyond Europeans' gaze. Everywhere people with access to imported weapons attacked less well-connected sources of captives who might restock devastated populations. One of the few peoples, for example, able to fight the Iroquois to a draw in the mid-seventeenth century were the Susquehannocks, whose homes were in what is now central Pennsylvania and Maryland, near the mouth of Chesapeake Bay. They were recent migrants to that location, having moved southward from areas nearer today's New York State border sometime in the sixteenth century. Archaeological evidence suggests that they displaced—and probably absorbed as war captives—a culturally distinct indigenous population, and that their primary motive for relocating was to gain freer access to the still-rare European prestige goods filtering into the continent from the Chesapeake and other coastal areas. All of this occurred at least a generation before the establishment of Jamestown—and helps to explain why a party of Susquehannocks was so eager to meet John Smith when he explored the upper Chesapeake in 1608.

Susquehannocks, like their Haudenosaunee foes, gained substantial access to trade goods and weapons only in the 1620s, after Dutch traders arrived. In 1624, the West India Company established Fort Nassau on the Delaware River at today's Gloucester, New Jersey, only to abandon the post between 1627 and 1633. Meantime, in 1630, a Virginia English trader named William Claiborne purchased Kent Island in Chesapeake Bay from the Susquehannocks and began supplying them with imported goods in exchange for furs. In 1634 the arrival of colonists in Maryland (which claimed Kent Island but, because of the Susquehannocks' military might, could not eject their supplier Claiborne) provided additional sources of trade goods. Then, in 1638, the New Sweden Company—despite its national affiliation, really a renegade operation by Nieu Nederlandt's ex-director Peter Minuit and other disgruntled components of the Dutch WIC—established Fort Christina on the site of Wilmington, Delaware, a location easily reached from the Susquehannocks' country.

All of these points of access to European goods briefly gave the Susquehannocks regional dominance. With firm control of hunting territories throughout much of the Susquehanna River watershed, they prospered for a generation. In about 1645, at the peak of their power, they relocated to a new, heavily fortified town near the Susquehanna. There, three thousand to five thousand people, many of them no doubt war captives, lived in a flourishing economy dependent on trade for weapons, tools, cooking utensils, and countless other everyday goods. From the Susquehannock town, goods also moved northwestward through a trading network that included, for a time, such Great Lakes Iroquoian people as the Eries and the Wendats. Still, for all their advantages, the Susquehannocks' position remained precarious. War with Native neighbors to the north and south was almost constant—Susquehannock defenders bloodily repulsed a massive Seneca Iroquois assault on their town in 1663, for instance—and epidemics, particularly smallpox in the early 1660s, struck multiple times, as they did everywhere in Native North America. By about 1665, the Susquehannock population, like all others, was plummeting.

So there really were no winners in the brutal Indian wars of the seventeenth century—only survivors. We know far less about the details of what happened farther south and west, where a handful of Spanish priests and colonists in La Florida and Nuevo México left only spotty records of events in the interior that they little understood. Everywhere, however, formerly densely settled territories were virtually emptied, as through warfare and voluntary resettlement people gathered together in new and often smaller towns. The political configurations that came to be known as Creeks, Cherokees, Chickasaws, and many others took shape during the nightmare of disease, warfare, captivity, and resettlement unleashed by the arrival of traders from Europe.

These processes are far better documented for one last area of the continent: the region that John Smith christened, and English-speakers since have called, "New England." There, dozens of rivalrous local Algonquian-speaking chiefdoms of the Ninnimissinouk (again the term means something like "the People") competed for the benefits of trade and alliance with the axemakers.

The pre-epidemic population of the Ninnimissinouk may have been as high as two hundred thousand. From their perspective, there could have been little unusual about the 1620 arrival on Cape Cod of the 102 English colonists who came to be known much later as "Pilgrims." Dutch traders and settlers had already been active in the Connecticut and Hudson valleys and around Long Island Sound for several years, and even they were latecomers. For over a century, the same European fishing and trading ships that sailed to the Grand Banks had frequently headed farther south along the coast and made the people of this region familiar with Europeans and their goods.

In 1602, near Cape Cod, Bartholomew Gosnold's expedition encountered "six Indians, in a Baske-shallop with mast and saile, an iron grapple, and a kettle of copper . . . , one of them apparelled with a waistcoat and breeches of blacke serdge . . . , [and] hose and shoes on his feet." Though "all the rest (saving one that had a paire of breeches of blue cloth) were all naked," clearly these were people who knew far more about Europeans and their technology than Gosnold did about his potential trading partners. Elsewhere, the Gosnold expedition found Native people well equipped with copper—which the Englishmen apparently did not suspect might have originated in Europe—and eager to trade furs for knives and other goods. One man even was able to repeat English phrases "so plaine and distinctly, as if he had been a long scholar in the language," no doubt because he had indeed chatted with English-speakers before. What, then, must Native people have made of Englishmen who visited three years later and thought it was necessary to demonstrate the supposed novelty of "knives and their use, by cutting of stickes and other trifles," particularly when these same Ninnimissinouk showed up a few days later to trade "40 good Beavers skins, Otters skins, Sables, and other small skins" obviously stockpiled for just such an opportunity?[12]

Nor was the Plymouth Colony the first English attempt to establish a lasting settlement in the region. Nor was it even the first called "Plymouth." In 1607, the Plymouth Company of Virginia had attempted to establish its equivalent of Jamestown at Sagadahoc in Maine. Colonists there found Natives who treated their arrival as an almost everyday occurrence, using "many french words" to demand what the English considered "over muche" in exchange for beaver skins.[13] One of the few accomplishments of the Sagadahoc colony was—at whatever price—to trade for a sizable stock of furs. Numerous other English visitors did likewise in the first two decades of the seventeenth century.

Many but not all of these interlopers were sent by the Plymouth Company, in which the dominant investor was an English West Country noble-man named Sir Ferdinando Gorges. After his organization collapsed in 1619, Gorges became the leading figure in its successor, the Council for New England, which in 1620 received a royal patent for the entire area between 40 and 48 degrees of latitude (stretching from today's Pennsylvania to Newfoundland). This grant was in the works but had not yet been officially sealed when the "Pilgrims" sailed. Shortly after the Plymouth colonists had settled into their first starving winter on Cape Cod, the leaders of the project received a charter from Gorges's council, to replace their original grant from the Virginia Company of London for lands farther south near Jamestown. In this, they were among many actual and aspirational colonists whom the Council for New England dispatched to the region. At any given time in the 1620s, there were five or six struggling bands of English people attempting to make a go of it in Ninnimissinouk territory.

English, French, Dutch, and Basque people thus were familiar enough that at least some Native people could not only speak a bit of one or more of their languages, but could tell the various nationalities of axemakers apart. At least in the region around Cape Cod, the English had recently developed a particularly nasty reputation as slave raiders—or, as Native people no doubt saw it, enemies who had committed the defining act of war by seizing captives. In 1611, three men were kidnapped from Chappaquiddick. In 1614, John Smith's associate Thomas Hunt seized twenty-seven people and tried to sell them in Málaga, Spain, where they were ransomed by Franciscan priests. Among this group was the man the Plymouth colonists came to know as Tisquantum, or Squanto. He somehow found his way to the British Isles, learned some English, come to the attention of the Gorges circle, and made at least two trips to New England as an interpreter, before returning home to find his entire village destroyed by the great epidemic of 1616–1618. These exploits perhaps explain the title by which Squanto made himself known to the English: "Tisquantum" was the name of a particularly powerful other-than-human person in the Ninnimissinouk pantheon.

The reputation of the English as military enemies, along with the social chaos among local Native people still reorganizing after the first great onslaught of disease, explains how difficult it was for the Plymouth colonists to make contact with the local population in the first few months after their landing. Apart from one brief bloodless skirmish in which the English fired their muskets and the Native people their brass-tipped arrows, there was much watching from afar (and one daring theft of a set of English tools), but no direct encounter with the sick and starving colonists. It is possible that more was at work than simple Native wariness toward those who spoke and looked like people who had proven themselves enemies. The English, without quite knowing what they were doing, had settled at the abandoned village site where all of Squanto's kin and townspeople had recently perished. They had kept themselves alive by unearthing buried stocks of corn that the dead had left behind, and they had plundered prestige goods from several graves of high-status people, despite an early vow to leave them "untouched, because we thought it would be odious unto them to ransacke their Sepulchers."[14] All of this must have further made the English appear not just odious but dangerous to the Ninnimissinouk who observed them from afar.

No wonder, then, that when the local chief Massasoit decided to make an overture, he sent not one of his own people but a Wabanaki visitor known as Samoset, who had learned a little English, and probably got the name he used (a variation on "Somerset") from some of Gorges's men. And no wonder that three days of purging ceremonies were necessary before Samoset could strip himself for war, carry two arrows, and strut unannounced right into the heart of the newcomers' settlement, where, as the astonished colony governor William Bradford put it, "out of his boldnesse, hee saluted us in English, and bad us well-come."[15] No wonder, too, that, having survived the encounter, Samoset quickly asked for a beer.

With none to be had, he enjoyed instead aquavit, sea biscuits, cheese, a slice of duck, and a coat to shelter him from the March wind. But personal food, drink, and clothing were not the point of his visit. Massasoit—like Powhatan and many others—had every incentive to make an alliance with the Englishmen and their goods. The recent epidemic had hit Massasoit's people, the Wampanoags, with particular force. Earlier European visitors had estimated that the many autonomous villages in the area around Cape Cod, Nantucket, and Martha's Vineyard could send three thousand men into battle. If one in five people was a warrior, that would imply a total population of fifteen thousand. By 1619, probably no more than one thousand Wampanoag men, women, and children remained alive on the mainland, and Samoset told the Plymouth colonists that the Pokanokets, Massasoit's chiefdom (or, as it was locally termed, his sachemship), had only sixty men.[16] Compounding the disaster, the Wampanoags' neighbors to the west, the Narragansetts, whose principal chiefs were named Miantonomi and Canonicus, had apparently escaped almost unscathed and so were able to force Massasoit to cede territory and pay tribute to them. Unlike Powhatan, then, Massasoit was operating from a position of weakness, within which an alliance with the English could make all the difference to his people's future.

The Plymouth colonists, of whom only about fifty had survived the winter, were in no stronger position and can hardly have seemed much of a military threat to Massasoit, despite their demonstrated gunpower and the presence of their own battle-hardened equivalent of Jamestown's John Smith: the Low Country war veteran Miles Standish. In short, when Samoset introduced the English to Squanto, who in turn announced an imminent diplomatic visit from Massasoit, each side needed the other. A standoff, reminiscent of the turf struggle prior to Powhatan's coronation, occurred: Massasoit stood on a hilltop with all sixty of his warriors and declined to enter the English village, while Plymouth governor John Carver refused to go out to meet him. Finally, the two sides met halfway at a brook, from which Massasoit was escorted with drums and trumpets into one of the colonists' buildings.

There, the parties agreed to a treaty. Massasoit promised—or at least the English wrote down—"that neither he nor any of his should injure" the English and that, if trouble should arise, "he should send the offender, that they might punish him." The English pledged that "if any did unjustly war against him, they would aid him," in exchange for a commitment that "if any did war against them, he should aid them." Furthermore, Massasoit was to "send to his neighbors . . . to certify them of this, that they might not wrong . . . [the English], but might be likewise comprised in the conditions of peace."[17] This treaty—celebrated a year after at what, much later, Americans would call the First Thanksgiving—was less a reflection of godly Pilgrims making peace with the Indians than of a hard-headed, divide-and-rule English strategy of which any conquistador would have approved.

Yet it was just as hard-headed and practical on the part of Massasoit. The Wampanoags gained a valuable trading partner and ally. A few months after the treaty was made, a delegation from Plymouth visited Massasoit's capital bearing gifts of a copper chain and a red English coat. "Having put the Coat on his backe, and the Chayne about his necke, he was not a little proud to behold himselfe, and his men also to see their

King so bravely attyred," the visitors recorded. After promising to pro-
vide seed corn to feed his English tributaries, the sachem "made a great
Speech. . . . The meaning whereof was (as farre as we could learne) thus;
Was not he *Massasoyt* Commander of the Countrey about them?"[18]

Over the next few years, Massasoit and his people used their relationship with Plymouth not only to escape their tributary relationship to the
Narragansetts but to profit from the wampum trade and extract tribute
from their Indian neighbors, who had to deal with them before they could
deal with the English. Brokering these ties with the English, and relying
on the threat or reality of English military force against the Narragansetts
and others, Massasoit built a regional power base—an incipient paramount chiefdom—that never matched that of Powhatan to the south but
nonetheless was a major accomplishment. And like the Haudenosaunee,
but on a smaller scale, Massasoit assembled from the fragments of the
many autonomous disease-ravaged communities of today's southeastern
Massachusetts a new political entity, for there probably had never before
been anything like a centralized Wampanoag nation.

Some hint of the wealth and power that the Wampanoags' ties to the
English generated can be glimpsed from English traveler John Josselyn's
account of Massasoit's descendant and eventual successor, who visited
Boston in the early 1660s. "The *Roytelet* now of the *Pocanakets,* that is
the *Plimouth-Indians,* is Prince *Philip* alias *Metacom,* the Grandson of
Massasoit," Josselyn wrote. Philip walked confidently among the colonists
with "a Coat on and Buskins set thick with . . . [wampum] Beads in pleasant wild works and a broad Belt of the same," which Josselyn "valued at
Twenty pounds." Philip's self-presentation reflected the political skill and
personal connections that for centuries had been the hallmarks of a great
chief.[19]

The Plymouth colonists—whose leaders were good Calvinists—could
never so conspicuously display the fruits of their relationship with the
Wampanoags, but the profits were real. Squanto's lessons in fishing and
corn planting (which apparently included teaching these particular Englishmen the un-Algonquian English practice of using fish as fertilizer) are
well known. Less well known, but in many ways more important, was
Squanto's introduction of another practice familiar to other English people but not these: the trade of furs for imported cloth, tools, and weapons.
The colonists had arrived "altogether unprovided for trade," Bradford admitted. "Neither was there any amongst them that ever saw a beaver skin

till they came here and were informed by Squanto."[20] A few months after the 1621 treaty agreement, Squanto escorted a party of Plymouth colonists north to Massachusetts Bay, where the local Massachuset and Pawtucket populations were just as devastated by the recent epidemic as the Wampanoags and just as eager to establish trade with Plymouth. These ties in turn led, within a few years, to a thriving commerce between Plymouth and Wabanaki people farther up the coast in present-day Maine. By the late 1620s, the Plymouth people had established a trading post on the Kennebec River and were exchanging corn as well as imported goods with the Wabanakis for substantial numbers of furs; in this, the English stepped into a role traditionally played by Massachuset and other southern New England agriculturalists, who had apparently long traded foodstuffs to the hunter-gatherer Wabanakis. Despite a series of misfortunes, including the hijacking of one early shipment by Muslim North African pirates, Plymouth made this commerce the source of its most profitable export to Europe. In the years 1631–1636 alone, Bradford calculated, the colony shipped nearly £10,000 sterling worth of beaver pelts.[21]

The mutual profits and rivalries ran in several directions, among European as well as Native communities, creating a human landscape that must have been as bewildering to those who lived on it as it is to those today who try to comprehend its many unfamiliar names and places. On the Kennebec, the Plymouth traders competed with the French of Acadia and the fishing fleets of various nationalities that continued their annual pilgrimage along the northern route from Europe, while at the same time running afoul of Gorges's men and attempts by the Council for New England to enforce its alleged monopoly on the region's trade. Such a monopoly was no more enforceable for Gorges than it had been for French patentee Pierre du Gua de Monts a decade earlier. By the mid-1620s, under pressure from Gorges's competitors, Parliament revoked his exclusive privileges.

The cast of English characters in the region soon became even more diverse. In 1629 the first colonists sent by the newly chartered Massachusetts Bay Company arrived, followed a year later by John Winthrop's fleet of company colonists, who established Boston. Many others followed and planted a succession of towns, often on land that disease-stricken Massachuset people had left vacant (or so the colonists convinced themselves). By 1635, roughly ten thousand English people lived in scattered settle-

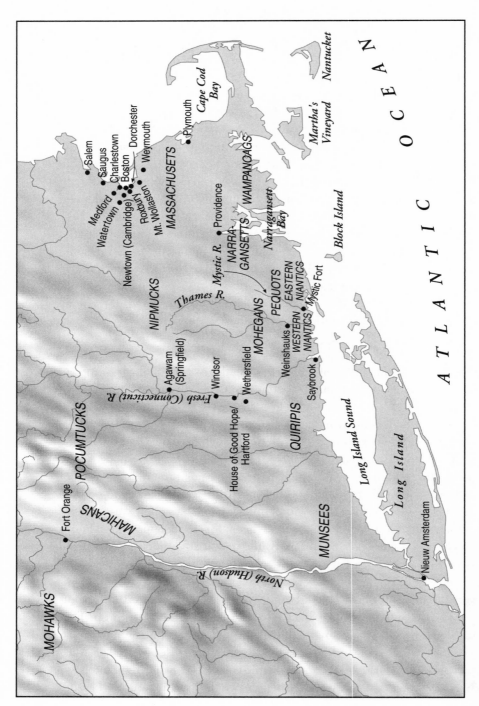

Southern New England, c. 1636.

ments between the Kennebec and Connecticut river valleys. This was, to be sure, a substantial number, but a mere one-twentieth of the Native population that the region had supported before the epidemics of 1616–1618 and 1633–1634. There is no particular reason to assume that the Ninnimissinouk initially saw these new arrivals, though they came by the hundreds, as fundamentally different from the many other Europeans who had come and gone in recent years. Dangerous as they might be as enemies, the English provided rising chiefs with sterling opportunities for trade alliances of the sort that Massasoit was so masterfully exploiting. Briefly, at least, the Narragansetts, for instance, saw the Massachusetts Bay Colony as a welcome counterbalance to the trade and diplomatic axis their Wampanoag rivals had built with Plymouth.

The few hundred Europeans settled in Nieu Nederlandt were demographically the smallest component in the southern New England mix, but for both Native and English people, their influence far outweighed their numbers. Dutch traders acquired as many as ten thousand beaver skins annually in the Connecticut Valley from 1614 to 1624.[22] Moreover, for at least a decade after 1627, these same traders supplied their Plymouth counterparts with most of the cloth, metal goods, and beads that they exchanged with the Wampanoags and Wabanakis. In the process, the Dutch introduced the Plymouth traders to shell beads. By the early 1630s, the English could not get enough wampum to satisfy the demand of Wabanaki and Massachuset people, who formerly, Bradford said, "had none or very little of it, but the sachems and some special persons that wore a little of it for ornament."[23] And the only major source of wampum was the Dutch, for Plymouth's alliance with Massasoit cut the colony off from the only serious alternative, his rivals the Narragansetts.

In the wampum trade, the Dutch were as dependent on their Native partners as Plymouth was on Nieu Nederlandt. Just as Massasoit exploited the arrival of the English at Plymouth to gain power over his rivals, the Pequot chief Tatobem had begun to use his relationship to the Dutch to build a paramount chiefdom in the Connecticut Valley and the Long Island Sound region. In 1622, a renegade trader named Jacob Eelckens (who had been a major figure in opening commerce with the Native people of the upper Hudson River) kidnapped a Pequot sachem, probably Tatobem himself, and held him for ransom. To gain his release, the Pequots paid one hundred forty fathoms of wampum, demonstrating to the Dutch both the high value that Native people placed on the shell beads and the massive supplies of them under Pequot control: strung end-to-end, forty fathoms of beads would have stretched nearly the length of a modern football field. Very soon, an official representative of the West India Company was back in Pequot country, not only to apologize for Eelckens's act but to offer Tatobem a virtual monopoly on Dutch imports in exchange for exclusive access to Pequot wampum.

Tatobem used his control of European goods to make the Narragansetts his tributaries and to impose an apparently unprecedented level of authority over many local chiefs on both sides of Long Island Sound, including those of the closely related people known as Mohegans. All supplied wampum in exchange for goods and military protection. None of this made Tatobem popular with his Native neighbors. By 1632, the Narragansetts, reinforced by their new links to the Massachusetts Bay colony, began a war against the Pequots, in alliance with several Mohegan chiefs. The next year, the WIC took advantage of Tatobem's distress to purchase from him a deed to a tract of land near today's Hartford, where they built a trading post on the Connecticut River called the "House of Good Hope." This threatened to eliminate the Pequots as middlemen in trade with other Native communities.

Finding nothing good about this Dutch hope, the Pequots, still at war with the Narragansetts, and desperately attempting to restore the power that came from control of the wampum trade, attacked one of the first groups of Indian customers who attempted to visit the post. The Dutch immediately retaliated by luring Tatobem aboard a sloop, holding him for a ransom that was quickly paid, and then executing him anyway. Under any circumstances, a paramount chief's death would throw his entire network of alliances, tribute, and exchange relationships into disarray. That Tatobem was killed by the very allies who were the source of the goods on which his power over subordinate chiefs rested seems to have placed his successor, named Sassacus, in an impossible situation.

With local chiefs already scattering to make their own alliances with the Dutch, the English, the Narragansetts, or each other, Sassacus was unable to mobilize much power beyond his own village to wage what was now a multisided struggle with both European and Native enemies. The horrific smallpox epidemic of 1634 soon compounded the troubles. As a result, the only immediate Pequot response to Tatobem's assassination was a small counterattack that Sassacus personally led on a trading vessel similar to the one that had kidnapped the sachem. Unfortunately, the nine victims turned out not to be Dutch at all, but instead a group of quasi-pirates led by a well-connected Englishman named John Stone, who had managed to become a wanted man in Nieuw Amsterdam, Plymouth, and Boston alike.

This case of mistaken identity symbolizes the confused landscape that the Ninnimissinouk territory had become in the 1630s. We tend now to think in terms of neatly drawn maps—Pequots to the west, Wampanoags to the east, Narragansetts in the center—all bracketed by clearly bounded Nieu Nederlandt on one side and Plymouth on the other, with newcomer Massachusetts Bay to the north and still-newer Rhode Island and Connecticut soon to take their middle places on Long Island Sound. But in 1633, no such tidy scene existed. Dozens of local sachems tried to rebuild disease-ravaged communities by making alliances with others and by controlling trade with the varied Europeans. To Native people, the newcomers appeared to live not in geographically coherent colonies, but in many local trading posts and settlements such as Plymouth, Boston, Dorchester, Nieuw Amsterdam, and Good Hope. All of these European settlements were just as rivalrous, and just as concerned to make ties of trade, alliance, and dominance over Native people, as were the sachems they dealt with. The first great sorting-out of this chaos into something resembling a coherent order was the event subsequently known as the "Pequot War."

In this remapping of the human landscape, Sassacus's Pequots were less the aggressor than the odd man out who became an easy target for outnumbered English military men desperate to prove their dominance. Having lost the power that came from the Dutch alliance, Sassacus found everyone turning simultaneously against him. As early as 1631, a group of dissident Pequot or Mohegan chiefs traveled to both Boston and Plymouth to invite English traders to settle in their country and break the Tatobem-Dutch monopoly. In 1633—just as everything was falling apart for the Pequots—Plymouth accepted the offer and planted a trading post a short distance upriver from the House of Good Hope. Two Dutchmen then leap-frogged still farther upriver, only to nearly starve to death as their Native hosts succumbed to the 1634 smallpox epidemic. At the same time that the Plymouth men were settling in on the Connecticut, a ship from Boston was cruising the river and Long Island Sound, trading for wampum. A few months earlier, an Englishman named John Oldham had traveled overland to the Connecticut Valley to barter with former tributaries of the Pequots, who seem to have heartily welcomed the visitor wherever he went.

Sassacus, meanwhile, made his own overtures to Boston in an attempt to restore his people's power. The result was a treaty in which Sassacus's emissaries gained a promise from Massachusetts Bay governor John Winthrop to mediate the conflict between the Pequots and the Narragansetts and to establish a trading center in the Connecticut Valley exclusively for Pequot customers. In return, Massachusetts received a tribute payment of four hundred fathoms of wampum, cession of what Winthrop called "all their right at Connecticut," and a pledge that the murderers of Stone and his men would be delivered up for trial.[24] In light of the fact that Stone had actually been banished from Boston after being charged with drunkenness and adultery, the last provision at first glance seems either inexplicable or cynical, but it cut to the heart of what the Boston government was about. Massachusetts would make the Pequots its legal subjects, if not its neo-feudal vassals. Imposing the power of life and death over criminals was the most important indicator of that domination. Conquistador habits died hard.

Sassacus's people comprehended tribute and subjection, although they probably saw (or desperately hoped to see) the relationship as an alliance that brought English power and goods into their orbit. Whether they understood English claims to their territory as anything more than an acceptance of a Native invitation to live on those lands and a confirmation of political loyalty is not clear. Moreover, whatever "all their right at Connecticut" meant, the Pequots' actual homes were along the Mystic River, well to the east of the Connecticut. Equally ambiguous was the business about delivering Stone's killers to English justice. Several of the perpetrators had died in the smallpox epidemic; the Native custom of tribute gifts should (in the Pequots' minds) have satisfied Stone's grieving kin; and Winthrop and other Bostonians had already expressed their personal distaste for the victim. As a result, the Pequots were unlikely to take the provision seriously.

Yet, as other Native people could have testified, the English were deadly serious about their right to enforce their jurisdiction. Had the Pequots not been at war with the Narragansetts, they might have asked the Narragansett sachems Miantonomi and Canonicus about a visit to Boston two years earlier, when the Massachusetts magistrates forced the chiefs to inflict a public beating on two Native men who had allegedly broken into an English house. Had smallpox not claimed the Massachuset sachem Chickatawbut, the Pequots might also have asked him about the occasion on which some of his people were judged guilty by a Massachusetts court "for assaulting some English of Dorchester in their houses, etc." According to Winthrop, "They were put in the bilboes [shackles], and Chicktabot required to beat them, which he did."[25]

The seriousness of the Massachusetts Bay English—and the dangerous mistake that Sassacus had made in trying to ally with them—became apparent in 1636, when another English trader, the same John Oldham who had been well received in Pequot country three years earlier, turned up dead on Block Island. The culprits were evidently Niantics, formerly subordinate to the Pequots but now in the Narragansetts' orbit. Miantonomi and Canonicus denied any involvement and rapidly made restitution for Oldham's goods. Still, everyone seemed to agree, as Winthrop put it, "that all the sachems of the Narragansett except Canonicus and Miantonomi were the contrivers of Mr. Oldham's death," perhaps because the Englishman was blamed for the smallpox epidemic, or, more likely, because, as Winthrop concluded, "he went to make peace and trade with the Pequots."[26] That the Pequots nonetheless became the target of English wrath, and the Narragansetts their allies in the resulting war, has caused many a historian to find something suspect, paranoid, or downright duplicitous in the conduct of the English.

With good reason, but there was a logic involved. It centered on the colonial government's proclaimed right to punish any Native person who killed an Englishman, whether that Englishman was a savory character or not. Despite the efforts of Miantonomi and Canonicus to resolve things according to Native principles, Winthrop, his councillors, and the political and religious leaders of the Bay Colony towns agreed that "doing justice upon the Indians for the death of Mr. Oldham" was essential. Ninety volunteers under the command of John Endecott sailed off with instructions "to put to death the men of Block Island, but to spare the women and children, and to bring them away," that is, to enslave them as prisoners in a just war. The troops were "to take possession of the island; and from thence to go to the Pequods to demand the murderers of Capt. Stone and other English, and one thousand fathom of wampom for damages, etc., and some of their children as hostages, which if they should refuse, they were to obtain it by force."[27]

At Block Island, Endecott's troops burned two abandoned villages to the ground, along with cornfields and stores of food and goods. But two and a half days of slogging across the island achieved nothing else. Sailing upriver to confront the Pequots, Endecott had even less success. A Pequot spokesman got the best of him in a verbal sparring match, utterly rejecting all English demands and claiming that no chiefs with any authority were available to speak with him. Endecott soon lost patience, and marched his troops toward a nearby village with flags flying. The Pequot residents not only refused to engage him in battle but shouted insults as they ran away. As he had done on Block Island—and as Richard Grenville had done at Roanoke fifty years earlier, and as many other frustrated conquistadores had done through the years—Endecott torched the village and its fields and headed home.

Pequots unleashed a series of counter-raids on the hundreds of English settlers who had poured into the region since their agreement with the Massachusetts Bay government and in the wake of the 1634–1635 epidemic. The first English had arrived in 1634 at what became Wethersfield, Connecticut. In 1635, others had settled at Hartford and Windsor, on lands the newcomers purchased from local sachems who were formally subordinate to the Pequots and were now eager to make their own connections to what they presumed were English traders. Others had installed themselves at Saybrook, at the mouth of the Connecticut River, under the leadership of Winthrop's son, John Winthrop Jr., and by the legal pretence of one particularly dubious example of the many patents issued from the Council for New England. The influx of colonists, combined with Endecott's invasion, seems to have rallied a number of local warriors and sachems back to Sassacus's side—particularly in light of the fact that, for several months, there was no effective English counterattack.

Certainly not won over were a relatively small number of Mohegans led by the sachem Uncas, one of many local chiefs who had broken away from the Pequot orbit after the assassination of Tatobem. From his perspective, the English were more than welcome allies against the Pequots; they were the means by which he would raise himself and his people to a paramount position in the Connecticut region. Uncas quickly offered the services of his seventy warriors to the Connecticut Valley English, along with the heads of five Pequots they had slain. For good measure, the Mohegans tortured and executed a sixth Pequot man inside the walls of Saybrook Fort. Slightly less eager allies of the English were Canonicus's and Miantonomi's Narragansetts, who, despite their ongoing quarrel with the Pequots, had a healthy distrust of the colonists' motives—and, with a population that still outnumbered all the English together, the power to act on that distrust. It took several months of diplomacy to bring the Narragansetts into the colonists' coalition.

In May 1637 an expeditionary force mobilized ninety Englishmen led by Low Country war veterans John Underhill of Massachusetts Bay and John Mason of the Connecticut outposts, seventy Mohegans led by Uncas, and five hundred Narragansetts. Its objectives were the two main forti- fied Pequot villages, on the Mystic River and at Weinshauks (present-day Groton, Connecticut), which was Sassacus's seat. As many as seven hun- dred Pequot men, women, and children were sleeping at Mystic Village when Mason and Underhill broke through the two gates of its palisades at dawn. The hundred and fifty or so who were warriors put up a fierce fight, killing two Englishmen and severely wounding twenty others. The battle became so intense that Mason and Underhill decided that hand-to-hand combat in the village's crowded streets could never be won. "We must burn them," Mason matter-of-factly concluded.[28] Fires were quickly set as the English withdrew to encircle the village, with their Mohegan and Narragansett allies forming a second ring in their rear. Most of the inhabi- tants were burned alive. The few who forayed outside the palisade or sim- ply tried to escape were picked off by English musketeers so trigger-happy that they killed and wounded some of their Narragansett allies in the process.

"Mach it, mach it!" the Narragansetts cried. "It is naught, it is naught, because it is too furious, and slays too many men" (and, they might have added, deprived Native victors of the opportunity to capture and enslave the vanquished).[29] Underhill admitted that it was "Great and dolefull . . . to see so many soules lie gasping on the ground so thicke in some places, that you could hardly passe along," but he did not consider the violence excessive.

It may be demanded, "Why should you be so furious (as some have said) should not Christians have more mercy and compassion?" But I would refere you to *David's* war, when a people is grown to such a height of blood, and sin against God and man, and all confederates in the action, there he hath no respect to persons, but harrows them, and saws them, and

puts them to the sword, and the most terriblest death that may bee: sometimes the Scripture declareth women and children must perish with their
parents; sometime the case alters: but we will not dispute it now. We had
sufficient light from the word of God for our proceedings.[30]

Bradford, contemplating the scene from the safety of Plymouth, agreed:

It was a fearful sight to see them thus frying in the fire and the streams of
blood quenching the same, and horrible was the stink and scent thereof;
but the victory seemed a sweet sacrifice, and they gave the prays therrof to
God, who had wrought so wonderfully for them, thus to inclose their enemies in their hands and give them so speedy a victory over so proud and insulting an enemy.[31]

Approximately one-quarter of the Pequot population of three thousand
died in the Mystic massacre and in a series of running skirmishes that followed. Although Underhill and Mason, nursing their wounded and largely
abandoned by their appalled Narragansett allies, were unable to follow up
with an attack on the town of Weinshauks, they had dealt Sassacus's people
a stunning blow. Moreover, they demonstrated to Pequots, Narragansetts,
Mohegans, Wampanoags, and all the rest of the Ninnimissinouk the utter
folly of crossing the English.

Sassacus's people soon dispersed from Weinshauks. A hundred or so
went to Long Island; about seventy surrendered to the Narragansetts; others tried to hide out closer to home. The largest contingent, including
Sassacus, headed west toward Mohawk Iroquois country, hoping to find allies and shelter there. A few months after the Mystic massacre, most of the
warriors in this latter group made a last stand against the English in a
swamp near what is now New Haven. Two hundred women and children
surrendered. Nearly all of the men put up a night-long fight but in the end
fell before English firearms. Meantime, English forces scoured the countryside, enslaving women and children, killing most men, and occasionally
displaying a sachem's head on a pole. Mohegans, Narragansetts, Long Island Indians, and others joined in, taking captives and sending Pequot
scalps, heads, and hands to the English as gruesome trophies and signs of
loyalty. Ultimately, these included the scalp of Sassacus and his closest advisors, supposedly sent to Connecticut by the Mohawks.

The killing and enslavement for the most part came to an end at Hartford in September 1638, with a treaty not between the English and their Pequot enemies but between the English and their Mohegan and Narragansett allies. The Mohegans and Narragansetts made an alliance with each other and agreed to submit all future disputes to binding English arbitration. They yielded any claims they might have had to Pequot territory and agreed to execute any Indians who had killed English people and to send their heads or hands to the English as proof. Some of the male Pequot captives whom the English had enslaved were distributed to the Mohegans and Narragansetts, in exchange for annual wampum tribute payments to the new Connecticut colony government that took over most Pequot territory. No specific arrangements were made for the many Pequot women and children who had been enslaved or adopted by the two Indian nations. Most of the other captives who had not yet been put to work in colonial households were sold to the West Indies and Bermuda. The surviving Pequots were forbidden to return to their homes or even to use the name "Pequot." Many lived in and around their homeland nonetheless, but the chiefdom that Tatobem had assembled through his control of the Dutch alliance lay in utter ruin.

In its place stood Uncas and his Mohegans. Welcoming Pequot survivors and others into their communities, the Mohegans, like the Wampanoags, became a new people whose power came from their alliance with the "Knive-men." After the war, Uncas crafted a relationship with the Connecticut colony that paralleled the alliance between Massasoit and Plymouth: he became trading partner, military ally, political broker, and collector of wampum tribute from neighboring sachems formerly in the Pequot orbit. Also like Massasoit, he used English connections against the Narragansetts, defending his own people's autonomy and pulling various native tributaries into his, rather than their, network of alliance.

The turning point came in 1643, when the Mohegans' conflict with the Narragansetts spilled into open warfare, and Uncas captured Miantonomi in battle. In the 1638 Hartford treaty, the Mohegans and Narragansetts had agreed to make the English the arbiters of any disputes. Accordingly, Uncas turned Miantonomi over to colonial officials, who promptly, if hardly evenhandedly, determined that the Narragansett sachem deserved death for breaking the peace and attempting to kill the Mohegan leader. But rather than exercise the sovereign power of execution that Massachusetts Bay Colony officials went to war to defend in 1636, they turned

Miantonomi over to Uncas to carry out the sentence on Mohegan land, which he promptly did, with English witnesses at hand. Uncas thus could argue that the English were *his* clients, not vice versa.

Out of the bloodshed and epidemic devastation that wracked Native America in the mid-seventeenth century, then, Uncas and Massasoit achieved something similar to what Powhatan had hoped to accomplish a generation earlier in Tsenacomoco. Asserting control over Europeans and their goods, they mobilized power for themselves and their communities—not through a personal monopoly on prestige goods but through a political arrangement that ensured their peoples more egalitarian access to English traders. At the same time, through the bloody work of John Endecott, John Mason, and John Underhill, the New England governments achieved something similar to what Christopher Newport had hoped to achieve by crowning Powhatan. Making Native chiefs subject to their authority, they imposed their rule on Native and English inhabitants alike. Beginning with the execution of Miantonomi in 1643, this power was exercised through an intercolonial alliance known as the New England Confederation, composed of the colonies of Massachusetts Bay, Plymouth, Connecticut, and New Haven, a separate government claiming part of the Long Island Sound shoreline around the modern city of that name. For the next three decades, this blend of exchange-based Native alliance and neo-feudal European domination—a mix of traders and conquistadors enacting a North American version of a medieval protection racket—kept an unstable intercultural peace in southern New England.

Trade with Native Americans as Europeans envisioned it, c. 1602.

The Power of Exotic Goods

29

30

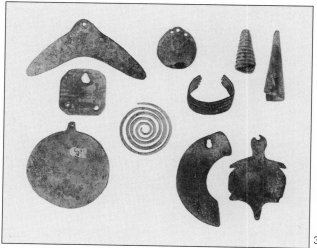

33

31

Clockwise from far left: Glass trade beads resemble gifts from powerful other-than-human persons dwelling underwater or beneath the earth. Sheet copper, long worn on the body to symbolize the power derived from alliance with its exotic sources, was reworked by Native craftspeople into many forms. Wampum (the French called it *porcelaine*), made with iron tools from the shells of quahog and whelk, epitomized the cultural creativity and political impact sparked by trade with Europeans; it was worn on the body like copper to demonstrate power and status, and woven in intricate belts and strings to preserve words and stories. Sheet copper was reworked by Native people into various symbolic and utilitarian forms.

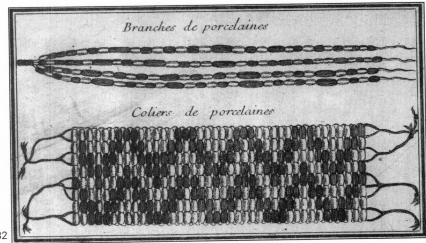

32

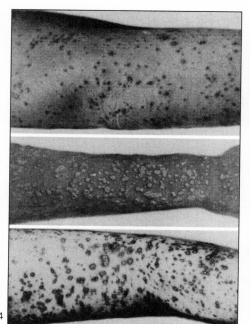

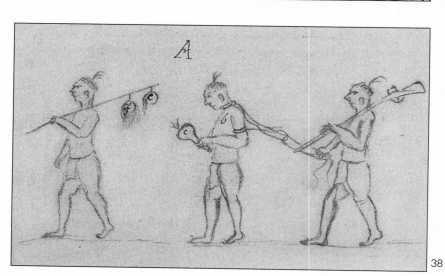

Clockwise: The ravages of smallpox, in twentieth-century and sixteenth-century images. Samuel de Champlain introduces northeastern Native people to firearms, 1608. Cartographer's depiction of the trading colony of Nieu Nederlandt, 1651. Native depiction of Haudenosaunee Iroquois warriors returning with a captive in the 1660s.

36

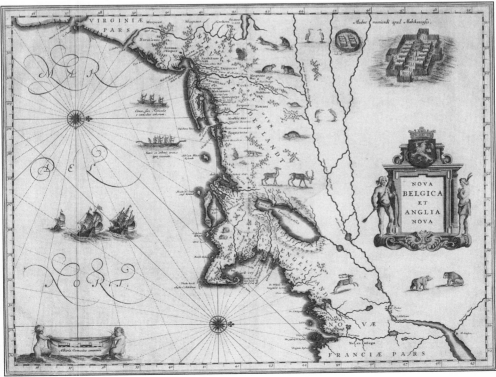

37

Clockwise: Targets for political, economic, and religious discontent included Archbishop William Laud, here wearing a priestly surplice; The Book of Common Prayer, scorned by English puritan satirists and by Scottish churchgoers; and King Charles I and his son James, duke of York, the future James VII and II.

39

42

Of God,   Of Man,   Of the Divell.

The least of these, the greatest ought to be.

The other two, of men and of the Devill. Ought to be rooted out for ere as evill.

40

The Arch-Prelate of St Andrewes in Scotland reading the new Service-booke in his pontificalibus assaulted by men & Women, with Cricketts stooles Stickes and Stones.

41

Planting English Patriarchy:
"Men of Small Meanes" in New England

43

44

46

Clockwise: Seal and Royal Charter of the Massachusetts Bay Company. New England Plantations, 1634. Planter's house and barn, Sudbury, Massachusetts.

The South part of New-England, as it is Planted this yeare, 1634.

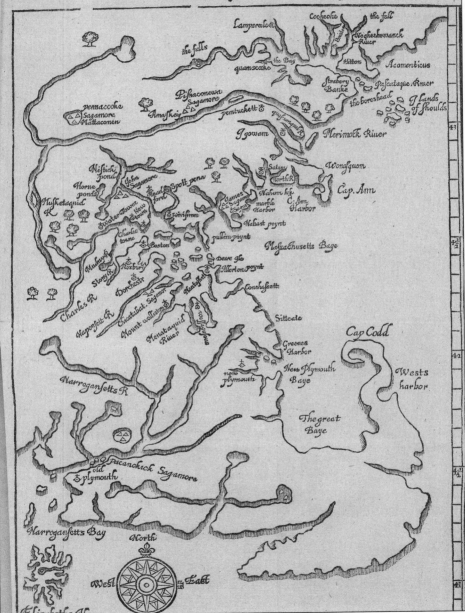

penmacooke Sagamore Mattacomen

Pissaconowa Sagamore

Amasheig

the falls

Lampereeloo

Cocheoho

the fall

Negherwwanch River

the Bay

quamscooke

Hitton

Acomenticus

Straberry Banke

Piscataque River

the boreshead

Ilands of shoulds

Pentuckett

Puyfunqu R

43

Igowam

Merimock River

Nistick pond

John Sagamore

Spott pona

Sateny North R

Wonasquom

Horne ponds

Read ford

James Sagamore

Nahum keg

Cap. Ann

Musketaquid R

Water Towne

New towne

Essex

marble Harbor

C. Ann Harbor

Winisimet

Charles towne

Boston

Nahant poynt

42½

Nahant poynt

pullim poynt

Massachusetts Bage

Mishewh

Roxbury

Deare yle

Allerton poynt

Charks R

Stony R

Dorchestr

Nantasket

Conchassett

Maponsett R

Chicatabot Sagamor

Mount wollston

Sittcale

Mattaquid River

Cap Codd

Greenes Harbor

new plymouth

New Plymouth Baye

42

Wests harbor

Narroganfetts R

The great Baye

41½

Pacanokick Sagamore

old plymouth

Narrogansetts Bay

North

West

East

41

Elizabeths Ile.

45

Planting English Patriarchy:
"Men of Small Meanes" in Virginia

47

50

48

Clockwise: Tobacco illustrated.
Governor Sir William Berkeley. An
atypical Chesapeake planter's
house—Governor Berkeley's
"Green Spring." A typical
seventeenth-century Chesapeake
planter's house (modern
reconstruction).

49

51

5

52

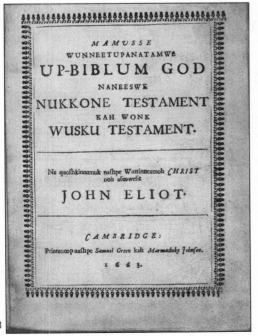

53

OLIVARIUS CRONVELIUS.
Reipublicæ Magnæ Britanniæ Protector:

Oliver Cromwell—Lord Protector of England, Scotland, and Ireland, sponsor of the "Western Design" to conquer Spanish America.

Planters

To PLANT. *v.a.* [*planto,* Latin; *planter,* French].
1. To put into the ground in order to grow; to set; to cultivate . . .
2. To procreate; to generate . . .
3. To place; to fix . . .
4. To settle; to establish: as, to *plant* a *colony.*
5. To fill or adorn with something planted; as, he *planted* the garden or the country.
6. To direct properly: as, to *plant* a cannon.

PLA´NTER. *n.s.* [*planteur,* French, from *plant*].
1. One who sows, sets or cultivates; cultivator . . .
2. One who cultivates ground in the West Indian colonies . . .
3. One who disseminates or introduces.

—Samuel Johnson, *A Dictionary of the English Language* (London, 1755)

SEVEN

Searching for Order in
New and Old England

WHEN JOHN UNDERHILL PUBLISHED his memoir of the Pequot War, he called it *Newes from America; Or, A new and experimentall discoverie of New England; containing, a true relation of their war-like proceedings these two yeares last past, with . . . a discovery of these places, that as yet have very few or no inhabitants which would yeeld speciall accommodation to such as will plant there.*[1] "Plant," "planter," and "plantation"— words long used for Irish conquests and North American dreams—were rough synonyms for "colonize," "colonizer," and "colony." Thus, William Bradford titled his account of his colony *Of Plymouth Plantation;* John Winthrop prayed "that men shall say of succeeding plantations: the lord make it like that of New England"; and an early published map was titled "The South part of New-England, as it is Planted this yeare, 1634."[2] In the sixteenth and early seventeenth centuries, such language had evoked large landed estates, manorial subordination of the native population, and importation of tenant labor—all in the name of cultivating English government, civility, and religion.

As Underhill's typically verbose seventeenth-century book title suggests, however, in New England, "plant," "planter," and "plantation" began to assume altered meanings—meanings glimpsed early on by John Smith. "Who can desire more content, that hath small meanes; or but only his merit to advance his fortune, then to tread, and plant that ground hee hath purchased by the hazard of his life?" Smith asked in his *Description of New England* (1616). "What to such a minde can bee more pleasant, then planting and building a foundation for his Posteritie, gotte from the rude earth, by Gods blessing and his owne industrie, without prejudice to any?"[3] The Pequot War demonstrated many things. Yet, perhaps most important, it marked the emergence of a new kind of small-landholder plantation colony and the kinds of land hunger it spawned—to the great prejudice (despite Smith's assurances) of the Pequots and their neighbors. Planters, more than conquistadores, were the real threat to the shared continent that Native and European traders were creating.

New England was the first place in North America where the new plantation regime—and the many new meanings of the verb "to plant"—took firm hold. The Pequot War was the event by which that regime made its presence known, but New England was hardly the only, or even the most important, place where men of "small meanes" left the British Isles to try to cultivate a new social order. Everywhere, it seemed, English people were in motion. Firm statistics are hard to come by, but conservative estimates are that, from 1630 to 1660, roughly twenty thousand migrated to New England, while thirty-three thousand emigrated to the Chesapeake colonies of Virginia and Maryland. A stream of migrants dwarfing these rode the great looping southern winds to Bermuda and the West Indies, which absorbed (and often killed with their diseases and working conditions) at least one hundred fifteen thousand more. Perhaps one hundred twenty thousand went to that old example and model of colonial planting, Ireland, if Scots as well as English are included in the figure. Many thousands more went to the European continent, primarily (as Plymouth's future colonists had done earlier) to the Netherlands. Meanwhile, countless thousands—probably more than a quarter million—left rural areas of England for burgeoning cities, especially London, unsanitary home to some three hundred fifty thousand crowded people in 1635.[4] It is clear that a combination of economic, political, and religious factors contributed to this massive population movement. Yet precisely what those factors were and how they operated to transport people from one side of the Atlantic are less easily sorted out.

At the root of much of England's economic distress was steady demographic growth. No appreciable advances in health, nutrition, or agricultural technology had occurred since the Middle Ages, and bubonic plague and other diseases continued to erupt regularly. Even so, the population of England and Wales roughly doubled during the hundred years before

1635, after which it plateaued at about five million for the rest of the seventeenth century.[5] Across the social spectrum, this growth caused turmoil. There were, commentators complained, simply too many people, too many mouths to feed, not enough land and work to go around. "There is nothing more daungerous for the estate of common-wealths, then when the people do increase to a greater multitude and number then may justly paralell with the largenesse of the place and countrey," one early promoter of the Jamestown colony observed, "for hereupon comes oppression, and diverse kinde of wrongs, mutinies, sedition, commotion, and rebellion, scarcity, dearth, povertie, and sundrie sorts of calumnities."[6] Such specters of doom were not confined to elite criticisms of those at the bottom of the pyramid. Gentry families found themselves with too many second, third, or even fourth sons who, while in no danger of becoming penniless, faced a land-impoverished future.

Yet far more than sheer numbers of people lay behind the problems England faced, for by 1640 its population had still not returned to late-medieval, pre-plague levels. One factor contributing to the sense of doom —exacerbated because no one understood it at the time—was the Little Ice Age, which was at its peak in the early seventeenth century. As in North America in the same period, the environment could not support the number of people it had sustained in a warmer era, and frequent droughts and crop failures only made things worse. Just as important was the decline of manorialism, the general loosening of hierarchical obligations, and the modest rise in the standard of living for ordinary people that had occurred since the fourteenth century. In an England already proud of its freedom, yeomen landholders, tenants whose leases guaranteed hard-won liberties, and even agricultural servants who worked on yearly rather than lifetime contracts would not put up with the serfdom and the starvation-level crop yields that their ancestors had endured.

At the same time this restive population was growing, much of the agricultural land abandoned during the Black Death remained out of cultivation. It had been turned instead into pasture for sheep, whose wool was the raw material for the textile production that gave England its primary export commodity. Even as the population rebounded, landowners continued to pull land from cultivation. By the late sixteenth century, the same loosening of manorial obligations that had gained ordinary people more freedom and made land increasingly difficult to lease led many large individual and institutional landowners to treat their estates in new ways. They managed them more as private property than as the collective domain of a village community for which they were responsible as lords of the manor. They raised rents to unprecedented levels and often expelled tenants from their leaseholds entirely. They erected fences and hedgerows to "enclose" formerly open common fields, frequently replacing oats or barley with sheep. Indeed, enclosure was perhaps the most immediate driving force behind England's great movement of population from the countryside to the cities and to the Atlantic colonies.

The suffering caused by these changes was very real. For a society in which most people received remuneration not in cash wages but in the form of food, shelter, and the right to work the land or a trade, it is difficult to quantify the distress. Nonetheless, it seems that the real wages of most ordinary English people fell by at least a third between 1550 and 1610.[7] Distresses multiplied after 1618, when the Thirty Years War on the European continent cut off many of the most important customers for English textiles and sent the nation's most profitable economic sector into decline. Yet talk of declining markets and real wages cannot capture the reality of what happened when people accustomed to the stability of lifetime agricultural leases, steady craft employment, and traditional understandings of what constituted a just wage and a fair price confronted a world in which none of those certainties existed any longer and in which one had to seek one's fortune far from home. The hard-luck vagabond storyline of what we now call fairy tales was the real experience of many early seventeenth-century people.

Elite English men fantasized that the distressed, displaced, and dangerous would find profitable new lives on American plantations. "The frye [offspring] of the wandringe beggars of England, that growe upp ydly, and hurtefull and burdenous to this realme, may there be unladen," Richard Hakluyt the Younger had argued in his 1584 "Discourse Concerning Western Planting."[8] Yet such schemes were at first inseparable from conquistador dreams of vast overseas landed estates peopled by happy peasant tenants—dreams unlikely to inspire the multitudes to take ship and embrace a life of plantation subjection when London or Bristol, for all their squalor, provided more tempting alternatives.

Hundreds of younger sons of the lesser gentry would indeed cross the ocean in the middle years of the seventeenth century and find ways to lure enough servants with them to place their stamp on Virginia, Barbados, and even New England. Yet these cannot begin to account for the multitude that left England during this period. Planters of what Smith called "small meanes" were neither the elite who dreamed of vast estates nor the rural poor who had been forced off the land. Indeed, the very fact that they had some "meanes" at all suggests that England's economic crisis had not crushed them as badly as it had many others. Material considerations figured in their decisions to migrate, but there was more to the story.

England's political turmoil is a similarly problematic factor in explaining the great migration. Like the kings of Spain and France, England's James I (James VI to his Scottish subjects) and Charles I tried to keep close tabs on the political loyalties of anyone who left their realm; understandably, they feared rivals who might win allies in foreign courts or set up independent power bases on West Indian islands or Virginian rivers. Thus, when the "Pilgrims" tried to emigrate to the Netherlands in 1607, they had to rely on an unscrupulous smuggler who betrayed them to the authorities after robbing them of most of their possessions. The next year, the male members of the party alone were able to board ship before officials in hot pursuit arrested the women and children, who only later, after much legal maneuvering, managed to join their husbands and fathers on the Continent. Almost everything we know about the identities and numbers of emigrants to the colonies in the early seventeenth century is the result of careful record-keeping designed to ensure that only the politically reliable boarded outbound ships. Of course, people stowed away, forged documents, bribed officers and captains, traveled incognito. Still, the regulations were effective enough to prevent a massive exodus of overt political dissidents.

Which is not to say that James (who reigned from 1603 to 1625) and his son Charles (reigned 1625–1649) lacked opponents, or that—even in a society where voting and other explicitly political acts were confined to a minority—discontents did not flourish across the social spectrum. For one thing, the Stuarts (or, as the name was spelled north of the border, Stewarts) were Scots, son and grandson of Mary Stuart and thus the closest living descendants of Henry VIII at the death of childless Elizabeth I. In Europe as a whole, mere foreignness and differences in language between monarch and people counted for little. Yet during the long reign of Elizabeth, the Englishness of the monarchy and the need to protect it from foreign interference had become deeply ingrained. The Lowland Scots language that James spoke (when people could understand his slurred speech at all) differed little more from London speech than did countless other dialects in the southern half of the island, and it was only during the Scotsman's reign that the translation of the Bible that bore his name helped to create a standard national language for the first time. Still, the presence of a foreigner on the English throne—and, for James's and Charles's Scottish subjects, the similar threat to national independence posed by the union of their Crown with that of the richer and more populous kingdom to the south—was a constant irritant.

Stuart foreign policy was more than just an irritant to many English people, particularly during the Thirty Years War, when James refused to ally with any of the Protestant contenders. Charles, meanwhile, during the last years of his father's reign, pursued spousal alliances with the two leading Catholic combatants, first in a diplomatic fiasco called the "Spanish Match" and then in his marriage to Princess Henrietta Maria of France. To the horror of English Protestants, she openly practiced her Catholicism at court and refused even to attend her husband's coronation because Protestant bishops were involved. As king, Charles approved several ill-conceived interventions in the Thirty Years War that, while directed at Catholic Spain and France, were rightly seen as a colossal waste of blood and treasure.

War and finance were the issues around which the early-modern nation-state coalesced. At bottom, the political issues that dominated the period of the great English migration were the familiar ones of centralizing monarchs attempting to consolidate authority and resources. James and Charles embraced the novel idea—just then taking hold in France and elsewhere on the Continent—of expansive personal royal power, or "Free Monarchy," as James called it in a book he published in Scotland in 1598 and in England in 1603. "The dutie, and alleageance of the people to their lawfull King," he proclaimed, "ought to be to him, as to Gods Lieutenant in earth, obeying his commands in all things" and "acknowledging him a Judge set by GOD over them, having power to judge them, but be judged onely by GOD." A king, James asserted, can "make daily statutes and ordinances . . . without any advise of parliament or estates: yet it lyes in the power of no Parliament, to make any kinde of lawe or statute, without his Scepter be put to it, for giving it the force of a law," because "the power flowes allwayes from himselfe."[9]

James only occasionally tried to act on the theories that flowed so grandiloquently from his pen, and he often retreated from their fullest implications. His son was far more vigorous, particularly as he sought funds for his continental military adventures. Most notably, from 1629 onward Charles determined to rule without summoning Parliament into session, a feat he was able to achieve for eleven years. Charles's efforts to find revenue, raise armies and navies, and centralize power in his court infringed on the traditional privileges of local grandees and common people all over his Three Kingdoms of England, Scotland, and Ireland. Extracting sizable forced loans made few political friends. Centralizing military organization to create a "perfect militia" undermined the authority of local gentry, who were used to raising troops for the king as they saw fit. So too did well-meaning efforts to respond to economic distress by imposing national standards for poor relief and requirements that local governments impose levies to pay for them.

Meantime, unable to raise new taxes without the consent of Parliament, Charles's government sought to reinvigorate old ones, by "Thorough" enforcement of privileges, that, however ancient and long-ignored, might yield revenue to the Crown. The corporate charters of cities came under attack through the legal writ of *quo warranto*—"by what warrant do you exercise a right?"—insisting that every jot and tittle of royal prerogative be observed. Royal legal courts of High Commission and Star Chamber found ways to further intrude on the purviews of local common law and manorial courts. Most controversial among many such aspects of "Thorough" was the attempt to extend the collection of "Ship Money," a traditional tax levied on port cities for their naval defense, to inland towns and boroughs, where they had never before been due.

Every lord of the manor, city council member, or rural grandee had his own story to tell about the ever-expanding tentacles of royal power. Still, similar stories could have been told in the days of Elizabeth or Henry, as well; there was nothing new in the rise of the centralized state. The toxic element in the mix was the way in which the political, and indeed the economic, distresses of England became inseparable from its internal struggles over religion. In his treatise on Free Monarchy, James VI and I asserted that the first oath of monarchs was "to maintaine the Religion presently professed within their countrie, according to their lawes, whereby it is established, and to punish all those that should presse to alter, or distrube [sic] the profession thereof."[10] Both he and Charles took that oath seriously and set out to impose uniform faith and practice on the diverse local religious environment that had grown up within the bundle of compromises that was the Elizabethan Church of England.

The varied "puritan" clergy and laity who considered Elizabeth's Church insufficiently reformed initially expected great things from James—for whatever else one might say about him, he was a good Protestant, placed as a boy on the northern throne by Calvinist nobles who wanted no part of his Catholic mother, Mary Stuart. In the last decades of Elizabeth's reign, these puritan forces—who referred to themselves simply as the "godly"—had achieved considerable influence, operating as a shadow church within the official ecclesiastical hierarchy. Oxford and especially Cambridge universities turned out a brilliant group of Calvinist theologians who preached to increasingly literate and intellectually sophisticated lay audiences. Despite the official uniformity envisioned by the Elizabethan Book of Common Prayer, many of these clergymen were able to operate with little supervision from bishops and government officials, because they were appointed to their positions by wealthy lay people who had acquired the right of "impropriation" along with the lands of a dissolved Catholic monastery. Urban puritan merchants were particularly active in these efforts. Dissident clergy "lectured" in a variety of venues to appreciative audiences of men and women, who in turn met in unauthorized "conventicles" and house meetings to pray, to read their Bibles, to discuss the mysteries of predestination and salvation by grace, and to compare conversion experiences with each other.

What set the diverse "godly" apart from their countrymen and -women was not their Calvinism, or their biblicism, or their moralism rooted in strict enforcement of the Ten Commandments. All of these were officially embraced by both the Church hierarchy and King James (who could cite Bible verses with the best of puritan divines), if not exactly by King Charles. Instead, at the core of the puritan movement was an intense emotionality—captured by the contemporary phrase "hotter sort of Protestant"—manifested both individually and collectively in local gatherings for prayer, study, and preaching. Anything that deflected attention from core experiential matters—like any doctrine that departed from the brutal Good News that God's free grace alone could save the predestined few from the eternal damnation assigned to the many—was a "remnant of popery," a survival of Roman Catholic error somehow still permitted to survive in the supposedly reformed Church of England.

Opinions varied on exactly how these core principles, or rather core

emotions, were to be put into practice. Only a small minority took the extreme, illegal, and possibly treasonous position that the Church, whose
head was the monarch, was hopelessly corrupt and that the godly must
separate themselves from it if they were to live as their Savior intended.
Among these "separatists" were the founders of Plymouth colony, whose
separation began with the founding of an illegal congregation in the English town of Scrooby, and continued with their illegal migration to the
Netherlands and their only slightly more legal relocation to Cape Cod Bay.
The majority of puritans, however, believed that the Church of England
could be transformed from within to conform to their ideals. They believed this because, in so many local cases at the turn of the seventeenth
century, their own congregations and clergy had been largely free to do as
they (or, rather, their god) pleased.

This began to change for puritans under James, and became nearly impossible for them under Charles. To understand how and why the Stuarts
considered puritans such a threat, spiritual, psychological, and theological
factors need to be joined with economic and political issues. The communal order that the godly desired among themselves stood in stark contrast
to the upheaval and economic distress they saw all around them. Tramping
hordes of the unemployed, greedy landlords carrying out enclosure, and
power-hungry royal officials were all signs of the sinful disorder of a people headed for damnation. In the midst of all this chaos, the godly hoped
to live together in lawful peace, pursuing their divine callings in this world
in hopes of salvation in the next. "God Almighty in His most holy and wise
providence hath so disposed of the condition of mankind, as in all times
some must be rich, some poor, some high and eminent in power and dignity, others mean and in subjection," puritan layman and former local justice of the peace John Winthrop told those bound for Massachusetts Bay
in 1630. This divine order was designed so "that every man might have
need of other[s] . . . for the glory of his Creator and the Common good of
the Creature, Man." The "City upon a Hill" that Winthrop evoked for his
audience could be envisioned for New England only because it had already been glimpsed in countless places in Old England before coming
under attack from the Crown.[11]

The many little cities upon England's metaphorical hills, with their outspoken preachers, their empowered lay women and men, and their de-
nunciations of the ungodly high as well as low, presented a profound political threat to the Crown. The order that the saints found in puritanism

appeared to the Stuarts and the bishops they appointed to be among the most dangerous *disorders* afflicting the realm. One of James I's earliest acts as king of England was to convene a meeting with puritan theologians at Hampton Court in response to the "Millinary Petition," supposedly signed by a thousand clergymen. While the monarch expressed sympathy with many points of theology raised in the meeting, it became clear that he had no interest in encouraging local initiative and challenges to hierarchy. Even the greatest achievement of the Hampton Court Conference, a plan for a new translation of the Bible, came to reflect this fact. When the Authorized or "King James" version was first published in 1611, it contained no explanatory notes conveying the Calvinist interpretation of its predecessor, the Geneva Bible; it came out in an expensive folio edition, and its elaborately decorated title page specified that it had been "Appointed to be read in Churches," and so by implication not in ordinary homes or small-scale meetings.[12]

The specific issues over which the battle between the Stuart government and the godly was fought were mostly symbolic matters of external conformity rather than high debates over theological principles. For the Stuarts and their bishops, external conformity was the key to good order—the least one could expect from diligent subjects of monarchs pledged "to maintain the Religion presently professed within their countrie." For the hotter sort of Protestants, such an emphasis on externals was precisely what was wrong with an institution that ignored the essence of religion and thus implicitly taught "works righteousness," rather than salvation by divine grace alone.

Few issues were more contentious than whether clergymen should be required to wear the garment known as the surplice, a medium-length white gown that distinguished them from ordinary parishioners. In a society where everyone wore intricately graded clothing to mark their status, the surplice made perfect sense as a sign that not just anyone had the right to preach and preside at the sacraments. But to puritans, this setting-apart marked the minister as a "priest" and was therefore unacceptable in a reformed Church that taught that *all* believers were priests. An extraordinary amount of energy fed this sartorial controversy, and an extraordinary number of popular clergymen were removed from their pulpits because they refused to be seen in white.

Also contentious was whether every meeting for worship should follow the wording scripted by the Book of Common Prayer and include a sermon verbatim from the Book of Homilies, or whether clergy were free to improvise, to pray as the spirit moved them, and, especially, to preach original sermons grounded in their biblical scholarship and their parishioners' spiritual needs. Again, it was a matter either of maintaining good order and suppressing rebelliously incorrect ideas, or of stressing hollow "papist" forms over genuine religiosity. It was the same with a host of other issues large and mostly small—whether one should make the sign of the Cross during the ritual of baptism, bow at the mention of the name of Jesus, kneel to receive Communion or sit around a table, place that table at the east end of the church and behind a rail or in the midst of the people, celebrate the unbiblical drunken winter holiday of Christmas or treat it as just another work day, set aside any days other than the Sabbath as "holy," allow the singing of humanly devised hymns and the playing of artificial instruments in addition to the chanting of biblical psalms by God-given voices. All evoked one basic, bitter debate.

Everything reached a climax during the reign of Charles I and his archbishop of Canterbury, William Laud, who differed with the puritans on theological fundamentals, not just on external manifestations of uniformity. Like many early seventeenth-century Protestants, Laud was sympathetic to the Dutch theologian Jacobus Arminius, who rejected the idea of predestination and, while continuing to stress the orthodox Christian position that God's grace is the only source of salvation, argued that human actions play a direct role in the rejection or acceptance of that grace. A decade before Laud became archbishop in 1635, edicts had come down that the Calvinist interpretation of predestination was no longer to be taught by Oxford and Cambridge professors.

Soon, bowing, kneeling, surplice wearing, prayer-book ritualizing, the rote reading of sermons (in 1623, the Book of Homilies was republished for the first time in three decades)—all the "remnants of popery" puritans detested—were enforced in nearly every parish in the realm. As if this were not enough, Charles insisted that *The Book of Sports,* an ill-advised attempt by James and his advisors in 1618 to find a compromise position on lawful Sunday behavior, be read from every pulpit in the land. Thus, authorities seemed to require, rather than merely permit, such ungodly activities as dancing, archery practice, and the erecting of Maypoles on the day that was to be kept holy. Ever more stringent efforts to make bishops deprive nonconforming clerics of their pulpits, suppress unauthorized sermonizing, and root out irregular religious meetings of any kind harassed

puritans at every turn and drove many prominent clergy, including Hugh
Peter and Thomas Hooker, into exile.

"When *England* began to decline in Religion," Massachusetts colonist Edward Johnson breathlessly recalled a little over twenty years later, "instead
of purging out Popery, a farther compliance was sought not onely in vaine
Idolatrous Ceremonies, but also in prophaning the Sabbath, and by Proclamation throughout Parish churches, exasperating lewd and prophane
persons to celebrate a Sabbath like the Heathen to *Venus, Baccus* and
Ceres; in so much that the multitude of irreligious lascivious and popish
affected persons spred the whole land like *Grashoppers.*" Fortunately, "in
this very time Christ the glorious King of his Churches, raises an Army out
of our *English* Nation, for freeing his people from their long servitude under usurping Prelacy; and because every corner of *England* was filled with
the fury of malignant adversaries, Christ creates a New *England* to muster
up the first of his Forces in." Small in number but powerful in grace, Johnson said, the godly heard the call: "Oh yes! oh yes! oh yes! *All you the people of Christ that are here Oppressed, Imprisoned and scurrilously derided, gather yourselves together, your Wifes and little ones, and answer
to your severall Names as you shall be shipped for his service, in the
Westerne World, and more especially for planting the united Collonies of
new England.*" Those colonies, Johnson concluded, were "the place where
the Lord will create a new Heaven, and a new Earth in, new Churches,
and a new Common-wealth together."[13]
    For hot Protestants steeped in the idea that the final battle between
Christ and the Antichrist was at hand—particularly for hot Protestants attempting to make sense of their decisions years later—the power of Johnson's crusading rhetoric cannot be discounted. England's social and political troubles came into sharp focus in their apocalyptic vision, and New
England's plantations became not mere refuges where they and their families could live and worship as their god commanded, but the front lines in
the great struggle against the Antichrist. "We shall find that the God of Israel is among us, when ten of us shall be able to resist a thousand of our
enemies, when He shall make us a praise and glory," Winthrop had said in
his 1630 sermon to the departing colonists, which Johnson had heard.[14]
    Like the conquistadores before them (if Johnson and Winthrop are to
be believed), the colonizers of New England were engaged in a holy

war. Native people were not the targets of that crusade—although some of them, as converts in the new heaven and earth, might be among its beneficiaries. Those who, like the Pequots, stood in the way of the saints had to be crushed. Nor would economic relations between the New Israel and the Indian Canaanites be the point of militant New England, although Johnson clearly understood the way in which it was built on a substratum of commerce. The "hope of a rich Trade for Bever-skins," he observed, "made some of our Countrymen make their abode in these parts, whom this Army of *Christ* at their comming over found as fit helps to further their designs."[15]

Still, the militant religion of Johnson, Winthrop, and the army of others who wrote in the same vein was inextricable from the social and political world that had shaped them. As Winthrop observed on another occasion, England had grown "weary of her Inhabitants, so as man which is most precious of all the Creatures, is here more vile and base than the earth they tread upon."[16] Plymouth's Bradford echoed that "the straitnes of the place"—its tight economic condition—"is such, as each man is faine to plucke his meanes as it were out of his neighbours throat." In England,

> The Towns abound with young tradesmen, and the Hospitals are full of the Ancient, the country is replenished with new Farmers, and the Almshouses are filled with old Laborers; many there are who get their living with bearing burdens, but more are fain to burden the land with their whole bodies: multitudes get their means of life by prating, and so doe numbers more by begging. Neither come these straits upon men always through intemperancy, ill husbandry, indiscretion, etc., as some think, but even the most wise, sober, and discreet men, go often to the wall, when they have done their best, wherein as God's providence swayeth all, so it is easy to see, that the straitnesse of the place having in it so many strait hearts, cannot but produce such effects more and more . . . : Let us not thus oppress, straiten, and afflict one another, but seeing there is a spacious Land, the way to which is through the sea, we will end this difference in a day.[17]

"Spacious Land"—in New England and also in Bermuda, Virginia, and the West Indies—lured not just puritans, but all sorts of men and women from the British Isles seeking relief from economic troubles, political upheaval, and religious oppression. For it was not only hot Protestants and Laudians who were at each other's religious throats. Despite puritans' overheated fears that popery was winning the day, under James and

Charles, England's remaining Roman Catholics endured even worse oppression from the same drive for uniformity and centralization that attempted to destroy hot Protestantism. And Catholics in Ireland faced un-
speakable hardships after their rebellions at the turn of the century.

In Lowland Scotland, meanwhile, the Church, or "Kirk," long admired
by English puritans as far more purely Calvinist than that of the southern
kingdom, confronted the same forces felt everywhere. Even before taking
the English throne, King James had tried to impose the centralizing authority of bishops on a Kirk organized in more decentralized "presbyteries," or representative courts of clergy. In 1618, he forced through the
Scottish Parliament "Five Articles of Perth," an unpopular set of anti-
puritan reforms requiring, among other things, that quintessential remnant of popery, kneeling at Communion. In 1637, Charles and his bishops
decreed that a Scottish version of the Book of Common Prayer must be
used. Opposition was so deep that a series of armed revolts known as the
"Bishops' Wars" broke out, inspired by a document called the "National
Covenant," which nearly every politically active Scot signed, either voluntarily or under duress, to show united support for the pure Calvinist Kirk.

In 1642, Charles had to call the English Parliament into session to raise
funds to suppress the Covenanters. But he rapidly dismissed what became
known as the "Short Parliament" when his opponents insisted on a range
of reforms as the price for new taxes. Underfunded royal troops then
failed to turn back an invasion of England by Scots who forced Charles
to negotiate and agree to their demand that he call a new English Parliament. Although no one imagined it at the time, this "Long Parliament,"
which first met in November 1640, would be the last one freely elected
for nearly twenty years. In 1642, Charles again tried to go to war on
his own, this time against rebels in Ireland. Parliament raised an army in
opposition to the king and began passing "ordinances" (rather than "laws")
without the king's approval—among other things, in 1645 banning use of
the Book of Common Prayer and ordering the execution of Archbishop
Laud. Bishops in general, who constituted a formidable voting block in the
House of Lords, could not be done away with entirely so long as that body
existed, but their real powers rapidly faded. Most of these efforts to purge
what puritans called "remnants of popery" came in response to the "Solemn League and Covenant" of 1643, which Charles's Scottish opponents
insisted all Englishmen must subscribe to as part of their joint struggle
against Charles and in favor of Calvinism.

Of course all Englishmen did not subscribe, and the struggles between Royalists and Parliamentarians, or "Cavaliers" (for their courtly airs) and "Roundheads" (for their severe puritan haircuts), only deepened. Both armies initially were throwbacks to the medieval era, dependent on local grandees who raised troops for the broader cause. In late 1644 and early 1645, parliamentary leaders made a series of decisions that, ironically, far outpaced anything Charles would or could have done to advance the State's capacity to centralize authority through a monopoly of force. A "Self-Denying Ordinance" required members of Parliament to resign all military posts, thus removing local nobles and other great men from the equation. A "New Model Army" then took shape, with a professional class of officers, a centrally raised and uniformly salaried body of troops, and a systematic campaign to indoctrinate those troops in the puritan values of the parliamentary cause. The New Model Army not only made quick work of royalist troops on the battlefields in Ireland and Scotland, as well as in England, but it also filled power vacuums to bypass parliamentarians and become the dominant political force. This was due not only to its armed might but to the fact that Parliament never found fiscal methods to match its military reforms, and thus soldiers were nearly constantly threatening to mutiny to receive their pay. With its ideologically fired troops, the army came to set the antiroyalist agenda. One of the few able to try to mediate the struggles among the army and various parliamentary factions was one of the handful of members of the House of Commons specifically exempted from the Self-Denying Ordinance: Oliver Cromwell. Thus, by default as much as by his own genius, he emerged as England's strong man.

By 1649, years of off-and-on fighting culminated in a military purge of the Long Parliament by those who rejected any further attempts to make peace with the king, who by this time had rallied to his side many Scots and Irish rightly fearful of England's domination. With Charles defeated and in prison, the "Rump" of remaining English parliamentarians tried him for treason, ordered his execution, and abolished both the monarchy and the House of Lords, declaring the former Three Kingdoms to be a united "Commonwealth," or republic. Yet stability remained elusive, and increasingly the only source of order was the army and Cromwell. Step by step, the three nations slipped into a unified military dictatorship: Ireland and Scotland by brute force, England by default. In 1653, adopting a title last used by the regent who had ruled during the minority of King Edward VI, Cromwell effectively abolished the Commonwealth and became

"Lord Protector," achieving a level of governmental centralization and lack of institutional restraint that James and Charles had never dreamed of.

These events, of course, created new hosts of political and religious dissidents, along with a proliferation of sects of the godly who took the ideas of the Reformation to ever more radical extremes. Among them were Baptists, Quakers, and others known by such colorful names (usually given them by their opponents) as Levellers, Diggers, and Ranters. But Cavaliers and bishops, too, became dissenters, joining thousands of moderates trying to make their way in what seemed a world turned upside down. At every step, new political, economic, and religious refugees were created, joining the great migrations to the Atlantic colonies. They did not so much escape the problems of the British Isles as take them along wherever they went. Few had the single-minded militant fervor of the leaders of New England, but all infused their new plantations with values shaped by the economic, political, and religious maelstrom of the mid-seventeenth century and were keenly aware of how that maelstrom remained relevant to their lives. As Winthrop said, "The eyes of all people are upon us."

EIGHT

Planting Patriarchy in
New England and Virginia

THE POLITICAL AND RELIGIOUS struggles that wracked the British Isles in the mid-seventeenth century ensured that, whatever John Winthrop hoped, the eyes of elite English, Scottish, and Irish people were in fact seldom focused on developments in the North American colonies. Yet those same ongoing struggles kept English immigrants' eyes firmly upon letters from kin and patrons still fighting and suffering at home. Through it all in the 1630s and 1640s, thousands of men of modest, "small meanes" transported themselves, along with their families and servants, across the Atlantic to work the land and to find the social order that eluded those they left behind. On the islands of Bermuda and Barbados, and most notably in Massachusetts Bay and in the reborn Virginia society that grew after the catastrophes of 1622, these people came to dominate the English mode of colonial expansion. Despite profound differences in religiosity, demography, climate, and economy, that mode imposed strong similarities on the two centers of English expansion in continental North America. In both New England and the Chesapeake, planters who were heirs to a downsized, sweat-of-the-brow version of the dream of patriarchal landed power superimposed themselves on—but did not obliterate—the colonial landscape created by conquistadores and traders.

The royal charter issued in 1629 to "the Governor and Company of the Massachusetts Bay in New-England" resembled other *adelantado* contracts issued by European crowns during the previous century and a half.

There was the ritual language reserving for the Crown "the fifth part of the . . . gold and silver which shall . . . happen to be found." Like many royal English city charters, and like later incarnations of the Virginia Company's several patents, the Massachusetts Bay document outlined a form of government for a corporation that resembled the "Citie of Ralegh" envisioned for Roanoke four decades before. A governor, deputy governor, and eighteen "Assistants" (we would say members of the board of directors) were to be elected annually by the "freemen" (stockholders), of which there were initially twenty-six. These directors were to meet at least four times a year in "Great and General Courts," with the power to admit new freemen, to appoint officers, and to "make laws and ordinances for the good and welfare of the said Company, and for the government and ordering of the said lands and Plantation . . . , so as such laws and ordinances be not contrary or repugnant to the laws and statutes of this our realm of England." To enforce its edicts, the company received authority

> for impositions of lawful fines, mulcts [penalties], imprisonment, or other lawful correction, according to the course of other corporations in this our realm of England, and for the directing, ruling, and disposing of all other matters and things whereby our said people, inhabitants there, may be so religiously, peaceably, and civilly governed, as their good life and orderly conversation may win and incite the natives of [the] country, to the knowledge and obedience of the only true God and Savior of mankind, and the Christian faith, which in our royal Intention, and the adventurers' free profession, is the principal end of this plantation.[1]

At least two crucial pieces of information failed to appear amid the long-winded legalese. First, except for the boilerplate about oversight of religion and conversion of the Natives, there was no hint that the company's investors were puritans who intended to create a utopia for the godly (and a dystopia for Church of England conformists, Catholics, Baptists, and Quakers). Second, unlike some similar documents, the Massachusetts Bay charter failed to specify where its General Court was to hold its meetings. (The Virginia Company of London, for instance, was so called for its meeting place.) A little over a year after the charter was issued, the principal investors slipped through this loophole and agreed that they themselves would emigrate to North America, take the charter with them, and hold all future courts there—thus achieving almost complete freedom from the prying eyes of royal and church officials and (their law-

yers could at least try to argue) perfecting a delaying tactic should King
Charles's familiar tactic of *quo warranto* proceedings against chartered institutions be initiated against them. The charter could not easily be produced in court if it was three thousand miles away.

Indeed, *quo warranto* proceedings began almost immediately after the
puritans' various critics made known what the company was up to. Meanwhile, some of the two hundred or so puritan clergy bound for New England had to smuggle themselves out of the country in order to avoid arrest.[2] "Thus disposed doth many Reverend and godly Pastors of Christ
present themselves, some in a Seaman's Habit" or other disguise, Edward
Johnson marveled. "What dolefull dayes are these, when the best choise
our Orthodox Ministers can make is to take up a perpetuall banishment
from their native soile!"[3] In 1637, the Court of King's Bench actually did
revoke the charter, and Charles I appointed Ferdinando Gorges, of the
Council for New England, as royal governor over the company's confiscated possessions. But the same empty royal coffers that would soon lead
to civil war prevented any funding to help the impoverished Gorges fulfill
his commission, and apparently the formal paperwork was never completed. The company went about its business in New England unhindered
from home, until its allies came to power there during the civil wars.

The Massachusetts Bay Company's business was made enormously
complicated, not only by the large numbers of immigrants who flooded
into the new colony but by the presence of so many very hot Protestants
among them. Observing from afar, an unsympathetic John Smith complained that "some could not endure the name of a Bishop, others not the
sight of a Crosse nor Surplesse, others by no meanes the booke of common Prayer." Smith assured his readers that Winthrop, "a worthy Gentleman both in estate and esteeme," had things under control and that "this
absolute crue, only of the Elect, holding all (but such as themselves) reprobates and cast-awaies now make more haste to returne to Babel, as they
tearmed England, than stay to enjoy the land they called Canaan."[4] Yet
even as some radicals left, others streamed in. At least a thousand immigrants arrived in Massachusetts in 1630, nine thousand more by 1635, an
additional eleven thousand by the outbreak of civil war in 1642, when the
flow virtually ceased and some even returned home to fight the Lord's battles there. This correlation between the fate of the puritan cause in England and the timing of migration to New England is the most persuasive
evidence that the religious motives articulated by the clerical and political

elite were widely shared by the ordinary men and women who made up the bulk of the colonists.

Those leaders phrased nearly every issue the colony confronted in apocalyptic religious terms, including, of course, their war with the Pequots. This religious vocabulary gave meaning to a whole cluster of political and economic issues rooted in the colonists' English experiences. The transfer of the charter, for instance, was plainly a device to achieve the leaders' religious goals. Yet just as plainly—perhaps even more plainly—it was an extreme expression of the localistic political reaction against Stuart centralization evident everywhere in the British Isles in the 1620s and 1630s. New England would be a political and economic as well as religious utopia, if its leaders could have their way.

For the charter was also—and most plainly, by the letter of its text—an economic document that made available millions of acres of land on which individual small planters could envision solutions to the economic straits in which they found themselves. The Massachusetts Bay charter explained that the company would hold its (or rather Ninnimissinouk) lands by the form of tenure known as "free and common Socage, and not in Capite, nor by knightes service"—a legalism that expressed the vital point that real estate could be bought, sold, and passed on to one's children unencumbered by feudal obligations.[5] Often, such formulaic words had been taken to apply only to the company as a collectivity or to its large-scale investors; for example, in another puritan colony founded at precisely the same time— Providence Island (now Providencia), off the coast of Nicaragua—a mere twenty aristocrats owned all the company stock and offered men of small means only tenancies rather than freeholds. In the spring of 1629, however, among the earliest decisions of the Bay Company was that "every person that shall goe over at his owne charge shall have fifty acres of land" and that "for such as transport servants, land shal be allotted for each servant, 50 acres to the master; which land the master is to dispose of at his discression."[6] Investors in the company received an additional fifty acres for each family member, but were not guaranteed larger estates. This early adoption of a limited version of Virginia's system of property distribution by "headrights" ensured that free and common socage would apply to thousands of small-scale planters, who could plan on bequeathing their modest estates to future generations.

Before migrating to Massachusetts, Winthrop and the other founders of the company had thought deeply about the moral, as well as economic, implications of private ownership of land expropriated from Native people. A document that he circulated among his coreligionists to make the case for emigration contained a passage that went through at least four ever-longer drafts while attempting to respond to the argument that "we have no warrant to enter upon that Land which hath been so long possessed by others." Winthrop's final version explained that "God hath given to the sons of men a double right to the earth; there is a natural right, and a Civil Right." The natural right applied

> when men held the earth in common, every man sowing and feeding where he pleased; then as men and their Cattle increased they appropriated certain parcels of Ground by enclosing and peculiar manureance, and this in time got them a Civil right. . . . As for the Natives in New England, they inclose no Land, neither have any settled habitation, nor any tame Cattle to improve the Land by, and so have no other but a Natural Right to those Countries. So as if we leave them sufficient for their use, we may lawfully take the rest, there being more than enough for them and us.

Not mere farming and house building on land owned by Indian kin groups, but private property, fences, and manure were what counted: these constituted what English planters called "improvement." Moreover, because Native people would "find benefit already by our Neighborhood, and learn from us to improve a part to more use then before they could do the whole," the result would be the equivalent of "a valuable purchase, for they have of us that, which will yield them more benefit, than all that Land which we have from them."[7]

In its emphasis on the virtues of small landholding, New England was just as utopian as in its religious and political dimensions. A remarkably small percentage of the immigrants had actually been farmers in England. If one scholar's careful analysis of nearly seven hundred of the best-documented migrants is representative, only about a third of the adult males had worked in agriculture on the eve of their departure. A quarter had worked in the cloth trades, a third in other artisanal occupations, and the rest in other urban callings. Moreover, 88 percent of the people migrated as part of complete family households, 43 percent were female, and among both sexes nearly half were under twenty years of age.[8] Traveling as complete households, often following a favorite puritan clergyman, these urban people self-consciously embraced a rural lifestyle, attempting to turn back the clock economically and socially as well as religiously and politically. New England was, as one modern study concludes, "a movement back to the land."[9]

This peculiar lure of land for urban planters wove seamlessly with puritan piety and political localism in the world the New Englanders created. All three strands became apparent even before the Winthrop fleet and the royal charter sailed in 1630 and, indeed, prior to the issuance of that charter in 1629. Operating under one of the many subgrants issued by Gorges's Council for New England, in 1628 the company sent one of the hottest Protestants among its investors, the same John Endecott who would later conduct the first campaign against the Pequots, to reinforce an existing fishing outpost at a place called Naumkeag. The settlement had originally been established under a grant from yet another company that included some of the same puritan investors. Rechristening the place with the biblical name "Salem," Endecott presided over a number of important decisions that would provide models for the much larger number of migrants soon to arrive. In 1629, when three hundred fifty more colonists, along with almost as many farm animals, arrived at Salem, Endecott sent nearly half of the people and cattle to plant a new settlement at Charlestown, on what would become known as Boston Harbor. Thus beginning a trend that would lead to the founding of twenty-three more towns within the next decade.

Each of these towns was also—and in puritan minds inseparably—a church, a body with distinctive institutional features first worked out at Salem in 1629. For all their criticisms of hierarchy and ceremony, most English puritans who had not declared themselves separatists had given little thought to how they might institutionalize their vision of a godly church community. Most apparently assumed that some presbyterian-style organization similar to that of the Scottish Kirk would replace the hierarchy of bishops, while leaving in place the idea that a parish church was defined more by geography than by voluntary association and that clergy would be ordained by external authority to preside in each locality. Accordingly, along with the other colonists of 1629, the company sent three clergymen to Salem to serve the spiritual needs of the colonists. One, Francis Bright, joined the group at Charlestown. Francis Higginson and Samuel Skelton remained at Salem, where they engaged in what must have been intense theological discussions with Endecott and other pious laypeople about the nature of a church and about the relationship between clergy and laity.

In the end, thirty Salem people—out of a population of several hundred—declared themselves a "congregation" and asked Higginson to draw up a written "covenant" for them to sign, a document in which they promised, "in the presence of God, to walke together in all his waies, according to how he is pleased to reveale himself."[10] The congregation then ritually ordained Higginson as its "teacher" and Skelton as its "pastor," taking upon itself a role previously reserved (except among separatists like those at Plymouth) for bishops or presbyteries. The core group, along with the clergy, then assumed the right to determine the spiritual qualifications of others to participate in the sacraments of Communion and baptism. Everyone else would be required to attend services and listen to preaching, but only the "gathered" elect were considered to be "members" of the "church." And only their members' definitions of a church would be considered legitimate. The fact that dissent would not be tolerated was demonstrated when a group of Salemites who disapproved of the proceedings began holding services using the Book of Common Prayer. Endecott sent them packing for England on the first available ship.

This was the "New England Way" of "congregationalism," which quickly became standard everywhere in the region. A core group—seven was generally considered the minimum number—signed a covenant, ordained its own ministers, and controlled future access to privileges reserved for the elect, or, to be precise, the "visible saints" (as they soon came to be called). No one but God could presume to know with certainty who was predestined for salvation and who was simply a masterful hypocrite. Those able to convince others that their conversion experiences were valid looked to be—were "visible" as—saints, and these constituted the church. The only legitimate external validation of these practices came from other, similarly gathered, churches. Thus, governor William Bradford and minister William Brewster had traveled from Plymouth to bestow approval from that colony's separatist congregation upon the Salem church. Those who disagreed with such proceedings had either to take their places quietly in the meetinghouse or, like the dissenters at Salem, face banishment from the community. The hot Protestant quest for religious purity, then, also produced a political form of religious organization that was localistic in the extreme.

A virtually identical process of localistic gathering characterized the formation of New England's town settlements, and here the religious and the political fused with the economic issue of the distribution of land. Individual granting of headrights seems to have ceased by early 1636, when the General Court ordered that the governor and assistants should "have power from time to time to dispose of the sitting downe of men in any newe plantation, and that none shall goe without leave from them."[11] Thereafter, it was impossible for an individual to acquire free and common socage real estate directly from the company government, as was the practice in Virginia. Land could be acquired only through corporate bodies of town proprietors, who functioned in the economic realm much as a gathered church did in the spiritual domain. New towns were formed by self-selected groups of men who applied to the General Court for a collective land grant several square miles in extent. The proprietors then laid out a settlement, assigning themselves house lots in the village core and, often, strips of farmland in common open fields that would have been familiar to their medieval ancestors. They reserved the vast majority of the town grant for future distribution to their children and grandchildren.

In this way, men of small means achieved their patriarchal landed dreams, while living modest Protestant lives that amassed few other kinds of riches in this world. Like visible saints, proprietors were free to admit others to their number, but, in almost every case, within a few years they declared the proprietorship closed. Newcomers would be welcome (although never automatically), but they could only purchase or be granted house and farm lots; like the unregenerate who were denied entry into heaven, they could not share in the great proprietary inheritance of future allotments. Thus, the New England town echoed the New England church; and because the initial proprietors tended also to be the initial saints who gathered the church, the echoes became even stronger. Politically, towns functioned on the same voluntaristic, participatory yet exclusivist, lines as church congregations. Drawing on, but not precisely replicating, practices in chartered English towns, New England's town proprietors, usually joined by all property-owning males, governed themselves through town meetings, which passed regulations of all sorts. Men of the towns annually chose individuals from among their number to serve as "selectmen"—and these selectmen, rather than centrally appointed mayors or sheriffs, administered affairs collectively between meetings.

The power that came from this deeply localistic form of government became evident when Winthrop and his assistants tried to extend their authority beyond the town of Boston under their transported charter. Soon after they arrived, the governor and assistants offered freemanship, and thus voting rights and participation in the General Court, to all adult male property owners. The first meeting of this expanded General Court then restricted the franchise to adult male church members, demonstrating both a determination that the godly should control the government and a rapid acceptance of Salem's innovative definition of the church. As freemen came to number in the thousands rather than the hundreds, however, obvious practical problems occurred in the structure of the General Court. In clear violation of the charter, Winthrop and his assistants argued that they alone would make all laws and decisions, with the role of the freemen-at-large limited to annual elections of the board of directors. Trouble erupted in 1634, when the governor and assistants started levying taxes without consulting the freemen. Not surprisingly, among people who at home had objected to Charles I's centralizing efforts to raise revenue, the freemen of the village of Watertown conducted their own version of a *quo warranto* proceeding. Demanding to see the company charter, they read in it their clear right to participate in legislation. A compromise finally allowed each town in the colony to elect two to three deputies, who would serve as representatives in the General Court. Thus, government in Massachusetts Bay became even more firmly rooted in the local power of its towns and churches.

In 1635 and 1636, on the eve of the Pequot War, a series of additional controversies—which elsewhere might have been tempests in teapots—rocked the young colony. As with the debates back in England over surplices and kneeling, these assumed an apocalyptic tone difficult for us to understand. But all in some way embodied themes of religious purity, political localism, and material access to land and patriarchal power.

The migrations of English people to the Connecticut Valley that helped spark the Pequot War were part of the process. Relatively minor points of theological disagreement with the Massachusetts version of the New England Way helped convince followers of the prominent English puritans Richard Hooker and John Davenport to emigrate, respectively, to Hartford and New Haven. Winthrop captured the mix of religious, political, and religious motives of those who founded Hartford:

The principal reasons for their removal were: 1. Their want of accommodation for their cattle, so as they were not able to maintain their ministers [financially], nor could receive any more of their friends to help them; and here it was alleged by Mr. Hooker as a fundamental error that towns were set so near each to other. 2. The fruitfulness and commodiousness of Connecticut, and the danger of having it possessed by others, Dutch or English. 3. The strong bent of their spirits to remove thither.[12]

Other localistic hivings-off from the Bay Colony were far less amicable, if just as much a product of strongly bent spirits. Among the many brilliant university-trained men who flocked to New England in the early 1630s was Roger Williams, a man who took the puritan quests for purity and local authority to their logical extremes, while raising uncomfortable questions about land and power. Soon after his arrival, he refused an appointment as pastor of the Boston church because the congregation would not formally declare its separation from the Church of England. During sojourns in Salem, Plymouth, and again in Salem, where he accepted a clerical post in 1633, Williams further developed the implications of his separatist ideals, which turned on an insistence that the workings of God's grace in the heart of a saint must not be constrained by ungodly human authority. This principle—which he would come to call "soul liberty"—went far beyond a technical insistence that a godly congregation must disavow any affiliation with the ungodly State Church. The saints, Williams preached, must not even meet together with unregenerate people for prayer or worship. Ultimately, he himself would refuse to pray with anyone but his wife, Mary—and one wonders whether even she always met his standards of religious purity. Certainly, he argued, there was no justification for, and much harm in, the Bay Colony's laws that required nonsaints to attend religious services. A similar logic led Williams to deny that secular authorities had any role at all to play in religious matters. In particular, he said, violations of the "First Table" of the Ten Commandments—injunctions against worshiping false gods, making graven images, taking the divine name in vain, and breaking the Sabbath—were utterly beyond the purview of officials who might be less than godly.

Here was the anarchy of Protestantism unleashed. Precisely because Williams's ideas flowed so logically from what the puritan magistrates and clergy of Massachusetts believed, he had to be suppressed. To compound the problem, Williams dared to challenge the right of the king, and thus

also of the royally chartered Massachusetts Bay Company, to assert ownership of Ninnimissinouk lands on free and common socage or any other
terms, because that land rightly belonged to its Native owners, Winthrop's
carefully parsed arguments to the contrary notwithstanding. Massachusetts leaders entreated Williams to keep his views to himself and both
pleaded with and threatened his Salem congregation, which was unwilling
to dismiss him. Finally, in late 1635, the General Court declared a sentence of banishment from the colony, beginning the next spring. When
Williams still refused to keep silent, the court ordered him placed on the
next ship bound for Laud's England, where someone of his outspoken beliefs surely would have been jailed, if not worse.

Rather than condemn Williams to that fate, Winthrop allowed him to
escape, first to Massasoit's village and then to a plot of land that the
Wampanoag sachem granted to him and several other exiles from Massachusetts, on the banks of the Seekonk River. Plymouth authorities soon
banished the refugees again, however, asserting that Massasoit had no
right to give them lands that belonged to the Bay Colony under its royal
patent. Williams and his associates moved farther west and south to accept
a gift of Narragansett land from Canonicus and Miantonomo, on which
he established a town he called Providence, and on which the sachems
pinned their hopes for a powerful alliance like the one Massasoit had
made with Plymouth. The cluster of exile communities came to be called
"Rhode Island and Providence Plantations" by its English residents and
the authorities who granted it an unprecedented parliamentary, rather
than royal, charter in 1644. Known as the "cesspool of New England" to
orthodox Congregationalists, it remained a thorn in the side of its larger
colonial neighbors. Its varied quests for religious purity, its example of the
fragmenting tendencies of localism, its commitment nonetheless to religious pluralism, and its blatant challenges to the right of men of small
means to claim title to Indian lands exposed tensions at the center of the
New England Way.

The other famous Boston banishment of the mid-1630s revealed the
same tensions, with an explosive component of gendered, as well as clerical and political, challenges to the right of some male saints to dictate the
terms on which others led their lives. Anne Hutchinson was, in many
ways, typical of the godly women who constituted a large portion of the
migrants to New England. Daughter of a Lincolnshire clergyman who encouraged her to become as learned in theology as any man, she and her

husband were devoted followers of the influential minister John Cotton. Like many of Cotton's flock (and like many women and men who were similarly devoted to other puritan clergymen), the Hutchinsons followed their spiritual leader to Boston shortly after he emigrated in 1633. In Boston, the Hutchinsons found a vibrant community eager to recreate the intense religious experiences that its members had left behind in England, and a community still tiny enough that nothing escaped anyone else's attention. This, a visitor said with only slight exaggeration, "was rather a Village, than a Town, there being not above Twenty or thirty houses" for its few hundred residents.[13] With Cotton's encouragement, Anne Hutchinson soon began holding regular meetings in her home to discuss the week's sermons and other matters—meetings that began to attract both sexes among a congregation where, as one scholar puts it, "hot Protestantism was finally free from the shackles of a hostile state and church hierarchy and was free to get as hot as it wanted." One of its members said, more simply, that Boston's was "the most glorious church in the world."[14]

Boston's church was also a nursery for politically as well as religiously dangerous ideas, particularly after the arrival of two charismatic Englishmen who, like Roger Williams and Anne Hutchinson, pushed the logic of puritanism to its hottest conclusion. One was a twenty-two-year-old aristocrat named Sir Henry Vane the Younger. Son of one of Charles I's privy counselors, he had decided to migrate to Massachusetts after concluding that he simply could not kneel to receive Communion. With his aristocratic title, his youthful good looks, and, especially, his connections at court at a time when the charter was under attack, the colony's freemen elected him governor a few months after his arrival, displacing Winthrop and others of distinctly smaller means from that office.

The other newcomer was Anne Hutchinson's brother-in-law, a very hot Protestant clergyman named John Wheelwright, who, with Vane, was quickly accepted as a visible saint by the Boston congregation and shaped many of its members' views. Like Cotton, but with even greater rigor, Wheelwright emphasized the unmediated power of God's free grace in transforming the life of a saint. His, and Hutchinson's and Vane's, opponents—who came to include most of the clerical and secular hierarchy of a colony in which many were disinclined to accept assertions of hierarchy—called these beliefs "antinomianism," the ancient Christian heresy that said saints were no longer subject to the Ten Commandments, because everything they did was by definition the product of divine grace. Oddly,

Williams, who really did come close to such an argument, was seldom tarred with the label "antinomian," while Hutchinson and her supporters, who believed no such thing, have ever since borne the name, and the upheaval they caused has become known as the "Antinomian Controversy."

The theological debate at the heart of the crisis turned on much finer points of Calvinist theology, and the whole affair should better be termed the "free-grace controversy."[15] One component of the emerging New England Way of Congregationalism was a consensus among most clergymen that, while God's free grace, rather than any human effort, effected salvation, people could nonetheless work to "prepare" their souls for a hoped-for infusion of divine power. They could do this through prayer, through reading the Scriptures, through diligent attendance at sermons, through efforts to live godly personal lives. Such a retreat from radical Calvinist doctrine served several useful functions. Most ministers considered "preparationism" the most compassionate advice they could give to poor souls who had not experienced an ecstatic infusion of divine grace: pray, study, conform, they counseled, and perhaps the Lord will come. Preparationism also served the more practical functions of keeping the unregenerate in meetinghouse seats and providing a reason for a trained clergy even to exist in its exalted role of preaching to the unconverted, while inculcating moral behavior in a population that otherwise might need to be kept in line by more forceful methods.

Hutchinson, Wheelwright, Vane, and apparently a majority of the Boston congregation would have none of it. Preparationism, they protested, was just another form of "works righteousness," which, like all of the heresies promulgated by William Laud and the pope, deluded people into thinking that their own good works could somehow earn them salvation. The free-grace faction began insisting ever more loudly that Wheelwright and Cotton were the only two clergymen in all of New England who proclaimed the pure Gospel. Everyone else was a false preacher.

In the rarefied air of a pre-Laudian Cambridge college, in an underground conventicle in late-1620s Lincolnshire, or even in the giddy early days of Boston's "most glorious church in the world," the debate over just how far to push the doctrine of free grace might have been one on which the godly could agree to disagree. Yet once a woman and a newly arrived male aristocrat attempted to turn the population of male voting church members against the fragile regime of men of small means who were fighting a morally questionable war against the Pequots for control of the

Connecticut Valley, the crisis of authority became acute. Like townspeople who refused to pay taxes to which they had not consented, like Williams who rejected secular authority over spiritual matters, like Pequots who dared thumb their noses at English demands, the free-grace faction was an intolerable threat precisely because it cut to the core of the New England Way.

So in March 1637, Wheelwright, like Williams before him, stood trial before the General Court. During the hearings, his sermons criticizing fellow ministers (which named no names) were twisted into proof of sedition against the government. Sentencing—presumed to be banishment—was postponed in hopes that Wheelwright would recant. But Wheelwright, Vane, Hutchinson, and their many supporters were not so easily gotten rid of. Vane, as governor, had technically presided over Wheelwright's trial, but had been outmaneuvered by Winthrop's faction and deprived even of the right to have his dissent from the verdict, and the dissents of two other people, officially recorded in the minutes. Vane thus began publicly questioning the legitimacy of the court's proceedings, compounding for Winthrop's faction the crisis of authority that they saw as being at the root of the whole affair. The threat was particularly acute in light of the possibility that Vane might return to England and his presumed connections at court. In a clear effort to hasten Vane from office (but not back to Britain), Winthrop's faction arranged to move the annual May elections from Boston to the presumably friendlier environment of Newtown (later renamed Cambridge). After a near-riot by a crowd of Vane supporters who walked from Boston to protest, the votes were tallied. Winthrop returned to the governorship, and Vane and his supporters lost out.

The crackdown then began. To prevent any further influx of newcomers with troublesome ideas, the General Court decreed that no immigrant could purchase land from a town or stay in the colony for more than three weeks without authorization from the magistrates. The Court summoned a synod—a meeting of the colony's clergy, also attended by magistrates, prominent laypeople, and representatives of Plymouth and Connecticut—to settle theological disputes once and for all. When that body met, it outlined eighty-two theological errors, many of them attributed to Hutchinson and her supporters, which it condemned. Conventicles in private homes, such as those held by Hutchinson, were discouraged. Congregants were not permitted to ask questions after sermons. Magistrates were to enforce the decisions of church bodies to discipline their members.

Wheelwright was banished, and so, after a long show trial, was Hutchinson. Pequot war hero John Underhill stood at the head of a list of sixty of Hutchinson's Boston supporters who, along with dozens elsewhere, were disarmed for fear they would lead a revolt.[16] Vane left voluntarily for England, probably unaware that the company charter had already been revoked, and certainly unaware that rebellion in Scotland had already begun and would make the revocation moot. Underhill soon left the colony as well, to publish his *Newes from America* in London. When he tried to return to New England, authorities quickly banished him for his religious and political views, and for alleged adultery. He settled first in what is now New Hampshire and then on Dutch Long Island, and never was able to rejoin the colony that his book did so much to celebrate. So much for the glorious flourishing of Protestantism in a free environment. Archbishop Laud could not have done a more efficient job of silencing dissent than did the rulers of Massachusetts. This, too, became the New England Way.

Such tortured religious controversies may make Virginia seem light-years, rather than just hundreds of miles, distant from New England. So too does the contrast between New England's cold winters and rocky soils and the Chesapeake's steamy summers and luxuriant tobacco fields. Yet in terms of migration, land hunger, and patriarchal local authority, the distinctions begin to fade, particularly for the period from about 1630 to 1660, after the collapse of the Chesapeake colony's initial tobacco boom and before its later embrace of race-based slavery. In Virginia, too, men of small means sought land and power in a way that confirmed their Protestant view of the world.

"Our first worke is expulsion of the Salvages to gaine the free range of the countrey for encrease of Cattle, swine etc. which will more then restore us," Virginia Governor Francis Wyatt wrote in the wake of the attack of 1622. "It is infinitely better to have no heathen among us, who at best were but as thornes in our sides, then to be at peace and league with them."[17] His words marked the death of the conquistador fantasy of a biracial hierarchy ruled by English lords of the soil. They also employed the kind of biblical language we tend to associate more with New Englanders than with tobacco planters. "The Lord spake unto Moses . . . , saying, Speake unto the children of Israel, and say unto them, When yee are come over Jorden to enter into the land of Canaan, Yee shall then drive out all the inhabitants of the land before you": Wyatt would have read this passage in the Geneva Bible. "If yee will not drive out the inhabitants of the land before you, then those which yee let ramaine of them, shall bee prickes in your eyes, and thornes in your sides, and shall vexe you in the land wherein yee dwell." Nonetheless, according to Scripture, Moses's successor "Joshua made peace with them, and made a league with them . . . and delivered them out of the hand of the children of Israel, that they slew them not." Thus having spared some of the Canaanites, "Joshua appointed them that same day to bee hewers of wood, and drawers of water for the Congregation, and for the altar of the Lord."[18] Refusing to hew and draw, the Powhatans got the expulsion they deserved.

And so, for a time, it seemed that the Virginia Canaan had averted the Lord's warning to Moses that, "if ye will not drive out the inhabitants of the land . . . , it shal come to passe, that I shal doe unto you, as I thought to do unto them."[19] Although the lives and livelihoods of hundreds of colonists (not to mention many more hundreds of Native people) had been destroyed in the decade-long war that began in 1622, and although death rates from disease remained frightful, until about 1630 a fortunate few English survivors extracted great wealth from the leaves of the tobacco plants that Pocahontas's husband, John Rolfe, had shown them how to grow. In some years, leaf sold in London for as much as three shillings per pound of weight; in others, for one shilling. In this experimental period, estimates of how much tobacco a planter could grow with his own hands varied. Some said five hundred pounds; others, as much as two thousand. At a price of one shilling, a thousand pounds of leaf would earn a little over £83 sterling, in an era when, amid falling wages in England, an agricultural labor might earn £5, a family farm £20, or a prosperous urban artisan £30 per year. Those able to put servants to work in their tobacco fields could expect an almost arithmetical increase in profits: one servant meant £166, five £498, ten (if one then stopped working oneself), a near-princely £830. In 1625, apparently as few as fifteen planters—most of them well-connected officials such as Governor Wyatt, Raphe Hamor, George Yeardley, or Abraham Piersey—oversaw as many as ten servants, but still the lure of growing smoke was obvious.[20]

And the connection with labor was virtually ironclad. Unlike maize, tobacco left to grow on its own was a mere weed. To yield smokable leaf, planters learned that they must painstakingly deposit seeds in hotbeds each January, laboriously hoe individual hills into which young plants

would be set in May, backbreakingly "top" and "sucker" to remove un-
wanted growth that otherwise would sap energy from primary leaves during the hot months of June and July, meticulously pull worms off the
plants throughout the summer, hurriedly cut the leaf and hang it to dry at
just the right moment in August, and carefully pack the final product in
shipping barrels in October, at the precise moment it was neither so dry it
would become powder nor so moist it would rot before arrival in England.
"*Tobacco* being once in the ground, is never out of hand till in the Hogs-
head," one of Virginia's many critics complained. "The poore Servant goes
daily through the rowes of *Tobacco* stooping to worme it, and being overheated he is struck with a Calenture or Feaver, and so perisheth."[21] All of
this work required not only killing toil by laborers, but considerable skill
on the part of the planter who judged the timing of each step. Once the
basics were perfected, there was little room for economies of scale.

The key factor, thus, was never the amount of land that one could put
into production (although, of course, excellent tobacco land with good access to water transportation was always at a premium). The critical element was the number of laborers one could put in the field. The headright
system that Virginia used to encourage migration—whereby a planter
gained fifty acres for each person whose passage into the country he
paid—reinforced the importance of labor. The more imported workers
one controlled, the more land one was entitled to own, even if it could
never all be put into tobacco production. In this way, the equation among
land, labor, and power—an interrelation deeply rooted in the medieval
European experience—took on a distinctive shape in the seventeenth-
century Chesapeake.

That shape endured even when tobacco prices plunged from shillings to
pennies. Overproduction in Virginia (and Barbados and Bermuda and
even England itself) was fundamentally to blame for the great market collapse after 1630, although perhaps it was more a matter of supply catching
up to a European demand that thereafter grew in lockstep with production, expanding from four hundred thousand pounds of leaf in 1630 to
nearly fifteen million by 1660. Three pennies per pound in a good year,
one penny in a bad one, remained the norm throughout that period; and a
thousand pounds of leaf now yielded, at best, a little over £12.

For English immigrants of small means, such a modest return continued to look good, particularly when combined with the profits to be made
from livestock, which could be left mostly to fend for themselves in the

woods until the meat could be shipped off to Connecticut, Barbados, or elsewhere. As colonial promoter John Hammond recognized in a tract published 1656, the importance of foodstuffs to Virginia's economy should not be underestimated. "From this industry of theirs," he wrote, "and [from] great plenty of Corn, (the main staffe of life) proceeded that great plenty of Cattel and Hogs, (now innumerable) and out of which not only *New England* hath been stocked and relieved, but all other parts of the *Indies* inhabited by Englishmen."[22] As Wyatt had foreseen, the expulsion of the Canaanites "gained the free range of the countrey for encrease of Cattle, swine etc."

The modest but real profits to be earned from tobacco and hogs help explain why, in the three decades after 1630, more than half again as many English people emigrated to Virginia and its neighbor Maryland (founded in 1634) as traveled to Massachusetts and points adjacent. It might be true that "*New-England,* is in a good Condition for livelihood," as a Virginia booster gloated. "But for matter of any great hopes but Fishing, there is not much in that Land; For its as *Scotland* is to *England* . . . : there is much Cold, Frost and Snow, and their Land so barren, except a Herring be put into the hole that you set the Corn or Maize in, it will not come up."[23]

Despite the contrast in opportunities, and although data for Chesapeake immigrants are far less complete than for New England, it appears that the approximately thirteen thousand people who paid their own way to Virginia (as opposed to being imported as servants) did not look much different from those who traveled to the more northerly colonies. A larger proportion of the self-financed Virginia immigrants seem to have been from the lower ranks of the titled nobility and the upper ranks of the gentry, and the average age was somewhat higher. Yet, as with the New England migrants, the vast majority were urbanites from the middling tiers of society, no more familiar than their northern counterparts with the toils of working a farm with their own hands—much less with the mysteries of cultivating *Nicotiana tabacum.* Few were Laudians or (later royalist myths notwithstanding) great supporters of Charles I. A substantial number were puritans or Quakers; slightly fewer were Roman Catholics who sought refuge in Lord Baltimore's manorial preserve of Maryland. But the majority in both Chesapeake colonies seem to have subscribed to the kind of broad Protestantism that had flourished in late Elizabethan and early Jacobean England. A lack of trained Church of England clergy, and, most of the time, a lack of commitment by officials to enforce religious uniformity, allowed diversity of opinion to survive—although sometimes bloody conflicts between Protestants and Catholics in Maryland, and occasional banishments of ministers who refused to use the Book of Common Prayer or Quakers who refused to keep quiet in Virginia, revealed tensions seldom far beneath the surface.

Two factors, however, distinguished the Chesapeake's population from the motley lot that collected in tolerant Rhode Island. First, remarkably few people migrated in families; a dearth of free children under age fifteen (3 percent as opposed to 30 percent in New England) explains the older age distribution of southern migrants, and a dearth of married women (free males outnumbered free females by more than two to one) explains much about the nature of the society that emerged from the tobacco fields. Well into the eighteenth century, Virginia and Maryland would remain overwhelmingly male, with household and family life further attenuated by a disease environment that made life expectancies perhaps twenty years shorter than in New England. It is difficult to avoid the conclusion that married women and men found the healthful and explicitly religious conditions of New England a more attractive milieu in which to raise their children than the Chesapeake, while single men whose experience and worldviews otherwise differed little from their Massachusetts-bound counterparts allowed the modest economic advantages of Virginia to win out.

The second difference between the population of the Chesapeake and that of New England was more dramatic. For each free immigrant, there were as many as four who were unfree. Of the unfree, roughly three-quarters were men, and nearly all were under age twenty-five. As late as 1660, only a tiny handful were Africans—no more than nine hundred in a total non-Indian population of about twenty-five thousand —although at least some English found even in such tiny numbers the promise of greater riches to come. "Of *Negroes* brought thither," one writer bragged in 1648, there were "three hundred good servants."[24] In this period, English planters lacked access to substantial numbers of the enslaved Africans who already toiled in great numbers in Spanish America. More readily available were Irish people transported as virtual slaves after rebellions in the British Isles. Still, the majority of Chesapeake servants, and thus a majority of the entire population, were the same kinds of displaced English rural folk and unskilled laborers who flocked to cities such as London and Bristol during the middle years of the seventeenth century. Their travels to Virginia or Maryland were just one more step in a long, often futile, and even fatal, quest to somehow better their lives.

The servitude they encountered in North America was unlike anything they might have experienced at home, either in the countryside or the city. It was not that servitude itself was strange. Unfreedom of one kind or another was an almost universal experience for older children and younger adults in England, and the primary model by which most work was organized. Within the patriarchal scheme of the household, servants stood in a relationship to their masters much like that of children to fathers, but with few of the privileges that went with ties of blood. No one— except, perhaps, for those tarred with such civil-war labels as "Leveller" or "Ranter"—believed that such "dependent" persons had anything like the same civil and political rights as their "independent" masters, or questioned the authority of patriarchs to discipline them harshly while extracting the fruits of their labors.

England's servants came in myriad forms, but most could be placed in one of three categories. Servants at husbandry were adult farm laborers who typically signed annual contracts providing a small cash wage in addition to the benefits of food and shelter. Apprentices and household servants, by contrast, were typically very young people, in theory learning a skill that would prepare them to become masters or housewives in their own right when they came of age. That training and perhaps "freedom dues," which might allow them to set themselves up on their own, provided their only compensation apart from room and board. Unlike such legally voluntary servants, orphans and paupers were bound out to masters who relieved society as a whole from the burden of supporting them. For the most part, this third category of English servants had no right to negotiate their own contracts, no influence over the kind of work to which they were assigned, no choice over whom they had to serve, and little expectation of profiting from their own labor.

Chesapeake servitude was a strange hybrid displaying the worst of each form. Like a servant at husbandry, an unfree immigrant to Virginia had a contract, in theory freely negotiated; this was the "indenture" that gave the institution its name. Instead of an annual wage, however, the indentured servant earned credit against the cost of his or her transportation to North

America, a debt that usually required four to five years' service to pay. Such a long term resembled the indentures signed in England on behalf of apprentices. So too did a standard feature of colonial contracts that provided for freedom dues in the unlikely event the servant lived long enough to collect them: some agricultural tools, a suit of clothes, a ration of foodstuffs, and a claim on the fifty acres of land the master had received for importing the servant in the first place. The latter, however, meant little because of the many fees and expenses involved in actually claiming a tract. As promoter Hammond admitted, contractual promises of land were "an old delusion, for there is no land accustomary due to the servant, but to the Master, and therefore that servant is unwise that will not dash out that custom in his covenant, and make that due of land absolutely his own."[25]

Few, however, were in any position to make such a demand, for the strongest resemblances between Chesapeake servitude and English precedents were features much like the powerless bondage imposed on English orphans and the poor. Having signed on with a ship's captain for transportation to America, an immigrant would simply be sold to the highest bidder at the destination. That bidder, who technically owned only the labor contract, in fact pretty much owned the servant's person for the next four to five years, was free to buy and sell him or her at will, could impose whatever work discipline and minimal subsistence seemed best, and could use the courts to extend the term of service should the servant have the temerity to run away, resist, or (if she were female) bear a child, even if that child was the product of rape by the master. Hammond tried to put a good face on it. Do not "let that brand of selling of servants, be any discouragement to deter any from going," he wrote, "for if a time must be served, it is all one with whom it be served, provided they be people of honest repute, with which the Country is well replenished."[26]

Such fine words notwithstanding, there is no way to minimize the ugliness of servitude in an economy where every body put into a tobacco field promised that much more production and profit. The exploitative value of servant labor is suggested even in the way the Chesapeake colonies calculated taxation. In New England, rates were initially levied on towns as collective entities, and even after a system of more individualized poll and property taxes was devised, towns continued to be the mechanism through which revenues were actually raised. Virginia and Maryland instead taxed "tithables"—individual workers, originally assumed to be male, yet later defined to include African and Native American women but not European female servants. The assumption was that a householder's ability to pay was best measured by the number of laborers he controlled. In theory, the planters of New England derived their responsibilities as taxpayers, as well as their rights as voting freemen of the corporation, from their visible sainthood—the key to membership in both the gathered church and the town with which it was coterminous. In practice, the planters of Virginia derived their responsibilities and rights from their control of labor.

In both plantations, land in free and common socage was the most important right of a free man. And the Chesapeake's headright system ensured that access to land, too, depended on control of labor. As in New England, it was possible to buy land from a colonist who already owned it; perhaps it was even possible to acquire it as freedom dues. But in both regions, the downsized manorial dream was best realized through a free grant of land from the colonial government that had ensured its initial expropriation from the Indians. Political connections, then, were crucial in both settings. Not just any group of godly New England men could declare themselves a town and receive a vast collective tract, and not just any Virginia planter could parlay the few hundred acres he received for importing himself and a handful of servants into a domain sprawling over several square miles.

In Virginia, the emphasis on individual mastery of labor inspired a particularly frantic sort of land grabbing. Whoever first "took up" a plot of choice riverfront ground with an abandoned Powhatan village and cornfields, hired a surveyor to mark its bounds, and paid the appropriate registration fees upon displaying official sanction for the appropriate headrights won the prize. Not surprisingly, a well-connected elite of government officeholders—mostly composed of men whose origins were little grander than the rest of the men of small means around them—rapidly and literally came to dominate the landscape, ensconcing themselves as so many local lords of the soil.

Also not surprisingly, English Virginia found itself at war with the Powhatans again in 1644. Opechancanough—said to be one hundred years old, nearly blind, and unable to walk unassisted—organized a reprise of the attack he had led in 1622. The root of the war was the relentless colonial pressure on Native land holdings from Virginia planters and the roaming herds of semi-domesticated animals that, by trampling the remaining Indian cornfields, had become as much a part of the English juggernaut as tobacco. Documentation on the Powhatans' campaign against the Virginians is sparse, but one chronicler said that for some time after the initial assault, "the *Indians* [were] Allaruming them night and day, and killing all their Cattell, as with ease they might doe, and . . . destroying in the nights, all their Corne Fields, which the *English* could not defend." He also explained that the attacks came when they did because Opechancanough had learned of the civil war wracking England and determined "that now was his time, or never, to roote out all the *English:* For those that they could not surprize and kill under the feigned masque of Friendship and feasting, and the rest would be by wants; and having no supplyes from their own Countrey which could not helpe them, be Suddenly Consumed and Famished." Nonetheless, two years of scorched-earth counter-raids by the English resulted in the death and enslavement of hundreds of Native people and, finally, the capture of Opechancanough in March 1646. Displayed in a cage at Jamestown, the man the chronicler called "that bloody Monster upon 100 yeers old" remained defiant until one of his guards shot him in the back.[27]

Contemporaries on both sides of the Atlantic gave Sir William Berkeley credit for turning the tide against the Powhatans, "which by the great mercy of God was done and effected," the chronicler proclaimed, "that the great God may have his due Glory, Honour, and Praise for ever and ever, *Amen, Amen, Amen.*"[28] A loyal courtier and advisor of Charles I, Berkeley had been appointed royal governor of Virginia in 1641 and, after returning to England—supposedly to seek aid in the war against the Powhatans, but actually to put in some time on the battlefield against parliamentary forces—he returned to lead the expedition that captured Opechancanough and to impose peace terms.

A treaty of 1646 required the surviving remnants of the paramount chiefdom to pay annual tribute to the colony, to cede much of their territory to the English Crown, to live on what was in effect a reservation north of the York River granted back to them by the Crown, and to refrain from unauthorized entry into English land on pain of death. Although the same treaty supposedly also prohibited the English from entering Indian territory, colonial land claims there almost immediately began to be approved. The unequal balance of power between English and Indians in Virginia thus came to resemble the one that took shape almost simultaneously far-

ther north with the formation of the New England Confederation, but
with far less room for the Native parties to maneuver.

The internal system of government over which Berkeley presided had
accreted from customary practices, local legislation, and occasional royal
decrees accumulated since the revocation of the company charter and the
imposition of royal rule in 1624. Like Massachusetts, Virginia had an
elected legislature: the House of Burgesses, which traced its origins to the
period of company rule and which, largely by default, continued to operate under the royal regime. Through a hodgepodge of local constituencies
with no pretense of equal representation among them, adult property-
owning men chose the legislature's membership, invariably consisting of
the most substantial planters in the colony—who thus, much like their
counterparts in Massachusetts, brought their intensely local interests to a
contentious central arena.

The House of Burgesses was the only part of the government in which
voting played any role. The governor appointed his council—analogous to
Massachusetts's assistants—from among the leading planters. Functions
handled in New England by town meetings were, in Virginia, assigned either to county courts, selected by the governor from the same circles of
planters who dominated the council and Burgesses, or to local parish
church vestries. Like the gathered church memberships of New England,
vestries were bodies of laymen who administered church affairs and appointed clergymen and determined their salaries. Unlike their northern
counterparts, vestries also levied taxes on tithables, controlled buildings
and property (New England meetinghouses belonged to the town), and
oversaw aid, such as it existed, for orphans and the poor. Freemen participated in elections to vestries exactly once, when a parish was first established; thereafter, all replacements were appointed by the sitting members—the same substantial planters who held all other positions.

So, just as thoroughly as a puritan elite dominated Massachusetts, a tightly
connected planter elite, fiercely jealous of its local privileges, dominated
Virginia. The basic elements of the system had evolved before Berkeley
arrived; but he perfected it during a reign of over thirty-five years, which
was only briefly interrupted during Cromwell's regime. Throughout that
period, when Berkeley was officially replaced by a series of former members of the council, he remained on the scene pulling strings. Theo-

retically the representative of the far-off Stuart monarchy he claimed to support—in 1649 he had the House of Burgesses pass legislation declaring even the mention of Charles I's execution to be treason—Berkeley actually presided as if he were the unchecked lord of his local domain. Imposing peace on the Indians, cultivating connections with the emerging planter elite, winking at that elite's various corruptions, welcoming carefully selected royalist exiles and second sons of the English gentry to emigrate with their families, servants, and retainers and join the ranks of the fortunate few, he built a circle of allies called the "Green Spring Faction," named for the manor house he built for himself a few miles outside Jamestown in 1645. A huge pile of brick and leaded windows that eclipsed both the one-room shacks of the vast majority of ordinary planters and the only slightly larger wooden houses of most of the elite, Green Spring epitomized the kind of power that land and labor bought in the Chesapeake. This was the Virginia way.

NINE

Dutch, French, Spanish, and
English Counterpoints

TO COMPREHEND THE NOVELTY of the societies that English planters created in New England and the Chesapeake—to appreciate how
truly odd those places were in global history—we need to look elsewhere
in North America and the Atlantic basin, where patterns laid down by
traders and conquistadores continued to prevail. In Nieu Nederlandt,
La Nouvelle-France, La Florida, and Nuevo México, few of the small-
scale landed dreams that captured English planters' imaginations were on
offer. There, relative handfuls of Europeans continued to envision a future
dependent on close ties with Native Americans, and Native Americans
continued sometimes to embrace profitably and sometimes to reject violently the ways in which colonizers tried to define those terms. Dutch,
French, Spanish, and Native ways contrasted profoundly with those of
New Englanders or Virginians and yet flourished simultaneously with
them, revealing the continued influence of older cultural forms even as
new ones grew atop them. Those continuing influences were not confined
to non-English-speakers, for a strain of conquistador spirit continued to
thrive among those who ruled the British Isles in the middle years of the
seventeenth century. Their contrasting vision of global power profoundly
threatened the interests of Dutch traders, Spanish colonizers, and, ultimately, English planters alike.

Men of small means would not have prospered in either Virginia or New
England, had not Nieu Nederlandt continued to build its trading networks while Englishmen swarmed to their new plantations. Nor would the

Dutch have thrived in North America without the agricultural products that English colonists fed into their commercial system. In colonial ports everywhere, Dutch ships were nearly as likely to be found as English ones, and colonists extended them a hearty welcome. On a December day in the late 1640s, for example, a Virginia planter counted "ten ships from *London,* two from *Bristoll,* twelve *Hollanders,* and seven from *New-England*" in the James River.[1] Observers in Boston, New Haven, or Providence might have found similar ratios. Lumber, foodstuffs, cattle, hogs, wampum, and furs moved up and down the Atlantic seaboard and to Europe and the Caribbean, largely on Dutch ships. The plantation regimes of the English superimposed themselves on a trading network dominated by the Dutch West India Company and its various affiliated and disaffected merchants.

Statistics are elusive, particularly in light of the fact that colonials from rival nations were not supposed to be trafficking with each other, but the Dutch carried substantial Chesapeake tobacco across the Atlantic. The "Dutch Masters" who once decorated ubiquitous North American cigar boxes were likely puffing English weed. By the 1650s, more value in tobacco than in furs was shipped from Nieu Nederlandt, and very little of it seems to have originated on Dutch soil. Some came from New England and the West Indies, but most was probably transshipped from the Chesapeake. Meantime, Dutch ships were carrying at least half as much leaf directly to the Netherlands. The Dutch merchants who dominated the New Sweden Company were also major handlers of English colonial tobacco— at least on the rare occasions when ships from Europe visited the colony of New Sweden, on the Delaware River. Transshipments weighing over fifteen thousand Swedish pounds left in 1644, over twenty-four thousand in 1647, and over thirteen thousand in 1654. In all, this was three to four times as much weight as was produced by the Nordic colony's own farmers, who seem to have virtually stopped growing tobacco themselves after 1646.[2] Recognizing the centrality of such trade to the fragile prosperity of Virginia planters, Virginia's governor, William Berkeley, was an outspoken supporter of commerce with the Dutch from his first arrival in the Chesapeake through his endorsement of a formal commercial treaty between Virginia and Nieu Nederlandt in 1660. In England, however, perhaps the only thing that royalist and Cromwellian government officials could agree on was that any such arrangement was a horrible idea. Every cask of tobacco carried to the Netherlands reduced revenue from customs duties on imports to England, revenue that otherwise would have to be extracted from the domestic population through direct Parliamentary taxation.

In addition to their English-exchequer-draining dominance in the carrying trade, the Dutch briefly became the Atlantic world's largest dealers in enslaved African labor. The wave of assaults on Spanish interests that launched the Dutch East India and West India companies extended to Africa, as well as to the Americas. In 1612, Dutch traders had established a post on the Gold Coast of present-day Ghana. In 1637, the WIC conquered the infamous Portuguese post of Elmina, and thus gained control of the largest single shipment point for enslaved people. By 1642, every major Portuguese West African trading center was in Dutch hands. Although ultimately Portugal regained control of many of these posts, at least forty thousand people left Africa enchained on Dutch ships in the two decades before 1660. Most of that labor went to the sugar plantations of Brazil, the northern half of which the WIC conquered and renamed "Nieuw Holland" in 1629. In 1645, revolts by the still largely Portuguese colonial population confined the Dutch to the area around their capital at Recife, which in turn surrendered to the Iberians in 1654. Thereafter the island of Curaçao, an agriculturally barren spot off the coast of present-day Venezuela that was long used as a transshipping port for slaves, became the focal point for Dutch slavers.

Throughout the period before 1660, English planters who wanted enslaved Africans had to rely on the Dutch. English slaving was haphazard, involving only occasional expeditions to the West African coast or privateering raids on Portuguese shipping. Not until 1651 did a group of English merchants called the Guinea Company build a fort on the Gold Coast, and even then precious metal rather than human labor was the main attraction. The first Africans recorded to have arrived in English Virginia came on a Dutch vessel in 1619; they had actually been seized from a Portuguese slaver by an English privateer working in partnership with the Dutch ship. Most of the small numbers of other Africans sold to mainland North American English planters before the Dutch established themselves on the African coast probably arrived by similarly tangled routes. Thereafter, Dutch vessels brought only a slightly larger number of slaves to the English mainland colonies, as first Brazil and then English Barbados consumed nearly every enslaved body the WIC could provide. Those who did reach the Chesapeake or New England were most often people who had already spent time further south, and who had been sold off because their masters regarded them as troublemakers.

So it was in Barbados, not Virginia, where English planters first determined that enslaved labor was more profitable than servitude and decided that skin color doomed certain men and women to the status of perpetual property. Established in 1627 as part of the same great spewing-out of English population that produced Massachusetts and a reinvented Virginia, Barbados had limped along for a quarter-century, attempting to grow cotton and a kind of tobacco that turned out to be far inferior to that produced in the Chesapeake. Then, after 1640, its largest planters (no more dominant and not even as well-off as their contemporaries in pre-Berkeley Virginia) suddenly switched over to the cultivation of sugar, an enormously profitable crop never before seriously grown by English people.

That they were able to make the transition was largely due to expertise, personnel, and enslaved African labor provided by the Dutch of Brazil and Curaçao. This seeming act of economic suicide in fact made perfect sense to the WIC and its fractious associates. Always far more interested in the profits to be made from trading in commodities than in their actual production, and well aware of the fragile hold they had on Brazil, Dutch merchants welcomed Barbados as an alternative source for a lucrative commodity and as an alternative market for enslaved Africans. The transformation of the Barbadian labor force was nearly complete by 1660, as two hundred to three hundred planters gobbled up nearly all of the land suitable for sugar, mobilized a workforce of some twenty-seven thousand Africans (who outnumbered the rapidly declining English population of twenty-six thousand), and focused so single-mindedly on profits that they became dependent on Virginia and New England to supply food for them and their workers.[3]

In exchange for foodstuffs, at least a few hundred enslaved Africans were shipped from Barbados to the Chesapeake, on Dutch and English ships. Perhaps more important, the *idea* of a planter class that based its power on enslaved labor arrived in the same vessels. Although the largest Chesapeake planters, with their paltry dozens of servants and sprinklings of slaves, as yet could only watch enviously as a handful of their counterparts in Barbados enriched themselves, the lessons were plain.

In the early 1660s, Africans constituted less than 4 percent of the population of the English Chesapeake but close to 20 percent of Dutch Nieuw Amsterdam. Virginia's 4 percent comprised about nine hundred people, however, while Nieuw Amsterdam's nearly 20 percent amounted to less than five hundred. A mere twenty-five hundred European and African people lived in Nieuw Amsterdam and only about nine thousand in the entire colony of Nieu Nederlandt, compared to twenty-five thousand in Virginia and Maryland to the south and thirty-three thousand in New England to the east. Among non-English North American outposts, however, Nieu Nederlandt's population was gigantic. Fewer than three thousand French people inhabited La Nouvelle-France. Probably no more than a thousand Spanish colonists lived in Nuevo México among the descendants of the Ancestral Puebloans, with perhaps half again that many in La Florida among descendants of the Mississippians. In 1660, English people outnumbered all other Europeans in North America by a factor of almost four to one, a ratio that would increase with each passing year. This statistic, better than any other, shows how atypical, how new under the sun, the English mode of planting was.[4]

While there was never any question that the primary purpose of Nieu Nederlandt was trade, first with Native people and then with English colonists, a substantial faction of the WIC's directors always envisioned a plantation colony populated by free immigrants, servants, and slaves producing agricultural commodities for export. Yet on both ends of the migratory equation—"push" factors in Europe and "pull" factors in North America—the Dutch case differed fundamentally from that of the English. At home, the Netherlands had traveled even farther than the English along the road that loosed people from their economic and social ties to rural village communities. The Low Countries contained a population just as mobile and able to pursue economic opportunities as its counterpart across the North Sea. But, even during the worst days of the Thirty Years War, conditions in the Netherlands remained favorable enough that few people looked beyond the region's cities for opportunity. A plantation colony "demands more people than our lands can supply," the directors of the WIC confessed in 1644, "not so much for want of population, with which our provinces swarm, as because all those who will labor in any way here, can easily obtain support, and therefore, are disinclined to go far from home on an uncertain outcome."[5] A prosperous economy was joined by a stable political order and a tolerant religious environment, where even Portuguese Sephardic Jews were relatively welcome in a Calvinist country. None of the push factors that drove so many English people from their homes were at work. On the contrary, thousands of English emigrants flocked to Dutch cities in search of opportunity.

Nieu Nederlandt exerted no such pull, for few of the factors that drew immigrants to English North America applied there. The colony had no clear religious vision (apart from its general anti-Spanish aims and the ill-fated efforts of its last director-general, Petrus Stuyvesant, to impose Calvinist orthodoxy on a diverse population), no clear agricultural mission, and, perhaps most important, no land policy comparable to those of New England or the Chesapeake. As the Virginia Company of London had done with its scheme of "particular plantations," the WIC did offer huge land grants to wealthy people. Such landowners, known as "patroons," pledged to populate their estates with employees and tenants. Only one of these patroonships developed in any serious way, however: Rensselaerswyck, surrounding modern-day Albany, and the Indian trade, rather than agricultural production, was its mainstay. The company also devised a variety of programs whereby retired company soldiers and employees or immigrant families who paid their own share of company-subsidized transport could obtain grants of heritable land, but under far less favorable conditions than in either Virginia or New England. Instead of multiple fifty-acre headrights or a share in a several-mile-square town tract, immigrants to Nieu Nederlandt appear to have received just enough land to support themselves.

As a result, only about half of the nine thousand residents of Nieu Nederlandt traced their roots to the United Provinces. The rest included Walloons (from what is now Belgium), Sephardim, German-speakers of various sorts, refugees from the collapse of Dutch Brazil, a few hundred Swedes and Finns in the Delaware Valley, and a sizable contingent of ever-restless English from New England, especially in a cluster of towns on Long Island whose governance was contested with the New Haven colony. Most residents were men of small means, but few pinned their hopes—as New Englanders or Virginians did—on becoming patriarchs of their own landed domains. The most effective spur to immigration that the West India Company came up with was to abandon its monopoly on the fur trade in 1640, granting all colonists the right to participate.

Meantime, small-scale landed patriarchal dreams hardly existed at all in La Nouvelle-France, where no such thing as free and common socage existed. All real estate was held in seigneurial tenure, although most of the medieval obligations associated with that system had been stripped away. As the Virginia Company had done with its particular plantations and the WIC with its patroonships, Les Cent Associés distributed large seigneuries—some several hundred square miles in extent—to a handful of major investors, who were expected to populate them with dozens if not hundreds of servants and retainers. The most significant seigneuries, however, went to the Jesuits, the Ursuline Sisters, parish churches, and other Catholic entities. Almost no one came to La Nouvelle-France outside the auspices of religious institutions, lay seigneurs, or the company itself. Barely three hundred people paid their own way during the entire history of the colony.[6]

Apart from priests, nuns, and the occasional shipment of young women intended as brides for a population that was even more overwhelmingly male (80 percent) than that of Virginia, the vast majority of immigrants came as indentured servants, or, as they were known in La Nouvelle-France, *engagés*. Compared to the situation of servants in the English colonies, an *engagé* enjoyed very attractive arrangements: a term of only three years, an annual wage in addition to room and board, and the virtual certainty of receiving a small tract of land from his seigneur when he gained his freedom. Seigneurs were also required, however, to provide round-trip transportation for their *engagés,* and more than two-thirds of servants seem to have found a return to their French villages far more attractive than the life of an *habitant* (small landholder) in Canada.

Neither pull nor push factors operated in any compelling way for immigrants to La Nouvelle-France. For a freed servant, little profit could be expected from the fur trade, despite the fact that in 1645 Les Cent Associés subcontracted their monopoly to a Compagnie des Habitants in which every landholder, in theory, held a share. Even less could be expected from a tiny plot of agricultural land in a colony that endured a short growing season, that had found no cash crop, and that lacked an Atlantic market even for exported foodstuffs, in large part because its thousand-mile-long river route to the east froze shut for much of the year. Meanwhile, rural France had its share of economic and political difficulties but, unlike England or the Netherlands, had almost no tradition of internal migration that made it a usual thing for young men or women to leave their homes permanently in search of better opportunities. To some degree, this was because many medieval obligations remained intact and because the legal tradition of partible inheritance ensured every male heir at least some subsistence.

But a strong cultural bias against emigration seems also to have been at work. "I find it strange to have a son whom I have cherished more than my own self but who has no thought for me," one French father wrote to a wayward *engagé*.

> I thought I would have the happiness of seeing him within four or five years of his departure. My dear son, I beg of you to try to find a way of coming back to France and of spending two to three months in your native town of La Flèche. I swear to you that you are your mother's heir and should you come to La Flèche you would have over 800 livres [in money]. . . . I ask for nothing except that you show me the respect owed father and mother. . . . Your uncle Lucas sends you his best, as do your aunt, his wife, and all your good friends in this good land of Anjou, where white wine costs a sol.[7]

Cheap wine, loving kin, a modest inheritance: What had Canada to compare to those?

The Jesuit missionary Claude Boucher put the comparison differently in 1660. "The Ocean which separates us from France sees, on its eastern side, only rejoicing, splendor, and bonfires; but, on its western, nothing but war, slaughter, and conflagrations," he wrote as he observed the Native American conflicts engulfing the heart of the continent. "Our invincible Monarch gives peace and life to all Europe, while our America seems to be reduced to extremities by the most cruel of all wars." Only a transcendent Catholic religious vision—one every bit as thrilling as its Protestant mirror-image in New England—made Boucher stay. "What consoles us is . . . knowing the vows, the prayers, the penances, and all sorts of good works, which are being performed almost everywhere for the conversion of our Savages; and learning of the good purposes with which God has inspired many persons of merit, for accomplishing the destruction of the Iroquois," he concluded. "Such an enterprise is worthy of the piety of those engaged in it, and quite consistent with the glory of the French name, which has never shone more brightly than it did in the holy wars and in the defense of Religion."[8]

New Englanders and Virginians could not have more eloquently evoked their god for a war of extermination. In contrast to New England's "city upon a hill," however, the Catholic New Jerusalem promised little relief from the land hunger that might inspire pious men of small means to join the crusade, although Boucher tried to put a good face on it. "It must be admitted that . . . the prospects of our French colonies would be excellent if the fear of the Iroquois did not render their stay dangerous," he observed. "The soil is very productive; and, if the husbandman who cultivates it only labors with diligence, in a few years he will see himself not merely out of need, but at his ease—he, his wife, and his children." Indeed, "We see many such men who, having received a grant,—which can here be had for the asking,—in less than five or six years harvest enough grain to feed themselves with all their family, and even to sell some."[9] How those men were to support themselves and their families in the meantime, and what prospects there might be for future inheritance or wealth beyond mere subsistence, he could not say.

Pious would-be patriarchs, then, found little in La Nouvelle-France. For some pious women, however—French analogues of Anne Hutchinson—the story was different. The experiences of Marie Guyart, for instance, were extraordinary, but on a lesser scale shared by dozens of nuns and lay sisters who, like their male Jesuit counterparts, crossed the ocean to build a New Jerusalem. At age twenty, Guyart, a widow with a two-and-a-half-year-old son, experienced a religious conversion of an emotional intensity any English puritan would have envied (if the puritan could have given this "papist" credit for genuine spirituality). A series of visions and direct visitations by the Holy Spirit of the sort that got Hutchinson banished from Massachusetts led Guyart to abandon her son and join an Ursuline convent, where she took the name "Marie de l'Incarnation." Then, battling the contrary advice of family and male church authorities, she migrated to Québec, where in 1639 she established a convent and school for French and Native girls. From behind the iron grill that theoretically separated her cloistered existence from the world at large, she brilliantly managed the Ursulines' agricultural seigneury, carried on an extensive correspondence with her reconciled adult son and many prominent French people, and advised those who governed the colony. In these and countless other ways, Marie de l'Incarnation epitomized the stark contrast between her colonial society and the variant that English Protestant planter patriarchs were establishing to the south.

Yet still farther south, another variant that highlighted the oddity of the English model took shape. La Florida had developed in fits and starts since the massacre of the French Huguenots in 1565, and had done so with a remarkably small European population. Francis Drake's sacking of San Agustín in 1586 dealt the Spanish a severe blow. The next year all troops and colonists consolidated at San Agustín, and the marginally more prosperous northern settlement of Santa Elena on Parris Island was abandoned. Since the death of the *adelantado* Pedro Menéndez de Avilés in 1574, the Crown had assumed direct rule of the colony, through a procedure not unlike the *quo warranto* writs that revoked the privileges of the Virginia Company in 1624 and that threatened the Massachusetts Bay Company in 1637.

In contrast to the English examples, however, La Florida's royal takeover brought with it direct financial support from the Crown, in the form of an annual subsidy called the *situado,* typically about sixty-five thousand pesos, or £13,500 sterling per year. This was more than the value of five years' worth of Plymouth colony fur exports in the 1630s, but nothing compared to the annual profit that English crews earned from their share of the Grand Banks fisheries. Almost the entire lay male Florida population of roughly two thousand *peninsulares* (Spanish-born) and *criollos* (born in México or other colonies, approximately two-thirds of the total) were either government officials, soldiers, or people imported specifically to support the state apparatus.[10] All of these *floridanos* were encouraged to bring with them wives, children, and enslaved Africans. In such a situation, the main promise of wealth lay not in acquiring land but in finding ways to defraud the royal treasury or one's fellow colonists, who had to purchase supplies from officials and other middlemen funded by the *situado.*

And as had long been the case everywhere in the Spanish colonial world, everything depended on Native people's labor and food supplies. With respect to the local Timucuan-speaking communities, Menéndez de Avilés had initially resumed the strategy of divide-and-rule where the French of La Caroline had left off, allying himself with Outina against Saturiba. By 1568, after a series of poorly documented scorched-earth campaigns, he had conquered Saturiba's chiefdom and made Outina's and other Timucuan chiefdoms in the zone around San Agustín tributaries to the Spanish. Under agreements that Spaniards took great pains to describe as voluntary, Native chiefs the Spanish called caciques pledged their vassalage to the king, supplied annual allotments of maize and laborers to harvest Spanish fields, and allowed Franciscan missionaries to bap-

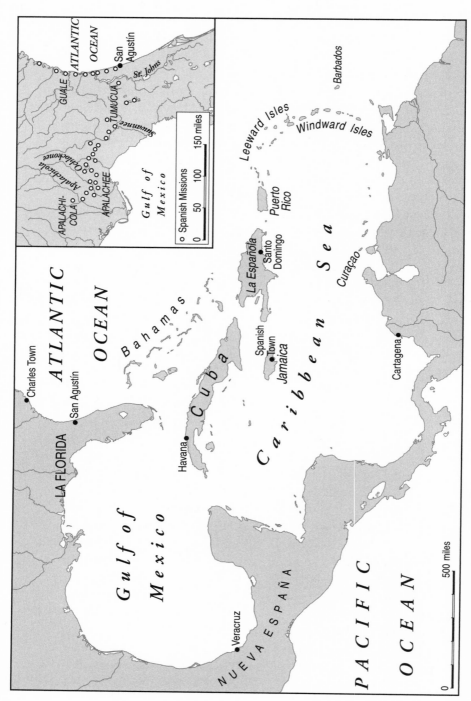

La Florida and the West Indies, c. 1670.

tize their people and instruct them in Christianity. The colonial governor distributed cloth, metal goods, beads, and other prestige goods in return, in effect inserting himself into the system as paramount chief.

Similar strategies—punctuated by the occasional brutal military campaign against "rebels" that made the later English campaigns against Powhatans and Pequots seem restrained—gradually extended the *pax hispanica* and Spanish paramountcy throughout the Timucuan-speaking area of the central Florida peninsula, northeastward to the Muskogean-speakers inhabiting what the Spanish called the province of Guale, and northwestward to what they called Apalachee and Apalachicola. Caciques profiting politically and economically from their ties with Europeans, manipulating military alliances to defeat their native enemies, and delivering material goods to their followers discovered independently the same successful strategies for working within a system of colonial power that counterparts such as Uncas and Massasoit were inventing at the same time a thousand miles to the north.

But in La Florida, it all took place on a much more massive scale than in New England. By midcentury, perhaps thirty-five thousand Native people had accepted, to one degree or another, Spanish suzerainty and Christianity in an arc of forty-four mission towns stretching from just south of today's Savannah, Georgia, to well west of today's Tallahassee, Florida.[11] La Florida's biracial colonial population, then, roughly equaled the European population of New England, yet with a far different demographic balance. As was the case nearly everywhere in Spanish America, the missions were run by the Franciscans, or Order of Friars Minor, founded by Francis of Assisi in the early thirteenth century. The gentle spirit of Christ-like poverty and respect for all God's creatures that Francis had taught had gone through many transformations over the centuries since the Middle Ages, and along the way Franciscans had become the constant companions of conquistadores, first in Iberia and then in Spain's Atlantic colonies. At their best, the Franciscans' insistence on the humanity of Native people and their zeal to spread the Gospel checked the excesses of *adelantados* and *encomienderos*. At their worst, their vows of poverty mutated into coerced material support from Native people and their piety into efforts to manage every detail of their converts' private lives and use floggings to enforce their moral demands. "Have you shown some part of your body to arouse in some person desires of lust or to excite them?" a manual for conducting confessions in a Timucuan language asked. "Have you had intercourse with someone contrary to the ordinary manner?"[12]

The enormous scale of the Franciscan enterprise in La Florida—a few dozen friars attempting to minister to tens of thousands of people speaking multiple languages spread over hundreds of miles—ensured that such intimate clerical control was usually impossible and that an overzealous padre was likely to inspire a violent revolt. In spiritual as well as temporal matters, the tiny number of Spanish colonizers, and La Florida's lack of a European agricultural economy with its accompanying land hunger, meant that, apart from occasional disputes over grazing ranges for Spanish cattle, Native people in La Florida could maintain their own agricultural and hunting practices and ignore many of the behavioral demands of missionary priests. Under these conditions, a colonial policy that envisioned a dominant *república de españoles* rigorously segregated from an inferior *república de indios* worked to empower local caciques—but only so far. Spanish military might was sufficient to brutally suppress rebellions against colonial rule that erupted in Guale in 1597 and 1645, in Apalachee in 1647, and in Timucua in 1656. As Native populations shrank steadily from disease, an uneasy truce between caciques and *floridanos* set in, epitomized by a series of Franciscan efforts to suppress the ceremonial ball play that Native people had performed since Mississippian times. Claiming to be convinced that Indians had stripped the practice of any spiritual significance, Spanish officials let the matter drop. Ball poles continued to share space with Crosses in Native towns.

A parallel story, but with a less peaceful ending, unfurled fifteen hundred miles to the west in what the Spanish called Nuevo México. Like La Florida, that colony began with a military conquest by a ruthless *adelantado,* Don Juan de Oñate. In the spring of 1598, the criollo Oñate led a little over one hundred troops, seven Franciscan missionaries, and more than three hundred fifty supporting colonists from México up the Río Grande Valley to the pueblos of diverse Keresan- and Tewa-speaking peoples. Here, as elsewhere in the Americas, dense concentrations of agricultural peoples living in towns promised a rich harvest of souls for the True Faith, a harvest difficult to imagine in the sparsely populated deserts of Northern Mexico. Legally, neither conquistadores nor the reading of the *requerimiento* still existed in the Spanish Empire, which since the promulgation of the New Laws of the Indies in 1542 had spoken instead of "pacification" and voluntary submission to Catholicism. Nonetheless, Oñate acted very much like his predecessors, assembling the leaders of pueblos to announce to them the virtues of submitting to Spanish authority and of embracing the Catholic religion, carefully recording what he claimed to be their serial agreements to become vassals of King Felipe II, and doling out *encomienda* labor rights to his fellow conquistadores.

Whatever Pueblo peoples may have made of these ceremonies, after Oñate took over one Tewa town as his headquarters, the Spaniards quickly wore out their welcome by stealing food and torturing, murdering, and raping all who got in their way. In this, Oñate's forces followed the footsteps of several previous criollo expeditions that, in recent years, had sought riches on México's far northern frontier—and explicitly violated viceregal instructions that emphasized peaceful conversion of the Natives. When people from Acoma Pueblo retaliated for the violence and the demands for food by killing Oñate's nephew and several other invaders, the *adelantado*'s men responded with a frontal assault on the high mesa on which Acoma stood. The Spaniards slaughtered eight hundred people outright, captured five hundred others, tried all those over age twelve for treason, sentenced the alleged rebels to slavery, and amputated one foot of each of the eighty adult males. This show of force—along with several others in the next couple of years—secured Spanish dominance, but the violence and Oñate's increasingly erratic behavior sent many colonists fleeing back to México. In 1606, the Crown took direct control of what was left of the colony and began a long legal proceeding that led to the revocation of all of Oñate's privileges in 1614.

Thereafter, under royal rule, Nuevo México became a landlocked, adobe-walled, weaker twin of La Florida. With an annual subsidy roughly half that of its eastern counterpart, and with supply lines stretching fifteen hundred miles overland to Ciudad de México (a six-month journey) rather than a short sail to Cuba, it would never in the seventeenth century be prosperous or secure. In about 1608—as English colonists were entering their second year at Jamestown and Samuel de Champlain was establishing Québec—the government relocated the Hispanic population from its occupied pueblo to a new settlement called Santa Fe. That town became Nuevo México's San Agustín, radiating diplomatic, economic, and religious influence outward to towns throughout the region. By 1630, some fifty pueblos, stretching along more than one hundred miles of the Río Grande, from Socorro in the south to Taos in the north, were to one degree or another under the Spanish hegemon. Intersecting the string of Río

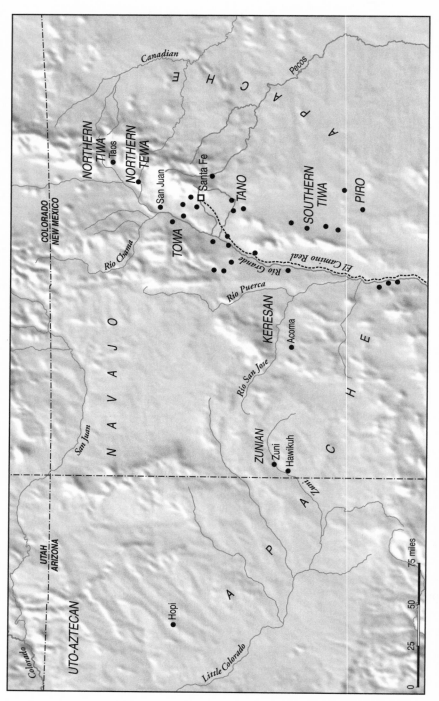

Nuevo México, c. 1670 (modern state boundaries are for orientation only).

Grande missions at midpoint, another line of missions ran, as one Franciscan missionary observed, like the base of a Cross two hundred fifty miles westward through Acoma and Zuni to Hopi. Santa Fe stood at the Cross's crowning eastern midpoint.

As was the case everywhere in mid-seventeenth-century Native America, the population of these communities declined rapidly from imported diseases. Of approximately eighty-six thousand Pueblos who met the Spanish in 1598, perhaps only thirty thousand remained alive in 1630 and only seventeen thousand by 1680. As in La Florida, the survivors owed labor and tribute payments to their priests, to the government, and to various colonists who had rights to *encomienda* and *repartimiento*. In exchange they received military protection, religious instruction, and the right to continue to live in their own homes. As one historian puts it, "intimidation was the key to Spanish authority."[13]

Confident of Spanish power, a Franciscan missionary took up residence in each major pueblo, inserted himself into the role of a Native shaman, and forced Native people into at least external conformity with Catholic notions of sexual and economic morality. Nuevo México's *república de indios* included an array of local Native officials in each pueblo—a *gobernadorcillo* (petty governor), a sheriff, church wardens, and others—but all tended to be handpicked by the priests. Like the Jesuits who spread out from La Nouvelle-France, and like their Franciscan counterparts in La Florida, the missionaries attracted such political followers because of their association with a valued European colonial power, because of their understanding of Native political structures, and, especially, because of the spiritual crisis provoked by warfare and epidemic disease.

Unlike the Jesuits, however, with a few notable exceptions the Franciscans of Nuevo México seldom bothered to learn Native languages (they relied on indigenous translators) and equally seldom hesitated to use force to impose their beliefs, smashing "idols," filling in kivas and building churches atop them, banning ball plays and sacred kachina dances, flogging the disobedient, and, ultimately, relying on the king's soldiers to ensure the triumph of the Faith. Local rebellions and even executions of friars—in 1632, 1639, 1643, 1647, and 1650—were always bloodily suppressed. Unsurprisingly, a Hopi term for a Spanish priest is *Tota'tsi*, meaning "tyrant," "dictator," "demanding person."[14] It is tempting to speculate that the entire experience summoned bitter memories of Chaco Canyon's tyranny.

Still, most Pueblo peoples, like their counterparts elsewhere, found economic and military reasons to continue their relationship with *nuevos mexicanos,* particularly as they confronted raids from Apache and Navajo enemies, who virtually surrounded them. Spaniards obliged by conducting slave-catching expeditions among the Pueblos' foes that provided the colony with its main profitable (if illegal) export to Ciudad de México. Yet the economic situation, and thus the basis of the relationship between Europeans and Indians, always remained perilous. At best, pack trains made the long journey to and from the south only once every three years, leaving outnumbered Hispanic colonists bereft of military support, perennially short of the goods that elsewhere bound Native people to European orbits, and embarrassingly impoverished apart from the food and cotton cloth they could extract from the Pueblos. Those extractions were oppressive indeed; beginning in 1643, the governor personally demanded a cotton blanket and roughly two bushels of maize from each adult, in addition to labor and tithes due to Franciscan friars and to various *encomienderos.* Such requisitions gave the Spanish control over nearly all food surpluses, leaving nothing for Native communities to exchange with each other.

The drain on Pueblo economic resources thus also disrupted their relations with neighboring Apache bands, with whom warfare had long alternated with exchanges of foodstuffs, medicinal herbs, hides, and prestige goods. At the same time that this trade was breaking down, the nomadic bands' increasing skill in taming horses (descended from animals long since escaped from México and gone feral) made their raiding more daring. For a time, poverty and fear of Apache raids opened space for Pueblo peoples to gain concessions and even to practice traditional rituals that the friars thought they had expunged. In light of their slave raiding, *nuevos mexicanos* were just as vulnerable to attack as were Pueblos, and so governors dared not push their subjects so hard as to drive them into the enemy's arms. Meantime, conflicts between governors and the clergy over the right to control Native labor paradoxically worked to the Natives' advantage.

The cumulative result was to erode the mystique of Spanish invulnerability on which the regime rested. Crisis stage arrived in the late 1660s and the 1670s. Beginning in 1666, four years of drought reduced Indians and Spaniards alike to starvation. Distress from the drought drove Apaches into ever-greater conflict with Pueblos; in 1673, for instance, raiders burned the Zuni community of Hawikuh to the ground, killing two hundred people and taking captive a thousand others, along with hundreds of domesticated animals. Hawikuh's friar also perished, as did several other missionaries in raids during the early 1670s, all with no effective Spanish response. Meantime, disease and famine continued.

In 1675, just as the Spanish regime was showing its inability to live up to its promises of protection in exchange for tribute and religious conformity, a new royal governor, Juan Francisco Treviño, arrived, intent on the final suppression of all forms of Native religious expression, from kachina dancing to gatherings in kivas, many of which he ordered destroyed. Three Pueblo holy men were tried and hanged for sorcery and sedition, another committed suicide before he could be executed, and forty-three others received public whippings and sentences of slavery. But even this show of force revealed the weakness of the Spanish regime. Shortly after the sentencing, seventy Native men—backed by many more hiding in the hills around Santa Fe—barged into Treviño's residence and threatened to kill him if he would not release the captives. When he gave in to their demands, he drove the last nail into the coffin of Spanish invincibility.

Among the men Treviño released was a figure from San Juan Pueblo known to his own people as "Pop'ay" and to the Spanish as "Popé." Moving to Taos, the northernmost pueblo and thus the farthest from Spanish authority, he and others began building a secret anti-Spanish coalition across thirty or more traditionally rivalrous communities. In bridging linguistic and political divides, Pop'ay and his allies drew upon three generations of common experiences with Franciscans and colonial governors, and the fact that at least some people in every pueblo spoke enough Spanish to communicate with each other. Mestizos and people of African descent may also have been involved. Because the colonizers did not learn of the plot until it had nearly matured, and because the plotters destroyed all of the parish records that held clues to political alignments in the pueblos, we will never know exactly who Pop'ay's followers were, whether indeed Pop'ay *was* the main leader or merely the one most visible to the Spanish, or what percentage of the population went along. We do know that assent was far from universal, both within and among the various communities. In at least two pueblos, the movement's opponents carried the day. Nonetheless, the basic outlines of the rebels' message were clear, and its appeal was widespread. Pueblo people, they said, must unite to "destroy the governor and all the Spaniards, so that the whole kingdom might be theirs" again; "they were saying that now God and Santa Maria were dead . . . and that their own God whom they obeyed had never died."[15]

Beginning on August 10, 1680—one day earlier than originally planned, because Pop'ay's opponents had revealed the plot to the Spanish—the rebels struck, burning ranches and churches, killing every Spaniard they could find, and paying particular attention to Franciscan friars, twenty-one of whom they executed. In at least one case, the executioners wore kachina masks to evoke the powers of the ancient spirits; in another, they forced a priest to ride naked on the back of a hog before they killed him. The total Hispanic death toll was about four hundred. Within a few days, more than two thousand Pueblo people laid siege to most of the surviving colonists at Santa Fe. The current governor, Antonio de Otermín, led a fierce assault that killed three hundred besiegers, captured nearly fifty more (all of them promptly executed), and sent the remainder fleeing. Nevertheless, nursing arrow wounds to his face and chest, Otermín realized that his situation was untenable and led a retreat that carried fifteen hundred people—most of them Indian servants, Native converts, and mestizos—to El Paso. For the next twelve years, as rebellions spread throughout Native communities on Spain's northern frontiers, Nuevo México ceased to exist as a colony, except on Spanish maps.

If Nuevo México was the weakest link in Spain's imperial domains, the Caribbean basin was its strongest. Yet a quarter-century earlier and thousands of miles away from Pop'ay and his followers, another religious zealot had imagined this space as the target of an even more audacious assault on Spanish Catholics, an even more dramatic transformation of Spanish cartography, and yet another counterpoint to the visions of New England's and Virginia's planters. In 1653, the hot Protestant Oliver Cromwell was at the height of his power in the British Isles. Four years of fighting had at last seemingly conquered all of Ireland, a goal that had eluded a century's worth of English kings, conquistadores, and planters. Also subdued were Scotland—where the political leadership had never acknowledged the legitimacy of the execution of King Charles I, and where his son Charles II had briefly sat on the throne—and opponents in England itself, with the dismissal of Parliament and the proclamation of Cromwell as Lord

Protector. Only one obstacle stood between him and a final assault on the current occupant of the throne, whom Protestants had long associated with the Antichrist: Felipe IV of Spain.

Since 1652, Cromwell's England had been at war with its fellow Calvinist and nonmonarchical power, the United Provinces of the Netherlands. The roots of the conflict between the two longtime allies in Europe's religious wars were complex. During the English Civil Wars, Frederik Hendrik, the Dutch stadtholder, had earned Cromwell's enmity by financially supporting Charles I. In large part, this was dynastic politics, for Frederik Hendrik's son and heir, the future Willem II of Orange, had been married to Charles I's daughter, Mary, when he was fourteen and she nine. The marriage was not consummated—the 1641 wedding night involved a bed equipped with multiple sheets and an elaborately stitched double pair of shirts that kept the teenage boy's virtue confined—until after the English civil wars began and young Mary fled to the Netherlands with her mother. After Frederik Hendrik's death, when Willem II attempted to transform the office of stadtholder into a military dictatorship (much as Cromwell was doing in England), his Dutch opponents sought the Lord Protector's aid, offering as an enticement vague talk of some sort of political union. Before Cromwell could respond, Willem II died, leaving as heir a posthumous infant son, also named Willem, who was thus a grandson of the deposed king of England.

Infants could hardly lead troops and thus could not be elected stadtholders—although the members of House Orange acted as if the office should be hereditary. Complicated political maneuvers in the various Dutch provinces in effect abolished the stadtholdership and turned the Netherlands into a confederation of republics that much resembled Commonwealth England before Cromwell became Lord Protector. With the Orange-Stuart alliance out of the way, the States General—the United Provinces' counterpart to England's Parliament—recognized England's revolutionary regime in 1651. Much to the surprise of the Dutch, Cromwell responded by sending a delegation to negotiate terms for a political union with the Netherlands, for a joint religious war against the Spanish Catholics, and for a carving up of the world's trades and colonies into an English sphere in the Americas and a Dutch sphere in Africa and Asia—a sort of Protestant version of the post-Columbian Treaty of Tordesillas, which had divided the earth between Spain and Portugal.

In this attempted anti-Catholic crusade, Cromwell envisioned himself as perhaps the last of the great conquistadores, seeking more to win the world for the Protestant god than merely to enrich the nation and his followers. When Dutch leaders—whose East India Company had already conquered much of the Portuguese empire, and whose West India Company was not about to yield its lucrative Atlantic carrying trades to the English—refused the deal, Cromwell and his allies in the Rump Parliament began to see the Netherlands as perfidiously addicted to wealth and insufficiently devoted to the Protestant cause.

Determined that England should carry on the anti-Catholic crusade alone, in 1651 the Rump passed an act entitled "For the Increase of the Shipping and the Encouragement of the Navigation of This Nation": no commodities produced in Asia, Africa, or the Americas were to be imported into England or its possessions except in ships owned by people of England or its colonies, and European goods could be imported only in English ships or in ships belonging to the country of the items' origin.[16] Since the Netherlands produced almost nothing of their own for export, this "Navigation Act" effectively banned Dutch merchants from the commerce of England and its colonial outposts. Cromwell demonstrated that he meant business by unleashing privateers around the globe. They seized more than a hundred Dutch vessels alleged to be violating the act. The sea war ended with the Treaty of Westminster of 1654, by which the Netherlands, on paper at least, agreed to respect the Navigation Act.

This truce allowed Cromwell and his English allies to refocus on the papists. In the negotiations leading up to the Treaty of Westminster, Cromwell had again unsuccessfully proposed union with the Netherlands, and as early as 1651 a printed defense of the Navigation Act had tried to emphasize the real hierarchy of England's foes. "It hath been a thing for many years generally received, That the Design of *Spain* . . . is, to get the Universal Monarchie of Christendom," its author wrote. "Nor is it a thing less true (how little soever observed) that our Neighbours [the *Dutch*] . . . have, likewise, for som years, aimed to laie a foundation to themselvs for ingrossing the Universal Trade, not onely of Christendom, but indeed, of the greater part of the known world."[17] For Cromwell, a Catholic "Universal Monarchie" was a greater threat than a Dutch "Universal Trade." Having dismissed Parliament, with its advocates of war with the Netherlands, and made the Treaty of Westminster, he returned to the main threat. A great blow against Spain would secure England's, and the world's, Protestant revolution once and for all.

With a combination of great secrecy and greater hubris, then, planning began for a "Western Design" that would expel Spanish papists from the Americas. The first step would be the conquest of the islands of La Española, Puerto Rico, and Cuba and of the mainland port of Cartagena, in what today is Colombia. All of this and more seemed possible in light of God's undoubted support for the undertaking, of the great victories won by Cromwell's New Model Army in the English, Scottish, and Irish civil wars, of the expectation that enslaved Africans would welcome the English as liberators, of the ease with which Francis Drake had conquered Spanish possessions two generations earlier, and of the relative success that English naval forces had enjoyed recently against the Dutch. So confident were the planners, that some officers and men brought their wives along to watch the glory unfold when God's Protestant servants, as former Plymouth colony governor Edward Winslow put it, "execute[d] his determined vengeance upon that tyrannous and idolatrous and bloudy nation that hath inflicted so many cruelties upon the nations of the earth."[18]

Winslow was one of five civilians whom Cromwell deputed to oversee the recolonization of the conquests, once the Western Design had been carried out. The military campaign was under the joint command of Admiral William Penn and General Robert Venables, who had distinguished themselves in Cromwell's Irish campaigns and in other ways as godly supporters of the Lord Protector's cause. In late 1654 and early 1655, Penn and Venables assembled more than fifty ships (sixteen of them seized from Dutch violators of the Navigation Act in the West Indies) and nine thousand men. About a third of the troops sailed from England. Most of the rest were recruited from landless small planters and servants, first from Barbados and then the English colonies in the Leeward Islands, where the armada was completed. Venables offered the servants freedom in exchange for enlistment. Like conquistadores before them, all probably hoped to be rewarded with their share of conquered land.[19]

In April 1655, the fleet of the Western Design reached its first and most important target, La Española. This was no poorly supplied and understaffed Nuevo México, but one of the most densely settled of Spain's possessions in the heart of its Caribbean domains, a place that combined the strengths of Spanish imperialism with those of the heavily populated colonies that the English were creating elsewhere. Probable failure became inevitable disaster when Penn misjudged his landing spot, requiring the army to march overland for several days with little food and water before even trying to attack the capital of Santo Domingo. "Those who took upon them to conduct the Army in the most commodious wayes and passages near water, proved but blinde guides, and deceived them," a contemporary complained. As a result, "some became exceeding faint, scant able to march, (others were necessitated to drink their own Urine) and all in generall so extreamly weakened, that it was wonderfull to behold." The same chronicler reported that, during the most deadly of several ambushes that the troops stumbled into during their attempts on the capital and a nearby fort, eight hundred men died and nearly three hundred were injured, "whereof many were past recovery, most of them all receiving their hurts in the back parts"—presumably because they ran from the battle. In three horrific weeks, a total of perhaps seventeen hundred men perished.[20]

At last, Venables gave up and decided to attack next-door Jamaica instead. Things hardly went much better on that lightly populated island, where most Hispanic residents dispersed to the hills and allowed the English to die of malnutrition and intestinal diseases. (Winslow succumbed en route to the island.) Within ten months, five thousand of the seven thousand English who had survived La Española perished on Jamaica, with little to show for it but control of the capital city, renamed "Spanish Town." The colony's governor quickly surrendered, but it would take five more years before the Hispanic population in the countryside could be expelled or pacified. The African slaves who were supposed to welcome the English as liberators instead often fought alongside the Spanish or fled into the hills, where they established "maroon" communities that the new rulers never did succeed in subduing.

Nonetheless, for all its failures, the conquest of Jamaica in 1655 "marked a signal moment in the development of an English imperial vision. For the first time the state captured the colony of a rival European power."[21] In the Western Design and through the Navigation Act, agents of the English government itself—not decentralized freelance *adelantados,* traders, or planters—articulated a new, and occasionally coherent, vision for an expansionist Atlantic empire of a sort only its Spanish rival had previously created.

Cromwell did not long outlive his failed but nonetheless transformative Western Design, nor could he have imagined the even more transformative developments that followed his death. Beginning in 1660, through a course of events no one in 1642 or even 1652 could have foreseen, the

Crown, the House of Lords, and the Church of England with its bishops and prayer books were all restored, with Charles II, son of the executed king, sitting on the thrones of his Three resurrected Kingdoms of England, Scotland, and Ireland. The overwhelming majority of the political elite seemed to have rejected everything that Cromwell and his revolution stood for. Much more than the Crown was restored in Restoration England—or so many hoped.

But at least one thing remained unchanged: the centralized approach to state-sponsored imperial expansion forged in Cromwell's Western Design. One of the first moves of the restored Crown and English Parliament was to pass a strengthened version of the 1651 Navigation Act, which added to the clauses restricting trade to English ships a short list of "enumerated goods"—commodities produced in the colonies that could be transported only to England, Ireland, or other colonial ports; among these were tobacco, sugar, cotton, and certain dyestuffs used for the production of textiles. In 1663, a "Staple Act" asserted similar control over commodities moving in the opposite direction. With a few exceptions, European products headed for the colonies were now to be transshipped from England, rather than exported directly.

That same year saw another direct English assault on Spain's colonial possessions. In September 1663, on the coast of La Florida not far from the site of ill-fated La Caroline, an exploratory party from Barbados encountered a group of Native people. The Indians spoke "many *Spanish* words, as *Cappitan, Commarado,* and *Adues*"; they were familiar with firearms; and they were "as little startled at the firing of a Peece of Ordnance, as he that hath been used to them many years." Reporting that "the nearest *Spanyards* were at St. *Augustins,* and [that] several of them had been there, which as they said was but ten days journey," they eyed the opportunities that trade with the newcomers promised.[22] Perhaps in 1655 and 1656 they had participated in a series of events sparked by Cromwell's Western Design but unknown to any of the English. Fearful that the English fleet would attack the mainland, Governor Diego de Robolledo had demanded that the Timucuas of the mission communities mobilize their warriors for La Florida's defense. Caciques incensed at receiving orders rather than being negotiated with—at being treated as inferiors rather than as members of the *república de indios*—rallied their people to armed resistance. As they had in the past, the Spanish governor's troops quashed the uprising and publicly executed its leaders. Caciques and *floridanos* returned to the uneasy truce that had long defined their relationship. But the Timucua revolt of 1656 demonstrated that, more than the English knew, La Florida was ripe for the picking.

The exploratory party from Barbados who met the Spanish-speaking Indians had been sent to pick that fruit. In 1663 the restored English king issued a patent to a group of eight proprietors for a huge tract of La Florida henceforth to be known as "Carolina . . . so called in honour of His Sacred Majesty that now is, *Charles the Second.*"[23] All of the grantees were being rewarded for their service to the Stuart family. The organizing force behind the project, prominent Barbadian planter Sir John Colleton, had fought in the civil wars before emigrating to the West Indies. Anthony Ashley Cooper (later known as the Earl of Shaftsbury) and George Monck, Duke of Albemarle, though prominent in the Cromwell regime, had been influential in returning Charles to the throne. Sir William Berkeley had recently regained the governorship of Virginia. Courtiers John Lord Berkeley, Sir George Carteret, Edward Hyde, Earl of Clarendon, and William Earl of Craven had remained with the royals throughout the Interregnum.

In 1669, Cooper and John Locke drafted a gloriously impractical document called *The Fundamental Constitutions of Carolina,* which utterly repudiated both the republicanism of the Cromwell regime and the social vision of the planter regimes created by men of small means elsewhere in North America. "That the Government of this Province may be made most agreeable to the *Monarchy* under which we live . . . and that we may avoid erecting a numerous *Democracy,*" *The Fundamental Constitutions* imagined a province dominated by three species of hereditary nobility. At the pinnacle would be the eight proprietors and their heirs, each bedecked with a suitably lofty title and ruling the colony collectively as the "Palatine's Court." (In medieval English law, a "palatine"—a high-level official attached to imperial courts since Roman times—ruled with virtually all the powers of royalty.) Beneath the Palatines would be one "Landgrave" and two "Cassiques" for each of twelve "Counties": the first title evoked Anglo-Saxon counts; the second, the Native chiefs of La Florida. The lands of each county would be divided into "eight *Signiories,* eight *Baronies,* and four *Precincts,*" with each of the latter in turn comprising "six *Colonies*" of twelve thousand acres. All the signiories would belong to the proprietors, the baronies to the landgraves and cassiques, and the precincts and their colonies to more common folk. Any commoner fortunate enough to acquire three thousand to twelve thousand acres might be designated lord of a manor and could claim—like the nobility—the right to "hold *Court-Leet* there, for Trying of all Causes both Civil and Criminal." Most fantastically, *The Fundamental Constitutions* imagined that ordinary immigrants would voluntarily enroll in a sort of hereditary serfdom that would be more restrictive than the forms of tenure that still prevailed on some English manors. As a *"Leet-man* or *Leet-woman,"* an immigrant of this type would be denied "liberty to go off from the Land of their particular Lord, and live any where else, without Licence obtained from their said Lord." Land in free and common socage for men of small means was nowhere in the picture. That privilege belonged only to the elite.[24]

Nor was the kind of religious regime that planters dominated in Massachusetts congregations or Virginia vestries. While pledging "to take care for the building of *Churches,* and the publick Maintenance of *Divines,* to be employed in the Exercise of *Religion,* according to the *Church of England,* which being the onely true and *Orthodox,* and the National *Religion* of all the King's Dominions," the authors of *The Fundamental Constitutions* envisioned a degree of religious toleration exceeded perhaps only by Rhode Island among the existing English colonies. "That *Jews, Heathens,* and other *Dissenters* from the purity of *Christian Religion,* may not be scared and kept at a distance from it, but . . . may by *good usage* and *perswasion* . . . be won over to embrace, and unfeignedly receive the *Truth,"* *The Fundamental Constitutions* proposed that "any seven, or more Persons agreeing in any *Religion,* shall Constitute a *Church* or *Profession,"* so long as the group registered with the authorities in their precinct. No one—not even an enslaved person—was to be persecuted for his or her religious beliefs, although it was also made clear that "no *Slave* shall hereby be exempted from that *Civil Dominion* his Master hath over him" and that "every *Freeman* of *Carolina* shall have absolute Power and Authority over his *Negro Slaves.*"[25]

The small number of English people who had already settled in Carolina eagerly embraced their authority over the bodies of the enslaved, but, caught up in alternative dreams of free and common socage, they resisted nearly every other aspect of *The Fundamental Constitutions.* The document never fully went into effect. Nonetheless, for all their extravagance, the proprietors' dreams for Carolina represented major currents in a new wave of imperialism unleashed by the restoration of the English Crown—currents that threatened not just the Spanish and Dutch empires, but the interests of English planters everywhere. The Restoration was no mere local phenomenon of the British Isles. It profoundly, violently transformed North America and its many peoples, natives and newcomers alike.

Imperialists

IMPE´RIAL. *adj.* [*imperial,* French; *imperialis,* Latin].
1. Royal; possessing royalty . . .
2. Betokening royalty; marking sovereignty . . .
3. Belonging to an emperor or monarch; regal; royal; monarchical.

IMPE´RIALIST. *n.s.* [from *imperial*]. One that belongs to an emperor.

— Samuel Johnson, *A Dictionary of the English Language* (London, 1755)

TEN

Monarchical Power Reborn

IN THE STREETS OF LONDON or the rooms of Whitehall Palace, as people plotted for power and status in the restored court of Charles II or
scurried to avoid imprisonment or death for their role in what was now
considered the murder of their legitimate king, the American colonies remained far from the center of anyone's attention. Nonetheless, the Restoration transformed North American power relationships among European
states, their colonial subjects, and their Native American neighbors. Beginning in the 1660s, England, rapidly followed by France, took steps that
Castilian monarchies had long since accomplished in their century-older
empire, subordinating freelance *adelantados* to centralized control by an
imperial state embodied in the person of the monarch. Novel as these
efforts were, they nonetheless spawned grand atavistic visions in which
English and French courtiers imagined themselves reaping wealth and
power from North American domains. The imperialists' visions clashed
with those of the English small-planter regimes already established in
North America. And imperialists and planters alike found themselves on a
collision course with Native American and Dutch traders and the relationships they had forged with each other. Everywhere earlier ways were under assault simultaneously from within and without, as a new monarchical
landscape began to form.

Those who dreamed of empire in Restoration England were often confused, when they were not contradictory. In some quarters—epitomized

by *The Fundamental Constitutions*—a fanciful ideal of hyper-feudalism took hold, inspired in part by the rediscovery of the legal writings of the thirteenth-century legal scholar Henry de Bracton, but largely by royalist reaction to the perceived democratic excesses of the Cromwellian era. As the complicated scheme of religious toleration proposed for Carolina suggests, spiritual questions that had bedeviled England for generations also were crucial. More often, however, hardheaded calculations about the exercise of power, the extraction of revenue, and the structure of the State took precedence.

Restoration-era imperialism found its roots in the politics surrounding the court of Charles II, where, as had been the case since the days of the conquistadores, state building and imperial expansion were inseparable. Religious uniformity, state centralization, and personal rule without Parliament—the central issues of Charles I's prerevolutionary reign—had not exactly been abandoned by his elder son, Charles II. They certainly were not by his younger son, James, duke of York and Albany, who would push the old Stuart agenda relentlessly during his brother's reign, and disastrously in his own brief kingship as James VII and II, from 1685 to 1688. Yet as the Stuarts navigated tricky political waters at home and tried to make decisions about England's North American colonies, it became clear that the old trinity of related issues had mutated almost beyond recognition since the 1640s.

When Charles II returned to power in 1660, he and many of his subjects may simply have been "longing that . . . wounds which have so many years together been kept bleeding, may be bound up." The phrase comes from the Declaration of Breda, issued on the eve of the king's triumphant reentry to his kingdoms, a document whose very existence showed the impossibility of pretending that Oliver Cromwell had never lived or that the pre-civil-war doctrine of a "free monarchy" could be restored. Despite a modest bow to divine right—"we can never give over hope in good time to obtain the Possession of that Right which GOD and Nature hath made our due"—the Declaration of Breda not-so-tacitly admitted that the Restoration occurred only at the sufferance of the reconstituted Parliament elected amid the chaos that followed Cromwell's death. Even the "full and generall Pardon" that Charles offered his wayward subjects had to exclude "such Persons as shall hereafter be excepted by Parliament." The same caveat applied to the second major promise made by the Declaration of Breda: that subjects would enjoy "a Liberty to Tender Consciences, and that no man shall be disquieted or called in question for differences of opinion in matters of Religion, which do not disturb the Peace of the Kingdom." Religious toleration, like royal pardon, depended on "an Act of Parliament . . . granting that indulgence."[1] And it would be an indulgence, not a right.

The vexed question of religious uniformity or toleration remained inseparable from countless other issues. Charles II's own religious views remained opaque. Many said he had none. Others suspected him of inheriting his mother's Catholicism and flirting with the Crown of France to bring England and Scotland back into the fold of Rome. The flirting did take place, although not until a decade after the Restoration. And Charles did convert to Catholicism at some point, although the official story was that he did so only on his deathbed in 1685. His brother James refused to take Communion in the Church of England at Christmas in 1672, openly converted to Rome in 1676, and made no secret thereafter of his intent to reintroduce "papist" worship to England. Yet in 1660, all this lay in the future. Whatever the case, Charles seems to have been sincere in his belief that, within limits, religious toleration was vital to political stability. In this, he and many of his closest advisors were embracing something like the status quo of Cromwell's Protectorate, in which a Calvinist state establishment unable to enforce a single mode of organization and practice had coexisted with liberty of conscience for most other kinds of Protestants, except those who publicly used the Book of Common Prayer.

There was little doubt that the Prayer Book would be reintroduced. It was republished in slightly revised form in 1662, with "King Charles Martyr" added to its calendar of saints as an unambiguous message to the puritans who had killed their monarch. Bishops, too, resumed their place both in the Church hierarchy and in the House of Lords. The same was true even in Scotland, where Charles insisted on reintroducing the hierarchy that had been so roundly hated by Covenanters in his father's time.

Yet if Charles imagined that somehow all of this could be made compatible with liberty of conscience, he would be thwarted at every turn by those in the English Parliament who disagreed with their monarch. The group that came to be known as "Anglican Royalists" were not exactly latter-day Laudians (they embraced a variety of viewpoints on the fine points of predestination theology), but they fervently insisted on conformity to the state Church and did everything in their power to stamp out Presbyterians, other puritans, Quakers, Baptists, and all the sectaries whom they blamed for all the chaos of the previous two decades. Such deluded people had, proclaimed one clergyman in 1662, led their country down a slippery slope. "At first they had only some small matter to object against our Bishops, our Liturgie, the manner of our Administring Baptisme, receiving the Holy Communion, and against our Ecclesiastical Discipline," he said. "In the end have not some or other of them come to that passe as to reject all manner of Ministers, all manner of Liturgies, even to the Lords Prayer, the Creed, and the ten Commandments; absolutely to condemn Infant Baptisme, and the Celebrating of the Lords Supper . . . : and finally (under pretence of maintaining their Christian liberty) to make themselves right *Independents* in all things?" No one had ever better summed up the anarchy inherent in Protestantism. And no one had ever more fervently called on the faithful to "wholly strip your selves of the spirit of contention" and "submit your selves with all humility unto that publick order which you find established in the Church of God in this Kingdome."[2]

So, despite the Declaration of Breda, persecution resumed of those who refused to use the Prayer Book, to see ministers wear the surplice while doing so, or to engage in other behaviors that puritans found so objectionable a generation earlier. A series of events after the Restoration accelerated the crackdown. In 1661, a religious radical named Thomas Venner, who had previously led an uprising against Cromwell, had sparked a four-day London revolt that allegedly wanted to replace King Charles with King Jesus. Venner and many of his followers were hanged, drawn, and quartered, but the lessons of too much religious liberty seemed plain. Four years later, one hundred thousand Londoners perished from bubonic plague; and a year after that, much of the city was consumed in the Great Fire of 1666. More than a few attributed the first disaster to God's punishment of his sinful disorderly people, and the second to some dark plot by Catholics.

All of these events played into the hands of those who wanted to stamp out heresy and ensure conformity to the state Church. In part, the Anglican Royalists waged a grudge match against their political and religious opponents. Many were also seriously convinced that the Stuarts wanted to use liberty of conscience to allow "papists" to infect the country. But mostly they believed, as their ancestors had done, that a single, coherent state Church was essential to social and political peace. Good order must be restored, in ceremony as well as soul, in church as well as state, in bishops as well as in kings. The hierarchical faith of the Anglican Royalists exceeded that of the royal family itself.

Yet, ironically, restoring the Church of England also promised to reverse some of the oppressive centralization of Cromwell's state by resurrecting the right of local grandees to appoint parish clergy, whose political messages they hoped to control. (In this, Anglican Royalists perhaps forgot how Elizabethan puritans had earlier used the same "impropriation" device to spread their subversion.) The purge of local dissent and vestiges of the Cromwellian regime went far beyond pulpits and pews. In 1661, Parliament passed the Corporation Act, which required officers of cities, boroughs, and other chartered political corporate bodies not only to swear allegiance to the king but to renounce the Solemn League and Covenant and to receive Communion according to the Book of Common Prayer at least once a year. This statute was followed in 1662 by the Act of Uniformity, which required all clergy to use the Book of Common Prayer and deposed nearly a thousand dissenters from their pulpits; the Conventicle Act of 1664, which outlawed unauthorized meetings of worshipers; and the Five Mile Act of 1665, which warned deposed dissenting clergy to move at least that far from their former postings. The latter two laws proved almost impossible to enforce, but clearly the Anglican Royalists had no intention of embracing the toleration promised by the Declaration of Breda, any more than they would allow a return of republicanism.

As had been the case under Archbishop Laud and Charles I, those who challenged the hard religious line—and they now included the royal family and its closest courtiers—transferred some of their hopes for relief to the Atlantic colonies. Thus *The Fundamental Constitutions of Carolina* envisioned a future where liberty of conscience might flourish without pesky interference from parliamentary representative institutions dominated by religious fanatics. Yet Restoration imperialism's focus on the colonies embraced far more than debates over toleration or conformity to the Book of Common Prayer.

Like all European kings, Charles II desperately needed independent sources of revenue. Unlike most European kings, he had few such sources at his disposal, despite lifetime parliamentary grants of £1.2 million in tax revenue from England and £40,000 from Scotland. In England, especially, most of the income from lands, fees, and perquisites that Charles I had milked through his "Thorough" policy of enforcing royal privileges had been swept away by the revolution and never restored. On the contrary, in

December 1660 Parliament passed an act that abolished all forms of land tenure other than common socage, along with all vestiges of feudal monetary obligations to the Crown. Meantime, dozens of courtiers who had stuck with the Stuarts during the Interregnum or paved the way for their return to the throne awaited proper rewards and repayment of loans and other debts. Great merchants in London—Anglican Royalists and especially those who were not—had to be kept happy if Parliament was to be managed, additional tax revenues raised, and the monarchy secured on its restored throne.

Thus, the royal family and politically influential groups all over the political spectrum came to embrace one of the great revenue-generating state-building projects of the despised Cromwellian regime: economic and military warfare against the Netherlands. The scramble to seize trade, wealth, and tax revenue from England's rival across the North Sea proved perhaps the only unifying political issue of the fractious Restoration period; despite their Cromwellian antecedents, the anti-Dutch Navigation Acts of 1660 and 1663 were almost universally acclaimed in the capital. The Crown adored them because customs revenues from foreign trade redirected from the Netherlands to the British Isles flowed directly to its coffers, and nothing prevented individual royal family members from engaging directly in trading companies granted Crown monopolies. Merchants whose profits from the trades seized from the Dutch would make the taxes more than worthwhile readily scrambled aboard, seeking their own monopoly privileges if possible, and hypocritically arguing for free trade when the privileges went to competitors. Anglican Royalists joined the cause by embracing the idea that the Dutch, with their pretensions to a universal monopoly on trade and their pernicious combination of nonmonarchical government and Calvinist religion, were the prime international threat to all that the Restoration stood for. That the current Willem of Orange—Charles I's grandson and Charles II's nephew—continued to be denied his rightful place as stadtholder compounded the Dutch republican crime.

England's Restoration empire, then, would not be built from scratch; it would be conquered from the Netherlands. No one understood the political and economic benefits of seizing Dutch wealth better than the king's brother, James, duke of York. And no source of that wealth seemed more lucrative than the trade in enslaved Africans that the Dutch had dominated for a generation. Charles II, in the year he took the throne, signed a charter for the "Company of Royal Adventurers into Africa," in which James, numerous other members of the royal family, and four future Carolina proprietors—the duke of Albemarle, the earl of Craven, John Lord Berkeley, and Sir George Carteret—were principal investors. Initially focused, like the Guinea Company before it, on the trade for gold that gave its name to the coins called "guineas," the Adventurers quickly turned to the commerce in human beings. In 1663, when the operation reorganized as the Royal African Company, with James as its governor, or chief executive, its new charter gave it a monopoly on "the whole entire and only trade . . . for the buying and selling bartering and exchanging of for or with any negroes slaves goods wares and merchandises whatsoever."[3] By 1665, at least a quarter of its revenues of £400,000 came from slaving, and this, said an official company document, was a good thing. "The trade of Africa is so necessary to England, that the very being of the Plantations depend upon the welfare of itt," the company argued, "for they must be utterly ruined, if they either want supply of Negro servants for their worke, or be forced to receive them at Excessive rates."[4] That the virtues of slaving were preached by the *Royal* African Company suggests the trade's role in generating revenue independently from Parliament. That the brother of the king and heir to the throne stood at the company's head testified to the importance of slave labor to royal power. So too did the brand "DY" said to be burned into the flesh of the people the duke of York's company sold.

But the African Company was only one of many ways in which the duke and his circle hoped to capitalize on Atlantic trade in general and competition with the Dutch in particular. In the 1660s, James was governor not just of the Adventurers into Africa but of another anti-Dutch enterprise called the Company of the Royal Fishery of England (of which five Carolina proprietors were also members). He was also a major investor in the English East India Company and Lord High Admiral of England, which further placed him in the front lines of the battle for control of seaborne trade. In March 1664, the duke took on one more important role in the cause when he became sole proprietor of a vast domain in North America that embraced, according to his patent from his royal brother,

all that part of the maine Land of New England, begining at a Certaine place called or knowne by the name of St. Croix next adjoyning to new

Scotland [Nova Scotia] in America, and from thence extending along the
Sea Coast, unto a certaine place called Petuaquine or Pemaquid, and so up
the River thereof . . . , to the River of Kinebequi, and so upwards by the
Shortest Course to the river of Canada Northward, And also all that Island
or Islands commonly called by the severall name or names of Matowacks
or Long Island . . . , together also with . . . Hudsons River and all the Land
from the west side of Conecticutt, to the east side of Delaware Bay, And
also all those severall Islands called or knowne by the names of Martins
Vinyard and . . . Nantukett.[5]

In other words, the duke now owned what Dutch trespassers on soil long
claimed by the English Crown presumed to call Nieu Nederlandt, and it
was his job to return it to its rightful possessors. As a committee advising
the king had put it in 1663, the nation could "no longer sustain the intolerable disgrace done to his Majesty . . . by the Intrusion of such monsters
and the exceeding damage to his subjects by this bold usurper," the Netherlands.[6]

English imperial bellicosity went far beyond such words. In 1663 and
1664, a Royal African Company fleet captured most of the Dutch West India Company's trading posts on the Gold Coast of West Africa. In 1664,
four ships carrying three hundred troops under the command of the
duke's lieutenant governor, Richard Nicolls (a member of the Royal African Company), sailed to what was now called New York. Reinforced with a
substantial militia from the English settlements on Long Island recruited
by Connecticut governor John Winthrop Jr., Nicolls soon surrounded the
town of Nieuw Amsterdam by sea and land. Dutch director general Petrus
Stuyvesant tried to prepare for battle, despite the handicaps of an ill-
maintained fort and a mere one hundred fifty trained soldiers at his command. But the population had little stomach for a fight that promised only
"misery, sorrow, conflagration, the dishonor of women, murdered children
in their cradles, and, in a word, the absolute ruin and destruction of about
fifteen hundred innocent souls."[7]

Nicolls offered generous terms, and, through the mediation of Winthrop, Stuyvesant surrendered without a shot being fired. Upriver from
the rechristened city of New York, at Fort Orange, a similarly bloodless
surrender allowed Nicolls's subordinate Sir George Cartwright to rechristen the place Albany, after one of the duke's hereditary titles. The only violence occurred at the other end of Nieu Nederlandt, along the Delaware

River. Disobeying Nicolls's orders, troops under Sir Robert Carr plundered the town of New Amstel (soon renamed New Castle) when its governor failed to surrender immediately. At least three people were killed and ten wounded, with the surviving Dutch soldiers apparently sold into slavery in Virginia.

By 1667, when the Second Anglo-Dutch War, which these actions in North America and West Africa provoked, ended with a treaty confirming England's possession of New York, several core principles of Restoration-era English imperialism had become clear: the capture of English colonial commerce through the Navigation Acts and the expulsion of the Dutch from North American ports so that, as King Charles put it in his instructions to Nicolls, they "may noe longer ingrosse and exercise that trade which they have wrongfully possessed themselves of"; the creation of a secure English source of enslaved African labor for plantation economies; the establishment of an unbroken line of North American colonies encroaching on the Spanish to the south and the French to the north; and, not least, the personal enrichment of the duke and the powerful circle of courtiers who formed the interlocking directorates of the various companies and proprietorships that carried out the program.[8] James himself anticipated substantial profits from his new proprietary colony, including at least £10,000 per year in customs revenues from the furs and other commodities exported from New York. This would be a drop in the bucket for a man who spent nearly a quarter-million per year to live in the way a king's brother should, but enough to make a significant dent in annual deficits approaching £30,000, particularly when combined with rents, fees, taxes, and other emoluments from the European colonists already living in New York.[9]

Still, James kept personally only a portion of his sweeping North American conquest. Several courtiers received potentially lucrative estates that —in acreage at least—outstripped anything previously bestowed on royal favorites in Ireland or elsewhere. John Berkeley and George Carteret were among the planners of the Nicolls expedition, and, even before it sailed, they had been rewarded with proprietary land rights to the portions of Nieu Nederlandt that became East and West New Jersey. Intended, as Carolina was later, to be peopled with obedient tenants, the Jerseys promised (although they would never deliver) wealth beyond measure. Such promises particularly appealed to a group of would-be Scottish lairds who purchased proprietary shares in East Jersey during the late seventeenth

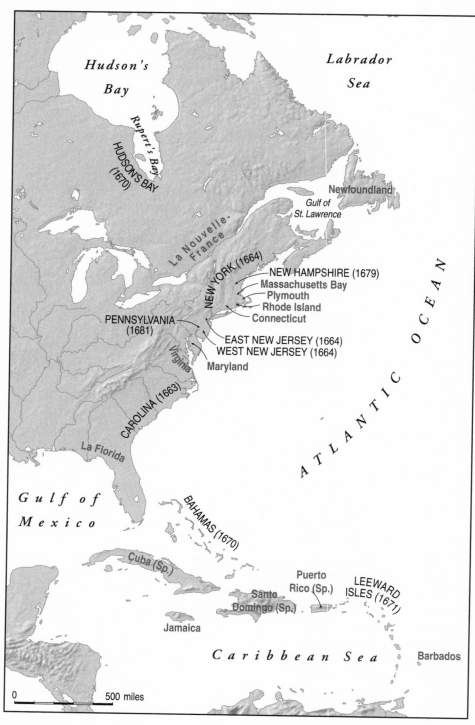

Hudson's
Bay

Labrador
Sea

Rupert's Bay

HUDSON'S BAY
(1670)

La Nouvelle-
France

Newfoundland

Gulf of
St. Lawrence

NEW YORK (1664)

NEW HAMPSHIRE (1679)
Massachusetts Bay
Plymouth
Rhode Island
Connecticut

PENNSYLVANIA
(1681)

Virginia

EAST NEW JERSEY (1664)
WEST NEW JERSEY (1664)

Maryland

CAROLINA (1663)

La Florida

ATLANTIC OCEAN

Gulf of
Mexico

BAHAMAS (1670)

Cuba (Sp.)

Puerto
Rico (Sp.)

LEEWARD
ISLES (1671)

Santo
Domingo (Sp.)

Jamaica

Caribbean Sea

Barbados

0   500 miles

England's Restoration colonies, 1664–1681.

century. Also like Carolina, the Jerseys offered the liberty of conscience denied in the British Isles. Thus, immigrants from both England and Scotland made East New Jersey a haven for Presbyterianism. Similarly, Quakers from both kingdoms sailed in even greater numbers for West New Jersey and, a few years later, for the new proprietorship of Pennsylvania.

That colony was named for Sir William Penn, the admiral whom Cromwell had disgraced for his part in the failure of the Western Design and who repaid the insult by helping to pave the way for the Restoration. Charles II rewarded Penn with several high offices, and Penn in turn loaned the Stuart family at least £16,000 before his death in 1670. In payment of that debt, in 1681 Charles granted Penn's son the portion of Nieu Nederlandt that lay west of the Delaware River, between the vaguely defined boundaries of Maryland and New York. The younger William—who, unlike his father, was a devout Quaker—received an opportunity to implement his own variant on feudal dreams: a fresh start and a "Holy Experiment" in religious toleration in Pennsylvania. But, with no sense of contradiction, he also expected to make substantial profits from land rents and other duties, to pay off not only the debt he had inherited from his father but also the estimated £12,000 he had spent in extracting his charter from the royal bureaucracy and launching the colony.

Restoration imperialism and its campaign of conquest against the Dutch, then, pursued revenue for the Crown and rewards in the form of landed estates for its most loyal courtiers. But it also pursued religious and political goals that Anglican Royalists and other great men prevented the Stuarts and their closest confidants from achieving at home. The royal patent for New York allowed James to govern his possessions in almost any way he wished, subject to boilerplate stating that his "Statutes, ordinances and proceedings be not contrary to, but as neare as conveniently may be Agreeable to the Lawes Statutes and Governments of this Our Realme of England" and that judicial decisions could be appealed to the Crown.[10] The issue of governance was complicated by the need to somehow manage a conquered Dutch-speaking population whose legal and political traditions differed vastly from England's and whose local governmental arrangements varied from place to place. Moreover, most of the existing English-speaking population lived in Long Island towns, organized in the New England planter fashion, over which the New Haven colony had claimed jurisdiction. In this fractious and potentially violent situation, an ideological preference for centralized authoritative rule merged with practical necessity.

The duke commissioned Nicolls, as his deputy governor, "to performe and Execute all and every the Powers, which are . . . granted unto me to bee executed."[11] No written directions from the duke about how the powers should be executed survive, perhaps because James thought none were necessary in a situation where old Stuart dreams of a "free monarchy" unencumbered by meddlesome parliamentary institutions might come to fruition in North America, if not in the British Isles. No elected legislature was to be part of the picture, as Nicolls made clear to the representatives that he summoned from the English towns on Long Island in early 1665. At the meeting, the deputy governor promulgated—rather than sought approval for—a manuscript document that came to be called "The Duke's Laws." Running to sixty-five pages when a historian finally printed it two hundred years later, this compilation of administrative, civil, and criminal regulations was largely silent on colony-wide affairs and enforcement of the Navigation Acts, for which all power, by default, remained in the hands of the deputy governor and his handpicked council of resident advisors.[12] On the local level, Nicolls improvised a patchwork of institutions— counties and townships on Long Island and in the lower Hudson Valley, chartered corporate municipalities for New York and Albany, quasi-feudal manors here and there—that reshaped existing English and Dutch governmental traditions, invariably in ways that minimized local authority and electoral choice while retaining a sufficient façade of consent to prevent rebellion.

Like personal rule without representative institutions, the religious toleration that the restored Stuarts were unable to achieve in the British Isles also took root under the Duke's Laws. No Christians were to "be disturbed in their private meetings in the time of prayer preaching or other divine Service, nor . . . molested fined or Imprisoned for differing in Judgment in matters of Religion." On paper, at least, such protection did not extend to Jews, who lived in the colony in substantial numbers, to Native Americans, who were not "Suffered to Powaw or performe outward worship to the Devil in any Towne within this Goverment," or to anyone who dared "by direct exprest, impious or presumptuous ways, deny the true God and his Attributes," which was a capital offense. Yet in each local parish a body of "overseers" (comparable to Virginia's vestries) could appoint a minister of nearly any Protestant stripe who had "Received Ordination either from some Protestant Bishop, or Minister within some part of his Majesties Dominions or the Dominions of any foreign Prince of the Reformed Religion." Baptists and Quakers, however, were excluded from pulpits by requirements that, respectively, ministers baptize children of Christian parents and offer Communion at least once a year. Moreover, religious minorities in any given locality would not be released from paying taxes to support a clergyman of the majority's persuasion. Nonetheless, the situation was vastly more tolerant than in either puritan Massachusetts or Restoration England.[13] In New York, as in Carolina—and in the Jerseys and Pennsylvania as well—religious pluralism became a hallmark of Restoration imperialism.

The Duke's Laws also reveal a racial order that James and his circle placed at the center of their imperial vision. Unsurprisingly, given the duke's role in the Royal African Company, the New York code safeguarded the enslavement of Africans. Borrowing language from a contemporary Massachusetts statute, the laws decreed that "no Christian shall be kept in Bondslavery, villenage or Captivity, Except Such who shall be Judged thereunto by Authority, or such as willingly have sould, or shall sell themselves," but added that "nothing in the Law Contained shall be to the prejudice of Master or Dame who shall by any Indenture or Covenant take Apprentices for Terme of Years, or other Servants for Term of years or Life." In the latter case, the covenant presumably need not include the consent of someone enslaved for life but sold into bondage by someone else, in Africa for instance. Whatever the case, non-Christians were fair game.[14]

Relations between colonists and Native Americans received more attention from the Duke's Laws. No land was to be purchased from Indians without prior permission from the governor and a personal appearance before him by both buyer and seller. Trade was to be strictly controlled by licenses, with particular attention to the sale of firearms, ammunition, and liquor. Colonists were required to assist Native people in building fences to protect their cornfields from wandering livestock, and "all injuryes done to the Indians of what nature whatsoever shall upon their Complaint and proofe thereof in any Court have speedy redress gratis." The impulse toward peaceful relations with Native people was genuine, yet it stemmed primarily from the need to create stable conditions for trade and for land transfers under the close supervision of, and with due revenue for, the

duke's government. The first entry under "Indians" suggests the priority:
"No Purchase of lands from Indians . . . shall be Esteemed a good Title
without leave first had and obtained from the Governour."[15] "Good title"
to real estate was something one would think planters and imperialists
could agree upon—but only if both agreed to the rules of Restoration imperialism. Many in the older English colonies did not.

To impose the racial, religious, economic, and political vision of the Duke's
Laws on the conquered territory of Nieu Nederlandt would seem to be
more than any human could accomplish, but Nicolls had been sent to
North America with a still-larger agenda. Along with Cartwright, Carr, and
Samuel Maverick, a long-time opponent of the Massachusetts Bay regime,
Nicolls held a commission to investigate conditions in the New England
colonies—which the king's territorial grant to the duke encircled and infringed upon just as surely as Carolina encroached La Florida. Today's
states of Maine, New Hampshire, and Vermont, a large chunk of Connecticut (whose domain supposedly extended to the Pacific), and the islands
off the Plymouth and Massachusetts shores were all, on paper, subject to
Nicolls's direct authority.

The commissioners let Connecticut off relatively easily. The assistance
of Governor Winthrop in conquering Nieu Nederlandt was rewarded by
an agreement that the boundary between his colony and New York would
be drawn at the midpoint between the Connecticut and Hudson rivers,
rather than at the west bank of the former, as decreed by the duke's charter. This expanded border ratified an understanding between Connecticut
and Nieu Nederlandt that had held since shortly after the Pequot War.
Connecticut and its neighbor Rhode Island were also favored by the fact
that each had recently voluntarily sought and received a charter from
Charles II, for the first time legitimizing their existence in the eyes of the
Crown—Connecticut having created itself in the Pequot War, and Rhode
Island having been established by various refugees from puritan intolerance and having operated since 1644 under a Parliamentary patent now
considered illegitimate. On paper, at least, these two colonies peacefully
joined the new monarchical order.

The real target of royal investigation was Massachusetts Bay, where
Maverick and others had reported (mostly accurately, if one-sidedly) that
the puritan regime balked at administering oaths of loyalty to the restored

Crown, oppressed its Native neighbors, harbored two judges who had participated in the execution of Charles I, ignored the Navigation Acts, and not only refused to practice religious toleration but banned the use of the Book of Common Prayer. Publicly, the commissioners were to make a show of objectivity. Privately, however, they were instructed to get their hands on the Bay Colony charter—which had been so carefully carried across the Atlantic and shielded from official recall—to scan it closely for violations. (That neither the commissioners nor their superiors in England had seen a copy is proven by their anachronistic insistence that religious "liberty of conscience" was expressly "provided for" in a document that could have said no such thing.)[16] At the very least, the commissioners were to pressure the colony's officials not only to answer the charges laid against them, but to agree to royal approval of future elected governors and to royal control of the militia.

The rulers of Massachusetts stood firm—in part because the commissioners made no effort to understand their point of view. Indeed, the investigators seldom left the house of a prominent critic of the Massachusetts regime, with whom they ostentatiously lodged rather than accept the accommodations officially offered them. Not that the magistrates had any intention of cooperating anyway: they waited weeks to arrange a formal meeting, alleged that the investigators' credentials lacked proper certification, and in general proved masters of legalistic delay. When the commissioners unsurprisingly recommended *quo warranto* proceedings against the Bay Colony charter, the magistrates not only refused a royal command to send their governor, Richard Bellingham, to England to explain things (he was, they said, too old to make the trip), but, for good measure, formally annexed several towns in Maine supposedly under the duke's government. Massachusetts Bay's rulers not only suffered no repercussions for these acts, but earned the king's thanks for the loyalty they showed in donating several large ships' masts to the Crown and foodstuffs for English forces in the Caribbean during the Second Anglo-Dutch War.

In the 1660s, then, the new English empire remained more vision than reality. The Second Anglo-Dutch War had on the whole been a financial and political disaster. Vast sums raised by Parliament for the war effort went unaccounted for, spent instead, most assumed, on the lavish courts and many mistresses of Charles and James. Meantime, in 1665, the Dutch retook most of the slaving forts the English had seized in 1663 and in the process nearly bankrupted the duke's Royal African Company. By 1667, on

the eve of the treaty that ended the war, the underfunded English navy
was mostly bottled up in its ports and left virtually defenseless when a
Dutch fleet sailed up the River Medway to Chatham, burned a dozen
ships, and captured the flagship *Royall Charles*. As Lord High Admiral,
the duke of York's reputation lay in tatters, and people began not-so-
secretly talking of the good old days under Oliver Cromwell, who at least
knew how to run a war. As one high government official told the diarist
Samuel Pepys, it was "out of possibility for us to escape being undone,
there being nothing in our power to do that is necessary for the saving us—a lazy prince—no council—no money; no reputation at home or
abroad."[17]

Abroad in North America, meanwhile, the Stuart monarchy clung tenuously to sprawling new territories extending from Maine to the Carolinas
that had been seized from Dutch, Spanish, and earlier English claimants.
In the new colonies, the Crown made itself dependent on the dreams of
courtier-proprietors to enforce its will, relying on personal and kinship
connections to supervise what threatened to become modern-day ungov-
ernable *adelantados*. In the oldest planter colony, Virginia, the Crown's
power similarly rested personally on the shoulders of Governor Sir William Berkeley, one of the Carolina proprietors and brother of John Berkeley, the courtier involved in so many of the duke's imperial projects. As
with much else associated with Restoration imperialism, Sir William's ability to translate plans into action and to govern stubborn local planters remained unproven. Despite fresh royal charters, Connecticut and Rhode
Island continued to be governed by elected legislatures and governors and
to escape direct proprietary rule by James and his favorites, although Connecticut governor John Winthrop Jr. was well connected at court, notwithstanding the puritanism of his deceased father. Meantime, the colony that
the father had founded, Massachusetts Bay, stood in open defiance of its
would-be royal masters. Through it all, an imperial agenda that mixed a
hard-headed assault on trades and labor sources controlled by the Dutch
coexisted uneasily with feudal fantasies of hierarchical regimes yielding
emoluments to a charmed slaveholding circle of noble landed proprietors
who enjoyed liberty of conscience.

At the same time that those around the duke of York were stumbling toward a new vision of empire, similar figures at the French court also tried

to seize Atlantic trade from the Dutch, impose more centralized authority on far-flung colonies, and expand a neo-feudal order in North America. In the 1620s and 1630s, French trading companies, like their English counterparts, had established colonial enterprises not only in North America but in the West Indies, on islands such as St. Christopher's, Guadeloupe, and Martinique. By the 1640s, French officials, like English ones, regularly complained that the bulk of the tobacco, sugar, and other products grown in these colonies sailed on Dutch ships. As in England, the ability to do anything about the situation was hampered by dynastic uncertainty (King Louis XIV had inherited the throne as a four-year-old boy in 1643, and assumed personal rule only in 1661), by domestic political upheaval (the civil wars known as the Fronde, which lasted from 1648 to 1653), and a war against Spain (from 1653 to 1659).

When the domestic situation calmed, Louis XIV, with his chief minister, Jean-Baptiste Colbert, issued a variety of decrees that sought to limit French colonial trade to French ships; these equivalents of the Navigation Acts later became known collectively as *le système exclusif*. Charters for a series of anti-Dutch trading companies soon followed—a West India Company in 1664, a Senegal Company in 1673, and a Guinea Company in 1685. Meantime, in 1663, the Crown revoked the existing charters of Les Cent Associés and the company's West Indian counterparts, reducing La Nouvelle-France, Martinique, and Guadeloupe to direct royal rule of the sort that Nicolls was simultaneously imposing on New York and hoped to establish over Massachusetts Bay.

From a reinvigorated base on the St. Lawrence, the French king's agents spread trading posts and Catholic missions into the continental interior. There, a French variant on the imagined world *of The Fundamental Constitutions of Carolina* took shape, with Native people, rather than hereditary tenants, as its fancied subjects. In June 1671, at Sault Sainte Marie, where Lake Superior and Lake Huron meet, an officer named Simon François Daumont de Saint Lusson summoned leaders from at least fourteen of the region's Native communities to "the most solemn ceremony ever observed in these regions." A Cross and a French royal flag were raised, "while the air resounded with the discharge of musketry and with repeated shouts of 'Long live the King!'" All of this, the chronicler claimed, occurred "to the delight and astonishment of all those peoples, who had never seen anything of the kind." In an Algonquian language that many of the bemused Native people did not understand, a priest gave a long sermon describing the power and majesty of Louis XIV. Next, Lusson explained through a translator "that he was sent to take possession of that region, receive them under the protection of the great King whose Pane-gyric they had just heard; and to form thenceforth but one land of their territories and ours." The festivities "closed with a fine bonfire, which was lighted toward evening, and around which the Te Deum was sung to thank God, on behalf of those poor peoples, that they were now the subjects of so great and powerful a Monarch."[18]

Thus, Frenchmen imagined into existence a great North American em-pire of peaceful conquest. Their king's alleged Native subjects saw things a bit differently. According to a skeptical observer, as the ceremonies at Sault Sainte Marie drew to a close, notaries drafted official reports of the transactions, some of which the Indians were asked to mark with the "in-signia of their families" and others of which only the Europeans signed. One of the papers was nailed to a cedar post behind an iron plate bearing the coat of arms of Louis XIV. Almost immediately, the Indians "drew out the nails from the plate, flung the document into the fire, and again fas-tened up the arms of the king—fearing that the written paper was a spell, which would cause the deaths of all those who dwelt in or should visit that district."[19]

Nonetheless, the French extended their claims to sovereignty ever fur-ther. In 1682, René Robert Cavelier, sieur de La Salle, completed the job with a voyage down the Mississippi River to its mouth, where his ex-ploits infringed on Spanish La Florida from the west and on the recently evacuated Nuevo México from the east. At several stops along the way downriver, he had "established a peace . . . and taken possession," while convincing himself that each local "chief acknowledged that the village be-longed to his Majesty." Elsewhere, La Salle's party passed through a Na-tive village "lately destroyed, and containing dead bodies and marks of blood," or so said a notary remarkably uncurious about what had produced the grisly scene. A few days later, at a spot in the delta far enough from the river's mouth to be presumed safe from flooding, the French delegation buried a lead plate, erected a cross and flag, named the place La Nouvelle-Orléans, and took "possession of this country of Louisiana, the seas, har-bors, ports, bays, adjacent straits; and all the nations, people, provinces, cities, towns, villages, mines, minerals, fisheries, streams, and rivers com-prised in the extent of said Louisiana, from the mouth of the great river St. Louis, on the eastern side, otherwise called Ohio, Alighin, Sipore, or

Chukagona, and this with the consent of the Chaouanons, Chikachas, and other people dwelling therein."[20]

France, like England, had dreams for glorious expansion in North America that coexisted with a more hard-headed economic crusade against the Dutch. Among the most important targets were the Haudenosaunee Iroquois people, whom the French perceived to be Dutch allies. As the traders and missionaries of La Nouvelle-France had hunkered down under the relentless midcentury campaigns that the Haudenosaunee waged against the colony's trading partners, Nieu Nederlandt frequently took the blame for all their woes. "Fifty Hiroquois are capable of making two hundred Frenchmen leave the country," missionary Paul Le Jeune had complained as early as early as 1641, but "fifty Frenchmen would rout five hundred Hiroquois, if the Dutch did not give them firearms."[21] In 1665, when French viceroy Alexandre de Prouville, sieur de Tracy, arrived in La Nouvelle-France after a grand tour of Guiana, where he reconquered a post taken by the Dutch, and of Martinique and Guadeloupe, where he installed new royal governments, he brought with him a thousand troops of the elite Carignan-Salières Regiment and orders "totally to exterminate" the Five Nations for the devastation that their Dutch-enabled raids had caused.[22]

Before Tracy reached North America, the English conquest of Nieu Nederlandt had transformed the situation. The resident Dutch traders of newly christened Albany remained in place, but their supply lines, and thus their ability to trade arms and other goods to the Iroquois, had been disrupted by the conquest and by the Anglo-Dutch war in the Atlantic sea lanes. Moreover, for the better part of a decade before the English invasion, Dutch traders had been unable to provision their Haudenosaunee customers in the way to which both had become accustomed. A major factor was a rapid inflation of the value of wampum against gold and silver in the account books of the North American colonists. Nieu Nederlandt saw its primary medium of exchange fall in value by as much 60 percent between 1641 and 1658 and by more than 200 percent during the following decade, particularly after 1660, when the beads ceased to be accepted for payment of taxes in the New England colonies. To the directors of the West India Company, Nieu Nederlandt appeared by then to be populated with hapless traders, unable to acquire either furs or trade goods, "sitting meanwhile on their boxes full of wampum."[23] The economic distress helps explain the alacrity with which Dutch colonists surrendered to Nicolls in

1664. And it placed Haudenosaunee people in a weak position with respect to their French and Native American enemies—so much so, that already in 1663 a Dutch colonist concluded that it was "not safe for the Indians" to travel to Fort Orange, "for one says that the French Indians are coming and another that the English are coming with Indians."[24]

For all the weakness of the Haudenosaunee, the French found it easier said than done to exterminate them. Of three attempts to invade the Mohawk Iroquois country in 1666, only the last reached its goal, and it could do no more than burn villages that had been abandoned by their forewarned inhabitants. Nonetheless, the loss to the Mohawks was devastating; the invaders destroyed enough preserved food "to nourish all Canada for two years," along with dozens of "well built and magnificently ornamented" houses.[25] These losses, in combination with uncertain trade at Albany and certain attacks by Native American enemies, convinced nearly all Mohawks to agree to a peace treaty with the French in 1667. The other four Haudenosaunee nations had already come to terms two years earlier.

During most of the ensuing decade, the Five Nations temporarily became part of the French sphere of influence in the St. Lawrence and Great Lakes region. French Jesuits set up missions in every major Iroquois village, sundering the Iroquois politically and siphoning off hundreds of people to resettle in mission villages on the St. Lawrence. This *pax gallica* is what allowed Lusson and La Salle to enact their dreams of empire in the Great Lakes and the Mississippi Valley, where former Native enemies of the Five Nations gathered under the political protection and economic auspices of the French Crown. Over time, a semblance of empire in fact emerged where once there had been only a dream.

Empire was no mere dream for Louis XIV elsewhere in the world, and everywhere both the Netherlands and England were in his sights. At Dover in 1670, Louis made a treaty with Charles II that was kept secret from England's Parliament. Under its terms, the two crowns jointly went to war against the Netherlands in 1672, in a globe-girdling conflict in which, for once, economic motives seemed to trump religion. Threatened on the European continent and on the high seas by the alliance of Catholic France with Protestant England, the Netherlands got crucial support from its former Catholic overlord, Spain, which, among other things, had become just as dependent on the Dutch to supply enslaved laborers for its colonies as were the French and the English. On the whole, the war became a fiasco for both Louis XIV and Charles II, who lost hundreds of ships to Dutch privateers and suffered major defeats on nearly every front. Among these was a bloodless reconquest of New York, which briefly again became Nieu Nederlandt in 1673.

Louis would slog on until the war reached a stalemate in 1678, but Charles made a separate peace with the Dutch in 1674, largely because his political opponents had revealed the embarrassing terms of his secret treaty of 1670 and made continued parliamentary support of the French alliance impossible. In an attempt to free himself from parliamentary revenue, Charles had accepted a £300,000 annual subsidy from Louis and made vague promises to convert publicly to Roman Catholicism and to extend toleration to his coreligionists, if not to create an outright English Catholic state establishment. Two royal actions seemed to confirm the grand design: a "Declaration of Indulgence" on the eve of war in 1672 that overrode Parliament's legal restraints on Protestant dissenters and Catholics, and the duke of York's marriage to Mary of Modena, a Catholic woman handpicked for him by Louis XIV in 1673. Because Charles had no heirs, and the duke and the duke's children would succeed him, the future of the monarchy now seemed to rest in French Catholic hands. Nonetheless, needing millions of pounds rather than Louis's hundreds of thousands, Charles had to call Parliament into session to raise taxes. Parliament's price for the revenue was a "Test Act" that voided the Declaration of Indulgence and required all officeholders—not just the local ones covered by the Corporation Act—to receive Communion according to the Book of Common Prayer once a year. Even James, duke of York, was not exempt. He had to resign his tattered post as Lord High Admiral, but not before commissioning a gaudy portrait of himself in the garb of Mars, the god of war.

To New England's puritan planters—and indeed to Protestant men of small means everywhere in English North America—these developments at home confirmed their deepest suspicions of the kind of governmental and spiritual regime the king and his brother, and agents like Nicolls and Maverick, were trying to impose upon them. Religious toleration, oddly, became associated not with freedom but with tyranny, something a Catholic monarch was determined to ram down the throats of good Protestant Englishmen as part of a general scheme to deprive them of local control of their own affairs and to subordinate them to a new hierarchy of great men claiming neo-feudal privileges as proprietors and seigneurs. By these lights, the fact that Charles's separate peace with the Netherlands returned New York to the duke was not good news.

If Protestant planters quivered, Native people trembled. Throughout much of eastern North America, the expansion of the reinvigorated French and English empires and the erasure of Nieu Nederlandt redrew the lines of power that European and Native traders had created earlier in the century. The prolonged conflict between the English and the Dutch left the Haudenosaunee economically and politically dependent on La Nouvelle-France. Shortages of trade goods at Albany during 1673 in particular, French Jesuit missionary Jacques Bruyas reported, caused "stuffs to be so dear, that our Iroquois are resolved to provide themselves with these at Montreal."[26] Bruyas chose the possessive pronoun deliberately, and for the time being there was little that Iroquois foes of the French could do about their people's subordination to La Nouvelle-France.

The economic threats to political autonomy spread far and wide in Indian country, everywhere that the Dutch commercial empire had stretched. The collapse of Nieu Nederlandt's wampum trade caused near-universal distress. Ironically, that collapse resulted from a brief triumph of Dutch power in North America: the conquest of the short-lived colony of New Sweden on the Delaware River in 1655. The Swedes had built their prosperous trade with the Susquehannocks largely upon imports of wampum obtained not directly from Dutch suppliers but second-hand from New Englanders, or, rather, third-hand, since the beads ultimately originated with Native peoples of Long Island Sound. Ships from New Haven colony in particular brought shell beads, firearms, and other trade items for Native people (along with grain and manufactured goods for the colonists), in exchange for the furs those items purchased from the Susquehannocks. The conquest of New Sweden seems to have almost completely halted New England's trade with the Delaware. The resulting glut of wampum in New England caused the value of the beads to plummet in Dutch and English colonies alike.

The Dutch and then English conquests of the Delaware Valley were particularly devastating developments for New Sweden's primary Native trading partners, the Susquehannocks. Already in 1652, after years of on-and-off warfare with English people on the Chesapeake, the Susquehannocks had made peace with Maryland (then tenuously governed as part of Virginia by the Commonwealth government that temporarily replaced Governor Berkeley). This was apparently to hedge their bets on the unstable Swedish trade, as well as to protect their southern flank during a period of heightened conflict with the Iroquois. The arrangement briefly gave the Susquehannocks access to Virginia trading posts at the head of the Chesapeake Bay, but collapsed in 1657 when Maryland regained its independence from Virginia. In 1661, the Maryland assembly, fearing the consequences for their frontiers should the Iroquois defeat the Susquehannocks, declared the latter "a Bullwarke and Security of the Northern parts of this Province" and authorized a Susquehannock-speaking defector from Nieu Nederlandt named Jacob Claeson to trade with them on their behalf.[27] From Claeson and other English and Dutch sources, the Susquehannocks acquired sufficient arms—including artillery reportedly manned by Marylanders—to repulse a major Iroquois attack on their main town in 1663.

That was only a year before the English conquest of Nieu Nederlandt threw all the trading connections of both the Susquehannocks and the Iroquois into disarray. In the Delaware Valley, tense hostility punctuated by occasional murders replaced peaceful trade as the norm for interactions between Europeans and Native people. "We are in a sad condition," local English officials complained to the duke's governor. "It is most uncertain living under the power of the Heathens," who "give for reason of their war that they threaten to make upon the Christians . . . [that] where the English come they drive them from their lands."[28]

The precise effect of these developments on the Susquehannocks is unclear, as their spokesmen appear only occasionally in European records during the early 1670s. The documentary silence suggests that Susquehannocks could carry on only limited trade with Europeans, and suffered considerably as a result. "Here live Christians and there live Christians," one of their frustrated spokesmen supposedly said to Lenapes who were pondering an escalation of violence against the Delaware Valley English. "As they were surrounded by Christians, if they went to war [against them], where would they get powder and ball?"[29] By 1675, the formerly dominant Susquehannocks had seemingly concluded that their only option was to throw in their lot with the Marylanders, who for twenty years had provided an alternative to the Swedes on the Delaware. In February of that year, what was reputed to be the entire surviving population of the nation arrived at St. Mary's City, Maryland's capital, and "some of the[ir] Great Men . . . desired to know what part of the Province Should be allotted for them to live upon."[30]

The Maryland government was unable to provide even the symbolic shelter that Louis XIV's coat of arms offered to Native peoples of the Great Lakes and Mississippi Valley. The Susquehannock refugees had hardly settled into an abandoned Piscataway village on the Potomac River when they found themselves at war with militiamen from Maryland and Virginia during the colonial political upheaval called "Bacon's Rebellion." Almost simultaneously, conflict between Native people and English planters also wracked New England, in the struggle known as "King Philip's War." Spain's North American colonies, too, fought with their would-be Indian subjects during these years—La Florida with periodic flare-ups, and Nuevo México with the cataclysmic Pueblo Revolt of 1680. All of these conflicts had particular local origins rooted in particular local jealousies and hatreds between Europeans and Natives. There are no direct links between the quarrels that Virginians and New Englanders, and *nuevos mexicanos* and *floridanos,* provoked with their Native neighbors. Yet all four local events were also inseparable from the transatlantic imperial systems in which they took place. Spain's empire—drifting under the leadership of those who governed in the name of the physically and mentally disabled King Carlos II, who took the throne at the age of four in 1665—was old and established, and so too were its problems with Native people. In England's fledgling empire—expanding under the bumptious politics of Charles II and his parliaments—the problems were new, and Bacon's Rebellion and King Philip's War cast a harsh light upon them.

ELEVEN

Planters Besieged

WHILE NOTHING DIRECTLY links Bacon's Rebellion and King Philip's War on the one hand and the Pueblo Revolt on the other, there is something compelling about the near-simultaneity of the violence between Indians and Europeans across the continent. In 1680, Native people utterly drove the Spanish from Nuevo México. In 1675–1676, the European populations of the Chesapeake and New England—far larger than those of the Spanish colony—inflicted more damage on Native people than they received. But nonetheless the cost in English blood, property, and wealth was immense. While the colonies physically survived, by the 1680s the planter regimes that had ruled for a generation were ruined almost as thoroughly as the Spanish Franciscan regime that perished in the Southwest. There were no winners anywhere. Efforts by agents of the English Crown to impose their imperialist vision on the chaos led only to more violence and to a series of internal rebellions in the colonies at the end of the decade.

Virginia's upheaval in 1675–1676 was exceedingly confusing, for those who lived through it no less than for those who have since tried to make sense of it. To the author of an aptly named 1677 pamphlet called *Strange News from Virginia,* "the only Cause and Original of All the Late Troubles in that Country" was a recent immigrant named Nathaniel Bacon, who gave those troubles their name. By contrast, one of Bacon's comrades attributed the chaos to "the frowardness avarice and french Despotick

Methods" of the colony's long-serving governor, William Berkeley. Royal
commissioners sent to investigate in 1677 found plenty of blame to go
around—in Bacon, in Berkeley, and in a deluded "giddy-headed multitude" who saw Bacon "as the onely Patron of the Country and preserver of
their Lives and Fortunes."[1]

An eyewitness account penned nearly thirty years after the events spied
more mysterious forces at work. "About the year 1675," Virginia planter
Thomas Mathews recalled, "appear'd three Prodigies in that Country,
which, from th' attending Disasters, were Look'd upon as Ominous Pres-
ages." The triple omens included a comet seen every night for a week,
"Flights of Pigeons in breadth nigh a Quarter of the Mid-Hemisphere, and
of their Length was no visible End," and the sudden appearance and disappearance of what were probably seventeen-year cicadas. More eerily,
during the events leading up to the rebellion, a "Papist" suggested that a
captured Native boy who lay in a coma had been bewitched by Indians
and that "Baptism was an Effectuall Remedy." Some tipsy Protestants
mockingly administered the sacrament according to the Book of Common
Prayer and "return'd to drinking Punch," only to learn that the boy did in
fact miraculously revive. "This," Mathews said, "was taken for a Convincing Proofe against Infidelity."[2]

Whatever may have been proved about Virginia infidels' lack of faith,
Mathews located the more secular origins of the troubles in the 1675 killing of two men who worked for him. One was an unnamed Native American who may have been a slave. The other was a "Herdsman" (most likely
a pig tender) improbably named Robert Hen, who, as he breathed his
last, blamed the Doeg Indians for the deed. These were an Algonquian-
speaking people who probably once had been part of Powhatan's chiefdom
but now lived on the Maryland side of the Potomac River. The word
"Doeg" was a rough equivalent of the people's name for themselves—
"Toags," or "Taux"—but must have reminded Protestant English planters
of the biblical character Doeg the Edomite, who "would surely tell Saul: I
have occasioned the death of all the persons of thy father's house."[3]

"From this Englishman's bloud," Mathews wrote of his herdsman Hen,
"did (by Degrees) arise Bacons Rebellion with the following Mischiefs
which Overspread all Virginia." Yet the murder was not the random act of
violence that Mathews pretended. Instead, it was one episode in a running
personal dispute with a group of Doegs who accused Mathews of not pay-

ing them for some goods he had received from them. In July 1675, they retaliated by confiscating some of his hogs. English militiamen pursued the Natives, reclaimed the animals, and killed some Doegs for good measure. Hen's death was in retaliation. In counter-retaliation, Virginia militiamen again marched into Doeg country, where, at daybreak, they surrounded two houses full of sleeping people. Outside one dwelling, when a man the Virginians took to be the chief tried to run away after claiming no knowledge of Hen's death, they shot him. Ten other Indians quickly perished in a hail of gunfire, and the boy who would soon fall into that mysterious coma was captured. At the second house, another firefight broke out, and fourteen Native men lay dead before a Native man grabbed the Virginia leader "by one Arm Saying 'Susquehanoughs Netoughs,' i.e. Susquehanaugh friends, and fled, Whereupon he ran amongst his Men, Crying out, 'For the Lords sake Shoot no more, these are our friends the Susquehanoughs.'"[4]

The case of mistaken identity was no small matter. Virginians had long been used to pushing around members of tiny groups like the Doegs. The Susquehannocks—despite the economic and military difficulties that had brought them to the banks of the Potomac—were a different story. This became clear when some one thousand freelance Virginia and Maryland militiamen (led by, among others, John Washington, great-grandfather to George) surrounded their main fortified town and, under the cover of negotiations to make amends for the misguided earlier attack, assassinated five of their chiefs. Understandably vengeful Susquehannocks then killed thirty-six Virginians in a single raid in January 1676, and subsequently were able to pick off colonists with impunity. The victims included two members of Bacon's household. Terror spread through the upper reaches of Virginia's watersheds. By February, only eleven of seventy-one plantations along the Rappahannock River were still occupied, and by March perhaps as many as three hundred Virginians lay dead.[5]

Berkeley initially responded to the Susquehannock onslaught by commissioning a militia army to counterattack, but quickly withdrew the order—partly because he was genuinely disgusted at the militiamen's treachery that had sparked the war, partly because the Susquehannocks were making peace overtures, partly because he realized that ill-trained Virginians had little chance of doing any real damage to Susquehannocks on the run, and partly because he remembered all too well the devastating general war between colonists and Indians in 1644–1646. Summoning the House of Burgesses into session, Berkeley pushed through a defensive rather than offensive program: building forts to protect interior plantations and raising taxes to pay for them, banning arms sales to Indians, and preventing the export of foodstuffs during the emergency. Panicked planters were enraged at what they considered Berkeley's insufficiently aggressive and expensively useless forts. The Susquehannocks, they complained, "quickly found out where about these Mouse traps were sett, and for what purpose, and so resalved to keepe out of there danger; which they might easely ennough do, with out any detriment to there designes."[6]

No one was more contemptuous of Berkeley's policies than Nathaniel Bacon, who, though he had arrived in Virginia only in 1674, already cut a major figure there. A Cambridge-educated thirty-something ne'er-do-well whose father had sent him packing to North America along with a spouse, two children, and a stake of £1,800, he was a relative of Berkeley's wife and of a long-time planter who also bore the name Nathaniel Bacon. Those connections—along with "great natural parts" and (when he wasn't hurling curses and skirting atheism) a reputation among "all that knew him, that he usually spoke as much sense in as few words, and delivered that sense as opportunely as any they ever kept company withal"—gained him a speedy appointment to the governor's council, as well as a substantial plantation called "Curles Neck." Forty miles upriver from Jamestown, this estate lay well within the Susquehannocks' line of fire.[7]

When the conflict erupted, Bacon repeatedly demanded that Berkeley issue him a commission to lead not just an offensive against the Susquehannocks and Doegs, but a preemptive strike against all Indians, including those protected by tributary relations with the colony. Berkeley just as repeatedly refused. Accounts differ on what happened next. Some say Bacon and neighboring planters methodically set a deadline by which they would proceed, with or without the governor's approval. Others refer to a conspiratorial pact signed with names in a circle to disguise the true leadership. Others stress a night of drinking, after which Bacon and his companions carried a boatload of rum to militiamen who happened to be gathered on the banks of the James River and who welcomed him as their leader with shouts of "a Bacon! a Bacon! a Bacon!"[8] In any event, Bacon soon led his Virginians in search of Indians to kill—by marching to the southwest toward the country of the Siouan-speaking Occaneechees, rather than north toward the Susquehannocks. This move derived from rumors that the southerners were providing aid and comfort to the planters' foes and from the Occaneechees' long-standing reputation for uppityness. As one Virginian had complained a few years earlier, they were "insolent for they are but a handful of people, besides what vagabonds repaire to them it being a receptackle for rogues."[9]

Berkeley publicly declared Bacon a rebel and ordered his arrest. Had not so many people—Indians and English—died in the following months, the tale would read like a bad comedy. Berkeley called elections for a new House of Burgesses. Bacon, despite the double disqualifications of being a member of the governor's council and a declared rebel, got elected to it. Sailing downriver with a sloop full of armed men, Bacon tried to take his assembly seat. Berkeley placed him in chains. After Bacon knelt before Berkeley to confess, the governor granted him a pardon, restored him to his council post, and even promised the long-sought commission to lead troops against the Indians. When the promise fell through, Bacon surrounded the statehouse with musketeers and demanded his commission from the governor and Burgesses meeting inside. This demand "Berkeley utterly refused, and rising from his chair of judicature came down to Bacon, and told him to his Face and before all his men that hee was a Rebell and a Traytor etc. and should have noe commission, and uncovering his naked Bosome before him, required that some of his men might shoot him, before ever he would be drawn to signe or consent to a commission for such a Rebell as Bacon."[10]

When no one replied, Berkeley drew his sword and challenged Bacon to a duel. The investigative report of the royal commissioners describes what ensued:

All the answer Bacon gave the Governor was, "Sir, I came not, nor intend to hurt a haire of your honor's head, and for your sword your Honor may please to putt it up, it shall rust in the scabboard before I shall desire you to drawe it. I come for a commission against the Heathen who dayly inhumanely murder us and spill our Brethren's Blood, and noe care is taken to prevent it," adding, "God damne my Blood, I came for a commission, and a commission I will have before I goe," and turning to his soldiers, said "Make ready and Present [arms]," which they all did. Some of the Burgesses looking out at the windows and seeing the soldiers in that posture of Firing cry'd out to them, "For God's sake hold your handes and forebear a little, and you shall have what you please."[11]

Document in hand, Bacon marched off to kill more Native people, and the colony plunged into civil war, with planters, servants, and even slaves taking up sides, the latter two groups encouraged by empty promises from each party that they would gain land and freedom in payment for their service. Armies traversed the countryside, plundering each other's homes—including Berkeley's Green Spring—when they were not plundering Indians. The capital of Jamestown—a pitiful "Metropollis" composed of "som 16 or 18 howses, most as is the Church, built of Brick, faire and large; and in them about a dozen Familles (for all the howses are not inhabited) getting there liveings by keepeing of ordnaries [taverns], at extreordnary rates"—changed hands three times.[12] When Bacon laid his final siege, he used some of his opponents' wives as human shields, and then burned the entire town to the ground to prevent Berkeley's forces from retaking it.

A few weeks later, Bacon died of "Bloody Flux" (probably dysentery), "accompanyed with a Lousey Disease."[13] His followers spirited away the body and buried a coffin full of rocks, to prevent the corpse from suffering exposure on a gibbet, which was the usual fate of a traitor. Nonetheless, Berkeley crowed that since Bacon's "usual oath . . . which he swore at least a Thousand times a day was God damme my Blood . . . [,] God so infected his blood that it bred Lice in an incredible number so that for twenty dayes he never washt his shirts but burned them. To those God added the Bloody flux and an honest Minister wrote this Epitaph on him: 'Bacon is Dead I am sorry at my hart / that Lice and flux should take the hangmans part.'"[14] The real hangman had plenty of work to do, as Bacon's followers scattered and Berkeley's men mopped them up, while confiscating their estates for themselves. Twenty-three men went to the gallows.

Through all the haze of these confused events, two themes repeatedly emerge. First is a mingled hatred and fear of Native people, Susquehannock or Doeg, unsuspecting friend or provoked foe—emotions that Bacon seems to have mobilized among planters who voiced "their reiterated prayers, first to him self, and next to Heaven, that he may become their Guardian Angel, to protect them from the cruelties of the Indians, against whom this Gentleman had a perfect antipathy."[15] Second was the bitter personal quarrel between Bacon and Berkeley, not just over policies toward Indians but over issues of power, status, and authority. And while the rebellion has long borne Bacon's name, in many ways Berkeley is the key to an understanding of the events of 1675–1676. As both a Virginia planter and a Restoration imperialist, he embodied the dual fountainheads of a flood that nearly swept the colony away.

As a planter, Berkeley had amassed considerable personal wealth and power, symbolized by his grand house, Green Spring, and by the thousand acres of prime tobacco land it dominated. Berkeley also owned at least two other sizable plantations and at least five of the often-vacant brick houses that semi-graced Jamestown. No records survive to document the exact number of servants and slaves whose labor made these possessions profitable, but they must have been numerous, and there is every reason to believe that the governor commanded one of the largest contingents of enslaved people in a colony that in 1670 still counted only about two thousand Africans in a non-Indian population of fewer than thirty thousand. The coterie of planters that Berkeley gathered around him at Green Spring shared his privileges of wealth, labor, and especially land. Manipulating their control of offices that dispersed real estate and exploiting the fifty-acre headrights they accumulated with each importation of a servant or slave, they amassed such huge estates that virtually no good potential tobacco land remained outside their grasp, except that held by Native people. Servants who had earned their freedom after long years of labor, and newcomers who lacked the kind of connections and familial wealth that Bacon had brought with him, could acquire real estate only under two legal conditions: they could try to purchase it from a great planter at a price few men of small means could afford, or they could become the tenants of such great men.

In all this and in many other ways, Berkeley the planter merged seamlessly with Berkeley the imperialist. Virginia seemed well on its way to becoming the kind of neo-feudal utopia envisioned by imperial dreamers. Particularly after the Restoration, Berkeley systematically recruited younger sons of the English aristocracy, who, like Bacon, saw Virginia as a place to gain the estates they could not acquire at home. Among these were people with names such as Byrd, Jefferson, Bland, and Culpeper—all of them related by marriage, well connected at court and at Jamestown, and able to import enough capital and servants to grab a substantial slice of the pie. As the governor wrote in a tract he published in London, "a small summe of money will enable a younger Brother to erect a flourishing

Family in a new World; and adde more Strength, Wealth, and Honour, to his Native Country, then thousands did before."[16]

The interests of Berkeley the planter and Berkeley the imperialist also aligned on the future role of slavery in Virginia. English Virginians had never considered Africans their equals, as shown by the nearly universal practice of attaching the word "Negro" or "Neger" to names in official documents and by the law of 1643 that declared African women, but not European females, to be tithables subject to taxation. Yet enslavement initially lacked any clear legal status. A substantial minority of midcentury Afro-Virginians gained their freedom, and some even acquired land of their own. After the Restoration, however, Berkeley's allies in the House of Burgesses began enshrining slavery in law, inspired by the Barbados colonial assembly, which passed an act "for the better ordering and governing of Negroes" in 1661. In 1662, the Virginia Burgesses declared that the free or enslaved status of a child must follow that of its mother; thus, they not only defined the hereditary status of slavery, but reserved the rights of patriarchal authority to English masters and silently relieved men who raped their slaves of parental responsibility for their offspring. A 1667 statute further eased moral qualms by pronouncing that Christian baptism did not release an enslaved person from earthly bondage. In 1669, "an act about the casuall killing of slaves" made it clear that masters had every right to punish enslaved people in any way they saw fit, even if death resulted.[17] A year later, the Burgesses removed another ambiguity by declaring that all non-Christian servants brought into the colony were slaves for life. Finally, drawing directly on the Barbados code, a 1671 law stated that, for purposes of inheritance, enslaved people were not to be considered chattel, or movable property, but something more akin to real estate, which could pass more certainly from one generation to another. Thus, for this period the term "chattel slavery" is technically a misnomer.

The legislature that passed these acts not only consisted of a band of elite planters consolidating their authority, but also reflected Restoration imperialism's disdain for representative institutions. In 1661, shortly after his reconfirmation as royal governor, Berkeley called elections for the House of Burgesses; but he did not do so again until forced to by the upheavals of 1675–1676. The members of what Virginians called their "Long Assembly" (in echo of England's Cromwell-era "Long Parliament") met frequently to pass laws and levy taxes, but became increasingly dependent on Berkeley and the privileges he dispensed and on the handsome salaries they voted themselves, rather than on the electors who had originally placed them in office. The distance became even greater in 1670, when the Burgesses stripped the vote from free men who did not own property.

Bacon may have been partly admitted to the charmed circle of rulers when he received a seat on the governor's council in 1674, but he struck a nerve among political outsiders when he questioned the basis of the elite's power and wealth. Noting that "some in Authority" who were "now wealthy" had not been so "when they came first in to the Country," Bacon asked "by what just ways, or means, they have obtained the same; and whether they have not been the sponges that have sucked up and devoured the common treasury?" Not surprisingly, Berkeley was said to have distrusted "Bacon's temper, as he appeared Popularly inclined; A constitution not consistent with the times."[18]

Bacon, of course, was even more critical of another imperial trend of the times: peaceful relationships with Native peoples. He even accused the governor of taking the Indians' side in "their quarrel (though never so unjust) against the Christian's rights and interests."[19] Berkeley's preference for tributary obligations over aggressive expansion matched the emphasis on humane treatment favored in the Restoration court. But more important, his policy suited the needs of the planter elite not only by protecting their estates, but by limiting the amount of land available to lesser men. Indeed, restraint on competing planters' desire to seize Indian territory artificially created the kind of scarcity that had empowered the slaveholding class of Barbados, which Berkeley and others so much admired. "To make a Parallel betwixt Virginia and our other Island Plantations in America, we will take the Mistresse of them all, *Barbadoes*," he wrote.[20]

Peaceful relations with Native people carried other great benefits. As with nearly everything else in Virginia, Berkeley and his circle kept for themselves the licenses required to engage in the trade in furs and hides —licenses that they denied to Bacon and several of his most prominent supporters. It is also likely that enslaved Indians were among the commodities the licensees bought from Native trading partners, who used the firearms they got in exchange to capture still more victims from their enemies. With slaves as well as land and wealth accumulating in a few fortunate hands, it is no wonder that Baconites suspected that the real reason Berkeley resisted taking the offensive was the "Avarice, to . . . which, he was (by the common Vogue) more than a little Addicted." According to

"Popular Surmizes and Murmurings," the governor meant to ensure "that no Bullets woud pierce Bever Skins" and that "Rebells forfeitures woud be Loyall Inheritances," when he got his hands on the property confiscated from Bacon's outlawed followers.[21]

Virginia's lopsided distribution of land and its popular pressure to allow a war against all Indians as a remedy became all the more pressing an issue because of some major ways in which the agenda of Berkeley's planters *failed* to mesh with those of Restoration imperialists. As one of the Carolina proprietors and as the brother of John Berkeley, Virginia's governor traveled in the circles of favored courtiers on whom Charles II bestowed vast North American possessions, but not in the innermost rings. Thus, in 1674 he was unable to prevent several courtiers—including some of his own kin—from transforming an old proprietary claim to land in the "Northern Neck" between the Rappahannock and Potomac rivers into a legal right to all the undeeded real estate of Virginia. If allowed to stand, this patent threatened to freeze everyone else out, whether member of the Green Spring faction or outsider, landed or landless. Yet when the burgesses passed a heavy tax of sixty pounds of tobacco per thithable to finance a mission to London to contest the patent, the delegation appeared to Berkeley's opponents to be yet another example of the Green Spring faction's defending its ill-gotten privileges at the expense of all others.

Even more of a problem than the Northern Neck proprietary were two core related programs of Restoration imperialism: the Navigation Acts and the Anglo-Dutch wars. From the time of his first arrival in the Chesapeake in the early 1640s, Berkeley, like all Virginia planters (indeed virtually all English colonists in North America and the West Indies), was an outspoken proponent of commerce with the Dutch, who paid decent prices for the colony's tobacco—thus the trade treaty he negotiated with Nieu Nederlandt in 1660, before he learned of the repassage of the Navigation Act. While admitting that his fellow English people had too often "suffered the *Dutch* to enrich themselves on our discoveries," Berkeley continued to argue against "confining the Planters to Trade only with the English." The result was "that forty thousand people should be impoverish'd to enrich little more then forty Merchants, who being the only buyers of our *Tobacco,* give us what they please for it, and . . . sell it how they please."[22] Yet the customs duties reaped from every pound of leaf imported to England were too profitable for the Crown to give up, and Berkeley's arguments fell on deaf ears.

It is doubtful whether greedy London merchants and hungry royal coffers alone were to blame, but there is no questioning the fact that thousands of Virginia tobacco planters faced economic ruin in the years after the passage of the 1660 Navigation Act and, especially, after the imposition of a 1673 Parliamentary statute that discouraged illegal commerce by levying "plantation duties" of one penny per pound of tobacco, payable before ships left the colonies. No simple explanation for Virginia planters' distress will do, and, as Berkeley also realized, overproduction was a major factor. Still, the success of the Navigation Acts in curbing the sale of tobacco to the Dutch and enforcing the payment of duties on tobacco sent to England had a substantial impact. Under the English-only regime, prices plummeted to a half-penny per pound of leaf in 1666, and hovered around one penny for the next decade—less than half of what they had been in the 1650s, when the Swedes and Dutch were major purchasers, and barely equal to the tax shippers owed to the Crown.

In 1667, English warfare with the Netherlands combined with Mother Nature to deepen the distress. A Dutch fleet sailed into Chesapeake Bay and captured a dozen ships loaded with cured leaf, and a hurricane destroyed much of what was growing in the field. In light of all this, among Berkeley's many worries was that, when warfare resumed in 1673, the "large part of the people" who were "so desperately poor" might welcome a Dutch invasion, "in hopes of bettering their condition."[23]

It was Nathaniel Bacon, not the Dutch, who briefly raised the hopes of what Berkeley called "a People wher six parts of seaven at least are Poore Endebted Discontented and Armed."[24] Many of them sought relief from their poverty not by growing less tobacco at a higher price but by finding a means to grow more—namely, by seizing lands from Native people. "The common cry and vogue of the Vulgar was . . . wee will have warr with all Indians," the royal commissioners concluded. "We will spare non, and [if] wee must be hang'd for Rebells for killing those that will destroy us, let them hang us, wee will venture that rather than lye at the mercy of a Barbarous Enemy."[25]

In the end, no one in Virginia won. Not Virginia's servants and slaves, whose hopes of land and freedom were dashed. Not Bacon's closest followers, who were lucky if they received pardons from Berkeley's executioners. Not Berkeley, who in 1677 sailed to England in disgrace and died within a year. (King Charles supposedly complained that "that old fool has hang'd more men in that naked Country, than [the king himself] . . . had done for the Murther of his Father.")[26] And not the Native people of the region. The Susquehannocks drifted back north in small bands. Now powerless against their Haudenosaunee foes, most resettled under duress in Iroquoia, as had thousands of others vanquished during the midcentury wars among the region's Native peoples.

The impact of the rebellion on the Native people of Tsenacomoco, descendants of Powhatan's great paramount chiefdom, can be glimpsed in the personal story of Cockacoeske, the woman the English called the "Queen of Pamunkey." She descended from the same female line as Opechancanough, and thus claimed Powhatan's title of *mamanatowick;* in Native America, as in Elizabethan England, sometimes women stepped in when no male heirs survived. Since Opechancanough's death and the treaties of 1646, her Pamunkeys had accepted a tributary relationship to the Virginia government, and occasionally supplied troops to support colonial raids into the interior. Among them was a disastrous campaign in which Cockacoeske's husband, Tatapamoi, and dozens of other men perished. During the chaotic session of the House of Burgesses that met during the early months of Bacon's Rebellion, a committee of the house summoned Cockacoeske to help again. As Mathews recalled the scene, the queen

> entred the Chamber with a Comportment Gracefull to Admiration, bringing on her right hand an Englishman Interpreter, and on the left her Son a Stripling Twenty Years of Age, She having round her head a Plat of Black and White Wampum peage Three Inches broad in imitation of a Crown, and was Cloathed in a Mantle of dress't Deerskins with the hair outwards and the Edge cut round 6 Inches deep which made Strings resembling Twisted frenge from the Shoulders to the feet; Thus with grave Courtlike Gestures and a Majestick Air in her face, she Walk'd up our Long Room to the Lower end of the Table, Where after a few Intreaties She Sat down; th' Interpreter and her Son Standing by her on either side as they had Walked up, our Chairman asked her what men she would Lend us for Guides in the Wilderness and to assist us against our Enemy Indians. . . . She after a little Musing with an earnest passionate Countenance as if Tears were ready to Gush out and a fervent sort of Expression made a Harangue about a quarter of an hour, often interlacing (with a high shrill Voice and vehe-

ment passion) these Words, *Tatpatamoi Chepiack*, i.e. Tatapamoi dead ... ;
for which no Compensation (at all) had bene to that day Rendered to her
wherewith she now upbraided us.

Her Discourse ending and our Morose Chairman not advancing one
cold word towards asswaging the Anger and Grief her Speech and De-
meanour Manifested under her oppression, nor taking any notice of all she
had Said . . . , He rudely push'd againe the same Question "What Indians
will you now Contribute" etc.? Of this Disregard she Signified her Resent-
ment by a disdainfull aspect, and turning her head half a side, Sate mute
till that same Question being press'd, a Third time, She not returning her
face to the board, answered with a low slighting Voice in her own Language "Six," but being further Importun'd She sitting a little while Sullen,
without uttering a Word between Said "Twelve," tho' she then had a hundred and fifty Indian men in her Town, and so rose up and gravely Walked
away, as not pleased with her Treatment.[27]

Whether or not those twelve, or six, men ever showed up for service
with the English, the Pamunkeys soon felt the wrath of Bacon's forces,
who sacked their main town, killed an unknown number of people, enslaved forty-five others, and plundered wampum, furs, imported cloth,
and "divers sorts of English goods (which the Queene had much value
for)." Cockacoeske, meanwhile, fled with a ten-year-old boy "into wild
woodes where shee was lost and missing from her owne People fourteen
dayes, all that tyme being Sustained alone onely by gnawing sometimes
upon the legg of a terrapin, which the little Boy found in the woods and
brought her when she was ready to dye for want of Foode."[28]

While there were many losers in Bacon's Rebellion, those who lost least
represented the forces of Restoration imperialism. The three royal commissioners sent to investigate arrived in early 1677, after Bacon was dead
and after most of the fighting and hanging were over. One of them was a
Virginia planter and one-time member of the Green Spring faction, Francis Moryson, who had been in England as the colony's successful agent in
the legal battle against the Northern Neck proprietors. The second was Sir
John Berry, commandant of a naval squadron that brought more than a
thousand troops under the command of the third commissioner, Colonel
Herbert Jeffreys. Jeffreys carried an appointment as lieutenant governor

and instructions to replace Berkeley one way or another. If Sir William was dead, he was to use his troops to depose Bacon and put down the rebels; if the great man was alive, he was to send him to England to explain himself. The troops were not necessary—and indeed succeeded only in alienating planters whose devastated houses and fields left them unable to provide the soldiers with food and shelter. In this and other ways, Berkeley and the Green Spring faction deeply resented this intrusion at the moment of their triumph, particularly when the commissioners insisted on trying to publish a royal pardon for nearly all the rebels, on halting the confiscation of Baconite estates, and on holding reasonably objective hearings to listen to popular grievances. At every turn, the imperial interlopers encountered resistance from the governor and his circle. To make their attitude clear, Lady Berkeley once arranged for the colony's hangman to drive the commissioners' ceremonial carriage.

Nonetheless, Berkeley did finally board ship to leave, and Jeffreys did convene a newly elected House of Burgesses. Jeffreys's troops, his royal commissions, and his contempt for Berkeley and the great planters who had enriched themselves around him—all represented a stark assertion of the power of the newly aggressive English imperial state over its colonial possessions and peoples. The power was more asserted than exercised, but, in addition to removing Berkeley from the scene, Jeffreys achieved at least one clear victory for royal authority. On May 29, 1677—which, not accidentally, was the king's birthday and the anniversary of the monarch's restoration to the throne—the new governor convened a treaty council with the Pamunkeys, with other surviving elements of the Powhatan chiefdom, such as the Appomattucks, Nansemonds, and Weanocks, and with additional peoples who had been caught up in the recent violence, such as the Siouan-speaking Monocans and Saponis and the Iroquoian-speaking Nottoways and Maherins. Conspicuously absent were representatives of the original targets of Virginians' wrath—Doegs, Susquehannocks, and Occaneechees—though the treaty did proclaim that all "Indians and English in the Province of Maryland are included in these Articles of peace." By those articles, the assembled chiefs declared "all Subjection to the great King of England" as their "now dread Soveraigne," and admitted that they held their lands not by natural right but "Patent under the Seale of this his Magesties Colony." For their part, the English acknowledged the "violent intrusions of divers English into their lands," which "the late unhappy Rebellion . . . in a great measure begunne and fomented." In order "that the said Indians be well Secured and defended in theire persons goods and properties against all hurts and injuries of the English," a three-mile buffer zone around each Native village was declared off-limits to colonists. Finally, the treaty restored Cockacoeske to her titular role as paramount chief over many of the tributary tribes.[29]

Like his French counterpart but on a much smaller scale, an English governor had created a paper empire of loyal Indian subjects. And like Christopher Newport three-quarters of a century earlier, Jeffreys's successor as governor, Thomas Culpeper, carried with him to Virginia a crown to be placed on a Native vassal's head; he also brought a robe, a silk dress, a silver medal, and other gifts. On his arrival, local grandees convinced him that Cockacoeske could receive some of her gifts but emphatically not the crown, for "such Marks of Dignity . . . must not be prostituted to such meane persons."[30]

The terms of the Virginia treaty and the insulting language of Virginia planters would have sounded painfully familiar to another Native leader, had he still been alive to learn of them. In June 1660, Wamsutta, heir to the Wampanoag chief Massasoit, had appeared, along with his brother Metacom, in front of the governor and legislature of Plymouth Colony to complain of the same kind of hurts and injuries that would later lead to Bacon's Rebellion. As with the Doegs in 1675, hogs and land were at the center of the trouble. Free-running swine from the English town of Rehoboth were destroying Wampanoag cornfields, and Englishmen allegedly paid a Narragansett sachem for a parcel of land that rightly belonged to Wamsutta's people. After the court gave the Wampanoags permission to impound offending pigs until their owners paid damages, and after it promised to look into the land deal, Wamsutta announced "that in regard his father is lately deceased," he was "desirous, according to the custom of the natives, to change his name"—to receive a title appropriate to his new status as Plymouth's principal Native ally—and that he hoped "the court would confer an English name upon him." Reaffirming their own little corner of English dominance, the colonial officials decreed "that for the future hee shalbee called by the name of Allexander Pokanokett; and desireing the same in the behalfe of his brother, they have named him Phillip."[31]

The official records do not say whether the Englishmen explained the titles to Wamsutta and Metacom, but the allusions were to Alexander the Great and his half-brother and successor, King Philip III. These ancient Macedonian names recalled a passage in the biblical Book of Acts in which the apostle Paul had a vision of Macedonians crying out to him, "Come over . . . and help us." Those who had seen the official seal of the neighboring Massachusetts Bay Colony would have conjured an image of a Gospel-starved Indian with the same words flowing from his mouth. Those who had a passing knowledge of classical history, however, would have recalled that King Philip was the supposedly mentally handicapped half-brother who succeeded King Alexander, only to be murdered while others fought over the breakup of the empire. In this sense, the naming ceremony was eerily prophetic. Sixteen years later, while Bacon's and Berkeley's forces were pillaging the houses of each other's supporters and of the Pamunkeys, Philip, who succeeded his brother as king of the Wampanoags and once strode the streets of Boston in buckskins and wampum, would lie dead, his body quartered, his hands and feet chopped off. The alliance that Massasoit had built, along with nearly all of Ninnimissinouk country and much of colonial New England, collapsed, like English Virginia, in smoldering ruins.

Bacon's followers were well aware of the parallels: when the "Vulgar" said they would rather be hanged "than lye at the mercy of a Barbarous Enemy," they also vowed not to "endure the calamity that befell New England."[32] The two calamities arrived by different routes, but both could be traced, in part, to the effects of Restoration imperialism. The erasure of Nieu Nederlandt affected southern New England Algonquians much the way it affected the Susquehannocks, and indeed the Virginia tobacco planters. The great wampum inflation, the demonetization of the beads in New England, the relentless pressure on the Indian land base from an expanding English population, and the removal of any possibility that a Dutch government might be played off against the English put Wampanoags, Narragansetts, and Mohegans in an almost impossible bind. Thus, in 1667 Plymouth officials had good reason to believe rumors that Philip had expressed "his readiness to comply with French or Dutch against the English, and so not only to recover their lands sold to the English, but enrich themselves with their goods."[33] And in 1665 it had been no rumor that Native people warmly welcomed the arrival of the royal commissioners sent to investigate the crimes of the Massachusetts government. The Narragansett chiefs hosted a treaty council with the commissioners and placed themselves, their people, and their lands under the direct protection of the king, rather than trusting to the planters whose overlordship they feared.

Economic distress and a shrinking land base were only part of the reason that Ninnimissinouk leaders were so eager to find a counterbalance to the planters' power. During the Cromwellian period, and with even greater vigor after the Restoration, a handful of clergymen—John Eliot and Daniel Gookin from Massachusetts Bay, Thomas Mayhew Jr. and Richard Bourne from Plymouth—began serious efforts to convert Native people to Christianity and to bring them under direct colonial government. Financial support for their efforts came from an organization called the New England Company for the Propagation of the Gospel, incorporated by Parliament a few months after the execution of Charles I in 1649 and rechartered after the Restoration under the leadership of the philosopher Robert Boyle. Inspired by tracts that Eliot and his colleagues published in London with titles such as *The Day-Breaking, If Not the Sun-Rising of the Gospell with the Indians in New-England* (1647) and *The Glorious Progress of the Gospel amongst the Indians* (1649), pious Protestants in the imperial capital (but almost no lay people in New England itself) supplied funds. Among other things, these contributions allowed Eliot, working with several of his Native proselytes, to translate the entire Bible into the Massachuset language, to purchase a new printing press with appropriate fonts, and in 1663 to produce more than a thousand copies of a twelve-hundred-page volume of the Scriptures. This was by far the most ambitious publishing project yet attempted in North America, but also evidence of new imperial forces emanating from London, where people still believed that Indians should submit to the humane government of Christians.

Eliot, along with a small corps of literate Native teachers and a handful of influential sachems, encouraged would-be converts to resettle in "praying towns"—controlled environments where, in theory at least, they would learn not just to worship like good English Christians but also to emulate them in their dress, farming methods, and houses. The Protestant message seems first to have gained a serious following during a smallpox epidemic in 1650, when, as Eliot put it, "the Indians who call[ed] upon God" were more likely to survive than "their profane neighbors [who] were cut off."[34] The first praying town, Natick, took root the next year. By 1674, approximately twenty-three hundred Native people lived in at least fourteen

Christian communities in Massachusetts Bay, and in several others in Plymouth, on Martha's Vineyard, and on Nantucket. While that figure represented only a little over 10 percent of a total Ninnimissinouk population of about twenty thousand, in Plymouth and eastern Massachusetts the proportion was more like 25 percent, and among the one thousand or so of Philip's Wampanoags, roughly six hundred had resettled in Christian communities. Although only about three hundred fifty Native people throughout New England had met the stringent puritan standards for baptism— "all those we call praying Indians are not all visible church members, or baptized persons," Gookin confessed—the trend toward Christian domination was clear.[35] King Philip almost certainly had never heard of Nuevo México, but his people seemed headed for a fate similar to that of Pop'ay's.

Yet in New England, in contrast to Nuevo México, Native people were far outnumbered by the sixty thousand European colonists who surrounded them and whose lust for free and common socage seemed boundless. *"Land! Land!* hath been the Idol of many in *New-England,"* Massachusetts clergyman Increase Mather complained. "Whereas the first Planters here that they might keep themselves together were satisfied with one Acre for each person, as his propriety, and after that with twenty Acres for a Family, how have Men since coveted after the earth, that many hundreds, nay thousands of Acres, have been engrossed by one man."[36]

The pressure on Indian land was particularly intense on two fronts. One—as the Wampanoags' controversies with Narragansetts and Rehoboth over real estate and hogs had already shown in 1660—was Philip's home territory, centered on his capital town of Sowams on Mount Hope Neck, near present-day Bristol, Rhode Island. Sowams, near the shores of a bay that the English had named "Narragansett" after Philip's rivals, occupied an ill-defined region on the boundary between Plymouth and Rhode Island, less than thirty miles from territory claimed by Massachusetts Bay to the north and Connecticut to the west. In these straitened circumstances, Philip complained that his people "had not so much land or money, that they were as good be killed as leave all their livelihood," and "had no hopes left to keep any land."[37] The other front was well to the north and west, in the upper Connecticut River Valley, where planters from Connecticut and Massachusetts Bay were converging on the lands of the Nipmucks, who had hitherto escaped the reach of English religious and political authority, but were well aware of what was happening to the Wampanoags.

Those who harbored any doubts about how seriously the balance of power was shifting away from Native people had only to listen to Philip recount his own experiences since he and his brother had received their new names in 1660. In 1662, Plymouth had demanded that Alexander appear in Plymouth to explain rumors of an Indian conspiracy against the English. When he refused, English troops captured him at gunpoint and arrested him for interrogation. Suffering from a fever and hardly able to stand, Alexander barely survived a lecture from Governor Thomas Prince. On the way back to Sowams, he died. Whether or not the English were directly responsible for Alexander's death—and Philip certainly blamed them— the naked display of power could not be ignored. In 1671, the message of domination was reinforced. Philip, having already been compelled to surrender a sizable cache of guns, but having resisted English demands for complete disarmament, was summoned to explain his "insolent carriages and expressions" in front of the governors of Plymouth, Massachusetts Bay, and Connecticut. The English forced him to sign a document acknowledging that he and his people were "subjects to his majestie the Kinge of England, etc., and the government of New Plymouth, and to theire lawes."[38] Philip probably insisted on inserting King Charles's name in the agreement to avoid admitting total dependence on the planters.

That the planters nonetheless meant what they said about Indians' being subject to their statutes became clear in 1675. For several years, Philip had employed a literate, bilingual Indian man named John Sassamon as his secretary and aide; before taking up this assignment, Sassamon had been one of the translators on Eliot's Bible project. When asked to draw up a will for Philip, Sassamon supposedly "made the writing for a great part of the land to be his" own at the leader's death, but cleverly made the document "read as if it had been as Philip would."[39] Because of this deceit, and because Philip had apparently more generally concluded that his aide was a spy for Plymouth, when Sassamon died mysteriously in early 1675, many Indians as well as English assumed the Wampanoag leader had had him killed. Sassamon's death seems to have been an occasion for Native Christian political opponents of Philip to move against him by fingering the alleged murderers and handing them over for trial and execution by the Plymouth government. The accused were all close advisors of the Wampanoag leader; the accusers included a Christian named William

Nahauton and an alleged eyewitness to the crime named Patuckson, who was apparently deeply in debt to one of the alleged murderers. The influence of Native Christians also became evident in the composition of the trial jury, which included six nonvoting praying Indians sitting with the twelve English colonists who made the real decisions.

Against this background, within a few days of the execution of Sassamon's presumed murderers in June 1675, a party of Wampanoags attacked the Plymouth town of Swansea and killed nine people. Whatever Philip may have been planning, these men seem to have acted on their own, and it is not clear that any Native people yet envisioned a general war against the English. As in Bacon's Rebellion, an unpredictable series of events unfolded, in which personal quarrels mixed with long-standing grievances and the eagerness of many colonists to use the conflict as an excuse to kill every Indian they could get their hands on. As in Virginia, English militias soon sprang into action to try to counter Indian attacks. The militias, however—unlike those in Virginia—had the full support of the colonial governments of Plymouth, Massachusetts Bay, and, belatedly, Connecticut, which by fall was under heavy assault from Nipmucks allied with Philip.

By that time, the Wampanoag leader had also recruited many other local sachems and a substantial number of Native people who had formerly lived in praying towns. Raids on colonists and their property often took an explicitly anti-Christian tone, with attackers using their English-language skills to mock the puritan god. At least one dead colonist was found with his stomach ripped open and a Bible inside, and the Natives apparently made a concerted attempt to burn every last printed copy of Eliot's Massachuset Scriptures: only a handful of these books survived the war. Nor were Christian Indians any more welcome among the English colonists. By October 1675, supposedly for their own safety, all who remained in Natick and the other praying towns had been locked up on an island in Boston Harbor. Indian hating was so widespread that it is possible that more of Eliot's Bibles were burned by colonists than by Indians.

In late 1675, as fall turned to winter, Philip and his allies seemed nearly invincible. Fifty of the roughly ninety English towns of New England were attacked and thirteen destroyed.[40] Among major Native groups, only Uncas and his Mohegans unambiguously sided with the English. Narragansett leaders struggling to remain neutral gathered as many as four thousand people in a fortification they built at the Great Swamp, near what is today Kingston, Rhode Island. In December 1675, New England troops made a preemptive strike on the fort. After suffering heavy casualties in an initial assault, the colonists reenacted the massacre of the Pequots thirty-eight years earlier. There are no accurate counts, but perhaps a thousand Narragansetts—the vast majority of them women and children—perished from flames and gunfire. Although the survivors plunged fully into the war, the tide began to shift toward the English, who waged a systematic campaign to destroy Indian food stores and villages and to keep their enemies on the run.

Philip and about two thousand of his people retreated to a winter encampment north of Albany, where they hoped to recover their health, replenish their weapons, and enlist additional allies. The Wampanoag leader apparently believed that by retreating to the jurisdiction of the duke of York, he could evoke the royal protection to which he and the Narragansetts had separately submitted in former years. Instead, Edmund Andros, the governor of the duke's recently reclaimed province of New York, attempted to assert royal authority over the refractory puritan planters by posing as their indirect military savior. He supplied arms and encouragement to a party of Mohawk Iroquois (long-time enemies of New England Algonquians), who in February 1676 attacked Philip's encampment and forced him and those who survived the attack back across the Hudson.

As the weather warmed during the spring of 1676, English forces, with significant assistance from praying Indians released from their imprisonment, relentlessly hunted down, killed, and enslaved their Indian enemies. In August, forces commanded by Benjamin Church caught up with Philip himself in a swamp near Sowams, where a praying Indian named Alderman shot the Wampanoag leader. According to a book with the disturbing title *Entertaining Passages Relating to Philip's War*, compiled from original diaries by Church's son, the commander announced

Philips death; upon which the whole Army gave Three loud *Huzza's*. Capt. *Church* ordered his body to be pull'd out of the mire on to the Upland, so some of Capt. *Churches Indians* took hold of him by his Stockings, and some by his small Breeches, (being otherwise naked) and drew him thro' the Mud unto the Upland, and a doleful, great, naked, dirty beast, he look'd like. Capt. *Church* then said, *That forasmuch as he had caused many an* English mans *body to lye unburied and rot above ground, that not one of his bones should be buried.* And calling his old *Indian* Executioner, bid him behead and quarter him. Accordingly, he came with his

Hatchet and stood over him, but before he struck he made a small Speech directing it to *Philip;* and said, *He had been a very great Man, and had made many a man afraid of him, but so big as he was he would now chop his Ass for him;* and so went to work, and did as he was ordered. *Philip* having one very remarkable hand being much scarr'd, occasioned by the splitting of a Pistol in it formerly, Capt. *Church* gave the head and that hand to *Alderman,* the *Indian* who shot him, to show to such Gentlemen as would bestow gratuities upon him; and accordingly he got many a Pen[n]y by it.[41]

A few weeks later, in another swamp, Church tracked down Philip's second-in-command, Annawon, and took him prisoner. As the two men spent a sleepless night waiting to travel back to Plymouth, Annawon, speaking in English, presented Church with what he described as *"Philip's* Royalties which he was wont to adorn himself with when he sat in State": a nine-inch-wide wampum belt, adorned with complicated images of flora and fauna, that was designed to be worn around the shoulders and long enough to stretch to Church's ankles; other belts to adorn the head an chest; two powder horns; a red blanket. *"The War is ended by your means,"* Annawon told Church, *"and therefore these things belong unto you."*[42] Only one act could more clearly symbolize the final end of the prestige-goods economy on which Massasoit and then Philip had built their people's prosperity: when Church left Plymouth for a visit to Boston, someone beheaded Annawon and a few other prisoners whose lives Church had spared.

For the Ninnimissinouk in general, the war was as great a catastrophe as the smallpox epidemics earlier in the century. The region's Native population fell by half, with at least two thousand killed in battle or executed, three thousand dead from hunger, disease, and other wartime privations, one thousand enslaved and sent to Bermuda and elsewhere, and two thousand permanently exiled. Those who tried to remain within the boundaries of Massachusetts Bay were informed that they must either live in one of four remaining praying towns or as servants in the houses of English families.

English loss of life was much smaller—fewer than a thousand, or less than 2 percent of the population—but nonetheless staggering. Moreover, the physical devastation was enormous. Towns in a western swath more than twenty miles square were completely abandoned, some not to be reoccupied for a generation. Property damages were estimated at

£150,000, and the direct costs of paying and feeding soldiers, procuring weapons, and the like at another £100,000. Those sums work out to approximately £21 per household—more than most families earned in a year, and the source of crushing tax burdens levied by increasingly unpopular legislatures.[43] As in Bacon's Rebellion, then, there were no clear winners, except perhaps the forces of empire. In 1677, Plymouth governor Josiah Winslow sent King Philip's wampum and other marks of office to London, as a gift for King Charles.

The next year, cataloging rumors of renewed trouble between planters and Native peoples everywhere from the Chesapeake to Connecticut, Governor Andros of New York complained that such problems were "what we must expect and bee lyable to, so long as each petty colony hath or assumes absolute power of peace and warr, which cannot bee managed by such popular Governments."[44] An experienced military officer and long-time member of the royal household, Andros addressed the chaos by improvising the first centralized English imperial policy toward Native North Americans. In that policy, many of the strands of Restoration imperialism came together: the rhetoric of peaceful relations with Native people, the distrust of representative institutions, the assertion of royal claims and prerogatives, the control of international trade, and the quest for royal revenue.

Because one of the New York government's main sources of income was a tax on beaver pelts shipped through Manhattan, Andros had instructions to revitalize commerce with the Haudenosaunee people and with other former partners of Dutch traders on the Hudson, who would thereby also presumably find common interest with the English regime. One of the governor's first acts after securing his authority over Manhattan was to travel to the outpost once again called Albany to convene a treaty council with factions among the Mohawks and the other four Haudenosaunee nations. Andros reported that the Native leaders were eager to escape the French imperial orbit and, "declareing there former Allyance, . . . submitted in an Extraordinary manner, with retitterated promises."[45] When the governor encouraged his new Mohawk friends to attack King Philip's forces in 1676, then, the tactic was part of a broader strategy to strengthen bonds with them—and to place those bonds at the center of a continent-wide approach to dealing with Native people.

But mostly Andros posed as peacemaker. After Philip's death, he invited hundreds of Algonquians to resettle under joint New York and Haudenosaunee protection at Schaghticoke, some twenty miles northeast of Albany—a move that happened to expand New York's claims in the direction of both New France and Massachusetts. Meanwhile, he made similar provisions for Susquehannocks migrating northward from the violence in the Chesapeake, brokering peace between long-time enemies while asserting royal authority far to the south and west of Manhattan. As these people resettled in the Susquehanna River watershed, they were joined by refugees from southern New England and by Shawnees, Nanticokes, and others who migrated from a variety of directions. At the opposite end of the duke's dominions—in the Maine territory disputed with Massachusetts Bay (and La Nouvelle-France)—Andros built a fort at Pemaquid in 1677 and convened a peace treaty in 1678 between several local Wabanaki bands and the English settlers who, Bacon-like, had provoked a local adjunct to King Philip's War as soon as they heard that fighting had broken out farther south. In these varied transactions lay the origins of the English-Indian alliances known as the "Covenant Chain," through which New York and the Iroquois attempted to broker relationships among the region's English colonies and Indian nations—and by which the English Crown acquired a paper empire resembling that of the French far more closely than did the small-scale one Virginia constructed with the uncrowned Queen of Pamunkey.

In the same letter that decried the individual colonies' handling of Indian relations, Andros complained that New England's "popular governments" were busy deeding away to planters the Narragansett lands which the 1664 royal commissioners' treaty had placed under direct royal protection, that they continued their open violation of the Navigation Acts, and that they still refused to administer oaths in the king's name—the same kinds of faults that had brought the commissioners down on them in the first place. The competing proprietary claims that were such an important feature of Restoration empire-making continued to be a problem as well. In 1676, the heir to an old patent to what is today's New Hampshire convinced royal officials to send his handpicked agent, Edward Randolph, to Massachusetts Bay to demand the colonial government's response, and, while he was at it, to revisit all the issues left unresolved after the previous investigation.

Randolph, who arrived while English forces were still in pursuit of

Philip and Annawon, was no more welcome in Boston than his predecessors. He returned to England with a scathing report and a recommendation that a fleet be dispatched to blockade the colony's trade until its leaders submitted to royal authority. He was overruled on the military expedition, but nonetheless made such an impression at court that in 1679 he came back to Boston as royal collector of customs, charged with enforcing the Plantation Duties and other provisions of the Navigation Acts. He also bore instructions to detach New Hampshire from Massachusetts Bay and to proclaim it a separate province under direct royal government. Resisted by Bay Colony officials much as the Virginia commissioners had been by the Green Spring faction, Randolph spent his time strengthening his case against the puritan planters and marshaling the forces of local opponents to the regime.

By the late 1670s, those opponents were diverse and numerous, although never as multitudinous as Randolph's reports made them sound. The insistence on puritan religious orthodoxy in the Bay Colony, in particular, came to seem increasingly odious not only to Randolph and critics in England, but to many New Englanders aware of the varieties of Protestant belief that had flourished in Britain during the Interregnum and the changed calculus of toleration there after the Restoration. No one in New England publicly embraced the connection between toleration and Roman Catholicism repeatedly pressed by Charles and James. Yet the overreaction of those in Parliament who insisted on conformity to the Church of England, and the difficulties that Protestant dissenters faced under the Anglican Royalists' debilitating Uniformity, Corporation, and Test acts, made at least some New Englanders aware of the need for religious compromise, even as it made their local rulers ever more adamant that bishops must never sneak their noses under New England's tent flaps. Revulsion in Massachusetts at the hanging of three Quakers in 1659 and 1660, the struggles of Baptists and other Protestant dissenters to win the right to worship openly, and the desire of the occasional newcomer to worship using the Book of Common Prayer all added voices to a local minority eager to gain Randolph's ear.

Religious discontents merged with political and economic problems. One of the few concessions that the Bay Colony's rulers had made to earlier royal complaints was to extend voting rights to a handful of individuals who were not church members but who met a rigorous property-tax requirement. For the most part, however, power at the colony level remained in the hands of the shrinking portion of the population who were male visible saints. Political participation on the local level apparently remained more nearly universal among property-owning male planters, but this distinction only made the narrow base of colony-wide politics more evident, particularly in light of the heavy central tax burdens imposed after King Philip's War. (The town of Dorchester, for instance, paid about £28 to the colony government in the prewar year of 1672, but more than £111 in 1678.)[46] A suspicious number of house fires, along with bad harvests, disease, and the international trade disruptions of the Third Anglo-Dutch War not only multiplied the economic woes but led puritan clergy to conclude that God was angry with the colony. "The people here as you know are generally very poore," New Englander Simon Bradstreet tried to explain to Randolph in 1684. "The Warr with the Indians and late great fyres have much impoverished this Country, and the unproffitableness of trade every where doeth much discourage."[47] Conditions were not quite as dire as in Bacon's Virginia, but there were real parallels.

When Randolph's campaign against Massachusetts finally succeeded and the long-threatened *quo warranto* came down in 1684, a substantial faction actually welcomed the change—among them colonist Joseph Dudley, sent to London to lobby in defense of the Bay Colony's charter, but disgusted by the unwillingness of the puritan regime to give him any real power to negotiate. When Dudley returned to Boston at the head of an interim royal government, he and many others hoped that compliance with the Navigation Acts and cooperation with political interests at court would allow the region's merchants to prosper in the Atlantic carrying trades taken from the Dutch. Such hopes were short-lived, however. The Massachusetts Bay charter was repealed only a few months before Charles II passed away. When James, duke of York, became King James II of England and James VII of Scotland, he set about reducing New England, along with the entirety of his personal holdings in New York, to the absolute form of government that he had advocated since the Restoration.

In a series of moves between 1686 and 1688, colony borders were essentially erased, including those of the proprietaries of East and West New Jersey, of recently established New Hampshire, of disputed Maine, of previously relatively compliant Connecticut, Rhode Island, and Plymouth, and, of course, of Massachusetts Bay. All, along with New York, were lumped together in a single entity called the "Dominion of New England." This was to be the first of as many as four North American and Caribbean supercolonies that would function like the viceroyalties that organized the vast holdings of the Spanish Empire. Over the Dominion, James placed his trusted agent Edmund Andros, who was instructed to reign without summoning elected assemblies, "to permitt liberty of conscience in religion to all persons," to promote the use of enslaved labor by giving "all due encouragement . . . to the Royall African Company," to keep peace with the Indians "that they may apply themselves to the English trade and nation," to place all militia forces under royal command, to grant land as he saw fit, and to fill the royal coffers with taxes, customs duties, and fees from real estate transactions.[48] Indeed, the planter elites that Andros confronted were hard pressed to decide which was worse: his denial of their privilege to tax and govern themselves (and others) through their legislatures, or his insistence that those who made land their idol pay for new patents under the king's name.

James was no more popular among the political elite of England than Andros was in Massachusetts Bay. The conflation of Protestantism with English nationalism that had prevailed since the era of Elizabeth I reached new heights of religious bigotry, as one alleged conspiracy after another attached itself to James and to the Catholics and presumed Catholics around him. In 1678, a onetime Church of England clergyman named Titus Oates had circulated a fantastic story that Jesuit spies were plotting to assassinate Charles II, place James on the throne, and start a reign of terror against Protestants. Although there was no truth behind the story of the "Popish Plot," it did unleash a reign of terror—against Catholics in London, some thirty-five of whom were tried and executed for their alleged role in the conspiracy. The uproar also led to the "Exclusion Crisis" of 1678–1681, in which James's foes in Parliament nearly passed legislation that would have banned him, or any other Catholic, from the throne. In such a charged environment, it is no surprise that in February 1685, brief rebellions against the new monarch broke out in each of his two primary kingdoms.

Still, carefully managed, if not rigged, parliamentary elections in England returned a house willing to put up with the king for what everyone assumed to be the few years until his death and the expected succession to the throne of his daughter by a previous marriage, Mary, who had been carefully snatched from the royal household to be raised as a Protestant.

In 1677—on the eve of the Exclusion Crisis and in the midst of the controversy over the Crown's relations with Louis XIV and the unstable peace
that ended the Second Anglo-Dutch War—Charles II had arranged for
her marriage to his nephew Willem of Orange, who had reclaimed the office of stadtholder during the war with France. Thus, the expectation of
many in England, and of Willem himself, was that the great military champion of Protestantism on the Continent was poised to become England's
king when his wife took the throne.

Despite the willingness of his English foes to wait him out, James
quickly managed to alienate nearly all factions. He built up his armies and
navies without parliamentary consent. Anglican Royalists who thought
they had safely reasserted control in their localities found that their positions as justices of the peace or lords lieutenant of the militia were under
assault, as James tried to replace them with his own appointees. Boroughs
and corporations were similarly "remodeled," to purge opponents of the
Crown and supporters of the Anglican Royalists' Corporation and Test
acts. Catholic Mass was publicly celebrated at court, and Catholic chapels
publicly opened, it seemed, everywhere in the country. Catholics put in
jail for their alleged role in the Popish Plot were released. Fears of papist
conspiracies and suspicion of what the Stuarts meant by religious toleration took on renewed life late in 1685. King Louis XIV of France revoked
the Edict of Nantes, which for nearly a century had provided some protection to his nation's substantial Protestant Huguenot population. As refugees streamed out of the European continent, James did his best to prevent any of them from resettling in England. Meanwhile, the new king
also pressed his argument that he could nullify legislation, in particular the
Test Act. He not only issued declarations of toleration for Catholics and
(he said and meant, despite the suspicions of his critics) all other Christians, but appointed professed Catholics to high offices, tried to rig an
election at an Oxford College to put a Catholic at its head, and encouraged
the pope to ordain bishops for the British Isles.

Such royal flouting of parliamentary authority on behalf of tolerance
ceased to be tolerable by June 1688, when James and his queen, Mary of
Modena, produced an infant son—who, in his maleness, trumped the
claim of James's daughter Mary to the throne and paved the way for a series of Catholic, absolutist, French-allied tyrants stretching long into the
future. Wild rumors circulated that the baby was not James's son at all, but
a pretender whom a midwife had smuggled into the birthing room to replace a stillborn royal. Within months, James's political opponents had of-

fered the throne of England jointly to James's daughter Mary and to her husband, Willem of Orange, vindicating their long-standing Protestant claim. But "offered" may be too strong a word. Willem was determined that England must not again ally with Louis XIV against the Netherlands, which was once again on the brink of war with France. In the fall of 1688, he mobilized one of the greatest armadas in history to invade England and, while rescuing its Protestants from a papist king, ensure that its military and financial resources would enter the war on the correct side.

As many as five hundred ships and forty thousand men crossed the North Sea under Willem's personal leadership and—taking advantage of a "Protestant wind" that speeded their progress and kept James's fleet bottled up in the Thames—they landed at Torbay, in the southwest of England. As many as forty thousand copies of the "Declaration" released on the eve of the invasion explained that Willem sought only to rescue England from the ill-advised policies of the "Evill Councellours" surrounding James II. Although, he said using the royal plural, "our Dearest and most Entirely Beloved Consort, the Princess, and likewise we Our Selves, have so great an Interest in this Matter, and such a Right, as all the world knows, to the Succession to the Crown," he denied any "other Designe, but to have a free and lawfull Parliament assembled, as soon as possible." The goal was to ensure "the Preservation of the Protestant Religion, the Covering of all men from Persecution for their Consciences, and the Securing to the whole Nation the free enjoyment of all their Lawes, Rights and Liberties, under a Just and Legall Government."[49]

Careful deployment of Dutch troops prevented open resistance as Willem made a triumphant, flag-waving procession through the countryside toward London. James II—having fled his palace and tossed the Great Seal of England into the Thames in a misguided effort to prevent any official governmental acts from taking place in his absence—made it all too easy for James's opponents to say that the thrones of the Three Kingdoms were vacant and now awaited their just claimants. With as little reference as possible to the fact that overwhelming military force had enabled a virtually bloodless coup, Willem of Orange became William III of England and Ireland and William II of Scotland. His allegedly equal co-monarch was called Mary II in all of her realms.

News of the "Glorious Revolution" reached North America in early 1689. Almost immediately, uprisings occurred in the twin capitals of the Dominion of New England. In Boston, crowds threw Randolph and other officials in jail and forced Andros to yield control of the city's fort and join his comrades in captivity. The victors reestablished their old charter government in the name of the new Protestant monarchs and packed the tyrants on a ship bound for England. In New York, a militia led by a colonist named Jacob Leisler similarly took control of the royal fort and induced lieutenant governor Francis Nicholson to flee for the British Isles. In Maryland, meanwhile, a group calling itself the "Protestant Associators" forced the Catholic Lord Baltimore's lieutenant governor from office and, like their counterparts in Boston and New York, justified their actions in the name of William and Mary. Restoration imperialism seemed dead, and the planters once again seemed firmly in control—if "control" was the right word to describe the fragile power of those who presided over the shattered economies and societies of New England and the Chesapeake.

TWELVE

Revolution, War, and
a New Transatlantic Order

"WHEREAS HIS LATE Majesty King William the Third, then Prince of Orange, did, with an armed Force, undertake a glorious Enterprize, for delivering this Kingdom from Popery and Arbitrary Power; and divers Subjects of this Realm, well-affected to their Country, joined and assisted His
late Majesty in the said Enterprize; and it having pleased Almighty God to
crown the same with Success, the late happy Revolution did take Effect,
and was established." Or so it looked from the year 1710, when members of the House of Lords voted to impeach a clergyman named Henry
Sacheverell for daring publicly to question the legitimacy of the events of
1688–1689.[1] Britons on both sides of the Atlantic would one day tell themselves that King William, patriotic subjects, and the Protestant god had
created a happy world of liberty and prosperity where people were free of
the twin evils of "Popery and Arbitrary Power."

Yet a closer look reveals much older forces at work—forces familiar to
progenitors, conquistadores, traders, planters, and imperialists alike: war
and the expansion of the imperial state. In many respects, imperialism after the Glorious Revolution looked much the same as before. Three major
factors made all the difference, however. The resolutely Protestant domestic and foreign policy of the new regime removed the ideological disso-
nance that had always rendered Stuart patriotism suspect. William's un-
questioned Protestantism led not only to a religiously congruent war with
France, but to a war that, because of the parallel tracks on which the two
empires had been running, quickly spilled over into North America. And
the nature of the French and Spanish empires in North America ensured

that Native peoples, north and south, would be in the thick of the fighting. This had the ironic consequence of creating a firm place within the imperial system both for a set of powerful Indian nations and for the English planter regimes that otherwise would just as soon have seen the Indians dead.

Looking back on it, one sees that there *was* much to find glorious in the "happy Revolution" begun in 1688. On receiving the crown of England, William and Mary agreed to a Declaration of Rights, which was subsequently incorporated into a Bill of Rights adopted by Parliament in 1689. Responding to a list of specific acts through which "the Late King *James* the Second, by the assistance of divers Evil Counsellors, Judges and Ministers Employed by him, did endeavour to Subvert and Extirpate the Protestant Religion and the Laws and Liberties of this Kingdom," the members of the Lords and Commons spelled out English men's "Ancient Rights and Liberties." Monarchs had no power to suspend or ignore acts of Parliament or to establish courts, levy taxes, or maintain standing armies without the consent of the Lords and Commons. Parliamentary debate had to be free, and elections frequent. "Subjects which are Protestants" had the right to bear "Arms for Their Defence suitable to their Conditions and as allowed by Law." All English men had rights to petition the king without fear of persecution for their opinions, to be allowed jury trials, and to be free of "Excessive Bail," "excessive Fines," and "Cruel and Unusual Punishments."[2]

Only by agreeing to protect these rights were William and Mary and their heirs entitled to assume the throne—or at least that was the official line. And, the same dogma insisted, only by the presumed freedom of Protestantism could English liberties be preserved. "Whereas it hath been found by Experience that it is inconsistent with the Safety and Welfare of this Protestant Kingdom to be Governed by a Popish Prince, or by any King or Queen Marrying a Papist," Parliament decreed "that all and every Person and Persons that . . . shall Profess the Popish Religion, or shall Marry a Papist, shall be Excluded and be for ever uncapable to Inherit, Possess or Enjoy the Crown and Government of this Realm." Moreover, should a future monarch go over to the side of the Antichrist, "the People of these Realms shall be and are hereby Absolved of their Allegiance," as if that monarch "were naturally Dead."[3]

"Popery and Arbitrary Power" thus became more strongly linked than ever in English minds, with England's Protestant liberty guaranteed by a novel contractual theory of monarchy that philosophers such as John Locke were busy codifying. The Bill of Rights defined the obligations of kings and queens to protect the liberties of their subjects, whose allegiance depended upon royal fulfillment of those obligations. The same contractual theory prevailed in Scotland, where William and Mary agreed to a "Claim of Right" drafted by the northern kingdom's parliament. This document outdid the English Bill of Rights both in its list of particulars and in its portrayal of the former king as a "profest *Papist*" who "did by the Advice of Wicked and Evil Counsellers Invade the Fundamental Constitution of this Kingdom, and Altered it from a Legal Limited Monarchy, to an Arbitrary Despotick Power."[4]

Just as integral to the Revolution as the Bill of Rights and the Claim of Right, and just as integral to what the revolutionaries understood to be their victory over Popery and Arbitrary Power, was the Toleration Act that the English Parliament passed in 1689. With Anglican Royalists discredited, this statute removed nearly all legal restraints from Protestants who behaved themselves, paid their taxes (including levies that supported the state Church establishment), and agreed not to "worship with the doors locked, barred, or bolted" (and thus not to hatch plots or celebrate Mass out of the sight of authorities and neighbors). All one had to do was to swear—or, if one was a Quaker or some other dissenter who thought oath taking was sacrilege, to declare publicly—that he would "be true and faithful to King William and Queen Mary" and "renounce, as impious and heretical, that damnable doctrine and position, That princes excommunicated or deprived by the Pope . . . may be deposed or murdered by their subjects," to "profess faith" in the Christian Trinity, and to "acknowledge the Holy Scriptures of the Old and New Testament to be given by divine inspiration."[5] These declarations did not exactly guarantee full religious liberty; Roman Catholics and Jews were defiantly excluded, and a Test Act continued to limit officeholding to communicants in the established Anglican Church. But English Protestants had at last declared something like the spiritual truce envisioned by the founders of Carolina—and by the detested Stuarts.

The fact that those detested Stuarts remained very much part of the picture was also an important aspect of the Revolution. A popular song bravely proclaimed that

> The Pillars of Popery now are blown down,
> One thousand six hundred eighty and eight,
> Which has frighten'd our Monarch away from his Crown,
> One thousand six hundred eighty and eight.
> For *Myn Heer* did appear, and they scamper'd for fear,
> One thousand six hundred eighty and eight.[6]

Those whom Heer William sent scampering settled with James in his court in exile, on a French estate provided by Louis XIV. The Sun King, like the pope and much of the rest of Catholic Europe, continued to recognize James VII and II—and after him his son James Francis Edward, the "Old Pretender" whose birth in 1688 had helped spark the Revolution—as the legitimate "Jacobite" claimants to the Scottish and English thrones. When William brought England into his War of the League of Augsburg, he linked the fate of the Revolution to military victory over the French. As in the days of Elizabeth I, England's national independence again became inseparable from hatred of Catholics.

If anything, the link was stronger in North America than in the British Isles. War, fear of war, and anti-Catholic bigotry had permeated the movements to overthrow the Dominion of New England and the proprietary government of Maryland. On the eve of the revolutions, memories of Bacon's Rebellion and King Philip's War were still fresh, and planters feared that surviving Indians would make common cause with the French to settle old scores. In this context, Restoration imperialism's concern for the rights of Native peoples put governors in the same unpopular position that William Berkeley had occupied in the 1670s, but with an added suspicion that a papist plot was behind it all. "We are every day threatned with the Loss of our Lives, Liberties, and Estates . . . by the Practices and Machinations that are on foot to betray us to the *French, Northern,* and other *Indians,* of which, some have been dealt withal, and others Invited to Assist in our Destruction," Maryland's revolutionaries complained in their printed "Declaration of the Reasons and Motives for the Present Appearing in Arms of Their Majesties Protestant Subjects."[7]

From places such as Maryland and New England, therefore, the Covenant Chain diplomacy of New York's Governor Andros, and his efforts to resettle Native refugees from the conflicts of the 1670s under Iroquois protection, looked deeply suspicious. Yet many people in the province of New York (before it became part of the Dominion) and in the villages of the Haudenosaunee nations saw things quite differently, at least until the mid-1680s. Not only did Andros's policies revive a mutually profitable trade between Albany and Iroquoia; they also helped the duke's governor build political support, both among Dutch- and English-speaking traders who reaped the profits and among Iroquois leaders who hoped to escape French hegemony. Emboldened and supplied by these alliances, in the early 1680s anti-French Iroquois resumed large-scale military campaigns against the Great Lakes nations whom the French considered part of their empire. Haudenosaunee people further declared their independence from the *pax gallica* by expelling Jesuit priests from their communities. In the summer of 1687, these acts provoked some two thousand French and allied Native troops to invade the country of the Senecas, the westernmost Iroquois nation, and sack all of its major towns.

Still knowing nothing of the revolution in the British Isles, English North Americans thus had their worst fears confirmed: French armies were on the move, and James's governors were doing nothing about it. Andros seemed to confirm these fears in a public council held at Albany in October 1688, when he urged the Iroquois to halt retaliatory strikes on La Nouvelle-France. "You have had notice of the truce made by our Great King [James] putting a stop to the French invading this Government, or annoying you further, or your continuing any acts of hostility towards them; which is punctually to be observed," he announced, with a surreal assurance that "you may go and hunt as formerly and need have no other regard to the French . . . then as they are our friends to do them no harm."[8] Similarly, the Dominion governor appealed for calm when he heard reports that French-allied refugees from King Philip's War had killed several English people on the upper Connecticut River. And when jumpy colonists and Wabanakis on the Maine frontier began capturing and shooting each other, he (rightly) laid most of the blame on the English. Andros then marched a six-hundred-strong army, dragooned from throughout southern New England to Maine, on what his critics called either a wild goose chase, an expedition too much inclined to talking with (rather than killing) Indians, or a fiendish plot to leave southern towns defenseless by taking their militiamen away from home. "We are again Briar'd in the Perplexities of another *Indian War;* how, or why, is a mystery too deep for us to unfold," the Boston revolutionaries wrote in the

printed justification of their actions. "The whole War hath been so managed, that we can't but suspect in it, a branch of the Plot, *to bring us
Low.*"[9]

There was nothing happy, then, about the mood of the North Americans who carried out their own versions of the Glorious Revolution in
1689. The mood was not confined to the three colonies that erupted
in open revolt. Restless Virginians, for instance, still recalling Berkeley's
"french Despotick Methods," had endured even more from their governor, Francis Howard, Baron Howard of Effingham. He arrived in 1684
and enacted a Stuart agenda of personal control of appointments to office,
government by royal proclamation, and rule without representative institutions; he dismissed the House of Burgesses in 1685. Virginians seem to
have refrained from joining the uprisings only because Effingham happened to have sailed for England shortly before word of the revolution
reached the colony, upon which the council ruling in his absence promptly
proclaimed the province's loyalty to William and Mary.

In Boston, New York, and St. Mary's City, meanwhile, the revolutionaries claimed that they had risen up only under the direst of circumstances,
and they explicitly linked their actions to those taking place across the Atlantic. "We did nothing against these Proceedings, but only cry to our
God," said the Bostonians, until "informed that the rest of the English
America . . . [was] Alarmed with just and great fears, that they may be
attaqu'd by the *French*," and "(though the *Governour* has taken all imagi-
nable care to keep us all ignorant thereof) that the Almighty God hath
been pleased to prosper the noble undertaking of the Prince of *Orange,*
to preserve the Three Kingdoms from the horrible brinks of Popery and
Slavery."[10]

Even more fevered rhetoric came from Maryland, where the revolutionaries recalled their "great Grief and Consternation, upon the first
News of the great Overture and happy Change in *England.*" But instead of
celebrating deliverance from arbitrary power,

> We found our selves surrounded with Strong and Violent Endeavours from
> our *Governours* here, being the Lord *Baltemore's* Deputies and Represen-
> tatives, to defeat us of the same.
>
> We still find all the means used by there very Persons and their Agents;
> *Jesuits, Priests,* and lay *Papists,* that Art or Malice can suggest, to divert the
> Obedience and Loyalty of the Inhabitants from Their Most Sacred *Maj-*

esties, to that height of Impudence, that solumn Masses and Prayers are used (*as we have very good Information*) in their *Chappels* and *Oratories* for the prosperous success of the *Popish* Forces in *Ireland,* and the *French* Designs against *England,* whereby they would involve us in the same Crime of Disloyalty with themselves, and render us Obnoxious to the Insupportable Displeasure of Their Majesties.[11]

Much of this language, of course, came from men desperate to ally themselves in print with the new regime across the Atlantic, in order to avoid being hanged as traitors. Yet the hope that the new monarchs would rescue their North American subjects from tyranny, popery, the French, and the Indians was genuine.

Everywhere, the broader target was the political and social order that had taken shape in the Restoration era—for which the shorthand phrase was "Popery and Arbitrary Power." *The Declaration, of the Gentlemen, Merchants, and Inhabitants of Boston, and the Countrey Adjacent,* written, probably by clergyman Cotton Mather, to justify the overthrow of Andros, reads like a conspiratorial critique of everything associated with Restoration imperialism—not just its Catholicism masquerading as religious toleration, but its disdain for representative assemblies, its imposition of the Navigation Acts, its schemes to enrich a well-connected few, its feudal dreams of a docile agricultural labor force, and its assaults on the privileges of small planters. The Bostonians traced all of these things to the same sources as the alleged Popish Plot to assassinate Charles II in 1678. In the spirit of that conspiracy, Edward Randolph ("a man for his *Malice* and *Fals-hood* well known unto us all") had engineered the repeal of the Massachusetts Bay charter, leaving the colony "without any liberty for an Assembly, which the other *American Plantations* have." Enforcement of the Navigation Acts served "to damp and spoyl" New England's trade, while in other ways "care was taken to load Preferments principally upon such Men as were strangers to, and haters of the People." Andros's minions allegedly believed "that the people in *New-England* were all *Slaves* and the only difference between them and *Slaves* is their not being bought and sold." And "because these things could not make us miserable fast enough, there was a notable Discovery made, of, we know not what *flaw* in all our *Titles to our Lands.*" Legal proceedings were "served on People; that after all their sweat and their cost upon their formerly purchased Lands, thought themselves *Free holders* of what they had." Having thus seized choice real estate, "the Governour caused the Lands . . . to be measured out, for his Creatures to take possession of."[12]

Given all this, the New Englanders believed they "ought surely to follow the Patterns which the Nobility, Gentry and Commonalty in several parts of the Kingdom have set before us, though *they* therein have chiefly proposed to prevent what *we* already endure."[13] As in England and Scotland, the revolution in Boston involved a major show of military force; and, as in Bacon's Virginia, that force was in the form of militias self-mobilized in the name of the people. After months of rumors, in early April 1689 a ship from the West Indies brought news that William had invaded England. Andros, seemingly confirming every suspicion about him, arrested the bearer of the tidings on charges of sedition. Within two weeks, apparently spontaneously but clearly with careful planning, more than a thousand armed men appeared in the streets of the city. A self-designated "Council of Safety"—composed of representatives elected under the former charter, a group of Andros's appointed council members who had defected, and several prominent merchants and clergy—maintained order while Andros, Randolph, the commander of a royal navy ship in the harbor, and two dozen other officials sat in prison. Within two months, the pre-Dominion system of government was back in business, awaiting the royal pleasure. By midsummer, the previous regimes in Connecticut, Rhode Island, and Plymouth had similarly reestablished themselves, though not always without internal controversy.

Whatever controversies there might have been in southern New England, they paled next to the bitter struggles that the Glorious Revolution spawned in New York, though the overthrow of James II's government occurred bloodlessly there as well. In New England, the form of government under the Dominion was an innovation that provoked virtually unanimous opposition among forces that otherwise were inclined to be at each other's throats. In New York, it grew organically from the conquest regime that Andros himself had created a decade and a half earlier. Much as Berkeley had previously done in Virginia, Andros and Thomas Dongan (who succeeded Andros before his return as governor of the Dominion and who was a professed Roman Catholic) had cultivated support among a sector of the local elite. This faction had profited from control of the fur trade, from a thriving market in other exports and imports, from land grants, from the perquisites of office, and from an economy more prosperous than it had been in the final days of the Dutch regime. Many of its members were recently arrived English-speakers, but some were longtime Dutch colonists who threw in their lot with the new regime. Opposing these "anglicizers" were others who considered themselves locked out of a political order dominated by English overlords. Like the general population of Nieu Nederlandt, this group included people from many different ethnic backgrounds. Among them were German-speakers such as the militia captain who emerged as the revolutionaries' leader, Jacob Leisler. But most identified with the Dutch language and the Calvinist Dutch Reformed Church, and thus felt a particular affinity with England's new Dutch Protestant king.

In June 1689, these "Leislerians" engineered New York's Glorious Revolution and, with a show of militia strength, forced Andros's lieutenant governor, Francis Nicholson, to surrender the government and the city's fort. While their actions resembled those of the Bostonians after whom they modeled themselves, the Leislerians encountered resistance at every step from anglicizer opponents, who came to be known by default as "Anti-Leislerians." New York's Glorious Revolution thus quickly turned into a struggle over which of two competing elites would win the new monarchs' approval. The terms of the struggle became clear when the anglicizers who controlled Albany refused to recognize the authority of Leisler's New York City Council of Safety. Calling themselves a "convention," the Albany leaders issued their own proclamation of loyalty to William and Mary and conducted their own diplomacy with the Haudenosaunee people, who were again vigorously fighting the common French enemy. Only in February 1690, when a French and allied Indian army destroyed the town of Schenectady a few miles away, were the Albany Anti-Leislerians frightened into a begrudging alliance with the Leislerians.

Maryland faced no such immediate French threat, despite wild rumors that the papists and the Seneca Iroquois were plotting an attack. Still, if there was anywhere that Protestant hatred of Catholics would seem to have a basis in reality, it was in this colony. Maryland's priests supposedly prayed for James's triumph, and its proprietary officials publicly refused to acknowledge the new monarchs even after William and Mary had been proclaimed king and queen in neighboring Virginia in April 1689. Maryland, chartered by Charles II in 1632 and in many ways the model for the proprietary colonies established after the Restoration, had never, strictly speaking, been a Catholic colony. The Calvert family, the Lords Baltimore, were themselves Catholics and certainly intended their territory to be a refuge for their English coreligionists. Yet the majority of planters and servants who emigrated to the colony were indistinguishable from those who had settled next door in Virginia. The usual mix of moderate Church of England conformists and varied hot Protestant dissenters had no sympathy with the proprietor's religious convictions, and they looked with suspicion on the private chapels where priests practiced rites outlawed in the British Isles. Religious, political, and economic strife had reached a peak during a chaotic mid-1640s period known as the "plundering time" and during the Cromwell era, when control, such as it was, slipped in and out of the Calvert family's hands.

After 1660, the proprietorship (held by Cecilius Calvert, Second Baron Baltimore, until his death in 1675, and thereafter by Charles Calvert, Third Baron Baltimore) ruled with the usual tendencies of Restoration imperialism. Religious toleration was the official policy—which inevitably led the Protestant majority to argue that papists were favored. A monumental Catholic church, constructed of brick in the capital of St. Mary's City during the late 1660s, drove home the message. Meanwhile, the representativeness and authority of the colony's elected legislature receded. In 1670, free men who did not own property lost the right to vote, as they did in Virginia the same year. A few years later, Cecilius Calvert unilaterally declared that only two representatives, rather than four, should be elected from each county. The proprietors, their lieutenant governors, and a small circle of appointed councillors ignored laws passed by the assembly and asserted powers similar to those that James II claimed at home. Like the Green Spring faction in Virginia, like the anglicizers in New York, and, indeed, like the puritan proprietors of New England's towns, this group monopolized officeholding and manipulated land grants and other resources for their own benefit—in a context of depressed tobacco prices and general poverty. Religious hatreds merely gave a harder edge to the kind of elite stranglehold on power that was familiar almost everywhere in English North America on the eve of the Glorious Revolution.

Even when Cecilius Calvert, issuing edicts from England, tried to rule in what he considered the interests of ordinary colonists, the arbitrariness of the proprietary system came to the fore. In 1666, Virginia's Berkeley had convinced a reluctant Maryland assembly and Charles Calvert (then Cecilius's lieutenant governor on the scene) to agree that both Chesapeake colonies would stop growing tobacco for a year, in hopes of raising prices for the leaf. Cecilius promptly vetoed the agreement, "haveing duely considered the greate Inconveniences which may follow from the same not onely to the *poorer* sorte of the planters within Our said Province, But alsoe to the Kings most Excellent Majestie in relation to his Majesties Customes." The pronouncement, "given under Our hand and Seale . . . in the 35th Yeare of Our Dominion over our said Province," led hypocritical members of Virginia's Green Spring faction to complain that the "absolute and Princely Tearmes" of Baltimore's Royal We language and Cecilius's "unlimited and (it appeares to us) Independent power and authority" left "his owne Province weithering and decaying in distresse and poverty."[14]

Against a background of many such episodes, hundreds of withered and distressed militiamen calling themselves "Protestant Associators" appeared in St. Mary's City in late July 1689. At their head, playing the role of Jacob Leisler or Nathaniel Bacon, was a longtime assembly representative and critic of the regime named John Coode. Playing the role of Edmund Andros—but emphatically not that of the trigger-happy William Berkeley—Charles Calvert's lieutenant governor William Joseph and his outnumbered troops surrendered without a shot. No one in the English-speaking world better articulated the contractual theory at the core of the transatlantic Glorious Revolution than the Maryland Associators, as they made their case in print. "Looking upon our selves, Discharged, Dissolved, and Free from all manner of Duty, Obligation, or Fidelity, to the Deputies, Governours, or Chief Magistrates here, . . . *They having Departed from their Allegiance* (upon which alone our said Duty and Fidelity to them depends) and by their Complices and Agents endeavoured the Destruction of our Religion, Lives, Liberties, and Properties, all which they are bound to Protect," Marylanders had been compelled "*to take up Arms, to Preserve, Vindicate, and Assert the Sovereign Dominion, and Right, of King* WILLIAM *and Queen* MARY."[15]

It was one thing for disaffected English Americans to rise up in the name of what they understood to be the principles of William and Mary. It was another to get those in power at the imperial center to accept the colonial rebels' assertions. And it was another thing entirely for a semblance of political stability to emerge out of the chaos in Boston, New York, and St.

Mary's City, or, for that matter, in London and Edinburgh. Little was certain in 1689 and early 1690, as the fragile new regimes in New York and Boston struggled to deal with the French and Indian attacks they had long feared, and as the silence remained deafening from an imperial center preoccupied with war and rebellion closer to home. Only after another chaotic quarter-century would the Revolution finally appear to be Glorious.

Nothing was more important in determining the fate of the transatlantic revolutions than the wars with the French empire that William III and II had begun on the European continent before invading England in 1688 and that the Haudenosaunee Iroquois had begun in North America several years earlier. William's War of the League of Augsburg (recalled in the colonies as "King William's War" and elsewhere as the "Nine Years War") continued until 1697. Five years later, and a few months after William died and the throne passed to Mary's sister Anne, England and the Netherlands again battled France in the War of the Spanish Succession ("Queen Anne's War"), which—provoked by the heirless death of Carlos II—did not end until 1714. On both sides of the Atlantic, the sheer length of these struggles between Protestant Britons and Catholic French burned the language of antipopery into Anglo-American consciousnesses, while the pressures of war forced quarreling factions to accept political arrangements that they otherwise might have resisted. In England, supporters and doubters of the Revolution alike—those who came to be called "Whigs" and Anglican Royalist-descended "Tories," respectively—had to compete for the titles of true patriots, true Protestants, true experts in managing the war, and, ultimately, true defenders of the political arrangements patched together in 1688 and 1689. In Ireland, war and revolution made a mockery of the liberties that the English so proudly proclaimed. In Scotland, the northern kingdom's parliament had to accept its own destruction and full union with England. And in the colonies, similarly, the pressures of war forced elites to acknowledge a degree of centralized imperial control that few could have anticipated in 1689.

As had been the case for centuries everywhere in Western Europe, the consolidation of state power became inseparable from the making of war. In England, conflicts at the turn of the eighteenth century strengthened the State in countless ways, while entrenching the regime created in 1688–1689. Most notable among these developments was an ever-stronger alliance between wealthy subjects and the government, epitomized by

Parliament's creation of the Bank of England in 1694. In return for an initial loan to the king of £1.2 million, a group of urban merchants and landed aristocrats led by the Scots financier William Paterson received a royal charter as the "Governor and Company of the Banke of England."[16] The bank did not formally receive a monopoly on such activities as "dealeing in Bills of Exchange or in buying or selling Bullion Gold or Silver," and would not for many decades acquire the functions we today associate with a nation's central bank. Indeed, "monopoly" was becoming a bad word among merchants who had chafed under James's many royal proprietaries and companies. But the bank's titanic capitalization (the loan to the government counted as its stock) and its income from annual government interest payments of a near-usurious 8 percent, payable quarterly along with various management fees, gave it an economic power almost no other English entity could match. England at last had a financial equivalent to the Dutch East India and West India companies.

Perhaps more important, the creation of the Bank of England set a pattern that the British state would follow throughout the eighteenth century. Massive loans made military exploits and other governmental activities possible; by the end of the War of the Spanish Succession, the total government debt stood at roughly £40 million. Creditors received both substantial return on their investments and the right to buy and sell at a profit the securities that carried the debt. The government in turn paid the interest on its loans through earmarked taxes approved by representatives of the investors in Parliament. (In 1694, for example, this tax was a complicated levy on the tonnage of merchant vessels; more frequently, excise taxes on particular goods paid the bills.) An iron circle thus took shape: the government got the resources it needed through loans funded by taxes voted by its creditors, who had a vital interest in the survival of the government and its system of debt and taxation. James II had collected about 3 percent of the national income in taxes. By 1715 the regime was reaping nearly 9 percent, and, while many grumbled, few with real power seriously complained. The fiscal-military state had at last solved the problem of the *adelantados:* subjects' impersonal money and credit, rather than their unpredictable personal service and private loans, now did the bidding of the king, who could enforce his (and Parliament's) will through something resembling a professional bureaucracy. War, debt, and taxes—rather than King William's arms, patriotic subjects, and the blessings of the Protestant god—secured the fate of England's late happy revolution.

Elsewhere in the British Isles, external conflict with the French merged with internal war against opponents of the new regime to create less happy outcomes—outcomes that would create new outflows of immigrants to North America, once relative peace returned. The deposed King James invaded Ireland in March 1689, with hefty military and financial support from Louis XIV. In July 1690, William III and II personally led the army that defeated the Jacobites at the Battle of the Boyne, but not before a deepened legacy of religious and political hatreds had been bequeathed to the island. In an attempt to rally support, James had summoned an Irish parliament, in which Catholics, who had been barred from sitting in the body since 1652, passed legislation confiscating the lands of the Protestants who had confiscated Catholic lands after the Cromwellian conquests. After William's victory, a new parliament—with its membership once again restricted to Protestants—undid these measures and, over the next several decades, passed increasingly punitive "penal laws" restricting the political, legal, and economic rights of the three-quarters of the population who were Catholic.

Meantime, England's parliament, determined that Ireland should never again provide a base for French and Jacobite threats, chipped away at the independence of the western kingdom and its already unrepresentative legislature. Under these conditions, nothing like religious toleration even for dissenting Protestants took hold in Ireland. Local power rested with a small elite among the 10 percent of the population affiliated with the legally sanctioned Protestant bishops of the Church of Ireland. The tens of thousands of dissenting Presbyterians who constituted a majority of the population in the northern province of Ulster fared better than their Catholic neighbors, but still remained ineligible to serve in their kingdom's parliament and in other ways suffered political, economic, and social marginalization.

In Lowland Scotland, it was Presbyterians who seized the right to label all other Protestants dissenters. One of the northern kingdom's first acts after the revolution was to abolish the on-again, off-again system of bishops that had been so controversial since the days of James VI and I and to affirm the Calvinist Presbyterian Kirk as the state Church. Surviving Scottish bishops and a dwindling band of their followers in what later came to be called the "Church of Scotland" found themselves in a legal limbo compounded by the suspicion that their real sympathies were with the Jacobites and Catholics. Gaelic-speaking Highland Scots, most of whom, like their Gaelic Irish counterparts, actually were practicing Catholics, were a more reliable and more numerous threat to the Protestant monarchy because of ancient prejudices and oppression by Scots-speaking Lowlanders.

As with Ireland, then, Scotland remained a constant source of worry to the English elite, which was busily marrying its economic future to a Protestant fiscal-military state. Pressure mounted for a formal union of the two kingdoms that had shared a common monarch (when there was one) for a century. Understandably, the Scottish parliament resisted these efforts, but ultimately the northern kingdom's failure to develop the kind of fiscal order that was taking hold in England forced its leaders to submit. The crisis came in 1707, after the spectacular collapse of an effort to establish an independent Scottish Atlantic empire. Hundreds of thousands of pounds, including most of the capital of the Bank of Scotland (organized in 1695 by the same William Paterson who masterminded the Bank of England) flowed into a turn-of-the-century scheme to plant a colony in the Darien region of the Isthmus of Panama. Done in by disease and by instructions from King William that English ships and colonial governors were not to provide aid, the vast majority of the thousands of colonists shipped there perished, and the Scottish state found itself virtually bankrupt. English parliamentarians' promise to assume the debt—along with handsome personal bribes to key Scottish legislators—led to the Act of Union that created the United Kingdom. In exchange for financial benefits and a modest number of seats in the houses of Commons and Lords, Scotland lost its parliament (for nearly three centuries, as things turned out) but retained its distinctive religious and legal systems. Popular discontent with the union contributed to the excitement attending the invasion of Scotland by James's now-adult son, the Old Pretender James Francis Edward, in 1715—but the "Fifteen," as the uprising came to be known, was quickly subdued.

By then, the successor to Queen Anne—the reliably Protestant George I, who had been imported from the German electorate of Hanover under the terms of a parliamentary Act of Succession—seemed secure on the throne not only of his Three Kingdoms but of his many provinces in North America and the West Indies. In the colonies, few of the financial issues that were so determinative in England and Scotland had much relevance, and nothing resembling a fiscal-military state would emerge before the twentieth century. Nonetheless, wars at the turn of the eighteenth century solidified a new political order in the western portion of Britain's Atlantic empire. After 1715, British North Americans too could look back on happy results of the Glorious Revolution. But only in blinkered hindsight could that possibly seem to be the case.

Whatever Leislerians, New Englanders, Associators, and other North Americans may have hoped for in 1689, those making decisions in the court of William and Mary approached the task of governing their empire in much the same way as had those at the courts of Charles II and James II. To a large degree, this was because many of the same people remained in charge, most notably William Blathwayt, longtime right-hand man of James as duke and king, the omnipresent Edward Randolph, and many members of the Lords of Trade, the committee that, since 1675, had held responsibility for advising the king on colonial affairs. Even the deposed Edmund Andros returned to North America, as governor of Virginia from 1692 to 1698 and of Maryland from 1693 to 1694. There was moderation in only two themes of Restoration imperialism—the disdain for elected assemblies and the penchant for handing out proprietary land grants to royal favorites—and these turned out to be important exceptions indeed. But on other matters, particularly increasing central control, strengthening the Navigation Acts, insisting on religious toleration, restraining colonial expropriation of Native lands, promoting enslaved African labor, and enriching royal coffers, the new regime was virtually indistinguishable from the old.

That the North American planters who rebelled in the name of William and Mary could hardly expect complete fulfillment of their dreams first became clear in New York. Among the three provinces that overthrew governors in 1689, this was the first to receive direct, if ambiguously interpreted, instructions from the imperial center. In December 1689, a packet dated nearly four months earlier arrived from the monarchs' privy council, addressed "to our loving friends Francis Nicholson Esquire their Majesty's Lieutenant Governor . . . And in his absence to such as for the time being take care for preserving the Peace and administring the Laws."[17] Leisler, fitting the latter description, opened the packet, followed its instructions to issue an official proclamation of allegiance to William and Mary, and took to calling himself their majesties' lieutenant governor.

That the packet was addressed to Andros's deposed underling should have given some indication that those in the imperial center were disinclined to approve of Leisler's actions and leaned toward the views of the Anti-Leislerians. Nicholson reinforced that disinclination when he himself reached London and filled the ears of the Lords of Trade with the Anti-Leislerian side of the story. The man Leisler belatedly sent to court as his agent—a Dutch-speaking mere ensign and tavernkeeper named Joost Stoll, who was introduced with a letter remarkable even by seventeenth-century standards for its poor spelling and odd syntax—had no credibility as a counterweight. Several weeks before Leisler opened his packet in New York, and several days before Stoll delivered his written case in London, the Crown had already named a career military man named Henry Sloughter as the new governor of New York.

A host of problems, including a shipwreck, kept Sloughter from taking up his post until March 1691. In the long interim, Leisler and his counterparts in New England did their best to manage the war that had broken out with the French. In early 1689, the court of Louis XIV, understanding more quickly than its English counterparts the potential importance of North America to the international struggle, approved a request from the governor of La Nouvelle-France for an expedition intended not only to crush the Iroquois, but to destroy their supply base at Albany as well. As with Sloughter's voyage, however, the transport of royal troops under the command of former and now-reappointed governor Louis de Buade, comte de Frontenac, endured endless delays. When the troops finally arrived, they were too few in number and too late in the fall to do the job. The only things that could be managed over the winter and spring of 1690 were three raids by French and allied Native forces. The one that sacked Schenectady in February was followed by assaults on Salmon Falls, New Hampshire, and Falmouth, Maine.

In retaliation—and to demonstrate, both to their own people and to anyone paying attention in London, their zeal for the Protestant cause—Leisler and his New England revolutionary counterparts planned a grand two-pronged invasion of La Nouvelle-France. While a New England fleet sailed down the St. Lawrence, thousands of New York, Connecticut, Massachusetts, and Iroquois forces were to march overland through the Lake Champlain Valley. The attempted invasion was nearly a complete disaster. A Massachusetts fleet captured Port Royal in Acadia from the French but bungled its assault on Québec, retreating with heavy losses. Meanwhile, fewer than half of the English troops pledged for the land assault reported for duty, and a smallpox epidemic kept all but a handful of Iroquois at home as well. Apart from much finger pointing among revolutionaries and their domestic opponents, the only result was a raid that destroyed the French settlement of La Prairie, near Montréal.

Amid these fiascos, horror set in among colonial populations already primed to see devilish papists and hostile Indians around every corner. In the Massachusetts hamlet of Salem Village, the climate of fear, along with the absence of an effective central government to restrain zealous locals, helped unleash a flurry of witchcraft accusations that tore the community apart in late 1691 and early 1692. It was not the witchcraft accusations themselves that were unusual; throughout the seventeenth century and on both sides of the Atlantic, unexplained illnesses or other strange goings-on occasionally led to accusations of witchcraft against a party deemed responsible. Frequently this was an elderly woman known for her outspokenness, cantankerousness, or perhaps even her control of property coveted by enemies. Salem Village—an outlying district of the seaport of Salem Town with a particularly unfortunate history of economic impoverishment, political infighting, and, most recently, a high death rate among soldiers in Andros's ineffective war against the Wabanakis—was the kind of troubled community in which witchcraft accusations might almost be predicted. That the minister of the equally troubled local church, Samuel Parris, had been a failure in everything he had previously done and was inclined to make the omnipresence of the Devil the main theme of his sermons only increased the fears and suspicions of his parishioners. The first two alleged victims of witchcraft were Parris's daughter and his niece, and the first alleged witch was his slave Tituba, a Native American woman who had been captured and sold away from papist Spanish domains, perhaps in La Florida. With her combination of links to Catholicism and Indians, and her presumed skill in satanic arts, she was almost a too-perfect embodiment of everything the villagers feared.

What was less predictable was how, over the next weeks and months, the accusations of witchcraft spiraled wildly out of control, to target well over three hundred people, inside and outside Salem Village, high and low on the social scale—all somehow or other embodying someone's personification of blame for a world spinning out of control.

In equally fearful New York City, a besieged Leisler insisted ever more zealously that he did have things under control and was merely awaiting further instructions from William and Mary. Finally, in February 1692, a regiment of English redcoats commanded by Richard Ingoldesby, a vet-

eran of William's Irish campaign, arrived at Manhattan expecting to find
the still-delayed Sloughter already in power. When Ingoldesby attempted
to occupy the city's fort in the name of his governor and his monarch,
Leisler demanded to see official instructions empowering him to do so.
Ingoldesby refused, and, within a few weeks, his and Leisler's troops were
shooting at each other—a situation that did not present a good first impression when Sloughter at last showed up. For two days after the governor's arrival, Leisler still refused to yield control of the fort unless he saw
appropriate royal paperwork. When the surrender finally did take place,
a hasty trial condemned Leisler and seven supporters to death as traitors. Sloughter—in a classic display of the mixture of mercy and terror
by which European rulers asserted their authority—pardoned six of the
condemned, but ensured that Leisler and his closest lieutenant, Jacob
Milborne, dropped from the gallows. Before they died, they were cut
down so they could be beheaded while still alive. Sloughter showed his
mercy by not carrying out the court's full sentence, which stipulated dis-
emboweling and burning the excised guts while the men were still alive
and quartering their headless corpses.

Despite the Anti-Leislerian sympathies of the Lords of Trade, Sloughter
had not been sent to mutilate traitors but to impose what would become
the template for future governments throughout British North America.
According to his official royal instructions, which carried the force of law,
his rank was "Captain General and Governor in Chief." These military titles gave him supreme authority over all of the province's military forces—
including the militias that had caused so much trouble elsewhere in recent
years—but placed strict limits on how that power could be used. On his
own initiative, a captain general could wage war only defensively, in response to aggression by Native peoples or foreign European powers. Offensive campaigns required explicit direction from the Crown. To assist
him in his military as well as civil duties, Sloughter was to nominate a small
group of the most prominent colonists to serve as his council, but the
nominations had to be forwarded to the Lords of Trade and the Crown,
which would make the actual appointments. "From time to time as need
shall require," the governor was "to summon and call generall Assemblies
of the Inhabitants being Freeholders," which was to say that property-
owning males had the right to elect representatives to a legislature.[18]
Members of the assembly, the council, and all other office holders had

to take the two oaths prescribed by the English Bill of Rights, ensuring religious toleration for all Protestants as well as loyalty to the Protestant monarchy. Laws and taxes were to be passed by the assembly, council, and governor jointly, with the governor having the power to veto any legislation and with the provision that all laws must not only "be (as near as may be) agreeable unto the Lawes and Statutes of this our kingdome of England," but also be submitted within three months for approval or disapproval by the Crown. The governor had the right to appoint all judges, and the obligation to establish a court of admiralty with jurisdiction over crimes involving seagoing vessels, including piracy and violations of the Navigation Acts. Subjects, meanwhile, had the right to appeal judicial decisions to the Lords of Trade and the Crown, and to petition the monarch directly on any matter.[19] These latter provisions, of course, flew in the face of Sloughter's hasty execution of Leisler and Milborne, and, had the governor not died only a few months after taking office, he might have been fired. The Lords of Trade were soon responding to petitions from New York by urging reconciliation between Leislerians and Anti-Leislerians. By 1695, these efforts convinced Parliament to pass a bill posthumously reversing the treason convictions.

Such transatlantic politicking was also a part of the new imperial order. Unlike their counterparts in New York, the revolutionaries of Massachusetts and Maryland sent savvy representatives to plead their cases before the Lords of Trade and to counter the arguments of critics such as Randolph and Charles Calvert. Nonetheless, they received governments that looked very much like the one Sloughter brought to New York. In 1691, Increase Mather won several major concessions in the new royal charter that replaced the one revoked in 1684—most notably the right for the legislature (rather than the Crown) to choose the governor's council, and for the Bay Colony to absorb Plymouth and Maine. Still, what was now known as "Their Majesty's Province of the Massachusetts Bay in New England" had to accept a royally appointed governor with the limited military powers of a captain general. The new charter provided for royal disallowance or veto of legislation, a franchise based on property ownership rather than church membership, and—bitterest pill of all for puritans—religious toleration.

As in New York, controversial judicial proceedings were among the first things on the new government's agenda. Royal governor Sir William Phips appointed a special court of Oyer and Terminer to deal with the Salem witchcraft accusations, a court that quickly mired itself in the legal morass of determining what kind of evidence could be used to "prove" witchcraft. With Increase Mather and many other leading Massachusetts clergy agreeing that the legal problems were insurmountable—if the Devil is by nature a liar, how could anything associated with him be proven true?—Phips was finally able to shut the trials down and to pardon all the surviving accused in early 1693. The process was long and messy, but Salem Village's local troubles ultimately found their resolution in the transatlantic political revolution that brought Phips to power.

The transition to royal government went smoothest in Maryland. With Coode and Calvert personally arguing their cases before the Lords of Trade, the colony did not receive a charter but instead became, like New York, a royal province. Maryland received an appointed governor (whose instructions were much like Sloughter's), an appointed council, an assembly elected by property owners, and a brand of toleration that extended liberty of conscience, though not voting rights, to Catholics. Although the Calvert family thus lost the power to govern its neo-feudal domain, it retained its property rights and much of the revenue that went with them.

This, too, became standard practice. At one time or another between 1689 and 1729, the proprietors of Pennsylvania, the Jerseys, and the Carolinas all had to accept royal government. Only the Calvert family (in 1715) and the Penn family in Pennsylvania (in 1694) ever regained their rights of government—and then only by accepting strict supervision by the Lords of Trade. By the early eighteenth century, a younger generation of both families had safely converted to the Church of England from Catholicism and Quakerism, respectively. In all these waves of administrative reform, only Connecticut and Rhode Island, with prerevolutionary charters still intact, escaped the imposition of royally appointed governors—but they, too, lost much of their earlier independence.

Such governmental arrangements sometimes intentionally, sometimes by happenstance, corrected many of the structural flaws that had produced so much trouble since the Restoration. The militias and private armies that started Indian wars and overthrew governments fell (at least in theory) under centralized discipline in the name of the monarch. The entrenched, narrowly based elites that everywhere monopolized power in mid-seventeenth-century English America were not tamed, but their ranks were opened a bit and, more important, alternative centers of power emerged to hear the voices of formerly excluded opponents. Governors

who owed their (usually short-term) status to the Lords of Trade were far
less likely than Berkeley, Andros, or an elected Massachusetts executive to
identify with a single faction. If they did, they were likely soon to be replaced by someone charged with cleaning things up—and inclined to side
with the previous administration's local opponents. Council appointments
that required transatlantic political connections as well as the ear of the
governor similarly broadened access to power. That these appointments
were usually for life provided a serious counterweight to both governors and assemblies. Meanwhile, toleration for all Protestants and frequent elections under a franchise determined by property qualifications
expanded basic political participation in Massachusetts, stabilized it in
Maryland and Virginia, and reliably established it for the first time in New
York. Everywhere, planters of small means secured a voice in colonial assemblies, which resumed control over powers of lawmaking and taxation that had so often been challenged in previous years. The potential
for royal disallowance of legislation, and for appeals and petitions to the
Crown, on the one hand checked the power of entrenched elites and on
the other provided a back channel for the aggrieved to be heard.

By 1699, New York's governor already bore witness to the cumulative
effect of all these reforms. In a letter to the Lords of Trade that was full of
complaints about squabbling between Leislerians and Anti-Leislerians in
the provincial assembly, he noted one incident in particular. "Upon reading a bill where were the words 'late happy Revolution,'" one representative "moved that the word 'happy' might be left out, for he said he did not
conceive the Revolution to be happy."[20] Yet the critic voiced his complaint
openly, without fear of reprisal, as an elected member of his majesty's assembly. A decade earlier, he probably would have had to take up a gun to
make his point—and would have feared hanging or worse as a consequence.

Still, the disgruntled New Yorker rightly found nothing much to be happy
about in the way the new governmental arrangements had taken hold. In
every case, the imposition of royal rule was justified—and colonials were
forced to acquiesce—by the need for strong military leadership against
the French and their Native allies. Perhaps the most important key to the
public acceptance of royal government in Massachusetts, for example, was
the fact that the first appointee was Phips, hero of the one bona fide colo-

nial victory in the revolutionary interregnum, the assault on Acadia's Port Royal. Although not a member of an old planter family, he was a longtime resident of Massachusetts and, while critical of the puritan regime in the days of Edward Randolph, he had recently converted to Congregationalism. Military issues took on particular urgency because of the general ineptitude of colonial militias and the mere handful of royal troops that governors were sometimes able to muster. Even Phips, after all, despite his victory at Port Royal, had not been able to conquer Québec and Montréal.

In northeastern North America, the War of the League of Augsburg was almost entirely a conflict fought by Native Americans. Backed by English arms and encouragement, the Haudenosaunee Iroquois continued their struggle against La Nouvelle-France and the many Indian peoples of the Great Lakes who had been carefully mobilized by French imperial expansion since the 1660s. Backed by French arms and encouragement, those Indian peoples meantime carried on their own long-term struggle against the Haudenosaunee nations, while in the east others—refugees and descendants of refugees from King Philip's War—resumed their struggle against New Englanders.

As English colonists feared the next Native raid, papered over their internal differences, and hoped that their new Protestant monarchs and governors would save them from the papist hordes, the war turned relentlessly against the outnumbered Haudenosaunee people. In 1701, at a grand conference in Montréal attended by nearly a thousand men, women, and children from more than a dozen Indian nations allied to the French, the Iroquois made a final peace with all their ancient enemies to the north, west, and east and pledged their neutrality in future wars between France and England. In exchange, the French guaranteed Iroquois rights to hunt for furs in the Great Lakes lands of their former foes. About a month earlier, another delegation of Haudenosaunee leaders had attended a council in Albany at which they reaffirmed their Covenant Chain alliance with the government of New York, while presenting the English Crown with a deed to the same lands in which the French Crown had promised to protect their hunting rights. In their befuddlement at this unexpected gift, the English never quite grasped that the Haudenosaunee people and La Nouvelle-France really were at peace and that the Iroquois, through their simultaneous negotiations with both European powers, had imposed upon the Great Lakes a regime of neutrality between the empires.

During the War of the Spanish Succession, as a result, governors and planters who understood the need somehow to convince the Iroquois to abandon neutrality and fight for them finally began to understand the value of centralized diplomacy in the hands of strong royal government, a lesson Andros had preached as early as the 1670s. Paradoxically, the lesson might not have sunk in quite so deeply if New York had in fact *had* strong royal government during these years. From 1701 to 1710, ten different men ruled as governor, lieutenant governor, or, in the death or absence of both, senior member of the royal council. The hope of royal military and diplomatic salvation thrived in part precisely because military execution was so weak, easing colonial acceptance of what might otherwise have seemed tyrannical royal authority.

The tangled threads came together in the later years of the War of the Spanish Succession. Twice, in 1709 and 1711, Anglo-American leaders attempted what they labeled the "Glorious Enterprise," a recycling of Leisler's plan for a land and naval conquest of La Nouvelle-France. Unlike Leisler's 1690 debacle, however, this was to be a genuinely imperial, transatlantic effort, utilizing Native and English troops from North America and a fleet from Great Britain, all under the full authority of Her Majesty's captains general and under the command of none other than Francis Nicholson, the lieutenant governor deposed by Leisler in 1689. In 1709, fifteen hundred New York, New England, and Iroquois troops (who had temporarily abandoned their neutrality because they believed the French were not upholding their commitments under the 1701 peace) massed north of Albany. They sat there for weeks, awaiting arrival of the British fleet, which, they finally learned, had long since been diverted to fighting off the coast of the Iberian Peninsula.

The next year, in hopes of trying again, Nicholson and New Yorker Peter Schuyler took four young Native men to London to carry out the most grandiose transatlantic political lobbying effort ever attempted. Passed off as the "Four Indian Kings" (although only one had any claim to hereditary title), the visitors were the toast of the town and of Queen Anne's court, where the "Glorious Enterprise" was enthusiastically embraced. Nearly sixty royal navy ships and a regiment of redcoats followed the delegation back to North America. That the fleet foundered on the rocks of the Gulf of St. Lawrence and that Nicholson was again left waiting at his land base (legend says he tore off his wig and stomped on it when he heard the news that the fleet had failed) confirmed British and colonial military incompetence. That so many political, military, and financial resources could be mobilized across thousands of miles of ocean and factional divides confirmed just as strongly how integrated British North America had become in the Atlantic empire created by the Glorious Revolution and a generation of warfare.

The interaction between warfare and the new Atlantic imperial order was even more convoluted in the southeast, where the feudal dreams of *The Fundamental Constitutions of Carolina* had long since produced little but chaos. Two distinct population centers, separated by some two hundred fifty miles of coast, had developed in the vast tract claimed by the Carolina proprietors. Immigration to what ultimately became the separate province of North Carolina came mostly from England's oldest surviving colony, Virginia. The much larger number who settled in and around the port city of Charles Town came primarily from England's most fully developed slave-based society, Barbados. Claiming supreme power over both regions were the rivalrous descendants of the eight original proprietors. Most of them resided in England, but, at varying times, some lived in Barbados, in the colony itself, and elsewhere. There was no established procedure for appointing an on-site governor to act in the proprietors' name. The results were not only rapid turnover in the office, but constant suspicions that whoever held the post had no certain right to it. Carolina's elected Commons House of Assembly was no clearer about the extent of its powers, but missed no opportunity to try to obstruct whatever those who claimed to speak for the proprietors wanted.

This was a society with politics too disorganized even to permit a proper Glorious Revolution in 1689. In 1686, a Spanish naval attack, a devastating hurricane, and the apparently unauthorized retirement of governor James West, who abruptly moved to New York, had left a power vacuum filled by James Colleton, a descendant of the founding proprietor Sir John Colleton of Barbados. James Colleton arrived in the colony with his household the same year that James West left. Bearing the second-level *Fundamental Constitutions* title of "landgrave," he had the highest feudal rank of anyone on the scene and started acting as governor. When the assembly refused to pass legislation that Colleton deemed necessary for defense against the Spanish, he declared martial law. The populace seethed until 1691, when a proprietary heir named Seth Sothell moved to the colony and evoked his higher rank as full proprietor and "palatine" to displace Colleton, who did not go quietly. Nor did Sothell when, a few months later, his fellow proprietors in London declared him a traitor and suspended his privileges.

This climate of virtual lawlessness shaped the kind of society that emerged in what became South Carolina. Whatever the other proprietors thought, the Colleton family always intended the region to be an extension of Barbados, a "colony of a colony" in which the sugar plantation regime they were perfecting there could be replicated on a much larger scale.[21] But as with every other orderly colonial feudal dream of Restoration imperialism, things did not quite turn out as planned. Wealthy Barbadans and their connections—who came to be known as "Goose Creek Men," for the location of their plantations—squared off against men of small means who had been pushed out of the Barbados economy as the great slaveowning planters consolidated their power.

Whatever these planters hoped to gain from relocating to Carolina, and whatever they thought of manorial grandees, they agreed with the Goose Creek Men that the enslavement of others was the key to their future prosperity. Stuck too far north to grow sugar, and confronted with the same difficulty in acquiring enslaved Africans that Virginians and other English mainlanders faced in the era when most of the Royal African Company's human cargoes went to the West Indies, the South Carolinians seized a lucrative, if—according to the high-minded declarations of the ineffectual proprietors—highly illegal, opportunity. They began to enslave and export Native people captured in wars among the region's Indians. Salem's Tituba may have been one of them.

Because the trade in Indian slaves was illegal, few records survive to document its scale, but the best estimates are that, between 1670 and 1715, thirty thousand to fifty thousand men, women, and children were shipped out of Charles Town to toil, and usually die, not only on Barbadian sugar plantations but in homes and farms in New England and the middle colonies. Unknown thousands more went to plantations in the Chesapeake and Carolina, where they constituted as much as a quarter of the enslaved population in the first decade of the eighteenth century. From a Native American perspective, what began as a profitable sideline to traditional patterns of wartime captivity evolved into regularized patterns of slave raiding for the market of Charles Town. The metal goods, cloth, and firearms that Indian people elsewhere on the continent received in exchange for animal furs and hides here were purchased with the living bodies of vanquished Native enemies. And no wonder, for the sale of one slave could earn the same return as two hundred deerskins.[22]

A grim pattern emerged in which one decade's Native victors became the next decade's victims, and Carolinians themselves seldom had to fire a shot. The Westos, the Great Lakes Iroquoian-speaking group forced southward during the conflicts in the continental interior at midcentury, appear to have been the first to sell large numbers of their war captives to the English. By the 1660s, the Westos were already battling the Carolina region's coastal Cusabos and selling the captives they took to Virginians. By the 1670s, as English immigrants arrived from Barbados, the Carolina newcomers joined in buying the people the Westos had to sell. With such a thriving market, by the 1680s only a handful of Cusabos survived, and the Westos were the next to be enslaved—by another group recently transplanted from the north, the Algonquian-speaking Savannahs, also known as Shawnees. In the 1690s, the Shawnees in turn fell victim to Siouan-speaking groups from the Carolina Piedmont. Meantime, the mission towns of La Florida also began to be raided for slaves, by the varied Muskogean-speaking peoples later known to the English as Yamasees and Creeks, both of whom had apparently long been resisting incorporation into the *pax hispanica* in the south just as the Iroquois had been resisting the *pax gallica* in the north.

At the same moment that the Haudenosaunee Iroquois disengaged from their disastrous involvement in European imperial wars, then, many Yamasees and Creeks leaped wholeheartedly into an alliance with South Carolinians in the War of the Spanish Succession. Spain had been on England's side during the War of the League of Augsburg, but in the new conflict the Spanish regal successor in question was allied with France's Louis XIV, and so Spain and La Florida became the open foe of England and of its colonies. The Creeks gained the first victory in this war, slaughtering and enslaving roughly half of a seven-hundred-man Spanish-Apalachee army sent against them in early 1702.

Later that year, Carolina's current governor of suspect credentials, James Moore, sought to bolster his position in the colony and in the imperial center—and to profit from slave raiding—by setting off to conquer Spanish San Agustín. This was precisely the kind of freelance campaign that the imposition of captains general on other colonies and schemes such as the Glorious Enterprise in the north were designed to prevent.

Piling a few dozen Englishmen and perhaps thirteen hundred Native allies into a small fleet of boats, Moore pillaged the Guale mission towns
along the coast before trying to lay siege to the stone fortress that defended the capital of La Florida. Unfortunately, he brought no mortars or
other equipment suited to the task, and, eight weeks later, he scuttled his
ships and returned home overland, having impoverished the colony treasury but enriched his Native allies (and presumably himself) with many
Indian slaves. In 1704, Moore led a second expedition to the captive-rich
mission towns of Apalachee. Creek and Yamasee attacks continued in the
meantime, and, by the end of the war of the Spanish Succession in 1713,
none of the towns of La Florida's *república de indios* survived. Thousands
of its former residents had been killed or enslaved, while others retreated
into the interior.

By that time, too, the Indian wars that Moore and other Carolinians had
so cleverly profited from had come home to roost. In 1711, one of the
Yamasees' other slave-raiding targets, the Tuscaroras of present-day interior North Carolina, responded to the intrusion of European settlers on
their lands by capturing and killing Carolina's provincial surveyor and then
conducting raids in which a hundred or more of the intruders perished.
The Carolina government coordinated retaliatory expeditions with the
Yamasees and other Indian rivals of the Tuscaroras. By 1713, most of the
Tuscarora villages had been burned, perhaps one thousand men, women,
and children had been killed, and seven hundred others had been enslaved. Nearly all of the twenty-five hundred Tuscaroras who survived
moved north to join the Haudenosaunee peoples as the Sixth Nation of
the Iroquois League.

But if the Yamasees thought their service in the Florida and Tuscarora
campaigns would secure their position in the Carolina trading universe,
they quickly learned otherwise. Among the many things that failed to
emerge in chaotic Carolina was an effective system of diplomacy with Native Americans. Despite the deep economic ties between colonists and Indians—which had expanded to include a sizable trade for deerskins as well
as for human beings—few of the ritual trappings that made exchange and
alliance comprehensible elsewhere on the continent took hold, except on
an individual level involving many private traders who established sexual
alliances with Native women and who in other ways adapted to local customs. The destruction of the last mission villages of La Florida, in a period
when the trade of La Louisiane (French Louisiana) remained at a rudi-

mentary level, suddenly left not just the Yamasees but all of the Native peoples of the southeast solely dependent on Carolinian officials who had not bothered to learn much about the politics of prestige goods and material alliance. Until 1707, for example, it had apparently been the norm that governors simply pocketed any diplomatic gifts they received from Native chiefs. Realizing that an exploitative system based on slave raiding for profit was inherently dangerous, the elected Carolina Commons House began passing statutes to impose some order. In 1707, a licensing act tried to regulate traders by placing them under the supervision of a full-time government agent. In 1710, a Board of Commissioners of the Indian Trade added a further layer of supervision. As always in Carolina, however, the result was further confusion, as two rivalrous characters, Thomas Nairne and John Wright, claimed the title of agent.

All of these developments—aimed exclusively at restraining the behavior of Carolina traders (and consolidating the economic benefits of trade in fewer hands), rather than at broadening diplomatic relations—seem to have been perceived by Native people as money-grubbing neglect of the cultural side of exchange relations. Many were deeply in debt to Carolina traders, who regularly enslaved defaulters. The cycle of debt worsened as the War of the Spanish Succession interrupted the international trade in deerskins and as changing fashions in Europe dried up the market for furs of all sorts, depriving Indians of salable nonhuman commodities. At the same time, Indians saw their lands on the Savannah River being overrun by planters and their free-ranging cattle.

After months of complaints from Native people, and months of no diplomatic initiatives whatever, Nairne and Wright held a council at the main Yamasee town in April 1715, where they apparently gave the assembled chiefs incompatible messages regarding English intentions. Both were gruesomely assassinated, and Native people from throughout the region began destroying Carolina plantations and killing English traders throughout the trading paths of the interior. "Mr. Wright said that the white men would come and . . . hang four of their head men and take all the rest of them for Slaves . . . , for he said that the men of the Yamasees were like women," explained a note the Yamasee leader known as the Huspaw King left for the English to find. "What he said vex'd the great Warrier's, and this made them begin the war, . . . and the Indians are all comeing to take all the Country."[23]

What has since been called the Yamasee War—misnamed, because it involved not just the Huspaw King's nation but Native people from towns throughout the region—reached a turning point when Carolinians persuaded many Cherokees, who primarily traded with Virginians and were seeking stronger ties with an alternative source of European goods, to attack the anti-English coalition. By early 1715, when the fighting subsided, vast areas of the Indian southeast were depopulated, some 7 percent of British Carolinians had perished, and the regional economy, including its Native American slave trade, was shattered.

The Tuscarora and Yamasee wars were Carolina's equivalent of Bacon's Rebellion and King Philip's War and led, finally, to its much-belated version of the Glorious Revolution. Writing from the ruins of their plantations, Carolinians flooded London with pleas to revoke the proprietors' charter and give the colony direct royal government. Equally fed up with the ineptitude of the proprietors, the imperial government had already been considering *quo warranto* proceedings for the better part of a decade, but faced vexing issues of how to disentangle the financial and political interests of the eight proprietary families. Sick of delays and panicked by rumors of a Spanish attack, in late 1719 militiamen appeared in the streets of Charles Town, bloodlessly deposed governor Robert Johnson, declared themselves a convention, and elected as interim governor (pending an appointment by King George) James Moore Jr., an architect of the Carolina victory over the Tuscaroras and the son of the elder Moore who had led the expeditions against La Florida in 1702 and 1704. The next year, in 1720, Moore Jr. yielded his place when the same Francis Nicholson who had been deposed in New York's Glorious Revolution and frustrated in the Glorious Enterprise arrived to preside as royal governor. From that point, although the proprietors' charter would not be formally revoked until 1729, South Carolina and the now separate government of North Carolina fully joined the eighteenth-century English Atlantic empire of Protestants united against Popery and Arbitrary Power.

Amsterdam receiving the tribute of four continents.

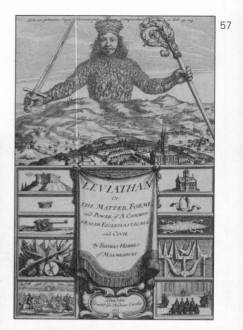

57

61

6

Clockwise from Figure 57:
Frontispiece from Thomas
Hobbes, Leviathan, with its
argument for sovereign
monarchical power. Charles II of
England (1630–1685), in
appropriate pose. Wedding
portrait of Mary, England's
Princess Royal, and Willem II,
Prince of Orange, parents of
Willem III, Prince of Orange—
the future William III of England
and William II of Scotland (1650–
1702). Carlos II of Spain (1661–
1700). Louis XIV of France, who
outlived and outreigned them all
(1638–1715).

63

62

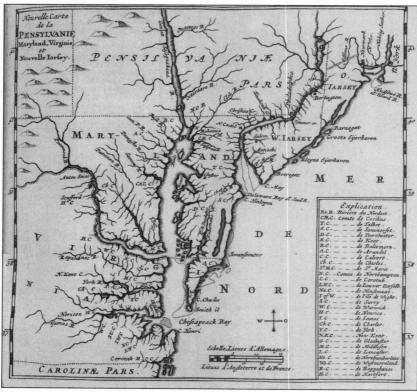

67

65

Clockwise: Seal of the Royal African Company: an elephant bearing a castle is flanked by two African men. James, duke of York, governor of the Royal African Company, proprietor of New York, and future King James VII and II, portrayed as Mars, the god of war. Sir George Carteret, proprietor of Carolina and East New Jersey, and member of the Royal African Company. John Lord Berkeley, proprietor of Carolina and West New Jersey, and member of the Royal African Company. William Penn, proprietor of Pennsylvania and West New Jersey. Proprietary North American domains conquered from Nieu Nederlandt.

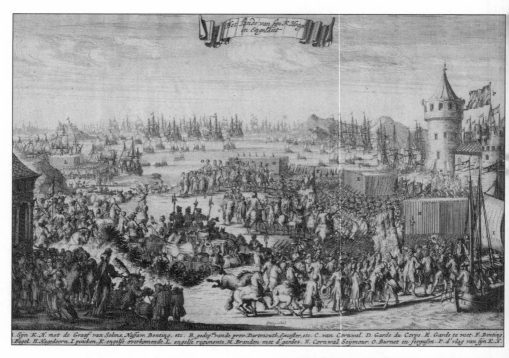

Syn K.N. met de Graef van Solms, Nassaw, Benting, etc. B. gedep."s van de prov. Dartmouth, Excester, etc. C. van Cornwal. D. Garde du Corps. E. Garde te voet. F. Benting Fagel. H. Nagedoorn. I. pincken. K. engelse overkomende L. engelse regimente. M. Brandon met d. gardes. N. Cornwal Seymour. O. Burnet en ferguson. P. d'vlag van syn K.N.

Clockwise: Willem of Orange invades England. Charles Calvert, Third Baron Baltimore, deposed governor of Maryland. Declaration of Maryland Revolutionaries. William and Mary banish "Popery and Arbitrary Power." Sir Edmund Andros, deposed governor of the Dominion of New England.

69

(i)

THE

DECLARATION

OF THE

REASONS and MOTIVES

For the PRESENT

Appearing in Arms

OF

THEIR MAJESTIES

𝕻𝖗𝖔𝖙𝖊𝖘𝖙𝖆𝖓𝖙 𝕾𝖚𝖇𝖏𝖊𝖈𝖙𝖘

In the PROVINCE of

MARYLAND.

Licens'd, *November 28th* 1689. J. F.

Lthough the Nature and State of Affairs relating to the Government of this Province, is so well and notoriously known
to all Persons any way concerned in the same, as to the
People and Inhabitants here, who are more immediately Interested, as might excuse any *Declaration* or *Apology* for this
present inevitable *Appearance* : Yet forasmuch as (by the *Plots, Con-
trivances, Infinuations, Remonstrances*, and *Subscriptions*, carried on,
suggested, extorted, and obtained by the Lord *Baltemore*, his Depu-
A   ties,

70

1

73

Clockwise: The Virginia House of Burgesses chamber echoes the British House of Commons. Newspapers created a transatlantic British cultural community. Capitol buildings in New York, Philadelphia, and Williamsburg embodied the balance of the British Constitution: on the lower floors were separate wings for Assemblies (the many) and for Councils (the few), bridged on the upper floor by chambers for the governor (the one). Satire of a boisterous Philadelphia election day.

December 27, 1759.   NUMB. 1618.

The PENNSYLVANIA   G A Z E T T E.

Containing the Fresheſt Ad-   vices, Foreign and Domeſtic.

75

77

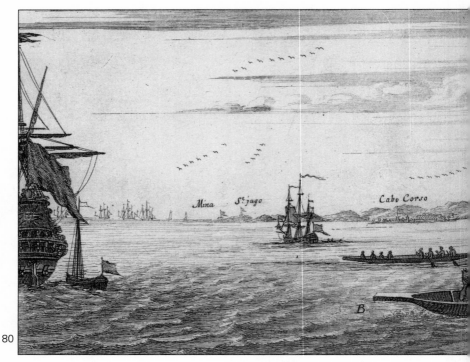

On Tuefday the 9th Inftant, George Philips of Byberry, in Philadelphia County, being in the Woods about to cut Timber, fell'd one Tree which lodg'd by the Top on another; he then cut a fecond to fall acrofs the firft, in order by the Weight of it to bring both down : but the Butt-End mounting up, fwung round and ftruck him on the Back of his Head, Neck and Shoulders, fo as to kill him inftantly.

Cuftom-Houfe, Philadelphia; Entred inwards.
Ship Amity, William Murray, from Jamaica.
Ship Boneta, Thomas Read, from London.

Entred Outwards.
Brig. Philadelphia Hope, George Spafford, to Weft-Indies.
Sloop Surinam, Henry Norwood, to Barbadoes

Cleared Out.
Sloop Adventure, Robert Rawle, for Surinam.
Ship Samuel and Ann, Thomas Glentworth, to Madera.
Brigt. Clementina, Jofeph Arthur, to Antigua.
Brigt. Henrietta, Samuel Farra, for Madera.
Ship Cupid, Stephen Pugh, for Gibraltar.
Ship Three Batchelors, William Spafford, for Barbadoes.
Ship Mary, Robert Sanders, for Ifle of Man.

Buried in the feveral Burying-Grounds fince the 4th Inftant.

Church	2.	Baptifts	0.
Quakers	1.	Strangers, Whites	0.
Presbyterians	0.	Blacks	0.

ADVERTISEMENTS.

JUft Imported in the Ship *Boneta*, Capt. *Thomas Reed*, Mafter, from *London*, (lying near the Market Wharff) a Parcel of very likely Servant Men and Boys, of fundry Trades, as well as Husbandmen : To be fold by *Edward Horne* and *William Rawle*, very Reafonable, (as alfo good *Newcaftle* Coal) for Cafh, Flower or Bread.

81

Clockwise: Enslaved people loaded on ships at Elmina Castle, West Africa.
Advertisements for sale of an enslaved African and for capture of a runaway Irish
servant. Advertisement for the arrival of the ship *Boneta,* which brought English
servant William Moraley to North America, and for his sale as an indentured
servant.

83

The bearer Hendrick the great *Sächem* or Chief of the Mohawk Indians, one of the Six Nations now in Alliance with & Subject to the King of Great Britain.

Prosperity from Atlantic trade transformed the material lives of North Americans and reinforced patriotism for the British Empire and its maritime might. Clockwise from far left: Flag carried by New England troops at the siege of Louisbourg, 1745. Tea drinking and its necessary equipage epitomized the eighteenth-century consumer revolution for Euro-Americans, as did imported clothing and weapons for such Native Americans as the Mohawk leader Hendrick Theyanoguin. Imported goods furnish a Georgian interior space. Pennsylvanian James Logan's Georgian house, "Stenton."

88

The British Conquest of La Nouvelle-France destroyed the delicate balances of power that had created the Atlantean World. This is Benjamin West's heroic depiction of the death of General James Wolfe during the assault on Québec in 1759.

Atlanteans

ATLANTEAN, *a.* (ætlæn'tiːən) [from Latin *Atlantē-us,* from *Atlant-:* see prec. and -EAN.]
Pertaining to, or having the supporting strength of, Atlas.

—*Oxford English Dictionary* (Oxford, 1989)

With Atlantean Shoulders, etc. Of vast Abilities, fit to undertake the weightiest Affairs of mightiest Kingdoms: *Atlas* was King of *Mauritania,* for his great skill in Astrology Fabled to support Heaven on his Shoulders.

—Patrick Hume, *Annotations on Milton's Paradise Lost* (London, 1695), 63

As my design was a dictionary, common or appellative, I have omitted all words which have relation to proper names.

—Samuel Johnson, *A Dictionary of the English Language* (London, 1755)

THIRTEEN

Producing and Consuming in
an Atlantic Empire

THE REVOLUTIONS OF 1688–1689 came to appear glorious—and the rights and liberties they proclaimed took hold—because an epoch of prosperity emerged from the tumultuous quarter-century that William III and II brought to the British Empire. Between 1715 and the middle years of the eighteenth century, the descendants of Native and English progenitors alike found themselves ever more bound not just to the imperial center of London but to places, things, and people throughout the North Atlantic basin. None of these people would have described themselves as "Atlantean," a term that referred to the mythical figure of Atlas, who bore the weight of the heavens on his shoulders and, having been turned to stone, survived in the form of Mount Atlas in North Africa. ("Atlantic" thus became the name of the western ocean off Africa's coast.) Still, the weighty global dimensions of the word "Atlantean" capture something of the lives of the peoples who lived in North America after the Glorious Revolution. Ships plying the ancient unifying winds and currents of the North Atlantic brought people from Europe, Africa, the West Indies, and America together. The consumer goods, agricultural products, and intellectual fashions that the vessels carried made the look and feel of daily life ever more similar from London to Boston, from Barbados to Philadelphia, from Creek country to Wabanakia.

The British Atlantean Empire may have begun in revolts against Popery and Arbitrary Power, but it always was, most fundamentally, an empire of commerce. In this respect, the empire had deep roots in the earlier historical stratum of traders. For North America's Native and European peoples alike, the structure of that commerce, and the relative peace and prosperity it brought, stemmed, like so much else, from decisions made in the imperial capital during and after the Glorious Revolution. The same alliance of financial and governmental forces that produced the Bank of England led Parliament to pass a revised Navigation Act in 1696. As with most imperial developments of the period, the act evolved, rather than departed, from Restoration programs to enrich the State through efficient collection of customs revenue and to enrich English merchants through control of commodities circulating in the Atlantic shipping lanes. Nonetheless, it brought unanticipated benefits to North Americans, many of whom settled prosperously into its restraints during the early eighteenth century. In a way few could have anticipated in 1660, the Navigation Acts made North America prosper.

Heavily influenced by the ubiquitous Edward Randolph, the Navigation Act of 1696 aimed primarily to strengthen existing regulations. It required governors to take solemn oaths to enforce all of the previous Navigation Acts, with a penalty of £1,000 for failure to do so. It placed colonial customs inspectors on a centralized royal payroll and gave them sweeping powers to collect taxes. It created colonial vice-admiralty courts, juryless institutions using military rules of justice to punish violators. It encouraged prosecutions by dividing fines collected from offenders equally among the whistleblower, the royal governor, and the Crown.

Shortly after King William approved the new Navigation Act, he enhanced enforcement by replacing the Lords of Trade with a new body, variously known as the Committee for Trade and Plantations, the Lords Commissioners of Trade and Plantations, or simply the Board of Trade. On paper, it had less authority than its predecessor, because it was no longer composed of members of the Privy Council and became merely an advisor to the cabinet minister who held the title of Secretary of State for the Southern Department. If information was power, however, the Board of Trade far outmatched its predecessor. Eight of its sixteen members remained courtiers who attended meetings only when they felt like it. But the other eight were chosen for their expertise in colonial affairs more than for their political connections. Each was paid the princely sum of £1,000 per year, and they included people such as longtime Stuart servant William Blathwayt. Although it would be too much to call them professional bureaucrats, by early eighteenth-century standards they came close. They collected and processed information of many kinds, drafted all-important instructions for royal governors, reviewed colonial legislation, coordinated the establishment of vice-admiralty courts and customs collectors, instigated a crackdown on piracy around the world, regularized a system by which colonies could appoint formal agents to represent them in London, and recommended legislation to Parliament and courses of action to the Crown. Negotiating interests from all sides of the Atlantic, the Board of Trade, more than anything else, made the early eighteenth-century British Empire work.

And particularly in time of peace, the name said it all: Board of Trade. For what the Navigation Acts had done was to create a transatlantic protected commercial zone, in which diverse merchants, producers, and consumers could thrive. Decades of political upheaval and international warfare obscured what became clear once peace took hold in the 1720s. Most North Americans were now better off under the Navigation Acts than their grandparents had been when the Dutch carried the bulk of their trade. The English imperial system had always been most burdensome to the planters of Virginia and Maryland, whose tobacco was not just on the list of Enumerated Goods but was the only item that the Navigation Acts taxed to raise revenue rather than just to corner a market. (The other entries on the short original list of enumerated items that could be shipped only to England had little effect on North Americans; sugar and cotton grew only in the West Indies, and dyestuffs came from exotic locales mostly not even under English control.) Yet in the new century, even the restrictions on the tobacco trade came to seem less onerous. After the War of the Spanish Succession, prices earned by planters rose slightly from their Bacon-era nadir to about two pence per pound of leaf. Moreover, demand at last seemed to synchronize with supply, particularly because of a booming reexport trade from Britain to the European continent.[1]

While this most distressed of commodities became modestly profitable under the Navigation Acts, other colonial products thrived. In 1700, the value of North American exports to England was approximately £302,000. By 1754, it had nearly tripled to £891,000; including exports to Scotland (absorbed into the system after the 1707 Act of Union), the figure rises to £1,076,000. The gains were real, although the statistics are somewhat misleading, as the European population of North America increased even faster, from 234,000 in 1700 to nearly one million in 1754.[2]

Yet the keys to eighteenth-century prosperity lay less in the commodities that North Americans exported to the British Isles than in other activities that the Navigation Acts made possible. The same provisions that prohibited colonists from trading with the Dutch or French created a sheltered environment in which they could trade with each other for goods that they might otherwise have purchased from foreigners. All of the North American mainland colonies found strong trading partners in the British Caribbean. By far the most valuable of enumerated commodities was West Indian sugar. A seemingly insatiable transatlantic British sweet tooth accompanied voracious tastes for the Asian tea, and later the West Indian coffee, that the sugar sweetened. Well before the end of the seventeenth century, this demand completed the transformation of Barbados and other islands into virtual monocultures, dependent on North Americans for most of the food and other things needed to support sugar processing and to minimally feed and clothe the enslaved people the endless work drove to early deaths.

Meantime, cattle, horses, fish, whale products, wheat flour, maize, rice, salted beef and pork, butter and cheese, lumber, barrel staves, and countless other mundane items moved from North American small farms, pastures, and woods to Boston, Newport, New York, Philadelphia, Charles Town, and thence to the West Indies. New Englanders also exchanged their various commodities for a byproduct of sugar production, molasses, which they distilled into potent, often nasty rum, a drink even more ubiquitous in the eighteenth-century Atlantic world than tea, although not nearly as profitable to those who sold (or drank) it. Similar trades in everyday items tied the various North American ports to one another as well, and indeed to non-British islands and the European and African continents. With the exception of rice, added to the enumerated list in 1704, North American foodstuffs were exempt from commercial restrictions and so could be shipped anywhere in the Atlantic basin, including continental Europe. This trade became so important that Thomas Paine could later quip that American farmers would "always have a market while eating is the custom of Europe."[3]

By 1720, the majority of colonial shippers employed small coastal vessels built and owned in North America. By 1750, these craft were joined by larger ships that carried transatlantic commerce. Here was the greatest opportunity that the Navigation Acts opened for British North Americans, who had the right to build, own, and sail their own ships on an equal basis with subjects in the British Isles. But in fact there was nothing equal about the situation, for North American shipbuilders had a major advantage over their British counterparts: an apparently limitless supply of oak timbers, pine masts, pine tar, pitch, and all the other "naval stores" that were the raw materials of the age of sail. (Only sailcloth usually had to be imported from England.) Because many of the American-built craft were small and never docked in the British Isles, statistics on their number are hard to come by, but shipbuilding's impact on the colonial economies—and on the ability of New Englanders, New Yorkers, and Pennsylvanians to seize control of their own carrying trades—was vast. By about 1760, at least a third of all of the ships registered with the insurer Lloyds of London had been manufactured in North America. The addition of naval stores to the enumerated list in 1705 did nothing to slow any of these developments; it only increased the market for a valuable colonial export. In effect, the colonists themselves were the ones who replaced the Dutch in carrying goods to and from North America and the West Indies, and they reaped the profits. As one eighteenth-century Philadelphian put it, "Carriage is an amazing Revenue."[4]

No one in England seems to have anticipated this explosion of colonial shipping. But in an age when expanding trade required all the vessels that could be set afloat, few complained, especially when American ships carried home the goods of British merchants. In part, this reflected one of the few major departures from the Restoration-era approach to imperial trade after the Glorious Revolution. Those who controlled Parliament, the Board of Trade, and the apparatus of the Crown tended to be hostile to great chartered trading companies, and particularly to the court-connected monopolies beloved of the Stuart monarchs. For all its economic might, the Bank of England proved the rule, for its charter granted it no formal monopolies. Great men of landed wealth and powerful merchant families held most of the levers of power. Yet by design as well as chance, the eighteenth-century British imperial economy belonged to thousands of smaller-scale traders and family networks, pooling their resources in varied ways to seek the main chance. Protected markets defined by the Navigation Acts, regularized transatlantic and global trade routes created by more than a century of experience, the ability of the British navy to provide protection from pirate and foreign attacks on commercial shipping, and increasingly sophisticated financial mechanisms made it all possible.

Those mechanisms appear to modern eyes incomprehensible in their primitive intricacy: a bewildering array of gold and silver coins issued by many nations; private bills of exchange, resembling paper money, that were drawn on the accounts of merchants thousands of miles away and traded many times before their final redemption; personal credit and debt arrangements of staggering complexity; connections among consignees, factors, and agents maintained by slow-motion letters trying to predict supply and demand; shipping insurance contracts that made underwriters somehow wealthy, shipowners and merchants somehow feel secure, and clients somehow complacent with endless lawsuits when insurers failed to pay for a loss. In all of these convoluted transactions, merchants and shipowners in Boston, New York, Newport, Philadelphia, and smaller ports may have been small fry compared to their counterparts in the trading houses of London, Bristol, or Glasgow. Yet apart from large-scale dealers in a few commodities such as tobacco and sugar, small fry were everywhere the norm. British North Americans had as good a chance to make a killing, or at least a living, as nearly anyone else.

Merchants, large and small, could profit only if they had something to trade, and sea captains only if they had something to carry. By the mid-eighteenth century, nearly every living person in eastern North America produced for the ever-expanding Atlantic market. That large-scale Chesapeake tobacco planters and their enslaved workers did so is obvious. That New England and Newfoundland fishermen fed much of Europe is clear. That South Carolina planters who turned their enslaved workforce to growing rice also did so is plain: production, which began only in the 1690s, reached 1.5 million pounds annually by 1710 and 20 million by 1730.[5] (Cotton would not become Carolina's main crop until nearly a century later.) Involvement with Atlantic markets is also obvious for the roughly 5 percent of British North Americans who lived in such port cities (or rather such large towns) as Philadelphia (its 1760 population was about 17,000), Boston (16,000), New York (13,000), Charles Town (8,000), or Newport, Rhode Island (7,500).[6] Most residents in these places and smaller ports made their living in crafts and other occupations directly or indirectly associated with shipping and trading. More easily overlooked are the efforts of men of small means everywhere, from the Carolinas to Maine, to work themselves, their children, their servants, and their slaves a bit harder to produce a small surplus of wheat, corn, or whatever else could, through many intermediaries, find its way to an oceangoing ship. The women who lived with those small planters churned butter, brewed beer, or spun textiles to be sold in local markets that ultimately fed into the Atlantic commercial maw.

Also easily overlooked is the great extent to which Native Americans produced for the Atlantic market. From the Ohio Valley northward, the main product continued to be beaver and other furs (added to Britain's enumerated list in 1721). The fact that oversupply on the one hand and overhunting on the other led to periodic economic hardship only emphasizes the deep interdependence of the Native American and Atlantic economies. From the Ohio Valley southward, the main Native product was deerskin, for which the appetite seemed infinite. On the eve of the Yamasee War, a wave of epidemics happened to decimate the cattle herds of continental Europe. The plagues returned repeatedly during the next few decades, creating voracious demand for alternative sources of leather. As diverse peoples resettled to become the Indian nations known as Creeks, Cherokees, and Chickasaws and reestablished relations with Carolina traders—whose royal governors now struggled to master the diplomatic niceties necessary for commerce to flourish—the regional economy shifted from slave raiding to deer hunting in order to meet the global demand. By the 1760s, perhaps a million does and bucks were falling victim annually to an operation of near-industrial scale.[7]

Just as the British replaced the Dutch as carriers of their own colonial products, then, they also replaced the Dutch as the primary trading partners of eighteenth-century Native Americans. Still, bitter experiences stretching from the Pequot War, through King Philip's War, through the disastrous entanglement of the Iroquois in King William's War, to the horrors of the Yamasee War had taught Native leaders the dangers of becoming solely dependent on English colonists for their economic livelihoods. The geo-strategic concerns of British governors seeking allies against the French and the Spanish mitigated the dangers somewhat, but every independent Native nation now kept its options open. In the far northeast, Wabanakis in the French orbit continued to trade with hated New Englanders. Haudenosaunee people traded with Albany but always maintained access to alternate markets in La Nouvelle-France; as an exasperated New York official explained, "To preserve the balance between us and the French is the great ruling principle of the modern Indian poli-

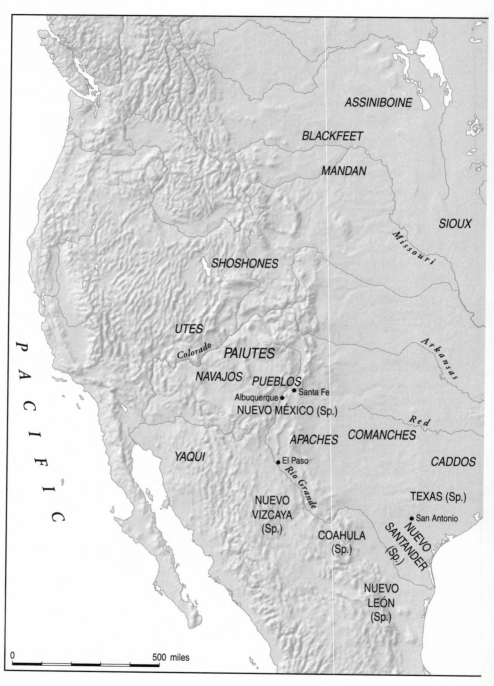

North America, c. 1730.

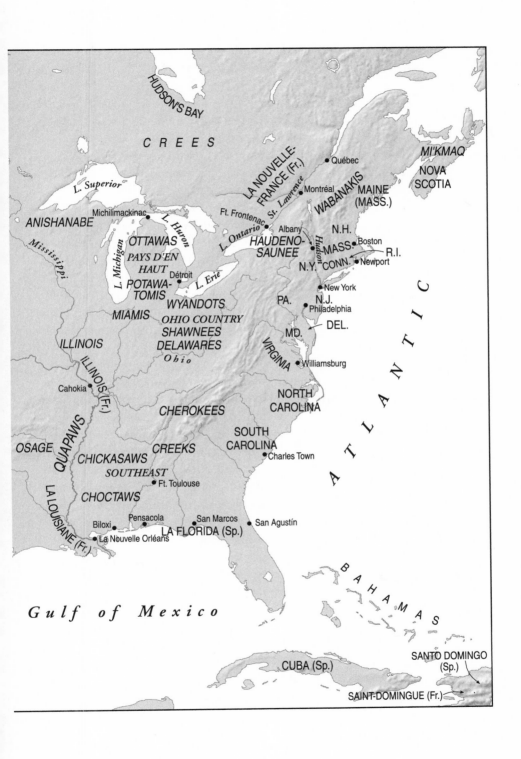

HUDSON'S BAY

CREES

L. Superior

ANISHANABE

Mississippi

Michilimackinac

L. Huron

OTTAWAS
PAYS D'EN
HAUT

L. Michigan

Détroit

POTAWA-
TOMIS

L. Erie

WYANDOTS

MIAMIS

OHIO COUNTRY
SHAWNEES
DELAWARES

Ohio

ILLINOIS

ILLINOIS (Fr.)

Cahokia

QUAPAWS

OSAGE

CHICKASAWS

SOUTHEAST

CHOCTAWS

LA LOUISIANE (Fr.)

Biloxi

Pensacola

La Nouvelle Orléans

CHEROKEES

CREEKS

Ft. Toulouse

San Marcos

San Agustín

LA FLORIDA (Sp.)

LA NOUVELLE-
FRANCE (Fr.)

Québec

MI'KMAQ

NOVA
SCOTIA

St. Lawrence

Montréal

WABANAKIS

MAINE
(MASS.)

Ft. Frontenac

L. Ontario

Albany

N.H.

HAUDENO-
SAUNEE

MASS.

Boston

R.I.

Newport

N.Y.

CONN.

Hudson

New York

PA.

N.J.

Philadelphia

DEL.

MD.

VIRGINIA

Williamsburg

NORTH
CAROLINA

SOUTH
CAROLINA

Charles Town

ATLANTIC

BAHAMAS

Gulf of Mexico

CUBA (Sp.)

SANTO DOMINGO
(Sp.)

SAINT-DOMINGUE (Fr.)

tics."[8] The same principle applied in the Great Lakes region, where trading partners of La Nouvelle-France flirted with New York, and in the southeast, where Cherokees, Creeks, and Chickasaws kept Carolinians guessing about their dealings with La Louisiane, French-allied Choctaws did the reverse, and all kept hoping that La Florida might somehow also become an alternative to British economic dominance.

That dominance never stretched as far west as Nuevo México. There, too, however, a complicated balance of European and Native powers defined trading relationships spanning continents and oceans. The establishment of La Louisiane, and the activities of French traders up and down the Mississippi, brought Atlantic trade goods and firearms to a variety of peoples on the Great Plains and ultimately to the enemies of the Pueblos. Raids by well-armed Comanches and others, meanwhile, became an increasing threat to the Spanish of northern México. In the early 1690s, colonial authorities responded by establishing a series of presidios and missions across Texas and by dispatching troops under the command of an experienced administrator named Diego de Vargas to reconquer Nuevo México.

There, Pop'ay had died shortly after the Pueblo Revolt of 1680, and old divides of language and community had reemerged among the peoples he had briefly and imperfectly unified. Many Pueblos seem genuinely, if warily, to have welcomed the return of the Spanish in hopes of military protection and access to trade goods. Still, the reconquest was brutal; Vargas's standard tactic was to line up resisters, instruct a Franciscan friar to pronounce a hasty absolution over them, and order them to be shot. By 1698, the bloodshed was mostly over. Thereafter, Vargas's successors ruled with a lighter touch, and with less influence from the Franciscans, than had their predecessors. While never truly prosperous or entirely peaceful, eighteenth-century Nuevo México found its place on the fringe of the Atlantean world. A small population of criollos and mestizos raised cattle and horses on ranches scattered along the Río Grande. The Pueblos meanwhile became centers for a far-flung commerce. Utes, Comanches, and others came to annual trade fairs at Taos and other pueblos, where nuevos mexicanos and Natives bartered guns, ammunition, horses, and crops for meat, buffalo hides, furs, and Indian slaves.

Elsewhere, however, the British controlled much of the trade with Native Americans, primarily because of the quality, quantity, and low price of the goods that England's Atlantic empire could supply. From north to south, and all points between, Native consumers purchased from English, or more often Scottish, traders a similar store of items, most of them specifically manufactured to Indian specifications. The brass kettles and iron axes that for more than a century had been vital to everyday life now came in sizes and shapes finely tuned to their users' tastes. Textile workers in Gloucestershire produced a specific kind of woolen cloth known as "strouds" in precise shades of blue, red, and gray for the Indian market. Gunsmiths similarly created lightweight trade muskets with advanced flintlock mechanisms that Native hunters demanded. Less specialized items of every sort—from needles, scissors, spoons, and hoes to linen shirts, glass beads, jewelry, and rum—became integral parts of a pan-Indian material culture. And all depended upon trade connections with Britons who turned them out more plentifully and cheaply than their French or Spanish competitors. These consumer goods integrated eighteenth-century Native people with the broader Atlantic imperial world. As a colonial official observed, "A modern Indian cannot subsist without Europeans."[9]

Nor could a modern British North American planter or city dweller. The motive behind all the small-scale producing, the scrambling to find something to sell, and the hustling for coin or credit was to be able to purchase an array of consumer goods that previous generations on either side of the Atlantic could hardly have imagined. In 1660, the households of even the wealthiest Virginians and New Englanders had been remarkably empty of material possessions—not because of puritanical self-restraint but because no one below the aristocracy could afford to live in any other way. A brightly painted chest protected linens handed down from mother to daughter as a form of wealth. These would not be used as table cloths, because the majority of households *had* no tables, and only about half owned even one chair on which to sit. Meals were served, if that was the word for it, on makeshift boards placed on movable trestles, while people relaxed on chests, on crude stools, or around the huge walk-in fireplace that dominated one end of the room and served as the kitchen. A few bowls probably made of wood or simple ceramic earthenware, a large wooden platter called a trencher, some metal spoons, one all-purpose knife, and a shared mug completed the eating equipment.

The main item of furniture would have been the bed on which the master of the house and his wife slept. In the eighteen-by-twenty-foot one-room houses in which a third to a half of the population lived, there would have been space for little else. If there were two rooms, doubling the floor space, the bed would take pride of place in the chamber called the "parlor," where what passed for peace and quiet could be found and where honored guests could be entertained, while seated, if anywhere, on the edge of the bed. All other activities took place in the "hall," a combination of kitchen, dining room, living room, and workspace, where some members of the household were also likely to sleep at night; others would place their mattresses on the floor of the loft above. Few surfaces inside or out were painted or whitewashed. Windows were few and small, and unlikely to be equipped with expensive glass panes.

Only part of this scarcity stemmed from the expense of importing manufactured goods from Europe and the undeveloped state of colonial economies. By some measures, material conditions were better in English North America than in the British Isles. Meat was an everyday staple rather than an occasional luxury; wood fires that no one in tree-poor England could afford kept people reasonably warm; and the same excess of lumber allowed common folk's houses to be built more sturdily, if less often of brick, than those across the ocean. But on the whole, conditions were not that different on the two shores of the mid-seventeenth-century Atlantic. In rural England, Scotland, and Ireland, the majority of the population—including many in the middling ranks—lived much the way their North American counterparts did, and much as their medieval ancestors had done.

Through a process that remains somewhat mysterious, all this began to change in England after the Restoration. The transformations began with the elite, who had always been able to afford households stocked with more material goods of better quality—but often not of fundamentally different nature—than could ordinary folk. At the time, at least some English people must have thought it was all part of the great popish plot, because many of the new fashions came from Catholic Italy and France and were somehow associated with the opulent courts of Charles II and James VII and II. But things were far more complicated than that. One of the most important new fashions, and one of the first to spread from the aristocracy to more common homes, arrived from the Protestant Netherlands in the form of Delftware, the bright blue-and-white ceramics that came in many forms, from wall tiles to large platters meant for display to individual plates, cups, and saucers. By the early eighteenth century, English craftspeople were making their own contributions to new household clutter with high-quality and relatively cheap salt-glazed Staffordshire ware and imitations of far more expensive Chinese porcelain.

Yet elite houses were not cluttered at all, because families with sufficient wealth were building a new style of dwelling, much larger and far differently laid out than the traditional hall-and-parlor model. Later and anachronistically called "Georgian," the house plan that spread rapidly across the British Isles and North America beginning in the reigns of William and Anne featured four symmetrical rooms on each of at least two floors, paired on either side of a central hall way and grand staircase. Every interior surface was plastered or paneled, painted or wallpapered. With cooking facilities banished to a separate kitchen in the basement or to an outbuilding, fireplaces shrank in size to heat rooms more efficiently and to display more effectively their elaborate mantelpieces. To illuminate these interior spaces, huge sashed multipaned windows replaced small leaded casements or wooden panels. These windows were symmetrically placed so that, from the exterior, two per story graced each side of the central door opening. The opulence of such a structure was obvious, but there had always been ways in which powerful men could display their prosperity through older cramped designs; Governor Berkeley's Green Spring was a controversial example. What was new, in addition to the particular fashion, was the number of nonaristocrats who had sufficient wealth from the new Atlantic trades to engage in similar display.

In the North American colonies, wealthy men connected with royal government and merchants and great planters profiting from the Atlantic trades started building Georgian houses only a few years after the style swept the British Isles. A handful of examples sprang up in New England in the closing years of the seventeenth century, but the spread of the new fashion is usually traced to the building of Virginia's new capital city of Williamsburg. Named for the Glorious Revolution's monarch, and laid out in 1699 as a deliberate symbol of imperial power (and a repudiation of the nightmares that had occurred a few miles away at largely abandoned Jamestown), Williamsburg was a proud expression of Virginia's integration into the British Empire. Its capitol building, begun in 1701, featured twin ground-floor wings, one each for the burgesses sitting as the legislative assembly and the Royal Council sitting as the provincial high court. A bridging upper story provided space where the governor and council sat together. This layout of separate spaces for what Britons called the "democratical," the "aristocratical," and the "monarchical" elements of the polity—the many (the assembly), the few (the council), and the one (the governor)—embodied the balanced constitution that protected British liberties. Meantime, Williamsburg's handsome Bruton Parish Church symbolized the power and stability of the Book-of-Common-Prayer order. Its College of William and Mary evoked both the heroes of the Glorious Revolution and the legacy of European learning. But its governor's palace, the finest example of Georgian architecture yet seen in North America, was its most influential structure of all. Within a few years, similar buildings were going up on plantations throughout Tidewater Virginia. By the 1730s, Georgian houses were becoming familiar sights throughout the colonies—visible examples of the common culture, and common wealth, that united the British Atlantean world.

Beyond its opulence, what would have struck everyone as most novel about a Georgian house was the size, openness, and brightness of its interior spaces. Although these spaces contained far more stuff than ever before—including dozens of the formerly rare chairs to sit on—it was possible to walk through the rooms without tripping over a bed, a linen chest, or a child napping on the floor. Indeed, a whole array of indoor behaviors suddenly became conceivable, and quickly became essential if one was to be deemed a respectable member of society. A visitor to a seventeenth-century house might have been ushered past the bustle of the hall into the sanctity of the dark parlor. There he might have perched on the side of a bed and perhaps chatted over a common cup of small beer before making a hasty exit to the outdoors or to the nearest tavern. By contrast, Georgian spaces were designed for entertaining guests, for ostentatious display, for visual enjoyment, for remaining delightfully indoors.

And especially for eating and drinking. Chairs, tables, chests, highboys, and lowboys filled the perimeters of the indoor spaces, but the most culturally important of the material goods in a Georgian house were food-related ceramics from Delft, Staffordshire, or China. Guests and family members seated in fine chairs at well-appointed tables discovered that they needed things that even the aristocracy had not deemed necessary a century before: an individual plate, bowl, cup, saucer, glass, knife, spoon, and fork (an ancient invention recently reintroduced to Britons from Italy). To use all of these tools properly, one had to learn a novel set of table manners, codified in countless advice books and now drummed into the heads of children and young men and women. Grand interior spaces required all sorts of rules of etiquette and manners for which there literally had been no room in the older living spaces. Men and women of refinement had to stand a certain way, move a certain way, dance a certain way, maintain a certain facial expression. All of it could be learned by buying the right books, hiring the right tutors. And of course one also had to dress the part, which required further expenditures. This spiral of material needs and desires—this insatiable urge to buy domestic and personal things no commoner had ever before needed—is what historians call the eighteenth-century consumer revolution.

A full Georgian house was beyond the means of the vast majority of Britons on either side of the Atlantic, but the consumer revolution that such buildings housed spread rapidly down in the social order, most notably through the purchase of ceramics. Benjamin Franklin, in one of the many perhaps apocryphal tales that populate his *Autobiography,* claimed to recall the exact moment when the consumer revolution struck his hitherto simple Philadelphia household in the 1730s:

We have an English Proverb that says,

> He that would thrive
> Must ask his Wife;

it was lucky for me that I had one as much dispos'd to Industry and Frugality as my self. . . . We kept no idle Servants, our Table was plain and simple, our Furniture of the cheapest. For instance my Breakfast was a long time Bread and Milk, (no Tea) and I ate it out of a twopenny earthen Porringer with a Pewter Spoon. But mark how Luxury will enter Families, and make a Progress, in Spite of Principle. Being call'd one Morning to Breakfast, I found it in a China Bowl with a Spoon of Silver. They had been bought for me without my Knowledge by my Wife, and had cost her the enormous Sum of three and twenty Shillings, for which she had no other Excuse or Apology to make, but that she thought *her* Husband deserv'd a Silver Spoon and China Bowl as well as any of his Neighbours. This was the first Appearance of Plate and China in our House, which afterwards in a Course of Years as our Wealth encreas'd augmented gradually to several Hundred Pounds in Value.[10]

For Franklin, it all began with a china bowl. But the vanguard of the consumer revolution in most ordinary eighteenth-century British American households was tea, or rather the complicated ceramic paraphernalia necessary to prepare, sweeten, and serve it in the proper way in the proper sort of room, even if that room could not be part of a full-scale Georgian house. Tea could not simply be slopped down like a bowl of morning porridge. It was a luxury item that cost twenty-four shillings per pound in Boston in 1720, and it had to be served in appropriate style. The necessary equipment included not just a teapot but containers for tea, cream, and sugar, a strainer, sugar tongs, special small spoons, cups and saucers for everyone likely to be present, and an elegant table on which to display it all. In 1722, one of the omnipresent sources of printed advice that taught manners to the British Atlantic world estimated that "a Tea Table worth its Equipage" could easily set one back £257, roughly ten times the annual wage of an urban laborer.[11]

Clearly, most women got by with a considerably smaller investment, but the combined pressures of emulation, status, and consumer desire were among the most compelling forces that pulled British North Americans into the imperial world of royal governors, Navigation Acts, and freedom from Popery and Arbitrary Power. And, as Franklin observed of his breakfast bowl, women were often in the forefront of the consumer revolution. Tea and its rituals were a distinctly gendered affair, the focal point of women-only early-evening gatherings, as well as of mixed assemblies in which a household's wealth, taste, and manners could be put on display.

Yet caffeine and crockery and all the other consumer delights were by no means confined to a female realm or to the domestic household. On the whole, exports from England and Scotland to North America and the West Indies nearly quadrupled between 1700 and 1750, from an estimated value of £364,000 to £1,374,000, comprising about 95 percent of all new exports during this period. For all the cultural importance of ceramics, textiles accounted for about half the value, and the array of other consumer items was vast. "Ships coming from afar bring all kinds of goods," including "various wines (Spanish, Portuguese, and German)" and "spices, sugar, tea, coffee, rice, rum (a spirit distilled from sugar and molasses), fine china vessels, Dutch and English cloth, leather, linen cloth, fabrics, silks, damask, velvet, etc.," marveled German sojourner Gottlieb Mittelberger when he first saw Philadelphia in 1750. "Already it is really possible to obtain all the things one can get in Europe in Pennsylvania."[12]

Items other than material goods were also obtainable. Books, ideas, fashions, and information of all kinds traveled in the many ships that sailed the Atlantic, tying Britons everywhere into a single cultural as well as material world. When Benjamin Franklin and his book-starved compatriots pooled their resources in 1731 to create the Library Company of Philadelphia, their initial order from London included editions of the classics and works on mathematics, chemistry, architecture, history, and other fields, but also the collected essays of London authors of the previous generation. Among these were Joseph Addison and Richard Steele's periodicals the *Tatler*, the *Spectator*, and the *Guardian*, and John Trenchard and Richard Gordon's series of essays entitled *Cato's Letters*, on such topics as liberty of conscience and freedom of speech. The subscription library that the Philadelphians created—like those soon founded elsewhere in North America—comprised the slightly-out-of date provincial version of the reading list of a British gentleman, or rather a citizen of the Atlantean world. With the establishment of the Library Company, "reading became fashionable," Franklin recalled in his *Autobiography*, "and our People having no public Amusements to divert their Attention from Study became better acquainted with Books, and in a few Years were observ'd by Strangers to be better instructed and more intelligent than People of the same Rank generally are in other Countries."[13]

Perhaps more important than books on the provincial reading list were the weekly newspapers that proliferated in the first half of the eighteenth century. Beginning with the Boston *News-Letter* in 1704 and the Philadelphia *American Weekly Mercury* and the *Boston Gazette* in 1719, they proliferated to include dozens of short-lived ventures. Among longer-lasting publications were the *New England Courant* (which Franklin left in order to escape his older brother's tyranny, afterward moving to Philadelphia and founding the *Pennsylvania Gazette* by 1729) and the *New York Weekly Journal*, which John Peter Zenger began in 1733. Usually printed on one large sheet folded to make four pages, these papers were stuffed with advertisements, lists of prices for items in diverse locales, and notes of the arrivals and departures of ships—the everyday diaries of the comings and goings of the goods that knit together the Atlantic world. But filling every additional inch of space were reprints of political essays and gossip from London, retreads of old pieces by Addison, Steele, or Trenchard and Gordon, and writings by local essayists aping the metropolitan style.

A reader who picked up the *New-York Weekly Journal* for April 14, 1740, for instance, would first see some imported "Verses occasion'd by the late united Address of the Lords and Commons to his Majesty" and,

before encountering an onslaught of ads, stumble through a locally produced poem entitled "Against Ambition." Stuffed between these political-
literary efforts were a letter from a reader describing a method of reviving
victims of suffocation, some four-month-old dispatches from Rome and
Madrid, a six-month-old report from Paris, and several breathless week-
old bulletins from elsewhere in North America that war had broken out
with Spain and that a copy of the royal declaration to that effect had just
arrived in Philadelphia. Three days later, a reader in Boston could read the
entire text of the king's war proclamation in her city's *Weekly News-Letter,*
along with more war-related reports from up and down the coast, more
months-old dispatches from Paris, and an account of the travels of evangelist George Whitefield in Georgia. The same day in Philadelphia, the
Pennsylvania Gazette led with a long letter from Whitefield criticizing
slavery, followed by the text of the war proclamation and a note that, in response to its public reading, "the People express'd their Joy in loud Huz-
zas; And the Cannon from the Hill, and the Ships in the Harbour, were
discharged." While toasts were raised to the monarch and assorted worthies, "plenty of Liquor was given to the Populace; and in the Evening
they had a Bonfire on the Hill."[14]

Through such marvels of seemingly random printed eclecticism—
passed from hand to hand and read aloud in taverns, coffeehouses, and
homes—British North Americans participated in a shared transatlantic
world. Although people in New York, Philadelphia, Boston, Charles Town,
London, Bristol, Glasgow, and Barbados lived in very different natural environments, spoke in more or less differing accents, and engaged in often strikingly different kinds of work, they read similar compilations of
what newspaper printers liked to call "the freshest advices, foreign and
domestick." And everywhere, British people drank the same tea, enjoyed
the same sugar, used the same crockery, read the same books, paid homage to the same monarch, gloried in the same tolerant Protestantism,
hated the same papists, and understood that their interdependent far-
flung locales were the joint sources of the material wonders they all enjoyed, or hoped to enjoy. They considered themselves Britons. But it
would be better to call them Atlanteans, for the Atlantic was the world in
which they lived, read, produced, and consumed.

The interconnectedness of the Atlantean world, the centrality of shipping,
trade, and the printed word to its existence, and the ways these reinforced

the British national patriotism forged during the Glorious Revolution crystallized in an odd scene in Britain's House of Commons in 1738. A sea captain named Robert Jenkins testified that, several years earlier in the West Indies, the Spanish coast guard had boarded his vessel, pillaged it of all its goods, and set it adrift. That the Spanish were entirely within their rights, and that the British would have done much the same had a Spanish ship violated the Navigation Acts by trading in Boston Harbor, made no difference. For Jenkins bore vivid evidence that the perfidious Spanish papists did more than just interfere with Atlantic commerce: he displayed for all to see a pickled human ear he claimed to have carried with him ever since the coast guard commander had cruelly sliced it from his head. As a Boston newspaper reported it, the Spaniard had "threatned to burn the Ship, and him and his People in it, for that they were obstinate Hereticks," and then "took hold of his Left Ear, and with his Cutlass slit it down; and then another of the Spaniards took hold of it and tore it off, but gave him the Piece of his Ear again, bidding him carry it to his Majesty King George."[15] War fever, fueled by Protestant bigotry and commercial greed, swept Parliament and public opinion on both sides of the Atlantic.

"The War of Jenkins's Ear" that began a year later—and of which reports officially reached American newspaper readers on those April days in 1740—was, if anything, a worse debacle than Cromwell's Western Design. Still, it revived a crusading spirit throughout Britain's Atlantic possessions, whose inhabitants saw themselves at the center, rather than on the periphery, of great imperial events. Hundreds of North American volunteers enlisted to sail with Admiral Edward Vernon in a grand effort to seize Spain's gold and trade routes, inspired by a royal proclamation that the Protestant monarch had "determined, by GOD's Assistance in so just a Cause, to vindicate the Honour of his Imperial Crown, to revenge the Injuries done to His Subjects, to assert their undoubted Rights of Commerce and Navigation, and by all possible Means to attack, annoy and distress a Nation that has treated his People with such Insolence and Barbarity."[16] In 1741, almost twenty-four thousand men in nearly two hundred vessels—by far the largest British fleet yet assembled—assaulted Cartagena, in what is now Colombia, a prize eyed ever since the days of Cromwell. Two months later, Vernon's fleet withdrew in defeat, having lost eighteen thousand men, most of them to disease. Among those who made it back to North America barely alive was a Virginia planter named Lawrence Washington. As he remodeled his version of a Georgian house, he patriotically named it "Mount Vernon," in honor of his commander.

FOURTEEN

People in Motion, Enslaved and Free

"RULE BRITANNIA! Britannia rule the waves," crowed a patriotic song first heard during the War of Jenkins's Ear; "Britons never, never, never shall be slaves!" Yet millions of Atlanteans *always* would be slaves. The prosperity of the Atlantic world rested squarely on the backs of enslaved Africans and their descendants, who came to constitute 20 percent of the population of British North America in general, and 40 percent or more in Virginia and the Carolinas. Even these workers could not satisfy a demand for labor that merged with the lure of eventual land ownership to draw tens of thousands of immigrants from continental Europe and the non-English parts of the British Isles. The movement of peoples created an ever more diverse, and ever more unequal, population. The mixture of peoples, cultures, and religions—which seems to us today so fully and completely American—was a measure of how thoroughly British North America focused the multiple energies of the eighteenth-century Atlantean world. Yet much of what many would now describe proudly as multicultural seemed deeply troubling to those who lived in that Atlantean world, Natives and immigrants alike.

Africans had toiled in North America since the earliest days of La Florida, but plantation regimes that relied primarily on slave labor were a phenomenon of the eighteenth century. A few numbers begin to tell the story. In 1680, shortly after Bacon's Rebellion, the African population of Virginia and Maryland—enslaved and free—was approximately 4,300, or about

7 percent of all non-Native Americans. By 1700 the number had nearly tripled, to about 13,000 (13 percent), but the number of free African Americans had shrunk to near invisibility, and non-African servants had become a minority in the tobacco fields. By 1730, enslaved Africans in the Chesapeake totaled more than 53,000 (27 percent of all non-Native Americans); and by 1750, nearly 151,000 (40 percent). South Carolina barely existed in 1670, but by 1700 its enslaved African population was nearly 2,400; by 1730, nearly 23,000; and by 1750 almost 40,000, representing a constant proportion of about 40 percent of the colonial population.[1]

Particularly in the Chesapeake and especially after 1730, much of the growth came from children born to mothers already in bondage, but forced immigration from Africa accelerated dramatically throughout the period as well. Only about 10,000 enslaved people arrived in all of British North America from 1676 to 1700; 37,000, from 1701 to 1725, and 97,000, from 1726 to 1750. All but about 10,000 of those imported from 1701 to 1750 went, in nearly equal numbers, to the Chesapeake and South Carolina. Large as these migration streams were, they were dwarfed by those funneling people to the sugar plantations of the British West Indies, where deaths from overwork, poor nutrition, and disease always substantially exceeded births. Roughly 182,000 African slaves went to the islands from 1675 to 1700 (95 percent of all British imports); 267,000, from 1701 to 1725 (87 percent); and 342,000, from 1726 to 1750 (77 percent). In any given year, Barbados, mother of British slavery, was in itself likely to absorb slightly more Africans than all of continental North America. Jamaica, the eighteenth-century British Empire's leading producer of sugar and coffee, chewed up twice as many.[2]

Several factors account for the rapid expansion of slavery in the eighteenth century. After the restoration of the British monarchy, for a number of reasons it became increasingly difficult to recruit English indentured servants. In the south and east of England, from which most early seventeenth-century servants had emigrated, the unemployment, low wages, and other distresses that had previously driven desperate English men and women to take their chances in North America fields had been replaced by relative prosperity. Population growth also slowed, and, after the Glorious Revolution, religious persecution eased. Yet there remained distress aplenty in the north of England, in Scotland, and in wretched Ireland, and indeed thousands did emigrate from those areas to other parts of the British Empire in the eighteenth century. A scarcity of European servants cannot entirely explain the shift to slave labor in the Chesapeake and South Carolina. Nor can the rapid decline in new British enslavement of Native Americans after the end of the Yamasee War.

More relevant is the increased supply of enslaved Africans that became available to planters everywhere in the Atlantic world. Within a decade of the formation of the Royal African Company, the English had already become the leading purveyors of enslaved people in Atlantic markets. The trade was so lucrative that the company could never keep up with the demand or enforce its legal monopoly. Even though it sold licenses to private traders to expand capacity, illegal operators carried up to a quarter of the slaves who left Africa in English ships before 1700. In 1698, the evident failure to meet demand, along with the era's general antipathy to monopolies, led Parliament to break the company's sole right to deal in slaves. Until 1712, any British trader willing to pay a 10 percent duty to the company could participate. Thereafter, the commerce was thrown open to all comers, under the general provisions of the Navigation Acts. Further incentive for British merchants and ship captains to enter the trade came in the 1713 peace treaty that ended the War of the Spanish Succession. For a term of thirty years, Spain granted Britain the *asiento de negros,* a contract to supply slaves to its empire. This right formerly had been held by the French Guinea Company, and before that by Dutch and Portuguese merchants.

The varied incentives for British subjects to expand their slaving ventures underlay the enormous growth in the supply of Africans available to North American and West Indian planters after 1700. But they do not entirely explain the metastasizing of slavery, which seems to have been driven less by mechanical supply and demand than by conscious choices made everywhere, from the highest levels of government to the households of elite, and would-be-elite, colonial North Americans. The British government's—and the royal family's—direct involvement in promoting slave labor continued unabated from the Restoration through the era of the Glorious Revolution. The official instructions that the Board of Trade drafted in the name of Queen Anne for New York governor Robert Hunter in 1709, for example, required him "to give all due encouragement and invitation to Merchants and others, who shall bring trade unto our said province . . . and in particular to the Royal African Company of England." Moreover, the instructions continued, "as we are willing to recom-

mend unto the said Company that the said Province may have a constant
and sufficient supply of Merchantable Negroes at moderate prices . . . so
you are to take Especial care that Payment be duly made, and within a
competent time."[3]

Everywhere, elite planters and elite town dwellers were making their
payments on time, and those payments were steep. For most of the first
half of the eighteenth century, the price for a young adult or teenage male
freshly arrived from Africa—such prime hands made up about 60 percent
of those purchased—averaged something like £35 sterling in New York or
Philadelphia, £30 in the Chesapeake, £25 in South Carolina, and £20 in
the West Indies. Prices for women and young children were somewhat
lower, but it is clear that planters of truly small means could not participate in the shift to slave labor, for, to them, the cost of a single worker
would amount to nearly an entire year's income.[4] Ownership of the bodies of enslaved people, then, became a mark of class privilege. Before Bacon's Rebellion, Virginia's elite—members of the Green Spring faction
and their counterparts among Bacon's followers—had already fully committed themselves to slavery. After the rebellion they also committed
themselves to removing the white "giddy-headed multitude" from the picture, primarily by ceasing to import unskilled European indentured servants who would gain their freedom, demand access to land, and challenge the rule of the few. Whatever economies of scale the shift to slave
labor may have provided for the Chesapeake's great planters, the political
advantages were even more substantial.

The transition took a long generation, but by the 1730s, when a handful
of great planter families began to enjoy the liberty and prosperity of the
British Atlantic empire and set their dozens of enslaved people to work
building and staffing their new Georgian mansions, their power was secure. Among the greatest of Virginia's great planters was William Byrd II,
who already in 1726 fancied himself "like one of the patriarchs." "I have,"
he declared,

> my flocks and my herds, my bond-men and bond-women, and every soart
> of trade amongst my own servants, so that I live in a kind of independence
> on every one, but Providence. However tho' this soart of life is without
> expence yet it is attended with a great deal of trouble. I must take care to
> keep all my people to their duty, to set all the springs in motion, and to

make every one draw his equal share to carry the machine forward. But then tis an amusement in this silent country, and a continual exercise of our patience and oeconomy.[5]

The desire for power, status, and authority—fantasies of becoming a modern-day patriarch—as much as sheer love of profitmaking, undergirded the vast expansion of slavery in the eighteenth century. The power that great men gained from owning large numbers of African people extended over lesser British people as well. In Virginia, for example, the elite used debt and credit to dominate the economic lives of the half of the white population of moderate means—those who owned a mere one to three slaves and a couple of hundred acres of land—and the remaining men of small means who could afford no slaves at all to work their common-socage plots or tenant holdings. In ways that would have been comprehensible to a medieval European lord, the great planters used their control of land and labor to dominate their society as well as to validate their manhood.

The political and social dimensions of enslavement become even more evident the farther one looks from the tobacco plantations of the Chesapeake. The Barbadians who dominated the early colonization of South Carolina created a society in which 40 percent of the population was enslaved *before* planters discovered a profitable crop to occupy the laborer's time; the colonists' social vision, perhaps more than their economic vision, was of a future in which the great displayed their power by enslaving others. North of Maryland, meanwhile, though enslaved people toiled in all sorts of occupations, a large percentage were domestics in the households of elite merchants, clergymen, and wealthy landowners. When such mighty men had their portraits painted, they sometimes made sure that the artist inserted a well-dressed black attendant among the accoutrements of wealth. When gentlemen died, their human possessions were often listed in wills and estate inventories alongside such other expensive items as race horses, clocks, and carriages. For such white Atlanteans, ownership of a slave was primarily a symbol of power—the ultimate consumer item that could be purchased in the markets of the Atlantic world.

Asserting humanity in a world where people were purchased as things was the central fact of black Atlanteans' everyday lives. Few would have been surprised at their enslaved condition, or at their masters' obsession with ownership as a measure of power. In most of West Africa's diverse societies, elite men owned slaves as private property and reckoned them as their primary source of wealth. By the early 1700s, the international slaving business in Africa was already two centuries old and, despite the brutality at its core, highly regularized. Slave raiders from African states near the coast captured people from weaker groups in the interior. The enslaved might change hands several times before an African broker brought them to fortified European trading posts on the shore. Principal among the British stations was Cape Coast Castle, a few miles east of the venerable Dutch stronghold of Elmina, on the Gold Coast of what is now Ghana. There, the same kinds of Atlantic world commodities familiar to North Americans changed hands: textiles, cooking utensils, firearms, gunpowder, alcohol. The typical total cost for acquiring a young man was about £6. Even given the substantial costs of transport and of the large crews needed to prevent rebellion during the Middle Passage, the profit from resale at three to five times that price in Barbados or Boston was substantial.[6]

Six distinct zones along the West African coast, from today's Senegal to Angola, shipped people to Atlantic markets. As a result, the diverse captives spoke hundreds of languages, came from centralized states as well as egalitarian village societies, and worshiped Catholic, Muslim, and indigenous deities. Yet the trading patterns that brought the same ships repeatedly to the same ports on both sides of the ocean tended to impose some homogeneity on the enslaved population of any given colony. West Africans from anywhere could be found anywhere in the Americas, but often people from a single region clustered in specific locales. The majority of people imported to South Carolina, for instance, were Angolans. Roughly half of those who went to tidewater Virginia were Igbos who sailed from the Bight of Biafra, and another quarter were Bantu-speaking people from West Central Africa.[7]

This ethnic clustering, and the intense bonds of friendship and fictive kinship forged in the miseries of the Middle Passage, provided the building material for human community among the enslaved. Those who were sold in a way that broke such connections suffered from the isolation. "I now totally lost the small remains of comfort I had enjoyed in conversing with my countrymen," wrote Olaudah Equiano, whose published life narrative preserves one of the few black voices to come down to us from the mid-eighteenth century. "The women too, who used to wash and take care of me were all gone different ways, and I never saw one of them afterwards." When he finally reached an isolated Virginia plantation, he "saw few or none of our native Africans, and not one soul who could talk to me."[8]

Equiano, whose story may draw on the experiences of other Igbos he knew, said that he spent only a few weeks in Virginia before being sold to a sea captain on whose ship he served for the next three years. Had he remained in the Chesapeake, he might well have continued his isolation indefinitely, for there were many small plantations with only a handful of slaves. More likely, however, is that he would have found himself in a dispersed network of people on neighboring plantations who spoke enough Igbo to communicate with him and teach him enough English to get by. From the 1720s on, a majority of these people were likely to have been born in Virginia and to have grown up speaking a creole dialect that mixed Igbo grammar with English vocabulary. The households that they grew up in of course enjoyed none of the fine Atlantic consumer goods that their labor allowed masters to enjoy. But in both the Chesapeake and South Carolina, roughly half of those who grew up on plantations with fifteen or more enslaved workers seem to have done so under the same roof as both of their parents. Most other children lived with their mothers.

Against all odds, then, enslaved people created family bonds, bonds always under assault from the threat that parents or children might be sold to a distant locale, that a planter would prevent a husband from visiting his wife and children on a neighboring plantation, that a master or a master's son would exercise the patriarchal privilege of raping his human property. The everyday struggle to maintain family ties, to find space to assert humanity in a society that labeled an individual a species of real estate, was the fundamental way that people resisted their enslavement—an everyday, every-hourly form of rebellion far more significant than the occasional violent outburst or desperate act of escape. When people did try to escape, they most often did so because they were searching for kin who had been sold away. That people did not run more often is less a testimony to the effectiveness of militia patrols and newspaper advertisements than to the power of kinship ties and familial obligations to keep an individual close to loved ones and to spare others the whippings and additional harsh collective punishments sure to follow an escape that was likely to fail. In some ways, the most courageous thing was to stay and fight quietly. "It is not that we would give less respect to . . . the many thousands who 'voted with their feet' for freedom," the most eloquent modern historian of slavery explained. "Rather, it is . . . to reach for the heart of a people whose courage was in their refusal to be brutes, in their insistence on holding themselves together, on acting, speaking, and singing as men and women."[9]

Nonetheless, runaways and individual outbursts of violence were commonplace, particularly among young men just arrived from Africa. But large-scale revolts were remarkably rare in British North America. The two most significant occurred in the 1730s, just as importations of African young men were reaching unprecedented proportions. In Virginia in 1730, after what appeared to be careful preparation, approximately three hundred enslaved men escaped from their masters and gathered in the Great Dismal Swamp on the border with North Carolina. The affair is poorly documented, and its scale may have been magnified by the fears of panicked masters, but it was ruthlessly suppressed, with at least twenty-four alleged conspirators hanged. The rebels seem to have believed a wild rumor that King George had issued an edict that Christian slaves must be freed, and many of them may have been Catholics from the Kingdom of Kongo.

The link between Christianity and freedom was clearer in a South Carolina uprising in 1739. Six years earlier, the Spanish Crown had devised a brilliant, if belated, response to the Carolina-inspired slave raiding that had destroyed the Indian missions of La Florida and rolled back effective Spanish control to little more than the immediate neighborhood of San Agustín. A royal decree offered liberty to any enslaved Africans who could escape from the English and reach the Spanish capital, and who would convert to Roman Catholicism. In 1738, several dozen escapees who appealed to Governor Manuel de Montiano for their freedom received grants of land, material assistance, and the offer of instruction by a Catholic priest at a new village called Pueblo de Gracia Real de Santa Teresa de Mose, a strategic spot two and a half miles north of San Agustín. In September 1739, when word of the existence of "Moosa" (and of the declaration of war against Spain) reached a group of about sixty enslaved men, they made a violent break for it, during which about twenty British Carolinians died along the Stono River, twenty miles from Charles Town. Over the next few months, a Carolina mop-up operation captured and executed nearly all the rebels, while a new Negro Act dramatically reduced the ability of enslaved people to move about on their own or hope for legal emancipation. Although nothing like the Stono Rebellion would be tried again, for decades, Moosa would continue to attract individual escapees.

Brave patriarchal words of men like Byrd to the contrary, masters everywhere feared that their slaves would rebel, and they lost many a night's sleep as a result. When a conspiracy was sensed, black people were killed, whether or not the rumors had any substance. White fears played out with particular brutality in New York City in 1741. The family and community networks that sustained enslaved people in urban areas were quite different from those of the Chesapeake or the Carolinas. Among the roughly 15 percent of New York's population who were black, the vast majority were enslaved but lived alone in the houses of their masters. The kinds of work they did—in craft shops and merchant stores, on the docks, as domestic servants, porters, and general laborers—took them out of those houses and allowed them to mingle with one another in public spaces and in the kind of low-end taverns that attracted white servants, day laborers, and others who were, in the eyes of the elite, the dangerous urban version of a giddy-headed multitude.

In February 1741, three enslaved people broke into a small shop and stole some snuffboxes, jewelry, and other imported consumer goods, which they apparently fenced at a nearby tavern that they frequented. While this crime was being investigated, the city's fort and the residence of the province's royal governor caught fire and burned to the ground. Several other blazes followed and were blamed, rightly or wrongly, on arson. In at least one case, a black man was said to have been seen running from an inferno. Somehow, all these events wound together to produce a fantastic theory that slaves conspired to burn down the city, that the tavern where the stolen goods were fenced was the epicenter of the plot, and that somehow the Spanish papists whom some five hundred New Yorkers had sailed off to fight at Cartagena were behind it all. A frenzy of kangaroo court judicial proceedings, extorted confessions, and hasty executions followed. When it was over, thirteen slaves had been burned at the stake, seventeen others along with four whites had been hanged after torture, and more than seventy others had been sold to the West Indies and elsewhere.

"That a plot there was, and as to the Parties and bloody Purpose of it, we presume there can scarce be a Doubt amongst us at this Time," wrote one of the judges who presided over the bloodletting. "The Ruins of his Majesty's House in the Fort, are the daily Evidence and Momento." In language that once could have been used to describe the Glorious Revolution, he proposed that

> we ought once a Year at least, to pay our Tribute of Praise and Thanksgiving to the Divine BEING, that through his merciful Providence and infinite Goodness, caused this inhuman horrible Enterprize to be detected . . . where by a Check has been put to the execrable Malice, and bloody Purposes of our Foreign and Domestick Enemies, though we have not been able entirely to unravel the Mystery of this Iniquity; for 'twas a dark Design, and the Veil is in some Measure still upon it![10]

Like all Britons, slaveowning New Yorkers would have been most familiar with the word "Atlantean" from their reading of John Milton's *Paradise Lost,* the epic poem that was never out of print in the eighteenth century and that, beyond the Bible, was one of a few works likely to be on the bookshelf of a prosperous family. Expelled from Paradise to Hell, Milton's fallen angels schemed

> To found this nether Empire, which might rise
> By pollicy, and long process of time,
> In emulation opposite to Heav'n.
> Which when *Bëëlzebub* perceiv'd, then whom,
> *Satan* except, none higher sat, with grave
> Aspect he rose, and in his rising seem'd
> A Pillar of State; deep on his Front engraven
> Deliberation sat and publick care;
> And Princely counsel in his face yet shon,
> Majestick though in ruin: sage he stood
> With *Atlantean* shoulders fit to bear
> The weight of mightiest Monarchies.[11]

No wonder masters, proclaiming the liberties that their monarch defended in their nether empire, seldom thought it was a good thing for the enslaved to be taught to read.

Britons were supposed never to be slaves, but at least one Englishman who arrived in Philadelphia in 1729 called himself exactly that. "Our

Cargo consisting chiefly of Voluntary Slaves, who are the least to be pitied, I saw all my Companions sold of[f] before me," wrote William Moraley, an impoverished onetime law student and apprentice watchmaker from Newcastle-upon-Tyne who had signed an indenture before boarding ship in London. "My turn came last, when I was sold for eleven Pounds."[12] Moraley was one of thousands of immigrants who accepted temporary bondage to pay for their passage across the Atlantic, although he was not exactly a typical case. A smooth talker and self-styled ladies' man, he somehow convinced the Burlington, New Jersey, farmer who bought him to shorten his contract from five years to three, despite the fact that he had run away and been caught, a crime for which the punishment normally was additional months or years of servitude. Moraley was also not typical—or perhaps he was more typical than we think—in that he was less interested in working hard, acquiring his own farm, and settling into modest prosperity than he was in finding a rich widow who could support him in the style to which he wanted to become accustomed. When things failed to work out, he went back to England and published his memoirs.

Moraley's book summed up the relationship between servitude, slavery, and agricultural prosperity for substantial planters who lived north of Maryland. "The first settlers," he asserted,

> not being sufficient of themselves to improve those Lands, were not only obliged to purchase a great Number of *English* Servants to assist them, to whom they granted great Immunities, and at the Expiration of their Servitude, Land was given to encourage them to continue there; but were likewise obliged to purchase Multitudes of Negro Slaves from *Africa,* by which Means they are become the richest Farmers in the World, paying no Rent, nor giving Wages either to purchased Servants or Negro Slaves; so that . . you will taste of their Liberality, they living in Affluence and Plenty."[13]

Moraley exaggerated, but his point is valid nonetheless, and nowhere more than for Pennsylvania. With Delaware and neighboring West Jersey, that province seems to have absorbed about half of the 111,000 or so people who emigrated as servants or paid their own way to North America as free people from 1700 to 1750. Chartered in 1681 as the last of the Restoration-era proprietaries, Pennsylvania was the great receiver of eighteenth-century immigrants, but this role was not necessarily foreordained. William Penn, like other colonial proprietors of his day, mixed utopian feudal fantasies with dreams of great wealth. Like them, he encountered immediate resistance from actual settlers unwilling to submit to his pretensions to govern as "True and Absolute Proprietary"—pretensions that did not survive the Glorious Revolution and his brief loss of his charter in the 1690s. And like other proprietors, Penn failed to reap great wealth; instead, he died deeply in debt. But unlike the others, he was astonishingly effective in recruiting people to migrate to his colony, and in ensuring that it bore some resemblance to his dream of a place where religious toleration would be taken to its logical extreme. According to the Quaker doctrine of the Inward Light, if souls were kept free of coercion from church and government authority, the divine spirit that lived within every man and woman would lead all to the same Truth and the same salvation. The Holy Experiment of Pennsylvania (named, Penn always insisted, in honor of his father and not himself) would be open to all who wanted to join.

Penn was a relentless salesman, and not just among fellow members of the Religious Society of Friends, as the Quakers preferred to be called. Within a year of receiving his charter, he persuaded six hundred "First Purchasers" to invest in land in his colony, and by 1684 some four thousand new emigrants had joined the thousand or so Swedes, Dutch, and English already living in what had been southwestern Nieu Nederlandt. The recruits were not just from England but from Wales, which had a substantial Quaker population, and from areas on the European continent that had become part of an international Quaker movement, particularly the Netherlands and German-speaking regions of what are now Switzerland and southwestern Germany. By 1700, a diverse lot of eighteen thousand people—most but not all Quakers and, even among Friends, nowhere near agreement on a single Truth, religious or otherwise—inhabited the colony. Three thousand of them clustered in the already thriving port of Philadelphia, where Quaker merchants maintained commercial relationships with their coreligionists throughout the Atlantic world.[14]

Surely these people flocked to Pennsylvania for its religious toleration, though for many it must have seemed an intolerant sort of liberty dominated by the consensual uniformity that Friends insisted upon. But just as surely the immigrants came for Pennsylvania's cheap and readily available land, carefully purchased—at least during William Penn's lifetime—by treaty from Lenape chiefs who ceded acreage that their disease-depleted populations no longer needed. Before 1720, prices were well below one shilling per acre, and real estate was remarkably easy to acquire, despite the fact that, in a system where all lands legally were held from a proprietor to whom quit-rents were due annually, free and common socage technically did not exist.

The ease of access stemmed from two fundamental problems that bedeviled the Penn family. First was the burden of debt; the Founder and his successors needed to throw open the doors to immigrants in hopes of somehow balancing the books. Second was the struggle among the Founder's heirs after his death in 1718. For years, the legal troubles virtually closed the colony's land office and made the collection of quit-rents almost impossible. This encouraged immigrants to take up lands on a more informal basis and to develop non-taxpaying habits that proved difficult to break even after Penn's sons Thomas, John, and Richard gained clear control over the family property. In 1732, Thomas Penn reorganized the land office, with elaborate plans to raise prices and quit-rents and reserve substantial tracts as Penn family manors. Eight years later, four thousand people had taken warrants to survey lands, but only five hundred of them bothered to file formal patents and thus pay all the appropriate fees.[15] If there was a Pennsylvania way, this was it: the scramble for land on the cheap.

And the cheap-to-free land in question was perhaps the richest on earth for growing the crops demanded by the British Atlantic world. "They have a saying there," groused Mittelberger: "Pennsylvania is heaven for farmers, paradise for artisans, and hell for officials and preachers."[16] Flax for Irish linenmakers, rye, wheat, barley, and oats to feed enslaved West Indians, cattle and hogs to feed the world, naval stores to help carry everything, and countless other products thrived in the soils of Penn's Woods and ensured the prosperity of those who could put a few hands to work growing them. "This Country produces not only almost every Fruit, Herb, and Root as grows in *Great Britain*, but divers Sorts unknown to us," Moraley wrote, echoing virtually every author who wrote about the province. "In short, it is the best poor Man's Country in the World; and, I believe, if this was sufficiently known by the miserable Objects we have in our [English] Streets, Multitudes would be induced to go thither."[17]

To appreciate the extraordinary attractiveness of Pennsylvania, one need only compare it to Georgia, chartered in 1732 specifically to be a poor man's country. Brainchild of a group led by the military officer, member of Parliament, and philanthropist James Oglethorpe, the colony fulfilled long-standing imperialist schemes to carve additional land out of La Florida and fill the gap left by the obliteration of Spanish mission villages during the wars of the early eighteenth century. But the project was also and primarily a charitable endeavor. "In America there are fertile Lands sufficient to subsist all the useless Poor in *England,* and distressed Protestants in *Europe;* yet Thousands starve for want of mere Sustenance," an early promotional tract explained. "The same Want that renders Men useless here, prevents their paying their Passage; and if others pay it for them, they become Servants, or rather Slaves for Years to those who have defrayed that Charge." With ample funding from Parliament— the only direct financial support it ever voted to establish a colony— Georgia's chartered trustees had a mandate to transport impoverished immigrants free of charge and "give them Necessaries, Cattle, Land, and Subsistence till such Time as they can build their Houses and clear some of their Land."[18] Unlike the proprietary lords of the previous century, Oglethorpe and the nineteen other trustees were forbidden to own any real estate in the colony themselves, and their regime would be strictly temporary, with the province reverting to a standard form of royal government after twenty-one years.

Yet like their predecessors, the trustees had a utopian vision for their colony. Impoverished immigrants would be carefully selected for their moral qualities. Settlement would be compact and defensible, beginning with the planned city of Savannah. Land grants would be no larger than five hundred acres, and could not be bought and sold. Slavery would be prohibited. All political decisions would be made in London, without an elected assembly on the ground. Offering no free and common socage, no easily exploitable labor force, and no vehicle for local planters to run their own affairs, the trustees unsurprisingly found few takers for their generous deal. Despite progressive weakening of restrictions, including permission for limited importation of enslaved labor, only a few thousand Europeans had populated the colony by 1752, when the trustees yielded their charter, a year early. Thereafter, under a standard form of royal government, and with all restrictions on property and slaveowning removed, the colony quickly prospered, replicating the plantation-based economy of its neighbor South Carolina.

Meanwhile, Pennsylvania and other northern destinations remained the overwhelmingly more popular destination for the poor and not so poor, both those who could afford to pay their own way and migrate as families and those who bound themselves as servants to work the land. Among the latter, William Moraley was atypical in more ways than one: only a minority of the indentured servants who made small planters affluent were En-

glish like him. Because of improved conditions at home, just 16,000 or so
of the 111,000 Europeans who emigrated to British North America in the
years between 1700 and 1750 came from England and 11,000 from Wales.
Among the English and Welsh, perhaps as many as 80 percent migrated as
servants, either with indentures or because they had been convicted of
a crime.[19] As had been the case a century earlier, most of these, like
Moraley, were young men down on their luck who had come to London
from elsewhere and then moved on to the colonies. And like Moraley,
many of them seemingly made the choice during a drunken conversation
with a newfound alleged friend. "After we had drank two Pints of Beer, he
paid the Reckning," Moraley recalled of his fresh acquaintance. "I absolutely agreed to go, and to that Intent we went before Sir *Robert Bailis,*
Lord Mayor, where I was sworn as not being a married Person, or an Apprentice by Indenture." Having thus verified that no legal obligations
bound Moraley to England, the recruiter took him to a stationer's shop,
where he had him sign an indenture and then personally escorted him to a
ship that had "on board 20 Persons, all Men, bound to the same Place, and
on the same Account."[20]

Similar stories could have been told in different accents by many of the
nearly forty thousand people who migrated from Ireland to North America between 1700 and 1750. More than half sailed from Dublin, Cork, and
other ports in the overwhelmingly Catholic and perennially impoverished
south of the island. Although there were no legal restrictions on Catholic
emigration—like all subjects of the British empire, the Irish could move
among its various provinces at will—there was little incentive for one to
advertise one's status as a papist anywhere in a virulently Protestant Atlantic empire. It is difficult to know, then, how many desperate Catholics
were able to escape Ireland in hopes of a better post-servitude life in
North America or how many kept their religious beliefs hidden once they
arrived; the best guess is that they made up about 30 percent of the total.
More certain is that the vast majority of those who left southern Ireland
were impoverished young men who, like Moraley, sold themselves into
bondage to pay their fare and sailed in small groups on ships that primarily
carried Irish linens and other consumer goods to the colonies. With frequent and cheap transport on established trade routes, there was always
room for ten or twenty servants to complete a cargo.

For the largely Protestant north of Ireland, the story is more compli-cated. There, too, many young men, both Catholic and Presbyterian, sold themselves into servitude in order to emigrate. But perhaps 80 percent of migrants—upwards of fifteen thousand people—paid their own way and traveled in family groups, replicating the pattern set by puritan planters a century earlier. As in that earlier period, a mix of religious and economic factors was at work. In the late 1710s and 1720s, controversies ripped Presbyterian congregations in Ulster. A faction called "New Lights" em-braced the ideas of personal freedom and religious toleration sweeping the British Empire as a whole, and hoped that appeals to liberty of con-science would win them exemption from the Test Act, which, in Ireland as in England, barred all but communicants in the established Church from officeholding. Their opponents, the "Old Lights," who clung ever more tightly to congregational supervision of personal morality and to formal as-sertions of Calvinist orthodoxy, focused on a campaign to require that all Presbyterians subscribe to the Cromwell-era Westminster Confession of Faith. They argued that the orthodoxy of this creed, shared with many Dissenters in England, was the best hope for relief from the Test Act. Nei-ther viewpoint prevailed with the parliaments of Ireland or England, al-though the Old Lights managed to defeat the New Lights for control of the regional presbyteries that governed their churches. Bitter feelings and disillusionment from the internal struggle and the failure of the campaigns against the Test Act led thousands of people to consider a fresh start in Pennsylvania, renowned not only for its toleration but also as the only North American province that already had a presbytery, established a gen-eration earlier by missionaries from Ireland.

But few would have actually boarded ships, had the religious controver-sies not coincided with economic distress. In the 1690s, after the defeat of James VII and II and his Catholic supporters, many Ulster Presby-terians—whether native to the region or relatively recent immigrants from Scotland and the north of England—had settled on lands vacated by Cath-olic tenants and leased by desperate landlords under attractive twenty-one-year terms. In the late 1710s, the leases began to expire and landlords began raising, or "racking," rents. These developments coincided with three years of disastrous harvests and a depression in the linen trade. More bad harvests—outright famines—struck both the north and south of Ireland in the late 1720s and in 1741, a horrific year when disease com-bined with hunger to kill upwards of three hundred thousand people.

Against this background, it is little wonder that families with sufficient means to pay their fare boarded boats for the "Best Poor Man's Country," often settling near friends, neighbors, and fellow church members they had known at home.

In Pennsylvania they were joined, a few miles down or up the road or just over the next ridge, by equally clannish enclaves of German-speaking immigrants from continental Europe. Nearly thirty-seven thousand arrived between 1700 and 1750, the vast majority after 1730. These, too, largely emigrated as intact families. Their individual stories varied greatly, but the broad forces that pushed them from their homes and attracted them to Pennsylvania—where about three-quarters of them settled—were similar to those of the northern Irelanders: in Europe, economic distress, the legacy of warfare, and religious controversies and persecutions; in America, religious toleration, cheap land, well-established trade routes, and welcoming kin and coreligionists who had already made the trip. About 90 percent of the German-speakers were members of one of the Lutheran or Reformed churches established according to the affiliation of local princes in the Holy Roman Empire. The remainder belonged to small Protestant sects—Anabaptists, and countless others with such colorful names as "Dunkers" and "Schwenkfelders"—who found in tolerant Pennsylvania the answer to their dreams of simply being left alone to worship their god as they saw fit. All of the Germans found further reason to see North America as the promised land after 1740, when the British Parliament passed legislation that regularized the process for non-British immigrants to gain the right to own land and vote; they needed only to reside in a British province for seven years, certify that they had received Communion in a Protestant church within the past three months, and take a version of the oaths required by the 1689 Toleration Act. (These provisions were soon revised to allow Quakers and Jews to enjoy the same benefits.)

The attractions of Pennsylvania, particularly once a handful of German-speakers from a particular principality or sect established a beachhead, were clear. But what made large-scale migration possible was a distinctive combination of recruiting, transportation, and financing arrangements that took shape by the 1720s. By then, the publicity campaign that William Penn had begun among German-speaking Quakers had exploded into a nonstop campaign of books, broadsides, and word of mouth, touting the wonders of Pennsylvania throughout the Rhine Valley, or, as it was often known, the "Palatinate." The campaign was managed by a small group of merchants who specialized in transporting Palatine Germans to North America from Rotterdam and Amsterdam, the Dutch seaports to which the Rhine flowed. Unlike the diversified shippers who included a handful of servants or families on merchant vessels sailing from the British Isles, the Dutch brokers popularly (or unpopularly) known as "Neuländer" packed one hundred fifty to two hundred emigrants at a time onto what resembled nothing so much as slave ships.

Their major innovation was to find a way for families who often had spent most of their savings simply traveling to the Netherlands to finance the remainder of their passage to Pennsylvania. Instead of forcing people to sell themselves into servitude before boarding ship, the Neuländer allowed them to travel on credit, with a fixed payment due within a short time after arrival at the destination. Emigrant families could then hope that kin already prospering in Pennsylvania might either pay the fare or arrange favorable terms of servitude for children to work off the debt, liberating the parents to make their way as free people. Many of these "redemptioners" thus still had to become bound laborers to pay for their transportation, but did so with far more freedom of action than Irish or English servants who were simply sold to the highest bidder.

Germans, Irish from north and south, and, in smaller numbers, Lowland Scots, Welsh, French Protestant Huguenots, and others joined many more enslaved Africans to make what had been English North America not only British but promiscuously Atlantean by the middle of the eighteenth century. Nowhere was this more true than in Pennsylvania and neighboring parts of New Jersey, Maryland, and Virginia. By 1750, not just Quakers but people of English descent in general were a distinct minority in the Penns' Province.

All of these immigrant peoples brought with them their diverse religious beliefs and disputes—disputes deepened by the wave of religious revivals that swept the European continent, the British Isles, and North America during what came to be known as the "Great Awakening" of the 1730s and 1740s. With university-trained clergy few and far between, the anarchic tendencies of Protestantism exploded in a cacophony of zealotry and pious experimentation. Outbreaks of enthusiastic religious conversion among local congregations of a kind long familiar to the hotter sort of Protestants combined in eighteenth-century minds to become a single "remarkable Revival of Religion" throughout the Atlantic world. Newspapers and other forms of widely circulated print created the story and centered much of it on the exploits of a charismatic handful of itinerant evangelists.

No itinerant was more famous than George Whitefield, who attracted tumultuous crowds wherever he went during North American tours in 1738, 1739–1741, 1751, 1754, and 1763. Throngs estimated at twenty thousand heard him in Boston and Philadelphia; a thousand or more heard him on at least sixty occasions.[21] A New England farmer named Nathan Cole captured the excitement:

> Now it pleased God to send Mr. Whitefield into this land; and my hearing of his preaching at Philadelphia, like one of the Old apostles, and many thousands flocking to hear him preach the Gospel; and great numbers were converted to Christ; I felt the Spirit of God drawing me by conviction; I longed to see and hear him, and wished he would come this way. . . . Then on a Sudden, in the morning about 8 or 9 of the Clock there came a messenger and said Mr. Whitfield preached at Hartford and Weathersfield yesterday and is to preach at Middletown this morning at ten of the Clock, I was in my field at Work, I dropt my tool that I had in my hand and ran home to my wife telling her to make ready quickly to go. . . . I with my wife soon mounted the horse and went forward as fast as I thought the horse could bear, and when my horse got much out of breath I would get down and put my wife on the Saddle and bid her ride as fast as she could and not Stop or Slack for me except I bad her . . . ; we improved every moment to get along as if we were fleeing for our lives; all the while fearing we should be too late to hear the Sermon, for we had twelve miles to ride double in little more than an hour. . . . On high land I saw before me a Cloud or fogg rising . . . [and] heard a noise something like a low rumbling thunder and presently found it was the noise of Horses feet coming down the Road and this Cloud was a cloud of dust made by the Horses feet; . . . and when I came within about 20 rods of the Road, I could see men and horses Slip[p]ing along in the Cloud like shadows and as I drew nearer it seemed like a steady Stream of horses and their riders, scarcely a horse more than his length behind another, all of a Lather and foam with sweat, their breath rolling out of their nostrils every Jump; every horse seemed to go with all his might to carry his rider to hear news from heaven for the saving of Souls.

Part entertainment, part spectacle, and so emotion-filled that even beasts of burden seemed to be moved by the spirit, Whitefield's appearances led many, at least temporarily, to encounter the divine. "When I saw Mr. Whitfield . . . he lookt almost Angelical," said Cole. "My hearing him preach, gave me a heart wound; By Gods blessing . . . I saw that my righteousness would not save me."[22]

When Whitefield moved on, others moved in, each leaving new traces of spiritual fervor and new divisions among followers of various doctrines. Meantime, those whose faiths were more conventionally orthodox or casually borne noted Whitefield's unangelical crossed eyes and mocked him as the "Reverend Dr. Squintum."[23] Especially in the mid-Atlantic region, the result of these many controversies and enthusiasms was a jostling patchwork of communities and beliefs, in which no group could impose its will on any other. Pennsylvania "offers people more freedom than the other English colonies, since all religious sects are tolerated there," the good Lutheran Mittelberger concluded in 1750 with considerable horror. "One can encounter Lutherans, members of the Reformed Church, Catholics, Quakers, Mennonites or Anabaptists, Herrenhüter or Moravian Brothers, Pietists, Seventh-Day Adventists, Dunkers, Presbyterians, New-born, Freemasons, Separatists, Freethinkers, Jews, Mohammedans, Pagans, Negroes, and Indians." Worse, "there are several hundred unbaptized people who don't even wish to be baptized."[24]

Mittelberger was not the only one who was worried about the great Atlantean mixing of peoples. In 1751, two men who lived a little over one hundred miles apart reflected on the migrants flooding the interior of North America. The name of the first is lost to us, but his words are recorded in the diary of Presbyterian missionary John Brainerd. Hoping to spread the Presbyterian gospel to Native people, Brainerd visited the Wyoming Valley—on the Susquehanna River near present-day Wilkes-Barre, Pennsylvania—where he encountered multiple obstacles. On the night he arrived, a Haudenosaunee war party passing through on its way south occasioned a "martial dance" that the clergyman found "terrible to behold." No sooner did the Iroquois leave, than preparations began for a council of Native people from miles around to discuss a young woman's recent prophetic message that "it was the mind of the Great Power that they should destroy the poison from among them." What that poison was, and what ex-

actly the young seer said about it, remained obscure, largely because the
Indians refused to discuss the details with outsiders. But a further difficulty was that Brainerd's interpreter—probably the Presbyterian Delaware Moses Tatamy—did not speak the principal local dialect. Most of the
residents seem to have been Nanticokes, who had only recently relocated
to Wyoming after British colonists had forced them from their homes on
the Delmarva Peninsula. These and other displaced groups settling in the
Susquehanna watershed were all too familiar with Europeans, their religions, and their languages. Brainerd observed that "there is but one in the
town that can speak English well, though sundry others can do considerable at it, and the most of them understood some."[25]

After Brainerd talked his way into the council convened to discuss the
young woman's prophecy, it was presumably that fluent English-speaker
who told him bluntly

> that the great God first made three men and three women, viz.: The In-
> dian, the negro, and the white man. That the white man was the youngest
> brother, and therefore the white people ought not to think themselves
> better than the Indians. That God gave the white man a book, and told him
> that he must worship him by that; but gave none either to the Indian or ne-
> gro, and therefore it could not be fit for them to have a book, or be any way
> concerned with that way of worship. And, furthermore, they understood
> that the white people were contriving a method to deprive them of their
> country in those parts, as they had done by the sea-side, and to make slaves
> of them and their children, as they did of the negroes; that I was sent on
> purpose to accomplish that design, and, if I succeeded and managed my
> business well, I was to be chief ruler in those parts, or, as they termed it,
> king of all their country, etc. They made all the objections they could, and
> raked up all the ill treatment they could think of that ever their brethren
> had received from the white people; and two or three of them seemed to
> have resentment enough to have slain me on the spot.

Over the next few days, other Native people told Brainerd's interpreter
that Native American Christians were welcome to join them at Wyoming
and practice their faith, but that their "minister must not come, because
he was a white man; that, if one white man came, another would desire it,
etc., and so by-and-by they should lose their country." The Wyoming Indians were convinced that "the great men in [New] York, Philadelphia, etc.
have laid a scheme to deprive the Indians of all their lands in those parts,

and to enslave them and their posterity; that the ministers are sent among them purely to accomplish that design."[26]

The Wyoming residents would have found little reassurance in the words of the second man who contemplated the mixing of peoples in 1751. In an essay called "Observations Concerning the Increase of Mankind, Peopling of Countries, etc.," Philadelphian Benjamin Franklin noted that "America is chiefly occupied by Indians," and that, "these having large Tracks, were easily prevail'd on to part with Portions of Territory to the new Comers, who did not much interfere with the Natives in Hunting, and furnish'd them with many Things they wanted." Yet, as Franklin saw it, something was wrong with the kinds of immigrants who were taking the Indians' place. "Why should the Palatine Boors be suffered to swarm into our Settlements, and by herding together establish their Language and Manners to the Exclusion of ours?" the Philadelphian asked. "Why should Pennsylvania, founded by the English, become a Colony of Aliens, who will shortly be so numerous as to Germanize us instead of our Anglifying them, and will never adopt our Language or Customs, any more than they can acquire our Complexion?" Consideration of the relative merits of Native people and British and German Atlantic immigrants led Franklin

to add one Remark: That the Number of purely white People in the World is proportionably very small. All Africa is black or tawny. Asia chiefly tawny. America (exclusive of the new Comers) wholly so. And in Europe, the Spaniards, Italians, French, Russians and Swedes, are generally of what we call a swarthy Complexion; as are the Germans also, the Saxons only excepted, who with the English, make the principal Body of White People on the Face of the Earth. I could wish their Numbers were increased. And while we are, as I may call it, Scouring our Planet, by clearing America of Woods, and so making this Side of our Globe reflect a brighter Light to the Eyes of Inhabitants in Mars or Venus, why should we in the Sight of Superior Beings, darken its People? Why increase the Sons of Africa, by Planting them in America, where we have so fair an Opportunity, by excluding all Blacks and Tawneys, of increasing the lovely White and Red? But perhaps I am partial to the Complexion of my Country, for such Kind of Partiality is natural to Mankind.[27]

Naturally or not, Franklin lumped people together as abstractions— "Palatine Boors," "Sons of Africa," "purely white people." Similarly, in Brainerd's account, none of the Native Americans—not even the interpreter with whom the missionary shared an arduous journey—merited a personal name. Nor, apparently, did the Wyoming residents distinguish among the nameless "minister," the "white people," and the provincial "great men." All, it would seem, had ceased being individuals and instead become stereotypes, faceless threatening competitors for the lands and resources of the continent. Once such thinking began to erase ambiguity and personal circumstances, murderous violence against those labeled enemies could easily come to the surface, as it did for the "two or three" Indians who wanted to kill Brainerd at Wyoming in 1751. By the middle of the decade, Indian rage at white land-grabbing would become nearly universal, and bloodshed on a scale the continent had not seen since the Tuscarora War would convulse the uneasy polyglot of Atlantean peoples.

FIFTEEN

Contending for a Continent

AT A TREATY CONFERENCE IN 1757, held at the height of the violence, a man named Teedyuscung, who had moved to the Wyoming Valley in 1754 and styled himself "King of the Delawares," tried to explain why he and his people had gone to war against neighboring Pennsylvania and other British provinces. The British delegation claimed not to fathom the complexities of his analysis, so Teedyuscung's interpreter put it more bluntly: "He said the meaning was this. The Land is the cause of our Differences, that is our being unhappily turned out of the land is the cause, and thô the first settlers might purchase the lands fairly yet they did not act well nor do the Indians Justice for they ought to have reserved some place for the Indians."[1] Three-quarters of a century earlier, during King Philip's War, Increase Mather had said that *"Land! Land!* hath been the Idol of many." And, he reminded his readers, "Idolatry brings the Sword."[2] For hundreds of years, descendants of medieval Europeans had equated power with the possession of land and the control of labor, while descendants of medieval North Americans equated power with alliances based on trade and reciprocity. For an eighteenth-century generation or so, the two configurations had uneasily coexisted; but as Teedyuscung and his interpreters tried to point out, by the middle of the 1700s coexistence no longer seemed possible. "Our differences have sprung from the land or earth . . . ," he said, "thô it was not the principal thing." The problem was not land idolatry alone, but idolatry so all-encompassing that it was blind to the needs of Native people for reciprocity and alliance. "If regular Methods had been

369

formerly taken for an habitation or residence for the poor Indians in this Land," Teedyuscung lamented, "this would not have come to pass."[3]

Teedyuscung's migration to the Wyoming Valley was part of a much larger movement of Native peoples—peoples who were just as much in motion as those who crossed the ocean as slaves, redemptioners, or free families. In the mid- to late seventeenth century, epidemics, warfare, and migration had virtually emptied the Indian country in what we today call central and western Pennsylvania and eastern Ohio. In the early eighteenth century, varied people had resettled the area. The Nanticokes whom Brainerd met were among many small communities who seemed constantly on the move; most Nanticokes stayed in the Wyoming Valley only a few years before moving on to new homes farther up the Susquehanna in present-day New York State, while others moved west. The villages at Wyoming then came to be dominated by bands of Lenapes and Munsees—collectively known as "Delawares"—who had been pushed out of lands farther east. Other Delawares settled farther south on the Susquehanna at Shamokin and Paxtang, others in the Juniata River valley, and many more in the Allegheny and upper Ohio River watersheds at places called Venango, Kittanning, and Logstown, in the region called the "Forks of the Ohio."

In all of these areas, sometimes in the same towns, sometimes in neighboring communities, were large numbers of Shawnees, whose ancestral homes were probably in today's states of Ohio and Kentucky but who had dispersed widely during the seventeenth-century Indian wars. Also numerous were Senecas and other Iroquois migrating south and west from the heartland of the Haudenosaunee. These groups—their decentralized political traditions accentuated by the stresses of migration—were joined by migrants from almost every point on the compass: Mahicans from the Hudson River valley; Ninnimissinouk from southern New England; Conoys, Piscataways, and others from the Chesapeake region; Tuscaroras and others who had fled slavers and Carolinians from the Southeast.

Some of these people were returning to lands on which their ancestors had lived. Some, defeated in conflicts with Euro-Americans or deprived of their homes by treaties they considered unjust, sought refuge wherever they could find it. Some came at the invitation of colonial governments; others at the invitation of Iroquois nations who claimed the Susquehanna Valley by right of conquest; some at the invitation of the French-allied

Wyandots who made similar claims to lands farther west; others sought no one's leave. Some settled in ethnically defined villages; some in mixed places that could be described only as "Indian." Many had spent time with missionaries, been baptized, bore Christian as well as Native names, and, like the people Brainerd encountered in the Wyoming Valley, spoke some English or German. But few of them recognized any central authority, Native or European. Precisely because they had relocated so often, none of them were in the mood to sell their lands and move again.

Many were, however, willing to grant privileges to European individuals and families who could profitably share the territory with them on indigenous terms. Traders with pack trains stocked by wealthy Philadelphia merchants followed Indian migrants from the Delaware and Susquehanna to their new homes in the west, and were soon joined by rivals from Virginia. Other colonists who were not so well connected followed. By midcentury the landscape was dotted with hundreds of cabins and farmsteads of Euro-Americans. Some settled with Indian permission, others not, but most seem to have been at least grudgingly tolerated. Some paid annual rents to Indian proprietors; others earned their keep through a small-scale trade in alcohol and other goods. Indians and Europeans saw each other daily and communicated as best they could in broken English, fractured German, or the time-tested Delaware Jargon. Native people, the white settlers reported, were "allmost dayly familiars at thair houses eat drank cursed and swore together were even intimate play mates."[4]

These Euro-Americans may have been tolerated by Indian neighbors and drinking partners, but not by the planters, merchants, and land speculators who controlled provincial and imperial governments. If immigrants made their own deals with Native people, speculators could gain no new estates, rents, or profits, and governments no new quit-rents, taxes, or other revenues. Instead, settlers had to buy their land from the proper British authorities, after those authorities extracted the land from its aboriginal owners. This relentless extraction is what the people of the Wyoming Valley meant when they told Brainerd's interpreter that "the great men in [New] York, Philadelphia, etc. have laid a scheme to deprive the Indians of all their land."[5]

Peter Wraxall, born in Bristol, England, but living in New York, where he attempted to make a career as a servant of the British Empire, came to much the same conclusion in 1756. "An unaccountable thirst for large Tracts of Land without the design of cultivation, hath prevailed over the

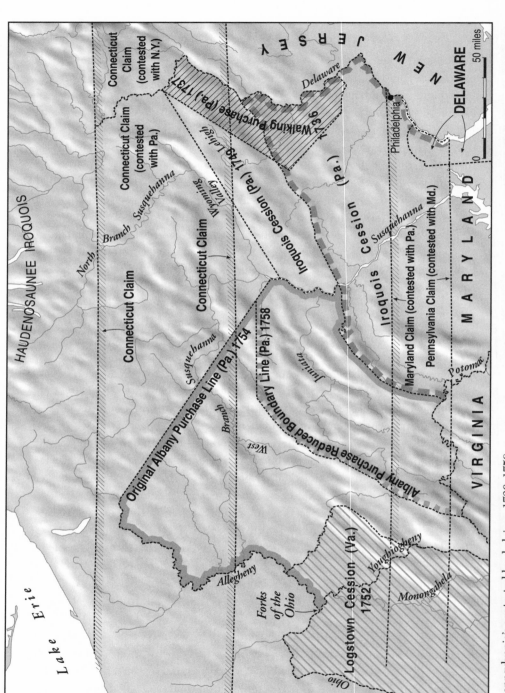

Pennsylvania's contested land claims, 1736–1758.

inhabitants of this and the neighbouring Provinces with a singular rage," he wrote. "Patents have been lavishly granted (to give it no worse term) upon the pretence of fair Indian purchases, some of which the Indians have alledged were never made but forged—Others bought of Indians who were no Proprietors, some by making two or three Indians Drunk and giving them a trivial consideration—They say also the Surveyors have frequently run Patents vastly beyond even the pretended conditions or limits of sale."[6] Such things had been going on for decades but achieved obscene audacity in precisely the decades when, and concerning precisely the territories where, Teedyuscung and others were settling in their new western homes.

The "thirst for large Tracts of Land" raged especially among the great men of Pennsylvania, first destination for so many European immigrants seeking free or cheap real estate. "As the numbers of these People encrease upon us, so will the Difficulties of settling them," provincial official James Logan complained as early as 1728.[7] Logan—the Penn family's longtime personal agent, secretary of the province and commissioner of property, and a land speculator and fur trader in his own right—knew that immigrant squatters were only one of many threats to his and his employers' pretensions to lands and revenue. Pennsylvania's claim, under its charter, to any territories south of the fortieth parallel (including even the city of Philadelphia, at 39°57′) were in dispute with Maryland, a dispute that would not be resolved until the 1760s, when Mason and Dixon surveyed their famous Line at 39°43′. Meantime, roughly the northern third of today's Pennsylvania was contested with Connecticut, whose royal grant stretched westward to the Pacific, encompassing, among other places, the Wyoming Valley. Similarly, Virginia's expansive charter supposedly gave it the Forks of the Ohio, along with much of the rest of the continent, and indeed Virginia was far more aggressive than Pennsylvania in asserting claims to the area around modern-day Pittsburgh. The French Crown, of course, had its own interpretations of how all of this territory should be divided among Europeans, drawing on its long-standing alliances with Native peoples to contest every British pretense to real estate west of the Appalachians.

Among the British, all agreed that conflicting European claims were best resolved by documented purchases from Native peoples. One of the legacies of Restoration-era imperialism had been the insistence that legitimate land titles must rest on such transactions. As a product of that era, as well as of his Quaker beliefs, William Penn had made this principle the cornerstone of his "resolution to live Justly peaceably and friendly with" Indian peoples. He also made deeds documenting Indian purchases central to his early territorial battles with Maryland. In 1683, for instance, he had given formal notice that he had purchased from a Lenape chief "all his Land lying between Delaware River, the Bay of Chesepeak . . . and Susquahannah River." On the basis of this purchase, Penn "warn[ed] all Persons, that they presume not to settle thereon without" permission from him, rather than from the Baltimore family.[8] By the same reasoning, if Logan and the younger Penns were to resolve the multiple dilemmas of squatters and colonial rivals, the vital step was to convince Native people to deed swaths of contested territory to Pennsylvania, which could then both sell the land to approved taxpaying settlers and rebut rival colonies' claims.

Yet who among the decentralized multiethnic Indian communities resettling the interior could or would sign the necessary documents? Logan's too-clever solution was to identify a central authority that, to his mind, could speak for all the Indians concerned—whether those Indians recognized that authority or not. The seventeenth-century wars of the Iroquois against inhabitants of the Susquehanna and Ohio countries allowed the Haudenosaunee nations to assert rights over their lands, an assertion bolstered by the fact that many (although hardly all) of the Indian refugees who had resettled the territories did so at Iroquois invitation. This logic produced two treaty documents in 1736, one made publicly during a ceremonial visit of Six Nations headmen to Philadelphia, and the other secured less decorously by Logan's agent Conrad Weiser at the Susquehanna Valley Indian town of Shamokin as the Iroquois delegation headed homeward. In the Philadelphia treaty, the Six Nations ceded all claims to lands on both sides of the Susquehanna River below North (or Blue) Mountain. By the second, private agreement, the Iroquois also released any claims between the Delaware and Susquehanna Rivers south of the same highlands—territory to which the Six Nations had actually never claimed ownership. Although the Iroquois made this fact clear to Weiser at the time, Logan and the Penns transmuted this paper release of nonexistent possession into a positive grant to their province.

The lands in question included a tract known to the Penns as the "Forks of the Delaware" and to a young Teedyuscung and other Lenapes who lived there as *Lechauwekink*, a word that colonists rendered as "Lehigh."

In recent decades, this area had become a main center for Lenapes who tried to remain within their ancient territory rather than migrate farther westward; leading figures in this group were chiefs named Nutimus, Tishcohan (Teedyuscung's maternal uncle), and Old Harris (his father). In 1700, William Penn had agreed with another Lenape chief upon terms for surveying lands previously purchased south of the Forks. An elaborate plan called for two Europeans and two Indians to stroll along a riverbank as far as they could in a day and a half—while making sure to stop for a leisurely lunch during which their pack horse was to be unloaded and then reloaded. At the end of the ramble, a line was to be drawn toward the setting sun to define the purchase boundary. Midway through the first afternoon of the walk, however, a dispute arose when Penn's men insisted on crossing into territory over which Nutimus claimed jurisdiction, and the survey party broke up with its work uncompleted. This affair constituted the first, and less controversial, Pennsylvania "Walking Purchase."

The lead-up to the second, and infinitely more contentious, Walking Purchase, began in 1732, when Thomas Penn claimed to have discovered in the province's papers an early draft of the original treaty. The document, which may well have been a forgery, omitted such important pieces of information as the date of the agreement and the direction in which the surveyors were to walk. Probably because Thomas Penn knew Nutimus could contradict him if he dated the document to 1700, he claimed that it referred to a land sale made between Lenapes and his father, William Penn, in 1686, long before Nutimus's time. Pennsylvania's story, then, was that the British merely planned to implement a half-century-old agreement by walking the boundaries originally agreed upon. Despite Nutimus's repeated objections, the Penns insisted that the walk take place. The 1736 documents by which the Iroquois ceded the territory gave the Penns the legal cover they needed for their scheme and—more important—robbed Nutimus of any political and diplomatic support he might have received from the Iroquois to resist. Meantime, the Penns sent scouting parties to blaze through the woods a trail most likely to take in the most territory in a day and a half.

In August 1737, when the walkers—or rather sprinters—hired by the province to carry out the charade completed their thirty-six-hour journey, they had enlarged Pennsylvania by something on the order of twelve hundred square miles. The territory encompassed all of the lands on which Nutimus's and Teedyuscung's people lived and the sites of today's cities of Bethlehem, Allentown, and Easton. The Penn family set apart only about sixty-five hundred acres around the village known as Nutimus's Town as a proprietary manor on which the Forks Indians could reside. Euro-American settlers quickly moved into the Walking Purchase, and by 1740, more than one hundred families had taken up residence, despite the Delawares' continued protests. A year later, the settlers were joined by the first of several German-speaking religious communities of the Unitas Fratrum, or Moravians, established at the place they called Bethlehem, the birthplace of their savior. These soon persuaded some of the Forks Indians to accept baptism and continue to reside in their homeland at the nearby mission community of Gnadenhütten ("Huts of Grace"). Among them, briefly, was Teedyuscung, whose baptismal name was "Gideon" until he and about seventy other converts relocated to the Wyoming Valley in 1754. For them, as for most other Lenapes, the diverse influx of European Atlanteans left little choice but to move on as part of the streams of Native peoples resettling the Susquehanna and Ohio watersheds.

The British great men's thirst for land followed them. In 1744, a treaty at Lancaster, Pennsylvania, extended the trail of obfuscatory Haudenosaunee paper transfers westward to the Ohio River watershed. For decades, southward-bound Iroquois war parties had scuffled with Marylanders and Virginians as they passed through the Cumberland and Shenandoah valleys on their way to raid southeastern Native foes. Most recently, a skirmish had left at least three Iroquois and eight Virginians dead. The Lancaster Treaty, brokered by Pennsylvania's Conrad Weiser and attended by commissioners from Virginia and Maryland, intended to restore peace and prevent further trouble by convincing Iroquois warriors to take a more westerly route. Invariably, the question of ownership of lands along that route came to the fore.

Negotiations with Maryland went fairly smoothly, with the Iroquois readily agreeing to sell the rights to a tract roughly corresponding to the western panhandle of today's state. Virginia was much harder to please, insisting that "the Great King holds *Virginia* by Right of Conquest, and the Bounds of that Conquest to the Westward is the Great [Pacific] Sea." When negotiators demanded that the Iroquois tell them specifically "what Nations of *Indians* you conquered any Lands from in *Virginia*," a Haudenosaunee spokesman complied and again rejected any rival British conquest claim to the territory. Nonetheless, in the end, a payment changed hands, and signatures were affixed to "a Deed recognizing the King's Right to all the Lands that are, or shall be, by his Majesty's Appointment in the Colony of *Virginia.*"⁹

Largely on the basis of this cession, members of some of Virginia's most powerful families—among them two elder brothers of fifteen-year-old George Washington—pooled their resources as the "Ohio Company" and in 1748 gained an order from the British Crown to Virginia governor Robert Dinwiddie to grant them five hundred thousand acres in the region, two hundred thousand of which were to be occupied and guarded by a fort as soon as possible. To speed things along, the investors made Dinwiddie himself a partner, along with various other government officials and great planters.

By signing over distant lands to British Pennsylvanians and Virginians, Haudenosaunee leaders seem to have hoped to fend off British New Yorkers who coveted territories closer to their homes. "We are now straitened . . . and liable to many other Inconveniences since the *English* came among us, and particularly from that Pen-and-Ink Work that is going on at the Table," an Iroquois spokesman complained at Lancaster, *"pointing to the Secretary"* who was writing up the proceedings.¹⁰ Indeed, the Walking Purchase and the Lancaster Treaty looked positively transparent compared to the multiplicity of patents that the great planters of New York had convinced royal governors to approve on the basis of fraudulent Indian deeds since the 1690s. The mother of all such travesties was the eight-hundred-thousand-acre Kayaderosseras Patent, which wrapped a spiral of paper dating back at least to 1703 around almost the entire homeland of the Mohawks, the easternmost of the Six Iroquois nations. Thankfully for the Mohawks, there were so many rivalrous New York Kayaderosseras claimants, so many contradictory documents, and so little evidence that even the ridiculously small sums alleged to have been paid them ever changed hands, that the entire matter tied up British courts on both sides of the Atlantic for decades.

But beginning in the mid-1730s—almost simultaneously with Iroquois involvement with the Walking Purchase—influential men pressed both the Mohawks and New York's royal governor to allow them to survey and resell portions of the Kayaderosseras grant. Meanwhile, complaints about the city of Albany's pretensions to a smaller tract known as the "Mohawk Flatts" led New York governor William Cosby publicly to burn a copy of an alleged deed at a treaty conference in 1733, after which the Mohawks signed another document entrusting the land to the British Crown, with the understanding that it would not be resold. Suits and countersuits among British claimants continued, however, and deeds with suspicious origins describing huge plots in vague terms continued to proliferate. In 1736, Mohawks forcibly turned back the surveyor general of New York when he tried to measure out some of these lands.

By June 1753, the leadership of the Mohawks—if not that of all of the Six Nations—had had enough. Hendrick Theyanoguin, longtime Mohawk spokesman and ally of the British, led a delegation to New York City to meet with the governor, George Clinton. "The indifference and neglect shewn towards us makes our hearts ake," Theyanoguin complained. Over the next few days, in public and private sessions, the Mohawks named names and listed specific grievances. Clinton, after a great show of consulting with advisors, perusing documents, and explaining legal difficulties, dismissed the complaints with assurances that the province's Commission for Indian Affairs—composed of Albany residents implicated in the shady deals—would investigate things further. "You tell us that we shall be redressed at Albany, but we know them so well, we will not trust to them, for they are no people but Devils," Theyanoguin responded. "As soon as we come home we will send up a Belt of Wampum to our Brothers the 5 Nations to acquaint them the Covenant Chain is broken between you and us." The imperial alliance that the duke of York's governor and Theyanoguin's ancestors had forged in the 1670s was dead. "So brother you are not to expect to hear of me any more, and Brother we desire to hear no more of you."[11]

Hendrick Theyanoguin made this dramatic pronouncement for a transatlantic audience—indeed, it is possible the whole affair was stage-managed to allow Clinton and his New York political allies to draw the Board of Trade's attention to the sorry state of British-Indian relations. Clinton enclosed the minutes of his conference with the Mohawks in a letter that renewed his long-standing request to be relieved of his post because of illness, and because of his exasperation with the relentless opposition he received from members of New York's fractious assembly when he tried to deal with Indian complaints or any other imperial concerns.

The Board of Trade, whose previously slumbering powers over colonial affairs were rejuvenating under the vigorous leadership of George Montagu Dunk, earl of Halifax, had already decided that Clinton had to go—among other things, ironically, for his mishandling of a land dispute between New York and Massachusetts—but its members certainly got Theyanoguin's message. "We cannot but be greatly concern'd and surprized that the Province of New York should have been so inattentive to the general interest of His Majesty's subjects in America . . . as to have given occasion to the Complaints made by the Indians," they wrote to Clinton's newly appointed successor, Halifax's brother-in-law Sir Danvers Osborne. As soon as possible after arriving in America, Osborne was told, he should convene a council with the Haudenosaunee to address their grievances, preferably at their capital of Onondaga rather than at devil-filled Albany. Representatives of Pennsylvania, Virginia, Maryland, New Jersey, Massachusetts Bay, and New Hampshire were also to participate. The goal was "one general Treaty to be made in his Majesty's name it appearing to us that the practice of each Province making a separate Treaty for itself in its own name is very improper and may be attended with great inconveniency to His Majesty's service."[12]

British officials were so worried because it seemed clear that armed conflict with France would soon reignite and that this was no time to lose what Britons considered their most reliable Native American military ally. The War of Jenkins's Ear—so disastrous militarily but so crucial politically in sealing the loyalty of British Americans to their transatlantic nation—had not so much ended as merged with another deadly dynastic struggle among Western Europe's monarchs, the War of the Austrian Succession, or, as North Americans later called it, "King George's War." The Austrian whose succession was contested was the Habsburg archduchess Maria Theresa, daughter of the Holy Roman Emperor Charles VI, who died in 1740. Technically, a woman could not be the Holy Roman Emperor, but Charles VI had negotiated an agreement called the "Pragmatic Sanction," which attempted to keep Maria Theresa on her varied thrones nonetheless. Among the many who disagreed with these arrangements were Friedrich II, king of Prussia (soon to be known as "Frederick the Great"), along with the crowns of France and Spain. This disagreement dragged the British into the conflict on the side of Maria Theresa against Spain and, ultimately, against Spain's ally France, which formally declared war against Britain in 1744.

North America remained a sideshow in the War of the Austrian Succession, which itself nearly became a sideshow to the final great Jacobite rebellion in Scotland that was brutally suppressed in 1745. But the "Forty-

Five," by highlighting Britain's problems in governing restive peoples on the near fringes of its empire, also drew attention to farther-flung possessions and to the importance of North America's Native and Euro-American people to the geopolitics of the larger Atlantean world. The most significant military victory by any side in North America was the capture in 1745 of the French fortress of Louisbourg on Cape Breton Island, which controlled entry to the St. Lawrence and thus to the Atlantic lifeline of La Nouvelle-France. The expedition was an intercolonial effort organized by London-born Massachusetts governor William Shirley and Maine-born Massachusetts provincial councilor and militia colonel William Pepperrell. Between them, they raised some forty-three hundred troops, mostly from Massachusetts and its district of Maine, but with substantial contributions from New Hampshire and Connecticut and material support from New York, Pennsylvania, and Rhode Island. Shirley, meanwhile, gained permission from England to enlist the aid of a small fleet from Antigua commanded by Peter Warren, an old acquaintance of Pepperrell and an Atlantean if there ever was one. Born a Catholic in County Meath, Ireland in 1703, he converted to the Church of England and joined the British navy as a young man. By 1730 he was based in New York City and, marrying into the prominent local De Lancey family, joined the great land-grabs of the era to acquire sprawling estates in the Hudson and Mohawk valleys. During the War of Jenkins's Ear, Warren participated in an unsuccessful siege of San Agustín and then sailed in the Caribbean with Edward Vernon in happier days before the latter's catastrophe at Cartagena.

With a mere four ships and forty-three hundred men, the fleet that attacked Louisbourg could not compare to Vernon's earlier doomed flotilla, but the expedition shared with its predecessor the patriotic fervor of provincial Britons crusading against a papist foe (and an extraordinarily high death toll from disease during a six-week siege). "It was a marvellous Thing, that when *this Province* had lately lost so *many Hundred* Men *Voluntiers* in the sad Expedition to *Carthagena,* . . . to see so many *Likely Men* . . . as *free Voluntiers,* to serve the God, their *King* and *Country,* in this hazardous Enterprize," a Boston clergyman declared in celebration of the victory. "Let us rejoice, not only in *our own Salvation,* the Salvation of *all our Colonies,* and some of the most important Branches of the *British Trade,*" he concluded, "but let our Joy rise higher, that hereby a *great Sup-*

port of *Antichristian* Power is taken away, and the *visible Kingdom* of CHRIST enlarged."[13]

Apart from its apocalyptic potential, the conquest of Louisbourg had two great implications. In 1748, when exhausted France and Britain came to the peace table (or rather the truce table, because nothing fundamental would be settled and everyone assumed the conflict would one day resume), the fortress became a bargaining chip. In the Treaty of Aix-la-Chapelle, Britain returned it to France in exchange for territories in the Netherlands and for Madras on the Indian subcontinent, which the French had conquered in 1746. British North American patriots were aghast at the betrayal. "Louisbourg—a place of equal importance to the nation with Gibraltar—Louisbourg gained at the expence of New England blood, and with the ruin of half the estates of the province, is again to return to its former masters, as an equivalent for the Netherlands, which is to our nation no equivalent at all," thundered an anonymous Bostonian who was probably twenty-six-year-old Samuel Adams.[14] In Massachusetts, at least, the sting was partly assuaged by the British House of Commons's agreement to reimburse the province's entire expenses for the campaign, to the precise tune of £183,649 2sh 7½d. This massive sum— the most concrete benefits that the fiscal-military state ever bestowed on North America—allowed Massachusetts to retire its entire public debt and refinance its hitherto shaky paper currency.[15]

With such sums in play, no one could pretend that North American military affairs were a minor concern to imperial officials, even if those officials refused to recognize Louisbourg's equivalence to Gibraltar. That concern deepened because of a second implication of the conquest of the Cape Breton fortress. With few other retaliatory tools at his disposal, Roland-Michel Barrin, comte de La Galissonière, the acting governor of La Nouvelle-France (the actual royal appointee had been captured by a British warship en route to his colony), encouraged old Native enemies of New England to raid outposts in Maine, while sending small joint forces of French and Indians against other targets on the frontiers of New England and New York. The most devastating attack destroyed the village of Saratoga, north of Albany. In response, Governor Clinton of New York began pressuring Haudenosaunee leaders to abandon their neutrality and take up arms against the French and their Indian allies. Yet neither the Euro-American traders at Albany—the men Theyanoguin would call "devils" in a few years—nor most Iroquois were much interested in a wider war.

To break the impasse, Clinton bypassed the Albany traders, and the Commissioners for Indian Affairs they dominated, by transferring their duties to William Johnson. Johnson was an Irish émigré and a nephew of Peter Warren, whose New York estates he first managed in the uncle's wartime absence and then used as the basis for acquiring huge personal tracts of his own, while building a thriving trade with his Iroquois neighbors. Johnson's main Native partner in all these activities was Hendrick Theyanoguin. In 1746 and 1747, he and Johnson had successfully recruited many Mohawks—but only a few other Haudenosaunee people—to fight against the French. The recruitment effort succeeded partly because Johnson spoke Mohawk and occasionally donned war paint and breechclout in public, but mostly because he channeled massive diplomatic presents and military subsidies through Theyanoguin to the Mohawks. Unable to convince the New York Assembly to reimburse his wartime expenses, Johnson resigned his post in 1751, returning the Albany devils to power. Theyanoguin, meantime, had to explain to his people not only why nothing was being done about their grievances over land, but also why the British largesse he had channeled to them during the war had been replaced by neglect of the most basic of diplomatic niceties, such as a ritual to confirm the end of the war with the French. "You have put the Hatchett into our hands and we Mohawks have taken and used it against your enemies," Theyanoguin told Clinton at New York in 1753, but "you have never taken the Hatchett out of our hands so that we still have it."[16]

While Theyanoguin thus declared that the Covenant Chain with the British was broken, many Native peoples' connections to the French were in no better condition. In 1747, the loss of Louisbourg and thus of access to Atlantic trade had caused severe shortages at French posts in the Great Lakes region, at the same time that traders from Virginia and Pennsylvania were spreading out from the Ohio country with larger and cheaper selections of goods. The most active was a Pennsylvanian named George Croghan, who seemed ubiquitous between Lake Erie and the Ohio River and who set up a thriving base for his fellow traders at the Indian town of Pickawillany on the Great Miami River. Rumors spread that Croghan's Native trading partners would force the French and their missionaries from their territories once and for all. How much of this talk was French paranoia and how much empty threats from Indians trying to get their

European allies' attention is unclear, but several French traders lost their lives in skirmishes with angry customers. In 1748, when ships from France made it past Louisbourg to Québec with news of the peace treaty, Galissonière, now governor in his own right, recognized the danger that frayed alliances with Native people posed to French claims on the continent. Like his counterpart Clinton, he wrote a long report to officials in Paris explaining what must be done to avert a crisis.

And thus eyes on both sides of the Atlantic, in Paris and London, in Québec, in New York City, in Philadelphia, in Williamsburg, in Onondaga, in Shamokin, in Logstown, and in Detroit, focused on the contested ground of the Ohio country. No sooner had word of the Treaty of Aix-la-Chapelle arrived than Galissonière sent two hundred thirty men under the command of Pierre-Joseph de Céloron de Blainville from Montréal through the Ohio country to Detroit, to reinvigorate Native alliances and reassert French sovereignty. When Céloron found Pennsylvanians trading at one Shawnee village, he sent them home with a stern note to their governor. "I have been much surprised to find traders belonging to your government in a country to which England never had any pretension," he wrote. "I hope, Sir, that you will be so good as to prohibit that trade in future." Far from rallying Indian trading partners against British interlopers, however, Céloron's expedition alienated those who insisted that the French had no more right to their land and exclusive commerce than the British—especially after the Frenchman and his troops made a point of ceremonially hanging metal plaques on trees and burying lead plates at strategic spots to assert Louis XV's claims, much as their predecessors had done at Sault Sainte Marie or La Nouvelle-Orléans decades earlier. At Logstown, a spokesman informed Céloron that the land belonged to Native people, not to the French, and that while there was any Indians in those Parts they would trade with their Brothers the English."[17] At another town, Shawnees ripped down and trampled Céloron's placards.

For most of the next two years, there was little follow-up, as Galissonière left North America to resume his naval career and affairs drifted under his short-term replacement. Yet when the new governor, Ange Duquesne de Menneville, marquis de Duquesne, took office in 1752, he had royal instructions to take a much firmer stance. Almost immediately—and perhaps not exactly carrying out Duquesne's orders—a party of

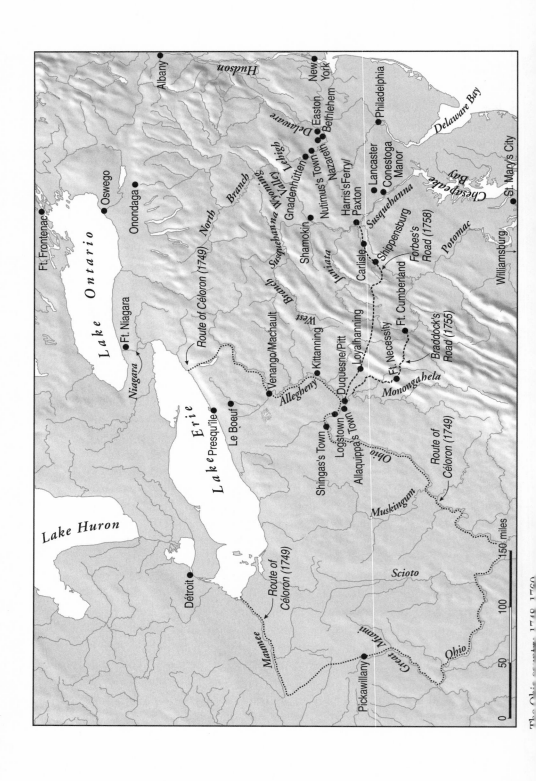

The Ohio country, 1748–1760.

French, Ottawas, and Ojibwas from Detroit attacked the center of British trade at Pickawillany. Before they left the town in ashes and carried its surviving Indian residents into captivity, they executed its leader, Memeskia—known as "Old Briton" for his imperial preference—"who," according to an English survivor of the raid, "they boiled and eat him all up."[18]

Meantime, with less violence but just as much resolve, Virginia governor Robert Dinwiddie and his fellow Ohio Company investors were making their move. In 1749, as Céloron was planting his plates, the company built a fort and staging base on the Monongahela River, at present-day Cumberland, Maryland. In 1750 and 1751, to the alarm of many Ohio country Indians, the company dispatched a Maryland surveyor named Christopher Gist to scout settlement locations. In 1752, a few weeks before the assault on Pickawillany, Gist worked with Croghan to negotiate a treaty with the Ohio country Indians at Logstown, in order to reconfirm the company's paper title to its lands and gain permission to build a fort at the Forks of the Ohio.

The Logstown Treaty reenacted all of the sleazy trends of the previous fifteen years. The negotiators representing Governor Dinwiddie were instructed to deal with the Six Nations Iroquois on what was formally to be a reconfirmation of the 1744 Lancaster Treaty cession. Yet this land was not Haudenosaunee territory. Furthermore, the only person remotely claiming to speak for the Six Nations at Logstown was a man named Tanaghrisson, whom many called the "Half-King" for his claim to rule there on behalf of the Iroquois. He was one of many Ohio country chiefs trying to provide leadership for the fractious Iroquois, Delawares, Shawnees, and other people of the region, and, for whatever reason, he had decided to cast his lot with the Virginians against the French. (Pennsylvanians had rejected his earlier offer to build a post at the Forks of the Ohio.) If the records left by the Virginia commissioners are to be trusted, at the public Logstown treaty sessions, Tanaghrisson somehow managed to convince the Delawares and Shawnees to let him do all the talking in the name of the Six Nations, whose council at Onondaga he said he would have to consult before making any final agreements. Although publicly he denounced the Virginians' expansive land claims and granted them permission only to build a small post at the Forks, in private he was somehow convinced to sign a document granting the Ohio Company everything it asked for.

Fort building then commenced. The Ohio Company built one on the Monongahela. The French built three, on Lake Erie at Presqu'île and on the Allegheny River at Le Boeuf and Machault, where they displaced the British traders who had called the place Venango. In 1754, a small party of Virginians were the first to reach the Forks where the Monongahela and Allegheny joined to form the Ohio. But before they could complete their work, a much larger French force chased them off and burned their half-finished structure. They replaced it with one named Fort Duquesne, in honor of their governor, and soon equipped it with earthen walls, moats, bastions, cannon, and at least five hundred troops, with many more on the way.

The Virginians fled just as reinforcements were en route, in the form of about one hundred sixty ill-trained troops led by George Washington. Just twenty-two years old, Washington had essentially inherited his officer position (along with the house at Mount Vernon and a major stake in the Ohio Company) from his deceased brother Lawrence. He traveled a familiar route toward the Forks, having a year earlier delivered Dinwiddie's written demand that the French vacate Fort Le Boeuf and having returned to Virginia with the commander's written refusal. On both trips, Washington had been welcomed and guided by Tanaghrisson and a handful of his Ohio Indian followers.

In 1754, as his mission unexpectedly shifted from reinforcing a Virginia fort to assaulting a French one, a panicked and inexperienced Washington camped at a place called the Great Meadows, and considered what to do. He apparently let Tanaghrisson, who was anything but panicked and inexperienced, convince him to attack a French patrol as it awoke from a night's encampment. According to an eyewitness, as the smoke cleared and several Frenchmen lay dying, Tanaghrisson approached their wounded commander, Joseph Coulon de Villers de Jumonville, said, "'Thou art not yet dead, my father,' and struck several hatchet blows with which he killed him."[19]

If, as seems likely, at "Jumonville's Glen" Tanaghrisson intended to start a war between his French "father" and his British "brothers," he succeeded beyond his wildest dreams. If he did so hoping somehow to use the conflict to pry the Ohio country loose from the competing European empires and return it to Native control, he failed beyond his wildest nightmares.

But he would never know the outcome. Giving up on Washington and despairing of winning over Ohio Indians to his point of view, he moved his family east and died from disease—some said witchcraft—within a few months. Meantime, troops from Fort Duquesne forced Washington to surrender the hastily constructed palisades at the Great Meadows that he called "Fort Necessity." They made him sign a document confessing that his troops had not just killed Jumonville in a skirmish, but had assassinated a peaceful emissary of the French Crown. Lucky to escape with their lives, Washington and his bedraggled men started home on July 4, 1754.

SIXTEEN

Gloomy and Dark Days

IN U.S. HISTORY, the conflict that began in Jumonville's Glen has usually been called the "French and Indian War." That term not only obscures the identity of the enemy that the French and Indians were fighting, but also assumes a unity of purpose between La Nouvelle-France and Native peoples that did not exist. Many Indian residents of the Susquehanna Valley, the Ohio country, and the Great Lakes denied any unity of purpose with the French, whom they trusted no more than the British. Be that as it may, although the war started in the Indian country of North America in 1754, it became a truly global conflict which involved several European empires and for which the name "French and Indian War" is nonsensical—except perhaps with reference to South Asia, which was one of the major combat zones. Thus, a better name might be the one that subsequently took hold in Europe, the "Seven Years War." But that antiseptic term conveys none of the violence that ripped North America's Atlantean peoples apart. Nor do the seven years in question line up in the conflict's varied theaters. In North America, fighting between French and British people began in 1754 and ended in 1760. In Europe, the span between official declaration of war and peace treaty was 1755 to 1763. In Indian country, the chronology was far less clear—as epitomized by the career of Teedyuscung, who moved to the Wyoming Valley in 1754, took up arms against English, Irish, and German immigrants in 1755, and labored mightily to make peace in 1757–1758. In 1763 he was murdered in his sleep, an act that reignited the massacres and counter-massacres that had begun at Jumonville's Glen, had paused in 1758, and would not subside until 1766. In North America, the "Seven Years War" was at least twelve years long.

Perhaps the best name for the conflict came from Teedyuscung: in 1757, he spoke of the war as "gloomy and dark days" that had "proceeded from the earth."[1] The darkness claimed many victims, Natives as well as colonists, British as well as French, women and children as well as fighting men. What briefly seemed a stunning British victory redrew the map of the continent, removing the French empire from the equation, redefining the Spanish possessions massively, and leaving Natives east of the Mississippi to face Britons alone in a newly racialized landscape. In the cataclysm, accumulated stresses transmitted from progenitors to conquistadores, traders, planters, and imperialists broke loose. Native American traditions of property, land, trade, and power smashed against those of Europeans, in turn setting land-grabbing creole planters against imperial officials. The final victim was the fragile unity of the Atlantean world.

When reports of the events of Jumonville's Glen reached Paris and London, the two imperial governments found their excuse to renew the conflict suspended in 1748. In the dynastic diplomacy of the European continent, some of the major players had switched sides—Prussia was now allied with Britain, and Spain loosely with France through the family ties of Bourbon monarchs—but the core Anglo-French imperial rivalry remained intact. In France, officials urged Governor Duquesne to continue to try to win back the trade and friendship of Ohio country and Great Lakes Indians and to maintain a defensive posture toward the British, while mobilizing four thousand regular troops to reinforce North American forts. In Britain, the government of Thomas Pelham-Holles, duke of Newcastle, also hoped for better relations with Native Americans while shipping troops across the Atlantic.

Yet Newcastle's plan for New York's governor, Danvers Osborne, to convene an intercolonial treaty with Native people at the Haudenosaunee capital of Onondaga was already a shambles. In October 1753, two days after arriving at New York City, Osborne, who had apparently long been suffering from depression, hanged himself. His temporary successor was James De Lancey, the president of the provincial council, an old political enemy of Clinton and Johnson, and a close ally of the Albany commissioners. De Lancey immediately began scheming to hold the conference in the usual Albany location, to demote representatives from other provinces to subordinate roles, and use the occasion not to placate the Iroquois but to extract more land from them. He scheduled what became known as the Albany Congress for June 1754—as it would turn out, precisely when Washington would be building his Fort Necessity.

While New Yorkers schemed to undermine the spirit of the Newcastle government's plan, in Philadelphia, Benjamin Franklin took that spirit in an entirely new direction. Since at least 1751, Franklin had been advocating a "Plan of Union," which would place Indian affairs under the control of a legislature comprising delegates from all the provinces and of a governor general appointed by the Crown for all North America. Alarmed by word that the French had settled in at Fort Duquesne, Franklin convinced at least some of those involved that the provincial delegations to the Albany Congress should discuss his plan—which they did at odd moments when they weren't drafting contradictory speeches to be delivered to the Indians or participating in treaty ceremonies. After contentious debate, the Congress hammered out a text for a Plan of Union and agreed to present it to their various governments. Those governments promptly killed it, in some cases by neglect, in others by overwhelming negative votes in assemblies unwilling to yield power to a continent-wide body. Virginia, militarily the most crucial element in any scheme for concerted action, did not even send a delegation to Albany and so never considered the Plan at all. Before the Congress convened, Franklin had published a cartoon in his *Pennsylvania Gazette* that has often been associated with his Plan of Union but actually was intended to spur the fractious colonies to united military action against Fort Duquesne. "JOIN, or DIE," it said beneath a sketch of a snake cut into sections labeled with the initials of the British colonies.[2] There would be a lot of dying before there was any joining.

The treaty negotiations with the Iroquois that were the inspiration for the Congress—and that consumed much more of the delegates' time and energy than did Franklin's plan—showed no evidence that the provincial delegates were capable of united action. They bickered endlessly over the text of speeches to be delivered to the Indians in public and, when they could not agree, gave separate orations on behalf of their own provinces. The façade of unity collapsed entirely as, sometimes in public, sometimes in secret, the provincials tried to extort more of the land deeds that had caused the crisis in British-Indian relations in the first place. As for the Iroquois delegates, barely two hundred even bothered to show up—far fewer than the five hundred to seven hundred who would normally attend such a major treaty conference. Almost half those who participated were Mohawks, and the majority of those were close allies of Theyanoguin. Only a handful of Onondagas, Cayugas, and Senecas attended—a measure of how alienated most Iroquois were from the British in general and New York in particular.

At the Albany Congress, Theyanoguin's speeches alternated between histories of the former glories of the Covenant Chain and stinging rebukes of New York's past behavior. But in the end, he seemed to conclude that the sole benefits he and his people could hope for from the Congress were material. He not only collected his part of the handsome official diplomatic gifts distributed at the end of the treaty, he and his compatriots affixed their names to several deeds conveying territory near their own homes to New Yorkers, and to two documents yielding much larger tracts considerably farther away. The Susquehanna Company, based in Connecticut, gained title to the Wyoming Valley, within the zone where their colony's claims overlapped with Pennsylvania's. Pennsylvania, meanwhile, walked away with a title to nearly all the territory between the Susquehanna and Allegheny rivers. These lands were precisely the ones that Delawares, Shawnees, and other residents were determined to keep from European control. The Newcastle government's plan to address Indian grievances with a grand unified treaty council had only made the situation infinitely worse.

The same was true of the British government's military response to events in the Ohio country, which took shape before news of the Albany Congress and its Plan of Union reached the British Isles. The Newcastle government showed even less interest in the Albany Plan than did the provincial legislatures. Indeed, the news from America, when it did arrive, only reinforced a conclusion that assemblies and governors would never act in concert, and that the only solution was to appoint a single commander-in-chief to take charge of military affairs and Indian relations. The man chosen for the post was a veteran named Edward Braddock, known more for his reputation as a stern administrator than for his battlefield experience, which was slight. In 1755 he sailed to Virginia with two understaffed Irish regiments and ambitious plans to requisition troops and funds from multiple colonies, follow the route that Washington had trav-

eled toward Fort Duquesne, and, after conquering that post, use it as a
base to sweep the French from the continental interior. None of this
worked out.

Whatever Braddock's administrative skills, he proved a wretched politician. As the owner of the house where Braddock did much of his planning
concluded, he was "a Man . . . of Week understanding, Positive, and Very
Indolent, Slave to his Passions, Women and Wine, As Great an Epicure as
could be in his Eateing, Tho' a brave Man."[3] Braddock endlessly criticized
the quality of the provincial troops that insufficiently filled his ranks.
Meanwhile, he swept aside Dinwiddie's and others' objections that provincial legislators jealous of their rights could not simply be ordered to vote
funds and troops to support his expedition, and that in any case it would
be next to impossible to move a large army with cannon and supply trains
from Virginia to the Forks of the Ohio.

Braddock's crowning political blunder was to rebuff six Ohio country
chiefs who—despite all that had happened in recent years—still had some
hopes for a good outcome to the struggle between the French and the
British. As their leader, a Delaware known as Shingas, recalled several
years later, the Indians

> had applied to General Braddock and Enquired what he intended to do
> with the Land if he Could drive the French and their Indians away. To
> which General Braddock replied that the English Shoud Inhabit and In-
> herit the Land, on which Shingas asked General Braddock whether the In-
> dians that were Freinds to the English might not be Permitted to Live and
> Trade Among the English and have Hunting Ground sufficient To Support
> themselves and Familys as they had no where to Flee Too. . . . On which
> General Braddock said that No Savage Should Inherit the Land.[4]

Nearly every British action in recent years had driven that same message
home. Now the Native people had it straight from a Briton's mouth.

In a story long enshrined U.S. folklore, Braddock went on to ignominious
defeat before reaching the Forks of the Ohio, his troops ambushed and
more than two-thirds slaughtered, his corpse buried in the road his men
had cleared, and his aide-de-camp George Washington leading another
retreat across the mountains. Braddock's debacle unleashed all the seeth-
ing violence that had been building against the British in Native commu-

nities. Because the enemies knew each other so well—because Indian and non-Indian people used many of the same material goods, hunted in the same woods with the same kinds of weapons, wore similar clothes, spoke the same German or Celtic-inflected English tongues—the war became deeply personal, and therefore bloodily brutal. Despite all the stereotyped talk in the Wyoming Valley or in Philadelphia, it would be nothing like an abstract battle of "French and Indians" against nameless "British" foes. Or it might be better to say that only a transcendent level of violence could reduce individual human beings to the inhuman category of nameless enemy.

When Delawares, Shawnees, and others took up arms, they engaged neither in random blows nor broad strategic sweeps. They probably killed and captured fewer than five hundred people in two years of raids. For the Delawares, the targets were very specific: particular homesteads of Euro-Americans who had settled on the lands that the Six Nations had sold out from under them to Pennsylvania in the Walking Purchase of 1737 and, especially, the Albany Treaty of 1754. Often Indians attacked people whose names they knew and against whom they had specific personal resentments—resentments they explained in German or English before they executed their foes or took them captive. Corpses were not just scalped in accordance with long tradition, but often brutally mutilated in ways that were both morally transgressive expressions of rage and symbolic messages to those who would discover the devastation. Shawnees also had particular grievances that inflamed more general concerns over land. In 1753, a war party headed for Catawba country had been captured by Carolinians and thrown in jail in Charles Town, where a prominent leader named Itawachcomequa died (or, as the Shawnees probably saw it, was murdered). Protracted intercolonial negotiations over release of the remaining prisoners convinced many Shawnees that Virginia and Pennsylvania officials were no more to be trusted than Carolinians. Virginia settlers, in particular, were targets for their wrath.

Euro-Americans returned the violence in kind—scalping Indian women and children, desecrating corpses, venting revenge on what they had seen done to their neighbors and kin—but seemed to do so in less focused ways, finding *any* Native American an appropriate target on the rare occasions they could locate one. The random brutality was a perversely unintended byproduct of Pennsylvania's history of Quaker pacifism. Although most prominent Friends had resigned from public participation in government in 1755, allowing the nonpacifist non-Quakers who now dominated the provincial assembly for the first time to vote funds to build frontier forts, raise troops, and supply arms, Pennsylvania's lack of any existing military infrastructure or supervised system of local militia forced western settlers to devise their own cruder, ad hoc means of striking back. A bounty the Quaker-free provincial government offered for each Indian scalp in 1756 validated the pattern. A male trophy earned 130 Spanish dollars, a female 50.[5]

Thus, racial violence ripped apart the mixture of peoples who had defined the Atlantean world, and left "red" and "white" facing each other across a deep cultural divide. A few on either side tried to remain above the carnage, but those who advocated peace were vilified and pressured to choose. After repeated threats from Native kin, for example, the forty or so Christian Indians who remained within the Walking Purchase at the Moravian mission town of Gnadenhütten had to flee to Bethlehem in late 1755, when non-Christian Delawares destroyed their town. Similarly, among Euro-Americans, the Moravians became increasingly suspect for their sheltering of Indians and their unwillingness to fight. Quakers, too, became suspect, especially when Israel Pemberton and coreligionists among prominent Philadelphians formed a "Friendly Association for Regaining and Preserving Peace with the Indians by Pacific Measures," which often worked at cross-purposes with the proprietary government and the bloodthirsty frontier folk who fled to eastern towns and plotted revenge.

While Indians and colonists killed each other in 1755 and 1756, Braddock's successor and second-in-command, Massachusetts governor William Shirley, mismanaged an already ill-advised plan that Braddock had concocted to invade Canada by way of Lake George and Lake Champlain. Shirley's successor, John Campbell, earl of Loudoun, proved, if anything, a worse politician than Braddock, alienating virtually every North American he encountered. In 1756, the French seized the only significant British post on the Great Lakes: Oswego, on Lake Ontario. And Britain's disasters were transatlantic. A series of military setbacks on the European continent, including an ignominious defeat at Minorca, led first to the fall of Newcastle's government, and then to an extended period of political confusion in Whitehall. Meantime, in North America, British military successes were few, far between, and costly. William Johnson's successful defense of Fort Edward on Lake George in late 1755, for example, consumed the lives of more than two hundred British and their Mohawk allies. Among the dead was Hendrick Theyanoguin.

The most dramatic defeat—which, thanks to James Fenimore Cooper's *Last of the Mohicans,* is as encrusted with legend as Braddock's debacle— was at Fort William Henry on Lake George in 1757. After a six-day siege, about twenty-three hundred British and provincial troops surrendered to a force of six thousand French and Canadians and two thousand Native Americans. Half came from Catholic missions and other towns in the St. Lawrence region. The rest were Ottawas, Ojibwas, and many others who had traveled hundreds of miles from all over the *pays d'en haut* to do battle with their enemies, expecting, according to the rules of Native combat, their share of captives, scalps, and booty. Following instead the chivalric rules of European combat, the French commander, Louis-Joseph, marquis de Montcalm, allowed the British forces the "honors of war"—the right to march out under their flags and to keep their arms and possessions in exchange for a pledge not to fight again for eighteen months. Native fighters, not to be denied what they considered rightly due them as victors, attacked the British as they left the fort, plundered most of their goods, killed perhaps one hundred eighty-five, and captured as many as five hundred.

Montcalm, like his counterparts Braddock and Loudoun, was a stubborn military professional who tangled with royal governors (in his case, the Canadian-born Pierre de Rigaud de Vaudreuil) and who had little use for provincials and less for Native Americans as allies. The events at Fort William Henry convinced him that Indian forces must never again be a major part of his plans. The disgruntled warriors from the *pays d'en haut* returned the favor and never again volunteered in large numbers. Thus, after 1757, the French—whose North American empire had always rested on Native American alliances—ironically adopted the go-it-alone British strategy that had led to Braddock's disaster.

At the same time, the British in Whitehall and in North America were moving in the opposite direction, responding to overtures from Teedyuscung and a few other Delawares who sought to end the bloodshed if the British would address the underlying issue of land. Negotiations began in late 1756 and continued through the Easton Conference of 1757, where Teedyuscung explained "the cause of our Differences." Multiple parties, often working at cross-purposes, tried to patch things together: Johnson, Croghan, and their Haudenosaunee allies, seeking to reestablish their pretensions to authority over Teedyuscung's and all the other peoples who were driving Europeans out of Indian country; the Friendly Association and the Moravian missionaries, who were far more sympathetic to the Delawares' grievances; Ohio country Delawares who did not acknowledge Teedyuscung's leadership; the Penn family and its governor, William Denny, who were trying to make the best of a bad situation and who built houses in the Wyoming Valley for Teedyuscung and his followers to demonstrate their commitment to satisfying Delaware land claims.

In October 1758, in a treaty at Easton, the Pennsylvania government agreed to prohibit further Euro-American settlement "Northward and Westward of the Alleghany Hills" and surrendered most of the land acquired in the 1754 Albany purchase. Ironically, the surrender came in the form of the same kind of real estate deed that had caused the war in the first place—although now the beneficiaries were Native people.[6] Significantly, however, the recipients of the deed were the Six Nations, not the Delawares and other Indians who lived on the land and who had fought so hard to regain it. Teedyuscung's Wyoming settlement was said to belong to the Delawares merely at the pleasure of the Haudenosaunee.

Even this unsatisfactory arrangement became possible only because the military balance between the empires had by then tilted decisively away from the French. In June 1757, Newcastle returned to power in Whitehall, as part of a new coalition with the charismatic parliamentary orator William Pitt. As Secretary of State for the Southern Department, the minister in charge of colonial affairs, Pitt shifted military resources toward the war in North America, which he saw as the key to global victory. At the end of 1757, he dismissed Loudoun and assumed personal command over a new set of North American generals, including Jeffrey Amherst, John Forbes, and James Wolfe, relatively young men with few political connections but demonstrated administrative skills. Pitt also committed massive funds to the American war, borrowing upwards of £1 million to help pay the bills. Freed of the former commanders' incessant demands that British North Americans tax themselves to pay their own troops, provincial assemblies as well as royal governors suddenly became far more cooperative, and a reasonably efficient, relatively united, British-American war machine took shape.

When that happened—and when the war became one primarily be-

tween rival empires, their colonial populations, and their European-style
armies, rather than between Indians and Britons—the French had little
chance, if only because of the wealth and manpower of the British provinces. There were roughly seventy thousand French Americans, compared
to 1.5 million British Americans. The entire military-age male population
of La Nouvelle-France barely totaled sixteen thousand. Under Pitt's new
policies, nearly fifty thousand British provincials turned out for campaigns
in 1758.[7]

In the summer of that year, led by many thousands of troops from
the British Isles, those forces conquered two vital points in French supply lines. In July, Amherst and Wolfe, with a fleet of forty ships and
nearly ten thousand troops, retook Louisbourg, once again cutting off La
Nouvelle-France from Atlantic trade. The same month, the last of the
generals from the Loudoun era, James Abercromby, assembled fourteen
thousand troops on Lake George to attack Fort Ticonderoga. This was the
first step in a planned invasion of Canada. Abercromby's incompetence allowed a vastly outnumbered Montcalm to repulse the assault and send
the panicked British who survived fleeing toward Albany. As the forces
regrouped, Abercromby's subordinate John Bradstreet led a contingent
westward to Lake Ontario for an assault on Fort Frontenac, the key distribution point for all French trade in the *pays d'en haut* and the Ohio country. Bradstreet's surprisingly easy victory there yielded as booty a horde of
goods intended for the Indian trade, and virtually assured that the French
would have nothing to sell or give to their remaining Native allies. This
fact, as much as anything, explains why the Ohio country Delawares were
willing to make peace at Easton in 1758. It also explains why, a few months
later, French forces had to withdraw from Fort Duquesne as an army led
by Forbes approached the Forks of the Ohio and prepared to rechristen
the site "Fort Pitt."

With Native people almost entirely out of the war, the British juggernaut prepared its final assaults in 1759. In July, Niagara fell to provincial
troops aided by Johnson and nearly a thousand Iroquois, who had suddenly rallied to the winning side, further tipping the scales against the
French. At about the same time, as Amherst mobilized another assault on
Lake George, the French destroyed their own forts in that previously
unconquerable corridor and retreated to Montréal. While all this was
happening, Wolfe and some eighty-five hundred troops had sailed from
Louisbourg up the St. Lawrence and laid siege to the citadel of Québec.

Throughout the month of July, the British shelled the city to no effect and endured huge losses in the one frontal assault they made against outlying lines of defense. In August, Wolfe turned to terror to try to force the French to submit. His troops raped and scalped their way through the countryside, burning at least fourteen hundred farms and destroying as many churches, mills, and other public buildings as possible. Still, Montcalm and the city held out. In September, in a desperate move, Wolfe sent some forty-five hundred men up a steep cliff and arranged them at dawn on the Plains of Abraham, west of the city walls. The British lines were potentially exposed to cannon fire from the fortress and vulnerable to some three thousand French reinforcements stationed a few miles away. Inexplicably, rather than wait for these troops to arrive, Montcalm led his army out of the city to make a frontal assault on the British lines and was soon routed.

Neither general survived the epic battle, but, as Wolfe lay bleeding, he was able to utter something resembling the stirring last words since attributed to him: "Now, God be praised, I will die in peace." At the time, the *Pennsylvania Gazette* reported two variants. In the first, Wolfe, when told "we had gained a compleat Victory, replied *'Then I die in Peace.'"* The second is a little more dramatic:

> The brave General WOLFE had three Balls shot through his Body, which brought him to the Ground. An Officer standing by, immediately caught him in his Arms, and supported him; to whom the Hero said, 'Tell me, Sir, do the Enemy give Way? Tell me, for I cannot see'; (his Eye-sight failing him, being then in the Agonies of Death) the Officer replied, 'They are beat, Sir, they are flying before you.' The General then said, 'I am satisfied, my Boys,' and expired in a few Moments.[8]

Whatever the phrasing, there was no denying the *Gazette*'s conclusion that "the most remarkable Success which it has pleased Heaven to afford unto His Majesty's Arms, in the Reduction of QUEBEC, the Capital of CANADA . . . has entirely broke the French power in America." It would be another year before Amherst's troops would finally take Montréal and accept a formal surrender of all La Nouvelle-France, but the British American victory was complete. Or so it seemed as the global imperial war moved elsewhere, to the Caribbean, to Gibraltar, to India, and even to the Philippines, where British forces piled up stunning victories against the French and against Spain, which formally entered the war against Britain only in early 1762 and then promptly lost Manila and Havana. There, as in North America from 1758 to 1760, in the imperial conflict between Britain and France, European fleets and European armies employing tactics in use since the days of the conquistadores won the war.

·No such clear victory ended the gloomy and dark struggle for land between Native Americans and British provincials. With few exceptions, provincials had been hapless against foes who seemed able to strike anywhere, anytime, and the British had yielded enormous tracts as the price of peace at Easton in 1758. Only well to the south of the Ohio country—and only well after Native people had lost their supply lines to the French—did anything like a British victory occur. In late 1759, Carolina governor William Henry Lyttelton launched an inconclusive preemptive attack on the Cherokees, who, like the Iroquois, had been deeply divided over how to respond to accumulating grievances against the British. Subsequently, Cherokees defeated a second invasion and attacked settlers from the Carolinas and Virginia. In 1761, freed from battles elsewhere, British regulars and provincials invaded Cherokee country a third time and torched some fifteen towns. In the treaty that ended the fighting, Cherokees ceded substantial territory and acknowledged British sovereignty.

Farther north, however, it was the British who had ceded territory, and the British were anything but sovereign in practice. "The Success of his Majestys Arms . . . gives rise to an Opinion generally received in the Army, that We have conquered the Continent," George Croghan wrote in early 1760. "It is True We may say We have beat the French." Yet there was "nothing to boast from the War with the Natives."⁹ Jeffrey Amherst (who had succeeded Abercromby as commander-in-chief) pretended nonetheless that British victory over the French was also British victory over the Indians, and that the British victory over the Cherokees was a lesson to those Native people who might think otherwise. "Any attempt to Disturb Us," he wrote in early 1762, "must only End in their own Destruction."¹⁰

Like Braddock and indeed Montcalm before him, Amherst had little use for Indians and their diplomatic ceremonies, and no understanding of the importance that chiefs attached to prestige goods as markers of power and alliance. "You are sensible how averse I am, to purchasing the good behavior of Indians, by presents," the commander-in-chief wrote to Johnson on the eve of a major treaty with the peoples of the *pays d'en haut* at Detroit in September 1761. "I think, it much better to avoid all presents in future, since that will oblige them to Supply themselves by barter, and of course keep them more Constantly Employed by means of which they will have less time to concert, or Carry into Execution any Schemes prejudicial to His Majesty's Interests."[11] Thus, the Detroit treaty became more like a forced surrender than a peace negotiation, as the British insisted on the unceremonial, unconditional, and uncompensated return of Euro-American war captives, who often had been adopted into Native families. British commanders acted with similar hauteur in the Southeast. Choctaws, for example, learned that henceforth they were not to "run from one nation to another to carry and receive mischievous speeches," and that only chiefs who "deserve[d] them" would receive diplomatic gifts.[12]

Having refused to purchase Indian allegiance, Amherst ensured that he would not receive it voluntarily. Choctaws responded to the new regime by attacking English traders and confiscating their goods. From Fort Pitt, Croghan reported that "all the Indian Nations were . . . become verry Jealous of the English, who had erected so many Posts in their Country, but were not so generous to them as the French, and particularly gave them no Amunition, which was the chief cause of their Jealousy and Discontent."[13] The jealousy multiplied as Amherst imposed severe new restrictions on trade. Over the objections of Johnson and others who understood the situation better than he, Amherst decreed that commerce was to take place only at British army posts—Detroit, Fort Pitt, Niagara, Michilimackinac, and about a dozen smaller garrisons—and that only licensed provincials who adhered to official price lists were to trade there. Rum was, in theory, completely banned, while gunpowder and lead would purposely be kept "scarce, . . . since nothing can be so impolitick as to furnish them with the means of accomplishing the Evil which is so much Dreaded."[14] Meantime, unlicensed traders ignored Amherst's regulations and flocked into Native villages bringing oceans of rotgut rum and high-priced shoddy goods. Such blatant lawlessness, combined with shortages of officially sanctioned alcohol and of the ammunition crucial for hunting, conveyed an impression of British mean-spiritedness, if not outright aggression.

But, as always, key issues involved land. At least since the Treaty of Easton, British officials had pledged that colonists would be barred from territory west of the Appalachians and had denied any plan to establish military posts at strategic spots formerly held by the French. In Philadelphia in 1762, a military spokesman assured a group of Delawares that "the English have no intention to make settlements in your hunting country beyond the Allegheny hills, unless they shall be desired for your conveniency to erect some store houses in order to establish and carry on a trade." Yet one of Amherst's first acts after the conquest of Niagara two years earlier had been to grant ten thousand acres there to subordinate officers, without so much as a nod to Indian owners. The Board of Trade ultimately annulled the grants, but the damage had been done, and Amherst showed no change of heart. In apologizing to the board for any misunderstanding, he completely ignored its warning that allowing the grants to stand would "be of the greatest prejudice to your Majesty's interests and the welfare of your colonys, by giving offence to the confederated Nations of Indians."[15] Moreover, as troops dug in not only at Niagara but at garrisons from Fort Pitt to Detroit to Michilimackinac, it also became clear that Amherst had no intention of fulfilling the promise to withdraw from western forts once the fighting ended. The Indians "say We mean to make Slaves of them, by Taking so many Posts in their Country," the commandant at Detroit reported in April 1763. They had convinced themselves "that they had better Attempt Something now, to Recover their Liberty, than Wait till We were better Established."[16]

No one—whether Britons, Indians, or the ordinary French colonists and traders left behind when their king's troops withdrew—knew conclusively under whose regime that establishment would take shape. The British had returned Louisbourg to France at the peace table once before and might do so again, this time including all of La Nouvelle-France. Croghan reported as late as April 1763 that Native people "always expected Canada would be given back to the French on a peace," and that they insisted "the French had no right to give up their country to the English."[17] With no peace treaty between the Crowns yet signed, rumors circulated that a Gallic fleet was on its way to reconquer North America. People dreamed—desperately but not irrationally—that if only French residents and Indians took matters into their own hands, Louis XV and his ministers would welcome the reconquest of lost territories and send the troops necessary to defend them.

These dreams assumed all the more power as European squatters returned to lands near Fort Pitt and elsewhere in territory supposedly restored to Indian ownership. Meantime it seemed that everywhere the thirst of great men for Indian real estate had resumed as if the gloomy and dark times had never happened. "All Canada haveing . . . submitted, the People thought themselves safe from both French and Indians; and the Inhabitants every where return'd to their habitations," New York's governor, Cadwallader Colden, wrote to the Board of Trade in 1762. "In the Spring following numbers gave in Petitions for licenses to purchase Lands of the Indians on the Frontiers."[18] The Susquehanna Company continued to eye the Wyoming Valley, while the Ohio Company redoubled its efforts to patent lands supposedly guaranteed to Indians near Fort Pitt. George Washington and other Ohio Company investors pooled resources for projects in the Great Dismal Swamp of North Carolina and elsewhere. Still other speculators eyed the Mississippi Valley. New combinations abounded, including groups designed to tug on wartime patriotic heartstrings; Croghan and investors who called themselves the "Suffering Traders" of Pennsylvania angled to exchange lands in the Ohio country for tracts in the Mohawk Valley, while a Connecticut "Company of Military Adventurers" pleaded as veterans for a share of conquered territories.

The thirst for land was so unslakable that in April 1763 one wag planted a notice in the *Newport Mercury* that "A Proposal is now on Foot, for settling a very extensive colony upon the finest part of the Ohio, which is to be called *NEW-WALES*, in honour of his Royal Highness the Prince of Wales, who is to be sole Proprietor." Four thousand settlers were "to march in two Divisions, and are to compose two Cities or Towns, for the more CONVENIENCE of laying out the Land round each." The article was reprinted in other newspapers and inspired at least one Boston copycat, who alleged a Philadelphia byline and specified the colony's dimensions as nine degrees of longitude by nine degrees of latitude—nearly thirty thousand square miles. Readers not tipped off to the joke by the impossible numbers might have noted that the Prince of Wales (the future George IV) was a mere eight months old when he supposedly took charge of this capacious domain.[19]

The Board of Trade, seeing little humor in North Americans' thirst, drafted instructions to royal governors that no new purchases should take place without approval from Whitehall. As the Secretary of State concluded in May 1763, while "it may become necessary to erect some Forts in the Indian Country with their consent, yet his Majesty's Justice and Moderation inclines him to adopt the more eligible Method of conciliating the minds of the Indians by the mildness of His Government, by protecting their persons and property, and securing to them all the possessions rights and Privileges they have hitherto enjoyed and are entitled to . . . against any Invasion or Occupation of their hunting Lands, the possession of which is to be acquired by fair purchase only."[20]

That very month, Native people were taking their rights and privileges into their own hands. At Detroit, the Ottawa war chief Pontiac led a coalition of several hundred Native warriors from throughout the region to lay siege to the fort. He was inspired by the teachings of a Delaware holy man named Neolin, who for years had traveled far and wide to spread a militant version of the teachings that Brainerd had heard at the Wyoming settlement in 1751. In a vision, Neolin had visited the Master of Life. "This land where ye dwell I have made for you and not for others," the Creator said. "Whence comes it that ye permit the Whites upon your lands? . . . Drive them out, make war upon them."[21] Inspired by the prophet's teachings, and only loosely (if at all) affiliated with the chief whose name has since been attached to "Pontiac's War," Native people took control of nearly every fort in *pays d'en haut* and the Ohio country. Only Niagara, besieged Detroit, and an equally besieged Fort Pitt remained in British hands.

At the same time, raids against European squatters on lands supposedly returned at Easton resumed with even more fury in 1763 than in 1755 and 1756. Many of the raiders were inspired by Neolin, but the immediate provocation for their attacks seems to have been Teedyuscung's murder. When persons unknown—they were probably working for the Connecticut Susquehanna Company—came to his home while he slept, burned the house Pennsylvania had built for him, and set fire to the rest of the village, whatever remaining trust the Indians had in British guarantees of Native land claims also went up in smoke. Over the next few months, throughout territories bordering Pennsylvania southward toward Virginia and the Carolinas, colonists who had squatted in Indian country or settled under patents that Indians did not recognize were slaughtered or sent fleeing to the east.

"Every Day, for some time past, has offered the melancholy Scene of poor distressed families driving downwards, through this Town, with their

Effects, who have deserted their Plantations, for Fear of falling into the cruel Hands of our Savage Enemies," wrote a resident of Frederick, Maryland. "Never was Panic more general or terrible than that of the Back Inhabitants, whose Terrors, at this Time, exceed what followed on the Defeat of General Braddock."[22] Among those slain were ten people foolhardy enough to remain at a settlement that the Susquehanna Company had planted at the Wyoming site within weeks of Teedyuscung's murder. In gruesome symbolism of what Neolin's followers thought of the British and their coveted consumer goods—especially those used to build houses and farms on Indian lands—the Wyoming intruders were "most cruelly butchered; the Woman was roasted, and had two Hinges in her hands, supposed to be put in red hot; and several of the Men had awls thrust in their Eyes, and Spears, Arrows, Pitchforks, etc., sticking in their Bodies."[23]

As in 1756–1757, the violence was not only bloody but personal. The mutilated Wyoming corpses were discovered by a party of militia from Paxton township, east of the Susquehanna River, near today's Harrisburg. Much of their subsequent rage focused on a man known as Toshetaquah or Will Sock, a onetime Native diplomatic envoy for the British who, the militiamen were convinced, not only consorted with enemy Indians but had himself killed and captured Pennsylvanians—if not at the Wyoming settlement, then elsewhere. The truth of these allegations is doubtful; Toshetaquah may simply have been a close-by and easy target, for he lived near Lancaster at Conestoga Manor, a tiny hamlet of twenty or so inhabitants of mixed Indian ancestry, to whom the Penn family had granted land.

With wartime hatreds running high, pretensions to a special relationship with the Pennsylvania government only made the Conestoga people more threatening. In mid-December 1763, men from Paxton burned Conestoga and killed all six people they found sleeping there. To protect the fourteen survivors, local officials lodged them in the Lancaster workhouse. A few days later, a well-organized mob broke in and slaughtered them all. "Knowing that the little Commonwealth of Indians at Conestoga that pretended to be our Friends, had done us much Mischief, and were in Reality our most dangerous Enemies," those known as the "Paxton Boys" explained, "a Number of Persons living amongst us, who had seen their Houses in Flames, their Parents and Relatives butchered in the most in human Manner determined to root out this Nest of perfidious Enemies; and accordingly cut them off."[24]

Next, marching toward Philadelphia and picking up numerous reinforcements along the way, the Paxton Boys turned their attention to another supposedly treacherous group of Indians who consorted with the enemy. Pennsylvania officials had relocated two Moravian Indian mission communities to the capital to protect them from such hotheaded militiamen. As the marchers approached, Benjamin Franklin and governor John Penn, normally political foes, hastily mobilized a thousand Philadelphia residents to oppose them. (The best estimates are that many thousands more—perhaps three-quarters of the city's population—sympathized with the militiamen.) At Germantown, a few miles outside the capital, Franklin and several other prominent Philadelphians negotiated with the Paxtonians and got them to turn back in exchange for an agreement to publish their grievances and place them before the provincial assembly.

As the political crisis—but certainly not the racial hatreds—spawned by the Paxton Boys calmed, the wars inspired by Neolin also wound down. Amherst, having shifted the bulk of his forces to the West Indies, had been in no position to carry out his threats to "extirpate or remove that Vermin" by means ranging from the use of hunting dogs to the distribution of smallpox-infected blankets—a tactic actually used at Fort Pitt in June 1763. Still, the commander-in-chief mustered enough troops to allow Colonel Henry Bouquet to reach besieged Fort Pitt. For their own reasons, the Indians surrounding the post then withdrew without a serious fight. A few weeks earlier, another British force reached Detroit but failed to dislodge Pontiac. At the end of October 1763, conclusive news of a treaty between the empires arrived, dashing Pontiac's hopes for support from French forces and leading him to lift his siege. Meanwhile, smallpox—whether or not exacerbated by the biological warfare at Fort Pitt—combined with continued shortages of arms and ammunition to undermine the ability of Neolin's disciples to wage new offensives.

As the war settled into a stalemate, Amherst learned that he had been fired. The Board of Trade had concluded that the commander-in-chief's decisions were "the causes of this unhappy defection of the Indians" and that "nothing but the speedy establishment of some well digested and general plan for the regulation of our Commercial and political concerns with them can effectually reconcile their esteem and affections."[25] In 1764 and 1765, the diplomatic approach that Amherst had scorned gradually brought an uneasy peace to the continental interior. The racial hatreds spawned by twelve years of conflict, however, festered beneath the surface calm.

As they nursed their wounds and enmities, all the peoples of North America struggled to understand the implications of two documents signed in Europe that transformed the formal map of North America: the Treaty of Paris and the Proclamation of 1763. The Paris Treaty between Britain and France, along with related negotiations between France and Spain, confirmed one of the greatest military triumphs of all time and established Great Britain as what seemed the dominant power on earth, with huge new claims in India. Nowhere were the territorial gains greater than in North America. Apart from the two tiny islands of St.-Pierre and Miquelon, which provided access to the fisheries off Newfoundland, France yielded all its claims in North America, in exchange for the British return of one West Indian island, Martinique, whose sugar plantations yielded far more revenue than all of La Nouvelle-France. (Britain retained its conquest of the three neighboring islands of St. Lucia, St. Vincent, and Grenada.) Britain returned Cuba to Spain, but gained in return all of La Florida—after France separately agreed to yield to Spain New Orleans and its environs on the east bank of the Mississippi, and all of Louisiana on the west bank.

So with a few strokes of the pen, the ability of Native North Americans to play one imperial power off against another—a defining characteristic of the eighteenth-century Atlantean world—virtually ceased to exist. East of the Mississippi, there was only the British; west of the Mississippi, only the Spanish. Because Spanish control of territories north of New Orleans remained tenuous for many years, even those Native people fortunate enough to border the Mississippi had few opportunities to seek alternative markets and alliances. At New Orleans and in the Illinois country of the upper Mississippi Valley, a substantial French *population* remained, but no French *government* or trading connections provided a counterbalance to British hegemony. In La Florida, no appreciable Spanish-speaking population—*peninsular, criollo, indio católico,* or free or enslaved *africano*—remained. All *floridanos* had been evacuated to Havana or other parts of the Spanish Empire.

Yet when news of the ratification of the Paris Treaty reached British

North America, few were in a mood to celebrate—in stark contrast to the patriotic elation with which Britons had greeted the victory at Québec in 1759. In the fall of 1762, Pitt had fallen from power, victim of byzantine struggles that surrounded the rise to the throne of George III in 1760, at age twenty-two. The new monarch detested Pitt and hoped to put his closest confident, the wildly unpopular John Stuart, earl of Bute, in his place. Out of office, Pitt, in speeches reported in many American newspapers, had unfairly but persistently criticized the preliminary articles of peace, negotiated by his successors, as a sellout to the French and a betrayal of everything he and his countrymen had fought for.

More important, British North Americans learned of the treaty and of the outbreak of Pontiac's War almost simultaneously. The disjuncture between formal peace and renewed violence was nowhere more evident than in the *Pennsylvania Gazette*'s issue of August 4, 1763. The front page printed a proclamation by Pennsylvania's lieutenant governor James Hamilton, calling for a public day of prayer and thanksgiving, "whereas our most gracious Sovereign, from . . . a sincere and humane Desire of putting a Stop to the Effusion of Christian Blood, hath been pleased to make, ratify and confirm, a Treaty of Peace and Friendship with their Most Christian and Catholic Majesties." Yet by turning the page, readers learned what Philadelphians were really praying about: "On Sunday last Sermons were preached in most of the Congregations of this City, in Favour of the distressed Back Inhabitants, and Collections are now making for them from House to House." Another article reported that the town of Shippensburg alone—well east of Indian country—struggled to house 1,384 war refugees, "many of whom were obliged to lie in Barns, Stables, Cellars, and under old leaky Sheds, the Dwelling-houses being all crowded."[26] There certainly had been no "Stop to the Effusion of Christian Blood."

Occupying more column inches than either the official peace proclamation or the war reports was a subject that might at first glance seem irrelevant. This was the latest news surrounding John Wilkes, the political firebrand (and ally of Pitt) who was making life miserable for Bute, King George, and all in the government. "Mr. W—s has of late been the topic of conversation in all companies, every one is eager to learn his most minute transactions, either in public or private life," a reader wrote to the *Gazette*. "Hardly any thing else is talked of, but his commitment, his enlargement, his privilege, his letters, his speeches, his principles, and his popularity."

Referring to the constitutionally questionable warrants that Wilkes's opponents had used to gather evidence to convict him of a crime, the letter
writer added that "Much too has been said of his stolen goods."

The Wilkes affair consumed so much space in American newspapers
because it seemed to speak so directly to the basic issues of the day. As
British Americans read of London crowds shouting "Wilkes and Liberty!"
and devoured reprints of their hero's scathing critiques of government tyranny in his *North Briton* newspaper, they confirmed a disturbing picture
of king's ministers who had not only thrown away the fruits of victory, who
were not only wildly out of touch with North American wartime realities,
but who were—in the words of Wilkes's most famous tract, *The North
Briton*, no. 45—"tools of corruption and despotism." Recalling the Glorious Revolution while playing on Bute's Scottish last name, Wilkes noted
that "the *Stuart* line has ever been intoxicated with the slavish doctrines of
the *absolute, independent, unlimited* power of the crown."[27]

Suspicions about the intentions of the ministry toward its loyal British
North American subjects deepened when those subjects pondered the
royal Proclamation of 1763. Although the edict was issued a few days after Whitehall learned about Pontiac's War, it had been in the works for
months before the ministry knew anything about the troubles in the Great
Lakes and Ohio country. The ministry was now dominated neither by Bute
nor by Pitt, but by George Grenville and Halifax, for whom the Proclamation was integral to the imperial administrative reforms that had been interrupted by the war and by Pitt's regime.

Accordingly, the document begins not specifically with a discussion of
lands belonging to Indians but, more broadly, with consideration of "the
extensive and valuable Acquisitions in *America,* secured to Our Crown by
the late Definitive Treaty of Peace." From those acquisitions, the Proclamation created four new provinces: Grenada in the Caribbean and East
Florida, West Florida, and Quebec in North America. All were placed
under military government, a reasonable decision for dealing with conquered populations, but worrisome to British Americans, who treasured
representative institutions and were immersed in the Wilkes controversy.
Next comes a scheme for distributing lands to war veterans in both new
and old colonies; Newfoundland and the Floridas were the focus, rather
than any of the western lands on which North American great men had
pinned their hopes. Not quite as an afterthought, the final third of the
proclamation declared that "the several Nations or Tribes of *Indians,* with

whom we are connected, and who live under Our Protaction, should not be molested or disturbed in the Possession of such Parts of Our Dominions and Territories as, not having been ceded to or purchased by Us, are reserved to them . . . as their Hunting Grounds." Royal and proprietary governors must not issue "any Patents for Lands beyond the Bounds of their respective Governments" or "beyond the Heads or Sources of any of the Rivers which fall into the *Atlantick* Ocean from the West and North-West, or upon any Lands whatever, which, not having been ceded to or purchased by Us as aforesaid, are reserved to the said *Indians.*" British subjects "who have either wilfully or inadvertently seated themselves upon" the reserved lands were "forthwith to remove themselves."[28]

Despite that directive, the Proclamation of 1763 was mostly meaningless to squatters who intended to return to Indian country as soon as war subsided. But it was quite a different matter for the provincial great men who coveted huge western tracts. Under the terms of the proclamation, speculators could not obtain legal title to those territories and, just as important, faced tough questions about their titles to lands east of the Proclamation Line purchased from Indians under questionable circumstances. Yet the great men were patient. "The majority of those who get lands, being persons of consequence in the Capitals, . . . can let them lye dead as a sure Estate hereafter," observed Johnson. "Tho' Proclamations are issued, and orders sent to the several Governours[,] experience has shewn that both are hitherto ineffectual and will be so, whilst the Gentlemen of property and Merchants are interested in finding out evasions or points of Law against them."[29]

Points of law and lines on maps—all seem abstractly formalistic, but these things traced profound fissures in the Atlantean world. The Proclamation of 1763 divided Native Americans from British Americans. Yet it just as surely divided British Americans from those who governed the Empire, who seemed to be rewarding Indians for the violence of Pontiac's War. One dare not openly oppose a proclamation by the King's Sacred Majesty, but from the perspective of many provincials, to accept the Proclamation of 1763 was to throw away the most precious fruits of the victory gained on the Plains of Abraham and at the peace table in Paris: the Indian lands that had been the main goal of the conflict from the beginning. "I am surprised to find it repeatedly asserted in the English Newspapers, that the present insurrection has been occasioned by the Indians having been cheated of their lands by the English in America," New York gover-

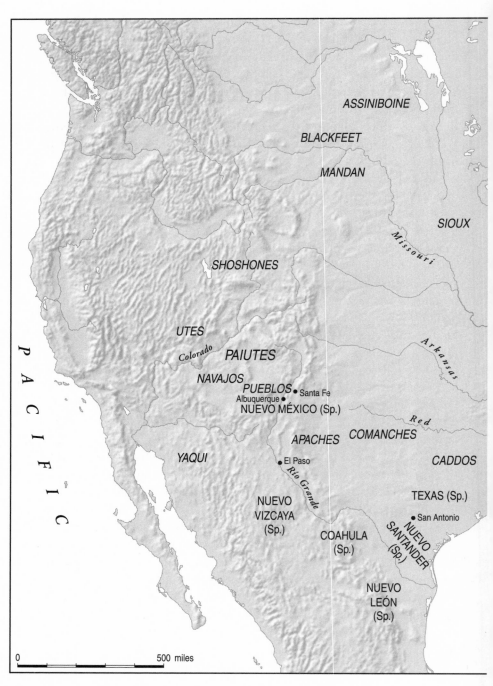

ASSINIBOINE

BLACKFEET

MANDAN

SIOUX

Missouri

SHOSHONES

UTES

Colorado

PAIUTES

Arkansas

NAVAJOS

PUEBLOS • Santa Fe
Albuquerque •
NUEVO MÉXICO (Sp.)

Red

APACHES   COMANCHES

YAQUI

CADDOS

• El Paso

Rio Grande

TEXAS (Sp.)

NUEVO
VIZCAYA
(Sp.)

COAHULA
(Sp.)

• San Antonio

NUEVO
SANTANDER
(Sp.)

NUEVO
LEÓN
(Sp.)

P A C I F I C

0   500 miles

North America, 1763.

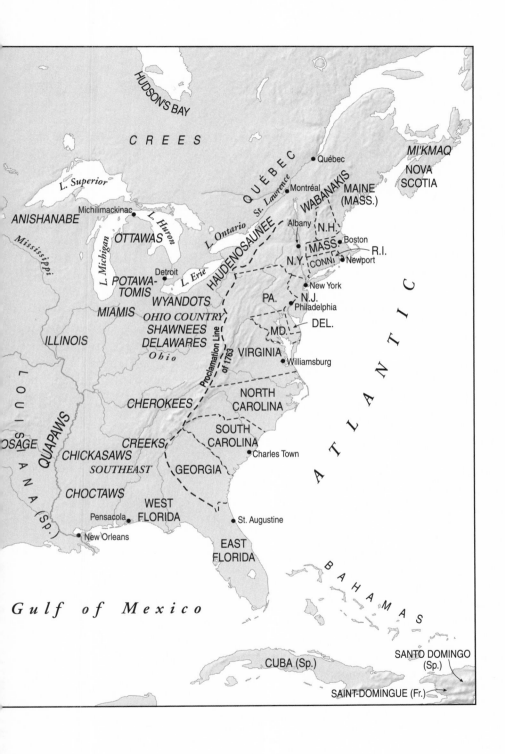

nor Cadwallader Colden disingenuously insisted to the Board of Trade during Pontiac's War. "I can assure your Lordships that there is not the least ground for this assertion and that, as to this Province it has happened without any provocation on our part so far as I have heard at least, and I believe to be true."[30] Most New Yorkers, most other British Americans, and all Native people knew better. And on paper, at least, the proclamation placed the British Crown squarely on the side of Native Americas. Copies of the document, paired with cautiously approving wampum belts, soon circulated throughout Indian country.

When the great men of New York, Pennsylvania, Virginia, and elsewhere learned about the Proclamation Line and about the systems of military government intended for the new colonies set aside for future population growth, both seemed part of a broader plan by Grenville to rein in the privileges of the provincial governments that those great men controlled. The divide between Whitehall and British North America yawned wider as a financial reckoning for the war commenced. Britain's national debt—normally a good thing for the health of the fiscal-military state—had nearly doubled during the war, leading to unsustainable levels of taxation in the British Isles just to fund interest payments to bondholders. Faced with rioting in the streets at home among taxpayers whose burden was approximately twenty-six times higher than that of most North Americans, the Grenville government logically decided that the pain had to be spread more equally.

Memories stretching back long before the Albany Congress convinced them that new revenue would never come voluntarily from the obstreperous legislatures of the various colonies. Instead, Grenville pushed through the parliamentary legislation known as the American Revenue or Sugar Act of 1764 and the Stamp Act of 1765. British North Americans' near-unanimous resistance to these taxes can be fully understood only in the context of the profound disillusionment that surrounded the Peace and Proclamation of 1763.

For Boston's James Otis Jr., for example, problems with the ministry's policies went beyond obvious issues of the rights of Englishmen to tax themselves through representative institutions, central as those rights were. In his 1764 pamphlet *The Rights of the British Colonies Asserted and Proved,* Otis took it as a given that the British "constitution is the most free one, and by far the best, now existing on earth: That by this constitution, every man in the dominions is a free man: That no parts of his

Majesty's dominions can be taxed without their consent." Yet a deeper grievance running throughout his pamphlet is a sense that those making decisions in Whitehall simply failed to comprehend the loyalty of British North Americans and the sacrifices they had made during the gloomy and dark days of the Seven Years War. Like Wilkes, Otis evoked the Glorious Revolution. "The deliverance under God wrought by the prince of Orange, afterwards deservedly made King William 3d, was as joyful an event to the colonies as to Great-Britain," he observed. "They all immediately acknowledged King William and Queen Mary as their lawful Sovereign. And such has been the zeal and loyalty of the colonies ever since . . . that I believe there is not one man in an hundred (except in Canada) who does not think himself under the best national civil constitution in the world." British North Americans' "loyalty has been abundantly proved, especially in the late war."

> The New England Colonies in particular, were not only settled without the least expence to the mother country, but they have all along defended themselves against the frequent incursions of the most inhuman Salvages, perhaps on the face of the whole earth, at *their own* cost. . . . Behold, an extensive territory, settled, defended, and secured to his Majesty, I repeat it, *without the least expence to the mother country,* till within twenty years past![31]

A gulf opened not just between North America and the British Isles, but between the mainland colonies and their erstwhile brothers and sisters in the West Indies. While British North Americans were fighting the Indians whom the Proclamation Line inexplicably coddled, "the *sugar colonies* have born little or no share in" the war. Otis admitted that West Indians "indeed sent a company or two of *Negroes* and *Molattoes,* if this be worth mentioning, to the sieges of Gaudaloupe, Martineco and the Havanna," but he could "not recollect any thing else that they had done; while the flower of *our* youth were annually pressed by ten thousands into the service, and there treated but little better, as we have been told, than hewers of wood and drawers of water."[32]

Similar contempt for Caribbean planters had dripped from a letter to the *Boston Evening Post* a few months earlier. The proposed Sugar Act, "if rigorously carried into execution, must, if not totally destroy, yet, greatly decrease the trade of this, and the neighbouring provinces," the anonymous author fumed.

And to what was all this sacrifice made? To the aggrandizement of the planters of our sugar colonies; who, notwithstanding they have become so opulent, that upwards of forty of them have seats in the House of Commons, and numbers have formed alliances with some of the noblest families in the kingdom, do yet complain for want of further encouragement. *Oh fatal Policy! Error irretrievable!*

This view is painful: Let us turn our eyes to a fairer portrait of Great-Britain, and contemplate her, exulting in the effects of an extended commerce, diffusing blessings to her colonies, and felicity to the whole world.[33]

The view *was* painful, and it is hard to say how many British North Americans as yet shared it in 1763 and 1764. But Otis, the Boston letter writer, and many others were beginning to suspect that their concerns, and their societies, had somehow radically diverged from the rest of the Atlantean world just at the moment of what should have been the greatest triumph of the transoceanic British Empire. Or, rather, they began to sense that the triumph of the British Empire was not the quite the same triumph that British North Americans had sought. "Alas, we have been long led away by ancient prejudices, and made large sacrifices to superstition," Thomas Paine would write in a few years. "We have boasted the protection of Great-Britain, without considering that her motive was *interest* not *attachment;* that she did not protect us from *our enemies* on *our account,* but from *her enemies* on *her own account.*"[34] Britain's enemies were rival European empires, but, said Paine, "France and Spain never were, nor perhaps ever will be our enemies." He did not say who the real foes of British Americans were, but the experience of gloomy and dark days and the hatred between the now irreconcilable descendants of two medieval progenitors made the answer clear. As Braddock had thundered, "No Savage Should Inherit the Land."

Epilogue

PAST. *n.s.* Elliptically used for past time.

ELLI´PSIS. *n.s.* [ἔλλειπσις].
1. A figure of rhetorick, by which something is left out necessary to be supplied by the hearer.

> —Samuel Johnson, *A Dictionary of the English
> Language* (London, 1755)

Present Pasts

THOMAS PAINE WAS Atlantean to the core. Born in 1737 in Thetford, England, he came to Philadelphia in 1774 bearing a letter of introduction from Benjamin Franklin, whom he had gotten to know in London. In 1787, a little over eleven years after Paine published *Common Sense,* and when he was well embarked on a transatlantic career as a revolutionary pamphleteer, he left the United States, it seemed for good. He went first to Britain, and then in 1792 to France, where he was initially welcomed as a champion of liberty but within a year was imprisoned for opposing the radical Jacobins. By then, he had also been declared an outlaw in his native England. He finally returned to the United States in 1802, hailed in some circles and reviled in most others for the radical ideas he had published in *The Rights of Man* (1791–1792), *The Age of Reason* (1794), and *Agrarian Justice* (1797). Many citizens of the United States who remembered his post–*Common Sense* career at all learned to revile him as the man Theodore Roosevelt later called "the filthy little atheist."[1] When he died in 1809, only six people attended his funeral. The disconnect between Paine's life and that of the nation he helped to launch in 1776 reveals the distance between his eighteenth-century Atlantean world and the subsequent history of the United States. Equally at home in Philadelphia, London, and Paris—or rather equally *ill at home* enough to preach revolution to each—he was the product of a cultural stratum that the floods of those revolutions submerged.

Yet just as earlier layers determined the contours of Paine's world, so his world continues to shape ours. Descendants of immigrants from England,

417

Ireland, and Germany have long since made peace with one another, and few today use the hierarchical language of masters and servants. But eighteenth-century tensions of ethnicity and class transmit their subterranean shivers to the present, when the grandchildren of older immigrants sometimes heap blame on newer arrivals for economic developments directed by great forces in global capitals—and forget the troubled layers of Spanish-speaking pasts that lie beneath the more recent English-language conquest of the continent. Two and a half centuries ago, Benjamin Franklin described German immigrants in language that echoes today everywhere from the borders of New Mexico to small towns in Pennsylvania. "Those who come hither are generally of the most ignorant stupid sort of their own Nation," he wrote. "Unless the Stream of their Importation could be turned from this to other Colonies . . . , they will soon so out number us, that all the advantages we have will not in my Opinion be able to preserve our Language, and even our Government will become precarious."[2]

Just as German-speakers and English-speakers have made peace, Lutherans and Presbyterians, Congregationalists and Episcopalians, Quakers and Baptists have long since come to terms. Yet Gottlieb Mittelberger's horror at the mingling of "Separatists, Freethinkers, Jews, Mohammedans, Pagans, Negroes, and Indians" still strikes a familiar chord. Citizens of the United States have long since ceased singing "Rule Britannia" and "God Save the King" (although many retain a peculiar fascination with the current royals and the replacement lyrics of "My Country 'Tis of Thee"). Yet those who would combine a crusading spirit with patriotism in the name of conquest still evoke, as did George II in 1739, "GOD's Assistance in so just a Cause, . . . to assert their undoubted Rights of Commerce and Navigation, and by all possible Means to attack, annoy and distress a Nation that has treated his People with . . . Insolence and Barbarity."[3] A crusading strain of Christianity linked to the expansion of state power—and persistent efforts to label both as necessary qualities of those who love freedom—lies deep in the historical bedrock of the twenty-first-century United States.

Even deeper lie patterns of racial exploitation. Enslavement of those whose speech, religion, and appearance differed from one's own was an ancient pattern on both sides of the Atlantic before Columbus; for Europeans, Native Americans, and West Africans alike, it was inherent in war and conquest. Unsurprisingly, the coerced labor of captive people early wove itself into the fabric of colonial experience. Yet only in the late seventeenth and early eighteenth centuries—under a perverse alchemy of the incessant demands of transatlantic labor markets, the interlocking quest for power by monarchs, merchants, and planter elites, and the emerging belief that Europeans themselves must never be slaves—did the Western world conceive the distinctively modern, capitalistic idea that African human beings, and only African human beings, were a commodity that could be bought and sold in a global market. Though eighteenth-century Atlanteans had not yet fully worked out a theory that categorized humankind by color, they had assembled all the ingredients for the subsequent tortured history of race relations in the United States and throughout the modern world.

That Native Americans, too, were enslaved—and still more that they themselves had a history as enslavers—lies more deeply buried in the continental past. So do the millennium-old North American patterns of warfare, the contests for political power, and the webs of economic relations in which European conquistadores, traders, planters, and imperialists embedded themselves. Nowhere were Native people passive victims of the colonizers, and nowhere did the colonizers—despite their own occasional fantasies of beginning the world over again and the grim realities of disease and warfare—impose themselves on a blank landscape of their own making. Everywhere, Native people not only resisted European domination in such cataclysmic struggles as the Pueblo Revolt and the Yamasee War but, more often, manipulated Europeans as trading partners, military allies, and sources of political power. Among the many features of the old Atlantean world that the revolutions of the late eighteenth century swept away were the constant rivalries among European North American empires that Native leaders had so skillfully exploited to maintain their independence. As a Seneca Iroquois spokesman explained to leaders of the newly independent state of New York in 1798, "The late contest between you and your father, the Great King of England, . . . threw the Inhabitants of this whole Island into a great tumult and commotion, like a raging whirlwind which tears up the trees, and tosses to and fro the leaves so that no one knows from whence they come or where they will fall."[4] When, after the War of 1812, the expansionist United States stood alone as imperial power south of the Great Lakes, east of the Rocky Mountains, and north of Texas, Native Americans truly faced a world in which they would have to begin over again.

It was a world in which an agricultural, economic, and political order spawned in Europe's Middle Ages seemed on the brink of erasing the one born in North America's. "What good man would prefer a country covered with forests and ranged by a few thousand savages to our extensive Republic, studded with cities, towns, and prosperous farms, embellished with all the improvements which art can devise or industry execute?" President Andrew Jackson would ask in 1830—erasing at a stroke not just the ancient North American economy but the very memory that it had ever involved a productive form of agriculture.[5] Still, Jackson's white farmers cultivated varieties of maize and beans descended from those developed by North America's agricultural revolution. And in the very act of ruthlessly exploiting the land for gains that no medieval European could have remotely imagined possible, they set about repeating on a far grander scale the ecological sins that probably caused the downfall of the great medieval North American civilizations. As we enter another global warm period, one can only wonder what Noquilpi, the Great Gambler said to have enslaved the doomed people of Chaco Canyon, might think.

Navajo stories condemn the tyranny of Noquilpi. Cherokee tales celebrate the overthrow of the oppressive *Aní-Kutâni*. And indeed, amid all the violence, exploitation, oppression, and enslavement of the continent's buried pasts, the contours of similarly hopeful stories live on in our present day. The same Franklin who mocked "ignorant Stupid" immigrants and called for "excluding all Blacks and Tawneys" also published the first German-language newspaper in North America, and in his old age called for the abolition of slavery. The same planters who ruthlessly exploited the environment and subordinated servants, slaves, and women to their quest for power also tenaciously resisted the efforts of greater men, of would-be feudal lords, and of the imperial state to subordinate them. Their efforts bequeathed a language and practice of liberty no less inspiring today than in their own time. The same patterns of European economic, political, and religious oppression on the one hand, and of colonial promises of opportunity and relentless demands for labor on the other, that transported hundreds of thousands of diverse Europeans to North America also forced those people to find ways to accommodate religious, linguistic, and cultural diversity. The same British imperial state that traced its origins to the conquests of medieval kings and that imposed slavery and death throughout the Atlantic world also spread institutions of representative government, a system of legal and constitutional rights, a doctrine, however limited, of religious toleration, and a paradoxical distrust of concentrated power that spawned the revolutions that would sweep that imperial state away.

The paradoxes of power and freedom, land hunger and economic independence, bigotry and religious liberty, ethnic hatred and national pride leap from the pages of North American newspapers published during the Seven Years War. A widely printed sermon by Boston clergyman Jonathan Mayhew conjured a "horrid scene" should British Americans shirk their martial duty:

> Do I behold these Territories of Freedom, become the Prey of arbitrary Power? Do I see the motly Armies of French and painted Savages taking our Fortresses, and erecting their own, even in our Capital Towns and Cities! Do I behold them spreading Desolation thro' the land! . . . Do I see Christianity banish'd for Popery! the Bible for the Mass book! the Oracles of Truth for fabulous Legends! . . . Do I see all Liberty, Property, Religion, Happiness chang'd, or rather transubstantiated, into Slavery, Poverty, Superstition, Wretchedness! And, in fine, do I hear the miserable Sufferers (those of them that survive) bitterly accusing the Negligence of the publick Guardians! and charging all their Calamities, less upon the Enemies, than upon the Fathers, of the Country![6]

The unholy crusade that Mayhew called for did, of course, come to pass. Yet amid the patriotic clamor of 1754—as amid the clamors of our own time—a few calmer voices, shouted down but not silenced forever, urged their compatriots to think long and hard about the fate of freedom in a regime devoted to war. One anonymous letter writer urged readers of the *Pennsylvania Gazette* "to consider seriously the true State of the Case . . . and not suffer themselves to be amused or frighted out of their Liberties, lest they should thereby bring on themselves burthensome Taxes, and real Evils; and instead of preserving their Country, Fortunes and Families, be the unhappy Instruments of their Ruin. Gentlemen, please to remember a Liberty once lost is hard to be regained."[7]

The same Atlantean society that produced the crusaders also produced this prophetic voice. Its words, and the struggles of ordinary women and

men, Native Americans and African Americans, enslaved and free ripple through the accumulated layers of the past to inspire us still. "After
all," wrote black Atlantean Olaudah Equiano quoting the prophet Micah,
"what makes any event important, unless by its observation we become
better and wiser, and learn 'to do justly, to love mercy, and to walk humbly
before God'?"[8]

NOTES

FURTHER READING

CREDITS

ACKNOWLEDGMENTS

INDEX

NOTE. *n.s.* [*nota*, Lat. *notte*, Fr.]
14. Explanatory annotation.
The best writers have been perplexed with *notes*, and obscured
with illustrations.   *Felton on the Clatsicks*

—Samuel Johnson, *A Dictionary of the English
Language* (London, 1755)

Notes

Reference notes are provided only for direct quotations and for specific quantitative information. When works exist in multiple editions with the same date, standard bibliographic identifiers, such as those used in *Early English Books Online, Early American Imprints,* and *Eighteenth-Century Collections Online,* are provided in square brackets. For a guide to the published scholarship on which these chapters rest, see the section entitled "Further Reading," below.

To convey a flavor of historical voices, quotations from English-language sources usually preserve the original spelling, capitalization, and italicization. I have silently modernized punctuation, uses of the formerly interchangeable letters *i* and *j* and *u* and *v,* and instances of *ff* and *vv* (antique forms of *F* and *w*). The Old English letter *thorn* (often rendered as *y* and for centuries used as shorthand for *th*) has also been modernized, because no one *ever* would have read y^e *olde shoppe* aloud as "yee oldee shoppee." They would, however, probably have added a slight puff of breath to emphasize the final sounds of the words *old* and *shop,* and so the additional letters there are worth retaining. Superscripts in usages such as ye were a form of shorthand. These and other abbreviations have been expanded or replaced with modern equivalents (*the* for y^e, *that* for y^t, *Mr.* for M^r, *nation* for *naĉon, and* for *&*). In words taken from French-language sources, the symbol often rendered as 8 (actually a *u* perched atop an *o*) has been replaced by *ou* or *w* to conform to modern usage. The Dutch *ij* has similarly been replaced with *y.* On a few occasions, comprehensibility has required modernization of particularly creatively spelled English quotations; these instances are always flagged in the notes.

Prologue: Layered Pasts

1. [Thomas Paine], *Common Sense: Addressed to the Inhabitants of America* (Philadelphia, 1776 [Evans no. 14959]), 43, 14.
2. Genesis 7:23, 8:1 (New Revised Standard Version).
3. Samuel Johnson, *A Dictionary of the English Language* (London, 1755), s.v. "Ancient."

4. Paine, *Common Sense*, 15.
5. Matthew 24:38–29 (New Revised Standard Version).

1. Legacies of Power from Medieval North America

1. Matthew W. Stirling, *Origin Myth of Acoma and Other Records*, Smithsonian Institution Bureau of American Ethnology Bulletin, 135 (Washington, D.C., 1942), 75.
2. Charles Hudson, *The Southeastern Indians* (Knoxville, Tenn., 1976), 60–62.
3. W. James Judge, "Chaco Canyon–San Juan Basin," in Linda S. Cordell and George J. Gumerman, eds., *Dynamics of Southwest Prehistory* (Tuscaloosa, Ala., 2006), 234, 245.
4. Brian M. Fagan, *Chaco Canyon: Archaeologists Explore the Lives of an Ancient Society* (New York, 2005), 21–21, 117.
5. Jared M. Diamond, *Collapse: How Societies Choose to Fail or Succeed* (New York, 2005), 149.
6. Steven A. LeBlanc, *Prehistoric Warfare in the American Southwest* (Salt Lake City, 1999), 164.
7. Stephen H. Lekson, *The Chaco Meridian: Centers of Political Power in the Ancient Southwest* (Walnut Creek, Calif., 1999), 158.
8. Stephen Plog, *Ancient Peoples of the American Southwest* (London, 1997), 102–108. Working ten-hour days, 365 days a year, it would take 8.2 people to accomplish 30,000 hours. Brian Fagan and other archaeologists argue that this is a relatively modest labor investment and "that thirty people could have completed the eleventh-century construction at Pueblo Bonito by working forty hours a week for ten years, distributed over a forty-five-year period" (*Chaco Canyon*, 142–144). Eight-to-ten-hour days and forty-hour work weeks, though, seem never to have existed, even among enslaved peoples, anywhere in the world before the nineteenth century. However one looks at it, the labor demands were extraordinary.
9. LeBlanc, *Prehistoric Warfare*, 176.
10. John R. Swanton, *Myths and Tales of the Southeastern Indians*, Smithsonian Institution Bureau of American Ethnology Bulletin, 88 (Washington, D.C., 1929), 76.
11. Christina Snyder, *Slavery in Indian Country: The Changing Face of Captivity in Early America* (Cambridge, Mass., 2010), 27–28.
12. Vernon James Knight Jr., "The Institutional Organization of Mississippian Religion," *American Antiquity*, 51 (1986), 677.
13. Brian M. Fagan, *Ancient North America: The Archaeology of a Continent*, 3d ed. (New York, 2000), 454.

14. Mary W. Helms, "Political Lords and Political Ideology in Southeastern Chiefdoms: Comments and Observations," in Alex W. Barker and Timothy R. Pauketat, eds., *Lords of the Southeast: Social Inequality and the Native Elites of Southeastern North America*, Archaeological Papers of the American Anthropological Association, 3 (1992), 187–188.

15. Thomas E. Emerson, *Cahokia and the Archaeology of Power* (Tuscaloosa, Ala., 1997), 17–18.

16. Ramón A. Gutiérrez, *When Jesus Came, the Corn Mothers Went Away: Marriage, Sexuality, and Power in New Mexico, 1500–1846* (Stanford, Calif., 1991), 23.

17. Stephen H. Lekson, "Chaco Matters: An Introduction," in Lekson, ed., *The Archaeology of Chaco Canyon: An Eleventh-Century Pueblo Regional Center* (Santa Fe, N.M., 2006), 29.

18. Timothy R. Pauketat, *Ancient Cahokia and the Mississippians* (Cambridge, 2004), 139–140.

2. Legacies of Conquest from Medieval Europe

1. Robert A. Scott, *The Gothic Enterprise: A Guide to Understanding the Medieval Cathedral* (Berkeley, Calif., 2003), 23–25, 11.

2. Charles Parain, "The Evolution of Agricultural Technique," in M. M. Postan, ed., *The Cambridge Economic History of Europe*, vol. 1: *The Agrarian Life of the Middle Ages*, 2d ed. (Cambridge, 1966), 125–142.

3. Kathy L. Pearson, "Nutrition and the Early-Medieval Diet," *Speculum*, 72 (1997), 12.

4. Edward Peters, *Europe and the Middle Ages*, 3d ed. (Upper Saddle River, N.J., 1997), 124; Pearson, "Nutrition and the Early-Medieval Diet," 17–18; Denys Delâge, *Bitter Feast: Amerindians and Europeans in Northeastern North America, 1600–1664*, trans. Jane Brierley (Vancouver, B.C., 1993, orig. publ. in French, 1985), 47; Sissel Schroeder, "Maize Productivity in the Eastern Woodlands and Great Plains of North America," *American Antiquity*, 64 (1999): 499–516.

5. Robert Fossier, "Rural Economy and Country Life," in Timothy Reuter, ed., *The New Cambridge Medieval History*, vol. 3: *c. 900–1024* (Cambridge, 1999), 58.

6. Chris Wickham, "Society," in Rosamond McKitterick, ed., *The Early Middle Ages: Europe 400–1000* (Oxford, 2001), 84.

7. Peters, *Europe and the Middle Ages*, 170.

8. Revelation 20:12–13, 15 (New Revised Standard Version).

9. Wendy Davies and Paul Fouracre, eds., *Property and Power in the Early Middle Ages* (Cambridge, 1995), 2.

10. D. A. Carpenter, "The Plantagenet Kings," in David Abulafia, ed., *The New Cambridge Medieval History*, vol. 5: *c. 1198–c. 1300* (Cambridge, 1999), 324–325, 347.

11. Ibid., 269.

12. Oliver J. Thatcher, and Edgar H. McNeal, eds., *A Source Book for Medieval History* (New York, 1905), 517.

13. Brian Tierney and Sidney Painter, *Western Europe in the Middle Ages, 300–1475* (New York, 1970), 210–211.

14. Ian Kershaw, "The Great Famine and Agrarian Crisis in England, 1315–1322," *Past and Present*, 59 (1973), 11.

15. Quoted ibid., 14.

16. Brian Fagan, *The Little Ice Age: How Climate Made History, 1300–1850* (New York, 2000), 81–83; Michael Jones, "Introduction," in Jones, ed., *The New Cambridge Medieval History*, vol. 6: *c. 1300–c. 1415* (Cambridge, 2000), 9; Christiane Klapisch-Zuber, "Plague and Family Life," ibid., 131.

17. Steven A. Epstein, "Urban Society," in David Abulafia, ed., *The New Cambridge Medieval History*, vol. 5: *c. 1198–c. 1300* (Cambridge, 1999), 27–28.

18. M. S. Anderson, *The Origins of the Modern European State System, 1494–1618* (London, 1998), 22–23.

19. Quoted ibid., 7.

20. Magnus Magnusson and Hermann Palsson, trans., *The Vinland Sagas: The Norse Discovery of America* (Baltimore, Md., 1965), 47–105.

3. Crusades of the Christ-Bearers to the Americas

1. Oliver Dunn and James E. Kelley Jr., trans. and eds., *The "Diario" of Christopher Columbus's First Voyage to America, 1492–1493, Abstracted by Fray Bartolemé de las Casas* (Norman, Okla., 1989), 17–18.

2. Samuel Eliot Morison, *Admiral of the Ocean Sea: A Life of Christopher Columbus* (Boston, 1942), 356–357.

3. Richard Hakluyt, *The Principal Navigations, Voyages, Traffiques and Discoveries of the English Nation* (London, 1599–1600), vol. 1, 212–213.

4. Matthew Restall, *Seven Myths of the Spanish Conquest* (New York, 2003), 68–69.

5. Quoted in Felipe Fernandez-Armesto, *Before Columbus: Exploration and Colonization from the Mediterranean to the Atlantic, 1229–1492* (Philadelphia, 1987), 234.

6. Quoted in Morison, *Admiral of the Ocean Sea*, 105.

7. Quoted ibid., 391.

8. Ibid., 481–495, 566–568; Irving Rouse, *The Taino: Rise and Decline of the*

People Who Greeted Columbus (New Haven, Conn., 1992), 150–155; J. H. Elliott, *Imperial Spain, 1469–1716* (New York, 1964), 59–64.

9. J. H. Elliott, *The Old World and the New, 1492–1650* (Cambridge, 1970), 60; Niall Ferguson, *The Ascent of Money: A Financial History of the World* (New York, 2008), 23 (quotations).

10. Charles Gibson, ed., *The Spanish Tradition in America* (Columbia, S.C., 1968), 59–60.

11. Charles E. Bennett, *Laudonnière and Fort Caroline: History and Documents* (Tuscaloosa, Ala., 2004; orig. publ. 1964), 80.

12. Hakluyt, *Principal Navigations,* vol. 3, 5.

13. Ibid., 36.

14. W. J. Eccles, *France in America* (New York, 1972), 2.

15. Richard Eden, trans., *The Decades of the Newe Worlde or West India . . . Wrytten in the Latine Tounge by Peter Martyr of Angleria . . .* (London, 1555), preface (unpaginated; spelling modernized).

16. Richard Eden, trans., *The History of Travayle in the West and East Indies . . . Newly Set in Order, Augmented, and Finished by Richarde Willes* (London, 1577), 458r–458v (spelling modernized).

17. Eden, trans., *Decades of the Newe Worlde,* preface (spelling modernized).

18. Ibid. (spelling modernized).

4. Crusades of the Protestants to New Worlds

1. Quoted in Conrad Russell, *The Crisis of Parliaments: English History, 1509–1660* (New York, 1971), 114.

2. Lucien Febvre and Henri-Jean Martin, *The Coming of the Book: The Impact of Printing, 1450–1800,* trans. David Gerard (London, 1976), 291.

3. Romans 3:20, 23–24 (New Revised Standard Version).

4. Charles E. Bennett, *Laudonnière and Fort Caroline: History and Documents* (Tuscaloosa, Ala., 2004; orig. publ. 1964), 82.

5. René Laudonnière, *Three Voyages* (1586), trans. Charles E. Bennett (Tuscaloosa, Ala., 2001; orig. publ. 1975), 29.

6. Ibid., 117.

7. Ibid., 124.

8. Bennett, *Laudonnière and Fort Caroline,* 38.

9. Ibid., 133–134.

10. *Collections of the Massachusetts Historical Society,* 4th ser., vol. 9 (1871), 7.

11. Richard Hakluyt, *The Principal Navigations, Voyages, Traffiques and Discoveries of the English Nation* (London, 1599–1600), vol. 3, 144.

12. Carlos Slafter, ed., *Sir Humfrey Gylberte and His Enterprise of Colonization in America,* Publications of the Prince Society, 29 (1903), 95–96.

13. Carole Shammas, "English Commercial Development and American Colonization, 1560–1620," in K. R. Andrews, *The Westward Enterprise: English Activities in Ireland, the Atlantic, and America, 1480–1650* (Detroit, 1979), 158–160.

14. E. G. R. Taylor, ed., *The Original Writings and Correspondence of the Two Richard Hakluyts* (London, 1935), vol. 2, 330.

15. Ibid., 332.

16. Quoted in Karen Ordahl Kupperman, *Roanoke: The Abandoned Colony* (Totowa, N.J., 1984), 74.

17. Michael Leroy Oberg, *The Head in Edward Nugent's Hand: Roanoke's Forgotten Indians* (Philadelphia, 2008), 96–98.

18. Kupperman, *Roanoke,* 118.

19. Quoted in David Beers Quinn, *Set Fair for Roanoke: Voyages and Colonies, 1584–1606* (Chapel Hill, N.C., 1985), 291.

20. Quoted ibid., 147.

21. Quoted in Nicholas P. Canny, "The Ideology of English Colonization: From Ireland to America," *William and Mary Quarterly,* 3rd ser., vol. 30 (1973), 588.

22. Quoted ibid., 582 (spelling modernized).

23. Quoted ibid., 588–589 (spelling modernized).

24. Quoted in David B. Quinn, *The Elizabethans and the Irish* (Ithaca, N.Y., 1966), 115.

25. Quoted in Canny, "Ideology of English Colonization," 593.

26. Thomas Hariot, *A Briefe and True Report of the New Found Land of Virginia* (Frankfort-am-Main, 1590), 24–25, E1r.

27. William Waller Hening, *The Statutes at Large: Being a Collection of All the Laws of Virginia,* vol. 1 (New York, 1823), 58.

28. William Crashaw, *A Sermon Preached in London before the Right Honorable the Lord Lawarre, Lord Governour and Captaine Generall of Virginea, and Others of His Majesties Counsell for That Kingdome, and the Rest of the Adventurers in That Plantation* (London, 1610), G3v (spelling modernized).

29. Stanley L. Engerman and Robert E. Gallman, eds., *The Cambridge Economic History of the United States,* vol. 1: *The Colonial Era* (New York, 1996), 261.

30. W[illiam] S[ymonds], *The Proceedings of the English Colonie in Virginia since Their First Beginning from England in the Yeare of Our Lord 1606, till This Present 1612* (Oxford, 1612), 45.

31. Ibid., 237 (spelling modernized).

32. Susan Myra Kingsbury, ed., *The Records of the Virginia Company of London,* vol. 3 (Washington, D.C., 1933), 14–15 (spelling modernized).

33. Raphe Hamor, *A True Discourse of the Present Estate of Virginia, and the Success of the Affairs There till the 18 of June, 1614* (London, 1615), 6–11, 54.

34. Ibid., 13–14.

35. Alden T. Vaughan, *American Genesis: Captain John Smith and the Founding of Virginia* (Boston, 1975), 111; Edmund S. Morgan, *American Slavery, American Freedom: The Ordeal of Colonial Virginia* (New York, 1975), 100–101.

36. J. Frederick Fausz, "Opechancanough: Indian Resistance Leader," in David G. Sweet and Gary B. Nash, eds., *Struggle and Survival in Colonial America* (Berkeley, Calif., 1981), 21–37.

37. Samuel Purchas, *Purchas His Pilgrimes* (London, 1625), vol. 4, 1813 (spelling modernized).

5. Native Americans and the Power of Trade

1. The following ten paragraphs are adapted from Daniel K. Richter, "Tsenacommacah and the Atlantic World," in Peter C. Mancall, ed., *The Atlantic World and Virginia, 1550–1624* (Chapel Hill, N.C., 2007), 29–65.

2. Clifford M. Lewis and Albert J. Loomie, *The Spanish Jesuit Mission in Virginia, 1570–1572* (Chapel Hill, N.C., 1953), 13.

3. Ibid., 133, 131, 118.

4. Ibid., 131–133.

5. [John] Smith, *A True Relation of Such Occurrences and Accidents of Noate as Hath Hapned in Virginia since the First Planting of That Collony* (London, 1608), C2v, C4v–D1; W[illiam] S[ymonds], *The Proceedings of the English Colonie in Virginia since Their First Beginning from England in the Yeare of Our Lord 1606, till This Present 1612* (Oxford, 1612), 54 (spelling modernized in both quotations).

6. Mark Nicholls, ed., "George Percy's 'Trew Relacyon,'" *Virginia Magazine of History and Biography,* 113 (2005), 244–245, 247; William Strachey, *The Historie of Travell into Virginia Britania (1612),* ed. Louis B. Wright and Virginia Freund (London, 1953), 85–86 (spelling modernized in both quotations).

7. Raphe [Ralph] Hamor, *A True Discourse of the Present Estate of Virginia, and the Success of the Affaires There till the 18 of June, 1614* (London, 1615), 41–45 (spelling modernized).

8. John Smith, *The Generall Historie of Virginia, New-England, and the Summer Isles* (London, 1624), 123.

9. Symonds, *Proceedings of the English Colonie,* 17.

10. Roger Williams, *A Key into the Language of America* (London, 1643), 38.

11. Harold Adams Innis, *The Cod Fisheries: The History of an International Economy* (New Haven, Conn., 1940), 16; David B. Quinn, *North America from Earliest Discovery to First Settlements: The Norse Voyages to 1612* (New York, 1977), 517, 528; George Louis Beer, *The Origins of the British Colonial System, 1578–1660* (New York, 1908), 288–292.

12. Reuben Gold Thwaites, ed., *The Jesuit Relations and Allied Documents: Travels and Explorations of the Jesuit Missionaries in New France, 1610–1791* (Cleveland, Ohio, 1896–1901), vol. 6, 295–297.

13. H. P. Biggar, gen. ed. and trans., *The Works of Samuel de Champlain* (Toronto, 1922–1936), vol. 2, 96, 129.

14. René Laudonnière, *Three Voyages* (1586), trans. Charles E. Bennett (Tuscaloosa, Ala., 2001; orig. publ. 1975), 117.

15. Thwaites, ed., *Jesuit Relations*, vol. 10, 75.

16. Quoted in W. J. Eccles, *France in America* (New York, 1972), 38.

17. Thwaites, ed., *Jesuit Relations*, vol. 7, 239–241.

18. Ibid., 255.

19. Ibid., vol. 10, 27; vol. 15, 157.

20. Engel Sluiter, "The Dutch Archives and American Historical Research," *Pacific Historical Review*, 6 (1937), 26n. Exchange values are calculated from John J. McCusker, *Money and Exchange in Europe and America, 1600–1775: A Handbook* (Chapel Hill, N.C., 1978), 44, 52.

21. J. Franklin Jameson, ed., *Narratives of New Netherland* (New York, 1909), 18.

22. Thwaites, ed., *Jesuit Relations*, vol. 1, 287.

23. Charles T. Gehring and William A. Starna, trans. and eds., *A Journey into Mohawk and Oneida Country, 1634–1635: The Journal of Harmen Meyndertsz van den Bogaert* (Syracuse, N.Y., 1988), 4.

24. John W. De Forest, *History of the Connecticut Indians: From the Earliest Known Period to 1850* (Hamden, Conn., 1964; orig. publ. 1851), 70.

25. Daniel Gookin, *Historical Collections of the Indians of New England: Of Their Several Nations, Numbers, Customs, Manners, Religion and Government, before the English Planted There* (1674) (Boston, 1792), 12; Jameson, ed., *Narratives of New Netherland*, 176.

6. Epidemics, War, and the Remapping of a Continent

1. Thomas Hariot, *A Briefe and True Report of the New Found Land of Virginia* (Frankfort-am-Main, 1590), 24–30.

2. Reuben Gold Thwaites, ed., *The Jesuit Relations and Allied Documents: Travels and Explorations of the Jesuit Missionaries in New France, 1610–1791* (Cleveland, Ohio, 1896–1901), vol. 3, 103.

3. Quoted in Helen C. Rountree, *Pocahontas's People: The Powhatan Indians of Virginia through Four Centuries* (Norman, Okla., 1990), 64.

4. William Bradford, *Of Plymouth Plantation, 1620–1647,* ed. Samuel Eliot Morison (New York, 1952), 270.

5. Thwaites, ed., *Jesuit Relations,* vol. 15, 41.

6. Adrian van der Donck, "Description of the New Netherlands," trans. Jeremiah Johnson (2nd ed., 1656), *New York Historical Society Collections,* 2nd ser., vol. 1 (1841), 183.

7. Ibid., vol. 19, 89–91.

8. Thwaites, ed., *Jesuit Relations,* vol. 28, 111; vol. 22, 305.

9. Isaac Jogues to Charles-Jacques Hualt de Montmagny, 30 June 1643, in Felix Martin, *The Life of Father Isaac Jogues, Missionary Priest of the Society of Jesus . . . ,* trans. John Gilmary Shea (New York, 1885), 134.

10. Joyce Marshall, trans. and ed., *Word from New France: The Selected Letters of Marie de l'Incarnation* (Toronto, 1967), 255.

11. Henry R. Schoolcraft, *Notes on the Iroquois; Or, Contributions to the Statistics, Aboriginal History, Antiquities, and General Ethnology of Western New York* (New York, 1846), 29.

12. Henry S. Burrage, ed., *Early English and French Voyages Chiefly from Hakluyt, 1534–1608* (New York, 1906), 330, 339, 368, 371.

13. Ibid., 403.

14. [William Bradford, Edward Winslow, and Robert Cushman], *A Relation or Journall of the Beginning and Proceedings of the English Plantation Setled at Plimoth in New England* (London, 1622), 6.

15. Ibid., 32.

16. Neal Salisbury, *Manitou and Providence: Indians, Europeans, and the Making of New England, 1500–1643* (New York, 1982), 101–105.

17. Bradford, *Of Plymouth Plantation,* 80–81.

18. Bradford et al., *Relation or Journall,* 45.

19. John Josselyn, *An Account of Two Voyages to New-England* (London, 1674), 146, 143.

20. Bradford, *Of Plymouth Plantation,* 94.

21. Ibid., 330.

22. Michael Leroy Oberg, *Uncas: First of the Mohegans* (Ithaca, N.Y., 2003), 37.

23. Bradford, *Of Plymouth Plantation,* 203.

24. Richard S. Dunn and Laetitia Yeandle, eds., *The Journal of John Winthrop, 1630–1649,* abridged ed. (Cambridge, Mass., 1996), 75.

25. James Kendall Hosmer, ed., *Winthrop's Journal: "History of New England"* (New York, 1908), vol. 1, 89.

26. Dunn and Yeandle, eds., *Journal of John Winthrop,* 98.

27. Ibid., 99.

28. Quoted in Alfred A. Cave, *The Pequot War* (Amherst, Mass., 1996), 150.

29. Quoted in Francis Jennings, *The Invasion of America: Indians, Colonialism, and the Cant of Conquest* (Chapel Hill, N.C., 1975), 223.

30. John Underhill, *Newes from America* (London, 1638), 39–40 (spelling modernized).

31. Bradford, *Of Plymouth Plantation*, 296.

7. Searching for Order in New and Old England

1. John Underhill, *Newes from America* (London, 1638).

2. William Bradford, *Of Plymouth Plantation, 1620–1647*, ed. Samuel Eliot Morison (New York, 1952); *Winthrop Papers*, vol. 2 ([Boston], 1931), 295; Richard S. Dunn and Laetitia Yeandle, eds., *The Journal of John Winthrop, 1630–1649*, abridged ed. (Cambridge, Mass., 1996), 10; William Wood, *New England's Prospect*, ed. Alden T. Vaughan (Amherst, Mass., 1977), 16.

3. John Smith, *A Description of New England* (London, 1616), 31.

4. Figures compiled from Henry A. Gemery, "Emigration from the British Isles to the New World, 1630–1700: Inferences from Colonial Populations," *Research in Economic History*, 5 (1980), 197, 204–205; E. A. Wrigley and R. S. Schofield, *The Population History of England, 1541–1871* (Cambridge, Mass., 1981), 219–224; Bernard Bailyn, *The Peopling of British North America: An Introduction* (New York, 1986), 25–26; Russell R. Menard, "British Migration to the Chesapeake Colonies in the Seventeenth Century," in Lois Green Carr, Philip D. Morgan, and Jean B. Russo, eds., *Colonial Chesapeake Society* (Chapel Hill, N.C., 1988), 105; and Alison Games, *Migration and the Origins of the English Atlantic World* (Cambridge, Mass., 1999), 14.

5. Wrigley and Schofield, *Population History of England*, 208–209.

6. Robert Gray, *A Good Speed to Virginia* (London, 1609), B3v.

7. Wrigley and Schofield, *Population History of England*, 208–209.

8. *Collections of the Maine Historical Society*, 2nd ser., vol. 2 (1877), 160–161.

9. [James VI and I], *The True Lawe of Free Monarchies; Or, The Reciprock and Mutuall Dutie Betwixt a Free King, and His Naturall Subjects* (London, 1603), [C5r–v], [C7v–C8r], D1r.

10. Ibid., B3v.

11. Dunn and Yeandle, eds., *Journal of Winthrop*, 1–2, 10.

12. *The Holy Bible, Conteyning the Old Testament, and the New . . . Appointed To Be Read in Churches* (London, 1611).

13. [Edward Johnson], *A History of New-England* (London, 1654 [i.e. 1653]),

1–3. This book is usually known by the title on its first page of text, "Wonder-Working Providence of Sions Saviour, in New England."

14. Dunn and Yeandle, eds., *Journal of Winthrop*, 10.

15. Johnson, *History of New England*, 16.

16. *Winthrop Papers*, vol. 2, 114.

17. [William Bradford, Edward Winslow, and Robert Cushman], *A Relation or Journall of the Beginning and Proceedings of the English Plantation Setled at Plimoth in New England* (London, 1622), 70–71 (spelling modernized).

8. Planting Patriarchy in New England and Virginia

1. Nathaniel B. Shurtleff, ed., *Records of the Governor and Company of the Massachusetts Bay in New England*, vol. 1 (Boston, 1853), 5, 1–12, 17 (spelling modernized).

2. Virginia DeJohn Anderson, *New England's Generation: The Great Migration and the Formation of Society and Culture in the Seventeenth Century* (New York, 1991), 18n.

3. [Edward Johnson], *A History of New-England* (London, 1654 [i.e., 1653]), 27. This book is usually known by the title on its first page of text, "Wonder-Working Providence of Sions Saviour, in New England."

4. John Smith, *Advertisements for the Unexperienced Planters of New-England, or Any Where* (London, 1631), 29.

5. Shurtleff, ed., *Records of Massachusetts Bay*, vol. 1, 5.

6. Ibid., 37b, 43.

7. *Winthrop Papers*, vol. 2 ([Boston], 1931), 140–141 (spelling modernized).

8. Anderson, *New England's Generation*, 222–226.

9. T. H. Breen and Stephen Foster, "Moving to the New World: The Character of Early Massachusetts Immigration," *William and Mary Quarterly*, 3rd ser., vol. 30 (1973), 216.

10. Quoted in Francis J. Bremer, *The Puritan Experiment: New England Society from Bradford to Edwards* (New York, 1976), 58–59.

11. Shurtleff, ed., *Records of Massachusetts Bay*, vol. 1, 167.

12. Richard S. Dunn and Laetitia Yeandle, eds., *The Journal of John Winthrop, 1630–1649*, abridged ed. (Cambridge, Mass., 1996), 70.

13. John Josselyn, *An Account of Two Voyages to New-England* (London, 1674),19–20.

14. Michael P. Winship, *Making Heretics: Militant Protestantism and Free Grace in Massachusetts, 1636–1641* (Princeton, N.J., 2002), 60, 63.

15. Ibid., 1.

16. Shurtleff, ed., *Records of Massachusetts Bay*, vol. 1, 211–212.

17. "Letter of Sir Francis Wyatt, Governor of Virginia, 1621–1626," *William and Mary Quarterly*, 2nd ser., vol. 6 (1926), 118.

18. *The Bible Translated According to the Ebrew and Greeke, and Conferred with the Best Translations in Divers Languages* (London, 1607 [STC no. 2201]), Numbers 33:50–52, 55; Joshua 9:15, 26–27.

19. Ibid., Numbers 33:55–56.

20. Edmund S. Morgan, *American Slavery, American Freedom: The Ordeal of Colonial Virginia* (Chapel Hill, N.C., 1975), 108–130; James Horn, *Adapting to a New World: English Society in the Seventeenth-Century Chesapeake* (Chapel Hill, N.C., 1994), 259–260.

21. William Bullock, *Virginia Impartially Examined . . .* (London, 1649), 11.

22. John Hammond, *Leah and Rachel; Or, The Two Fruitfull Sisters Virginia and Mary-land: Their Present Condition, Impartially Stated and Related* (London, 1656), 5.

23. *A Perfect Description of Virginia* (London, 1649), 12 (spelling modernized).

24. Horn, *Adapting to a New World*, 36–38; John J. McCusker and Russell R. Menard, *The Economy of British America, 1607–1789* (Chapel Hill, N.C., 1985), 136; *Perfect Description of Virginia*, 1 (quotation).

25. Hammond, *Leah and Rachel*, 8.

26. Ibid., 7.

27. *Perfect Description of Virginia*, 11, 6.

28. Ibid., 11.

9. Dutch, French, Spanish, and English Counterpoints

1. *A Perfect Description of Virginia* (London, 1649), 15.

2. Albert Cook Myers, ed., *Narratives of Early Pennsylvania, West New Jersey and Delaware, 1630–1707* (New York, 1912), 96–97, 120, 157n; Stellan Dahlgren and Hans Norman, *The Rise and Fall of New Sweden: Governor Johan Risingh's Journal, 1654–1655, in Its Historical Context* (Uppsala, 1988), 185–187; Amandus Johnson, *Swedish Settlements on the Delaware, 1638–1664* (Philadelphia, 1911), 317–318, 332, 516.

3. Richard S. Dunn, *Sugar and Slaves: The Rise of the Planter Class in the English West Indies, 1624–1713* (Chapel Hill, N.C., 1972), 46–83; John J. McCusker and Russell R. Menard, *The Economy of British America, 1607–1789* (Chapel Hill, N.C., 1985), 151, 153.

4. Oliver A. Rink, *Holland on the Hudson: An Economic and Social History of Dutch New York* (Ithaca, N.Y., 1986), 160–164; Ira Berlin, *Many Thousands Gone: The First Two Centuries of Slavery in North America* (Cambridge, Mass., 1998), 18–22, 29, 50–51; McCusker and Menard, *Economy*

of British America, 136, 103; Jaap Jacobs, *New Netherland: A Dutch Colony in Seventeenth-Century America* (Leiden, Netherlands, 2005), 313; Andrew L. Knaut, *The Pueblo Revolt of 1680: Conquest and Resistance in Seventeenth-Century New Mexico* (Norman, Okla., 1995), 133–135.

5. Quoted in Jacobs, *New Netherland,* 47.

6. Peter N. Moogk, "Reluctant Exiles: Emigrants from France in Canada before 1760," *William and Mary Quarterly,* 3rd ser., vol. 46 (1989), 497.

7. Quoted in Louise Dechêne, *Habitants and Merchants in Seventeenth-Century Montreal,* trans. Liana Vardi (Montreal, 1992), 25–26.

8. Reuben Gold Thwaites, ed., *The Jesuit Relations and Allied Documents: Travels and Explorations of the Jesuit Missionaries in New France, 1610–1791* (Cleveland, Ohio, 1896–1901), vol. 45, 181–183.

9. Ibid., 190.

10. Amy Turner Bushnell, *Situado and Sabana: Spain's Support System for the Presidio and Mission Provinces of Florida,* Anthropological Papers of the American Museum of Natural History, 74 (1994), 44, 47; John McCusker, *Money and Exchange in Europe and America, 1600–1775: A Handbook* (Chapel Hill, 1978), 100–103; Theodore G. Corbett, "Migration to a Spanish Imperial Frontier in the Seventeenth and Eighteenth Centuries: St. Augustine," *Hispanic American Historical Review,* 54 (1974), 414–430.

11. Paul E. Hoffman, *Florida's Frontiers* (Bloomington, Ind., 2002), 110.

12. Quoted in David J. Weber, *The Spanish Frontier in North America* (New Haven, Conn., 1992), 109.

13. Knaut, *Pueblo Revolt,* 17.

14. Kurt E. Dongoske and Cindy K. Dongoske, "History in Stone: Evaluating Spanish Conversion Efforts through Hopi Rock Art," in Robert W. Preucel, ed., *Archaeologies of the Pueblo Revolt: Identity, Meaning, and Renewal in the Pueblo World* (Albuquerque, N.M., 2002), 118.

15. Quoted ibid., 9–10.

16. Henry Scobell, *A Collection of Acts and Ordinances of General Use, Made in the Parliament* (London, 1658), 176.

17. [Benjamin Worsley], *The Advocate* (London, 1651), 1–2 (brackets in original).

18. Quoted in Karen Ordahl Kupperman, "Errand to the Indies: Puritan Colonization from Providence Island through the Western Design," *William and Mary Quarterly,* 3rd ser., vol. 45 (1988), 93.

19. Carla Gardina Pestana, *The English Atlantic in an Age of Revolution, 1640–1661* (Cambridge, Mass., 2004), 178, 202.

20. I.S., "an eye-witnesse," *A Brief and Perfect Journal of the Late Proceedings and Successe of the English Army in the West-Indies, Continued until June the 24th 1655* (London, 1655), 13, 16–17.

21. Carla Gardina Pestana, "English Character and the Fiasco of the Western Design," *Early American Studies*, 3 (2005), 1.

22. William Hilton, *A Relation of a Discovery Lately Made on the Coast of Florida* (London, 1664), 2–3.

23. *A Brief Description of the Province of Carolina on the Coasts of Floreda . . .* (London, 1666), 1.

24. *The Fundamental Constitutions of Carolina* ([London, 1670]), 1–6.

25. Ibid., 20–23.

10. Monarchical Power Reborn

1. *King Charles II, His Declaration to All His Loving Subjects . . . , the 4/14 of April 1660* (Edinburgh, 1660).

2. *The Book of Common Prayer* (London, 1662 [Wing no. B3622A]), n.p.; John Durel, *The Liturgy of the Church of England Asserted in a Sermon* (London, 1662), 10, 36.

3. Cecil T. Carr, ed., *Select Charters of Trading Companies, a.d. 1530–1707* (London, 1913), 180.

4. P. E. H. Hair and Robin Law, "The English in West Africa to 1700," in Wm. Roger Louis, ed.-in-chief, *The Oxford History of the British Empire*, vol. 1: *The Origins of Empire*, ed. Nicholas Canny (Oxford, 2001), 255–256; Company of Royal Adventurers Trading into Africa [to the King], [1665], C.O. 1/17, no. 110, The National Archives, Kew, England.

5. Peter R. Christoph and Florence A. Christoph, eds., *New York Historical Manuscripts: English: Books of General Entries of the Colony of New York, 1664–1673* (Baltimore, 1982), 1.

6. Quoted in Robert C. Ritchie, *The Duke's Province: A Study of New York Politics and Society, 1664–1691* (Chapel Hill, N.C., 1977), 13 (spelling modernized).

7. Quoted ibid., 21–22.

8. E. B. O'Callaghan and B. Fernow, eds., *Documents Relative to the Colonial History of the State of New York* (Albany, N.Y., 1853–1887), vol. 3, 57.

9. Ritchie, *Duke's Province*, 17.

10. Christoph and Christoph, eds., *New York Historical Manuscripts, 1664–1673*, 2.

11. Ibid., 4.

12. *The Colonial Laws of New York, from the Year 1664 to the Revolution*, vol. 1 (Albany, 1896), 6–71.

13. Ibid., 24–26, 42, 20.

14. Ibid., 18.

15. Ibid., 40–42.

16. O'Callaghan and Fernow, eds., *Documents Relative to New York,* vol. 3, 58.

17. Robert Latham and William Matthews, eds., *The Diary of Samuel Pepys* (Berkeley, Calif., 1970–1983), vol. 5, 286.

18. Reuben Gold Thwaites, ed., *The Jesuit Relations and Allied Documents: Travels and Explorations of the Jesuit Missionaries in New France, 1610–1791* (Cleveland, Ohio, 1896–1901), vol. 55, 105–113.

19. Emma Helen Blair, ed. and trans., *The Indian Tribes of the Upper Mississippi Valley and Region of the Great Lakes* (Cleveland, Ohio, 1911–1912), vol. 1, 347.

20. B. F. French, ed., *Historical Collections of Louisiana, Embracing Many Rare and Valuable Documents Relating to the Natural, Civil and Political History of That State,* Part 1 (New York, 1846), 45–50.

21. Thwaites, ed. *Jesuit Relations,* vol. 21, 117.

22. O'Callaghan and Fernow, eds., *Documents Relative to New York,* vol. 9, 25–26.

23. John J. McCusker, *Money and Exchange in Europe and America, 1600–1775: A Handbook* (Chapel Hill, N.C., 1978), 157, 157n; O'Callaghan and Fernow, eds., *Documents Relative to New York,* vol. 14, 450.

24. A. J. F. Van Laer, trans. and ed., *Correspondence of Jeremias van Rensselaer, 1651–1674* (Albany, N.Y., 1932), 325–326.

25. Joyce Marshall, ed. and trans., *Word from New France: The Selected Letters of Marie de l'Incarnation* (Toronto, 1967), 317–328.

26. Thwaites, ed., *Jesuit Relations,* vol. 57, 25.

27. Quoted in Francis Jennings, "Glory, Death, and Transfiguration: The Susquehannock Indians in the Seventeenth Century," *Proceedings of the American Philosophical Society,* 112 (1968), 27.

28. O'Callaghan and Fernow, eds., *Documents Relative to New York,* vol. 12, 493–494 (spelling modernized).

29. Victor Hugo Paltsits, ed., *Minutes of the Executive Council of the Province of New York: Administration of Francis Lovelace, 1668–1673* (Albany, N.Y., 1910), vol. 2, 502.

30. William Hand Browne, ed., *Archives of Maryland,* vol. 2 (Baltimore, 1883), 428.

11. Planters Besieged

1. *Strange News from Virginia: Being a Full and True Account of the Life and Death of Nathanael Bacon Esquire, Who Was the Only Cause and Original of All the Late Troubles in That Country* (London, 1677); Charles M. Andrews, ed., *Narratives of the Insurrections, 1675–1690* (New York, 1915), 40, 108–111.

2. Andrews, ed., *Narratives of the Insurrections,* 17–18.

3. Ibid., 26; 1 Samuel 22:22 (King James Version).

4. Andrews, ed., *Narratives of the Insurrections,* 16–18.

5. Ibid., 107–108.

6. Ibid., 50.

7. *Strange News from Virginia,* 8.

8. Andrews, ed., *Narratives of the Insurrections,* 110–111.

9. Quoted in Paul Kelton, *Epidemics and Enslavement: Biological Catastrophe in the Native Southeast, 1493–1715* (Lincoln, Neb., 2007), 115.

10. Andrews, ed., *Narratives of the Insurrections,* 116.

11. Ibid., 116–117.

12. Ibid., 54, 70.

13. Ibid., 139.

14. Wilcomb E. Washburn, ed., "Sir William Berkeley's 'A History of Our Miseries,'" *William and Mary Quarterly,* 3rd Ser., vol. 14 (1957), 412.

15. Andrews, ed., *Narratives of the Insurrections,* 52 (spelling modernized).

16. [William Berkeley], *A Discourse and View of Virginia* (n.p., 1663?), 9.

17. Quoted in Edmund S. Morgan, *American Slavery, American Freedom: The Ordeal of Colonial Virginia* (New York,, 1975), 312.

18. Andrews, ed., *Narratives of the Insurrections,* 58–59, 52 (spelling modernized).

19. Ibid., 59 (spelling modernized).

20. Berkeley, *Discourse and View of Virginia,* 11.

21. Andrews, ed., *Narratives of the Insurrections,* 20.

22. Berkeley, *Discourse and View of Virginia,* 6–7.

23. Quoted in James Horn, *Adapting to a New World: English Society in the Seventeenth-Century Chesapeake* (Chapel Hill, N.C., 1994), 156. John J. McCusker and Russell R. Menard, *The Economy of British America, 1607–1789* (Chapel Hill, N.C., 1985), 123, warns against attributing too much influence to the Navigation Acts in the fall of tobacco prices. Nonetheless it seems clear that many people at the time made precisely that attribution.

24. Quoted in T. H. Breen, "A Changing Labor Force and Race Relations in Virginia, 1660–1710," *Journal of Social History,* 7 (1973–1974), 4.

25. Andrews, ed., *Narratives of the Insurrections,* 113.

26. Ibid., 39–40.

27. Ibid., 25–27.

28. Ibid., 127–128.

29. *Virginia Magazine of History and Biography,* 14 (1907), 291–292.

30. Quoted in Martha W. McCartney, "Cockacoeske, Queen of Pamunkey," in Gregory A. Waselkov, Peter H. Wood, and Tom Hatley, eds., *Powhatan's*

Mantle: Indians in the Colonial Southeast, rev. ed. (Lincoln, Neb., 2006), 254.

31. David Pulsifer, ed., *Records of the Colony of New Plymouth in New England* (Boston, 1855–1861), vol. 3, 192.

32. Andrews, ed., *Narratives of the Insurrections,* 113.

33. Pulsifer, ed., *Records of the Colony of New Plymouth,* vol. 4, 164 (spelling modernized).

34. Henry Whitfield, "Strength Out of Weaknesse; Or, A Glorious Manifestation of the Further Progresse of the Gospel among the Indians of New-England" (1652), *Collections of the Massachusetts Historical Society,* 3d ser., vol. 4 (1834), 165.

35. Daniel Gookin, *Historical Collections of the Indians of New England: Of Their Several Nations, Numbers, Customs, Manners, Religion and Government, before the English Planted There* (Boston, 1792; orig. pub. 1674), 40–67 (quotation from p. 42); Alden T. Vaughan and Daniel K. Richter, "Crossing the Cultural Divide: Indians and New Englanders, 1605–1763," *Proceedings of the American Antiquarian Society,* 90 (1980), 33–35.

36. Increase Mather, *An Earnest Exhortation to the Inhabitants of New-England* (Boston, 1676), 9.

37. Charles H. Lincoln, ed., *Narratives of the Indian Wars, 1675–1699* (New York, 1913), 9–11 (spelling modernized).

38. Pulsifer, ed., *Records of the Colony of New Plymouth,* vol. 5, 76, 79.

39. Lincoln, ed., *Narratives of the Indian Wars,* 7.

40. Douglas Edward Leach, *Flintlock and Tomahawk: New England in King Philip's War* (New York, 1958), 243.

41. [Benjamin Church], *Entertaining Passages Relating to Philip's War* (Boston, 1716), 45.

42. Ibid., 52.

43. Leach, *Flintlock and Tomahawk,* 243–244; James D. Drake, *King Philip's War: Civil War in New England, 1675–1676* (Amherst, Mass., 1999), 168–169.

44. E. B. O'Callaghan and B. Fernow, eds., *Documents Relative to the Colonial History of the State of New York* (Albany, N.Y., 1853–1887), vol. 3, 271–272.

45. Ibid., vol. 3, 254.

46. T. H. Breen, *Puritans and Adventurers: Change and Persistence in Early America* (New York, 1980), 88.

47. Quoted ibid., 89.

48. O'Callaghan and Fernow, eds., *Documents Relative to New York,* vol. 3, 543–549.

49. *The Prince of Orange His Declaration: Showing the Reasons Why He Invades England* (London, 1688 [Wing no. 2231]), 12–13.

12. Revolution, War, and a New Transatlantic Order

1. House of Lords Journal, January 12, 1710, www.british-history.ac.uk/report.asp?compid=29796 (accessed December 12, 2010).
2. *Anno Regni Gulielmi et Mariæ, Regis et Reginæ . . . On the Sixteenth Day of December, Anno Dom. 1689 . . . This Act Passed the Royal Assent* (Dublin, 1695), 3–6.
3. Ibid., 12–13.
4. *The Declaration of the Estates of the Kingdom of Scotland* (Edinburgh, 1689), 3.
5. Andrew Browning, ed., *English Historical Documents, 1660–1714*, 2nd ed. (London, 1966), 401–403.
6. *Poems on Affairs of State, from 1640, to This Present Year 1704: Written by the Greatest Wits of the Age* ([London?], 1704), vol. 3, 317.
7. *The Declaration of the Reasons and Motives for the Present Appearing in Arms of Their Majesties Protestant Subjects in the Province of Maryland* (London, 1689), 6.
8. "Propositions to Indians of New York, 29 Apr. 1688," New York Colonial Manuscripts, vol. 35, folio 148, New York State Archives, Albany (trans. A. J. F. Van Laer, on file with the New Netherland Project at the New York State Library, Albany); E. B. O'Callaghan and B. Fernow, eds., *Documents Relative to the Colonial History of the State of New York* (Albany, N.Y., 1853–1887), vol. 3, 428–430, 558 (spelling modernized in both quotations).
9. *The Declaration, of the Gentlemen, Merchants, and Inhabitants of Boston, and the Countrey Adjacent* (Boston, 1689), n.p.; O'Callaghan and Fernow, eds., *Documents Relative to New York*, vol. 3, 738.
10. *Declaration of Boston*, n.p.
11. *Declaration of Reasons and Motives*, 6–7.
12. *Declaration of Boston*, n.p.
13. Ibid.
14. "Instrument of Cecil Lord Baltimore, Nov. 24, 1666," C.O. 1/20, no. 181, The National Archives, Kew, England; "Answer of the Governor and Council of Virginia" [1667], C.O. 1/21, no. 65, ibid.
15. *Declaration of Reasons and Motives*, 7.
16. "An Act for Granting to Theire Majesties Severall Rates and Duties, 1694," www.british-history.ac.uk/report.asp?compid=46414 (accessed December 12, 2010).

17. O'Callaghan and Fernow, eds., *Documents Relative to New York,* vol. 3, 605.

18. Ibid., 623–629.

19. Ibid.

20. Ibid., vol. 4, 508.

21. Peter H. Wood, *Black Majority: Negroes in Colonial South Carolina from 1670 through the Stono Rebellion* (Chapel Hill, N.C., 1974), 13.

22. William L. Ramsey, *The Yamasee War: A Study of Culture, Economy, and Conflict in the Colonial South* (Lincoln, Neb., 2008), 36–37.

23. Ibid., 228.

13. Producing and Consuming in an Atlantic Empire

1. John J. McCusker and Russell R. Menard, *The Economy of British America, 1607–1789* (Chapel Hill, N.C., 1985), 119–125.

2. Jacob M. Price, "The Imperial Economy, 1700–1776," in Wm. Roger Louis, ed.-in-chief, *The Oxford History of the British Empire,* vol. 2: *The Eighteenth Century,* ed. P. J. Marshall (Oxford, 2001), 103; McCusker and Menard, *Economy of British America,* 54.

3. [Thomas Paine], *Common Sense; Addressed to the Inhabitants of America* (Philadelphia, 1776 [Evans no. 14959]), 15.

4. Quoted in McCusker and Menard, *Economy of British America,* 73.

5. Ibid., 175–176.

6. Gary B. Nash, *The Urban Crucible: Social Change, Political Consciousness, and the Origins of the American Revolution* (Cambridge, Mass., 1979), 407–408, concerning Philadelphia, Boston, New York; Carl Bridenbaugh, *Cities in Revolt: Urban Life in America, 1743–1776* (New York, 1955), 5, concerning Charleston and Newport. Bridenbaugh's widely cited but inflated estimates for Philadelphia (24,000) and New York (18,000) suggest that his figures for Charleston and Newport are also too high (McCusker and Menard, *Economy of British America,* 252).

7. Kathryn E. Holland Braund, *Deerskins and Duffels: Creek Indian Trade with Anglo-America, 1685–1815* (Lincoln, Neb., 1993), 69–71.

8. Peter Wraxall, *An Abridgment of the Indian Affairs Contained in Four Folio Volumes, Transacted in the Colony of New York, from the Year 1678 to the Year 1751,* ed. Charles Howard McIlwain (Cambridge, Mass., 1915), 219n.

9. Quoted in Braund, *Deerskins and Duffels,* 30.

10. Leonard W. Labaree et al., eds., *The Autobiography of Benjamin Franklin* (New Haven, Conn., 1964), 145.

11. Quoted in David S. Shields, *Civil Tongues and Polite Letters in British America* (Chapel Hill, N.C., 1997), 114.

12. Jacob M. Price, "The Imperial Economy," in Marshall, ed., *Oxford History of the British Empire*, vol. 2, 87, 103; P. K. O'Brien and S. L. Engerman, "Exports and the Growth of the British Economy, from the Glorious Revolution to the Peace of Amiens," in Barbara L. Solow, ed., *Slavery and the Rise of the Atlantic System* (New York, 1991), 186; Gottlieb Mittelberger, *Journey to Pennsylvania*, ed. and trans. Oscar Handlin and John Clive (Cambridge, Mass., 1960, orig. publ. 1756), 37.

13. Albert J. Edmunds, "The First Books Imported by America's First Great Library: 1732," *Pennsylvania Magazine of History and Biography*, 30 (1906), 300–301; Labaree et al., eds., *Autobiography of Franklin*, 142.

14. *New-York Weekly Journal*, April 14, 1740; *Boston Weekly News-Letter*, April 17, 1704; *Pennsylvania Gazette*, April 17, 1740.

15. *American Weekly Mercury*, September 30, 1731.

16. *Boston Weekly News-Letter*, July 10, 1740.

14. People in Motion, Enslaved and Free

1. John J. McCusker and Russell R. Menard, *The Economy of British America, 1607–1689* (Chapel Hill, N.C., 1985), 136, 172; Philip D. Morgan, *Slave Counterpoint: Black Culture in the Eighteenth-Century Chesapeake and Lowcountry* (Chapel Hill, N.C., 1998), 61.

2. David Elitis, "The Transatlantic Slave Trade: A New Census," *William and Mary Quarterly*, 3rd ser., vol. 58 (2001), 45; Morgan, *Slave Counterpoint*, 59.

3. E. B. O'Callaghan and B. Fernow, eds., *Documents Relative to the Colonial History of the State of New York* (Albany, N.Y., 1853–1887), vol. 5, 136.

4. James G. Lydon, "New York and the Slave Trade, 1700 to 1774," *William and Mary Quarterly*, 3rd. ser., vol. 35 (1978), 393; Allan Kulikoff, *Tobacco and Slaves: The Development of Southern Cultures in the Chesapeake, 1680–1800* (Chapel Hill, N.C., 1986), 134; Peter Mancall et al., "Slave Prices and the South Carolina Economy, 1722–1809," *Journal of Economic History*, 61 (2001), 619; David Eltis, *The Rise of African Slavery in the Americas* (New York, 2000), 152.

5. Quoted in Kenneth A. Lockridge, *The Diary, and Life, of William Byrd II of Virginia, 1674–1744* (Chapel Hill, N.C., 1987), 123.

6. William St Clair, *The Door of No Return: The History of Cape Coast Castle and the Atlantic Slave Trade* (New York, 2007), 202–208.

7. Philip D. Morgan, "The Black Experience in the British Empire, 1680–1810," in Wm. Roger Louis, ed.-in-chief, *The Oxford History of the British*

Empire, vol. 2: *The Eighteenth Century,* ed. P. J. Marshall (Oxford, 2001), 476; Lorena S. Walsh, "The Chesapeake Slave Trade: Regional Patterns, African Origins, and Some Implications," *William and Mary Quarterly,* 58 (2001), 159–167.

8. Olaudah Equiano, *The Interesting Narrative of the Life of Olaudah Equiano, or Gustavus Vassa, the African,* 2nd ed. (London, 1789), vol. 1, 89–90.

9. Nathan Irvin Huggins, *Black Odyssey: The Afro-American Ordeal in Slavery* (New York, 1977), xiv.

10. [Daniel Horsmanden], *A Journal of the Proceedings in the Detection of the Conspiracy Formed by Some White People, in Conjunction with Negro and Other Slaves, for Burning the City of New-York in America, and Murdering the Inhabitants* (New York, 1744), 205.

11. John Milton, *Paradise Lost: A Poem Written in Ten Books* (London, 1667), Book 2, lines 296–307.

12. Susan E. Klepp and Billy G. Smith, eds., *The Infortunate: The Voyage and Adventures of William Moraley, an Indentured Servant,* 2nd ed. (University Park, Pa., 2005), 28 (brackets in original).

13. Ibid., 57.

14. Susan E. Klepp, "Encounter and Experiment: The Colonial Period," in Randall M. Miller and William Pencak, eds., *Pennsylvania: A History of the Commonwealth* (University Park, Pa., 2002), 61–65; Aaron Spencer Fogleman, *Hopeful Journeys: German Immigration, Settlement, and Political Culture in Colonial America, 1717–1775* (Philadelphia, 1996), 5.

15. Fogleman, *Hopeful Journeys,* 135.

16. Gottlieb Mittelberger, *Journey to Pennsylvania,* ed. and trans. Oscar Handlin and John Clive (Cambridge, Mass., 1960, orig. publ. 1756), 48.

17. Klepp and Smith, eds., *The Infortunate,* 52–53.

18. *Some Account of the Designs of the Trustees for Establishing the Colony of Georgia in America* (London, 1732), 1–2.

19. Aaron S. Fogleman, "Migrations to the Thirteen British North American Colonies, 1700–1775: New Estimates," *Journal of Interdisciplinary History,* 22 (1992), 698; idem, "From Slaves, Convicts, and Servants to Free Passengers: The Transformation of Immigration in the Era of the American Revolution," *Journal of American History,* 85 (1998), 71.

20. Klepp and Smith, eds., *The Infortunate,* 16–17.

21. Frank Lambert, *Inventing the "Great Awakening"* (Princeton, N.J., 1999), 4 (quotation), 7.

22. Leonard W. Labaree, "George Whitefield Comes to Middletown," *William and Mary Quarterly,* 3rd ser., vol. 7 (1950), 590–591.

23. John Harman, *The Crooked Disciple's Remarks upon the Blind Guide's*

Method of Preaching, for Some Years: Being a Collection of the Principal Words . . . Made Use of by the Reverend Dr. Squintum (London, [1761]).

24. Mittelberger, *Journey to Pennsylvania*, 41.

25. Thomas Brainerd, *The Life of John Brainerd, the Brother of David Brainerd, and His Successor as Missionary to the Indians of New Jersey* (Philadelphia, 1865), 232–234, 233n.

26. Ibid., 234–239.

27. [Benjamin Franklin], "Observations Concerning the Increase of Mankind, Peopling of Countries, etc." (1751), in [William Clarke], *Observations on the Late and Present Conduct of the French, with Regard to Their Encroachments upon the British Colonies in North America* (Boston, 1755), 2–3, 13–15.

15. Contending for a Continent

1. E. B. O'Callaghan and B. Fernow, eds., *Documents Relative to the Colonial History of the State of New York* (Albany, N.Y., 1853–1887), vol. 7, 301.

2. Increase Mather, *An Earnest Exhortation to the Inhabitants of New-England* (Boston, 1676), 9.

3. O'Callaghan and Fernow, eds., *Documents Relative to New York*, vol. 7, 301.

4. Quoted in David L. Preston, *The Texture of Contact: European and Indian Settler Communities on the Frontiers of Iroquoia, 1667–1783* (Lincoln, Neb., 2009), 128–130.

5. Thomas Brainerd, *The Life of John Brainerd, the Brother of David Brainerd, and His Successor as Missionary to the Indians of New Jersey* (Philadelphia, 1865), 239.

6. O'Callaghan and Fernow, eds., *Documents Relative to New York*, vol. 7, 17.

7. James Logan to John Penn, Penn Papers, Official Correspondence, vol. 2, 21, Historical Society of Pennsylvania, Philadelphia.

8. Mary Maples Dunn and Richard S. Dunn, eds., *The Papers of William Penn* (Philadelphia, Pa., 1981–1987), vol. 2, 129; "Declaration of William Penn, Oct. 18, 1683," C.O. 1/53, no. 11, The National Archives, Kew, England.

9. *A Treaty, Held at the Town of Lancaster, in Pennsylvania . . . in June, 1744* (Philadelphia, 1744), 20, 29.

10. Ibid., 12.

11. O'Callaghan and Fernow, eds., *Documents Relative to New York*, vol. 6, 781–788.

12. Ibid., 800–801.

13. Thomas Prince, *Extraordinary Events the Doings of God, and Marvellous in Pious Eyes* (Boston, 1745), 23, 34.
14. *Independent Advertiser,* Nov. 14, 1748, reprinted in J. Revel Carr, *Seeds of Discontent: The Deep Roots of the American Revolution, 1650–1750* (New York, 2008), 337.
15. Andrew McFarland Davis, *Currency and Banking in the Province of Massachusetts-Bay,* Part 1: *Currency* (New York, 1901), 224.
16. O'Callaghan and Fernow, *Documents Relative to New York,* vol. 6, 782.
17. Ibid., 532–533.
18. Quoted in Charles A. Hanna, *The Wilderness Trail; Or, The Ventures and Adventures of the Pennsylvania Traders on the Allegheny Path* (New York, 1911), vol. 2, 292.
19. Quoted in Fred Anderson, *Crucible of War: The Seven Years' War and the Fate of Empire in British North America, 1754–1766* (New York, 2000), 57.

16. Gloomy and Dark Days

1. E. B. O'Callaghan and B. Fernow, eds., *Documents Relative to the Colonial History of the State of New York* (Albany, N.Y., 1853–1887), vol. 7, 301.
2. *Pennsylvania Gazette,* May 9, 1754.
3. W. W. Abbot, ed., "General Edward Braddock in Alexandria: John Carlyle to George Carlyle, August 15, 1755," *Virginia Magazine of History and Biography,* 97 (1989), 212.
4. Beverly W. Bond Jr., ed., "The Captivity of Charles Stuart, 1755–57," *Mississippi Valley Historical Review,* 13 (1926), 63.
5. Francis Jennings, *Empire of Fortune: Crowns, Colonies, and Tribes in the Seven Years War in America* (New York, 1988), 267–268.
6. James Sullivan et al., eds., *The Papers of Sir William Johnson* (Albany, 1921–1965), vol. 10, 43–48.
7. Fred Anderson, *Crucible of War: The Seven Years' War and the Fate of Empire in British North America, 1754–1766* (New York, 2000), 235–236.
8. Quoted ibid., 791n; *Pennsylvania Gazette,* October 25, 1759.
9. Sullivan et al., eds., *Papers of Johnson,* vol. 10, 134.
10. Ibid., 400.
11. Ibid., vol. 3, 515.
12. Quoted in Stephen P. van Hoak, "Untangling the Roots of Dependency: Choctaw Economics, 1700–1860," *American Indian Quarterly,* 23 (1999), 116.
13. Sullivan et al., eds., *Papers of Johnson,* vol. 10, 634.
14. Ibid., vol. 3, 515.

15. O'Callaghan and Fernow, eds., *Documents Relative to New York,* vol. 7, 503, 508–510.
16. Sullivan et al., eds., *Papers of Johnson,* vol. 4, 95.
17. Ibid., vol. 10, 659–660.
18. Ibid., 491.
19. *Newport Mercury,* April 25, 1763; *Boston Post-Boy,* May 2, 1763. For reprints of the first article, see *Providence Gazette,* April 30, 1763; and *Georgia Gazette,* June 9, 1763.
20. O'Callaghan and Fernow, eds., *Documents Relative to New York,* vol. 7, 520–521.
21. [Robert Navarre?], *Journal of Pontiac's Conspiracy,* ed. M. Agnes Burton, trans. R. C. Ford (Detroit, [1912]), 28–30.
22. *Pennsylvania Gazette,* August 11, 1763.
23. Ibid., October 27, 1763.
24. John R. Dunbar, ed., *The Paxton Papers* (The Hague, 1957), 193.
25. O'Callaghan and Fernow, eds., *Documents Relative to New York,* vol. 7, 567.
26. *Pennsylvania Gazette,* August 4, 1763.
27. Ibid.; John Wilkes, *The North Briton, XLVI Numbers Complete* (London, [1772]), vol. 2, 256, 259.
28. Sullivan et al., eds., *Papers of Johnson,* vol. 10, 977, 982–983.
29. O'Callaghan and Fernow, eds., *Documents Relative to New York,* vol. 7, 881.
30. Ibid., 590.
31. James Otis, *The Rights of the British Colonies Asserted and Proved* (Boston, 1764), 65, 32.
32. Ibid., 57.
33. *Boston Evening-Post,* November 21, 1763.
34. [Thomas Paine], *Common Sense; Addressed to the Inhabitants of America* (Philadelphia, 1776 [Evans no. 14959]), 15.

Epilogue: Present Pasts

1. Theodore Roosevelt, *Gouverneur Morris* (Boston, 1896), 289.
2. Albert Henry Smyth, ed., *The Writings of Benjamin Franklin,* vol. 3 (New York, 1905), 139–140.
3. *Boston Weekly News-Letter,* July 10, 1740.
4. Quoted in Alan Taylor, *The Divided Ground: Indians, Settlers, and the Northern Borderland of the American Revolution* (New York, 2006), 310.
5. James D. Richardson, *A Compilation of the Messages and Papers of the Presidents, 1789–1897* (New York, 1896–1917), vol. 2, 521.

6. *Pennsylvania Gazette,* August 29, 1754.

7. Ibid., September 19, 1754.

8. Olaudah Equiano, *The Interesting Narrative of the Life of Olaudah Equiano, or Gustavus Vassa, the African,* 2nd ed. (London, 1789), vol. 2, 268, quoting Micah 8:6.

Further Reading

A book of this scope must rely on an entire library of studies by other scholars. This brief discussion can only highlight some of the most influential. Works relevant to multiple chapters are mentioned only once, and articles in scholarly journals are not included. Among previous surveys of the general terrain, several deserve special mention: Gary B. Nash, *Red, White, and Black: The Peoples of Early America,* 5th ed. (Upper Saddle River, N.J.: Pearson Prentice Hall, 2006; orig. publ. 1974); Alan Taylor, *American Colonies* (New York: Viking, 2001); James Axtell, *The Invasion Within: The Contest of Cultures in Colonial North America* (New York: Oxford University Press, 1985); Jack P. Greene, *Pursuits of Happiness: The Social Development of Early Modern British Colonies and the Formation of American Culture* (Chapel Hill: University of North Carolina Press, 1988); W. J. Eccles, *The French in North America, 1500–1763,* rev. ed. (East Lansing: Michigan State University Press, 1998; orig. publ. 1972); J. H. Elliott, *Empires of the Atlantic World: Britain and Spain in America, 1492–1830* (New Haven, Conn.: Yale University Press, 2006); David J. Weber, *The Spanish Frontier in North America* (New Haven, Conn.: Yale University Press, 1992); Colin G. Calloway, *Once Vast Winter Count: The Native American West before Lewis and Clark* (Lincoln: University of Nebraska Press, 2003); and Ira Berlin, *Many Thousands Gone: The First Two Centuries of Slavery in North America* (Cambridge, Mass.: Harvard University Press, 1998).

Progenitors

The most accessible introduction to medieval North America is Charles C. Mann, *1491: New Revelations of the Americas before Columbus* (New York: Knopf, 2005). For collections of scholarly perspectives, see Alvin M. Josephy Jr., ed., *America in 1492: The World of the Indian Peoples before the Arrival of Columbus* (New York: Vintage Books, 1992); and Bruce G. Trigger and Wilcomb E. Washburn, eds., *The Cambridge History of the Native Peoples of the Americas,* vol. 1: *North America* (Cambridge: Cambridge University Press, 1996). A broad survey of climate change in this period is Brian Fagan, *The Little Ice Age: How Climate Made History, 1300–1850* (New York: Basic Books, 2000). On developments in the Southwest, see Fagan, *Chaco Canyon: Archaeologists Explore the Lives of an Ancient Society* (New York: Oxford University Press, 2005); Stephen H. Lekson, *The Chaco Meridian: Centers of Political Power in the Ancient Southwest* (Walnut Creek, Calif.: AltaMira Press, 1999); and Steven A. LeBlanc, *Prehistoric Warfare in the American Southwest* (Salt Lake City: University of Utah Press, 1999). Works on the Mississippians include Charles Hudson, *The Southeastern Indians* (Knoxville: University of Tennessee Press, 1976); Mark W. Mehrer, *Cahokia's Countryside: Household Archaeology, Settlement Patterns, and Social Power* (De Kalb: Northern Illinois University Press, 1995); Thomas E. Emerson, *Cahokia and the Archaeology of Power* (Tuscaloosa: University of Alabama Press, 1997); and Timothy R. Pauketat, *Ancient Cahokia and the Mississippians* (Cambridge: Cambridge University Press, 2004).

Sound introductions to the social, economic, and cultural histories of medieval Europe are found in two massive collections: Paul Fouracre et al., *The New Cambridge Medieval History* (Cambridge: Cambridge University Press, 1995–2005); and M. M. Postan et al., eds., *The Cambridge Economic History of Europe,* vols. 1–4 (Cambridge: Cambridge University Press, 1965–1967). On agricultural developments, the foundational study is Georges Duby, *Rural Economy and Country Life in the Medieval West,* trans. Cynthia Postan (Columbia: University of South Carolina Press, 1968). On epidemics, see William H. McNeill, *Plagues and Peoples* (Garden City, N.Y.: Anchor Press, 1976); and John Kelly, *The Great Mortality: An Intimate History of the Black Death, the Most Devastating Plague of All Time* (New York: Harper Perennial, 2006). On the rise of new monarchies, see M. S. Anderson, *The Origins of the Modern European State System, 1494–1618* (London: Longman, 1998); and Jan Glete, *War and the State in Early Modern Europe: Spain, The Dutch Republic and Sweden as Fiscal-Military States, 1500–1660* (London: Routledge, 2002).

Conquistadores

An encyclopedic yet opinionated survey of European seaborne expansion is Samuel Eliot Morison, *The European Discovery of America*, 2 vols. (New York: Oxford University Press, 1971, 1974); see also J. H. Perry, *The Age of Reconnaissance* (Berkeley: University of California Press, 1981). Early developments are traced in Felipe Fernandez-Armesto, *Before Columbus: Exploration and Colonization from the Mediterranean to the Atlantic, 1229–1492* (Philadelphia: University of Pennsylvania Press, 1987). On the origins of the trade in enslaved Africans, see John Thornton, *Africa and Africans in the Making of the Atlantic World, 1400–1680* (New York: Cambridge University Press, 1992). On the conquest of the West Indies, see Irving Rouse, *The Tainos: Rise and Decline of the People Who Greeted Columbus* (New Haven, Conn.: Yale University Press, 1992). Ideological developments may be traced in Patricia Seed, *Ceremonies of Possession in Europe's Conquest of the New World, 1492–1640* (Cambridge: Cambridge University Press, 1995); Anthony Pagden, *Lords of All the World: Ideologies of Empire in Spain, Britain, and France, c. 1580–c. 1800* (New Haven, Conn.: Yale University Press, 1995); Andrew Fitzmaurice, *Humanism and America: An Intellectual History of English Colonisation, 1500–1625* (Cambridge: Cambridge University Press, 2003); and Matthew Restall, *Seven Myths of the Spanish Conquest* (New York: Oxford University Press, 2003).

Notable among the many studies of early English colonization are Kenneth R. Andrews, *Trade, Plunder, and Settlement: Maritime Enterprise and the Genesis of the British Empire, 1480–1630* (New York: Cambridge University Press, 1984); David Beers Quinn, *Set Fair for Roanoke: Voyages and Colonies, 1584–1606* (Chapel Hill: University of North Carolina Press, 1985); Quinn, *The Elizabethans and the Irish* (Ithaca, N.Y.: Cornell University Press, 1966); Jorge Cañizares-Esguerra, *Puritan Conquistadors: Iberianizing the Atlantic, 1550–1700* (Stanford, Calif.: Stanford University Press, 2006); Karen Ordahl Kupperman, *Roanoke: The Abandoned*

Colony, 2nd ed. (Lanham, Md.: Rowman and Littlefield, 2007; orig. publ. 1984); Kupperman, *The Jamestown Project* (Cambridge, Mass.: Harvard University Press, 2007); Peter C. Mancall, ed., *The Atlantic World and Virginia, 1550–1624* (Chapel Hill: University of North Carolina Press, 2007); and Alison Games, *The Web of Empire: English Cosmopolitans in an Age of Expansion, 1560–1660* (New York: Oxford University Press, 2008).

Traders

Studies of Tsenacomoco's relations with the English include Frederic W. Gleach, *Powhatan's World and Colonial Virginia: A Conflict of Cultures* (Lincoln: University of Nebraska Press, 1997); Margaret Holmes Williamson, *Powhatan Lords of Life and Death: Command and Consent in Seventeenth-Century Virginia* (Lincoln: University of Nebraska Press, 2003); and Helen C. Rountree, *Pocahontas, Powhatan, Opechancanough: Three Indian Lives Changed by Jamestown* (Charlottesville: University of Virginia Press, 2005).

On the development of the Newfoundland fisheries and early Native-European trade, see David Beers Quinn, *North America from Earliest Discovery to First Settlements: The Norse Voyages to 1612* (New York: Harper and Row, 1977). French-Indian relations are dissected in Olive Patricia Dickason, *The Myth of the Savage and the Beginnings of French Colonialism in the Americas* (Edmonton: University of Alberta Press, 1984); Bruce G. Trigger, *Natives and Newcomers: Canada's "Heroic Age" Reconsidered* (Kingston, Ontario: McGill–Queen's University Press, 1985); and Denys Delâge, *Bitter Feast: Amerindians and Europeans in Northeastern North America, 1600–1664,* trans. Jane Brierly (Vancouver: University of British Columbia Press, 1993), which also deals comparatively with the Dutch and English. Other studies of Dutch trade and colonization include C. R. Boxer, *The Dutch Seaborne Empire, 1600–1800* (New York: Knopf, 1965); Allen W. Trelease, *Indian Affairs in Colonial New York: The Seventeenth Century* (Ithaca, N.Y.: Cornell University Press, 1960); Donna Merwick, *The Shame and the Sorrow: Dutch-Amerindian Encounters in New Netherland* (Philadelphia: University of Pennsylvania Press, 2006); and Paul Otto, *The Dutch-Munsee Encounter in America: The Struggle for Sovereignty in the Hudson Valley* (New York: Berghahn Books, 2006).

Studies of seventeenth-century North American epidemics include Alfred Crosby, *The Columbian Exchange: Biological and Cultural Consequences of 1492* (Westport, Conn.: Greenwood, 1972); Ann F. Ramenofsky, *Vectors of Death: The Archaeology of European Contact* (Albuquerque: University of New Mexico Press, 1987); and Noble David Cook, *Born to Die: Disease and New World Conquest, 1492–1650* (Cambridge: Cambridge University Press, 1998). On warfare among Native peoples, see Bruce G. Trigger, *The Children of Aataentsic: A History of the Huron People to 1660* (Montreal: McGill–Queen's University Press, 1976); Daniel K. Richter, *The Ordeal of the Longhouse: The Peoples of the Iroquois League in the Era of European Colonization* (Chapel Hill: University of North Carolina Press, 1992); José António Brandão, *"Your Fyre Shall Burn No More": Iroquois Policy Towards New France and Its Native Allies to 1701* (Lincoln: University of Nebraska Press, 1997); Paul Kelton, *Epidemics and Enslavement: Biological Catastrophe in the Native Southeast, 1492–1715* (Lincoln: University of Nebraska Press, 2007); and Christina Snyder, *Slavery in Indian Country: The Changing Face of Captivity in Early America* (Cambridge, Mass.: Harvard University Press, 2010).

Early European-Indian relations and the Pequot War in New England are examined in Alden T. Vaughan, *New England Frontier: Puritans and Indians, 1620–1675,* 3rd ed. (Norman: University of Oklahoma Press, 1995; orig. publ. 1965); Francis Jennings, *The Invasion of America: Indians, Colonialism, and the Cant of Conquest* (Chapel Hill: University of North Carolina Press, 1975); Neal Salisbury, *Manitou and Providence: Indians, Europeans, and the Making of New England, 1500–1643* (New York: Oxford University Press, 1982); William Cronon, *Changes in the Land: Indians, Colonists, and the Ecology of New England* (New York: Hill and Wang, 1983); Kathleen J. Bragdon, *Native People of Southern New England, 1500–1650* (Norman: University of Oklahoma Press, 1996); Alfred A. Cave, *The Pequot War* (Amherst: University of Massachusetts Press, 1996); and Michael Leroy Oberg, *Uncas: First of the Mohegans* (Ithaca, N.Y.: Cornell University Press, 2003).

Planters

Books on seventeenth-century English Atlantic migration include E. A. Wrigley and R. S. Schofield, *The Population History of England, 1541–1871* (Cambridge, Mass.: Harvard University Press, 1981); David Cressy, *Coming Over: Migration and Communication between England and New*

England in the Seventeenth Century (Cambridge: Cambridge University Press, 1987); Virginia DeJohn Anderson, *New England's Generation: The Great Migration and the Formation of Society and Culture in the Seventeenth Century* (New York: Cambridge University Press, 1991); Alison Games, *Migration and the Origins of the English Atlantic World* (Cambridge, Mass.: Harvard University Press, 1999); Carla Gardina Pestana, *The English Atlantic in an Age of Revolution, 1640–1661* (Cambridge, Mass.: Harvard University Press, 2004); and Susan Hardman Moore, *Pilgrims: New World Settlers and the Call of Home* (New Haven, Conn.: Yale University Press, 2007).

The best introduction to the vast historical literature on transatlantic puritanism is Francis J. Bremer, *The Puritan Experiment: New England Society from Bradford to Edwards*, rev. ed. (Hanover, N.H.: University Press of New England, 1995; orig. publ. 1976). More specialized studies of religious, social, and political developments in the British Isles include Conrad Russell, *The Crisis of Parliaments: English History, 1509–1660* (London: Oxford University Press, 1971); Lawrence Stone, *The Causes of the English Revolution, 1529–1642* (New York: Harper and Row, 1972); Christopher Hill, *The World Turned Upside Down: Radical Ideas during the English Revolution* (New York: Viking, 1972); Patrick Collinson, *The Birthpangs of Protestant England: Religious and Cultural Change in the Sixteenth and Seventeenth Century* (London: Macmillan, 1988); Mark Kishlansky, *A Monarchy Transformed: Britain, 1603–1714* (New York: Penguin, 1996); and Margo Todd, *The Culture of Protestantism in Early Modern Scotland* (New Haven, Conn.: Yale University Press, 2002).

A sampling of works on seventeenth-century New England society includes Edmund S. Morgan, *The Puritan Dilemma: The Story of John Winthrop* (Boston: Little, Brown, 1958); Kenneth Lockridge, *A New England Town: The First Hundred Years, Dedham, Massachusetts, 1636–1736* (New York: W. W. Norton, 1970); Laurel Thatcher Ulrich, *Good Wives: Image and Reality in the Lives of Women in Northern New England, 1650–1750* (New York: Knopf, 1980); Charles Lloyd Cohen, *God's Caress: The Psychology of Puritan Religious Experience* (New York: Oxford University Press, 1986); David D. Hall, *Worlds of Wonder, Days of Judgment: Popular Religious Belief in Early New England* (New York: Knopf, 1989); and Michael P. Winship, *Making Heretics: Militant Protestantism and Free Grace in Massachusetts, 1636–1641* (Princeton, N.J.: Princeton University Press, 2002).

Studies of the development of Virginia in the seventeenth century include Edmund S. Morgan, *American Slavery, American Freedom: The Ordeal of Colonial Virginia* (Chapel Hill: University of North Carolina Press, 1975); Lois Green Carr, Philip D. Morgan, and Jean B. Russo, eds., *Colonial Chesapeake Society* (Chapel Hill: University of North Carolina Press, 1988); James Horn, *Adapting to a New World: English Society in the Seventeenth-Century Chesapeake* (Chapel Hill: University of North Carolina Press, 1994); Kathleen M. Brown, *Good Wives, Nasty Wenches, and Anxious Patriarchs: Gender, Race, and Power in Colonial Virginia* (Chapel Hill: University of North Carolina Press, 1996); and April Lee Hatfield, *Atlantic Virginia: Intercolonial Relations in the Seventeenth Century* (Philadelphia: University of Pennsylvania Press, 2004). On Virginia's neighbor to the north, see Gloria L. Main, *Tobacco Colony: Life in Early Maryland, 1650–1720* (Princeton: Princeton University Press, 1982). The best general survey of the early English Caribbean remains Richard S. Dunn, *Sugar and Slaves: The Rise of the Planter Class in the English West Indies, 1624–1713* (Chapel Hill: University of North Carolina Press, 1972).

Nieu Nederlandt is the subject of Oliver A. Rink, *Holland on the Hudson: An Economic and Social History of Dutch New York* (Ithaca, N.Y.: Cornell University Press, 1986); and Jaap Jacobs, *The Colony of New Netherland: A Dutch Settlement in Seventeenth-Century America* (Ithaca, N.Y.: Cornell University Press, 2009). Works on La Nouvelle-France include Louise Dechêne, *Habitants and Merchants in Seventeenth-Century Montreal,* trans. Liana Vardi (Montreal: McGill–Queen's University Press, 1992); Allan Greer, *The People of New France* (Toronto: University of Toronto Press, 1997); and Peter Moogk, *La Nouvelle France: The Making of French Canada—A Cultural History* (East Lansing: Michigan State University Press, 2000).

On La Florida, see Amy Turner Bushnell, *Situado and Sabana: Spain's Support System for the Presidio and Mission Provinces of Florida* (Athens: University of Georgia Press, 1994); Paul E. Hoffman, *Florida's Frontiers* (Bloomington: Indiana University Press, 2002); and Robert C. Galgano, *Feast of Souls: Indians and Spaniards in the Seventeenth-Century Missions of Florida and New Mexico* (Albuquerque: University of New Mexico Press, 2005). Among important studies of Nuevo México are Ramón A. Gutiérrez, *When Jesus Came, the Corn Mothers Went Away: Marriage, Sexuality, and Power in New Mexico, 1500–1846* (Stanford, Calif.: Stanford University Press, 1991); Andrew L. Knaut, *The Pueblo Revolt of 1680:*

Conquest and Resistance in Seventeenth-Century New Mexico (Norman: University of Oklahoma Press, 1995); and James F. Brooks, *Captives and Cousins: Slavery, Kinship, and Community in the Southwest Borderlands* (Chapel Hill: University of North Carolina Press, 2002).

Imperialists

Varied perspectives on English imperial developments in the late seventeenth century are provided by J. M. Sosin, *English America and the Restoration Monarchy of Charles II: Transatlantic Politics, Commerce, and Kinship* (Lincoln: University of Nebraska Press, 1980); Stephen Saunders Webb, *1676: The End of American Independence* (New York: Knopf, 1984); Ian K. Steele, *Warpaths: Invasions of North America* (New York: Oxford University Press, 1994); Steven C. A. Pincus, *Protestantism and Patriotism: Ideologies and the Making of English Foreign Policy, 1650–1668* (Cambridge: Cambridge University Press, 1996); Tim Harris, *Restoration: Charles II and his Kingdoms, 1660–1685* (London: Allen Lane, 2005); and the essays in Wm. Roger Louis, gen. ed., *The Oxford History of the British Empire*, vol. 1: *The Origins of Empire*, ed. Nicholas Canny (Oxford: Oxford University Press, 1998). Robert M. Weir, *Colonial South Carolina: A History* (Millwood, N.Y.: KTO Press, 1983), gives an introduction to the founding of that colony; and Robert C. Ritchie, *The Duke's Province: A Study of New York Politics and Society, 1664–1691* (Chapel Hill: University of North Carolina Press, 1977), details the conquest of Nieu Nederlandt. On New England's uneasy relationship with the Restoration regime, see Michael G. Hall, *Edward Randolph and the American Colonies, 1676–1703* (Chapel Hill: University of North Carolina Press, 1960); and Richard R. Johnson, *Adjustment to Empire: The New England Colonies, 1675–1715* (New Brunswick, N.J.: Rutgers University Press, 1981).

French imperial policies may be traced in Kenneth J. Banks, *Chasing Empire across the Sea: Communications and the State in the French Atlantic, 1713–1763* (Montreal: McGill–Queen's University Press, 2002); and James Pritchard, *In Search of Empire: The French in the Americas, 1670–1730* (Cambridge: Cambridge University Press, 2004). Impacts of imperial developments on Native peoples are discussed in Francis Jennings, *The Ambiguous Iroquois Empire: The Covenant Chain Confederation of Indian Tribes with English Colonies, from Its Beginnings to the*

Lancaster Treaty of 1744 (New York: W. W. Norton, 1984); and Stuart Banner, *How the Indians Lost Their Land: Law and Power on the Frontier* (Cambridge, Mass.: Harvard University Press, 2005).

Among analyses of Virginia in the period of Bacon's Rebellion are Wilcomb E. Washburn, *The Governor and the Rebel: A History of Bacon's Rebellion in Virginia* (Chapel Hill: University of North Carolina Press, 1957); T. H. Breen and Stephen Innes, *"Myne Owne Ground": Race and Freedom on Virginia's Eastern Shore, 1640–1676* (New York: Oxford University Press, 1980); Allan Kulikoff, *Tobacco and Slaves: The Development of Southern Cultures in the Chesapeake, 1680–1800* (Chapel Hill: University of North Carolina Press, 1986); Anthony S. Parent Jr., *Foul Means: The Formation of a Slave Society in Virginia, 1660–1740* (Chapel Hill: University of North Carolina Press, 2003); and Warren M. Billings, *Sir William Berkeley and the Forging of Colonial Virginia* (Baton Rouge: Louisiana State University Press, 2004).

Major studies of King Philip's War include Douglas Edward Leach, *Flintlock and Tomahawk: New England in King Philip's War* (New York: Macmillan, 1958); Jill Lepore, *The Name of War: King Philip's War and the Origins of American Identity* (New York: Knopf, 1998); James D. Drake, *King Philip's War: Civil War in New England, 1675–1676* (Amherst: University of Massachusetts Press, 1999); and Jenny Hale Pulsipher, *Subjects unto the Same King: Indians, English, and the Contest for Authority in Colonial New England* (Philadelphia: University of Pennsylvania Press, 2005).

Crucial works on the Glorious Revolution include Jonathan I. Israel, ed., *The Anglo-Dutch Moment: Essays on the Glorious Revolution and Its World Impact* (New York: Cambridge University Press, 1991); Tim Harris, *Revolution: The Great Crisis of the British Monarchy, 1685–1720* (London: Allen Lane, 2006); Lisa Jardine, *Going Dutch: How England Plundered Holland's Glory* (New York: Harper, 2008); Steve Pincus, *1688: The First Modern Revolution* (New Haven, Conn.: Yale University Press, 2009); and David S. Lovejoy, *The Glorious Revolution in America* (New York: Harper and Row, 1972). On subsequent political developments, see John Brewer, *The Sinews of Power: War, Money, and the English State, 1688–1783* (New York: Knopf, 1989); Linda Colley, *Britons: Forging the Nation, 1707–1837* (New Haven, Conn.: Yale University Press, 1992); David Armitage, *The Ideological Origins of the British Empire* (Cambridge: Cambridge University Press, 2000); Bernard Bailyn, *The Origins of Amer-*

ican Politics (New York: Knopf, 1968); Jack P. Greene, *Peripheries and Center: Constitutional Development in the Extended Polities of the British Empire and the United States, 1607–1788* (Athens: University of Georgia Press, 1986); Alison Gilbert Olson, *Making the Empire Work: London and American Interest Groups, 1690–1790* (Cambridge, Mass.: Harvard University Press, 1992); Patricia U. Bonomi, *The Lord Cornbury Scandal: The Politics of Reputation in British America* (Chapel Hill: University of North Carolina Press, 1998); Richard R. Beeman, *The Varieties of Political Experience in Eighteenth-Century America* (Philadelphia: University of Pennsylvania Press, 2004); and Brendan McConville, *The King's Three Faces: The Rise and Fall of Royal America, 1688–1776* (Chapel Hill: University of North Carolina Press, 2006).

On the turn-of-the-eighteenth-century imperial and Euro-Indian wars, see Douglas Edward Leach, *Arms for Empire: A Military History of the British Colonies in North America, 1607–1763* (New York: Macmillan, 1973); John Demos, *The Unredeemed Captive: A Family Story from Early America* (New York: Knopf, 1994); Evan Haefeli and Kevin Sweeney, *Captors and Captives: The 1704 French and Indian Raid on Deerfield* (Amherst: University of Massachusetts Press, 2003); Ann M. Little, *Abraham in Arms: War and Gender in Colonial New England* (Philadelphia: University of Pennsylvania Press, 2007); Alan Gallay, *The Indian Slave Trade: The Rise of the English Empire in the American South, 1670–1717* (New Haven: Yale University Press, 2002); Steven J. Oatis, *A Colonial Complex: South Carolina's Frontiers in the Era of the Yamasee War, 1680–1730* (Lincoln: University of Nebraska Press, 2004); and William L. Ramsey, *The Yamasee War: A Study of Culture, Economy, and Conflict in the Colonial South* (Lincoln: University of Nebraska Press, 2008).

Atlanteans

Among important studies of eighteenth-century Atlantic economy and society are John J. McCusker and Russell R. Menard, *The Economy of British America, 1607–1689* (Chapel Hill: University of North Carolina Press, 1985); Ian K. Steele, *The English Atlantic, 1676–1740: An Exploration of Communication and Community* (New York: Oxford University Press, 1986); Kathryn E. Holland Braund, *Deerskins and Duffels: Creek Indian Trade with Anglo-America, 1685–1815* (Lincoln: University of Nebraska Press, 1993); Cathy Matson, *Merchants and Empire: Trading in Colonial*

New York (Baltimore: Johns Hopkins University Press, 1998); and Serena R. Zabin, *Dangerous Economies: Status and Commerce in Imperial New York* (Philadelphia: University of Pennsylvania Press, 2009). The consumer revolution is treated in Richard Bushman, *The Refinement of America: Persons, Houses, Cities* (New York: Knopf, 1992); and Cary Carson, Ronald Hoffman, and Peter J. Albert, eds., *Of Consuming Interests: The Style of Life in the Eighteenth Century* (Charlottesville: University of Virginia Press, 1994). On the British Empire more generally, see Wm. Roger Louis, ed.-in-chief, *The Oxford History of the British Empire*, vol. 2: *The Eighteenth Century*, ed. P. J. Marshall (Oxford: Oxford University Press, 2001).

Important works on enslaved people in the eighteenth century include Peter H. Wood, *Black Majority: Negroes in Colonial South Carolina, from 1670 through the Stono Rebellion* (Chapel Hill: University of North Carolina Press, 1974); Philip D. Morgan, *Slave Counterpoint: Black Culture in the Eighteenth-Century Chesapeake and Lowcountry* (Chapel Hill: University of North Carolina Press, 1998); Herbert S. Klein, *The Atlantic Slave Trade* (New York: Cambridge University Press, 1999); David Eltis, *The Rise of African Slavery in the Americas* (New York: Cambridge University Press, 2000); Marcus Rediker, *The Slave Ship: A Human History* (New York: Viking, 2007); and Stephanie E. Smallwood, *Saltwater Slavery: A Middle Passage from Africa to American Diaspora* (Cambridge, Mass.: Harvard University Press, 2007). On indentured servitude, see David W. Galenson, *White Servitude in Colonial America: An Economic Analysis* (Cambridge: Cambridge University Press, 1981); and Sharon V. Salinger, *"To Serve Well and Faithfully": Labour and Indentured Servants in Pennsylvania, 1682–1800* (Cambridge: Cambridge University Press, 1987).

Eighteenth-century immigration is surveyed briefly in Bernard Bailyn, *The Peopling of British North America: An Introduction* (New York: Vintage, 1988); and extensively in David Hackett Fischer, *Albion's Seed: Four British Folkways in America* (New York: Oxford University Press, 1989). On German immigration, see A. G. Roeber, *Palatines, Liberty, and Property: German Lutherans in Colonial British America* (Baltimore: Johns Hopkins University Press, 1993); Marianne Wokeck, *Trade in Strangers: The Beginnings of Mass Migration to North America* (University Park: Pennsylvania State University Press, 1999); and Aaron Spencer Fogleman, *Hopeful Journeys: German Immigration, Settlement, and Political Culture in Colonial America, 1717–1775* (Philadelphia: University of Pennsylvania Press, 1996). On immigration from Ireland, see Patrick Griffin, *The People with No Name: Ireland's Ulster Scots, America's Scots Irish, and the Creation of a British Atlantic World, 1689–1764* (Princeton, N.J.: Princeton University Press, 2001). On migrants from Scotland, see Ned C. Landsman, *Scotland and Its First American Colony, 1683–1765* (Princeton, N.J.: Princeton University Press, 1985); and Colin G. Calloway, *White People, Indians, and Highlanders: Tribal Peoples and Colonial Encounters in Scotland and America* (New York: Oxford University Press, 2008).

The magisterial study of the Seven Years War is Fred Anderson, *Crucible of War: The Seven Years' War and the Fate of Empire in British North America, 1754–1766* (New York: Knopf, 2000). Important additional works are Francis Jennings, *Empire of Fortune: Crowns, Colonies, and Tribes in the Seven Years War in America* (New York: W. W. Norton, 1988); Richard White, *The Middle Ground: Indians, Empires, and Republics in the Great Lakes Region, 1650–1815* (New York: Cambridge University Press, 1991); Michael N. McConnell, *A Country Between: The Upper Ohio Valley and Its Peoples, 1724–1774* (Lincoln: University of Nebraska Press, 1992); Gregory Evans Dowd, *A Spirited Resistance: The North American Indian Struggle for Unity, 1745–1815* (Baltimore: Johns Hopkins University Press, 1992); Dowd, *War under Heaven: Pontiac, the Indian Nations and the British Empire* (Baltimore: Johns Hopkins University Press, 2002); Eric Hinderaker, *Elusive Empires: Constructing Colonialism in the Ohio Valley, 1673–1800* (New York: Cambridge University Press, 1997); Timothy J. Shannon, *Indians and Colonists at the Crossroads of Empire: The Albany Congress of 1754* (Ithaca, N.Y.: Cornell University Press, 2000); Matthew C. Ward, *Breaking the Backcountry: The Seven Years' War in Virginia and Pennsylvania, 1754–1765* (Pittsburgh: University of Pittsburgh Press, 2003); Richard Middleton, *Pontiac's War: Its Causes, Course and Consequences* (New York: Routledge, 2007); Peter Silver, *Our Savage Neighbors: How Indian War Transformed Early America* (New York: W. W. Norton, 2008); and David L. Preston, *The Texture of Contact: European and Indian Settler Communities on the Frontiers of Iroquoia, 1667–1783* (Lincoln: University of Nebraska Press, 2009).

Credits for Illustrations

1. Hans Holbein the Younger, *Design for a Stained-Glass Window for Christoph von Eberstein* (1522), detail. Ashmolean Museum, University of Oxford.

2. Samuel de Champlain, *Les Voyages du Sieur de Champlain, Capitaine Ordinaire, pour le Roy en la Nouvelle France ès années 1615 et 1618* (Paris, 1619), 87v, detail, retouched by Matthew C. Robbins. Robert Dechert Collection, Rare Book and Manuscript Library, University of Pennsylvania.

3. Mississippian effigy pipe, photograph by David H. Dye. Dr. Kent and Jonnie Westbrook Collection, Little Rock, Arkansas.

4. Limbourg Brothers, *Les Très Riches Heures du duc de Berry* (1415), Ms. 65, d, 3c, photograph by R. G. Ojeda, Musée Condé, Chantilly, France, Réunion des Musées Nationaux / Art Resource, N.Y.

5. John White, *Secoton* (1585), detail. Copyright © The Trustees of the British Museum.

6. [Theodor de Bry], *Wunderbarliche, doch warhafftige Erklärung, von der Gelegenheit und Sitten der Wilden in Virginia . . .* (Oppenheim, 1620), plate XXI (image originally published 1594). Library of Congress, Rare Book and Special Collections Division, The Hans P. Kraus Collection of Sir Francis Drake.

7. Interior of Salisbury Cathedral, photograph by Andreas Järgensmeier. Image ID 23794120, Shutterstock Images LLC.

8. Hartmann Schedel, *Liber Chronicarum* (Nuremberg, 1493). Rare Book and Manuscript Library, University of Pennsylvania.

9. William R. Iseminger, *Areal Perspective of Cahokia Mounds, circa a.d. 1150–1200.* Reproduced by permission of the artist.

10. Shell gorget with eagle dancer motif, Late Mississippian period, circa 1450 C.E. Copyright © Frank H. McClung Museum, The University of Tennessee, Knoxville.

11. Unknown engraver, *The Reformation* (late sixteenth century). NPG D23051, copyright © National Portrait Gallery, London.

12. *The Bible Translated According to the Ebrew and Greeke* (London, 1599), title page. Rare Book and Manuscript Library, University of Pennsylvania.

13. Areal view of Pueblo Bonito. Image 25462, courtesy Chaco Culture National Historical Park Museum Collection.

14. Ancient ruins at Chaco Canyon, photograph by Josemaria Toscano. Image ID 38735206, Shutterstock Images LLC.

15. Ruins of St. Andrews Cathedral, Scotland, photograph by Karolai Marek, Image ID 49450228, Shutterstock Images LLC.

16. Theodor de Bry, *Das vierdte Buch von der Neuwen Welt* . . . (Frankfurt am Main, 1613), plate IX. Library of Congress, Rare Book and Special Collections Division, The Hans P. Kraus Collection of Sir Francis Drake.

17. Pietro M. de Anghiera, *The Decades of the Newe Worlde,* trans. Richard Eden (London, 1555), title page. Reproduced by permission of The Huntington Library, San Marino, California.

18. Walter Bigges, *A Summarie and True Discourse of Sir Frances Drakes West Indian Voyage* (London, 1589). Reproduced by permission of the Rare Book Department, Free Library of Philadelphia.

19. Unknown artist, *Wedding Portrait of Fernando of Aragon and Isabel of Castile* (1469). Monastery of the Augustine Nuns at Madrigal de las Altas Torres, Spain.

20. Theodor de Bry, *Americae pars sexta* . . . ([Frankfurt am Main], 1596), plate III. Library of Congress, Rare Book and Special Col-

lections Division, The Hans P. Kraus Collection of Sir Francis
Drake.

21.   Walter Bigges, *A Summarie and True Discourse of Sir Frances
      Drakes West Indian Voyage* . . . (London, 1589). Reproduced by
      permission of the Rare Book Department, Free Library of Phila-
      delphia.

22.   Theodor de Bry, *Der ander Theil, der newlich erfundenen Land-
      schafft Americae* (Frankfurt am Main, 1603), plate VIII. Library of
      Congress, Rare Book and Special Collections Division, The Hans P.
      Kraus Collection of Sir Francis Drake.

23.   Map of Virginia (1608), detail. N.P. y D IV-66, España Ministerio
      de Cultura, Archivo General de Simancas.

24.   Powhatan's Mantle. Ashmolean Museum, University of Oxford.

25.   Unidentified artist, *Pocahontas,* probably after Simon van de Passe
      (after 1616). NPG.65.61, National Portrait Gallery, Smithsonian In-
      stitution; gift of the A. W. Mellon Educational and Charitable
      Trust.

26.   John Smith, *A Description of New England* (London, 1631), detail
      from map. Reproduced by permission of The Huntington Library,
      San Marino, California.

27.   Theodor de Bry, *Continuatio Americanae* . . . ([Frankfurt am Main,
      1627]), 42 (detail). Reproduced by permission of The Huntington
      Library, San Marino, California.

28.   Matthaeus Merian, *Decima tertia pars Historia Americae* (Frank-
      furt, 1634), 5. The Rooms Provincial Archives Division, MB 168.3,
      St. Johns, Newfoundland and Labrador.

29.   Glass trade beads. Jamestowne Image 126, Courtesy Preservation
      Virginia.

30.   John White, *A Chiefe Herowan* (1585). Copyright © The Trustees
      of the British Museum.

31.   Unknown artist, *Native American Sachem* (c. 1700), photography
      by Erik Gould. Courtesy of the Museum of Art, Rhode Island
      School of Design, Providence.

32. [Claude Charles Le Roy] Bacqueville de La Potherie, *Histoire de l'Amérique septentrionale* (Paris, 1722), vol. 1, facing p. 334. Robert Dechert Collection, Rare Book and Manuscript Library, University of Pennsylvania.

33. Brass objects made from pieces of trade kettles. State Museum of Pennsylvania, Pennsylvania Historical and Museum Commission.

34. George Henry Fox, *A Practical Treatise on Smallpox* (Philadelphia, 1902). Courtesy of the Historical Medical Library of the College of Physicians of Philadelphia.

35. Bernardino de Sahagún, *Florentine Codex* (c. 1540–1585). Biblioteca Medicea Laurenziana, Florence, ms. Med. Palat. 220, c. 460v, sue concessione de Ministero per i Beni e le Attività Culturali.

36. Samuel de Champlain, *Les Voyages du sieur de Champlain Xaintongeois . . .* (Paris, 1613), facing p. 232. Robert Dechert Collection, Rare Book and Manuscript Library, University of Pennsylvania.

37. Willem Blaeu, *Nova Belgica et Anglia Nova* (1662). Lawrence H. Slaughter Collection, The Lionel Pincus and Princess Firyal Map Division, The New York Public Library, Astor, Lenox and Tilden Foundations.

38. French copy of Iroquois pictograph (c. 1666). Colonies, C11A2, folio 263, Archives nationales d'Outre-Mer, Aix-en-Provence, France.

39. After Sir Anthony Van Dyck, *William Laud* (c. 1636). NPG 171, copyright © National Portrait Gallery, London.

40. Unknown engraver, *No Simple Cleric* (c. 1640), photo by Hulton Archive / Getty Images, file 4636455, iStockphoto LP.

41. [John Vicars], *A Sight of the Trans-actions of These Latter Yeares Emblemized with Ingraven Plats, Which Men May Read without Spectacles* ([London, 1646]), 5. Shelfmark E.365(6), copyright © The British Library Board.

42. Sir Peter Lely, *Portrait of King Charles I, with James, Duke of York* (1648). Photographic Survey, The Courtauld Institute of Art, London, Collection of the Duke of Northumberland.

43. *At a General Court Held at Boston the 16th of March 1680/1* (broadside). Courtesy of the American Antiquarian Society.

44. Charter of the Governor and Company of Massachusetts Bay in New England (1629), detail. SC1/Series 23X, Massachusetts Archives at Columbia Point, Boston.

45. William Wood, *New Englands Prospect* (London, 1634). Reproduced by permission of The Huntington Library, San Marino, California.

46. Sumner Chilton Powell, *John Ruddick House and Barn, 1661*, from *Puritan Village: The Formation of a New England Town,* following p. 124. Copyright © 1963 by Wesleyan University Press, reprinted by permission of Wesleyan University Press.

47. Mathias de L'Obel, *Plantarium, sev Stirpium historia,* vol. 2, 252. The Academy of Natural Sciences, Ewell Sale Stewart Library, Philadelphia.

48. Hariotte Lee Taliaferro, *Sir William Berkeley,* after an original by Sir Peter Lely, owned by Mrs. Marguerite du Pont Lee. The Library of Virginia.

49. Benjamin Henry Latrobe, *Greenspring, Home of William Ludwell Less, James City County, Virginia* (1797). Image ID 1960.108.1.2.33, courtesy of The Maryland Historical Society.

50. Godiah Spray Tobacco Plantation (reconstruction). Image courtesy of Historic St. Mary's City, Maryland.

51. Unknown artist, *France Bringing Faith to the Hurons of New France* (late seventeenth century). Musée des Ursulines de Québec, Collection du Monastère des Ursulines de Québec.

52. Arnoldus Montanus, *De Nieuwe en Onbekende Weereld, of Beschryving van America* (Amsterdam, 1671). Rare Book and Manuscript Library, University of Pennsylvania.

53. *The Holy Bible . . . Translated into the Indian Language . . .* (Cambridge, Mass., 1663), second title page. Reproduced by permission of The Huntington Library, San Marino, California.

54. Exterior of reconstructed church, Mission San Luis. Florida Division of Historical Resources.

55. Anonymous, *Olivarius Cronvelius, Reipublicae Magnae Britanniae Protector* (c. 1670). Fairclough Collection, David Wilson Library, University of Leicester.

56. [Olfert Dapper], *Historische Beschryvinghe van Amsterdam* (Amsterdam, 1663), title page. Amsterdam City Archives.

57. Thomas Hobbes, *Leviathan; Or, The Matter, Forme, and Power of a Commonwealth Ecclesiasticall and Civil* (London, 1651), title page. Rare Book and Manuscript Library, University of Pennsylvania.

58. John Michael Wright, *King Charles II in Coronation Robes.* RCIN 404951, The Royal Collection, copyright © 2010 Her Majesty Queen Elizabeth II.

59. Anthony van Dyck, *The Future Stadholder Willem II (1626–1650), Prince of Orange, and His Bride Princess Mary Stuart (1631–1660), Daughter of Charles I of England* (1641). SK-A-102, Rijksmuseum Amsterdam.

60. Juan de Miranda Carreno, *König Karl II von Spanien.* Kunsthistorishes Museum, Vienna.

61. Hyacinthe Rigaud, *Louis XIV, King of France* (1701), photograph by Hervé Lewandowski. Louvre, Paris, Réunion des Musées Nationaux / Art Resource, N.Y.

62. Cloth Seal of the Company of Royal Adventurers of England to Africa (c. 1670). 429539, copyright © Museum of London.

63. Henri Gascar, *James Duke of York* (1672–1673). BHC2797, National Maritime Museum, London.

64. Sir Peter Lely, *George Carteret* (n.d.). Collection of Seigneur Philip Malet de Carteret, used by permission.

65. George Perfect Harding, *John Berkeley, First Baron of Stratton* (c. 1825–1850). NPG D20130, copyright © National Portrait Gallery, London.

66. S. A. Schoff (engraver), *William Penn* (n.d.). Society Portrait Collection, The Historical Society of Pennsylvania.

67. Richard Blome, *Nouvelle carte de la Pensylvanie, Maryland, Virginie, et Nouvell Jarsey* (1688). Lawrence H. Slaughter Collec-

tion, The Lionel Pincus and Princess Firyal Map Division, The New York Public Library, Astor, Lenox and Tilden Foundations.

68. Bastiaen Stopendael or Daniel Stopendael, *The Landing of His Royal Highness in England* (etching, c. 1689). NPG D22617, copyright © National Portrait Gallery, London.

69. Godfrey Kneller, *Charles Calvert, Third Lord Baltimore.* Courtesy of Enoch Pratt Free Library, Maryland's State Library Resource Center, Baltimore, Maryland.

70. *The Declaration of the Reasons and Motives for the Present Appearing in Arms of Their Majesties Protestant Subjects in the Province of Maryland* ([London] 1689), 1. Courtesy of the John Carter Brown Library, Brown University.

71. Jakob Van der Schley, after Hubert-François Gravelot (né Bourguignon), *King William III, Queen Mary II* (line engraving, mid-eighteenth century). NPG D10672, copyright © National Portrait Gallery, London.

72. Mary Beale, *Sir Edmund Andros* (n.d.). Acc. no. 1966.23, Virginia Historical Society.

73. Capitol Building, House of Burgesses Chamber. Image D2002-BKT-0618-025, The Colonial Williamsburg Foundation.

74. John Pine, *A View of the House of Commons* (line engraving, 1749). NPG D11092, copyright © National Portrait Gallery, London.

75. *Pennsylvania Gazette*, December 27, 1759. Rare Book and Manuscript Library, University of Pennsylvania.

76. David Grim, *Plan and Elevation of the Old City Hall Formerly Standing in Wall Street in the City of New York as It Was in the Years 1745 & 1746 & 1747 . . .* (drawing, 1818). Negative 27567, Collection of The New-York Historical Society.

77. Independence Hall, Philadelphia. Courtesy Independence National Historical Park.

78. Aerial View of the Capitol. Image K2001-DMD-52, 15s, The Colonial Williamsburg Foundation.

79. Anonymous, *The Election: A Medley, Humbly Inscribed to Squire Lilliput Professor of Scurrility . . .* (cartoon, [1764]). The Library Company of Philadelphia.

80. Awnsham Churchill, comp., A *Collection of Voyages and Travels* . . . (London, 1732), vol. 5, plate 9. Rare Book and Manuscript Library, University of Pennsylvania.

81. *Pennsylvania Gazette,* July 4, 1751. The Library Company of Philadelphia.

82. *Pennsylvania Gazette,* December 9, 1729. The Library Company of Philadelphia.

83. William Effingham De Forest, *The Louisbourg Journal* (New York: The Society of Colonial Wars, 1932), 174. Reprinted by permission of The Society of Colonial Wars in the State of New York.

84. Richard Collins(?), *Man and Child Drinking Tea* (c. 1720). Accession 1954-654, image TC93-9, The Colonial Williamsburg Foundation.

85. Unknown engraver, *The Brave Old Hendrick the Great Sachem or Chief of the Mohawk Indians* (c. 1740). Accession 2001-761, image DS2001-413, The Colonial Williamsburg Foundation.

86. Queen Anne Dining Room. Winterthur Museum and Country Estate, Winterthur, Delaware.

87. "Stenton," House of James Logan. Courtesy of The National Society of the Colonial Dames of America in the Commonwealth of Pennsylvania at Stenton, Philadelphia.

88. Benjamin West, *The Death of General Wolfe* (1771), detail. Transfer from the Canadian War Memorials, 1921 (Gift of the Second Duke of Westminster, England, 1918), National Gallery of Canada, Ottawa, photo copyright © National Gallery of Canada.

Acknowledgments

This book owes its beginnings to two scholars: Sean Wilentz, who suggested that I write it, and the late Francis Jennings, who proposed in *The Invasion of America* that we look to the Middle Ages for the origins of American history. But equal credit must go to twenty-five years' worth of undergraduates at Dickinson College and the University of Pennsylvania who, in multiple iterations of my class in Colonial North American History, heard, challenged, and refined most of the ideas that appear here. A substantial share must also go to participants in the Friday seminar of the McNeil Center for Early American Studies, who for more than a decade provided an ongoing education in colonial history while being the most supportive group of intellectual companions anyone could hope for.

I was privileged to share portions of the work-in-progress with several audiences who provided excellent comments. Among them are the seminar of the Early Modern Studies Institute sponsored by the Huntington Library and the University of Southern California; the Early Modern Studies group at the University of Pennsylvania; the Princeton University History Department; the Zuckerman Salon; and the American History reading group at the University of Sydney. Two seminars' worth of University of Pennsylvania graduate students also provided feedback on much of the manuscript. Gregory Ablavsky, Andrew Lipman, Laura Keenan Spero, and Patrick Spero deserve particular thanks for their contributions. Brian Rouleau, Katherine Paugh, and Simon Finger offered research assistance and astute critiques; they made the book much better. Philip Schwartzberg translated my rough ideas into the original maps that grace the volume; Kristin Sperber performed similar wonders with the photo essays. Aro Velmet provided efficient assistance acquiring illustrations, and Jean-Robert Durbin scrambled to provide two last-minute images.

Many colleagues read and improved one or more chapters. I particularly thank Virginia Anderson, Francis Bremer, Kathleen Brown, Tim Duggan, Antonio Feros, Peter Mancall, Geoffrey Plank, Robert Preucel, Christina Snyder, and Margo Todd. I am especially grateful to Fred Anderson and Karen Kupperman, who read the entire manuscript twice, corrected many errors, suggested countless improvements, and, on the whole, were wonderfully supportive. Maria Ascher untangled countless sentences and saved me from many errors. Joyce Seltzer believed in the project from the start and helped it, and me, through some gloomy and dark days. Her assistant, Jeannette Estruth, was always helpful.

This is the first book I have written, start to finish, with the marvelous new online research tools available to those of us fortunate enough to teach at major research universities. Most notable among these are the *Colonial State Papers* series from the National Archives and *Early English Books Online*, published by the Chadwyck-Healey division of ProQuest LLC; *Early American Imprints* and *American Historical Newspapers*, published by the Readex division of Newsbank; and *Eighteenth Century Collections Online*, published by the Gale division of Cengage Learning. I am grateful to the librarians at Penn—most notably intrepid History bibliographer Nick Okrent—for fighting to make these resources available. And I can only hope that the subscription costs of these services will soon become affordable to a broader range of scholars and students.

None of my work for this book (or for much of anything else professionally) would have happened without the assistance of Amy Baxter-Bellamy, Alla Vilnyansky, Barbara Natello, Joan Plonski, Deborah Broadnax, and Susan Cerrone. For moral and other kinds of support I thank Richard Dunn, Mary Maples Dunn, David Farley, Karen Hart, Steve Keiser, Walter Licht, Robert Lockhart, Michelle McDonald, Roderick McDonald, Michael McDonnell, Philip Morgan, John Murrin, Carla Pestana, Kathy Peiss, Mary Richter, Tommy Richter, Richard Ruff, Robert Blair St. George, Wendy White, Michael Zuckerman, and the members of the Chester Avenue Dog Park. As always, Sharon Richter has been there as editor, critic, guide, friend, and love of my life.

Index

473